THE THEORY OF QUANTITATIVE ECONOMIC POLICY WITH APPLICATIONS TO ECONOMIC GROWTH, STABILIZATION AND PLANNING

STUDIES
IN MATHEMATICAL AND
MANAGERIAL ECONOMICS

Editor

HENRI THEIL

VOLUME 5

1973

NORTH-HOLLAND PUBLISHING COMPANY–AMSTERDAM · LONDON

THE THEORY OF
QUANTITATIVE ECONOMIC POLICY
WITH APPLICATIONS TO
ECONOMIC GROWTH,
STABILIZATION AND PLANNING

Second, revised edition

KARL A. FOX
Distinguished Professor of Economics,
Iowa State University

JATI K. SENGUPTA
Professor of Economics and Statistics,
Iowa State University and Senior
Professor, Indian Institute of
Management at Calcutta

ERIK THORBECKE
Professor of Economics
Iowa State University

1973

NORTH-HOLLAND PUBLISHING COMPANY–AMSTERDAM · LONDON
AMERICAN ELSEVIER PUBLISHING COMPANY, INC.–NEW YORK

Library of Congress Catalog Card Number: 70 - 134648
ISBN North-Holland: 0 7204 3076 3
ISBN American Elsevier: 0 444 10544 1

PUBLISHERS:

NORTH-HOLLAND PUBLISHING COMPANY–AMSTERDAM
NORTH-HOLLAND PUBLISHING COMPANY, LTD.–LONDON

SOLE DISTRIBUTORS FOR THE U.S.A. AND CANADA:

AMERICAN ELSEVIER PUBLISHING CO., INC.
52 VANDERBILT AVENUE, NEW YORK, N.Y. 10017

1st edition 1966

PRINTED IN THE NETHERLANDS

INTRODUCTION TO THE SERIES

This is a series of books concerned with the quantitative approach to problems in the behavioural science field. The studies are in particular in the overlapping areas of mathematical economics, econometrics, operational research, and management science. Also, the mathematical and statistical techniques which belong to the apparatus of modern behavioural science have their place in this series. A well-balanced mixture of pure theory and practical applications is envisaged, which ought to be useful for Universities and for research workers in business and government.

The Editor hopes that the volumes of this series, all of which relate to such a young and vigorous field of research activity, will contribute to the exchange of scientific information at a truly international level.

THE EDITOR

PREFACE

In recent years, the governments of many countries have assumed major responsibilities for economic stabilization and growth. Along with these responsibilities has come an increased awareness of the interrelatedness of different sectors of a national economy and of the need for coordination of policies which had previously been debated in terms of their direct impacts on individual sectors.

In attempting to describe their economies, economists in many countries have applied certain models which are by now widely known. Almost every country now has a set of national income and product accounts. Many countries have developed input-output models of the well-known open-static type, some for one year only and others for a number of bench-mark years or even annually. A more limited number of countries have experimented with econometric models of the type pioneered by Tinbergen in the 1930's—models primarily designed to shed light on the probable effects of economic policies on a year-to-year or even quarter-to-quarter basis. These are short-term models, with a stabilization focus. Finally, many countries are experimenting with growth models, development planning models and "decision models" as a basis for anticipating or planning the cumulative effects of investment and other policies over a period of a decade or more.

The need for certain kinds of frameworks or models is now so widely recognized that in many cases government agencies have assumed responsibility for maintaining national income and product accounts, input-output models and models for development planning. Only a few governments have taken responsibility for the development and maintenance of econometric models with a stabilization focus; therefore, much of the work in this field has been done by the economists associated with universities or private research agencies. The Netherlands has probably gone the farthest in governmental sponsorship and use of short-run econometric models.

Stabilization models have been of greatest interest in advanced economies which have relatively sophisticated data networks in the traditional sense—published time series on a host of commodity prices, outputs, employment in different industries and the like. There are many economists who have achieved considerable sophistication in short-run economic forecasting of major economic aggregates (gross national product, employment and consumer prices, among others) or for particular sectors of the economy. Some of these economists are also well versed in fields such as fiscal policy and monetary policy.

Until recently, there have been sharp differences of opinion between proponents of formal econometric models and those who feel that they have been operating quite successfully without such aids. The traditional view appears to be that all economic relationships should be dealt with on an intuitive level—that no tangible mechanism should intervene between the raw material (individual time series) and the finished products (economic forecasts and/or policy recommendations). This requires an act of faith on the part of both the giver and the receiver of economic advice. The newer view is that the policy implications of a host of raw time series can be made clear if they are organized into an econometric model—a system of equations which translates the concept of interrelatedness into an explicit, quantitative, reproducible form. Communication between econometricians and other economists has improved considerably in recent years; econometricians are perhaps more modest about the adequacy of their *present* models, and others are willing to concede that models of increasing realism and sophistication may become increasingly useful as aids to economic forecasting and policy.

This is not in essence a book about economic models. Economic models are simply positive or descriptive unless they are supplemented by something else. That something else is the theory of quantitative economic policy. Readers who are familiar with Tinbergen's *On the Theory of Economic Policy* (1952–1955) and Theil's *Economic Forecasts and Policy* (1958–1961) will need no further elaboration, though it must be stressed that this book is much more than simply an elaboration or codification of the Tinbergen and Theil approaches.

The theory of quantitative economic policy approaches any kind of model of an economy from a policy point of view. In the very simplest terms, this involves adding to the economic model itself a criterion or objective function by means of which alternative policies can be compared and appraised. This means that alternative positions of the economy or, if you will, alternative sets of values of major economic variables are to be evaluated in terms of some kind of preference scale. This evaluation does not assume that the utilities of different individuals can be aggregated. It does mean that the policy maker is required to set values upon unit increases or decreases in the various economic magnitudes (employment, price level, income and others) which he believes measure or reflect the performance of the economy. Different policy makers will, of course, attach different relative weights to such variables as the level of employment, on one hand, and the rate of increase in the price level, on the other. Certain economic policies can be determined on the assumption that the policy maker can make only ordinal judgments about the "utility" (as he sees it) of alternative policies; problems involving uncertainty can be handled more definitely and elegantly if we assume a policy maker with a cardinal "utility" function. One may even conceive of a policy maker as motivated by a "vote-fare" function in which alternative economic policies, leading to alternative positions of the economy, are to be evaluated in terms of expected numbers of votes for the party in power at the next election. The linear and quadratic objective functions used in programming models of individual firms and of military situations have close affinities with the possible forms of objective functions which may be used in economic policy models.

It is our view that the theory of quantitative economic policy provides a unifying focus within which to study a very wide range of economic problems which have heretofore been presented in isolation from one another. This book does not replace any specialized texts or manuals on such recognized topics as econometrics, national income accounting, economic development, linear and quadratic programming, statistical decision theory, business cycles, monetary policy or fiscal policy. However, we feel very strongly that our book will provide new insights to economists and students of economics in all of the fields mentioned.

Part I presents the basic theory of quantitative economic policy. It has grown out of ten years experience with a graduate seminar or workshop in economic policy at Iowa State University. During this time, each of the authors had opportunities to contribute to the common subject matter of the course. Part I is designed primarily for use as a text at the advanced graduate level. It assumes that the students will have had a first-year graduate course in economic theory, a good basic course in economic statistics or econometrics and some acquaintance with matrix algebra. Particular deficiencies could, of course, be made up by means of special lectures or assigned readings by the professor in charge of the course. Part I could also be used as a text for students who propose to terminate their formal education at the master's degree level. In this case, the instructor might find it necessary to skip certain topics requiring advanced mathematics or to do a considerable amount of interpretation of them.

Part II is intended to supply motivation and empirical content for the theory presented in Part I. Thus, particular econometric or stabilization models are discussed from a policy point of view. Other sections illustrate how the theory of quantitative economic policy might be extended into regional subdivisions of a national economy, to political jurisdictions below the national level or to particular economic sectors, such as agriculture. Part II also contains rather extensive discussions of economic growth and development planning models and a description of the planning models and methods used in a variety of countries. The whole of Part II can be assimilated by students with rather limited formal training in economic theory and statistics; it would be a useful adjunct to existing texts, particularly in the field of economic development.

We believe that economists in government agencies throughout the world will find this book a useful reference work and an introduction to related literature (some of it in fields such as control engineering and management science) on particular topics. Particular chapters or sequences will also be of interest as supplementary readings for courses in many standard fields, including monetary theory and policy, fiscal policy, economic development, econometrics and macroeconomic theory.

There is always a possibility that an attempt at synthesis will range too widely among different specialties and disciplines to meet the perceived needs of any one group. However, we believe the theory of quantitative economic policy is sufficiently coherent as a result of the omnipresence of a cluster of problems and methods which makers of economic policy (and their advisers) must confront as part of their daily responsibilities. They cannot refrain from dealing with complicated sets of economic policies. Given their basic responsibilities, they can ignore the use of quantitative economic models and methods for their evaluation only at considerable current hazard to the consistency of their policy decisions and the future risk of successful demonstration of superior policy design and performance on the parts of political competitors who will take advantage of the modern methods.

Since the first edition of this book important progress has been made in at least three related areas; (1) the improvement in the informational and data base and in computer technology; (2) the increasing number and sophistication of empirical applications of various aspects of quantitative economic policy and planning; and, (3) the developments of new methods such as optimal and adaptive control theory which can be applied to economic policy.

The new edition incorporates major revisions. Three chapters have been entirely rewritten, i.e. those dealing with (a) optimal and adaptive control methods in economic policy; (b) economic policy models for development planning; and, (c) models of stabilisation in developed economies: the case of the US. In addition, in practically every chapter new sections have been added to reflect the new contributions to the state of the arts since the first edition. Thus, new sections have been written on applied estimation methods, forecasting methods and models, programming models, decision models under risk, growth theory, regional models, national policy models in developed economies (i.e. the FIFI model used in the preparation of the French Sixth Plan and a model used in Hungarian planning), and sectoral agricultural models.

The authors are indebted to the National Science Foundation for generous grants to study the formulation and use of quantitative economic models, which provided them with research time. Some of the results generated by the above study have been incorporated in various parts of the book.

The book has been in every sense a joint and cumulative product as was the graduate seminar, and workshop from which it grew initially. We have enjoyed our continuing collaboration, and we hope we have produced something of value to economists and students of economic policy.

Geneva, 17 November 1972
Karl A. Fox
Jati K. Sengupta
Erik Thorbecke

CONTENTS

PART I

THE THEORY OF QUANTITATIVE ECONOMIC POLICY

PART II

APPLICATIONS TO ECONOMIC GROWTH
STABILIZATION AND PLANNING

LIST OF TABLES

LIST OF FIGURES

PART I

THE THEORY OF QUANTITATIVE ECONOMIC POLICY

Chapter 1

INTRODUCTION TO QUANTITATIVE ECONOMIC POLICY

1.1. Economic Theory and Economic Policy

Scientists and engineers who design space vehicles are in an enviable position. They start from theories which the layman would find uncanny and apply mathematical transformations which he would find incomprehensible. But in the end they orbit a vehicle which shines like a star; it appears in the night sky when and where they say it will; and their success is visibly evident not only to the layman himself but to his five-year-old child!

The economist who creates a new theory with the aid of advanced mathematics is respected by his own colleagues. But the layman remains smugly impervious to policy prescriptions derived therefrom: "It may be all right in theory, but it won't work in practice." This verdict is rendered with such complete self-assurance as to imply that an economic prescription which is right in theory is *ipso facto* wrong in practice. As communication is clearly impossible, this usually terminates the dialogue between economist and layman. Though this be true for the moment, the economist should fire a parting shot which might open the way for genuine communication later on: "Are you saying that every economic prescription which is *wrong* in theory is *ipso facto right* in practice?"

This book is written for economists. It will not be opened by laymen. However, working economists in government and business are usually called upon to operate in specialized contexts, each of which calls for the use of a limited range of economic concepts and a limited degree of abstraction. Even in university life, few economics professors feel the need for rigorous mathematical formulations in the specialized teaching and research which occupies most of their time. They are reassured by the expectation that the professors responsible for the advanced graduate courses in economic theory, econometrics and mathematical economics will be able to help them out when some facet of their research calls for abstraction and rigor. An economics faculty is well balanced if the required communication can be effected either directly or in not more than two stages. The economics profession as a whole may be relatively well balanced even though as many as three or four stages of communication are necessary to adapt the new results of the creative theorist to the applied work of economists with bachelors' or masters' degrees.

Even among economists, the words *theory* and *policy* suggest very different levels of abstraction, degrees of reliance upon mathematical tools and rosters of personnel. The "policy man," so-called, is an economist who knows the names and numbers of every major player in a particular cluster of government agencies and special interest organizations. He, of course, knows the policy men in his speciality at other major universities, and he is up-to-date on rumors concerning which government or trade association officials are about to resign and by whom they are to be replaced.

These attributes of the policy man are prerequisites for the exercise of a certain kind of leadership and influence, but they are not the essence of economic policy. The essence of economic policy is the quality of the advice which the economist is able to deliver *after* he has made his basic investment in establishing channels of communication and in learning the nuances of interpersonal and interagency politics. The quality of his policy advice *as an economist* must still rest on the quality of the body of economic theory upon which he draws and the thoroughness with which this theory has been related to empirical (often quantitative) evidence concerning the structure and performance of the economic subsystems on which he professes to advise.

Only in recent years have significant numbers of economists become convinced that improvements in economic policy must be based upon rigorous use of economic theory and econometrics in conjunction with more refined and accurate basic data. Large-scale econometric models are still very new; the first relatively large-scale and sophisticated econometric model of the United States (the Brookings-SSRC econometric model) was only published in full in 1965. The number of first-rate economic theorists whose names are associated with seriously intended empirical models of national economies is still quite small—until recently few names other than Tinbergen, Leontief, Klein and Stone would have stood out. Frisch also made impressive contributions by carrying economic theory and mathematical programming techniques to the point at which it became clear that various kinds of operational models could be manipulated successfully, given the requisite data.

At present, *management science* is beginning to acquire prestige. Results of interest to a particular firm are in some cases as convincing as the space scientist's orbiting satellite. In some industrial circles, it is coming to be recognized that mathematics and statistics may be directed toward maximizing a net revenue function just as they can be used in devising guidance systems for missiles or in optimizing the performance of an oil refinery or an assembly line.

It may be that the prestige which mathematical tools are acquiring in management science will within a few years be extended to macroeconomics as well. However, such applications will encounter much resistance from the layman and also the policy economist in the traditional sense. The individual elements of the production line in a factory have been carefully designed to perform their particular roles in the complete system. This is obviously not so of the microunits of the economy at large.

Is it reasonable to represent our neighbor's behavior and our own by means of stochastic equations and to aggregate these microequations, building our behavior and that of many other people into an econometric model? And is it reasonable to take this macromodel, far removed as it seems from the visible world of houses, schools and shopping centers, and test its stability properties with the aid of a computer?

Suppose we find that the equation system of such a model contains within it the potential for explosive oscillations—is this discovery true or significant with respect to the real world? As a matter of fact, an economy characterized by such an equation system would not have a national income oscillating between zero and infinity. If oscillations became very severe, political pressures would be set up which *de facto* set bounds on the oscillatory process, even though the nature of the oscillatory mechanism might be but dimly understood by the policy makers. (Without real understanding, of course, the cure adopted might be needlessly drastic and short-sighted, such as mobilizing an economy for war to "solve" an unemployment problem.)

It is in the nature of pure mathematics to develop its demonstrations in ideal forms. Ideal forms are in many cases extreme forms—they are maxima or minima or they involve the convergence of a power series to a limit within less than any previously assigned epsilon, however small. The policy man tends to be wary of extrema, whether they imply absolute stability or absolute instability. Something always happens to disturb an equilibrium, and something is always done eventually to dampen explosive oscillations.

Mathematical analysis of economic models, then, tells us what will happen to the variables in a model if specified initial conditions are given and if nothing is done to modify future developments. At the same time, mathematical analysis will generally provide us with insights as to what kinds of interventions in the process or changes in the structure of the model would be necessary to change the performance of the system in specified ways. If the undesirable feature of the mathematical model is a tendency toward explosive oscillations, the structure of the model usually suggests that some instruments or interventions look more promising than others for avoiding or dampening the oscillations.

By implication, we have been urging that the policy man not underestimate the practical importance of mathematical and econometric models as a basis for policy. However, the theorist has some responsibilities for reassuring the practical man on this score. Thus, the economic theorist should point out from time to time during his abstract presentations that the signs and orders of magnitudes of the parameters which lead to certain kinds of developments over time are indeed characteristic (or probably characteristic) of certain kinds of economic systems.

When we import new techniques from other sciences and areas of application, we have some obligation to express our beliefs or anticipations concerning their eventual fruitfulness in economics. However, it seems appropriate in a new and rapidly developing field such as the theory of quantitative economic policy to present some ideas which we think represent significant insights even though we are not prepared to certify that they will, without further modification, have important empirical uses in economics.

Some of the mathematical techniques presented in Part I have not been tested empirically on economic data. Many of them have, though often in an exploratory manner. We must put the reader on his own mettle to relate some of these demonstrations to the real economy or economies with which he is familiar.

1.2. Economic Structure and Economic Policy

Most readers of this book will have had a considerable amount of undergraduate training in economics. Some, perhaps, will also have had considerable instruction in mathematics and statistics. In any event, we believe it will help us relate the theoretical demonstrations to potential practice if we have in mind some rather tangible economic structure as we read.

To this end we will outline some aspects of the structure of the economy of the U.S. For U.S. readers, at least, the fruitfulness of the theory of quantitative economic policy will depend upon their ability to adapt it to policy problems which arise in connection with this economic structure.

1.2.1. *Regional Delineation for Economic Policy*

In general, economists who have written about macroeconomics and the theory of economic policy have given little attention to the spatial aspects of the economies with which they have dealt. Often, conventional political boundaries (provinces, states or administrative districts) have been accepted without question.

It seems clear to us, however, that some patterns of regionalization for economic models and policy are better than others. In virtually all countries of considerable geographic extent economic activities have reallocated themselves spatially from decade to decade without much regard for traditional political subdivisions. We feel confident that in most countries there are major and serious discrepancies between the boundaries of states or provinces and the *functional economic areas* which describe the face-to-face economic interaction spaces of their citizens. This is particularly true of the smaller political subdivisions, such as *counties* in the case of the U.S.

It seems quite fruitful to view the U.S. economy as made up of perhaps 400 *functional economic areas*, each covering from perhaps 3,000 to as many as 8,000 square miles of territory. As a first approximation, these functional economic areas could be delineated by determining a sixty-minute isochrone or "equal travel time" contour line, around either the central business district or the major factories and other places of employment on the outskirts of the central city of the area, whichever measuring point gives the longest reach in a given direction. The sixty-minute isochrone is an approximation of the maximum normal distance over which workers will commute on a daily basis and over which shoppers will travel for those goods and services which require personal selection or presence. The translation of minutes into miles depends on the prevailing mode of transportation as well as on local factors (quality and pattern of the road system, speed limits for motor vehicles, terrain, natural barriers, traffic congestion and the like). Further details are presented in Chapter 12.

Each functional economic area is relatively self-contained or "closed" with respect to a major class of economic activities, which may be called *residentiary*, as they are oriented toward serving residents of the area. The remaining activities constitute the *export base* of the area, linking it with other areas into an interregional trading system which constitutes the truly national portion of the economy.

1.2.2. *A Logical Division of Labor Between National and Regional (Local) Policy Makers*

Each functional economic area contains virtually all of those state and local government service units which are used by area residents. Thus, the desires of area residents for such services could be readily focused on an area basis, and the costs and benefits of these public services could be more accurately measured and related to one another on this basis than on the basis of small "open" economies in which many local taxpayers work and shop in other political jurisdictions.

If local governments were coextensive with functional economic areas, local policy makers would logically concern themselves with the set of residentiary activities, with respect to which the area is very nearly self-contained. *National* policy makers alone would be concerned with the macrofunctioning of the larger system of industries (extractive, manufacturing, transportation, communication, etc.) which operate on a national or multiarea basis. National policy makers also have access to various instruments (such as personal income taxes or grants-in-aid to state and local governments) which impinge directly upon the residentiary sectors of all areas.

1.2.3. *Integrating National and Regional Policy Models*

Directly or indirectly, national policies affect the welfare of residents of all areas. Therefore, an econometric model of a functional economic area, containing the variables which are ends (targets) and means (instruments) for both local and national policy makers, should be enlightening to both groups. An illustrative model is discussed in Chapter 12. A set of such models for all functional economic areas could be integrated, for analytical purposes, with a macromodel of the national economy as a whole. In principle, the national or interregional trading sectors of the economy could be given more or less aggregative formulations, allowing for interregional input-output relations and/or spatial equilibrium phenomena.

Different models might require different sequences of aggregation. Thus, one could aggregate all imports and exports from a given region into money values. This might be appropriate in international trade, in which balance-of-payments considerations are quite important. Or, emphasis could be placed upon aggregating *establishments* in each area along industry lines, looking toward a national input-output model partitioned by area and industry. Certain federal policies impinge on *firms*, so that aggregation by firms should take precedence over aggregation by establishments in some cases.

1.2.4. *Basic Models, Derived Models and Identification*

Economic models or systems of equations representing an advanced economy should reflect with adequate realism industrial, spatial and transactor phenomena of the sort we have been describing. When we speak of economic stabilization in a prescriptive context, we should have in mind the reaction times of consumers, firms and local governments as well as their behavioral propensities. When we speak of economic policy models for growth or for development planning, we should also have in mind the planning horizons of businesses and of state and local governments. The fruitfulness of particular kinds of mathematical models for prescriptive economic policy in the next decade will depend upon the capacity of the mathematical models to encompass and flexibly represent these propensities and time horizons.

We may note in passing that a realistic appraisal of reaction times of consumers to changes in prices and their own incomes should enable us to anticipate whether and to what extent certain types of identification problems are likely to arise in econometric models based on different time units. Empirical investigation and appraisal of the ordering policies and the hiring and firing policies of business firms are also helpful in determining whether an econometric model (or a submodel of it) is fully recursive, almost recursive, or highly interdependent under any given selection of the basic time unit of observation.

1.2.5. *Aggregation: The Bridge Between Microanalysis and Macroanalysis*

It appears that little practical use has been made of Theil's insights concerning the principle of "perfect aggregation." The usefulness of this concept should be examined further. Although the basic theoretical problem is to aggregate microrelations relating to individual households or firms into aggregates of many consumers or firms, its operational usefulness might be more immediate in connection with aggregation over occupational and income groups of households within and between functional economic areas and aggregating (say) consumption functions for all households in one functional economic area with those for households in all others.

So far, the bridges between microrelations and macrorelations have been relatively weak elements in economic policy models. Many economic policies operate by changing (1) the incentives or the budget constraints of individual firms or consumers or (2) the general environment for firms and consumers in such a way that their decisions are affected in ways which are desired from the standpoint of national macroeconomic policy. It is exceedingly important, in our judgment, to improve our knowledge concerning the ways in which macroeconomic policies influence individuals and firms and ramify through the economy. Such knowledge would certainly heighten the sense of responsibility of officials responsible for national economic policy and would lead them to a more realistic appraisal of the social costs of using different policy instruments.

Some very famous models have dealt with two-sector economies. Such models are useful for elucidating the basic principle or kernel of an important new idea. Two-sector or other extremely small models also enable the teacher of theory to present a considerable number of basically different models in a short time. However, such models can hardly advance to the prescriptive level unless they are capable of generalization to considerable numbers of industrial sectors and regions.

Policies to stabilize employment must deal with sharp differentiations of "the" employment problem by regions, occupations and educational levels. Policies to stabilize the level of real consumption expenditures per capita also have regional, occupational and age-group dimensions. Longer-term policies for economic growth or development planning have regional, occupational and industrial dimensions.

Like other teachers before us, we will use small-scale and simplified examples for pedagogical purposes. But we urge the reader to consider at the end of each demonstration the extent to which the simple model might be modified and extended to deal with realistic levels of disaggregation.

The mathematics in Part I will at times be rather exacting. The mathematically trained reader may find this pleasing for his own sake. For the reader who finds it difficult, we hold out the expectation that at least some of the methods demonstrated will provide valuable insights into the structures of economic policy problems—insights which will increase his competence to deal with them on the applied level. We firmly believe that explicit theory is requisite to defensible policies and reproducible outcomes in the real world.

1.3. Use and Scope of Economic Policy Models

The first nine chapters of this book present the core of the analytical theory of economic policy by means of a systematic survey of the logic involved in quantitative decision-making with the aid of some form of policy model. The remaining chapters extend and illustrate the theory of quantitative economic policy by relating it to recognized practical problems of achieving economic growth and stabilization.

Recently, increasing numbers of countries—both developed and under-developed—have been pursuing a policy of furthering economic development in one form or another. In most cases, some kind of analytical model, crude or sophisticated, has provided an initial logical basis for studying the implications of alternative policies. In some underdeveloped countries the quantitative models of development planning have been addressed to specific problems, such as the optimum allocation of investment between sectors over time. In other countries, questions of institutional change, such as agrarian reform in its various dimensions, have provided the most important areas of concern for analyzing the implications of alternative policies. In developed countries, where limitations of statistical data are less severe, greater emphasis has been placed on developing more comprehensive econometric models which can be utilized for different types of national policy goals, and particularly for stabilization of the economy.

The growth and the stabilization applications of quantitative economic policy models will be emphasized both in our presentation of analytical material and in the later chapters of the book, which are mainly of an applied nature.

The theory of economic policy is concerned with the analysis of decision situations and policy problems, using that part of general economic theory which can be quantitatively applied to economic data in some operational sense. Such a quantitative analysis may be usefully divided into three interrelated parts;

(i)   Characterization of the policy problem: specification of the preference function, the quantitative model and the constraints or boundary conditions.

(ii) The selection problem: classification of variables by their properties, such as randomness, direct or indirect controllability and time-dependence.

(iii) The steering problem: derivation of optimum decision rules in static and dynamic senses and the flexibility of optimal decision-making procedures under changing conditions associated with risk, uncertainty and the sequence of new information.

This analytical framework has been used implicitly or explicity in other contexts which are not economic in any conventional sense. For instance, control engineers and communications systems analysts, in developing the theory of servomechanisms and the principles of automatic control of a complex physical system, start by describing the "laws of motion" of the existing physical system by a set of differential or difference equations involving variables which are controlled (inputs) and other variables which are the effects or outputs. Comparisons are made between alternative outcomes over time when the controlled variables are completely absent from the system and when they are present at different assigned levels. A set of optimal controls is then chosen which in some sense provides the best possible outcome, e.g., which optimizes a given performance integral in a feedback control in the servomechanism theory.

As a second example, we might refer to problems of quality control where questions of statistical decision functions are directly involved. Here, at each stage of the sample inspection plan one has to decide whether to accept a given hypothesis, to reject it or to go on taking additional samples. As a third example, we may refer to the management models of operations research, e.g., inventory control, programming models of resource allocation, management games and simulation of alternative decision processes.

If the reader feels any uneasiness about references to control systems engineering in a book on economic policy, we hasten to reassure him. The mathematical principles of maximization and minimization which are so essential to the exposition of economic theory had a long history of application in the physical sciences before they were found to be relevant to certain problems in economics. The theory of least squares and matrix algebra were developed without thought of economic applications. They were applied to economic problems when persons with mathematical training perceived that the *logical structures* of certain economic problems were similar to those to which these methods had been applied successfully in other disciplines.

Here, and in certain other passages in Part I, we are simply saying that the logical structures of some problems of economic policy are formally analogous to problems of decision making and stabilization or "steering" in other fields. Economists are participating along with engineers, statisticians, mathematicians, physicists and computer scientists in developing such fields as operations research and management science. These are areas of intense current activity. We feel free to draw on developments in these fields to the extent that they illuminate or illustrate (often in a simple and tangible form) the logical structures of policy problems in economics and the mathematical principles by which such problems may be clarified or solved.

Our examples from systems engineering, quality control and management science show the extremely wide range of applicability of what might be called a "general theory" of decision making and policy. In our presentation of the theory of economic policy we will introduce at one stage or another aspects of the statistical theories of estimation and decision functions, aspects of the principles of adaptive and automatic control used in systems engineering and some specific cases of operations research or programming models useful in management decisions.

The theory of economic policy has a wide range of applications within economics, e.g., macrodynamic policy making, development programming, evaluating the efficiency of alternative monetary and fiscal policies for economic stabilization and growth, alternative cost calculations for inoptimal decision making at different stages of a multistage policy model or in different regions of a multiregion model and analysis of the predictability of outcomes of a particular economic policy applied by (1) a centralized policy maker or (2) a group of decentralized policy makers.

1.4. Analytical Framework

There are certain differences in analytical approach and implications between the theory of economic policy and conventional uses of economic theory. Tinbergen [12, Chapter 1–3], in his discussion of the theory of economic policy, made a distinction between "target variables" (*effect* variables in a broad sense) and "instrument variables" (*cause* variables in a broad sense). He emphasized that conventional economic theory takes the values of the instrument variables to be given and analyzes their economic effects, whereas the theory of economic policy (at least in a fixed-target model) takes the desired values of the target variables to be given and calculates the constellation of values of the instrument variables required to attain the given targets.

This proposition of Tinbergen's may be interpreted in two different ways. One is that conventional economic theory neglects the problem of specifying the preference function of a policy maker and hence the alternative profiles of "shadow prices" or costs associated with the use of particular constellations of instrument variables. It only analyzes the positive economic model which connects the instrument and target variables and does not examine the diversity of solutions which might result from different preference functions that express different barter terms of trade between the target variables. An example from microtheory may be helpful. In conventional theory, we never ask how the input policy of a firm would change if, instead of trying to maximize profits it should seek to maximize a linear function of two target variables, e.g., a fixed or desired rate of profits and a fixed or desired rate of capacity expansion. In other words, we do not ask about the "consistency" of the two targets, the "policy degrees of freedom" and the specification of the static and dynamic aspects of the preference function of the policy maker, in this case a single firm.

A second possible interpretation of the so-called inverse relation between target and instrument variables in the theory of economic policy is that a policy model must be something more than an ordinary econometric model used for forecasting: it must contain additional features necessitated by the steering problem mentioned before, which follows directly from the problem of selection and classification of variables. Some of these additional features are that the instrument variables cannot be passive (merely projected from past trends) and that the preference function may change; even some variables which were targets in the past may turn out in the future to be instrument variables under the control of the policy maker.

As Frisch [4] has emphasized, we must distinguish between the selection problem and the steering problem. The first is the problem of classifying all the constellations of values of the variables that are possible within the system with its given degrees of freedom and to describe how desirable these various constellations are in terms of certain standards (social values, practical considerations, etc.) which themselves do not form part of the model but which are, so to speak, superimposed on the model (e.g., the objective of maximizing national income). The second problem, that of steering the economy, arises when the ground has been prepared through a selection study. The problem is how to achieve a constellation of values of the economic variables which comes close to one that has been recognized as an optimum constellation. The questions now are (1) what variables can be considered as instruments of government policy and (2) how the values of these instruments must be fixed in order to induce the system as a whole to take on the desired constellation of values.

The theory of economic policy also differs from conventional economic theory in that we have not merely to optimize some objective but also to determine such things as the reliability of the optimum policy and the flexibility of specified suboptimal policies by using the theories of statistical decision functions, process control and information sequence. This aspect of our problem is very similar to an aspect of statistical and engineering-control theory, where a distinction is frequently made [1] between *empirical* feedback and *technical* feedback. Empirical feedback occurs when we can specify a simple decision rule which describes unequivocally what action should be taken and what new information ought to be collected in every conceivable situation. In technicical feedback, however, we have the sequence of information from observed data interacting with the technical knowledge of the technician and the policy maker to lead to some form of action.

A third distinctive feature of the theory of economic policy is the study of the problem of decomposition of an over-all model into a set of submodels, i.e., aspects of efficient decentralization of quantitative economic decisions. The elements of risk and uncertainty play a special role in the actual computation and estimation of the optimum system comprising optimum subsystems. The concept of recursiveness plays a highly significant role in this scheme of decomposition. The mathematical analysis required for this situation may sometimes go beyond the principles of variational calculus and dynamic programming to the extent that it involves considerations of random differential or integral equations and optimal control problems with restricted phase coordinates [9].

Although Tinbergen and his associates initiated the application of quantitative methods to economic policy per se, methods and techniques developed in areas such as the theory of engineering control systems have also contributed to the theory of economic policy. The problem of deriving a decision rule or line of action from an analytical model and testing the sensitivity of the rule to slight variations in the coefficients of the model had been posed by technicians dealing with cybernetics and reliability engineering, where in some cases absolute precision in measurement is difficult to obtain.

To illustrate the application of decision rules primarily developed in other areas than economics, let us consider a simple example from the multiplier principle of macroeconomic theory, where we discuss alternative policies for economic stabilization within a short-run Keynesian model. This is a simplified version of the stabilization policy model presented by Phillips [7].

$$\text{Demand:} \quad Y_d = (1 - s) Y + G,$$
$$\text{Supply:} \quad dY/dt = \dot{Y} = - \lambda (Y - Y_d), \quad Y \neq Y_d, \qquad (1.1)$$
$$\text{hence,} \quad dY/dt = - \lambda s Y + \lambda G.$$

Here G subsumes all autonomous expenditure on investment and consumption which can be varied by government policy, and the lagged response of aggregate supply (Y) to aggregate demand (Y_d) is assumed to be of the continuous exponential type with speed of response $\lambda > 0$. The linear homogeneous saving function is characterized by the saving coefficient s, which is assumed to be fixed in the short run. Other implicit assumptions are constant prices and a less than full-employment situation for which the model specified by the equation system (1.1) is assumed to hold.

Suppose now that the objective or target of the central policy maker (the government) is to achieve a full-employment level of national income Y^*, which is assumed to be a fixed constant for this short-run model. The problem is to select the level of government expenditure G in such a way that the target Y^* is attained. Since the target variable here is a fixed constant, it is purely a translation factor and does not complicate the solution of the system. Hence, there is no loss of generality in assuming Y^* to be zero and rewriting the final equation of the system (1.1) in terms of deviations $y = Y - Y^* = Y$ as

$$dy/dt = - s\lambda y + \lambda G. \qquad (1.2)$$

Our target now is to reach $y = 0$, i.e., zero deviation from the full-employment level, by an appropriate choice of the instrument variable G.

Three very simple types of linear decision rules have been suggested for this kind of economic policy model by Phillips and others, incorporating principles of automatic control from control system theory. These three decision rules or policies (which are by no means exhaustive) are:

$$\text{Proportional control:} \quad G = - f_p y,$$
$$\text{Integral control:} \quad G = - f_i \int y \, dt,$$
$$\text{Derivative control:} \quad G = - f_d (dy/dt),$$

where the f's are nonnegative constants.

For each of these very simple cases we can write the three complete solutions of the system (1.2) as follows):

$$\text{Proportional:} \quad y = y_0 \left[\exp \{ - \lambda t (s + f_p) \} \right],$$
$$\text{Integral:} \quad y = A_1 \exp (\mu_1 t) + A_2 \exp (\mu_2 t),$$
$$\text{Derivative:} \quad y = y_0 \exp \left[- s\lambda t / (1 + \lambda f_d) \right],$$

where y_0, A_1, A_2 are constants of integration and μ_1, μ_2, are the roots of the characteristic equation

$$\mu^2 + s\lambda\mu + \lambda f_i = 0.$$

The integral policy generally involves a second-order differential equation. Hence, aside from the effects of initial conditions, the time series of income y resulting from such a policy can be any one of the following: monotone equilibrating, cyclical equilibrating, cyclical with constant amplitude, cyclical explosive and monotonic explosive. By itself none of these five types of time series generated by the integral stabilization policy might be adequate. A more detailed analysis would be needed of the shocks and constraints underlying the system before policy decisions would be realistic. It would also be necessary even in the linear class of decision rules to consider in some cases a mixed policy combining the three types of rules we have mentioned.

Another kind of stabilization policy is the so-called "bang-bang" type of control in which G can take either of two values $\pm k$, where G is measured as a deviation from some desired value G^*. This is essentially the mechanism of a thermostat. There are other types of nonlinear control policies which have different types of stability over time. The desirability of a particular type of control policy depends on several properties, such as its stability, its flexibility and in some cases the ease with which it can be simulated for any large problem of the real world.

These different types of control policies show the need for specifying a preference function (or a *performance integral*, as it is called in the theory of control engineering) for ordering the efficiencies of alternative controls. And if the target $y=0$ for $t \geq 0$ cannot be attained precisely, to what sub-optimal levels can this target be approximated?

In actual economic systems the problems of optimal policy making are more complicated, first, because the equations (1) defining the economic system may contain random or stochastic elements and, second, because there may be lags between actual control (G) and the planned or potential control $(\bar{G})$, where the latter may be subject to upper and lower limits for each period of time. In a long-run model we must also introduce the condition that the target Y^* be not a fixed constant but a certain time function.

The net effect of all these real-world complications is that we have to supplement exact or deterministic models with the statistical aspects of estimation and the theories of decision functions and control techniques. However, we are writing as economists, and our criterion for applying such methods must be their demonstrated or expected usefulness in formulating or dealing with problems of economic policy.

We have tried to emphasize an operational approach in our presentation. In current economic literature the word "operationalization" has acquired two different meanings. In its *normative* sense, an operational model involves an optimal choice among a number of alternative combinations of the means or instrument variables. This requires that the relevant economic variables of the model must be quantitative and that the policy model must have one or more open ends or degrees of freedom. In its *positive* meaning an operational model need not necessarily have any "open ends" that may be useful for policy purposes, but it must be capable of being refuted. This criterion of refutability may be applied either to the model as a whole or to certain hypotheses derived therefrom.

In analyzing the logical basis of scientific inference, Karl Popper [8] has mentioned the criterion of falsifiability, which is more general in its philosophic content than the criterion of refutability. In his view a completely generalized model is not testable at all because it can never be falsified. This does not mean that a generalized model is not useful. So long as some basic hypotheses deduced from the completely generalized model are falsifiable on either economic, statistical or empirical grounds, the former may prove more useful than other specialized or partial models.

Although our operational approach is mainly oriented to the economic aspects of policy making, we are aware of the interdependence of other non-economic aspects of policy which must be considered as the implicit qualitative constraints of any economic policy system we analyze. This is very similar to the standpoint of Richard Stone [11], who has emphasized the common point felt by many:

> The model builder who wants to see his models put to practical use commits himself to a life of working with others. The idea that economic models can be useful is a comparatively new one and is resisted by many people from some vague apprehension that, once accepted, the models would begin to run their own lives.

Such apprehension has little foundation, in our opinion, so long as the models are explicitly stated, along with the data, assumptions and estimation procedures which would render the models reproducible and in some respects falsifiable. Far more dangerous to human freedoms are slogans, shibboleths and unanalyzed preconceptions about economic policy which are not quantified and tested against data.

REFERENCES

[1] Box, G. E. P., and Jenkins, G. M. "Some Statistical Aspects of Adaptive Optimization and Control," *Journal of Royal Statistical Society*, Series B, XXIV (1962), 297–343.

[2] Fox, K. A. *Econometric Analysis for Public Policy*. Ames: Iowa State University Press, 1958.

[3] Frisch, R. "From National Accounts to Macroeconomic Decision Models," in *Income and Wealth*, Series 4 (International Association for Research in Income and Wealth). Edited by Gilbert and Stone. London: Bowes and Bowes, 1955, 1–24.

[4] ——. "The Mathematical Structure of a Decision Model: The Oslo Submodel," *Metroeconomica*, VII (December, 1955), 111–136.

[5] HANSEN, B. *Economic Theory of Fiscal Policy*. Translated by P. Burke. Cambridge, Mass.: Harvard University Press, 1958.

[6] MARSCHAK, J. "Economic Measurements for Policy and Prediction," in *Studies in Econometric Method* (Cowles Commission for Research in Economics, Monograph 14). Edited by W. C. Hood and T. C. Koopmans. New York: John Wiley & Sons, 1953.

[7] PHILLIPS, A. W. "Stabilization Policy in a Closed Economy," *Economic Journal*, LXIV (June, 1954), 290–323.

[8] POPPER, K. *The Logic of Scientific Discovery*. Revised edition. Hutchinson, London: 1961.

[9] PONTRYAGIN, L. S., *et al. The Mathematical Theory of Optimal Processes*. Translated from Russian. New York: Interscience, 1962.

[10] SCHOUTEN, D. B. J., and LIPS, J. "National Accounts and Policy Models," in *Income and Wealth*, Series 4 (International Association for Research in Income and Wealth) Edited by Gilbert and Stone. London: Bowes and Bowes, 1955, 78–89.

[11] STONE, R. "Models of the National Economy for Planning Purposes," *Operational Research Quarterly*, XIV (1963), 51–59.

[12] TINBERGEN, J. *On the Theory of Economic Policy*. Amsterdam: North-Holland Publishing Co., 1952; revised edition, 1955.

Chapter 2

TINBERGEN'S APPROACH TO THE THEORY OF ECONOMIC POLICY AND ITS GENERALIZATIONS

2.1. A General Outline

The theory of economic policy developed by Tinbergen can be simply presented and analyzed in two interrelated parts: First, in terms of the logic of his operational approach, and second, in terms of the technical problems which arise in applying his approach. Tinbergen has emphasized a pragmatic and sometimes *ad hoc* attitude in specifying the logical structure of a "quantitative policy" model. He separates "quantitative policy" sharply, at least for theoretical analysis, from "qualitative policy," such as the nationalization of an industry or the creation of a monopoly where a competitive market existed before. Mathematically, of course, this distinction is important, because ordinary difference or differential equation systems cannot very easily incorporate perturbations which are large.

Similarly, in the classification of variables into targets and instruments he has emphasized a practical approach depending on the judgments of the technical experts and the policy maker. One consequence of this is that linearizations have frequently been advocated to facilitate the understanding of the interrelationships of a policy model. Carried to its logical conclusion, this tendency leads to the application of simulation techniques and heuristic methods to very complicated situations.

The three basic ingredients of his quantitative economic policy model are as follows; a welfare function W of the policy maker, which is a function of I target variables y_i and J instrument variables z_j; a quantitative empirical (econometric or otherwise) model M, which sets up a statistical or empirical relationship essentially between the I target variables and the J instrument variables, and a set of boundary conditions or constraints on the target, the irrelevant and the instrument variables. The policy model may be a fixed target or a flexible target model; in the former, W contains fixed target values, but in the latter, such target values are chosen as optimize (maximize or minimize) the welfare function W.

The model M specifies the set of quantitative relations (or equations or inequalities) between the variables. Such relations in their "original form," as distinct from the "reduced form," are called structural relations, and their coefficients are called structural coefficients. These structural relations may be divided into three groups; behavioristic, technical and definitional. The most important equations are the behavioristic ones, which contain essentially quantitative theories and hypotheses about empirical economic behavior, for example demand or supply relations or the reactions of economic groups to risk and uncertainty.

The variables of the model M, which may be discrete or continuous but "measurable" in the sense of measure theory, may be classified into four different types, the "target" variables (y_i), which are to be purposefully (though indirectly) influenced by the policy maker; the "instrument" variables (z_j), which are the means available to the policy maker; the "data" (u_k), which are not subject to control by the policy maker, and the "irrelevant" variables (x_s), which are the side effects in which the policy maker is not interested.

If for *ad hoc* reasons we regard some economic variables (x_s) as irrelevant for a given policy decision, we can in most cases eliminate them from a complete model by algebraic means, leaving a set of equations containing

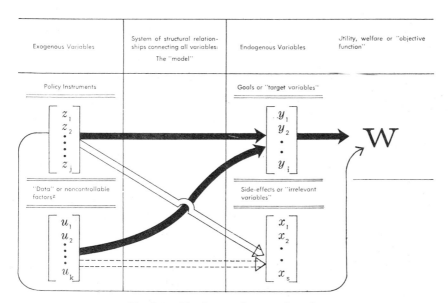

Fig. 2.1.   The theory of economic policy

only policy instruments and targets (plus the effects of strictly noncontrollable variables). Figure 2.1 may help to clarify the classification of variables in the Tinbergen-type policy model. The random components of the policy model are not explicit in the diagram. Furthermore, the light arrow running from the instrument vector to the welfare function W probably understates the importance of this connection because a cost imputation on the basis of either shadow prices or direct monetary expenditure can in most cases be made for the instrument variables used by a policy maker. In any case, the welfare function W can incorporate as elements instrument variables in addition to the target variables as such.

There are two useful ways of looking at these different variables of economic policy. From the standpoint of econometric theory, the "endogenous" variables comprise the targets and the irrelevant variables, while the "exogenous" variables comprise the instrument variables and the "data." Thus the unknowns are the endogenous variables, whose values are to be estimated from known values of the exogenous variables. In the theory of economic policy, however, the unknowns of the problem are the instrument variables and the irrelevant variables, whereas the knowns are the targets and the data.

One consequence of this difference in standpoint is best understood in terms of the concept of consistency in the policy sense as distinct from an equational sense. Suppose the policy model consists of N independent structural equations which contain I target variables, J instruments, K data (or noncontrollable) variables and S irrelevant variables. *Equational* consistency requires that the total number of endogenous variables (i.e., dependent or unknown variables) should equal the number of independent structural equations, i.e., $N = I + S$. Consistency in the policy sense, for a *fixed target* policy model, requires that the number of instrument variables should equal that of the targets, i.e., $J = I$. By combining these we get $J + S = N$, which gives us the necessary condition to solve for all the unknowns of our policy problem.

We must note that for a *flexible target* policy model it is not necessary to satisfy the consistency condition $J = I$. It is also necessary to emphasize here that *statistical* consistency requires a different condition, i.e., that the vector of instruments tend asymptotically to approach (a linear function of) the vector of targets in a large sample sense.

Similarly, we must distinguish between different uses of the concept of *degrees of freedom*. In a policy model, the term "degrees of freedom" refers to the excess (if any) of the number of instrument variables over the number of targets, i.e., $J > I$. In the mathematical sense, degrees of freedom refers to the excess (if any) of the number of endogenous variables over the number of equations, i.e., $I + S > N$. *Statistical* degrees of freedom in this context would refer to the number of independent sample observations (minus the number of coefficients estimated directly from the sample) on the basis of which we state the probabilistic convergence of the instrument vector z to the target vector y.

Following Frisch, we may further add the concept of "functional" degrees of freedom to the economic policy model, which specifies the extent to which the functional forms of structural equations are allowed to vary and, hence, the extent to which the optimum solutions of a policy model are sensitive or "robust." In a dynamic policy model where even the constraints or boundary conditions may be time-differential constraints and the preference function may be an integral over time, such questions of sensitivity of solutions would be fundamental. In the theory of control engineering a very detailed attempt is made to apply Lyapunov conditions and other theorems (discussed in Chapter 8) to test the robustness and stability of the time paths of the control vector when the latter is nonlinear and complicated.

Assuming linearity and eliminating the vector (x) of irrelevant variables, an economic policy model may be very simply specified in terms of three systems of equations:

$$\text{Optimize } W = a'y + b'z \text{ (preference function)} \qquad (2.1)$$

under the conditions

$$Ay = Bz + Cu \text{ (the model } M), \quad \text{and} \qquad (2.2)$$

$$\begin{cases} y_{min} \leq y \leq y_{max} \\ z_{min} \leq z \leq z_{max} \end{cases} \text{(boundary conditions)}, \qquad (2.3)$$

where A, B and C are matrices of coefficients of appropriate orders and y, z and u are appropriate column vectors of targets, instruments and data. If the matrix A is square and nonsingular, the "reduced form" of the model M in (2.2) can be obtained by multiplying both sides of equation (2.2) by the inverse of A:

$$y = (A^{-1}B)z + (A^{-1}C)u. \qquad (2.2.1)$$

For purposes of statistical estimation of the structural coefficients, the reduced-form equations (2.2.1) play a fundamental role, because (in some cases to be discussed later) least-squares theory can be very easily applied to the reduced form but not to the original system (2.2).

Since for the policy problem our unknown is the vector z of instruments, we solve for z from equation (2.2);

$$Bz = Ay - Cu. \qquad (2.2.2)$$

If the matrix B has constant elements and is square and nonsingular, the inverse of B exists and hence the vector of instruments z can be uniquely solved from equation (2.2.2) by premultiplying both sides by B^{-1}, i.e.,

$$z = (B^{-1}A)y - (B^{-1}C)u = Gy + Hu. \qquad (2.2.3)$$

The nature of the dependence of z upon y is associated with different types of structures [34, Chapter 4] of the matrices B and A:

(i)   If B and A are strictly *diagonal* matrices, then to each target there corresponds one and only one instrument and vice versa. There is no simultaneity in the relationship between the instruments and the targets. The practical implication would be that the policy maker could pursue each target with a single highly specific instrument. Or, he could afford to assign responsibility for each target and its unique instrument to a different cabinet officer or agency head without providing any mechanism for coordination or even communication among these officials!

(ii) If the matrices B and A are strictly *triangular* and of similar dimensionality, the policy model given by equation (2.2.2) is called recursive (or correspondingly consecutive). In this case we have a "pure causal chain" model, to use a concept developed by Wold [40] in his theory of estimation. The two-way simultaneity of relations between the vectors z and y (i.e., z affecting y and y affecting z) can be reduced to a unilateral dependence.

We must emphasize that z and y are *vectors*:

$$z = \begin{bmatrix} z_1 \\ z_2 \\ \cdot \\ \cdot \\ z_j \end{bmatrix}, \qquad y = \begin{bmatrix} y_1 \\ y_2 \\ \cdot \\ \cdot \\ y_i \end{bmatrix}.$$

Even if most of the z_j's were unilaterally dependent on certain of the y_i's, the *vectors* z and y would be interdependent (or show two-way simultaneity) if any one (or more) of the y_i's depended on one or more of the z_j's.

If the matrices A and B are strictly triangular, the first element z_1 of the vector z will depend only on the single element y_1 of vector y and other data (u). The second element z_2 will depend on z_1, y_1, y_2 and other data, but since z_1 has already been solved in terms of y_1, we have z_2 depending only on y_1, y_2 and other data. Similarly, the third element z_3 will depend finally on y_1, y_2, y_3, and not on any y_i higher than $i = 3$. Apart from the advantages of this pattern for statistical estimation, such a strictly recursive model allows a very simple policy interpretation. Specifically, if each equation were assigned to a different policy maker, the system of equations would specify a hierarchy such that a policy maker in a given position need not look at the instruments selected by those who are *below* his position in the hierarchy of equations in order to determine his own optimal policy.

(iii) If many of the elements of the matrices B and A are not different from zero (which sometimes occurs in practice in input-output models and in investment planning) [4], it may happen that such matrices are *quasi-diagonal* or *block-diagonal* rather than strictly diagonal. This means that each matrix contains square submatrices which, after appropriate arrangement of rows and columns, form blocks on the principal diagonal, the off-diagonal elements being zero.

In this case of a block-diagonal policy model, the over-all model could be split (or decomposed) into two or more independent parts depending on the number of blocks in the block-diagonal form. A centralized plan (model) could thus be decentralized into "relatively independent" subplans (submodels) which would permit efficient decentralized decision making.

(iv) Again, if the matrices B and A are *quasi-triangular* or *block-triangular*, i.e., triangular in blocks of submatrices, the set of instruments corresponding to any given block can be solved for without any knowledge of other instruments belonging to blocks which are *lower* in the hierarchy. In this case the over-all central plan (or model) could be split into separate "unilaterally dependent" plans (or models). Detailed examples of these types will be found in later chapters.

For clarity of exposition, we have presented these four kinds of matrix structures as pure cases. As will be shown later, some very practical policy models or submodels do indeed appear to be strictly triangular or block-triangular. In other cases, a few nonzero elements (or, in a very large model, blocks of elements) appear above the diagonal. This does not vitiate the insights and practical implications provided by the pure triangular cases, but it does require us to take cognizance of those specific elements of simultaneity which do exist in (1) solving for the instrument vector z and (2) providing for coordination not among *all* agency heads but among those in whose equations or blocks the interdependencies appear.

In each of the above cases we have assumed that the matrix B is non-singular. If so, the I target values y_i can be fixed arbitrarily and the solution in terms of z_j can be easily computed from (2.2.3). Suppose the number of targets equals the number of instruments $(I=J)$ but the matrix B is singular, i.e., its determinant is zero. Equational degrees of freedom now come into the picture.

As an example, suppose that at least one minor of the determinant of B is nonzero, although B is singular. This means that we can arbitrarily fix any finite values for the I targets and for any one of the J instruments. We say in this case that the equational system has $(I+1)$ degrees of freedom; the remaining instruments $(J-1)$ will have unique values. But if *all* the minors of the determinant of B are zero, we examine the minors of the subdeterminants of the original determinant of B. If at least one of them is nonzero, then we know that we have $(I+2)$ degrees of freedom, i.e., we can arbitrarily fix I targets and any two of the J instruments, but the remaining instruments will be uniquely determined. The procedure could be extended if need be to models having $(I+3)$ or more equational degrees of freedom.

So far we have assumed implicitly, if not explicitly, that we are discussing a fixed-target policy model; we may presume that some welfare function W lies behind the selection of target values, but W itself is not specified. In fact, however, a Tinbergen-type policy model may be fixed, flexible, random or mixed. In the *flexible* case we select the instruments to optimize the welfare function W (i.e., minimize or maximize values of some target variables) subject to the conditions of the model. In the *random* case we optimize the expected value (or some appropriate deterministic equivalent such as the variance or the probability that W takes a particular value or falls within a particular confidence interval) of the preference function. The randomness in the model may enter either through errors of statistical estimation of the model M from past observational data or because the targets set may have random components (or intervals within which random variation will be tolerated). A model is *mixed* when some targets are fixed, some are flexible and still others are random. Various other combinations are possible, e.g., some targets may be allowed to take only integral values, some may be continuous except at some "jump points," etc.

The boundary conditions indicated in equation (2.3) have three specific roles to play in the theory of economic policy: First, the error in specification of the model M is generally assumed to be a random term—a catch-all for everything important left out in specifying the model. Varying the end points of the boundary conditions has the effect of reducing some of the rigidity of the catch-all term. Second, the set of optimal solutions (i.e., optimal values of instruments) may be varied considerably from one subset to another by merely varying the boundary conditions, while the econometric model M remains unchanged. Third, for nonautonomous differential or difference equation models (i.e., when time t does not enter explicitly along with the vector functions dy/dt, dz/dt and y, z) the boundary conditions may be expressed as time-differential constraints, which allow the system to move as it were from one phase to another.

Last, but not least important, is the concept of "efficiency" used in the theory of economic policy [36]. This concept is applicable to a flexible target policy model and also to the random and mixed cases. Suppose for simplicity we write the welfare function W as a scalar function of the target variables, the instruments and random terms (v); that is, $W = W(y_1, y_2, ..., y_I; z_1, z_2, ..., z_J, v)$ after appropriate substitutions through the model. Then, assuming differentiability and other regularity conditions, we may state that the optimum set of instruments would be given by solving the following set of partial differential equations which are the necessary conditions for an extremum (optimum):

$$\frac{dW}{dz_j} = \sum_i \frac{\partial W}{\partial y_i} \cdot \frac{\partial y_i}{\partial z_j} + \frac{\partial W}{\partial z_j} = 0, \tag{2.4}$$

provided the random term v is identically zero and the second-order condition for a maximum or minimum is fulfilled. The term $(\partial y_i/\partial z_j)$ expresses the effectiveness of the instrument z_j in inducing a change in the value of the target y_i when all other instruments are kept constant. Hence, the term $\sum_i (\partial y_i/\partial z_j)$ expresses the sum of all "marginal" (i.e., partial) effects of a unit change in the given instrument z_j. The efficiency of the instrument z_j is specified by the term $\partial W/\partial z_j$ (and additionally by the second partial derivative), subject, of course, to the boundary constraints.

These efficiency indicators, which are partial measures of impact of the use of instruments, may be used to construct numerical tables to indicate the rates of substitution between different instruments. It should be noted that these indicators are not in terms of elasticities, hence comparisons of effectiveness of different instruments are not free from the units in which these instruments are measured.

When the vector of optimum instruments $z = z^*$ is finally computed, it is natural to expect that it will satisfy the efficiency requirement given in (2.4). However, if W is a nonmonotonic and nonlinear function, the condition may be satisfied only locally and not globally and hence we should distinguish between a locally efficient instrument vector z^* and a globally efficient instrument vector z^{**}. The difference between z^* and z^{**} may be eliminated through a trial and error process.

The concept of statistical efficiency arises when, due to the presence of the random term v in the welfare function W, we have to ask whether there exists a vector of instruments which *on the average* fulfills the condition $\partial W / \partial z_j = 0$ with minimum variance in a local sense, if not globally. Convergence in the mean square sense is implied in this statement.

2.2. Illustrative Examples

As a simple example let us consider a linear macroeconomic model[1] with two fixed targets: a given value of balance of payments ($B = B^*$) and a given volume of employment ($N = N^*$) and two instruments: government expenditure for consumption (G_c) and for investment (G_i). The model is

$$\text{Domestic output:} \quad Y = C + I + X + G_c + G_i \text{ (definition)},$$
$$\text{Imports:} \quad M = a_1 C + a_2 I + a_3 X + a_4 G_c + a_5 G_i$$
$$\text{(behavior equation)},$$
$$\text{Consumption:} \quad C = bY \text{ (behavior equation)},$$
$$\text{Employment:} \quad N = eY \text{ (technical relation)},$$
$$\text{Balance of payments:} \quad B = p_x X - p_m M \text{ (definition)}.$$

The boundary conditions on each of the variables are that they must belong to the real nonnegative interval $(0, \infty)$, which is closed at the left end but open at the right end. Here we have

$$\text{Endogenous variables:} \quad 5: \ Y, M, C, B, N,$$
$$\text{Exogenous variables:} \quad 4: \ I, X, G_c, G_i,$$
$$\text{Target variables:} \quad 2: \ B = B^*, N = N^*,$$
$$\text{Instrument variables:} \quad 2: \ G_i, G_c,$$
$$\text{Data variables:} \quad 2: \ I, X,$$
$$\text{Irrelevant variables:} \quad 3: \ Y, M, C.$$

After rearrangement of terms and appropriate substitution, we get

---

[1] This has been adapted from Theil [32].

$$N = N^* = b_1(I + X) + b_1 G_c + b_1 G_i,$$
$$B = B^* = p_x X - g_2 I - g_3 X - g_4 G_c - g_5 G_i, \tag{2.5}$$

where the constant coefficients are $b_1 = e/(1-b)$ and $g_i = p_m a_i + p_m a_1 b/(1-b)$ for $i = 2, 3, 4, 5$.

Since the data variables I, X are not controlled by the policy maker, they must be either forecast from past data (projected) or replaced by judgment estimates. We denote these values by I_0 and X_0. Substituting these known values in system (2.5), we can check the system for mathematical consistency in the sense of the existence of solutions. Since the number of targets equals the number of instruments in this case we can solve for "unique" values of the instruments G_i, G_c, if their coefficient matrix is nonsingular, i.e.,

$$\begin{bmatrix} G_i \\ G_c \end{bmatrix} = \begin{bmatrix} b_1 & b_1 \\ -g_4 & -g_5 \end{bmatrix}^{-1} \begin{bmatrix} N^* - b_1(I_0 + X_0) \\ B^* - (p_x - g_3)X_0 - g_2 I_0 \end{bmatrix}. \tag{2.6}$$

Suppose we reduce our two instruments to only one, i.e., $G = G_i + G_c$, by defining $a_4 = a_5$ and hence $g_4 = g_5$. We cannot now achieve the two arbitrarily fixed targets in general, because the system (2.5) now defines two equations in one unknown (G). However, if we reduce the two equations to one by defining $W = w_1 N + w_2 B$ where $W = W^*$ is the value of the fixed target, we again have consistency in the policy sense and under the usual regularity conditions the policy model can be solved. We note that the nonnegative weights w_1, w_2 specify the barter terms of trade between the two objectives N and B, which together specify the preference function of the policy maker. Further, it should be noted that a special case of the flexible policy model can be incorporated in the solution (2.6) of our policy model if we impose the condition that B^* must take the minimum possible value, zero.

Consider as a second example the two-sector model of development planning for India, which is formalized by Mahalanobis [25] and extended by a number of writers [31]. The planning model distinguishes two sectors, one producing investment goods (I_t) and the other consumption goods (C_t) on the assumption of a closed economy. The increase of real national output depends on the allocation of investment to each sector. The main policy problem is how to determine the optimal allocation of investment between the two sectors (the λ's being the investment allocation ratios) under alternative planning horizons and alternative sets of values of the output-capital coefficients (the B's).

The two-sector Mahalanobis model may be specified as

$$I_t = I_{t-1} + \lambda_i B_i I_{t-1},$$
$$C_t = C_{t-1} + \lambda_c B_c I_{t-1}, \qquad \lambda_i + \lambda_c = 1, \qquad (2.7)$$
$$Y_t = C_t + I_t.$$

This model can be applied to a fixed or flexible target policy problem. In the former case, for instance, the system would be solved in terms of the investment allocation ratios (the λ's, which are the instrument variables), given a fixed predetermined level of income at some future date. In this sense the problem reduces itself to a simple one-instrument one-fixed-target problem. (Even though there are two allocation ratios, there is only one effective instrument, since $\lambda_i + \lambda_c = 1$.)

Alternatively, if national income (Y) is a flexible target, the policy problem consists of maximizing Y, given a time horizon τ.

After solving the equations for consumption (C_t) and investment goods (I_t), the final income (Y_t) equation can be written as

$$Y_\tau = Y_0 + I_0 \left(\frac{\lambda_i B_i + \lambda_c B_c}{\lambda_i B_i} \right) [(1 + \lambda_i B_i)^\tau - 1] \qquad t = 0, 1, \ldots \tau. \qquad (2.8)$$

An optimal value of λ_i which would maximize Y_t for a given planning horizon can be easily computed from (2.8). With an estimate of the parameters $B_i = 0.2$ and $B_c = 0.3$, the value of the proportion of total investment to be allocated to the investment goods sector (λ_i) which maximizes income over a 15-year period (i.e. $\tau = 15$) is equal to one-third ($\lambda_i = 1/3$).

The Mahalanobis model and a four-sector version of it are further discussed in Chapter 9—in dynamic linear programming terms and in Chapters 10 and 13.

2.3. A Critical Appraisal of Tinbergen's Approach

Two types of generalization of the Tinbergen-type approach have been attempted in recent years. One is the generalization of estimation methods and forecasting techniques [33] so far as the economic model is concerned. Second, the empirical levels of application have been considerably widened to include different types of policy making agencies, in some of which the specification of the welfare function itself is a very difficult task and methods of heuristic programming and surrogates for uncertain decision problems have been suggested, e.g., the certainty equivalence theorem under a quadratic criterion function and the equivalence of certain nonlinear programming to some linear programming forms. However, in other areas of policy making considerable research has been done on methods of characterizing and incorporating various types of probability distributions which may generate risk and uncertainty, on the different types of stability of time paths of dynamic and stochastic control and on the basic interrelationship of control theory with information theory.

Broadly speaking, Tinbergen's approach to the theory of economic policy belongs to the *characterization* phase of the policy problem. Although he has made a number of suggestions concerning the organization, execution and supervision of (governmental) economic policy, e.g., emphasizing the needs for decentralization [38, Chapter 3] and accounting prices (shadow prices) and the process of planning by stages and approximations [37, Chapters 1, 8], he has not pushed very far the idea of relating and extending his theoretical apparatus to the *selection* and *steering* phases of the economic policy problem. His immediate responsibilities in the late 1940's and early 1950's as an economic adviser to government may be partly responsible for his pragmatic emphasis. This emphasis has certainly made the basic ideas of his theory of economic policy accessible at an early date to many economists in government agencies and (directly or indirectly) to many policy makers who would have been repelled by more rigorous and refined discussions of the selection and steering phases.

References to recent developments relevant to policy making in other contexts, such as business management decision making and inventory control, programming situations under uncertainty and parametric variations and learning models with adaptive control, are quite understandably absent from Tinbergen's cited works.

Arrow, in his review [3] of Tinbergen's approach to economic policy, emphasized that in the steering phase of the policy problem the sequential analysis of statistical data as more and more information is available and the designing of a flexible policy which has a learning process of adapting to changing circumstances assume a very critical role. It is already known from inventory theory that a policy which incorporates the future possibilities of learning (and adjustment) into account will be qualitatively different from one which neglects them.

There are many different ways of introducing the learning mechanism into a policy model; as a simple example, consider G_t as that part of total government expenditure (an instrument variable) which cannot be explained by time trend or any other systematic factors, and let $\bar{G}_t$ be the forecast of G_t on the basis of information available through the $(t-1)$st period. A simple learning mechanism would be to change the forecast values from one period to the next by an amount proportional to the latest observed error, i.e.,

$$\bar{G}_t = \bar{G}_{t-1} + r(G_{t-1} - \bar{G}_{t-1}), \qquad 0 \le r < 1.$$

(Its similarity with the proportional control mechanism discussed in Chapter 1 may be noted.)

A second important point regarding the quantitative approach of Tinbergen is that it does not go very deeply into the why and how of the specification of the preference function in its alternative parametric forms or of the classification of variables into targets and instruments. The economic justification of governmental policy as a balancing factor (or otherwise) to the free-market system is never detailed, nor are the interactions between the public and the private sectors which may have some common and some conflicting objectives.

As Arrow has pointed out in his review, Tinbergen does not take much account of the two classic justifications of welfare economics for government interference: economies of scale and the absence of markets to mediate external effects in certain areas. The former leads to the questions of natural monopolies which may be met by nationalization. This leads into the whole area of evaluating products of nationalized enterprise which has occupied a prominent role in the theoretical literature of welfare economics and some, particularly among the French writers such as Massé, Boiteux and Allais, on the practical side. To what extent may the presence of external economies and indivisibility affect the characterization of a policy model involving investment decisions? To what extent could the optimization of a nonscalar (i.e., vector) welfare function be introduced to analyze the multidimensional facets of a multivariable dynamic system? These are very basic questions which are not pushed very far.

One of the reasons for this may be the exclusion of qualitative policy, where the institutional structure and the techniques of economic control are themselves changed either discretely or continuously over time. Some changes in policy do not involve drastic reforms of the fundamental economic order but do involve a switchover, e.g., from one type of taxation scheme to another or one type of technique of production to another, within the existing institutional framework. The analytical framework of the policy model is not extended to include such very important changes.

Recent researches into the theory and application of control techniques have emphasized in this context the methods of evolutionary (or nonstationary) control with changing means and variances over time (e.g., the problem of switchover and changing regimes from one phase to another). To indicate the sequential nature of the method of evolutionary control, consider a simple situation in which the statistical data are available at discrete but equal time intervals (e.g., quarterly), a fixed number of intervals being called a phase. We suppose further that the situation remains constant during a phase but may change from one phase to another. We denote the instrument vector used in the k-th phase by $z(k)$. Now suppose the desired level of welfare W^* is given, as well as the statistical data acquired during the k-th and previous phases. The question is how best to change the control variables from $z(k)$ to $z(k+1)$ so that the loss during the $(k+1)$-th phase is minimized. One solution is that we estimate from our past data, both actual and predicted, the optimum value of the instrument vector to be expected in the $(k+1)$-th phase and then set $z(k+1)$ equal to it. In this case it is largely a problem of efficient prediction.

2.4. Technical Appraisal

From a technical standpoint the theoretical framework developed by Tinbergen is not complete without a study of the decision rules it might lead to under conditions of risk and uncertainty. Improved methods of statistical estimation of the model part (M) are now available, but to some extent these methods may not be very appropriate in those applications of an economic policy model where the boundary conditions are binding and they are changed from the observation period to the period during which the policy model would apply.

We note that this general framework leads to a statistical (or stochastic) programming problem because the error of estimation of the economic model introduces risk and uncertainty in the decision-making process and the additional boundary conditions on the instrument and target variables impose a programming structure. There are different methods of solving such policy problems of programming under risk and uncertainty (which will be discussed later). However, to indicate how the Tinbergen-type policy framework would look, we might consider here one method of approach which is based on the ideas of sampling theory.

Maxime

$$W = W(y, z), \tag{2.8}$$

subject to

$$Ay \leq Bz + Cu,$$
$$y_{min} \leq y \leq y_{max}; \qquad z_{min} \leq z \leq z_{max}.$$

We assume that the coefficient matrices A, B and C have random components, and we have sample observations for the triplet (A, B, C), where altogether we have N observations. For each observed sample value of the triplet (A, B, C) we compute (max W) which is assumed to be bounded and finite. Hence, we obtain N values of max W, which we denote as $(\max W)_n$, $n = 1, 2, ..., N$ and then derive a probability distribution based on these maximum values.

There are different lines of action possible. One may be to consider the expected value (95 per cent confidence interval or any other characteristic, depending on the nature of each specific problem) of the probability distribution. Other lines of action would be to consider some specific feasible pairs of (y, z) and consider the probability distribution of (max W) for each fixed pair. Then, on comparing the different probability distributions for different pairs, one might select the one which is in some sense the best according to a given risk-ordering principle.

A more basic question raised by the theory of general economic policy which is not concerned with very specific targets and like situations, as in Tinbergen, is the specification of preference functions consistent with "efficient" activities of an economic organization which may be centralized, decentralized or of varying degrees of centralization. The advantages of a decentralized solution (e.g., informational autonomy, computational efficiency, efficient division of functions between the central agency and the decentralized units, etc.), as against the centralized one, have been recently shown to be derived from the precise "adjustment rules" of the decentralized system which guarantee convergence to the desired equilibrium point. Considering differential equation systems to specify time paths of the variables $q_1, q_2, ..., q_n$ (activity levels which may be either instruments or targets) and their shadow prices $p_1, p_2, ..., p_m$ $(m \leq n)$, assume that the solution of a decentralized economic system (e.g., a decentralized firm) converges to a value $Q = (q_1, q_2, ..., q_n)$, which maximizes a profitlike scalar function, $f(Q)$ say, subject to some constraints $q_i \geq 0, i = 1, ..., n$ and $g_j(Q) \geq 0, p_j \geq 0, j = 1, 2, ..., m$. Then it is known that [26] if f and g_j are concave, a decentralized system would converge to a desired equilibrium point from any nontrivial initial point and this would be equivalent to a system converging to the saddle point of the function

$$F = f + \sum_{j=1}^{m} p_j g_j$$

where the saddle point maximizes the function F with respect to vector Q

and minimizes it with respect to the price vector $p = (p_1, ..., p_m)$ under the constraints of the decentralized system [6].

We may also note that the steering problem, which is less emphasized in the development of the Tinbergen-type theory of economic policy, is very closely related to the selection phase of the economic policy problem, e.g., it is concerned with specific problems of ensuring the convergence of the actual instrument (control) variable $z(t)$ and the optimal one $z^*(t)$ (say) by specifying, for example, criteria of control inaccuracy, by analyzing the probability-generating mechanism with new information becoming available and by studying the alternative ways of decomposing [7] an over-all model so as to permit efficiency in decentralized decision making. From the last-mentioned standpoint we might refer to Frisch, who in his 64-equation Oslo model (with 14 degrees of freedom) has constructed three hierarchic systems of possibilities arranged in decreasing order with respect to the amount of direct controls required by the government.

Another example would be how to define the best decision rule over time in a dynamic probabilistic model, where a number of alternative deterministic equivalents (e.g., mean, median, max probability, etc.) could be constructed and a reliability analysis (e.g., analysis of errors and control inaccuracy) needs to be performed. We may also mention here the basic problems of representation of the conflict between static and dynamic objectives (e.g., short-run stability and long-run growth) in the preference function, the apparent asymmetry in imputing weights to the target and instrument variables in the preference function and even the effects of truncating the planning horizon of the policy maker.

2.5. Generalizations of Tinbergen's Approach to Economic Policy

Two of the fundamental concepts in Tinbergen's approach to the theory of economic policy, which need to be generalized for both theoretical and practical purposes, are the concept of "independence" of the target and the instrument vectors and the concept of "optimality" implied by solving the system for a given welfare function.

The concept of interindependence of the targets in a given fixed policy model which is consistent in the policy sense has the important practical implication that it shows the condition under which policy solutions may be unique, in either a linear or a nonlinear model. To this extent the apparent inconsistency in setting nonindependent targets (and/or nonindependent instruments) by the policy maker may be easily identified and, if necessary, modified. It may also show that in certain situations when the statistical estimates of the parametric coefficients in a policy model lead to a non-independent set of targets we have to modify some of the statistical estimates in order to secure uniqueness of policy solutions.

Consider the matrix equation of a fixed target linear policy model M containing the instruments z_j, the targets y_i and the data u_k,

$$Bz = Ay - Cu. \tag{2.9}$$

We define the augmented matrix (B_1) associated with the coefficient matrix (B) of our unknown instrument vector (z) as

$$B_1 = [B \vdots Ay - Cu],$$

where y takes any arbitrary set of fixed values. Similarly, we can define the augmented matrix (A_1) associated with the coefficient matrix (A) of the target vector y as

$$A_1 = [A \vdots Bz + Cu],$$

where z is assumed to take a fixed set of values as in economic theory. A necessary and sufficient condition that none of the individual equations of system (2.9) are contradictory or incompatible to one another is stated by the following Kronecker-Capelli theorem.

Theorem A. Given the system (2.9), there must exist a solution for z, unique or otherwise, if and only if the rank of B equals that of B_1. Similarly, a necessary and sufficient condition that y could be solved, either uniquely or otherwise, for a given set of z and u values, is that the rank of A equals that of A_1.[2]

An important corollary of this theorem is that if B and A are square matrices of full rank and so B^{-1} and A^{-1} (i.e., their inverses) exist uniquely, the system (2.9) is necessarily compatible or solvable for either z or y.

Suppose that the number of targets (I) equals that of instruments (J) and so $i, j = 1, 2, 3, ..., N$ where $I = J = N$ (i.e., the model (2.9) is consistent in the policy sense) and further the matrices A and B are square matrices of order N. If y is given, a fixed set of values denoted by y^0 and B^{-1} exists; it is then obvious from the system (2.9) that the instrument vector z could be *uniquely* solved as

$$z = B^{-1}Ay^0 - B^{-1}Cu. \tag{2.10}$$

---

[2] For proof, see Aitken [1] and Hohn [16].

Similarly, if z is assigned a fixed set of values denoted by z^0 and A^{-1} exists, the target vector y can be *uniquely* solved as

$$y = A^{-1}Bz^0 + A^{-1}Cu. \tag{2.11}$$

If both the equations (2.10) and (2.11) hold simultaneously it is obvious that there is a one-to-one mapping of the vectors z and y, i.e., given any fixed set of y_i we can uniquely (one and only one way) determine another set of z_j and conversely (for $i, j = 1, 2, ..., N$). In this case the target vector and the instrument vector are both said to be *independent*. If B^{-1} exists but A is singular (i.e., A^{-1} does not exist), the instruments z_j $(j = 1, 2, ..., N)$ are all independent (i.e., unique) but not the targets. Similarly, if B is singular but A is nonsingular, it follows from (2.11) that the targets y_i $(i = 1, 2, ..., N)$ are mutually independent (i.e., unique) but not the instruments. This result is perfectly general and can be applied to any system linear or nonlinear. Hence, we state the following theorem of Jacobi[3] for any given system of implicit equations.

Theorem B. If the N implicit equations

$$f_n(z_1, z_2, ..., z_j; \quad y_1, y_2, ..., y_i; \quad u_1, ..., u_k) = 0,$$
$$i - 1, 2, ..., N,$$
$$j = 1, 2, ..., N \quad \text{and} \quad I = J = N,$$
$$n = 1, 2, ..., N,$$

are such that the functions f_n are real single-valued analytic functions of the instrument variables z_j and the target variables y_i and that the Jacobians of f_n with respect to z_j and y_i (i.e., the determinants below) are denoted, respectively, by G and H

$$G = \left| \frac{\partial (f_1, f_2, ..., f_N)}{\partial (z_1, z_2, \quad , z_N)} \right|,$$

$$H = \left| \frac{\partial (f_1, f_2, ..., f_N)}{\partial (y_1, y_2, ..., y_N)} \right|,$$

both the instrument vector z and the target vector y will be independent and unique (i.e., the N functions f_n will be independent) in a certain domain, if and only if the Jacobians G and H exist (are nonsingular) for that domain and the product GH equals unity. If only the Jacobian G exists (i.e., G being nonsingular) but not H, only the instruments are independent but not the

---

[3] For proof, see Frazer, Duncan and Collar [10].

targets. Similarly, if only a nonsingular H exists (but not a nonsingular G), the targets alone are independent (but not the instruments).

It is easy to check the validity of this theorem in the special case of a linear model when equations (2.10) and (2.11) above hold simultaneously. In that case $G=|B^{-1}A|$ and $H=|A^{-1}B|$ and, hence, GH equals $|B^{-1}AA^{-1}B|=|I|=1$, where $I=$ identity matrix. An important corollary of this result is that there is a unique transformation (mapping) from the N-tuple vector $(z_1, z_2, ..., z_N)$ to the vector $(y_1, y_2, ..., y_N)$. In this situation the contrast between the unknowns and the knowns in the policy sense and in the sense of traditional economic theory vanishes.

This theorem is also applicable when the functions f_n are functions of variables z_j and y_i, where some of these z_j's and y_i's are themselves time derivatives of other static variables, but in this case the domain of applicability may be somewhat restrictive [20].

It may sometimes happen in the policy application and implementation phase that some of the instruments which were previously directly under the control of the policy maker are no longer controllable and become targets. Similarly, some targets may be converted into instrument variables depending on the controllability factor (e.g., the wage rate as a target variable may turn into an instrument variable for the government as a policy maker when a direct wage control is introduced). Our next theorem states the condition under which all solutions of the linear policy model would be unique against all interchanges of targets into instruments or instruments into targets.

Theorem C. For a given linear fixed-target model, consistent in the policy sense

$$Bz + Ay + Cu = 0 \qquad (i,j = 1, 2, ..., N),$$

the solutions of unknowns (either in the policy sense z, or in the sense of usual economic theory y) will be unique for all interchanges between target variables and instrument variables, if and only if the following two conditions hold.

(i) The matrices B and A are nonsingular (consistence in the policy sense implies that B and A are square matrices), i.e., there are N linearly independent columns of B and A denoted by B_r and A_r ($r=1, 2, 3, ..., N$), respectively.

(ii) The independent columns of B and A are such that none of the columns of B (or A) could be expressed as a linear combination of less than N independent columns of A (or B).

Proof. For simplicity we give an outline of the proof for the case where

$N=3$, which can be easily extended to any arbitrary but finite N. Suppose z_1 is converted to y_1^o and y_1 is converted to z_1^o, where the superscript indicates the change in the status of the variable. If the z variables are the unknowns in the policy sense, the new coefficient matrix associated with (z_1^o, z_2, z_3) is

$$(A_1, B_2, B_3),$$

but since $A_1 = c_1 B_1 + c_2 B_2 + c_3 B_3$, where c_1, c_2, c_3 are arbitrary constants, none of which can be zero by our condition (ii), the rank of the matrix (A_1, B_2, B_3) equals the rank of the matrix (B_1, B_2, B_3) which is $N=3$, since a finite number of elementary transformations does not alter the rank of a matrix. Hence, (z_1^o, z_2, z_3) can be uniquely solved. Similarly, the uniqueness could be proved for the case where the y variables are the unknowns, as in a typical economic theory model where the intent is to explain the movements of the set of targets. The proof is similar in the general case when for any N any number of instruments and targets are interchanged.

Conversely, if for all possible interchanges of target and instrument variables the solutions are unique, any three ($N=3$) of the column vectors of the augmented coefficient matrix

$$(B_1, B_2, B_3, A_1, A_2, A_3)$$

must be nonsingular and of rank $N=3$. Hence, the conditions (i) and (ii) as stated in Theorem C follow.

Next, the principle of optimality underlying the Tinbergen approach is considered. Two of the basic questions in this connection are, first, the extent to which the welfare function can be endogenously derived from the specification of the model equation M, rather than arbitrarily specified by "imaginary interviewing" [39] of the policy maker, and second, the extent to which the planning horizon enters as an essential element in the specification of optimal paths in a dynamic model.

The welfare function (W) can be written as the following functional in a dynamic model

$$W = \int_0^T F(y, \dot{y}, z, \dot{z}, u, t)\, dt, \qquad (2.12)$$

defined over a certain planning horizon T. In equation (2.12) the function F is a scalar function of the instrument and the target vectors—(z) and (y), respectively—and their time derivatives denoted by dots. As an example we may assume the integrand F in (2.12) to be a simple quadratic function as before and specify the following generalized version of a simple Tinbergen-type policy model, consisting of one target and one instrument.

$$\text{Minimize } W = (2T)^{-1} \int_0^T a(t) \cdot [w_1(y_1 - y_1^*)^2 + w_2(z_1 - z_1^*)^2] \, dt \qquad (2.13)$$

subject to the model

$$\dot{y}_1 = -\lambda s y_1 + \lambda z_1 + c, \qquad (2.14)$$

where s, λ, c are assumed to be positive constants, c representing the exogenous data (as, for instance, the autonomous components of private consumption and investment demand), w_1, w_2 being nonnegative weight constants ($w_1 \neq 0$) and $a(t)$ being a time-discounting function. y_1^* and z_1^* are the desired values of the single instrument and the single target, which are assumed to be constant in this short-term stabilization policy model. Regarding the specifications (2.13) and (2.14), we may note two very basic differences of Tinbergen's approach from that followed in control system engineering. First, the control system theory, which basically employs the same type of equations as (2.13) and (2.14), interprets the performance integral (i.e., W) on a physical basis, depending on the physical characteristics described in the model equation (2.14). Second, since physical experiments can be conducted to see how far the performance integral is an accurate specification of the desired objective, the best alternative can be selected out of a set of different specifications of the performance integral, assuming that a large number of experiments could, in principle, be conducted. In other words, the performance integral can be endogenously specified in control system engineering (e.g., minimizing the integral of square of error, maximizing entropy, etc.) such that the weights w_1, w_2 in (2.13) can be changed in an adaptive way according to whether high, medium or low values of the plant coefficients s, λ are considered. The usual definition of an adaptive control policy, as distinct from a nonadaptive control, has three basic characteristics in control engineering terminology [2, 5].

(i)   Continuous measurement of the dynamic performance of the system when the latter is operating.

(ii) Means of converting this measure of performance into a number (i.e., a metric) that describes how good the performance is.

(iii) Readjustment of system control parameters on the basis of steps (i) and (ii).

2.6. Implications of Control Theory

Until very recently the theory of automatic control and servomechanism did not have the basic adaptive characteristics (ii) and (iii); instead, it relied on the analysis of dynamic stability properties of control policies determined on an *ad hoc* basis as were the proportional, integral and derivative policies. The recent advance of control system theory in the last half decade has emphasized, however, that the stability alone, which may be a necessary requirement of a good system design and for which the criteria of Routh, Hurwitz and Nyquist have been applied in linear and nonlinear servodesign theory, does not necessarily guarantee a suitable and optimum design. It has been increasingly stressed that an admissible control must have an optimizing character in some sense, e.g., minimizing the error of the system under control or satisfying certain specifications of accuracy and speed of performance of the system under control. For example, once we are given that the model in equation (2.14) specifies appropriately the dynamic response of a physical system except for an additive error term v on the right-hand side and assuming the error term v to have a zero mean, we can usually define an endogenous welfare function by observing how (v^2) changes with experiments. In that case (2.13) can be replaced by

$$\text{Minimize } W = \int_0^T E(v^2)\,dt, \tag{2.13.1}$$

where E is the expectation operator, when (2.14) is written as (2.14.1) $\dot{y}_1 = -s\lambda y_1 + \lambda z_1 + c + v$. Similarly, another very plausible performance integral which has a direct physical meaning is the concept of entropy (E_0) defined as

$$E_0 = -\int_0^T f(v) \log f(v)\,dv, \qquad 0 < v \le T, T \to \infty, \tag{2.13.2}$$

where $\log \int f(v) = 0$ by definition and $f(v)$ is the probability function of the random variable v. The optimal instrument z_1 in this case is given by that z_1^0 which maximizes E_0 in (2.13.2) subject to the dynamic model given in (2.14.1).

This does not mean, however, that control engineering has solved the problem of uniquely deriving a performance integral endogenously from the dynamic response equations of a system, although the experimental nature of physical systems has considerably narrowed the class of reasonable performance measures. The situation in nonlinear control systems which are probabilistic is still very complicated. To quote from a recent survey [30] in control system theory by Schultz and Rideout:

> The application of performance measures to adaptive systems increases the difficulty of choosing a performance measure. We must consciously think about measuring the performance of the chosen performance measure, and perhaps even consider mechanizing this second-order measure...
>
> All of this may seem discouraging to anyone seeking definite answers on performance measures. It seems apparent that there is no one magic formula, but that rather we are faced with a problem which is basically unanswerable. Nevertheless, engineers *must* choose performance measures, striving on the one hand to keep intuitive procedures from smotering the growth of more solidly based principles of measurement and yet attempting to keep mathematical complexity from hiding simple meanings.

One field of application in economic policy which would appear to lend itself to the use of performance measures of the above type is that of built-in stabilizers, as subsequently discussed.

2.7. Theoretical Approach in Control System Analysis

The recent development of the theory and application of control system engineering, to use the latter term in a very broad sense, may perhaps indicate several new lines of generalization of the Tinbergen approach to economic policy which are yet to be attempted.

One of the most interesting attempts in recent years has been to consider the various types of stability of control policies, especially in nonlinear models. The idea that control policy differs according to whether it is applied in a stable region of the state space or in an unstable region led to numerous theoretical and applied investigations about the qualitative theory of stability of differential equations. Specifically, the second method of Lyapunov [17] constructs a function, known as the Lyapnuov function, which is used to test the stability of behavior of solutions in an arbitrarily small region of the state space about the equilibrium position.[4] This result has been extended to control policies which include large deviations from equilibrium by means of the "canonic transformation" of the original dynamic system [17]. On the practical side, the theory of optimal nonlinear control led to the development of simulation (and numerical) methods to analyze the implications of control

---

[4] For definition, see Chapter 8.

policies in different regions of the state space of unequal degrees of stability. As an economic attempt in this line, one may refer to the stabilization policy model used for simulating the U.S. economy during the last recession [9]. The performance of the existing built-in stabilizers (such as progressive personal income taxes and unemployment compensation) in dampening the effects of (simulated) recessions of different degrees of severity was tested with the help of an econometric model describing the behavior of the U.S. economy in a recession setting.[5]

The second important line of work is in the area of optimal stochastic control, by assuming various types of probability structure of the error in the system design [24]. The recent emphasis is to introduce considerations of evolutionary stochastic processes of different types and analyze the reliability or effectiveness of alternative control policies in terms of their failure pattern or observed inaccuracy. As a natural consequence this has led to the application of statistical decision function ideas and information theory in the area of control system analysis and application.

The mathematical basis of the characterization of the optimum systems in control theory has been considerably generalized and unified through the development of Pontryagin's maximum principle, discussed in Chapter 8, the extension of variational calculus in terms of Bellman's functional equation technique and the application of singular optimal-control policies in nonlinear problems. However, the application of dynamic nonlinear programming is limited to economic problems of small dimensionality.

The most striking feature of these new developments in control system theory is its taxonomic and, hence, operational approach, especially in characterizing the different types of probability-generating mechanisms. The theory of economic policy is yet to develop to its fullest extent this taxonomic idea in its different manifestations.

2.8. Taxonomic Approach and Its Critiques

From a methodological viewpoint, Tinbergen's approach to economic policy, characterized by its numerous applications to different specific economic situations, raises two fundamental questions: (1) the extent to which the classification of variables into targets and instruments is absolute and (2) the extent to which the taxonomic approach limits the development of fruitful new hypotheses of greater generality. The first question is directly

---

[5] For a further discussion of this study, see Chapter 9 and, more specifically, Table 9.2.

related to the dichotomy in standpoints in the means-ends controversy between Robbins and Myrdal. With Robbins, the "ends" (targets) are given magnitudes and the social welfare function is a function only of ends (targets); the "means" (instruments), on the other hand, have no value connotations per se, and the role of the economist as a social scientist is limited to specifying the number of alternative combinations of means (and their consequences) to achieve the given ends [29]. Myrdal's position [27] in the means-ends continuum is that means are not always "neutral," i.e., free from value judgments, and, hence, means and ends may not be actually separable ("programs and prognosis are inseparable just as the physicist's case of the observer being affected by the thing observed"), and, further, that ends themselves change over time from empirical appraisal and prognosis of events, a fact which is not specifically considered by modern welfare economics in both its Paretian and Bergsonian versions.

Tinbergen's position in this controversy may be characterized as essentially pragmatic and operational. The differences in the above viewpoints appear to be related to the following factors: (1) A social welfare function may be very difficult to specify uniquely and unequivocally; (2) certain variables, either the instruments or targets, may not be quantifiable (e.g., they may contain value connotations which are not expressed in market categories) and, last but not the least important, (3) due to limitations of statistical data and other related empirical knowledge it may be difficult to discriminate between alternative model specifications for the same economic reality. It is possible, if not likely, that some targets may themselves be means to higher level targets, as in a hierarchy, but this may require, according to Tinbergen and Frisch, only different submodels related by an over-all general model.[6] Flexibility and the possible revision of the specifications of a policy model with increasing information have always been emphasized by the strictly operational attitude of Tinbergen. Thus, the inseparability of ends (targets) and means (instruments), if it is not due to inadequate disaggregation and nonquantifiable elements of measurement, can always be reduced if not eliminated altogether. For concrete and specific economic problems which do not involve very directly the fundamental social and philosophical ends, this operational approach is perhaps the most useful one insofar as practical questions of decision making are concerned (e.g., management decisions, area development, etc.).

A somewhat different line of criticism is that the approach of Tinbergen

---

[6] See Chapters 10 and 13 for a more detailed discussion and examples of this question.

is taxonomic, which implies at least three different characteristics basically different from, if not opposed to, the positive approach to economic theory. The three characteristics of a taxonomic approach are:

(i) A specific classification of variables, such as between the targets and instruments in Tinbergen, or endogenous, exogenous and predetermined in the Cowles Commission approach, the optimal solution (or optimal policy) depending on the particular classification scheme adopted.

(ii) A specification of a model in an *ad hoc* way, such that the model has a number of equations which are normative and not positivistic. The normative aspect is introduced in a taxonomic approach either through an *ad hoc* welfare function which is not in general endogenous or through a particular behavior equation in a model M. As an example of the latter case, consider the following Keynesian model, where an explicit consumption function is lacking:

$$Y = aK + bL,$$
$$L = L_0 \exp(nt), \qquad (2.15)$$
$$Y = C + I = C + dK/dt.$$

We can now either introduce a positive consumption function $C=f(Y)$ or derive a normative consumption function C^0 by imposing, for example, the following optimizing objective.

$$\text{Maximize} \left[\int_{t_1}^{t_2} \log C \, dt \right]; \qquad C > C_0, \qquad (2.16)$$

$C_0 = $ Minimum social level of consumption

subject to the model (2.15).

Denoting Y^0 as the optimal income path satisfying (2.16), the normative consumption-income relation can be derived by the Euler-Lagrange method as:

$$(Y^0/C^0) = (B/A - at) + (L_0 bn/A(n-a)) \exp((n-a)t) \qquad (2.17)$$

where A and B are two independent constants of integration.

In general, this normative path would be different from the observed consumption path.

(iii) A third characteristic of the taxonomic approach is the inadequate emphasis on the predictive quality of a policy model, since the normative relationships may not be empirically refutable (or "falsifiable," a concept due to K. Popper). In other words, if the realism of the assumptions made in constructing a normative policy model is emphasized at the expense of judging the predictive power of a model, this may be a serious stumbling block to the process of continuous interaction between the observed universe and hypothesis formulation and modification (i.e., theory), which is so essential for the development of new knowledge and scientific discovery as exemplified by the history of progress of physical and natural sciences. According to Friedman [11]:

the ultimate goal of a positive science is the development of a "theory" or "hypothesis" that yields valid and meaningful (i.e., not truistic) predictions about phenomena not yet observed ... (page 7) ...

The relevant question to ask about the "assumptions" of a theory is not whether they are descriptively "realistic" for they never are, but whether they are sufficiently good approximations for the purpose in hand. This can be seen by working out whether the theory yields sufficiently accurate predictions. (page 15)

A similar viewpoint is upheld by Johnson [18], another opponent of the taxonomic approach.

Referring to the distinction we have drawn between economic theory and the theory of economic policy in Chapter 1 and the proof of Theorem C above, it is apparent that the classification scheme (i.e., taxonomy) in a policy model has a definite role to play. In many respects it is similar to the classification scheme adopted in other applied branches like control engineering, servomechanism and cybernetics and even electrical network analysis. It may be possible to prove some "invariant" relations between the known and unknown variables[7] which are independent of a particular taxonomic classification, but this does not mean that we can determine optimal decision rules in specific operational situations of decision making without classifying variables according to their domain of controllability. As A.C.L. Day [8, pp. 70–71] has pointed out:

The difficulty [about using a model in policy analysis] ... is that many different relationships may conceivably be regarded as important in economic analysis, and it is very difficult to check how important they are and how serious would be the shortcomings of a model as a basis for analysis of real problems if a particular relationship were omitted.

The first stage in which taxonomy can be useful in economics is, therefore, at the stage of pure theory: the stage at which hypotheses are set up .... Only very broadly ... can the economist test directly

---

[7] For example, Theorem C and the certainty equivalence theorem stated in Chapter 6.

whether his hypotheses fit with reality. At this stage, taxonomy can organize the assumptions of different theories ....

The next stage in the process of economic analysis is the department of the applied economist, who receives from the pure theorist, via the tool-setter, an organized set of possible interactions of relationships which may be important. His task is to look at the real world and attempt, as far as possible, to find out what are the actual facts about the relationships.

It can be said in defense of the criticism that Tinbergen-type models are partial in character and therefore necessarily less useful that this is only an expediency necessitated by limitations of data. We should note that the types of Tinbergen models to characterize and approach policy problems at different levels—regional, national or international (e.g., monetary fund and other agencies)—are manifold and varied. In this connection Frisch [12, 13] has shown that it is possible to relax the rigid structure in model "specification" by constructing submodels belonging to a general model in such a way that there may be a one-way (or recursive) relation (approximately or exactly) between the submodels, each submodel being, however, a closely interdependent (i.e., nonrecursive) model except perhaps for a few variables. A good example of this type of model specification is provided by the Brookings-SSRC econometric model of the U.S. economy, which is discussed in Chapter 11.

The point that normative relationships in a Tinbergen-type policy model may not have the refutability (or falsifiability) property in the same way as the hypotheses of the positive economic approach appears to be only of very limited consequence for the following reasons: First, the operational framework of Tinbergen's approach requires us to adopt the best available methods of statistical estimation and the best available information from existing economic theory. Second, the nonexperimental nature of empirical data which, for the economist, has to be taken as given—and which, incidentally, distinguishes an economic hypothesis from a hypothesis in the physical and natural sciences—introduces a probabilistic element into almost all the hypotheses describing economic behavior. Probabilistic statements, as such, are not falsifiable in the same sense as deterministic statements are. To quote Karl Popper, [28, pp. 191–192] as a mathematical logician on the subject:

> Probability statements are not falsifiable. Neither, of course, are they verifiable, and this for the same reasons as hold for other hypotheses, seeing that no experimental results, however numerous and favourable, can ever finally establish that the relative frequency of 'heads' is $\frac{1}{2}$ and

will *always* be $\frac{1}{2}$ ... From the non-falsifiability and non-verifiability of probability statements it can be inferred that they have no falsifiable consequences, and that they cannot themselves be consequences of verifiable statements. But the converse possibilities are not excluded. For it may be (a) that they have unilaterally verifiable consequences (purely existential consequences or there-is-consequences) or (b) that they are themselves consequences of unilaterally falsifiable universal statements (all-statements).

The probabilistic hypotheses, owing to their special nature, have to be characterized by the types and implications of different probability distributions, and in this situation the taxonomic approach is almost essential. This is because the parameters of multivariate and/or mixed distributions (e.g., Poisson-normal, binomial-Poisson, mixed geometric, etc.) are usually very difficult to estimate from given empirical data, even by the latest available statistical techniques, ranging from the method of moments to the method of scoring used for solving maximum likelihood equations [15, 21, 22]. Some approximation method is almost a necessity if the policy problem is to be solved at all. Indeed, it can be argued that the concept of operationalism in statistical physics has an identical role to play as in the theory of applied economic policy. This role is both useful and unavoidable, until some more refined techniques are discovered.

2.9. Recent Developments in Control-Theoretic Methods for Economic Policy

Recent developments in modern control theory and their use in various economic models have raised a number of interesting issues in the theory of economic policy and its operational applications to problems of economic growth, stabilization and development planning. Some of these issues are discussed in technical terms in Chapter 8 using the methods of "the maximum principle" developed by Pontryagin and his associates [59]. In this section we describe briefly three aspects of the recent trend in using control-theoretic methods which seem to us to be of some importance in the specification and evaluation of alternative feasible policies defined in a quantitative economic model. These three aspects include the following areas: (1) how to introduce (short-run) monetary and fiscal policy in an optimum growth model [48, 63] which seeks to specify an optimal path of capital accumulation under certain production constraints by maximizing a discounted sum of dynamic utility functions suitably defined over a time horizon? (2) how to compute and interpret the optimal control solutions in various phases, particularly regarding their instability and oscillations and the behavior of the imputed prices (also called adjoint variables in Pontryagin's maximum principle) which are like dynamic shadow prices, that are dynamic versions so to say of the Lagrange multipliers in a static framework? (3) how to analyze the sensitivity of the optimal trajectory defined by the optimal time-paths of the state and the control variables, when parts of the dynamic equations of the economic model are econometrically estimated?

2.9.1 *Introducing Monetary and Fiscal Policy in Control Theory Models*

The first question basically concerns itself with methods for specifying operational linkages between a consistency model without any explicit optimization criterion and a control-theoretic optimization model with an explicit intertemporal objective function. From an operational viewpoint three attempts have been discussed in the current literature.

First, one may refer to the two-step method of introducing monetary and fiscal instruments by Uzawa [63] in an optimum growth model under a two-sector neoclassical framework (e.g., private and public sectors each having separate production functions with constant returns to scale). In the first step one computes a long run optimum solution satisfying the adjoint equations of Pontryagin's maximum principle and this specifies the long run optimum share of private sector output in gross national product and the long run optimal proportion of total private sector output to be invested. Denote these ratios by $\alpha(k(t))$ and $\beta(k(t))$ respectively, where $k(t)$ denotes per capita capital stock which changes over time. One asks in the second step: how to use a detailed short run model including monetary variables and competitive factor market conditions for the purpose of choosing by the public sector appropriate instrument variables such as tax rate variation (θ_1) and the rate of deficit financing (θ_2) such that the short run values of $\alpha(k(t))$ and $\beta(k(t))$ denoted by $\hat{\alpha}$ and $\hat{\beta}$ are as close as possible to the long run optimal values? If one restricts to the stationary solution of the optimum system of adjoint equations satisfying Pontryagin's maximum principle and thereby determines the long run equilibrium values α^* and β^* (assuming such a solution exists), then the short run policy problem is to choose the control variables (θ_1, θ_2) such that they satisfy the following equations.

$$\hat{\alpha} = \hat{\alpha}(\theta_1, \theta_2) = \alpha^*$$
$$\hat{\beta} = \hat{\beta}(\theta_1, \theta_2) = \beta^*.$$

If these equations can be solved for feasible values of the instruments θ_1, θ_2

we may say that the long run stationary solution is controllable or attainable. If, however, the solutions do not exist or the values of the instrument variables are very extreme (e.g., tax rate becoming 100 per cent), the controllability and attainability may fail to hold. The idea of controllability [55, 62] has been given great emphasis in recent developments of control theory, along with the concept of "observability" [62], where the latter specifies in effect a rule of statistical identification or estimability [52]. It is interesting to note that these concepts from control theory are reappearing in optimal growth models. Note also that this approach allows the flexibility of using detailed econometric models in the short run in order to determine the controls which should be applied to converge to the desired values α^*, β^*. It is clear also that unlike the input-output models based on input-coefficients for a single year, the short run model used here is an econometric model using parameter estimates and emphasizing consistency, whereas the long run model is one of optimization with an ordinally specified objective function.

A second formulation about the linkage between the short and the long run in the theory of economic policy under optimal growth is due to Arrow and Kurz [41]. In this formulation only one of the two parts of the maximum principle of Pontryagin (e.g., the first part satisfying the canonical or adjoint differential equations and the second part specifying the condition of maximization of the current value Hamiltonian with respect to the control variables) i.e., the second part is taken to define a short run equilibrium and the deviations from this equilibrium are analyzed for stability or otherwise in terms of the slopes of the relevant demand and supply functions which depend on the adjoint variables (i.e., dynamic shadow prices). If the short run equilibrium has global stability in a certain domain, then we know that the sequence of short run equilibrium converges to a long run equilibrium. Now if it has only local stability but not global stability, then we have to make sure first of all, by changing the initial conditions if necessary, that we are in the particular phase where there is local stability and then one can define a convergence to a local equilibrium solution. It is clear that sometimes one has to introduce appropriate jump conditions for changing from one phase to another [42]. Note that the introduction of monetary and fiscal instruments have to be done here in the specification of every short run equilibrium. Unlike the first case, it is the successive sequence of short run equilibria which are examined here for convergence to the long run equilibrium and not the other way round.

A third formulation basically utilizes the dynamic aspects of decomposi-

tion or decentralized decision processes. In the static models of decomposition [44, 54] one usually identifies two levels of decision making, the
central and sectoral. Any allocation of resources which are common to
different sectors (i.e., also called central resources which are distinct from
sectoral resources specific to individual sectors only), if it is feasible in terms
of the restrictions defines a set of sectoral submodels along with a set of
shadow prices known to the center. Given the shadow prices of the central
resources predetermined by the center, the sectoral submodels specify
partial equilibrium models. Successive revisions of the shadow prices of the
central resources may lead in this framework to changes in sectoral input
and output-mixes. For dynamic intertemporal problems, these revisions and
intersectoral adjustment processes may be of several types, e.g., tâtonnement,
nontâtonnement, quota-cum-pricing adjustment, etc. [51, 56]. Note that in
this framework the central model may only perform a coordinating role,
whereas the sectoral submodels display the various adjustment problems.
A number of applications [57, 60] of this method to problems of growth and
planning in different fields of economics and operations research has been
reported in the current literature.

2.9.2. Computational Problems

The second question concerns the computation [46] and interpretation of
optimal control solutions in reasonably large economic models. Except for
linear models, the problems of computation are quite substantial, e.g., even
in problems where control variables are four, say, with an equal number of
state variables and inequality constraints in the state space. For continuous
time multivariable control problems, two computing methods have found
some success in recent investigations; e.g., the conjugate gradient method
[47] and the Davidon method [45]. Although there is some computational
evidence to suggest (and our experiences with computing optimal growth
paths in a class of two-sector models [53] confirm this) that the Davidon
method performs better than the conjugate gradient and other computing
methods in the nonlinear case, yet the sensitivity of the computing algorithm
to the terminal constraints and hence its associated penalty functions is
generally unknown; also the effects of uncertainty in some of the parameter
estimates in terms of error propagation are not generally known [62]. This
suggests the need for more computing experiments and attempting approximate solutions. One approximate solution which is frequently referred to
in optimal growth models is the steady state solution [63] defined by the
adjoint equations of the Pontryagin principle with the proviso that the time

derivatives of the state and adjoint vectors are zero. Although the steady-state equilibrium solution, which in effect is derived from algebraic equations corresponding to the adjoint differential equations of the Pontryagin principle, considerably simplifies the computational difficulties associated with the numerical methods for solving differential equations, two basic objections can be raised against this approximating procedure. First, the time taken to reach the steady state may be quite long and under arbitrary initial conditions the steady state equilibrium may not be attainable; i.e., may not be controllable [62]. Second, it may be very difficult to check the realism of the assumptions underlying the derivation of the steady state solution. This point has been strongly emphasized recently by Frisch [49] as follows: "What is the economic relevance of intrinsic paths and turnpike type of theorem of the kind I have mentioned? To be quite frank, I feel that the relevance of this type of theorem for active and realistic work on economic development, in industrialized or underdeveloped countries is practically nil. The reason for this is that the consequences that are drawn in this type of theorem *depend so essentially on the nature of the assumptions made.* And these assumptions are frequently made more for the convenience of mathematical manipulation than for reasons of similarity to concrete reality" [49, p. 161–162].

A second kind of approximate solution to the optimal trajectory is to settle for a feedback type of feasible controls which need not necessarily be optimal. This defines a kind of second best solution and simulation methods [62] are sometimes applied to compare alternative feasible controls.

A more difficult problem arises in the interpretation of the optimal values of the adjoint variables; i.e., the dynamic shadow prices, even when the optimal control solution can be computed. Although these prices can be interpreted as competitive prices, though these are imputed prices, the fact remains that these are not market prices and hence the relationship between these two sets of prices has to be explicitly spelled out. Although it is reasonable to expect that there is a very high degree of correlation between these two sets of prices, one observed and the other imputed, the direction of causality and hence controllability is not very apparent.

2.9.3. *Methods of Simulation*

The third question concerning the sensitivity of the optimal trajectory and the related optimal control paths to parameter estimates and their errors has led to direct and indirect methods of simulation which provide in some sense a modification of the optimal growth path in cases where there is some kind of instability in the stochastic space. As an example of the indirect type of simulation one may refer to the Brookings' quarterly econometric model of the U.S. economy by Fromm and Taubman [50] for evaluation of the relative desirability of a set of monetary and fiscal policy instruments. They noted that the method of optimum growth defined in a Ramsay-type framework of maximization of a utility functional over a horizon is not applicable to cyclical paths; moreover, it ignores the disutility due to variances of arguments (e.g., consumption, etc.) in the utility function. They proposed a utility functional as the sum of two components $u_1(x_1, \ldots, x_n)$ and $u_2(1/\text{var } x_1, \ldots, 1/\text{var } x_n)$, where x_i denotes instrument variables like consumption, government expenditure, etc., with their variances denoted by var x_i. Note, however, that in this approach the utility functional having two components as above is not optimized explicitly to derive the time paths of the instrument variables, but the functional is used only to provide ranking among alternative policies.

A more direct method of simulation would be to introduce stochastic processes in the specification of the dynamic model and then analyze the sensitivity of the optimal trajectory in terms of the characteristics (e.g., the various moments) of the resulting statistical distribution of the utility functional. A number of stochastic applications in this field is now available [61, 62]. A somewhat restricted view of the direct method of simulation is followed by Naylor and his associates [58] in their simulation experiments. For example, we have here in the simplest case one instrument variable represented by government expenditure which is assumed directly proportional to national income and the factor of proportionality is varied to characterize alternative policies. The instability associated with any policy is measured by the estimate of average variance computed on the basis of simulated samples generated by random drawings from a normal universe. It is clear that more stable policies are preferred here, although there is some trade-off between stability and optimality.

REFERENCES

[1] AITKEN, A. C. *Determinants and Matrices.* Edinburgh: Oliver and Boyd, 1954.

[2] ANDERSON, G. W., *et al.* "A Self-adjusting System for Optimum Dynamic Performance," *1958-IRE National Convention Record,* Part 4, pp. 182–190.

[3] ARROW, K. J. "Tinbergen on Economic Policy," *Journal of American Statistical Association,* LIII (March, 1958), 89–97.

[4] BARNA, T. (ed.). *Structural Interdependence and Economic Development.* London: Macmillan and Co., 1963, Chap. 4 (Fox, K. A., "The Food and Agricultural Sectors

in Advanced Economies") and Chap. 5 (Sengupta, J. K., "Models of Agriculture and Industry in Less Developed Economies").

[5] BELLMAN, R., and KALABA, R. "On Adaptive Control Processes," *IRE Transactions on Automatic Control*, Vol. AC-4, No. 1 (November, 1959), 1–9.

[6] CHARNES, A., and COOPER, W. W. *Management Models and Industrial Applications of Linear Programming.* New York: John Wiley & Sons, 1961, Vol. 1, Chap. 9.

[7] DANTZIG, G. B., and WOLFE, P. "The Decomposition Principle for Linear Programs," *Operations Research*, VIII (February, 1960), 101–111.

[8] DAY, A. C. L. "The Taxonomic Approach to the Study of Economic Policies," *American Economic Review*, XLV (March, 1955), 64–78.

[9] DUESENBERRY, J. S., *et al.* "A Simulation of the U.S. Economy in Recession," *Econometrica*, XXVIII (October, 1960), 749–809.

[10] FRAZER, R. A., DUNCAN, W. J., and COLLAR, A. R. *Elementary Matrices.* Cambridge: Cambridge University Press, 1960.

[11] FRIEDMAN, M. *Essays in Positive Economics.* Chicago: University of Chicago Press, 1959.

[12] FRISCH, R. "From National Accounts to Macroeconomic Decision Models," in *Income and Wealth*, Series 4 (International Association for Research on Income and Wealth). Edited by Gilbert and Stone. London: Bowes and Bowes, 1955, 1–24.

[13] ———. "The Mathematical Structure of a Decision Model: The Oslo Submodel," *Metroeconomica*, VII (December, 1955), 111–136.

[14] ———. "A Survey of Types of Economic Forecasting and Programming and a Brief Description of the Oslo Channel Model," *Memorandum of the Institute of Economics.* Oslo: University of Oslo, May, 1961.

[15] HELMER, O., and RESCHER, N. "On the Epistemology of the Inexact Sciences," *Management Science*, VI (October, 1959), 25–52.

[16] HOHN, F. E. *Elementary Matrix Algebra.* New York: The Macmillan Co., 1958.

[17] INGWERSON, D. R. "A Modified Lyapunov Method for Nonlinear Stability Analysis," *IRE Transactions on Automatic Control*, Vol. AC-6, No. 2 (May, 1961), 199–210.

[18] JOHNSON, H. G. "The Taxonomic Approach to the Study of Economic Policy," *Economic Journal*, LXI (December, 1951), 812–832.

[19] JOHR, W. A., and SINGER, H. W. *The Role of the Economist as Official Adviser.* London: Allen & Unwin, 1955, Chaps. 1–5.

[20] KAPLAN, W. *Ordinary Differential Equations.* Reading, Mass.: Addison–Wesley, 1958.

[21] KENDALL, M. G. "Natural Law in the Social Sciences," *Journal of Royal Statistical Society*, Series A, CXXIV, Part 1 (1961), 1–19.

[22] ———, and STUART, A. *The Advanced Theory of Statistics*, Vol. II. London: C. Griffin & Co., 1961.

[23] KLEIN, L. R. "The Use of Econometric Models as a Guide to Economic Policy," *Econometrica*, XV (April, 1947), 111–151.

[24] LANING, J. W., and BATTIN, R. H. *Random Processes in Automatic Control.* New York: McGraw-Hill Book Co., 1956.

[25] MAHALANOBIS, P. C. "The Approach of Operational Research to Planning in India," *Sankhyā*, XVI (1955), 3–130.

[26] MARSCHAK, T. "Centralization and Decentralization in Economic Organizations," *Econometrica*, XXVII (April, 1959), 399.

[27] MYRDAL, G. *Value in Social Theory.* London: Routledge & Kegan Paul, 1958, Chaps. 2, 10, 11, Postscript, 137–240, 259–262.

[28] POPPER, KARL R. *The Logic of Scientific Discovery.* Revised edition. London: Hutchinson, 1961, pp. 191–192.

[29] ROBBINS, L. *Nature and Significance of Economic Science.* London: Macmillan and Co., 1932.

[30] SCHULTZ, W. C., and RIDEOUT, V. C. "Control System Performance Measures: Past, Present, and Future," *IRE Transactions on Automatic Control*, Vol. AC-6, No. 1 (February, 1961), 22–35.

[31] SENGUPTA, J. K., and TINTNER, G. "On Some Economic Models of Development Planning," *Economia Internazionale*, XVI (February, 1963), 34–50.

[32] THEIL, H. "On the Theory of Economic Policy," *American Economic Review*, Papers and Proceedings, XLVI (May, 1956), 360–366.

[33] ——. *Economic Forecasts and Policy.* Amsterdam: North-Holland Publishing Co., 1958; 2nd revised edition, 1961.

[34] TINBERGEN, J. *On the Theory of Economic Policy.* Amsterdam: North-Holland Publishing Co., 1952, 1955.

[35] ——. *Economic Policy, Principles and Design.* Amsterdam: North-Holland Publishing Co., 1956.

[36] ——. *Centralization and Decentralization in Economic Policy.* Amsterdam: North-Holland Publishing Co., 1954.

[37] ——, and BOS, H. S. *Mathematical Models of Economic Growth.* New York: McGraw-Hill Book Co., 1962, Chaps. 1–2.

[38] ——. *The Design of Development.* Baltimore: Johns Hopkins Press, 1958.

[39] VAN EIJK, C. J., and SANDEE, J. "Quantitative Determination of an Optimum Economic Policy," *Econometrica*, XXVII (January, 1959), 1–13.

[40] WOLD, H. "Causal Inference from Observational Data: A Review of Ends and Means," *Journal of Royal Statistical Society*, Series A, CXIX (1956), 28–61.

[41] ARROW, K. J., and KURZ, M. *The Public Investment, the Rate of Return and Optimal Fiscal Policy.* Baltimore: Johns Hopkins Press, 1970.

[42] BRUNO, M. "Optimal Accumulation in Discrete Capital Models", in *Essays on the Theory of Optimal Economic Growth.* Edited by K. Shell. Massachusetts: MIT Press, 1967, Chapter 11.

[43] BURMEISTER, E., and DOBELL, A. R. *Mathematical Theories of Economic Growth.* New York: Macmillan and Co., 1970.

[44] DANTZIG, G. B. "Large-Scale Linear Programming", in *Mathematics of the Decision Sciences.* Part I, Lectures in Applied Mathematics, Volume 11. Rhode Island: American Mathematical Society, 1968.

[45] DAVIDON, W. C. "Variable Metric Method for Minimization", *Argonne National Laboratory Report ANL 5590.* Revised, February, 1966.

[46] DOBELL, A. R. "Optimization in Models of Economic Growth", in *Studies in Optimization,* Part 1. Philadelphia, Pennsylvania: SIAM, 1970, pp. 1–27.

[47] FLETCHER, R., and REEVES, C. M. "Function Minimization by Conjugate Gradients". *Computer Journal,* Volume 7, 1964, 149–154.

[48] FOLEY, D. K., and SIDRAUSKI, M. *Monetary and Fiscal Policy in a Growing Economy.* London: Macmillan Co., 1971.

[49] FRISCH, R. "Econometrics in the World of Today", in *Induction, Growth and Trade.* Edited by Eltis, W. A., Scott, M. Fg. and Wolfe, J. N., Oxford: Clarendon Press, 1970, Chapter 11.

[50] FROMM, G., and TAUBMAN, P. J. *Policy Simulations with an Econometric Model.* Amsterdam: North-Holland Publishing Co., 1968.

[51] HAHN, F. H., and NEGISHI, T. "A Theorem on Non-Tâtonnement Stability", *Econometrica,* Volume 30, 1962, 463–469.

[52] KALMAN, R. E. "Mathematical Description of Linear Dynamical Systems". *SIAM Journal on Control,* Volume 1, 1963, 152–192.

[53] KELLER, E. A., Jr., and SENGUPTA, J. K. "Relative Efficiency of Computing Optimal Growth by Conjugate Gradient and Davidon Methods". Paper submitted for publication (1972).

[54] KORNAI, J., and LIPTAK, Th. "Two-Level Planning". *Econometrica,* Volume 33, 1965, 141–169.

[55] LEE, E. B., and MARKUS, L. *Foundations of Optimal Control.* New York: John Wiley, 1967.

[56] MALINVAUD, E. "Decentralized Procedures for Planning", in *Activity Analysis in the Theory of Growth and Planning.* Edited by Malinvaud, E. and Bacharach, M. O. L. New York: St. Martin's Press, 1967.

[57] MESAROVIC, M. D., PEARSON, J. D., and OTHERS. "A Multi-Level Structure for a Class of Linear Dynamic Optimization Problems". *Preprint of Technical Papers, Joint Automatic Control Conference.* Volume 6, 1965, 93–99.

[58] NAYLOR, T. H., WERTZ, K., and WONNACOTT, T. H. "Methods for Evaluating the Effects of Economic Policies Using Simulation Experiments". *Review of International Statistical Institute,* Volume 36, 1968, 184–200.

[59] PONTRYAGIN, L. S., BOLTYANSKII, V. G., GAMKRELIDZE, R. V., and MISHCHENKO, E. F. *The Mathematical Theory of Optimal Processes.* New York: Interscience, John Wiley and Sons, 1962.

[60] SENGUPTA, J. K. "Economic Problems of Resource Allocation in Nonmarket Systems", in *Economic Analysis for Educational Planning.* Edited by K. A. Fox. Baltimore: Johns Hopkins Press, 1972, Chapter 6.

[61] SENGUPTA, J. K. "Economic Policy Simulation in Dynamic Control Models Under Econometric Estimation". To be published in *Essays in Honor of Jan Tinbergen,* edited by W. Sellekaerts. New York: Macmillan International, 1972 (in press).

[62] TINTNER, G., and SENGUPTA, J. K. *Stochastic Economics: Stochastic Processes, Control and Programming.* New York: Academic Press, 1972.

[63] UZAWA, H. "An Optimal Fiscal Policy in an Aggregative Model of Economic Growth", in *The Theory and Design of Economic Development.* Edited by Adelman, I., and Thorbecke, E. Baltimore: Johns Hopkins Press, 1966, Chapter 5.

Chapter 3

IDENTIFICATION, ESTIMABILITY
AND CAUSAL INTERPRETATION OF
ECONOMIC POLICY MODELS

3.1. Identification

3.1.1. *Types and Implications of Identification*

If we define a set of objects (i.e., configuration Q) having components (i.e., elements q_i belonging to the set Q) which are interdependent in their functional behavior, i.e.,

$$f(q_1, q_2, ..., q_n) = f(q) = 0 \qquad (f = \text{vector function}), \qquad (3.1)$$

then any quantitative model of economic objects (i.e., variables) q_i can be represented by choosing a special form of the vector function f in equation (3.1). For example, assuming linearity, a model derived from equation (3.1) can be of the form

$$Aq - b = 0 \qquad (i, j = 1, 2, ..., n), \qquad (3.2)$$

where A is a square matrix a_{ij} of constant coefficients (or parameters), while q, b are n-component column vectors and the elements b_i are constant coefficients (or parameters). The *model* specified in equation (3.2) can be viewed as a set S of *structures* S_k defined by

$$S_k = \{(A, b)_k \text{ such that } A_k q = b_k\}, \qquad (3.3)$$
$$S = \{S_k, \text{ for all } k \text{ belonging to the index set } I_0\}.$$

Here $(A, b)_k$ and A_k, b_k indicate that a specific choice has been made of the pair (A, b) out of all possible choices of the coefficients, and this generates a specific structure S_k, which is assumed to be admissible. The set of all such structures, when the index $k \in I_0$ takes all admissible integral values from 1 to N, for instance, defines a model M, which is denoted here by S. For any fixed k, the structure S_k will have a number of structural equations, each of which will contain a number of coefficients or parameters. Since identifia-

57

bility is a property of distinguishability within a model, we can talk of identifiability (or nonidentifiability) of any "structure" within a model, of any equation (or equations) within a given structure and of any coefficient (or coefficients) in a given equation (or equations). If all the coefficients and all the equations in a given structure are identifiable, the given structure is identifiable.

There are at least three basic reasons for emphasizing the necessity of identification in an economic policy model. The first is that the model builder in economics is concerned with nonexperimental data, unlike the physical and natural scientists, who can generate experimental data through controlled experiments. With nonexperimental data, one has to know, for instance, on an *a priori* basis whether one obtains a supply function or a demand function by statistical fitting to a set of observed price-quantity data. Second, identification of economic relationships in a model is necessary under conditions of structural change, which is generally envisaged as a consequence of policy making. This would be the case, for example, when one is required to make predictions on the assumption that the economic behavior pattern itself will have undergone a change as compared with the past during which the historical information was obtained. Third, identification in one of its specific statistical senses (e.g., nonidentifiability of a set of coefficients in a given equation, due to multicollinearity) is necessary in order to avoid nonuniqueness and even indeterminacy of statistical estimates of parameters.

It is essential to emphasize that the concept of identification is not restricted only to statistical or probabilistic models, although in econometrics the concept was developed primarily in relation to statistical estimation in an interdependent model. The statisticians have, however, used the concept of "estimability" of coefficients (or their linear functions) derived from single-equation regression models, primarily with reference to the singularity or nonsingularity of the normal equations. In a more general sense, the logicians and mathematicians [17] (e.g., Kuratowski, Borel, Tarski) have long been concerned with developing a theory of hierarchies with properties of equivalence of structures within the model and with properties of distinguishability within the model. Hence, it may be convenient to characterize the concept of identification at three different levels: (i) on a logic-cum-mathematical basis, (ii) on a statistical or probabilistic basis and (iii) on a computational basis, arising in the application of iteration methods to specific estimation techniques, such as the method of scoring in maximum likelihood technique which is used in approximating a set of estimates of nonlinear parameters or the condition of identifiability in the second stage of a two-stage least-squares estimation.

3.1.2. *Properties and Criteria of Identification*

Consider first the logicomathematical basis of identification of a given structure within a model. Let S_1 and S_2 be two structures defined by equations (3.3) and (3.2) such that their coefficient structures (A_1, b_1) and (A_2, b_2) are related by a nonsingular transformation T in the following way:

$$A_2 = T A_1; \; b_2 = T b_1. \tag{3.4}$$

As we *define* it, any two structures S_1 and S_2 that belong to the same model S are identically *equivalent* if the set of solutions generated by S_1 and S_2 is identical for all possible transformations T allowed for A_1, b_1. Thus a given structure S_k for a fixed k ($k \in I_0$ and $S_k \in S$) is *uniquely* and *completely* identifiable within the model S if and only if there is no other structure in that model equivalent to S_k. In this case, the only transformation matrix T allowed in equation (3.4) is the identity matrix $I = T$, and so equivalence is strict and unique. This situation is appropriate for physical experiments in natural science, where because of the particular nature of the problem it can safely be assumed that the physical instruments have no error of any kind and hence that there may be only one structure S_k permitted in the model which is uniquely and completely identifiable. If the structure S_k in S is nonunique (i.e., weakly identifiable), identification is said to be incomplete if the coefficient matrix A_1 is not a strictly diagonal nonsingular matrix. In other words, the structure S_1 is *weakly* and *completely* identifiable if the transformation matrix T is a nonsingular diagonal matrix and the matrix A_1 is a strictly nonsingular diagonal matrix. In this case, the systems (A_1, b_1) and (A_2, b_2) differ only by a normalization factor. Denoting structures which are equivalent except for normalization factors as k-equivalent structures, we might say that any given structure S_1 belonging to the model S is weakly but completely identifiable if there are no other structures in the model S except the k-equivalent structures.

The above concepts of identification are applicable to situations (ii) and (iii) of the preceding section, i.e., to statistical estimation and approximation by iteration methods. Following Koopmans [9], [1] we shall call two structures

---

S_1, S_2 (where each structure is defined as the combination of the statistical distribution of the latent [or random] variables and a complete set of structural equations) observationally equivalent, if the two conditional distributions of endogenous variables generated by S_1 and S_2 are identical for all possible values of the exogenous variables. We shall call a structure S_k permitted by the model uniquely identifiable within that model, if there is no other structure equivalent to S_k which is contained in the model. A certain parameter b of a structure S_k is uniquely identifiable within a model, if that parameter has the same value for all structures equivalent to S_k contained in the model. Finally, a structural equation is identifiable, if all its parameters are identifiable.

Similarly, suppose we are approximating a well-behaved nonlinear single-valued analytic function $f(x)$ when x takes a set of values X, called the domain of x and $f(x)$ takes another set of values Y, called the range of x. Let a particular rule of approximation be given, and let S_1 and S_2 now stand for two linear approximations for this function, each of which contains, say, n fixed parameters b_i (i.e., constants defining the intervals of approximation). Then the two approximations are empirically equivalent, (or ε-equivalent) if the two approximating functions generated by S_1 and S_2 are identical (or identical within a range $\pm \varepsilon$, for a fixed preassigned small $\varepsilon > 0$, i.e., ε-identical). We might call a structure S_k permitted by a given rule of approximation and the given function $f(x)$ uniquely identifiable within that range and that domain of the function and that given approximation rule if there is no other approximation equivalent to S_k in that range and that domain of the function. A certain parameter b_i belonging to any given approximation S_k is uniquely identifiable if that parameter b_i has the same value for all approximations S_i, which are equivalent to S_k in the sense defined above.

We note that identification is not only the property of distinguishability of structures within a model. It also implies, in a certain sense, the property of nonsingularity. For instance, assume that for a certain choice of $k = 1, 2$ the square matrices A_k are singular and denote the corresponding structures by $\bar{S}_1$ and $\bar{S}_2$, which, unlike S_1 and S_2 in equation (3.3), are either not defined or not unique. Now we cannot talk of equivalence or even distinguishability of $\bar{S}_1$ and $\bar{S}_2$, because the inverse matrices of A_k are not uniquely defined. A similar problem exists when in the least-squares theory of linear statistical models the so-called linear normal equations (or any other optimizing equations such as the likelihood equations in maximum likelihood methods) are not uniquely solvable for their parameters because of the singularity of the coefficient matrix. The same problem exists in approximation theory—certain paths of approximation to obtain the solution of the nonlinear (maximum) likelihood equations $\partial L/\partial b_i = 0$, $L = \log$ of the joint likelihood function, $b_i =$ parameters, by the method of scoring which may or may not be possible to carry out after a certain point in the approximation space—if the so-called "information matrix" which has to be inverted at each stage of iteration is not strictly "positive-definite" (i.e., "nonsingular"). Those paths of approximation are said to be nonidentifiable.

The third property of identification, which is interrelated with the first two, consists, for example, in the distinguishability of two equations within a given structure by means of the presence of outside independent variables in each such equation. Thus, when we have a demand equation $q_d = f_d(p)$ and a supply equation $q_s = f_s(p)$ and, further, the equilibrium condition, or identity $q = q_d = q_s$, relating quantity (q) and price (p) of a single commodity, if the two functions are of the same form (e.g., linear) they are not identifiable or distinguishable because the observed quantity q does not distinguish between q_d and q_s. Suppose we now introduce income (y) as an exogenous variable in the demand equation, i.e., $q_d = f_d(p, y)$, and weather (x) as an exogenous variable in the supply equation, i.e., $q_s = f_s(p, x)$, such that x and y are statistically independent, then even under the condition $q = q_d = q_s$ the demand equation q_d is distinguishable from the supply equation q_s and both equations are identifiable. This same property is applied in a more specific sense when, for example, a pair of estimated coefficients in a given equation, which are not identifiable (i.e., estimable in the terminology of the statisticians) due to multicollinearity of independent variables, are made to be identifiable uniquely by imposing an extraneous estimate for one of the coefficients to be estimated and then solving uniquely for the other. Similarly, in some situations, identification of an equation within a structure can be secured by a set of specific restrictions on the form of the equations allowed in the structure. For example, suppose in a Keynesian model containing a savings function $S = S(Y)$ and an investment function $I = I(Y)$ we have the identity $S = I$; the savings function $S(Y)$ is identifiable if it is known that the investment function is nonlinear and that the savings function is linear. Note that the investment function is not identifiable unless the investment-income relation $I(Y)$ is strictly nonlinear, i.e., it does not contain any linear part, not even a constant intercept. Thus, identification refers to the imposition of a specific set of restrictions in various alternative ways, namely, through the admissible or allowable set of transformation T, through the structure of A_1, A_2, through the nonsingularity of normal equations, and through the imposition of specific restrictions on the algebraic form of the equations belonging to a structure.

3.1.3. *Equational Errors and Identification*

It may be useful to characterize some of the different phases at which the statistical problem of identification may arise. Thus, we may distinguish three types of identification problems according to whether they arise in (a) a system containing equational errors only, (b) a system having errors in the variables and (c) a system which is restricted by some peculiarities, such as by linear inequalities of a programming model or conditions upon the underlying stochastic process (Wold's *conditional causal chains*).

For the statistical estimation of a linear simultaneous equation model with only equational errors we can state, following Koopmans, the rank and order conditions of identifiability. A necessary and sufficient condition for the identifiability of a single structural equation within a linear model having G independent equations, restricted only by the exclusion of certain variables from certain equations, is that we can form at least one non-vanishing determinant of order $(G-1)$ out of those coefficients properly arranged with which the variables excluded from that structural equation appear in the $(G-1)$ other structural equations. This necessary and sufficient condition can also be specified in terms of the coefficient matrices of the "reduced form" equations.

A necessary but not sufficient condition which is easy to apply for a single equation belonging to a linear model in its original form, is given by the following rule: Let G be the total number of independent structural equations in the entire system and let K be the total number of variables, either endogenous or exogenous in the *entire system*. Let R be the total number of variables present in a *single equation* belonging to the system. Then the difference $(K-R)$ is called the number of "excluded variables" in the particular equation. The rule for just-identification or overidentification for that single equation is that

$$K - R \geq G - 1,$$

i.e., if $K-R=G-1$ we have just-identification and if $K-R>G-1$ we have overidentification. Obviously, if $K-R<G-1$, the particular equation is underidentified. To see how this necessary (order) condition is actually applied to a single equation in a linear simultaneous system, let us denote the column vectors of endogenous and exogenous variables by $y(t)$ and $x(t)$,

respectively, and specify a linear simultaneous (interdependent) equation model as

$$Ay(t) + Gx(t) = u(t); \quad \begin{array}{l} A: M.M, \\ G: M.N, \\ y(t): M.1, \\ x(t): N.1, \end{array} \tag{3.5}$$

and its reduced form as

$$y(t) = H_1 x(t) + v(t); \quad H_1 = -(A^{-1}G); \quad v(t) = A^{-1}u(t) \tag{3.6}$$

assuming the nonsingularity of the square matrix A. It is assumed that the column vector $u(t)$ is uncorrelated with the vector $x(t)$, which means that the residuals are assumed uncorrelated with all exogenous variables $x(t)$. In addition, only noncontemporary residuals are assumed to be mutually uncorrelated. In other words, contemporary residuals in different equations of the system (3.5) can be mutually correlated. Now any single equation belonging to the system (3.5), which need not contain all the endogenous and all the exogenous variables, may be written as

$$y = Y\alpha + X_1\beta + u; \quad \begin{array}{l} y: T.1, \\ Y: T.m, \\ \text{(after appropriate normalization)} \quad \alpha: m.1, \\ X_1: T.n, \\ \beta: n.1, \end{array} \tag{3.7}$$

where y is the column vector of T observations on the single dependent variable and α, β denote column vectors of m and n parameters ($m+1 \leq M$ and $n \leq N$), respectively, which are to be estimated. The matrix Y indicates that m other dependent variables are present in the equation and the matrix X_1 denotes that there are n exogenous variables in the equations (which include predetermined variables by definition). Applying the necessary (order) condition, we see that for the entire system (3.5) the total number of structural equations is M and the total number of variables is $N+M$, of which M are endogenous and N exogenous. In the particular equation (3.7), there are $(m+1)$ endogenous variables and n exogenous variables; hence, the total number of "excluded variables" in that particular equation is $(N+M-m-n-1)$. Hence, the particular equation (3.7) is overidentified, just-identified or underidentified according as

$$N + M - m - n - 1 \gtreqless M - 1,$$

i.e.,

$$N \gtreqless m + n.$$

In other words, equation (3.7) is said to be overidentified or just-identified in the structure of system (3.5), according as N exceeds or equals $(m+n)$. In case $N < m+n$ we have underidentification or nonidentifiability. If the equation (3.7) is just-identified by the sufficient condition also, the ordinary least-squares method can be applied to estimate the coefficients of the reduced-form model (3.6) and there is a unique (nonsingular) transformation relating the structural coefficients in the original model and the coefficients of the reduced form.

The above criteria of identification can be used in selecting a specification form for an economic model which can be statistically estimated. However, two critical comments are in order. First, the order and rank criteria of identification hold only for linear systems; however, if we view a linear system such as (3.5) as an approximation of a certain type of nonlinear system, the above conditions hold *locally*. Global criteria could be defined only when we consider all possible Jacobians for all linear approximations and if in each case the rank and order test is satisfied. In that case we have a globally identified system. One basic difficulty which might arise here is that the same linear system could be obtained by approximation from more than one nonlinear system. Obvious economic examples are (a) that the Domar-type growth model may be derived [11] from the Solow-type growth model in more than one way and (b) that the linear dynamic Leontief system of differential equations could be obtained [13] from mixed difference-differential equations or nonlinear differential equations.

A second comment is that the Bayesian approach, which emphasizes setting restrictions on the coefficients through a priori information, has not been much utilized in devising criteria of identification, which are suitable for situations that are only partly statistical. For example, it is frequently necessary for the econometrician in development planning [2] strategy to combine a sectoral input-output table for a year which is not statistically estimated with a behavioristic model of the Tinberg type, the latter being based on time-series data. [2]

It is possible that intuitive criteria of identification are necessary, for such combined or mixed models,[3] which have not as yet been formulated.

Further, we should note that the identification problem is not resolved by

---

[2] See Chapter 13 for concrete applications.

[3] Some intuitive criteria have, of course, been applied before, e.g., it has been known that in a demand-supply model, if demand is more stable in terms of variance than supply, the observed price-quantity data would identify the demand function, but not the supply function.

increasing the sample size. We may impose conditions of normality and independence of errors without necessarily making the system identifiable. Kendall [6] has observed that identifiability conditions require us to know what specifications on the disturbances (i.e., errors in the equations) are obeyed equally by linear functions of them. However, normality is not the only distribution which is reproduced by linear functions. The Cauchy and Poisson distributions have the same property. It may be said that the normal distribution is the only continuous distribution having finite second moments with the property of stability. Thus, we may say that if we postulate that the disturbances are idependent and do not follow a stable law the system is identifiable. Unfortunately this is not of much help, because in most cases we do not know anything about the statistical distribution function under-lying an empirical system. Hence, we have to fall back on those criteria of identifiability which do not depend on the restrictions imposed on the disturbances.

3.1.4. *Identification and Errors in the Variables*

The above results on the necessary and sufficient conditions for identification have been specified so far only in relation to a linear simultaneous model with errors in equations exclusively. Recently it has been shown by Konijn [8] and others that analogous conditions hold for the case of errors in the variables as well. This can be followed through fairly easily in our approach, because in our logical characterization of the identification problem at the outset we have seen that identification criteria are essentially derived from the conditions (i.e., criteria) we set up for defining equivalent classes (or equivalent structures within the model).

For instance, we assume now that instead of the linear model (3.5), which contained equational errors only, we have the observed variables $y(t)$, which are subject to errors $e(t)$ with a fixed nonsingular statistical distribution such that "the true parts" $r(t) = y(t) - e(t)$ of the observed variables, to-gether with other nonstochastic variables $x(t)$, satisfy M linearly indepen-dent equations

$$Br(t) + Cx(t) = 0 \; ; \quad \begin{array}{ll} B: & M.M\,, \\ r(t): & M.1\,, \\ C: & M.N\,, \\ x(t): & N.1\,, \end{array} \qquad (3.8)$$

where $r(t) = y(t) - e(t)$.

Here the statistical distribution of the observed endogenous variables $y(t)$ is generated through the observational error $e(t)$ for any given set of exogenous error-free variables $x(t)$. Let F denote this class of feasible statistical distributions of $y(t)$. Then the statistical *model* corresponding to equation (3.8) may be viewed as a set S of structures (i.e., component sets) S_k defined by

$$S_k = \{(B, C, F)_k \text{ such that equation (3.8) is satisfied}\},$$
$$S = \{S_k, \text{ for all } k \text{ belonging to the feasible set indexed by} \quad (3.9)$$
$$\text{the set of positive integers } I_0\},$$

where, as in equation (3.3) above, $(B, C, F)_k$ indicates that a specific choice has been made of the triplet (B, C, F) out of all possible choices and this generates a specific structure S_k which is assumed to be defined (S_k must be feasible or admissible) which requires nonsingularity of the appropriate coefficient matrices and of the statistical distributions of the error variables). Consider now any two structures S_1 and S_2 belonging to the set S which defines the *model*. S_1 and S_2 are called observationally equivalent if they generate identical distributions of the endogenous variables. With this definition we may say that a given structure S_k for a fixed k permitted by the model S is uniquely identifiable within that model if there is no other structure in that model observationally equivalent to S_k. In particular, any functional θ over the admissible set S denoted by $\theta(S)$ is identifiable within that model if $\theta(S_1)=\theta(S_2)$ for all observationally equivalent pairs S_1 and S_2 belonging to the model S. In this way, our necessary and sufficient conditions applicable in the errors-in-equations model carry over quite easily to the case of errors in the variables.

3.1.5. *Identification Under Other Constraints*

Although identification is not related to sample size, it has some relation to the presence or absence of equilibrium conditions in a simultaneous equations model. An example may clarify this point. Consider an interdependent model containing quantities demanded $q_d(t)$ and supplied $q_s(t)$ at time t and price $p(t)$ at time t.

$$q_s(t) = a_1 + b_1 p(t) + u_1(t),$$
$$q_d(t) = a_2 - b_2 p(t) + u_2(t), \quad (3.10)$$
$$q_d(t) = q_s(t) = q(t).$$

Here the disturbances $u_1(t)$, $u_2(t)$ are such that only noncontemporary values are assumed to be mutually uncorrelated, though contemporary values in different equations can still be correlated. The third relation which is an identity makes the problem of distinguishability of the demand and supply equations difficult. For we can multiply the first equation by a nonzero constant α_1 and the second by a nonzero constant α_2 and construct another system of "pseudofunctions". Then, if $u_1(t)$, $u_2(t)$ are assumed to be normal variates, $[\alpha_1 u_1(t) + \alpha_2 u_2(t)]$, which is a linear function of them, would also be normal. In other words, the assumption of normality would not help resolve the problem of distinguishability (i.e., identification) of the original functions and the pseudofunctions. Adding independence to the assumption of normality would not ordinarily make the system identifiable, since it is possible to have values of α_1 and α_2 depending on the variances of $u_1(t)$ and $u_2(t)$ such that the linear function $[\alpha_1 u_1(t) + \alpha_2 u_2(t)]$ is also distributed normally and independently. Consider, however, a transformation of the system (3.10) to a new system (3.11), which replaces the identity by an equation relating to adjustment of stocks arising out of demand-supply disequilibrium

$$
\begin{aligned}
q_s(t) &= \alpha_1 + \beta_1 p(t-1) + v_1(t), \\
p(t) &= p(t-1) + \gamma_1 [q_d(t-1) - q_s(t-1)] + v_2(t), \qquad (3.11) \\
q_d(t) &= \alpha_2 - \beta_2 p(t) + v_3(t).
\end{aligned}
$$

Here each equation is a behavioral relation containing disturbances $v_1(t)$, $v_2(t)$, $v_3(t)$. The statistical data required for this system are much more varied than those required for the system (3.10). We need separate data on quantity demanded and quantity supplied and, hence, their difference, i.e., stocks and inventories. Noting that the lagged endogenous variables $p(t-1)$, $q_d(t-1)$, $q_s(t-1)$ are predetermined (or exogenous) variables, which by assumption are independent of the disturbances $v_i(t)$, $i = 1, 2, 3$, we have the necessary condition for each equation of the system (3.11) to be just-identified. This is because the number of "excluded variables" in each equation is equal to $G-1$, where G stands for the number of structural equations, which is evidently three here. In Wold's terminology [20] the system (3.11) represents a purely causal chain (PCC) system, whereas we have an interdependent (ID) system in (3.10). We will discuss them in later sections in some detail. [4] We may only note at this point that a system which is intermediate between the ID and PCC models has been constructed by Wold and is called a conditional causal chain (CCC) model. The fact that there can be more than one type of conditioning of the underlying stochastic process generating the CCC models leads to an identification problem of a kind different from any we have discussed so far [10].

---

[4] See, for instance, Chapters 12 and 14.

A more difficult problem of identification arises when a complete model is specified in terms of a programming model with stochastic variations of the coefficients. The characterization of such a problem can be made in terms of the approach outlined at the beginning of this chapter. However, any operational specification of simple criteria becomes very difficult. Consider, for example, the following model of stochastic linear programming.

$$\text{maximize } z = (\bar{c} + \gamma)'x, \tag{3.12.1}$$

under the conditions

$$(\bar{A} + \alpha)x \lessgtr (\bar{b} + \beta), \tag{3.12.2}$$
$$x \geqq 0,$$

where x is an n-component column vector containing the instrument variables and the target variables in appropriately scaled units, $A = \bar{A} + \alpha$ is an m by n matrix of coefficients having an exact part $\bar{A}$ and a random part α, $c = \bar{c} + \gamma$ is an n-component column vector with $\bar{c}$ as the exact part and γ as the random part. The same applies to the m-component column vector $b = \bar{b} + \beta$, where the vector β is random. We assume that the probability distribution Prob (A, b, c) is nondegenerate. A set of points P belonging to Prob (A, b, c) and satisfying the system (3.12) is defined to be admissible, i.e., they must be feasible and nondegenerate in terms of the model. These points define a statistical distribution for the maximum value of z, i.e., of max z. Then the statistical model corresponding to the system (3.12) may be viewed as a set S of structures S_k defined by

$$S_k = \{\max z \mid (x, P\in(A, b, c))_k \text{ such that (3.12) is satisfied}\}, \tag{3.13}$$
$$S = \{S_k, \text{ for all } k \text{ belonging to the index set } I_0\},$$

where, as in our equation (3.9) before, $(x, P\in[A, b, c])_k$ indicates that a specific choice has been made of the admissible set $(x, P\in[A, b, c])$ out of all possible choices and this generates a specific structure S_k. We now define that any two structures S_i and S_j $i \neq j$ belonging to the statistical model S are observationally equivalent if they generate identical statistical distributions of the variable max z in the system (3.12). We may then characterize that a given structure S_k for a fixed k permitted by the statistical model S is uniquely identifiable if there is no other structure belonging to the model S that is observationally equivalent to it. However, it is difficult to lay down precise rules of identification in this case, although intuitively it appears evident that the set of optimal basic solutions corresponding to (3.12.2) is a set of equations to which the order and rank conditions of identification may be appropriate under some modifications. The difficulty, of course, lies precisely in defining the "appropriate modification," because the solutions of a parametric set of linear programming models need not be connected or continuous, and so the determinantal criterion, (i.e., the rank condition) is of little use.

There are other formulations for linear programming under random variations. They are surveyed in some detail in Chapter 9.

3.2. Estimability and Causal Interpretation

An important question in policy models—besides that of statistical identification discussed above—is the nature of the structure of the model and, particularly, of the relationship between targets and instruments. It must be strongly emphasized that such questions can be answered only when it is realistic to suppose that the econometric model holds even *after* the instruments are applied by the policy maker; that is, the changes must be relatively small and of a short-run nature. When policy instruments alter the "basic foundations" of an economy, as, for instance, in agrarian reform policy, which is discussed in Chapter 15, it is necessary to know the structure of the relations both before and after the reforms are applied. A major problem is that it is extremely difficult to obtain on an *ex ante* basis the new structure resulting from such reforms, although comparison with the experiences of other countries with more or less similar types of reforms or changes may provide bench marks.

Assuming, therefore, the existence of an environment within which quantitative economic policy can be exercised, a fundamental question which arises is the extent to which the concept of causality could be applied or used with respect to the two sets of variables in a policy model—the targets and the instruments. The concept of causality in its philosophical and physical content has a long history which should not concern us here. At the same time, it is obvious that the existence of causal relationships within and between the sets of instruments and targets has very important operational implications from the standpoint of the formulation of economic policy.

We may distinguish between at least two different characteristics of a causal relation between the target and the instrument variables: (a) irreversibility of relations and (b) recursive ordering of relations. Consider a fixed-target policy model

$$Ay = Bz + Cu, \tag{3.14}$$

and assume that the coefficient matrices A and B associated with the target (y) and the instrument (z) vectors are square. If A and B are both nonsingular, the relations of the model (3.14) are reversible, i.e., both y and z could be solved uniquely. If, however, A is singular and B is nonsingular, we know from our theorems in Chapter 2 that the different components of the instrument vector are mutually independent (but not the targets). Hence, given y, the vector z could be solved uniquely (assuming, of course, that the data variables Cu are given, which in any way are beyond the control of the policy maker). In other words, given z we cannot compute y in the same unique sense, since A^{-1} does not exist; the relation in this case may be said to be irreversible. Similarly, if A is nonsingular but B is not, the unknown y could be solved uniquely, given z, but not vice versa. In this sense one might say that z causes y, the causality here being equated definitionally to the nonexistence of the determinant of the coefficient matrix of the instrument vector. This result would also hold in the case of models which are not linear, as in equation (3.14), in view of our theorem on implicit functions mentioned in Chapter 2 (p. 37). As an example, consider a two-sector version of the long-term Dutch model (1950–1970), which is adapted from Verdoorn [19] and slightly modified to make it a fixed-target model:

Demand for capital (K_d) : $K_d = k_1 Y^{k_2}$,
Demand for labor (L_d) : $L_d = Y^r$,
Supply of capital (K_s) : $dK_s/dt = \alpha Y$,
Supply of labor (L_s) : $L_s = \exp(\pi t)$.

Assume that two fixed targets are to keep the demand-supply relations at fixed ratios θ_1, θ_2, respectively,

$$K_d = \theta_2 K_s ., \left(\frac{dK_d}{dt} = \theta_2 \frac{dK_s}{dt}\right)., \qquad L_d = \theta_1 L_s ;$$

and let the two instruments be the saving-income ratio (α) and the intensity of demand for labor (r). By substitution we obtain

$$k_1 k_2 Y^{k_2-1} \frac{dY}{dt} - \theta_2 \alpha Y = 0 = f_1, \text{ say}$$

$$Y^r - \theta_1 \exp(\pi t) = 0 = f_2, \text{ say}$$

we compute the Jacobians

$$J\left(\frac{f_1, f_2}{\theta_1, \theta_2}\right) = \begin{bmatrix} \dfrac{\partial f_1}{\partial \theta_1} & \dfrac{\partial f_2}{\partial \theta_1} \\[2mm] \dfrac{\partial f_1}{\partial \theta_2} & \dfrac{\partial f_2}{\partial \theta_2} \end{bmatrix} = \begin{bmatrix} 0 & -\exp(\pi t) \\[2mm] -\alpha Y & 0 \end{bmatrix} \neq 0$$

$$J\left(\frac{f_1, f_2}{\alpha, r}\right) = \begin{bmatrix} \dfrac{\partial f_1}{\partial \alpha} & \dfrac{\partial f_2}{\partial \alpha} \\ \dfrac{\partial f_1}{\partial r} & \dfrac{\partial f_2}{\partial r} \end{bmatrix} = \begin{bmatrix} -\theta_2 Y & 0 \\ 0 & Y^r \log Y \end{bmatrix} \neq 0.$$

Hence, the nonlinear relations in the model are reversible; there is intra-independence between the targets and also between the instruments, although the production function underlying the model is strictly complementary.

Consider now the recursive ordering of relations by which we refer to either a causal chain model developed by Wold, where the coefficient matrix of the endogenous variables is completely triangular with unit elements in the principal diagonal or a sequence of causal ordering developed by Simon [15]. Following Wold, a completely recursive linear system, i.e., a purely causal chain (PCC), can be written as

$$A_0 y(t) + B y(t - \phi) + C z(t) = u(t), \tag{3.15}$$

where $y(t)$ is the column vector of M endogenous variables, $y(t-\phi)$ and $z(t)$ are column vectors of N_1 lagged endogenous variables and N_2 exogenous variables, respectively. The coefficient matrix A_0 is assumed to be strictly triangular with unit elements in the principal diagonal. The recursiveness in coefficient structure of A_0 allows one to treat in each equation the $y_i(t)$ variable with the unit coefficient as the resultant variable and $y(t-\phi)$ and $z(t)$ as causal variables.

It is well known that a recursive (causal chain) model which may also be dynamic and nonlinear has a number of features which are convenient for economic policy models. It permits, for example, an explicit causal interpretation of the economic behavior relations in the sense of a stimulus-response relationship such that it allows an easy changeover when some dependent variables (i.e., targets) turn out to be amenable to direct control by the policy maker through other outside predetermined variables. At the end of this chapter and in Chapter 14, Section 14.2.1 concrete examples of recursiveness and interdependency in policy models are given. In other words, the relations of a purely recursive (PCC) system are designed as behavior relations for as many decision-making units as there are independent equations; hence, the behavior of the i-th decision-making unit can be given a stimulus-response or cause-effect interpretation in terms of the i-th equation of the system. A second advantage of such a system is that predictive inference is always possible, in terms of the parameters of either the original system or the reduced form, since the structural relations take the form of conditional expectations when we assume that residuals in each equation, whether lagged or nonlagged, are uncorrelated with the regressor variables and also uncorrelated mutually. Under such circumstances the estimation procedures turn out to be very simple, and the ordinary least-squares regression of the effect variable on the causal variables retains some of its desirable properties. Most important is that such estimates are asymptotically unbiased and equivalent to maximum-likelihood estimates when the joint distributions of the error terms are normal and the underlying stochastic process is ergodic.

On the other hand, an interdependent model of a simultaneous equations system does not ordinarily permit in its original form any causal interpretation of its relations, unless this is viewed as an approximation to the corresponding recursive system. Moreover, from the estimational viewpoint there always is a dichotomy between the estimation of parameters in the reduced form and in the original model, except in the just-identified case.

However, the interdependent (i.e., nonrecursive) model does enable us to predict the effects on the y variable resulting from the controlled variations in the exogenous variables.

Herbert Simon has developed the second type of causality, which has been also called "vector causality" [16]. If in equation (3.15) the vector $y(t)$ is partitioned into, for example, four column vectors y_1 to y_4, such that the coefficient matrix A_0 can be conformably partitioned into a block triangular matrix, i.e.,

$$A_0 y(t) = \begin{bmatrix} A_{11} & 0 & 0 & 0 \\ A_{21} & A_{22} & 0 & 0 \\ A_{31} & A_{32} & A_{33} & 0 \\ A_{41} & A_{42} & A_{43} & A_{44} \end{bmatrix} \begin{bmatrix} y_1 \\ y_2 \\ y_3 \\ y_4 \end{bmatrix} \qquad (3.16)$$

where A_{ij} are appropriate submatrices, this system defines, according to Simon, a relation of asymmetry or precedence in time that has a causal characteristic. Thus, according to this notion, the subvector y_1 may be said to be caused by the vectors $y(t-\phi)$ and z, the subvector y_2 caused by y_1 and z and so on till the subvector y_4 is caused by y_1, y_2, y_3 and z. It is easy to note that Wold's concept of causal chain is more strict and explicit, because it can be viewed as a special case of Simon's concept of causal ordering in terms of vector causality. There are at least three characteristics underlying Simon's concept which emphasize the recursiveness: (a) a basis of asymmetry between the subvectors y_1 to y_4 in relation (3.16), (b) causality is defined in a very strong sense, and is as such, independent of time, and (c) ordering of subvectors of endogenous variables in terms of the information content (i.e., a block-triangular coefficient matrix).

An example of a fixed-target model may clarify this point further. Consider the following simple Tinbergen model:

$$X = Y + E - M, \tag{3.17.1}$$

$$X = X_0 + bY, \tag{3.17.2}$$

$$M = mY, \tag{3.17.3}$$

$$D = M - E, \tag{3.17.4}$$

which relates to total expenditure X, exports E, imports M, balance of payments deficit D and domestic income Y. Assume that autonomous (public) expenditure X_0 is the only instrument and the fixed target is to attain a full-employment level of income $Y = Y_F$. Putting the known variables on the left-hand side and the unknown variables on the right-hand side, we may rewrite the system (3.17) as

$$Y_F = (1/m) M + 0.X + 0.D + 0.X_0 \tag{3.17.3}$$

$$Y_F + E = 1.M + 1.X + 0.D + 0.X_0 \tag{3.17.1}$$

$$E = 1.M + 0.X - 1.D + 0.X_0 \tag{3.17.4}$$

$$Y_F = 0.M + (1/b) X + 0.D - (1/b) X_0 \tag{3.17.2}$$

i.e.,

$$\begin{bmatrix} Y_F \\ Y_F + E \\ E \\ Y_F \end{bmatrix} = \begin{bmatrix} 1/m & 0 & 0 & 0 \\ 1 & 1 & 0 & 0 \\ 1 & 0 & -1 & 0 \\ 0 & 1/b & 0 & -1/b \end{bmatrix} \begin{bmatrix} M \\ X \\ D \\ X_0 \end{bmatrix}. \tag{3.18}$$

From the above rewritten system it is apparent that equation (3.17.3) has precedence over equations (3.17.1) and (3.17.4), since equation (13.17.1) for example, presupposes the value of M known from (3.17.3). Similarly, equation (3.17.1) precedes equation (3.17.2). Using the notation $\rightarrow$ to indicate "has precedence over," we may also say for the variables that

$$M \longrightarrow X \longrightarrow X_0$$
$$\searrow$$
$$D$$

and

$$(3.17.3) \longrightarrow (3.17.1) \longrightarrow (3.17.2)$$
$$\searrow$$
$$(3.17.4)$$

Simon defines those self-contained subsets of a linear structural model that do not contain proper subsets the minimal self-contained subsets of the structure. The order of a minimal subset (or subsystem) is specified by the stage of obtaining a derived structure (i.e., more information) from a minimal primary system (or subsystem) of lowest order. For the above example we have the following arrow diagram for causal ordering.

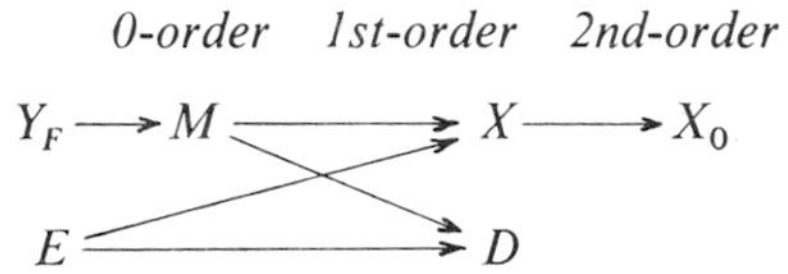

Diagram 3.1

Here ordering is according to an increasing sequence of information, i.e., a lower triangular coefficient matrix. A more detailed analysis[5] of the causal ordering scheme for a realistic model like the recent Social Science Research Council econometric model of the U.S. economy and its agricultural sub-model is found in Chapter 11.

One great advantage of constructing a causal ordering scheme, for a large model especially, is that ordering the equations and variables according to their "precedence and causal relations" shows the logical network of impact of the unknown policy variables.

However, two points may be made. First, the concept of vector causality is not invariant under all linear transformations, and so the problem of identification is not entirely resolved for all the equations (or subsets) of the entire system. Second, the presence of singularity which characterizes irreversibility of relations defined before may make the direction of causality in Simon's sense somewhat vague, if not altogether undefined.

The above model is recursive in terms of Simon's definition; yet it is interdependent (i.e., not recursive) if Wold's criterion is used (see equation (3.15)). It can, indeed, easily be verified that the coefficient matrix of the (nonlagged) endogenous variables is not triangular in (3.17).[6]

Another example is presented below to illustrate the concept of recursiveness (and causal chain) according to the Wold criterion.

---

[5] For a causal ordering scheme of the Central Economic Plan (1961) of the Netherlands, see Fox and Thorbecke [4]. See also Chapter 14, Section 14.2.1, of this book where the above model is presented and its causal aspects analyzed.

[6] The coefficient matrix of the endogenous variables in model (3.17) is:

$$\begin{bmatrix} 1 & -1 & -1 & 0 \\ b & -1 & 0 & 0 \\ -m & 0 & 1 & 0 \\ 0 & 0 & -1 & 1 \end{bmatrix} \begin{bmatrix} Y \\ X \\ M \\ D \end{bmatrix} = \begin{bmatrix} -E \\ -X_0 \\ 0 \\ -E \end{bmatrix}$$

Model A

Given the following policy models:[7]

$$Y = C + I + G + E - M,\qquad (3.19.1)$$
$$X = Y - T_i,\qquad (3.19.2)$$
$$C = a + bY,\qquad (3.19.3)$$
$$M = c + dY,\qquad (3.19.4)$$
$$I = kY_{(t-1)},\qquad (3.19.5)$$
$$T_i = f + hY,\qquad (3.19.6)$$
$$B = E - M.\qquad (3.19.7)$$

Model B

Same as above except for different consumption and import functions

$$C = a' + b'Y_{(t-1)},\qquad (3.19.3')$$
$$M = c' + d'Y_{(t-1)},\qquad (3.19.4')$$

where Y = national income at market prices,
X = national income at factor costs,
C = private consumption,
I = private investment,
E = exports,
M = imports,
G = government expenditures,
T_i = indirect taxes,
B = balance of payments surplus (deficit),
$Y_{(t-1)}$ = national income in year $t-1$,
f = autonomous level of indirect taxes.

Assume that there are two policy targets which are fixed and given, namely, full employment (X^F) and balance of payments equilibrium (B^E), and two instruments: government expenditures (G) and the autonomous level of indirect taxes (f). Furthermore, E and $Y_{(t-1)}$ are assumed to be given exogenously.

The policy problems are solved with respect to the two models A and B. An important point which comes to light in the following analysis is that the proper identification of a policy problem (i.e., whether a unique solution exists in a fixed target model) is completely independent of the structure of

---

[7] These models are rather trivial from a policy standpoint. The only purpose here is to illustrate the concept of causality and recursiveness à la Wold.

the model itself, that is, whether the model is recursive or interdependent in Wold's sense.

Model A

Endogenous Variables	*Exogenous Variables*
Targets: X^F, B^E	Instruments: f, G
Irrelevant	
Variables: Y, C, M, I, T_i	Data: E, $Y_{(t-1)}$

The reduced form can be easily obtained by a substitution process. X^F and B^E can, thus, be expressed as functions exclusively of the exogenous variables, the data and the instruments.

$$X^F = \left(\frac{1}{1-b+d}\right)\left[(a-c+kY_{(t-1)}+E)(1-h)\right]$$

$$- f + G\left(\frac{1}{1-b+d}\right)(1-h), \tag{3.20.1}$$

$$B^E = E - c - \frac{d}{1-b+d}(a-c+kY_{(t-1)}+E) - G\left(\frac{d}{1-b+d}\right). \tag{3.20.2}$$

It can immediately be seen that B^E is influenced exclusively by G, whereas X^F is influenced by both G and f. Thus the policy maker can only use government expenditures (G) for balance of payments equilibrium purposes, the only effective instrument to control X^F being f. In the above example G can be obtained from equation (3.20.2) and substituted in equation (3.20.1) to solve for f.

It is evident that Model A is interdependent in Wold's sense, since, for instance, M and C are functions of Y, while at the same time Y is determined by M and C.

It can readily be seen that the coefficient matrix of the endogenous variables is not triangular.

I				$= kY_{(t-1)}$	(3.19.5)
	C		$-bY$	$= a$	(3.19.3)
		M	$-dY$	$= c$	(3.19.4)
		$M+B$		$= E$	(3.19.7)
$-I$	$-C$	$+M$	$+Y$	$= E+G$	(3.19.1)
			$-hY+T_i$	$= f$	(3.19.6)
			$-Y+T_i+X=0$		(3.19.2)

Notice that in the above form the endogenous variables appear on the left-hand side and the exogenous variables on the right-hand side. In matrix form:

$$
\begin{bmatrix}
1 & 0 & 0 & 0 & 0 & 0 & 0 \\
0 & 1 & 0 & 0 & -b & 0 & 0 \\
0 & 0 & 1 & 0 & -d & 0 & 0 \\
0 & 0 & 1 & 1 & 0 & 0 & 0 \\
-1 & -1 & 1 & 0 & 1 & 0 & 0 \\
0 & 0 & 0 & 0 & -h & 1 & 0 \\
0 & 0 & 0 & 0 & -1 & 1 & 1
\end{bmatrix}
\begin{bmatrix}
I \\ C \\ M \\ B \\ Y \\ T_i \\ X
\end{bmatrix}
=
\begin{bmatrix}
kY_{(t-1)} \\ a \\ c \\ E \\ E+G \\ f \\ 0
\end{bmatrix}
$$

Model B

Here again the values of the instruments can be found by obtaining the reduced form. Substituting, we obtain for Y

$$Y = \underbrace{a' + b'Y_{(t-1)} + kY_{(t-1)} + E - c' - d'Y_{(t-1)}}_{L} + G. \qquad (3.21.1)$$

Let L stand for the constant term to the right of the equality sign. Further substitution gives us

$$X^F = L(1-h) - f + G(1-h), \qquad (3.21.2)$$
$$B^E = E - c' - d'Y_{(t-1)}. \qquad (3.21.3)$$

From the above it is obvious that X^F is a function of both instruments, whereas B^E is influenced by neither, being completely predetermined by the data E and $Y_{(t-1)}$. Thus, instead of having a system of two unknowns (G, f) and two equations, we have two unknowns and one equation (3.21.2) and one policy degree of freedom. An arbitrary value can be assigned to one instrument to solve the equation for the equilibrium value of the other instrument.

Yet Model B is recursive, according to Wold's rule as can be seen by working out the coefficient matrix of the endogenous variables:

$$
\begin{aligned}
I && = kY_{(t-1)} && (3.22.5) \\
C && = a' + b'Y_{(t-1)} && (3.22.3) \\
M && = c' + d'Y_{(t-1)} && (3.22.4) \\
M + B && = E && (3.22.7) \\
-I \quad -C \;+M \quad +Y && = E + G && (3.22.1) \\
-hY + T_i && = f && (3.22.6) \\
-Y + T_i + X && = 0 && (3.22.2)
\end{aligned}
$$

or, in matrix notation:

$$\begin{bmatrix} 1 & 0 & 0 & 0 & 0 & 0 & 0 \\ 0 & 1 & 0 & 0 & 0 & 0 & 0 \\ 0 & 0 & 1 & 0 & 0 & 0 & 0 \\ 0 & 0 & 1 & 1 & 0 & 0 & 0 \\ -1 & -1 & 1 & 0 & 1 & 0 & 0 \\ 0 & 0 & 0 & 0 & -h & 1 & 0 \\ 0 & 0 & 0 & 0 & -1 & 1 & 1 \end{bmatrix} \begin{bmatrix} I \\ C \\ M \\ B \\ Y \\ T_i \\ X \end{bmatrix} = \begin{bmatrix} kY_{(t-1)} \\ a' + b'Y_{(t-1)} \\ c' + d'Y_{(t-1)} \\ E \\ E + G \\ f \\ 0 \end{bmatrix}$$

From the above matrix it is easy to derive the corresponding causal ordering scheme:

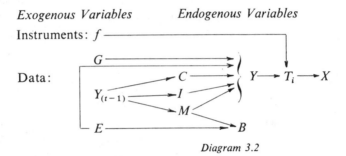

Diagram 3.2

It can be seen that B is not influenced by either instrument, as equation (3.21.3) indicated, while X is affected by both f and G. The policy maker has no way of controlling the balance of payments but has one instrumental (policy) degree of freedom with respect to his other target X^F.

REFERENCES

[1] BENTZEL, R., and HANSEN, B. "On Recursiveness and Interdependency in Economic Models," *Review of Economic Studies*, XXII (3), No. 59 (1954–55).

[2] CHENERY, H. B. "Development Policies for Southern Italy," *Quarterly Journal of Economics*, LXXVI (November, 1962), 515.

[3] FOX, K. A. *Econometric Analysis for Public Policy*. Ames, Ia.: Iowa State University Press, 1958.

[4] ——, and THORBECKE, E. "Specification of Structures and Data Requirements in Economic Policy Models," in *Quantitative Planning of Economic Policy*. Edited by B. G. Hickman. Washington, D.C.: The Brookings Institution, 1965, Chap. 3.

[5] JOHNSTON, J. *Econometric Methods*. New York: McGraw-Hill Book Co., 1963.

[6] KENDALL, M. G. "Regression, Structure and Functional Relationship," *Biometrika*, XXXIX (May, 1952), 96–108.

[7] KLEIN, L. R. *A Textbook of Econometrics*. Evanston, Ill.: Row, Peterson, 1953.

[8] KONIJN, H. S. "Identification and Estimation in a Simultaneous Equation Model with Errors in the Variables," *Econometrica*, XXX (January, 1962), 79–87.

[9] KOOPMANS, T. C. "Identification Problems in Economic Model Construction," in *Studies in Econometric Method*. Edited by W. Hood and T. C. Koopmans. New York: John Wiley & Sons, 1953.

[10] KSHIRSAGAR, A. "Prediction from Simultaneous Equation Systems and Wold's Implicit Causal Chain Model," *Econometrica*, XXX (October, 1962), 801–811.

[11] OTT, A. E. "Production Functions, Technical Progress and Economic Growth," *International Economic Papers*, XI (1962), 102.

[12] POPPER, K. *Logic of Scientific Discovery*. Revised edition. London: Hutchinson, 1961, Chaps. 6–7.

[13] SARGAN, J. D. "Lags and Stability of Dynamic Systems," *Econometrica*, XXIX (October, 1961), 659.

[14] SENGUPTA, J. K. "Specification and Estimation of Structural Relations in Policy Models," in *Quantitative Planning of Economic Policy*. Edited by B. G. Hickman. Washington, D.C., The Brookings Institution, 1965, Chap. 4.

[15] SIMON, H. "Causal Ordering and Identifiability," in *Studies in Econometric Method*. Edited by W. Hood and T. C. Koopmans. New York: John Wiley & Sons, 1953.

[16] STROTZ, R., and WOLD, H. "Recursive Versus Nonrecursive Systems: An Attempt at Synthesis," *Econometrica*, XXVIII (April, 1960), 417–427.

[17] TARSKI, A., and SUPPES, P. (eds.) *Logic, Methodology and Philosophy of Science*, Stanford, Calif.: Stanford University Press, 1962.

[18] TINTNER, G. *Econometrics*. New York: John Wiley & Sons, 1952.

[19] VERDOORN, P. J. "Complementarity and Long-Range Projections," *Econometrica* XXIV (October, 1956), 429–450.

[20] WOLD, H. "Construction Principles of Simultaneous Equation Models in Econometrics," *Bulletin of International Statistical Institute*, XXXVIII (1960), 111–138.

Chapter 4

ECONOMETRIC ESTIMATION OF QUANTITATIVE POLICY MODELS

4.1. The Logic of the Least-Squares Method

Econometric estimation may be viewed from two alternative standpoints: either as a part of statistical decision theory (which requires the specification of a function for the loss resulting from a given difference between the estimate and the true value of the unknown parameter) or as a technique of statistical inference (which has the general objective of developing optimum rules for discriminating among alternative possible situations on the basis of the given data). Since the approach of decision theory will be reviewed in its operational aspects in Chapters 6, 7 and 9, we consider estimation here only as in some sense the best method of making a statistical inference from the given data.

The single method of estimation which has proved most operational and useful in econometric estimation of simultaneous models is still the method of least squares with some appropriate modifications necessitated by economic data which are nonexperimental in nature. Situations which do not satisfy all the assumptions of least-squares theory in a strict sense require in most cases a "least-squares-like" or quasi least-squares method of estimation, because of the simplicity of calculation and a host of other valuable properties such as robustness and consistency. Examples of such quasi-least-squares methods for economic models are provided by the applications of (a) least squares to the reduced form of a linear interdependent model,[1] (b) two-stage and k-stage least squares to derive consistent estimates [2, 38], (c) stepwise and numerical procedures for nonlinear least squares [14] and (d) least squares under constraints in the parameter space [25].

---

[1] For a just-identified case a special case of this method called indirect least squares could be applied to each separate equation of the reduced form. See Johnston [17]. For the general approach see Haavelmo [13].

4.2. Single-Equation Least-Squares Method

It is useful to consider some of the important results of the classical least-squares method [17] when applied to a single equation model. Assume we have n observations for a single dependent variable and p independent variables related by a linear model

$$y = X\beta + e \quad \begin{array}{l} y : n.1 \text{ (vector of observations)}, \\ X : n.p \text{ (known constants)}, \\ \beta : p.1 \text{ (unknown constants)}, \\ e : n.1 \text{ (error vector)}, \end{array} \quad (4.1)$$

such that the joint distribution of the error vector e is independent of the ·explanatory variables and $E(e)=0$ and $E(ee')=\sigma^2 I_n$, where E stands for the expectation operator, prime denotes transposition and I_n means an identity matrix of order n. Further, σ^2 is a finite scalar constant, implying the assumption of homoscedasticity. Under these assumptions the least-squares method defines an estimator $\hat{\beta}$ by minimizing the scalar $(e'e)$, i.e.,

$$\underset{\beta}{\text{minimize}}\, Q(\beta) = e'e = (y - X\beta)'(y - X\beta),$$

and then set $\beta=\hat{\beta}$ to obtain the least-squares estimator $\hat{\beta}$. The minimizing equations, usually called normal equations, are given by

$$X'X\hat{\beta} = X'y. \quad (4.2)$$

The Gauss-Markov theorem on least squares has several important implications, some of which may be mentioned here without explicit proof:

(a) The normal equations given by (4.2) are always consistent mathematically for any y, since rank $(X'X)=$ rank $(X'X \vdots X'y)$; this is true even if the rank of $(X'X)$ is less than p. In case $X'X$ has rank p, the p-element column vector of estimates $\hat{\beta}$ is unique, i.e., $\hat{\beta}=(X'X)^{-1}X'y$.

(b) The least-squares estimator $\hat{\beta}$ is unbiased, i.e., $E\hat{\beta}=\beta$, and in the class of linear unbiased estimators it has the minimum variance, i.e., Var $(\hat{\beta})=(X'X)^{-1}\sigma^2 \leq$ Var $(\tilde{\beta})$, where $\tilde{\beta}$ is any other linear unbiased estimator. In other words, the least-squares estimate has b.l.u.e. (best linear unbiased estimate) properties in the sense defined. However, one should note that the reference set for comparison is the class of linear and unbiased estimators.

(c) If the joint distribution of the vector e be such that it is heteroscedastic, i.e., $E(ee')=\sigma^2 V$, where V is a nondiagonal and nonsingular (i.e., positive definite) variance-covariance matrix and other assumptions of the model

(4.1) hold, one could apply Aitken's method of generalized least squares i.e., since the symmetric matrix V is assumed positive definite there must exist a real nonsingular matrix T such that $TVT' = I_n$. In this case $\text{Var}(Te) = \sigma^2 I_n$, and so we can transform the model (4.1) as

$$(Ty) = (TX)\beta + (Te), \tag{4.1.1}$$

and so denoting $\bar{y} = Ty$, $\bar{X} = TX$ and $\bar{e} = Te$ we get

$$\bar{y} = \bar{X}\beta + \bar{e}, \tag{4.1.2}$$

which has all the properties and assumptions of ordinary least squares.

(d) The least-squares estimator $\hat{\beta}$ has its generalized variance less than that of any other estimator belonging to the class of linear unbiased estimators, where the generalized variance of random variables $u_1, u_2, ..., u_n$ is defined by the determinant of the variance-covariance matrix of $u_1, u_2, ..., u_n$.

Intuitively, it seems that this result accounts partly for the robustness of a least-squares estimate, i.e., its appropriateness in small sample situations and insensitivity to slight variations in some of the underlying assumptions. A proof[2] of this result may be instructive. Let $\hat{\beta}$ be the least-squares estimate, then

$$E(\hat{\beta} - \beta)(\hat{\beta} - \beta)' = E\left[\{(X'X)^{-1}X'e\}\{e'X(X'X)^{-1}\}\right]$$
$$= (X'X)^{-1}X'E(ee')X(X'X)^{-1} = \sigma^2(X'X)^{-1}$$

assuming homoscedasticity and the full rank case, i.e., rank $(X'X) = p$. Then the generalized variance of $\hat{\beta}$ is $(\sigma^2)^p |(X'X)^{-1}|$.

Let $\tilde{\beta} = A'y$ be any arbitrary linear unbiased estimate of β other than $\hat{\beta}$, where A is a constant matrix of n by p. Since $\tilde{\beta}$ is unbiased, therefore, $E\tilde{\beta} = A'Ey = A'X\beta = \beta$, i.e., $A'X = I = X'A$. Now

$$E\left[(\tilde{\beta} - \beta)(\tilde{\beta} - \beta)'\right] = E\left[\{A'(X\beta + e) - \beta\}\{A'(X\beta + e) - \beta\}'\right]$$
$$= E(A'ee'A) = \sigma^2 A'A\,;$$

therefore

$$\text{generalized Var}(\tilde{\beta}) = (\sigma^2)^p |A'A|.$$

We know that $\text{Var}(\hat{\beta}) < \text{Var}(\tilde{\beta})$, since the least-squares estimate has the b.l.u.e. properties. Denoting by λ a p-element column vector of nonzero

---

2 The following proof is taken from a set of lecture notes prepared by Professor George Zyskind for his course on General Linear Hypothesis at Iowa State University, 1963.

constants, it is easy to show from this that

$$\text{Var}\,(\lambda'\tilde{\beta}) > \text{Var}\,(\lambda'\hat{\beta}),$$

i.e.,

$$\sigma^2\lambda'A'A\lambda > \sigma^2\lambda'(X'X)^{-1}\lambda,$$

i.e.,

$\lambda'(A'A - (X'X)^{-1})\lambda \geqq 0$, with equality if and only if $\lambda = 0$.

As $(X'X)^{-1}$ is positive definite, real and symmetric there must exist a nonsingular matrix Q such that $Q'(X'X)^{-1}Q = I$. But $Q'A'AQ$ is symmetric, and so there exists an orthogonal matrix R such that $R'(Q'A'AQ)R = D = \text{diag}\,(d_1, d_2, ..., d_p)$, where d_i are the characteristic roots of the matrix $Q'A'AQ$. Now let us choose λ such that $\lambda = QR\gamma$. Then

$$\lambda'(A'A - (X'X)^{-1})\lambda = \gamma'R'Q'(A'A - (X'X)^{-1})QR\gamma = \gamma'(D - I)\gamma \geq 0$$

$$= \sum_{i=1}^{p} (d_i - 1)\gamma_i^2 \geq 0, \text{ with equality, if and only if } \gamma = 0.$$

Hence, $d_i \geq 1$ and not all $d_i = 1$. Therefore,

$$|D| = (d_1 d_2 ... d_p) = |R'Q'A'AQR| > 1 = |I| = |Q'(X'X)^{-1}Q|.$$

By the product rule for square determinants

$$|R'Q'A'AQR| = (|R|)^2 (|Q|)^2 |A'A|$$
$$|Q'(X'X)^{-1}Q| = (|Q|)^2 |(X'X)^{-1}|.$$

But $(|R|)^2 = 1$, since R is an orthogonal matrix and $|Q|$ is not zero by non-singularity. Hence, it follows that

$$|A'A| > |(X'X)^{-1}|.$$

Therefore

$$\text{generalized Var}\,(\hat{\beta}) < \text{generalized Var}\,(\tilde{\beta}).$$

(e) Another very important property of least-squares estimation is its robustness in terms of specification error [44]. Write equation (4.1) in a general form,

$$y_i = x_{i1}\beta_1 + x_{i2}\beta_2 + \cdots + x_{ip}\beta_p + e_i \qquad i = 1, 2, ..., n,$$

where i is the subscript for the number of observations. For a fixed i, we can rewrite this as

$$y = x_{(1)}\beta_1 + x_{(2)}\beta_2 + \cdots + x_{(p)}\beta_p + e. \tag{4.3}$$

Now if the "true" model has another term on the right-hand side of equation (4.3) such as $x_{(p+1)}\beta_p$, which has a significant role in explaining the variation in y, but instead we hypothesize an incorrect model like (4.3) and estimate β's, we commit a specification error. This is the most important matter, since the specification error will not tend to zero with the increased size of the sample; moreover, it might even distort the estimates obtained from a misspecified model, depending on the degree of misspecification. However, under ordinary conditions, the least-squares estimator $\hat{\beta}$ has a robust property, which states that [44] if (i) the disturbance term e in equation (4.3) has a small standard deviation $\sigma(e) \leq \theta_1$, where θ_1 is a preassigned small quantity, and (ii) it has small correlation coefficients with $x_{(1)}, \ldots, x_{(p)}$ (i.e., correlation $(e, x_{(i)}) \leq \theta_2 \sigma(e) \sigma(x_{(i)})$, where θ_2 is a preassigned small quantity); then, the least-squares regression estimates $\hat{\beta}_i$ ($i = 1, 2, \ldots, p$) approximate the true values β_i in model (4.3) within margins that are small of order $\theta_1 \theta_2$, i.e.,

$$\|\hat{\beta}_i - \beta_i\| < c \cdot \theta_1 \theta_2 \qquad (i = 1, 2, \ldots, p),$$

where $\| \ \|$ denotes the absolute value and the variable c does not depend on the error e.

(f) This robustness property of least-squares estimates is enhanced by the fact that least-squares estimation is relatively less sensitive to the presence of multicollinearity among the explanatory variables than other methods of estimation such as maximum likelihood, etc. Multicollinearity among the explanatory variables is frequently encountered in econometric models based on time-series data. In single-equation regression models, this leads to singularity in the variance-covariance matrix, and so the estimates of individual coefficients of the intercorrelated variables are either undefined or indeterminate. It is possible, however, to analyze the sensitivity and the existence of a limiting value of an estimated coefficient when the intercorrelation among the set of explanatory variables tends to be perfect, i.e., maximum multicollinearity. Recent investigations, both experimental or empirical [12] and theoretical [22], have shown that even in those cases where the limiting value of the estimated coefficients exists as the intercorrelation tends to its maximum, there is a marked difference in the sensitivity of alternative estimation methods to the presence of multicollinearity. The models which are recursive or very nearly so are the least sensitive to such problems of multicollinearity because the least-squares method is appropriately applicable to the model in its original rather than reduced form. The two-stage least-squares and (to an even greater extent) the limited-information methods of estimation have greater sensitivity than least squares to the presence of singularity resulting from multicollinearity, primarily because there is more than one stage of estimation procedure involved.

(g) The least-squares model we have discussed so far does not admit of any restriction on the parameter space which may be external or a priori. If the restrictions imposed on the parameters constitute a set of q *exact* linear equations, i.e.,

$$G\beta = k, \tag{4.4}$$

where G is a g by p nonsingular matrix of known constants and k is a q-component column vector of known constants, a simple transformation [19, 42] of the least-squares model (4.1) would resolve the problem of restricted least-squares regression. Let the matrix G and the vector β be partitioned such that

$$G\beta = [G_1 \vdots G_2] \binom{\beta_1}{\beta_2} = G_1\beta_1 + G_2\beta_2 = k,$$

where the inverse G_1^{-1} exists. Since we have

$$\beta_1 = G_1^{-1}(k - G_2\beta_2) \tag{4.5}$$

the linear model equation (4.1) becomes

$$y = [X_1 \vdots X_2] \binom{G_1^{-1}(k - G_2\beta_2)}{\beta_2} + e,$$

i.e.,

$$(y - X_1 G_1^{-1}k) = (X_2 - X_1 G_1^{-1} G_2)\beta_2 + e,$$

i.e.,

$$\bar{y} = \bar{X}\beta_2 + e, \tag{4.6}$$

where we denote

$$\bar{y} = y - X_1 G_1^{-1}k; \qquad \bar{X} = X_2 - X_1 G_1^{-1} G_2,$$

and assume that the matrix G_1 is square and nonsingular, i.e., appropriate partitioning of the matrix X and G is implied. We can obtain a straightforward least-squares estimate $\tilde{\beta}_2$ from equation (4.6) and then obtain an estimate of β_1 from equation (4.5). This provides a method of blending the internal and external restrictions on the parameter space. [3]

---

[3] See Section 4.6.

When the restriction is linear but not exact, an optimal method of blending the internal and external estimates can be easily devised. Suppose we have one set of observations for the model (4.1) and we have external information on the same parameters through another cross-section model (or prior information). When the extra information is in the form of extra observations on the y and the X-variables only, we can write the extra information as

$$r = R\beta + v \qquad \begin{array}{l} r\text{: } m.1 \text{ (}y\text{-variables)}, \\ R\text{: } m.p \text{ (}X\text{-variables)}, \\ \beta\text{: } p.1 \text{ (parameter)}, \\ v\text{: } m.1 \text{ (error)}, \end{array} \qquad (4.7)$$

where r is the vector of observations on the y-variable and R is the matrix of observations on the independent X-variables, although (4.7) is obtained through an alternative and *independent* source of information (i.e., v should be independent of e in (4.1)).

Following Theil [40], we may write the combined system, i.e., (4.1) and (4.7) in a single matrix equation

$$\left(\begin{array}{c} y \\ \hline r \end{array}\right) = \left(\begin{array}{c} X \\ \hline R \end{array}\right)\beta + \left(\begin{array}{c} e \\ \hline v \end{array}\right).$$

Hence, denoting

$$\left(\begin{array}{c} y \\ \hline r \end{array}\right) \text{ by } \bar{y}, \left(\begin{array}{c} X \\ \hline R \end{array}\right) \text{ by } \bar{X} \text{ and } \left(\begin{array}{c} e \\ \hline v \end{array}\right)$$

by $\bar{e}$ we get the transformed least-squares model

$$\bar{y} = \bar{X}\beta + \bar{e}$$

with all optimum properties. If in the original but separate models the least-squares estimate has b.l.u.e. properties, the combined estimate will also have b.l.u.e. properties. This sort of combination is sometimes called a mixed-estimation method, and it covers a class of estimation methods when at some stage or other the usual statistical estimation procedure has to incorporate extraneous information which may even be of an a priori (or subjective) rather than statistical (or objective) nature.

4.3. Singularity and Estimability

In our brief review of single-equation least-squares methods, we have not so far mentioned situations where some of the elegant results of least-squares theory may not hold. Two such situations which arise most frequently in economic models which are based on time-series data need some special attention. One is the case when some of the explanatory variables in the model (4.1) are lagged endogenous variables. The second is the problem of multicollinearity of the explanatory variables (already referred to), which may result in singularity or near-singularity of the coefficient matrix $(X'X)$ of the normal equations or the variance-covariance matrix of the least-squares estimates.

In the first case, when the independent variables include lagged endogenous variables along with other truly exogenous variables, the least-squares estimate is no longer a *linear* function of the observations, hence the b.l.u.e. property does not hold. So long as other conditions for a regular least-squares situation hold, the estimates obtained would have, however, the property of consistency or asymptotic unbiasedness. Kendall and Durbin[4] have attempted to define a criterion in terms of a best linear unbiased estimating *equation* in analogy with the best linear unbiased estimate. For example, consider the following simple two-variable linear regression models

$$y_t = \beta x_t + e_t, \qquad e_t \text{ and } v_t \text{ are random errors independently} \quad (4.8)$$
$$y_t = \alpha y_{t-1} + v_t, \qquad \text{distributed with } (0, \sigma^2). \quad (4.9)$$

In case (4.8) the least-squares estimate

$$\hat{\beta} = \left(\sum_t x_t^2 \right)^{-1} \left(\sum_t x_t y_t \right)$$

is a linear function of the observations and has b.l.u.e. properties under the classical assumptions mentioned before. In case (4.9) the least-squares estimate

$$\hat{\alpha} = \left(\sum_t y_{t-1}^2 \right)^{-1} \left(\sum_t y_t y_{t-1} \right)$$

is a ratio of two quadratic forms and, hence, nonlinear and, hence, not b.l.u.e. For case (4.9) the estimating equation is

$$\hat{\alpha} \sum y_{t-1}^2 - \sum y_t y_{t-1} = 0.$$

Replacing the estimate $\hat{\alpha}$ by the parameter α we get

$$\alpha \sum y_{t-1}^2 - \sum y_t y_{t-1} = 0.$$

Thus, suppose the estimator $\hat{\alpha}$ of a parameter α is given by the linear equation

---

[4] This section is based on Durbin [7].

of the form

$$T_1 \hat{\alpha} - T_2 = 0, \tag{4.11}$$

where T_1, T_2 are functions of observations (e.g., Σy_{t-1}^2 and $\Sigma y_t y_{t-1}$, respectively) such that T_2/T_1 is independent of the unknown parameter α and where $E(T_1 \alpha - T_2) = 0$. Then equation (4.11) is called a linear unbiased estimating equation. Suppose that $T_1 \tilde{\alpha} - T_2 = 0$ is an unbiased linear estimating equation such that

$$\text{Var } (T_1 \hat{\alpha} - T_2) \leqq \text{Var } (t_1 \tilde{\alpha} - t_2),$$

for all other unbiased linear estimating equations $t_1 \tilde{\alpha} - t_2 = 0$. Then equation (4.11) may be called b.l.u.e.e. (best linear unbiased estimating equation) by analogy with b.l.u.e.

However, the difficulty posed by multicollinearity is more complicated. Due to the presence of lagged endogenous variables as explanatory variables, there is more likely to be a very high intercorrelation among these variables, and so the matrix $(X'X)$ in the normal equation (4.2) is singular or very nearly so. But since the normal equation (4.2) is always consistent mathematically (i.e., existence of solution is proved), singularity of the coefficient matrix $(X'X)$ may be analyzed under two different cases:

(a) Case 1, when the solution of the normal equation (4.2) is not unique but a linear function of the parameters, e.g., $\lambda'\beta$ (where λ is a column vector of p elements) may be unique. (Other conditions of classical least squares are assumed to be fulfilled here.)

(b) Case 2, when the uniqueness of the estimates is obtained through either inequality restrictions on the set of feasible estimates or prior restrictions.

In Case 1 we have to follow what is known as the estimable-function approach in least-squares theory. In case of multicollinearity, an alternative approach to this is the method of principal components [23], where we replace the intercorrelated explanatory variables by a set of mutually orthogonal index numbers (constructed out of the correlation matrix of the intercorrelated explanatory variables). However, this may be of less practical use, if we are interested in the coefficients associated with the intercorrelated explanatory variables, because there is no unique transformation from the coefficients of the principal component variables back to the original coefficients.

In the estimable-function approach we seek to specify the conditions under which any linear function $\lambda'\beta$ of the parameter β would be estimable, and if the relevant normal equations involve a singular coefficient matrix, we impose certain normalizing conditions on the matrix to define a more generalized class of inverse, known as the Moore-Penrose-type inverse [31] (which characterizes even a matrix and its inverse which would ordinarily be regarded as singular).

A linear parametric function $\lambda'\beta$ is said to be linearly estimable from the observed data that are subject to the least-squares model (4.1), if and only if there exists a column vector μ independent of the actual values of β such that

$$\lambda'\beta = E(u'y) = E\left[\mu'(X\beta + e)\right] = \mu'X\beta$$

for all β, i.e., $\lambda' = \mu'X$. In other words, the vector λ' should be expressible as a linear function of the row vectors of the matrix X. Hence, if the arbitrary vector λ' of linear combination cannot be expressed as a linear function of the row vectors of the matrix of observations X, the function $\lambda'\beta$ is said to be nonestimable. It is not difficult to show from this that the number of linearly independent estimable parametric functions $\lambda'\beta$ is equal to the rank of the matrix X. If the linear function $\lambda'\beta$ is estimable, its estimate is given by

$$\lambda'\hat{\beta} = \lambda'(C^-X'y) = \lambda'C^-X'y,$$

where C^- is the generalized inverse (g-inverse) of $(X'X)$ defined as

$$C^- = \begin{cases} (X'X)^{-1}, \text{ if the ordinary inverse exists}, \\ g\text{-inverse, if the ordinary inverse is not defined}. \end{cases}$$

Following Rao,[5] a generalized inverse (i.e., g-inverse) of a matrix C of order m by n is defined to be a matrix of order n by m denoted by C^- such that for any column vector β for which the set of equations $C\beta = k$ is consistent we have the solution $\beta = C^-k$. Note that if $C = X'X$ and $k = X'y$ the result is directly applicable to our normal equation (4.2) before.

From this definition, two properties [33] of a g-inverse can be derived.

(i)   If C^- is a g-inverse, $CC^-C = C$ and the converse.

(ii) A g-inverse C^- exists for any matrix C, although it may not be unique and, further, it can be constructed in such a way that it has C itself as the g-inverse. In other words, it is possible to find C^- such that $CC^-C = C$ and $C^-CC^- = C^-$.

(iii) A general solution of $C\beta = k$, when this is consistent, is $[C^-k + (C^-C - I)z]$, where I is the identity matrix and the column vector z is arbitrary.

---

[5] This section is based on Rao [33].

(iv) A necessary and sufficient condition that a linear function $\lambda'\beta$ is *unique*, when β satisfies $C\beta = k$ is that $\lambda'C^-C = \lambda'$.

Applying these results to the least-squares theory, we see that if the normal equation system (4.2) is singular, i.e., $|X'X| = 0$, the solution of $\hat{\beta}$ is not unique but, however, a linear function $\lambda'\beta$ of parameters may be unique. Such a function is said to be estimable, and its estimate is given by $\lambda'\hat{\beta} = \lambda'C^-X'y$. Further, almost all the other properties of classical least-squares may be derived now with the help of the g-inverse, e.g.,

(i) $E(\lambda'\hat{\beta}) = \lambda'\beta$, if $\lambda'\beta$ is estimable,

(ii) $\text{Var}(\lambda'\hat{\beta}) = (\lambda'C^-\lambda)\,\sigma^2$,

(iii) $\text{Var}(\lambda'\hat{\beta}) \le \text{Var}(\mu'y)$ for any μ such that $E(\mu'y) = \lambda'\beta$, i.e., any linear unbiased estimate of the estimable function $\lambda'\beta$ other than the least-squares estimate $\lambda'\hat{\beta}$ has its variance higher than or equal to that of the least-squares estimate.

However, it is important to emphasize that the concept of g-inverse is not unique, and different methods have been suggested to impose the uniqueness property. For instance, Penrose defined a unique generalized inverse B of any arbitrary matrix A which satisfies the following four conditions, the first two of which we have mentioned before:

$$ABA = A, \; BAB = B, \; (AB)' = AB, \; (BA)' = BA.$$

Hence, the estimable-function approach has the practical limitation that, like the principal-component method, it introduces a rather artificial rule of scaling or normalizing the coefficient matrix of normal equations to break through its singularity. However, it is a great analytical improvement to prove the result that under regular conditions of classical least squares the singularity of the coefficient matrix of the normal equations does not violate any of the b.l.u.e. properties we have discussed before.

In Case 2, when we introduce a priori knowledge on the parameters, we generally convert the least-squares situation to one of quadratic programming. For example, assume we have a regular case (i.e., $(X'X)^{-1}$ exists) of normal equation (4.2) which gives us the least-squares estimate $\hat{\beta}$. This estimate $\hat{\beta}$ does not take account of any a priori knowledge, e.g., that the parameters β are nonnegative ($\beta_i \ge 0$) or that they are subject to inequality constraints

$$\left(\text{e.g.,} \sum_{i=1}^{p} \beta \le 1\right).$$

Hence, a more general case of the least-squares problem can be formulated as

$$\text{minimize } Q(\beta) = e'e = (y - X\beta)'(y - X\beta) \qquad (4.12)$$

under the linear constraints

$$R\beta \leqq q \, ,$$

where R and q are known by a priori knowledge (i.e., the matrix R and vector q specify all the inequality restrictions on the parameters β). Any vector which solves the quadratic programming problem (4.12) is called a restricted least-squares estimate (i.e., restricted by a convex parameter space) and denoted by $\tilde{\beta}$. To avoid trivial results we assume $\tilde{\beta}$ to be not equal to $\hat{\beta}$. We assume further that some form of algorithm for quadratic programming [4.6] has been applied to obtain $\tilde{\beta}$. What are the relations between the unrestricted least-squares estimate $\hat{\beta}$ and the restricted least-squares estimate $\tilde{\beta}$? We will mention an important result,[6] which may be useful for solving problems of multicollinearity later.

Theorem. The minimization of the residual sum of squares $Q(\beta)$ defined in (4.12) in the convex region S specified by the linear constraints is identical with determining that point $\tilde{\beta}$ in region S which is "nearest" to the least-squares estimator. The concept of "nearest" refers to the metric in which the elements of $\hat{\beta}$ are independently distributed with equal variance.

Proof. Considering the model (4.1) before

$$y = X\beta + e$$

and assuming $X'X$ to be nonsingular, let T of order p by p and U of order n by p be appropriately nonsingular transformations such that

$$T'X'XT = I_p = U'U \, .$$

Then the model (4.1) becomes

$$y = XTT^{-1}\beta + e = U\gamma + e,$$

where $\gamma = T^{-1}\beta$ and $U = XT$. With the usual assumption $E(e) = 0$, $E(ee') = \sigma^2 I$, the least-squares estimate $\hat{\gamma}$ of γ is

$$\hat{\gamma} = (U'U)^{-1}U'y = I_p U'y = U'y.$$

In the transformed parameter space, i.e., the γ-space, the quadratic form

---

[6] These results are taken from Lewish [25].

that is minimized is

$$Q_{LS} = (y - U\hat{\gamma})'(y - U\hat{\gamma}).$$

Denote by Q_p the quadratic form minimized for the system (4.12) by a quadratic programming algorithm, where $\tilde{\beta}$ is the vector of estimates. Then for the $\tilde{\gamma}$-system corresponding to $\tilde{\beta}$ we have

$$
\begin{aligned}
Q_p &= (y - U\tilde{\gamma})'(y - U\tilde{\gamma}), \\
    &= [(y - U\hat{\gamma}) + U(\hat{\gamma} - \tilde{\gamma})]'[(y - U\hat{\gamma}) + U(\hat{\gamma} - \tilde{\gamma})], \\
    &= \{(y - U\hat{\gamma})'(y - U\hat{\gamma}) + 2(y - U\hat{\gamma})'U(\hat{\gamma} - \tilde{\gamma})\} + (\hat{\gamma} - \tilde{\gamma})'U'U(\hat{\gamma} - \tilde{\gamma}), \\
    &= Q_{LS} + (\hat{\gamma} - \tilde{\gamma})'(\hat{\gamma} - \tilde{\gamma}), \text{ since } U'U = I_p.
\end{aligned}
$$

Since Q_{LS} is a constant, it follows from this relation that Q_p is a function of only $\tilde{\gamma}$ over the convex region S_γ and $\tilde{\gamma}$ appears only in the distance-squared term

$$(\hat{\gamma} - \tilde{\gamma})'(\hat{\gamma} - \tilde{\gamma}) = \sum_{i=1}^{p} (\hat{\gamma}_i - \tilde{\gamma}_i)^2.$$

(Note also that since $\gamma = T^{-1}\beta$, the estimate $\tilde{\gamma}$ lies in the plane of $\hat{\gamma}$.) Thus, minimizing Q_p is equivalent to minimizing the distance term. In other words, the quadratic programming technique selects from the acceptable region S (i.e., defined by the convex and linear constraints of the model (12)) that solution vector $\tilde{\gamma}$ that is nearest to the unrestrained least-squares solution vector $\hat{\gamma}$. However, this property of minimum distance applies only to a specific metric, which has been shown to be that metric in which $U'U$ is the identity matrix I_p. In this metric the elements of $\hat{\gamma}$ have equal variances $\hat{\sigma}^2$ and zero covariances. Using the above theorem, Lewish has further proved that if the parameter space S is convex and the true parameter β is in S, $|\tilde{\beta}-\beta|^2 \le |\hat{\beta}-\beta|^2$; this can be written as

$$\sum_{i=1}^{p} (\tilde{\beta}_i - \beta_i)^2 \le \sum_{i=1}^{p} (\hat{\beta}_i - \beta_i)^2.$$

Hence, taking expectations on both sides

$$\sum_{i=1}^{p} \text{MSE}(\tilde{\beta}_i) = E|\tilde{\beta} - \beta|^2 \le E|\hat{\beta} - \beta|^2 = \sum_{i=1}^{p} \text{Var}\,\hat{\beta}_i,$$

where MSE is the mean-square error. However, this does not imply a stronger statement that

$$\text{MSE}(\tilde{\beta}_i) \le \text{Var}(\hat{\beta}_i) \text{ for every } i$$

unless $p = 1$ or if $\beta_i (i = 1, 2, ..., p)$ are unrestricted.

In case of multicollinearity when the rank of $(X'X)$ is less than p, one may suggest an optimum method of combining the information in normal equations with that available through extraneous sources. A small example would perhaps illustrate the point. Suppose we have a three-variable least-squares model

$$y = \alpha_1 x_1 + \alpha_2 x_2 + e.$$

The normal equations are

$$\begin{bmatrix} \sum x_1^2 & \sum x_1 x_2 \\ \sum x_1 x_2 & \sum x_2^2 \end{bmatrix} \begin{pmatrix} \hat{\alpha}_1 \\ \hat{\alpha}_2 \end{pmatrix} = \begin{pmatrix} \sum x_1 y \\ \sum x_2 y \end{pmatrix}. \tag{4.13}$$

In case the coefficient matrix is of rank one (i.e., less than full rank), it is obvious that the least-squares estimates $\hat{\alpha}_1$, $\hat{\alpha}_2$ cannot be obtained uniquely; at most, one of them or a single linear relation between them (i.e., estimable function) could be obtained. If, however, we need both the coefficients, which might represent definite economic concepts, such as elasticity of demand or propensity to consume, etc., we must introduce some further conditions. Suppose these further conditions are available through external sources (or cross-section information), which we take for simplicity of the form

$$\begin{bmatrix} 1 & 0 \\ 0 & 1 \end{bmatrix} \begin{pmatrix} \hat{\alpha}_1 \\ \hat{\alpha}_2 \end{pmatrix} \leq \begin{pmatrix} k_1 \\ k_2 \end{pmatrix}, \tag{4.14}$$

where k_1, k_2 are fixed preassigned constants determined a priori. Introducing slack variables $\hat{\alpha}_3$, $\hat{\alpha}_4$, we can now rewrite the constraints (4.14) as equalities. If the solution lies on the boundaries, we have to consider $2 \times \binom{4}{2} = 12$ ways of selecting two variables out of $\hat{\alpha}_1$, $\hat{\alpha}_2$, $\hat{\alpha}_3$, $\hat{\alpha}_4$ when the coefficient matrix of (4.13) is of rank one. For each selection we compute the objective function $(e'e)$ and select one by a decision function criterion. A straightforward and simple case is one when it is possible to pick a pair $(\hat{\alpha}_1, \hat{\alpha}_2)$ that gives the minimum of $e'e = \Sigma e^2$,assuming singularity of the normal equations (4.13). In case the optimal pair turns out to be $(\hat{\alpha}_1, \hat{\alpha}_3)$, which includes a slack solution, we know that the preassigned upper-bound k_1 is not binding at all (i.e., it could be lowered). In other words, it is possible by this method to obtain at least an interval estimate for each of the coefficients α_1, α_2, when a point estimate is not available from the normal equations with a singular coefficient matrix. The computational efficiency of this method may, however be limited.

4.4. Simultaneous Estimation Techniques: A Brief Review

It is now possible to outline a brief review of econometric estimation techniques that have been discussed in current literature in relation to simultaneous linear equations.

From the standpoint of flexibility in statistical estimation it may be useful to subdivide the linear simultaneous-equations systems into two polar types, e.g., the recursive type and the nonrecursive type, the latter sometimes being called "an interdependent model." A complete recursive model [45], which is sometimes called "a pure causal chain model" (discussed in Chapter 3) may be very simply written in matrix form as

$$A_0 y(t) + B y(t - \phi) + C z(t) = u(t), \tag{4.15}$$

where $y(t)$ is the column vector of M endogenous variables, $y(t-\phi)$ and $z(t)$ are the column vectors of N predetermined variables (assumed to be free of observational errors), N_1 of which are the lagged endogenous variables $y(t-\phi)$ and the rest $(N-N_1)$ are exogenous variables $z(t)$. The coefficient matrices are denoted by A_0, B and C, where by recursive structure the matrix A_0 is assumed to be strictly triangular with ones in the principal diagonal. The $u(t)$ is an M-component column vector of stochastic residuals $u_i(t)$, which is assumed to be such that for every i-th element $u_i(t)$ is uncorrelated with the predetermined variables $y(t-\phi)$ and $z(t)$ and that all residuals $u_i(t)$, whether time-lagged or not, are mutually uncorrelated.

Under these assumptions[7] the method of ordinary least squares can be applied directly to the system (4.15) to give the asymptotically unbiased estimates of the coefficients. If, further, the joint distributions of the residuals $u_i(t)$ are assumed to be normal, the ordinary-least-squares estimates are identical with the usual maximum-likelihood estimates, which have their usual optimal properties. If, however, the joint distributions are not exactly normal but approximately so, the estimates derived by applying straightforward the maximum-likelihood method would indicate only quasi-maximum-likelihood estimates.

In case the assumptions for the application of the maximum likelihood method hold good, it is interesting to explore further the optimality properties of such estimates, especially in finite small samples and in situations where the very concept of efficiency in the sense of asymptotic variance of an estimate can be refined, if not improved, under large sample assumptions. In the first case (small sample) we have to look at the whole likelihood function, which may not be very difficult with the help of present computers. In the

---

[7] For consistent estimates it is also required that the underlying stochastic process must have the ergodic property.

second case (large sample) the concept of first- and second-order efficiency defined [32] with respect to the degree of closeness of approximation to the derivative of the log likelihood function may prove to be useful.

Although we could easily solve for $y(t)$ in system (4.15) to derive the reduced form, it is not necessary for estimation because the original form itself permits predictive and causal inference. It has been pointed out by Wold [44] that under certain general conditions the ordinary-least-squares method applied to (4.15) keeps the specification error of the model within limits of a very small order. We note, however, that owing to the presence of endogenous lagged terms $y(t-\phi)$ in (4.15) the best linear unbiased type of optimality criterion following from the usual Gauss-Markov theorem of ordinary-least-squares does not apply here, although one could apply [7] the concept of "best unbiased estimating equations" in some asymptotic sense at least.

An interdependent model can be represented by the same system (4.15), except that the triangular coefficient matrix A_0 has to be replaced by a general M by M matrix and the assumption about the residuals is slightly changed. For each residual $u_i(t)$ it is still assumed that it is uncorrelated with all predetermined variables and only noncontemporary residuals are assumed to be mutually uncorrelated. In other words, contemporary residuals in different equations of system (4.15) can now be mutually correlated. Under these assumptions, the ordinary-least-squares method applied to the original system is in general biased and not statistically consistent in the usual sense. Moreover, there is the usual problem of identification of each equation in the whole structure [42].

Using the notation $x(t)$ to denote the column vectors of all predetermined variables, whether exogenous or lagged endogenous, and the constant matrix G to denote its coefficient matrix which subsumes matrices B and C of system (4.15), we may represent the general structure of an interdependent model as

$$Ay(t) + Gx(t) = u(t) \begin{cases} A: M.M \\ G: M.N \\ y(t): M.1 \\ x(t): N.1 \\ u(t): M.1 \end{cases}, \quad (4.16)$$

and its reduced form as

$$y(t) = -A^{-1}Gx(t) + A^{-1}u(t) \\ = H_1 x(t) + v(t) \quad (4.17)$$

where the matrix H_1 of order M by N denotes $(-A^{-1}G)$ and $v(t) = A^{-1} u(t)$. Any single structural equation belonging to the system (4.16), which need not contain all the endogenous and all the predetermined variables, may be written as

$$y = Y\alpha + X_1\beta + u \left\{ \begin{array}{l} y: T.1 \\ Y: T.m \\ \alpha: m.1 \\ X_1: T.n \\ \beta: n.1 \end{array} \right. \qquad (4.18)$$

where y is the column vector of T observations on the single dependent variable and α and β denote column vectors, respectively, of m and n parameters $(m+1 \leq M, n \leq N)$, which are to be estimated. The matrix Y indicates that m other dependent variables are present in the equation, and the matrix X_1 shows that there are n predetermined variables in the equation. We note that this equation (4.18) is said to be overidentified or just-identified according as N exceeds or equals $(m+n)$. In case the equation (4.18) is just-identified, the ordinary least-squares can be applied to estimate the coefficients of the reduced-form model (4.17), and then there is a unique transformation relating the structural coefficients in the original model and the coefficients of the reduced form.

When the equation (4.18) is overidentified, which is the very usual case in most simultaneous models, a number of methods are available; the common point between most of them is that they indirectly overcome the difficulty caused by the lack of a unique transformation from the reduced-form coefficients to the original structural coefficients and that they define estimates which are consistent at the least.

The method of instrumental variables [21], when applied to estimate the parameters of equation (4.18) in case of overidentification $(N > m+n)$, selects as many predetermined variables in the system (which are not in the given equation) as there are unknown parameter coefficients of endogenous variables in equation (4.18). In our case of equation (4.18) we choose m such predetermined variables, say $x_{n+1}, x_{n+2}, \ldots, x_{n+m}$, and we had already n predetermined variables in the given equation, e.g., $x_1, x_2, \ldots, x_n$. Then we multiply these by each variable and solve the following system of as many linear equations as there are unknown parameters.

$$x_j'y = x_j'Y\alpha + x_j'X_1\beta, \qquad j = 1, 2, \ldots n, n+1, \ldots, n+m. \qquad (4.19)$$

The estimates of α and β obtained by this method are statistically consistent.

A generalization of this approach is provided by the limited-information method of estimation, which obviates the arbitrariness in selecting the predetermined variables outside the given equation, although belonging to the system. The limited-information method of obtaining maximum likelihood estimates consists in maximizing the likelihood function formed from the joint distribution of the residuals $v(t)$ in the reduced form (4.17) assuming the residuals to be distributed as the multivariate normal — subject to some restrictions on the parameters of the particular equation (4.18); these restrictions are constructed systematically by comparing the original model and the reduced form corresponding to the given equation. This method is less general and less precise than the full-information method of maximum likelihood, because it uses the restrictions on the particular equation only, i.e., utilizes only a part of the restrictions that the original set of structural equations imposes on the system. Both these (limited-information and full-information) methods of maximum likelihood estimation have to use some iterative procedure (e.g., method of scoring [9] when the residual-error terms have a heteroscedastic distribution (i.e., come from populations with unequal variances), and this is computationally not simple.

A different kind of estimation method (in case of overidentification) is provided by noting that the main difficulty in applying ordinary least squares to equation (4.18) is due to the presence of other dependent variables (i.e., matrix Y) as explanatory variables in the given equation. The method of two-stage least-squares [2, 38, 41] replaces, in the first stage, these other dependent variables (i.e., matrix Y) by their estimates obtained from the reduced form through ordinary least squares and then, at the second stage, it applies ordinary least squares to equation (4.18) after the above replacement in the first stage.

For instance, corresponding to Y in equation (4.18), which indicates the presence of m dependent variables, we can find, in the reduced-form system (4.17), equations containing precisely those m dependent variables. Let the latter equations be written as

$$Y = XH + \bar{V}, \qquad (4.20)$$

where H and $\bar{V}$ represent the true coefficient structure and the errors in the reduced form, respectively. The ordinary-least-squares estimate $\hat{H}$ of H and the estimate $\hat{V}$ of $\bar{V}$ can be obtained from (4.20) as $\hat{H} = (X'X)^{-1} X'y$ and $\hat{V} = Y - X(X'X)^{-1} X'y$, respectively. We note that $\hat{H}$ is a consistent estimator of H, since the reduced-form residuals by assumption are homoscedastic and have zero lagged covariances.

Now we can write equation (4.18) equivalently as

$$y = (Y - \bar{V})\alpha + X_1\beta + (u + \bar{V}\alpha).$$

In general, the true residuals $\bar{V}$ are not known. Hence, we replace this by its least-squares estimate $\hat{V}$ obtained before, and applying ordinary least squares to

$$y = (Y - \hat{V}X_1)\binom{\alpha}{\beta} + (u + \hat{V}\alpha), \qquad (4.21)$$

we obtain the two-stage least-squares estimator $\binom{\hat{\alpha}}{\hat{\beta}}$ as

$$\binom{\hat{\alpha}}{\hat{\beta}} = \begin{bmatrix} Y'Y - \hat{V}'\hat{V} & Y'X_1 \\ X_1'Y & X_1'X_1 \end{bmatrix}^{-1} \begin{bmatrix} Y' - \hat{V}' \\ X_1' \end{bmatrix} y$$

by solving the normal equations

$$\begin{bmatrix} Y' - \hat{V}' \\ X_1' \end{bmatrix} y = \begin{bmatrix} Y'Y - \hat{V}'\hat{V} & Y'X_1 \\ X_1'Y & X_1'X_1 \end{bmatrix} \binom{\hat{\alpha}}{\hat{\beta}}. \qquad (4.22)$$

The two-stage least-squares estimate is statistically consistent, and it is also unbiased if in equation (4.21) the true error residuals V are known rather than estimated. The estimate is also unique if the first matrix on the right-hand side of equation (4.22) is nonsingular.

However, there are two basic difficulties in this method. One is the implicit normalization assumption in going from system (4.16) to system (4.17), in which one dependent variable in each equation appears with unit coefficient. The second point is that when the sample size (T) is small relative to the total number (N) of predetermined variables in the system $(T<N)$, it may not be possible to obtain unique estimates $\hat{H}$, $\hat{V}$ by applying ordinary least squares at the first stage to the system (4.20). Reducing the number (N) of predetermined variables by using principal components may partly solve the latter difficulty. The advantages of the two-stage least-squares method are that it is computationally simpler than the limited-information method of maximum likelihood which has the same asymptotic variance-covariance matrix and that by iterative procedures [26] this method can be extended to include the restrictions not only on one equation but on all other equations of the system.

A generalization of the two-stage least-squares method is provided by the k-class estimator

$$\binom{\hat{\alpha}}{\hat{\beta}}_k.$$

obtained from the following system of estimating equations

$$\begin{bmatrix} Y' - k\hat{V}' \\ X_1' \end{bmatrix} y = \begin{bmatrix} Y'Y - k\hat{V}'\hat{V} & Y'X_1 \\ X_1'Y & X_1'X_1 \end{bmatrix} \begin{pmatrix} \hat{\alpha} \\ \hat{\beta} \end{pmatrix}_k, \tag{4.23}$$

where k is an arbitrary (scalar) number. With $k=0$, we have ordinary least squares, with $k=1$ we have two-stage least squares and with $k=1+\lambda$, where λ is the smallest root of the determinantal equation $|M_1 - (1+\lambda)M| = 0$ (M_1 and M being the moment matrices of the estimated residuals of all jointly dependent variables in (4.18)), we get limited-information maximum-likelihood estimates. Recent investigations [28] about the finite sample behavior of this k-class estimator have shown the remarkable result that under rather general conditions (assuming normality of $u(t)$ in (4.16)) the scalar k in the k-class estimator could be so adjusted according to

$$k = 1 + (N - m - n - 1)/T, \quad T = \text{total number of observations}$$

as to make the k-class estimator unbiased approximately to order T^{-1}. This suggests that efficiency of such estimates can be further improved by using higher order approximations through computers. One may ask whether the concept of first- and second-order efficiency mentioned earlier in connection with maximum-likelihood estimates can be fruitfully applied in this context with appropriate modifications.

A further generalization [27] of the k-class estimator is provided by the double k-class estimator

$$\begin{pmatrix} \hat{\alpha} \\ \hat{\beta} \end{pmatrix}_{k_1, k_2}$$

obtained from the following estimating equation

$$\begin{bmatrix} Y' - k_2\hat{V}' \\ X_1' \end{bmatrix} y = \begin{bmatrix} Y'Y - k_1\hat{V}'\hat{V} & Y'X_1 \\ X_1'Y & X_1'X_1 \end{bmatrix} \begin{pmatrix} \hat{\alpha} \\ \hat{\beta} \end{pmatrix}. \tag{4.24}$$

The ordinary k-class estimator can be obtained from this as a special case when $k_1 = k_2$.

These alternative estimators (although the list is by no means exhaustive) suggest the need, perhaps, for analyzing the exact distributions, so that they may be useful in small sample situations. The role of Monte Carlo methods of investigation may be very considerable in this respect.

An interesting line of further work would be to investigate the behavior of these alternative estimators when the predetermined variables are observed with error. Intuitively, it seems that such errors, when known or estimable extraneously, can be incorporated by adjusting the relevant variables of the system, but the case when such error structure is not known is more interesting from the standpoint of economic realism.

Another line of work which is also very important from an economic viewpoint is to investigate the impact of temporal but limited dependence of the residual terms $u(t)$ in situations when a Markov or other, simpler, processes can be assumed for $u(t)$. However, even in simple cases this leads to a nonlinear estimation problem such as that of autoregressive least squares and the computational task may be quite involved.

4.5. Methods of Nonlinear Estimation [8]

So far we have discussed methods of estimation on the tacit assumption that the parameters to be estimated enter linearly into the structure of the original form of the model. For most dynamic economic models which are nonlinear in parameters, an approximation by a corresponding linear model can be made either by an appropriate choice of the time interval or by an appropriate linearizing of the nonlinear relationship. It has been shown [16] that such linearizing treatment may not only prove to be a very good approximation for short-run purposes but may yield quasi-maximum-likelihood estimates that are statistically consistent under suitable hypotheses.

There are, however, two basic advantages of a nonlinear model, i.e., a model involving nonlinear equations. In the first place, it offers a wider range of choice of possible paths for a given linear economic relationship, and this is particularly helpful in constructing models for analyzing economic instability in the form of either cyclical fluctuations or an intermixture of trends and cycles. For instance, a linear difference (differential) equation must have at least two lags (second-order terms) to allow the possibility of cyclical behavior, whereas an appropriate nonlinear difference (differential) equation or equations with only one lag (first-order term) can do the job. Similarly, it is well known that the knife-edge stability of the income path in a Harrod-Domar type of growth model can be generalized in two different ways, e.g., either by admitting production functions (preferably nonlinear) more general than the linear and complementary type or by introducing capacity constraints such that certain parameters (or relations) of the structural equations change their regimes when the capacity constraint is violated.

A second advantage of a nonlinear model when it is appropriate is its

---

[8] This section is based on Sengupta [36].

capacity to throw considerable light on the sensitivity of solutions of the corresponding linearized model (or models) to the stochastic process underlying the model. Just as the correspondence principle [35] seeks to establish the stability properties of equilibrium in a static model by analyzing deviations from equilibrium by means of a corresponding dynamic model, one might analyze the different types of stability of a linear stochastic process model by considering its corresponding nonlinear generalizations.[9]

As a simple example, consider a stochastic process $X(t)$ with its expected value $M(t)$ and its standard deviation $V(t)$, each of which is a function of time in an evolutionary (i.e., nonstationary) sense. The relative fluctuation of the stochastic process is measured by the ratio of $V(t)$ to $M(t)$, i.e., the coefficient of variation. The interesting point about this statistical aspect of fluctuation is to study how the ratio changes over time when $M(t)$ rises to a higher and higher level. The nonlinear processes allow the most generalized study possible of the time behavior of this relative fluctuation. Economic models of cyclical growth which emphasize the inseparable intermixture of the phenomena of growth and cyclical fluctuations would belong to this category.

However, the chief difficulty of a nonlinear model is the problem of statistical estimation. If the structure of the nonlinear model is recursive, either completely or very nearly so, the least-squares method may be applicable in most stituations to each single equation of the model. Hence, for any given equation with m nonlinear parameters b_i to be estimated, we end with m nonlinear normal equations whose solutions would minimize the sum of squares of the error residuals, which may be assumed to be independently and normally distributed as usual.

Although there are some iterative methods of solving the normal equations of nonlinear least squares, it is not generally known whether the iterative solution so obtained is a local minimum or an absolute minimum, and it is only for the absolute minimum values that the asymptotic optimality properties apply in least-squares models which do not contain lagged endogenous variables. Hence, in such cases various methods [15, 18] of improving the efficiency of iterative calculations may have to be applied.

One suggestion which has some practical virtues is to divide all of the

---

[9] For a simple case of the Markov process known as the logistic process, it is well known that the expected value of the process is less than the deterministic solution of the corresponding logistic model. For *linear* birth and death process models, however, the expected-value solution of the evolutionary stochastic process model generally coincides with the solution of the corresponding deterministic model. See Bartlett [1].

observations into m equal (preferably disjoint and exclusive) groups and obtain by averaging for each group a total of m exact nonlinear equations which have to be solved to obtain a trial estimator of b_i. Under rather general conditions a trial estimator thus constructed is consistent. With this set of trial estimates as the starting value, the standard Gauss-Newton method of iteration can be applied for only a few steps to accomplish the minimization of the error residuals. If the first-stage trial estimates are consistent, the second stage requires only a very few iterations to improve efficiency of the estimate materially.

The difficulty in this approach is that obtaining a set of trial estimates which are consistent may not be very easy and that the convergence of the Gauss-Newton method of iteration is by no means assured unless certain conditions are fulfilled at each stage of iteration. In cases where it is known that the normality assumption for the error residuals is too restrictive (e.g., a certain type of demand may never be negative), one may have to define a particular type of nonnormal process (e.g., the Poisson process) and then apply maximum-likelihood methods to derive a set of equations which can again be iteratively solved by the standard Gauss-Newton method to obtain a set of estimates for the nonlinear parameters which are statistically consistent. The small sample behavior of such estimators is not well known.

It may be natural to suppose that things are more complicated when a given nonlinear equation in a recursive model contains either lagged endogenous variables as explanatory variables or error terms which do not have the same variance (heteroscedastic errors). In the former case it is not known whether the ordinary least-squares estimates, if they are obtainable, have the property of a best estimating function [7], although there is nothing sacrosanct about any best unbiased type of optimality criterion. In the latter case some methods are available which provide a correction, so to say, for the original least-squares estimates by incorporating the additional knowledge about the temporal dependence of the residual errors. It is interesting, however, to note [34] that under certain reasonable conditions applied to a linear equation model the asymptotic results on the efficiency of the ordinary least-squares estimate are fairly well satisfied for even small sample sizes, and the difference between the ordinary least-squares estimate and the Markov estimate (i.e., the estimate which incorporates the heteroscedastic variance structure) turns out to be very small in the numerical investigations. This may raise our hopes about the operational validity of the straightforward least-squares method even in nonlinear models of a recursive type.

For a nonrecursive simultaneous-equations model which is nonlinear, the situation is more complicated in that we have to apply our estimation techniques to the reduced form of our original model, although we are interested in the parameters of the original model. If the model is nonlinear only in its variables but not in its parameters or can be approximately taken to be so, we can still apply quasi-maximum-likelihood methods of estimation, assuming the residual errors to be mutually independently distributed approximately as the joint normal distribution. Frequently, however, an explicit solution of these maximum-likelihood equations would be difficult to derive, because the Jacobian of the transformation would contain unknown values of the variables.

It has been suggested [21, 43] that we should replace these unknown values by their observed sample means in order to obtain an explicit solution of the maximum-likelihood equations. This involves, of course, a linearization of the structural equations. An alternative method [4] that seems to be applicable in this case is to minimize, when feasible, the sum of squares of the reduced-form disturbances. The quasinormal equations that would be nonlinear in this case could be solved by an iterative procedure using the standard Gauss-Newton technique mentioned before. This method, sometimes called the method of simultaneous least squares, appears to be largely distribution-free and computationally less complicated.

The net effect of this discussion is twofold. First although it is easy to show that a first-order linear differential (difference) equation with real coefficients can never generate cyclical fluctuations, while its corresponding mixed difference-differential equation can [24], the statistical estimation problem involved in the latter is invariably nonlinear, and so we have to apply at some stage or another linearizing approximations. This holds good more appropriately in the case of a system of dynamic linear equations. The sensitivity of the nonlinear specification of the original model to the linearizing approximations necessitated by the estimation procedure will ultimately determine the econometric usefulness of the many nonlinear models of economic fluctuations available in the recent literature.

Second, if it is our objective to devise measures of control over economic instability, it is necessary and useful to analyze the efficiencies of alternative types of control, both linear and nonlinear, by studying systematically the time path of response of the endogenous variables to a unit shock in one single period [39] or to a shock which is sustained over time. Such a study, although it looks highly theoretical, may, in our opinion, offer dividends of immense practical significance, e.g., in deriving the optimum path of nonlinear control to achieve a certain type of stability and in challenging the very concept of economic equilibrium when confronted with statistical evidence from the out-of-equilibrium world.

4.6. Appendix

Multicollinearity and the Use of A Priori Information

Multicollinearity is generally recognized as a major problem in estimating structural equations from economic time series. It is quite pervasive in economies which are experiencing price and wage inflation as well as rapid growth in population, employment and production.

The input-output mechanism tends to produce multicollinearity among "real" variables. Consider the following two-sector model, in the form $X=(I-A)^{-1} Y$, where X is total gross output, Y is deliveries to final demand and $(I-A)^{-1}$ is the inverse matrix derived from the matrix (A) of technical input-output coefficients:

$$\begin{bmatrix} X_1 \\ X_2 \end{bmatrix} = \begin{bmatrix} 1.8 & 0.1 \\ 0.4 & 1.6 \end{bmatrix} \begin{bmatrix} Y_1 \\ Y_2 \end{bmatrix}.$$

In an expanding economy, both categories of final demand, Y_1 and Y_2, tend to increase strongly. Through the input-output mechanism, a unit increase in Y_1 tends to raise X_1 by 1.8 units and Y_2 by 0.4 units. Similarly, a unit increase in Y_2 tends to raise X_1 by 0.1 units and X_2 by 1.6 units.

In Table 4.1, Y_1 and Y_2 both follow exactly linear trends and are therefore perfectly correlated:

TABLE 4.1

Multicollinearity Produced by an Input-Output Mechanism: Perfect Correlation Between Total Gross Output (X_1, X_2) of Two Producing Sectors Generated by Perfect Correlation Between Two Components of Final Demand (Y_1, Y_2)

Year	Y_1	Y_2	$X_{1.1} + X_{1.2} = X_1$	$X_{2.1} + X_{2.2} = X_2$
0	10	20	$(18.0 + 2.0) = 20.0$	$(4.0 + 32.0) = 36.0$
1	11	21	$(19.8 + 2.1) = 21.9$	$(4.4 + 33.6) = 38.0$
2	12	22	$(21.6 + 2.2) = 23.8$	$(4.8 + 35.2) = 40.0$
3	13	23	$(23.4 + 2.3) = 25.7$	$(5.2 + 36.8) = 42.0$
4	14	24	$(25.2 + 2.4) = 27.6$	$(5.6 + 38.4) = 44.0$
5	15	25	$(27.0 + 2.5) = 29.5$	$(6.0 + 40.0) = 46.0$

The input-output mechanism causes X_1 to move according to the sum of two linear trends, $X_1 = X_{1.1} + X_{1.2}$, where $X_{1.1} = 1.8\ Y_1$ and $X_{1.2} = 0.1\ Y_2$.

Also, X_2 moves as the sum of the two linear trends, $X_{2.1} = 0.4\,Y_1$ and $X_{2.2} = 1.6\,Y_2$. The sum of the two linear-trend components of X_1 is a linear trend; the same is true in the case of X_2. The result is that X_1, X_2, Y_1 and Y_2 are *all* perfectly correlated; it is impossible to separate out (identify) the net effects of Y_1 and Y_2 upon X_1 and X_2, respectively, by any statistical technique!

If Y_1 and Y_2 have short-run deviations from trend which are not perfectly correlated, these deviations will be propagated through the input-output mechanism into X_1 and X_2. The deviation in X_1 will be $x_1 = 1.8\,y_1 + 0.1\,y_2$, and the deviation in x_2 will be $x_2 = 0.4\,y_1 + 1.6\,y_2$. The deviations in x_1 and x_2 will not be perfectly correlated with each other or with either y_1 or y_2. If there are errors of measurement or aggregation in all variables, the regression of x_1 on y_1 and y_2 may give a good approximation to the input-output coefficient connecting x_1 to y_1, but the net regression coefficient of x_1 upon y_2 might appear to be of borderline significance.

In the conventional input-output model, Y_1 and Y_2 are independent or exogenous variables and X_1 and X_2 are dependent or endogenous. The inverse matrix permits us to make conditional forecasts of X_1 and X_2 *given* Y_1 and Y_2. If we were free to choose sets of values of Y_1 and Y_2 which were completely uncorrelated with one another and which covered wide ranges (as in a designed experiment), we could regress the resulting values of X_1 and X_2 on the assigned values of Y_1 and Y_2 and obtain quite good estimates of all four coefficients of $(I - A)^{-1}$ along with their standard errors.

Alternatively, suppose that $(I - A)^{-1}$ has been obtained from a recent and accurate input-output study (for the moment, we assume no serious problems of aggregation and no changes in input-output coefficients between the year of the study and the year for which we must forecast). The coefficients of $(I - A)^{-1}$ then constitute a priori information; they do not have to be estimated from time series, and they are (by assertion) more accurate than any regression coefficients we could hope to estimate under the most favorable conditions.

If we do not know the $(I - A)^{-1}$ coefficients themselves but know that they will not change from (say) years 0–5 to year 6, for which we must make forecasts of X_1 and X_2, the fact that Y_1 and Y_2 are perfectly intercorrelated does not matter. We can regress X_1 and X_2 on either Y_1, or Y_2, or both — it is immaterial. But we should not assume that these regression coefficients have structural significance, and we should not use them for forecasting in a period in which Y_1 and Y_2 are no longer highly intercorrelated.

An actual case of multicollinearity encountered in working with U.S. data (quarterly) from 1947 through 1960 yielded the following correlation matrix for the four most highly intercorrelated variables in a consumption function which logically required the inclusion of eight variables:

TABLE 4.2

Multicollinearity Resulting From Upward Trends in Two Major Categories of Retail Prices, in Real (Deflated) Income Per Capita, and in "Time": Based on Actual Quarterly Data for the U.S., 1947–1960

Variable		Time	Retail price, nonfoods	Disposable personal income per capita (deflated)	Retail price, food crops
		t	P_{nf}	$\left(\dfrac{Y - T + T_r}{PN}\right)$	P_c
Time	t	1.0000	0.9926	0.9785	0.9330
Retail price, nonfoods	P_{nf}	0.9926	1.0000	0.9749	0.9406
Disposable personal income per capita (deflated)	$\left(\dfrac{Y - T + T_r}{PN}\right)$	0.9785	0.9749	1.0000	0.9003
Retail price, food crops	P_c	0.9330	0.9406	0.9003	1.0000

The value of the determinant is approximately 0.00009, a very near approach to singularity! (Recall that the determinant of a matrix with zero inter-correlation would have a value of 1.) If we assign a priori coefficients to three of these variables, we can estimate the coefficient of the fourth variable by statistical means. The intercorrelations of the other three explanatory variables among themselves and with the trend-dominated fourth were not unduly high.

An elaborate consumer demand matrix published by Brandow [3] provided a priori coefficients for three of the four trend-dominated variables and for one other (C_l/N). Hence, the combination of a priori and statistical infor-mation was sufficient to give us useful estimates of the net effects of all seven explanatory variables upon retail prices of food livestock products and per capita consumption of food crops.

The elasticity coefficients in Brandow's matrix looked reasonable in relation to some earlier results by Fox. Brandow's own-price elasticity of

−0.48 for food livestock products may be compared with Fox's estimates of −0.52 to −0.56 during 1922–1941.[10] Brandow's own-price elasticity of −0.34 for all food compares with Fox's 1922–1941 estimates of −0.34 to −0.37.[11]

In one version of the food livestock products consumption equation, the a priori coefficients were imposed in the following fashion:

$$P_1^* = P_1 - \left[-11.3177\left(\frac{C_1}{N}\right) \right.$$
$$\left. + 0.1222P_c + 1.2718P_{nf} + 0.2360\left(\frac{Y - T + T_r}{PN}\right) \right].$$

The adjusted variable P_1^* was regressed on its own value for the previous quarter, $(P_1^*)_{-1}$, on time (t) and on a dummy "inflationary period" variable (d_1), yielding the following equation:

$$P_1^* = 634.3751 - 0.2083t + 24.3988d_1 + 0.4504(P_1^*)_{-1} + u_1,$$
$$\quad (121.9413) \quad (0.1869) \quad (5.9470) \quad (0.1033)$$
$$R^2 = 0.7226; \quad \bar{S} = 15.3026; \quad \partial = 1.9788.$$

The expression in brackets (containing the four a priori coefficients) was then added to each side of the last equation to obtain the complete form:

$$P_1 = 634.3751 - 0.2083t + 24.3988d_1 + 0.4504(P_1^*)_{-1}$$
$$\quad (121.9413) \quad (0.1869) \quad (5.9470) \quad (0.1033)$$

$$+ \left[-11.3177\left(\frac{C_1}{N}\right) \right.$$
$$\left. + 0.1222P_c + 1.2718P_{nf} + 0.2360\left(\frac{Y - T + T_r}{PN}\right) \right] + u_1. \qquad (4.25)$$

No statistical technique could possibly extract meaningful structural coefficients from the eight time series in equation (4.25). The four coefficients within brackets are not, of course, known without error. Various methods have been suggested for assigning approximate standard errors to a priori coefficients, but we will not discuss them here. Our handling of the consumption function is a specific application of the model described in equations (4.4), (4.5) and (4.6).

---

[10] See Fox [11, p. 116].
[11] See Fox [10, p. 65].

4.7. Selected Recent Developments in
Applied Estimation Methods

The purpose of this section is to present a general outline of some of the recent developments in applied methods of statistical estimation which are relevant for economic models. This outline, however, is selective in the sense that only those aspects which are likely to be very important and relevant for economic policy models are included here. In particular, the following three areas are discussed: (1) Some recent methods for handling multicollinearity problems, (2) methods for analyzing the sensitivity of regression estimates, and (3) Estimation viewed in a decision-theoretic framework.

4.7.1. *Some Recent Methods for Handling Multicollinearity Problems*

In addition to the various methods for handling multicollinearity problems in regression models mentioned in earlier sections of this chapter, two other recent methods will be outlined here. One is to characterize multicollinearity problems arising from the singularity of the matrix $X'X$ (i.e., rank of the matrix is less than p in terms of the regression equation (4.1) mentioned in Section 4.2 before) as a subset of imprecise estimates [69] and then define a direction (or in some sense an optimum direction if there are more than one where imprecision of estimation could be relatively reduced (i.e., precision could then be improved). The second type of methods [55] suggest a procedure for selecting a subset from a given set of independent variables which do not give the smallest value of the sum of squares function (i.e., the $e'e$ function, where the error vector is given by equation (4.1) before) and are not unbiased but which are in a certain sense "stable" and provide smaller mean square error.

Consider the first method applied to the linear least squares (LS) model defined in equation (4.1) before:

$$y = X\beta + e \qquad \begin{matrix} X: n \cdot p \\ \beta: p \cdot 1. \end{matrix} \qquad (4.26)$$

It is well known [65] that when the matrix X does not have full rank (i.e., X has rank less than p), certain linear parametric functions, i.e., functions of the form

$$\lambda'\beta = \lambda_1\beta_1 + \lambda_2\beta_2 + \cdots + \lambda_p\beta_p$$

do not possess unbiased linear estimators. Indeed, we know from the estimable function approach mentioned already before that $\lambda'\beta$ possesses an unbiased linear estimator if, and only if, the row vector λ' can be expressed as a linear combination of the rows of X. An equivalent and in some sense more illuminating way of saying the same thing is this: the scalar function $\lambda'\beta$ is estimable if the vector λ can be expressed as a linear combination of the latent vectors of the matrix $X'X$ corresponding to its non-zero latent roots [64].

This result helps us to determine those linear parametric functions which can be estimated precisely and those which are estimable but can be estimated very imprecisely. To see this, we choose V, an orthogonal matrix whose columns are orthonormal latent vectors of $X'X$, i.e.,

$$X\beta = (XV)(V'\beta) = Z\gamma,$$

where $VV' = I$, $XV = Z$ and $V'\beta = \gamma$. It is clear that the columns of XV are orthogonal, since

$$(XV)'XV = V'X'XV = \text{diag}\{\theta_1, \theta_2, \ldots, \theta_p\},$$

where θ s are the latent roots of $X'X$. Again, if the matrix $X'X$ has the latent root zero of multiplicity j, then the j of the columns of XV are zero say, the last j. Then the last j components of the vector γ are not estimable from the observations. However, the remaining parameters, i.e., $(\gamma_1, \gamma_2, \ldots, \gamma_{p-j})$ or any linear combination of these are estimable. Hence, the function $\lambda'\beta$ is estimable if and only if it transforms into $(\mu_1\gamma_1 + \cdots + \mu_{p-j}\gamma_{k-j})$, that is, if and only if the last j components of the vector $V'\lambda$ are zero, since $\lambda'\beta = \lambda'VV'\beta = (V'\lambda)'\gamma$. Thus, by taking j orthonormal latent vectors $v_1, v_2, \ldots, v_j$ of $X'X$ corresponding to each of the nonzero roots $\theta_1, \theta_2, \ldots, \theta_j$ respectively, we can write

$$\lambda = \mu_1 v_1 + \mu_2 v_2 + \cdots + \mu_j v_j \tag{4.27a}$$

$$\text{var}(\lambda'\hat{\beta}) = \sigma^2 \cdot \left[\frac{\mu_1^2}{\theta_1} + \cdots + \frac{\mu_j^2}{\theta_j} \right] \tag{4.27b}$$

$$\leq \sigma^2 \cdot \frac{1}{\min(\theta_1, \ldots, \theta_j)} \tag{4.27c}$$

where $\hat{\beta}$ is the blue estimator of the Gauss-Markov theorem and the vector λ can be normalized to satisfy $\lambda'\lambda = 1$ thus implying $\Sigma\mu_i^2 = 1$.

It is clear from (4.27b) that relatively precise estimation is possible in those directions of the latent vectors of $X'X$ which correspond to large latent roots (i.e., different from zero); similarly the directions corresponding to small latent roots (i.e., very close to zero) specify the possibility of relatively imprecise estimation. Thus, for all practical purposes we have to find an

appropriate direction (which may not be unique, of course) by which multicollinearity may be reduced. For example, suppose that the matrix $X'X$ has
no zero latent roots but one small root θ, say, and other $(p-1)$ large roots.
This is a case of multicollinearity which is not extreme. It is clear that
estimation is relatively imprecise in the direction of a unit latent vector
corresponding to the small root θ. Let the latent vector corresponding to θ
be v and suppose we take an additional observation y_{n+1} at the values
$x'_{n+1} = (x_{1,n+1}, x_{2,n+1}, \ldots, x_{p,n+1})$ of the explanatory variables where
$x'_{n+1} = mv'$, where m is a scalar. Then the complete model is

$$\begin{pmatrix} y \\ y_{n+1} \end{pmatrix} = \begin{pmatrix} X \\ x'_{n+1} \end{pmatrix}\beta + \begin{pmatrix} e \\ e_{n+1} \end{pmatrix},$$

where it follows that

$$\left[\begin{pmatrix} X \\ x'_{n+1} \end{pmatrix}'\begin{pmatrix} X \\ x'_{n+1} \end{pmatrix}\right]v = [X'X + m^2vv']v = \theta v + m^2 v.$$

Thus, v is a latent vector of $X^{*'}X^*$, where $X^{*'} = [X'x_{n+1}]$ corresponding to
the latent root $(\theta + m^2)$. But even if θ is small, $(\theta + m^2)$ may be large. Thus, by
choosing the new observation vector x_{n+1} in the direction of v we improve
the precision of estimation in the direction for which it was previously most
imprecise.

An easy generalization of the above rule is to propose [69] that a new set
of values of the explanatory variables x_{n+1} be chosen, subject to the constraint

$$x'_{n+1}x_{n+1} \leqq m^2, m: \text{a nonzero scalar},$$

which satisfy some criterion of optimality, e.g.,

(a) choose the vector x_{n+1} of new observations in order to maximize the
minimum latent root of the new information matrix $[X'X + x_{n+1}x'_{n+1}]$;
(b) choose x'_{n+1} in order to maximize the determinant of $(X'X + x_{n+1}
x'_{n+1})$.

It may be noted that this is closely analogous to the method we proposed
at the end of section 4.3.

Now consider the second method applied to the linear model (4.26). If the
explanatory variables are correlated then the matrix $X'X$ becomes ill-
conditioned in the sense that the determinant $|C|$ of the correlation matrix
C obtained from X takes a very small value. When the matrix X is appropriately centered and scaled, denote by $C = Z'Z$, where Z indicates the

matrix X centered and scaled. Then it is clear that the matrix $C + \theta I$, where I is the identity matrix of order p, would be nonsingular for a suitable choice of the scalar θ; therefore, the estimate $\hat{\beta}(\theta)$ of parameter β of the system (4.26) would be given by

$$\hat{\beta}(\theta) = [C + \theta I]^{-1} Z' y.$$

If X is already scaled such that $C = X'X$

$$\hat{\beta}(\theta) = [C + \theta I]^{-1} X' y; \text{ for } \theta > 0.$$

Note that if $X'X$ is nonsingular, so that there is no multicollinearity, then the ordinary LS estimate $\hat{\beta}_{LS}$ can be obtained from above by simply taking $\theta = 0$, i.e., $\hat{\beta}_{LS} = \hat{\beta}(0)$. A plot of $\hat{\beta}_i(\theta)$ against θ (also called a "ridge trace") can be made for all the p parameter estimates and as θ is increased, the estimates $\hat{\beta}_i(\theta)$ $(i = 1, 2, \ldots, p)$ tend to become more stable. A suitable value of θ, say, θ^* is then selected. As in the first method, the choice of θ^* is not unique and several guidelines are suggested [56], e.g.,

(a) At a certain value of θ the system will stabilize and have the general characteristics of an orthogonal system;

(b) Coefficients with incorrect signs at $\theta = 0$ will have changed to have the proper signs (i.e., proper signs as expected from theoretical grounds);

(c) The residual sum of squares will not be unduly large relative to what would be a reasonable variance for the process generating the data.

The robustness of this procedure, which is unlike the LS method has much practical usefulness and in some basic sense it is very close to the method of generalized inverses indicated in previous sections.

4.7.2. *Analyzing Sensitivity of Regression Estimates*

One of the major problems of econometric estimation using observed non-experimental data is due to aggregation [72]. The problem of aggregation bias in estimation becomes very acute when aggregate relationships like the production function for manufacturing or agriculture [50] have to be estimated from national or international cross-section data. We do not intend to go into this topic in any details; instead we would outline in this section three of the most interesting operational methods for handling some aspects of the sensitivity of the regression estimates which may be due partly to aggregation and partly to structural change.

Consider first an example of a structural change. Suppose we intend to estimate price elasticity of supply in a certain less developed country by regressing supply in logarithmic terms (y) on price in logarithmic terms (x) on the basis of time series data for T years, which combine the periods before and after the so-called "green revolution", which resulted in a substantial yield improvement. It may be reasonable to expect that the price elasticity of supply is very likely to be different during the two periods, before and after the green revolution. How can one estimate the cut-off point t such that the two regression coefficients a_1, a_2 defined below

$$y = a_1 x + u_1 ; u_1 \sim N(0, \sigma_1^2); (t \text{ observations})$$

$$y = a_2 x + u_2 ; u_2 \sim N(0, \sigma_2^2); (T - t \text{ observations}),$$

(4.28)

may be said to belong to two different structural regimes? The same problem would arise if instead of time, another outside variable like the size of land holdings, for example, is used to order the output series and our objective is to test the hypothesis that the elasticity parameters a_1, a_2 belong to two different structural regimes, one represented by the small farmers and the other by the large (where the small and the large are determined in terms of the cut-off point in the size of landholding). For such problems, we have not one but two regression equations obeying a structural change of regimes. It is clear, therefore, that in the second case (where price elasticity of supply may be different for small and large farmers), the aggregate supply elasticity to be economically meaningful must be a weighted average of the two components elasticities, i.e., $a = w a_1 + (1 - w) a_2$, where w denotes the proportion of output produced by the small farmers and a denotes the aggregate supply elasticity.

For such problems of two regressions (4.28) obeying one (or more) change of regimes a very interesting method has been suggested [63] and empirically applied [66]. To illustrate assume that the errors u_1, u_2 in (4.28) are normally independently distributed; then the likelihood of the entire sample of two groups, the first containing t observations and the second containing $T - t$ observations can be easily computed as

$$L = L_1 \cdot L_2,$$

where

$$L_1 = (\sigma_1 \sqrt{2\pi})^{-t} \exp\left[-(2\sigma_1^2)^{-1} \sum_{i=1}^{t} (y_i - a_1 x_i)^2\right]$$

$$L_2 = (\sigma_2 \sqrt{2\pi})^{t-T} \exp\left[-(2\sigma_2^2)^{-1} \sum_{i=t+1}^{T} (y_i - a_2 x_i)^2\right].$$

Define $L_0 = \log L = \log L_1 + \log L_2$ and then, taking $\partial L_0/\partial a_i = 0$ and $\partial L_0/\partial \sigma_i = 0$ $(i = 1, 2)$, we obtain the maximum likelihood estimates $\hat{a}_i$, $\hat{\sigma}_i$ say. Putting these values in $L_0 = L_0(t)$, we get

$$L_0(t) = -T \log \sqrt{2\pi} - t \log \hat{\sigma}_1 - (T - t) \log \hat{\sigma}_2 - T/2.$$

Finally, we have to select other values of t, till we find by numerical or programming methods the optimum value t^* of t, where we have the maximum of the maximum likelihood function, i.e.,

$$L_0(t^*) \geq L_0(t^* \pm i); \; i = 1, 2, \ldots$$

An approximate but operational procedure would be to calculate the value of the $L_0(t)$ function above for three or four possible values of t within $[1, T]$ and select that value of t which corresponds to the maximum maximorum. Approximate statistical tests may be made by using the likelihood ratio $\lambda = L(\hat{w})/L(\Omega) = \hat{\sigma}_1^t \hat{\sigma}_2^T \, {}^t/\hat{\sigma}^T$, where $\hat{\sigma}$ is the standard error of estimate taking all observations, where $(-2 \log \lambda)$ for large T has the approximate distribution of a chi-square variate, although the exact conditions for this approximation are not applicable here.

It is clear that the above method can be generalized to more than two regimes and also to simultaneous equation systems. A closely related problem arises when the data are already grouped into two subgroups by some index of size and two separate regressions are run along with an aggregate regression based on the pooled data. In this case statistical tests from the theory of linear hypothesis can be applied to testing the homogeneity of the entire set (or a subset) of coefficients in two regressions [60]. For example, assume that we have two regressions

$$y_1 = X_1\beta_1 + e_1 \qquad e_1, y_1 : n \cdot 1; e_2, y_2 : m \cdot 1$$

$$y_2 = X_2\beta_2 = e_2 \qquad X_1 : n \cdot p; X_2 : m \cdot p$$

$$\beta_1 : p \cdot 1; \beta_2 : m \cdot 1$$

$$m > p,$$

where the second regression contains m additional observations of the dependent variable y_2 which became available after the first regression based on n observations y_1 was estimated. Since the above two regressions may be written equivalently as

$$\begin{pmatrix} y_1 \\ y_2 \end{pmatrix} = \begin{bmatrix} X_1 & 0 \\ 0 & X_2 \end{bmatrix} \begin{pmatrix} \beta_1 \\ \beta_2 \end{pmatrix} + \begin{pmatrix} e_1 \\ e_2 \end{pmatrix}$$

therefore, under the null hypothesis that the two regression vectors are equal (i.e., $H_0 : \beta_1 = \beta_2 = \beta_0$) the model becomes

$$\begin{pmatrix} y_1 \\ y_2 \end{pmatrix} = \begin{bmatrix} X_1 \\ X_2 \end{bmatrix} \beta_0 + \begin{pmatrix} e_1 \\ e_2 \end{pmatrix}.$$

It is known [65] that the sum of squares of the residuals under the null hypothesis H_0 is equal to the sum of squares of residuals under the alternative hypothesis (i.e., $H_a : \beta_1 \neq \beta_2$) plus the sum of squares of the derivations between the two sets of estimates of y under these two hypotheses. The ratio between the latter two sums, adjusted for their degrees of freedom follows an F distribution as follows if the null hypothesis is true:

$$F(p, m + n - 2p) = \frac{\|X_1 \hat{\beta}_1 - X_1 \hat{\beta}_0\|^2 + \|X_2(\hat{\beta}_2 - \hat{\beta}_0)\|^2}{\|y_1 - X_1 \hat{\beta}_1\|^2 + \|y_2 - X_2 \hat{\beta}_2\|^2} \cdot \frac{(m + n - 2p)}{p}.$$

This is the standard analysis-of-covariance test [60] when $m > p$. When $m \leq p$ we can test H_0 by the F ratio

$$F(m, n - p) = \frac{\|X_1 \hat{\beta}_1 - X_1 \hat{\beta}_0\|^2 + \|y_2 - X_2 \hat{\beta}_0\|^2}{\|y_1 - X_1 \hat{\beta}_1\|^2} \cdot \frac{(n - p)}{m}.$$

If the observed value of $F(n_1, n_2)$ exceeds or equals the 100 α per cent tabulated value $F_\alpha(n_1, n_2)$, then we reject the null hypothesis that the two regression coefficient vectors are identical. This test has been modified by Chow [52] to include comparisons between subsets of regression coefficients.

Consider now the second type of problems caused by aggregation bias which have led some authors [77] to emphasize the random coefficient model as a possible construct for cross-section observations, since it permits corresponding coefficients to be different for different individuals. Assume that for the kth economic unit we have the equation

$$y_k = X_k \beta_k + e_k \qquad\qquad (4.29)$$

$$k = 1, \ldots, N$$

$$X_k : n \cdot p \text{ or rank } p$$

$$\beta_k : p \cdot 1 \text{ vector,}$$

where β_k contains the p parameters to be estimated and e_k is an n-element column vector of error terms with mean zero and N is the number of economic units being considered here. Defining macro-variables by simple aggregation, i.e.,

$$y = \sum_{k=1}^{N} y_k \text{ and } X = \sum_{k=1}^{N} X_k$$

the aggregate regression equation may be defined as [72]

$$y = X\beta + e. \tag{4.30}$$

Note that the aggregate relationship (4.30) does not follow mathematically from (4.29) by applying a rule of aggregation, hence, as is expected, the expectation of the least squares estimate of β in (4.30) using only macro-data depends in general on all the micro coefficients β_k of (4.29) both corresponding coefficients and non-corresponding coefficients:

$$E\hat{\beta} = E(X'X)^{-1}X' \sum_{k=1}^{N} (X_k\beta_k + e_k) = \sum_{k=1}^{N} P_k\beta_k,$$

$$\text{where } P_k \equiv (X'X)^{-1}X'X_k.$$

A way out of this difficulty due to the apparent lack of consistency and correspondence between the macro and the micro coefficients is to consider the coefficients β_k of the model (4.29) to be random and then derive an estimate of the expected value of β_k, say $\bar{\beta}$. As Klein and others [73, 77] have pointed out this viewpoint may be very appealing in the analysis of cross-section data since it permits corresponding coefficients to be different for different individuals. To this end, we rewrite the model (4.29) as follows:

$$y_k = X_k(\bar{\beta} + u_k) + e_k \qquad k = 1, 2, \ldots, N,$$

$$\text{where } \beta_k = \bar{\beta} + u_k \text{ with } Eu_k = 0,$$

where u_k is a random vector with zero expectation. Summing over k this becomes

$$y = \Sigma y_k = X\bar{\beta} + \Sigma X_k u_k + e, \qquad e = \Sigma e_k,$$

which, in contrast to (4.30), is the macro-equation derived mathematically from the micro-relations. Thus, the macro least squares estimator $\hat{\beta}$ is an unbiased estimator of $\bar{\beta}$ the common mean of the micro-coefficient vectors β_k, i.e.,

$$\hat{\beta} = (X'X)^{-1}X'y = (X'X)^{-1}X'(X\bar{\beta} + \Sigma X_k u_k + e)$$

$$E\hat{\beta} = \bar{\beta}, \text{ since } E[(X'X)^{-1}X'\Sigma X_k u_k] = 0 \text{ and } E(X'X)^{-1}X'e = 0.$$

Hence, there is no aggregation bias. Note, however, that there are two sources of randomness in the sample estimate $\hat{\beta}$ above, one due to the u_k and the other from the macro-disturbance term $e = \Sigma e_k$. This approach can easily be generalized to simultaneous equation systems [77]. Some asymptotic efficiency properties of the estimator $\hat{\beta}$ above are available [71] under the simplifying assumption that the disturbances u_k and e_j are statistically independent.

An alternative approach to the case where the parameters are random is to consider an estimate $\hat{\beta}$ restricted to the class of linear unbiased estimates of β having the general form

$$\tilde{\beta} = By \qquad B: p \cdot n$$
$$y: n \cdot 1,$$

such that the matrix B minimizes a quadratic risk function as follows:

$$R(B) = E[(\tilde{\beta} - \beta)'W(\tilde{\beta} - \beta)], \qquad W: p \cdot p,$$

where the weighting matrix is arbitrary and only restricted to being positive definite. Under the following assumptions for the linear model $y = X\beta + e$ with random parameters β

$$Ee = 0 = Eey'; \; Eee' = V$$

$$Eyy' = H; \; E\beta y' = D; \; E\beta\beta' = F \quad V, H: n \cdot n \tag{4.31}$$
$$D: p \cdot n$$
$$F: p \cdot p,$$

it can be easily checked [76] that the risk function $R(B)$ reaches an absolute minimum for the choice of B as B_0, where

$$B_0 = DH^{-1}.$$

Hence, the minimum value of the risk function can be derived as

$$R(B_0) = \text{tr}[(F - 2DB_0' + B_0 H B_0')W]$$
$$= \text{tr}[(F - DH^{-1}D')W],$$

since H is symmetric, where tr denotes the trace of a matrix. It is clear that if estimates of F, D and H are available, then the estimator $\tilde{\beta}$ can be calculated as

$$\tilde{\beta} = B_0 y.$$

The weighting matrix W may also be chosen such that it minimizes the risk function and in that case it is known from the theory of weighted least squares [53] that the matrix W^{-1} should be the covariance function V required for the minimum variance estimate.

We consider now the third aspect of the problem of sensitivity of regression estimates which arises when we want to analyze the impact of departures from the assumption of normality for the disturbance terms. It is clear that if the disturbance term e in (4.26) is not normally distributed, then the usual t-test on the estimated regression coefficient may not be valid. Geary [58] and more recently Tukey [75] have shown that probabilities derived from the well-known analysis of variance and other small sample tables which postulate universal normality may differ seriously from true probability, when the universes are nonnormal even in some cases when the degree of nonnormality is not considerable. Two types of attempts are available for handling such problems. One is the use of nonparametric or distribution-free methods of estimation, for which we have a considerable amount of recent literature [62, 70]. Economic applications [68] are also reported more increasingly. A second method is to apply some kind of Monte-Carlo or other types of simulation based on specific near-normal distributions so that the robustness of the estimates can be better appraised [75].

4.7.3. *Estimation Viewed as Regulation*

The view of estimation as problems of prediction has come into contrast in recent years with the view of optimal control in a stochastic framework. In deterministic control theory, optimal controls are the instrument variables which satisfy a system of dynamic equations and also optimize a dynamic intertemporal scalar objective function (see Chapter 8 for some examples). It is clear that if there are random elements in the dynamic equations or in the objective function, the optimal controls become stochastic. Various methods are available [48, 49, 76] for handling such problems. In some cases (e.g., quadratic objective function, linear dynamic system with no constraints on the control vector) the problem reduces to a prediction problem, since the theorem of certainty equivalence [76] applies. In general, however, the problems of stochastic sensitivity of the optimal trajectory require analysis in terms of the characteristics of the underlying stochastic processes.

REFERENCES

[1] BARTLETT, M. S. "Some Evolutionary Stochastic Processes," *Journal of the Royal Statistical Society*, Series B, XI (1949), 211.

[2] BASMANN, R. L. "A Generalized Classical Method of Linear Estimation of Coefficients in a Structural Equation," *Econometrica*, XXV (1957), 77–83.

[3] BRANDOW, G. E. *Interrelations Among Demands for Farm Products and Implications for Control of Market Supplies*. University Park: Pennsylvania State University Agricultural Experiment Station Bulletin 680 (an interregional publication), 1961.

[4] BROWN, T. M. "Simultaneous Least Squares," *International Economic Review*, I (September, 1960), 173–191.

[5] CHRIST, C. "Simultaneous Equations Estimation: Any Verdict Yet?" *Econometrica*, XXVIII (October, 1960), 835–845.

[6] ——. "On Econometric Models of the U.S. Economy," in *Income and Wealth*, Series 6 (International Association for Research in Income and Wealth). London: Bowes and Bowes, 1957.

[7] DURBIN, J. "Estimation of Parameters in Time-Series Regression Model," *Journal of the Royal Statistical Society*, Series B, XXII (1960), 139.

[8] EZEKIEL, M., and FOX, K. A. *Methods of Correlation and Regression Analysis*. 3rd revised edition. New York: John Wiley & Sons, 1959.

[9] FISHER, G. "Iterative Solutions and Heteroscedasticity in Regression Analysis," *Review of the International Statistical Institute*, XXX, No. 2 (1962), 153.

[10] FOX, K. A. "Structural Analysis and the Measurement of Demand for Farm Products," *Review of Economics and Statistics*, XXXVI (February, 1954), 57–66.

[11] ——. *Econometric Analysis for Public Policy*. Ames: Iowa State University Press, 1958.

[12] ——, and COONEY, J. F. *Effects of Intercorrelation Upon Multiple Correlation and Regression Measures*. Washington, D.C.: U.S. Department of Agriculture, Agricultural Marketing Service, Bulletin, April, 1954, reissued October, 1959.

[13] HAAVELMO, T. "The Statistical Implications of a System of Simultaneous Equations," *Econometrica*, XI (January, 1943), 1–12.

[14] HARTLEY, H. O. "The Estimation of Nonlinear Parameters by Internal Least Squares," *Biometrika*, XXXV (June 1948), 32.

[15] ——. "The Modified Gauss-Newton Method for the Fitting of Nonlinear Regression Functions by Least Squares," *Technometrics*, III (1948), 269–280.

[16] HOOD, W. C., and KOOPMANS, T. C. (eds.). *Studies in Econometric Method*. New York: John Wiley & Sons, 1953.

[17] JOHNSTON, J. *Econometric Methods*. New York: McGraw-Hill Book Co., 1963.

[18] JORGENSON, D. W. "Multiple Regression Analysis of a Poisson Process," *Journal of the American Statistical Association*, LVI (1961), 235–245.

[19] KEMPTHORNE, O. *The Theory of Least Squares and the General Linear Hypothesis*. Ames: Iowa State University, Statistical Laboratory, 1960. (Dittoed.)

[20] KLEIN, L. R. "The Use of Econometric Models as a Guide to Economic Policy," *Econometrica*, XV (April 1947), 111–151.

[21] ——. *A Textbook of Econometrics*. Evanston, Ill.: Row, Peterson, 1953.

[22] ——, and NAKAMURA, M. "Singularity in the Equation Systems of Econometrics:

Some Aspects of the Problem of Multicollinearity," *International Economic Review*, III (1962), 274–299.

[23] KLOEK, T., and MENNES, L. "Simultaneous Equations Estimation Based on Principal Components of Predetermined Variables," *Econometrica*, XXVIII (January 1960), 45–61.

[24] LEONTIEF, W. "Lags and Stability of Dynamic Systems," with a reply by J. D. Sargan, *Econometrica*, XXIX (October 1961), 659–675.

[25] LEWISH, W. T. Linear Estimation in Convex Parameter Spaces. Unpublished Ph. D. dissertation, Iowa State University, 1963.

[26] NAGAR, A. L. "The Bias and Moment Matrix of the General k-Class Estimators of the Parameters in Simultaneous Equations," *Econometrica*, XXVII (July 1959), 575–595.

[27] ——. "A Monte Carlo Study of Alternative Simultaneous Equation Estimators," *Econometrica*, XXVIII (July 1960), 573–590.

[28] ——. "Double k-Class Estimators of Parameters in Simultaneous Equations and Their Small Sample Properties," *International Economic Review*, III (May 1962), 168–188.

[29] NATIONAL BUREAU OF STANDARDS. *Basic Theorems in Matrix Theory*. Washington, D.C.: Applied Mathematics Series No. 57, 1960.

[30] NEYMAN, J. "Two Breakthroughs in the Theory of Statistical Decision-Making," *Revue de L'Institut International de Statistique*, XXX (1962), 11.

[31] PENROSE, R. A. "A Generalized Inverse for Matrices," *Proceedings of Cambridge Philosophical Society*, LI (1955), 406.

[32] RAO, C. R. "Efficient Estimates and Optimum Inference Procedures in Large Samples," *Journal of Royal Statistical Society*, Series B, XXIV (1962), 46.

[33] ——. "A Note on a Generalized Inverse of a Matrix with Applications to Problems in Mathematical Statistics," *Journal of Royal Statistical Society*, Series B, XXIV (1962), 152.

[34] ROSENBLATT, M., et al. "Regression Analysis of Vector-Valued Random Processes," *Journal of Society of Industrial and Applied Mathematics*, X (1962), 89–102.

[35] SAMUELSON, P. A. *Foundations of Economic Analysis*. Cambridge, Mass.: Harvard University Press, 1947.

[36] SENGUPTA, J. K. "Specification and Estimation of Structural Relations in Policy Models," in *Quantitative Planning of Economic Policy*. Edited by B. G. Hickman. Washington, D.C.: The Brookings Institution, 1965, Chap. 4.

[37] THEIL, H. "Specification Errors and the Estimation of Economic Relationships," *Review of International Statistical Institute*, XXV (1957).

[38] ——. *Economic Forecasts and Policy*. 2nd revised edition. Amsterdam: North-Holland Publishing Co., 1961.

[40] ——, and GOLDBERGER, A. S. "On Pure and Mixed Statistical Estimation in Economics," *International Economic Review*, II (January 1961), 65–78.

[39] ——, and BOOT, J. "The Final Form of Econometric Equation Systems," *Review of International Statistical Institute*, XXX (1962), 136–152.

[41] ——, and KLOEK, T. "The Statistics of Systems of Simultaneous Economic Relationships," *Bulletin of International Statistical Institute*, XXXVII (1960), 345–368.

[42] TINTNER, G. *Econometrics*. New York: John Wiley & Sons, 1952.

[43] WILLIAMS, E. "Exact Fiducial Limits in Nonlinear Estimation," *Journal of Royal Statistical Society*, Series B, XXIV (1962), 125–139.

[44] WOLD, H. "Causal Inference from Observational Data: A Review of Ends and Means," *Journal of Royal Statistical Society*, Series A, CXIX (1956), 28–61.

[45] ——. "Construction Principles of Simultaneous Equation Models in Economics," *Bulletin of International Statistical Institute*, XXXVIII (1960), 111–138.

[46] WOLFE, P. "Methods of Nonlinear Programming," in *Recent Advances in Mathematical Programming*. Edited by R. L. Graves and P. Wolfe. New York: McGraw-Hill Book Co., 1963.

[47] AITCHISON, J. "Statistical Problems of Treatment Allocation", *Journal of Royal Statistical Society*, Series A, Volume 133, 1970, pp. 206–238.

[48] AOKI, M. *Optimization of Stochastic Systems*. New York: Academic Press, 1967.

[49] BOX, G. E. P. and JENKINS, G. M. "Discrete Models for Feedback and Feedforward Control", in *The Future of Statistics*, edited by Watts, D. G. New York: Academic Press, 1968.

[50] BROWN, M. (editor). *The Empirical Analysis of Production*. Volume 31, Studies in Income and Wealth, National Bureau of Economic Research, New York, 1967.

[51] CHAMPERNOWNE, D. G. *Uncertainty and Estimation in Economics*. Three volumes. San Francisco: Holden Day, 1969.

[52] CHOW, G. C. "Tests of Equality between Sets of Coefficients in Two Linear Regressions", *Econometrica*, Volume 28, 1960, pp. 591–605.

[53] DEUTSCH, R. *Estimation Theory*. Englewood Cliffs, N.J.: Prentice Hall, 1965.

[54] DHRYMES, P. J. *Econometrics*. New York: Harper and Rowe, 1970.

[55] DRAPER, N. R. and SMITH, H. *Applied Regression Analysis*. New York: John Wiley, 1966.

[56] DRAPER, N. R. and SMITH, H. "Methods for Selecting Variables from a Given Set of Variables for Regression Analysis", *Bulletin of International Statistical Institute*, Volume 43, 1969, pp. 7–13.

[57] FARRAR, D. E. and GLAUBER, R. R. "Multicollinearity in Regression Analysis: The Problem Revisited", *Review of Economics and Statistics*, Volume 49, 1967, pp. 92–107.

[58] GEARY, R. C. "Testing for Normality", *Biometrika*, Volume 34, 1947, pp. 209–242.

[59] JENKINS, G. M. and WATTS, D. G. *Spectral Analysis and its Applications*. San Francisco: Holden-Day, 1969.

[60] KEMPTHORNE, O. *The Design and Analysis of Experiments*. New York: John Wiley, 1952.

[61] KENDALL, M. G. *A Course in Multivariate Analysis*. London: Griffin and Co., 1957.

[62] MILLER, R. G., Jr. *Simultaneous Statistical Inference*. New York: McGraw Hill, 1966.

[63] QUANDT, R. E. "Tests of the Hypothesis that a Linear Regression System Obeys Two Separate Regimes", *Journal of American Statistical Association*, Volume 55, 1960, pp. 324–330.

[64] RAO, C. R. "The Theory of Least Squares when the Parameters are Stochastic and its Application to the Analysis of Growth Curves", *Biometrika*, Volume 52, 1965, pp. 447–458.

[65] SCHEFFE, H. *The Analysis of Variance*. New York: John Wiley and Sons, 1959.

[66] SENGUPTA, J. K. and TINTNER, G. "An Approach to a Stochastic Theory of Economic Development with Applications", in *Problems of Economic Dynamics and Planning: Essays in Honor of M. Kalecki*. Warsaw: PWN Polish Scientific Publisher, 1964.

[67] SENGUPTA, J. K. "Optimal Stabilization Policy with a Quadratic Criterion Function", *Review of Economic Studies,* Volume 37, 1970, pp. 127–145.

[68] SENGUPTA, J. K. and SANYAL, B. C. "Bounds for the Distribution of the Maximand in Stochastic Linear Programming" (Sent for publication, 1972).

[69] SILVEY, S. D. "Multicollinearity and Imprecise Estimation", *Journal of Royal Statistical Society,* Series B, Volume 31, No. 3, 1969, pp. 539–552.

[70] STEPHENS, M. A. "The Goodness-of-Fit Statistic V_N: Distribution and Significance Points", *Biometrika,* Volume 52, 1965, pp. 309–321.

[71] SWAMY, P. A. V. B. "Efficient Inference in a Random Coefficient Regression Model", *Econometrica,* Volume 38, March 1970, pp. 311–323.

[72] THEIL, H. *Linear Aggregation of Economic Relations.* Amsterdam: North Holland Publishing, 1954.

[73] THEIL, H. *Principles of Econometrics.* New York: John Wiley, 1971.

[74] TINTNER, G. and SENGUPTA, J. K. *Stochastic Economics: Stochastic Processes, Control and Programming.* New York: Academic Press, 1972.

[75] TUKEY, J. W. "The Future of Data Analysis", *Annals of Mathematical Statistics,* Volume 33, 1962, pp. 1–67.

[76] WHITTLE, P. *Prediction and Regulation.* London: English Universities Press, 1963.

[77] ZELLNER, A. "On the Aggregation Problem: A New Approach to a Troublesome Problem", in *Economic Models, Estimation and Risk Programming:* Essays in Honor of Gerhard Tintner, edited by Fox, K. A., Sengupta, J. K. and Narasimham, G. V. L. Berlin: Springer-Verlag, 1969, Chapter 16.

Chapter 5

THE MEANING AND IMPORTANCE OF FORECASTING IN ECONOMIC POLICY MODELS AND OF IMPERFECTIONS IN DATA AND DATA ADJUSTMENTS

The object of national economic policy may be viewed as that of wielding available instruments in such a manner as to approximate desired values and time paths of policy targets in the face of uncertainty concerning the future values of noncontrollable factors. The noncontrollable factors may be preponderantly favorable or preponderantly unfavorable to the policy maker's objectives at a given time; also, the noncontrollable factors in a given year may be favorable to the achievement of certain targets and unfavorable to the achievement of others. We cannot steer an economy successfully unless we can anticipate to some extent the values of major exogenous variables.

This chapter discusses the basic principles of forecasting and the factors which determine the accuracy with which we can predict future values of variables. The succeeding chapter (Chapter 6) outlines the derivation of decision rules for economic policy models. The irreducible levels of uncertainty surrounding future values of noncontrollable variables can be built into rules for steering an economy or at least for adjusting the instruments through which a policy maker hopes to steer the economy in a desired direction.

5.1. Introduction

The policy maker is not interested in the values of exogenous variables for their own sakes. If they are truly exogenous, his stance with respect to them must be one of "cooperating with the inevitable." Rather, he is concerned about the values of those endogenous variables (targets) which he considers important for the general welfare and with the values of those instrument variables to which important segments of the population attach welfare connotations.

The policy maker, then, would like to have *unconditional* forecasts of the target variables. The economic adviser, however, feels more comfortable in dividing the forecasting problem into two parts. First, he wishes to know how successful his economic model would be in predicting values of the endogenous variables *given* specified values of all of the exogenous ones. The resulting predictions of the endogenous variables may be called *conditional forecasts*—forecasts conditioned upon the emergence of specified values of all the exogenous variables. The second element of the economic adviser's problem is that of forecasting values of the exogenous variables which he cannot control. Some exogenous variables can be forecast with greater accuracy than others. In fact, some economies may be less stable than others because of the greater inherent variability of the exogenous variables with which they must contend.

It is also customary to distinguish between forecasting on the assumption of a constant economic structure and forecasting when confronted with a changing economic structure. Economists who have gone so far as to develop economic policy models of their national economies will be well aware of this distinction. For example, the structure of an economy may be deliberately changed by the introduction of a steeply progressive personal income tax or by a tax on corporate incomes. These built-in stabilizers will change the characteristic responses of such target variables as consumer expenditures to given exogenous shocks. The effects of unit changes in policy instruments upon the endogenous target variables may also be changed by these deliberate modifications of the economic structure.

Policy makers who are aware that their own actions are changing the economic structure should be able to avoid the naive empiricism which originally justified sermons from econometricians to "practical" economic forecasters in the 1940's.

From the policy maker's viewpoint, improved forecasts mean increased welfare. An error in forecasting a "datum" leads to errors in forecasting one or more target variables. These errors in turn lead to errors in setting various instruments. If the policy maker has projected desired time paths for the targets and for those instruments with welfare connotations, erroneous forecasts not only lead him to achieve suboptimal values of the target variables but also to deliberately choose what turn out to be suboptimal values of some of the instruments.

Other types of errors also result in welfare losses. These include errors of measurement in the *ex post* values of variables and aggregation or index number problems among others.

5.2. An Exposition in Terms of Price Forecasts[1]

Although our major concern in this book is with policy models of complete economies, the basic principles involved in forecasting can be illustrated quite concretely in terms of the economic outlook or forecasting work of the U.S. Department of Agriculture. This work was begun in 1922, and thirty years of experience with it had accumulated by 1952. During that year (1952), three major articles appeared relating to the accuracy of the outlook work. The first of these, by James P. Cavin [5], described methods used by the Bureau of Agricultural Economics in preparing forecasts of general economic conditions and appraised the accuracy of such forecasts made during 1946–1951. The other two, by John D. Baker, Jr. and Don Paarlberg [2, 3], appraised the accuracy of the Bureau's general demand forecasts and its forecasts of production and prices of wheat from 1922 to 1950.

A comparison of forecasts and actual outcomes gives us a measure of the accuracy which has been obtained in the past. To the farmer who acts, or considers acting, on the basis of outlook information, the historical record also offers the most credible evidence as to the level of accuracy which may be expected in the future. The record itself does not tell us why a particular level of accuracy was achieved, nor does it tell us how, or whether, the accuracy of future forecasts may be improved. To answer these questions, we must study the structure of economic and natural forces affecting the variable which is forecast and the accuracy and completeness of statistical information relating to both the forecast variable and the factors which affect it.

In general, price is the economic variable which farmers are most interested in anticipating. The outlook for various demand and supply factors is of value to farmers mainly, though by no means entirely, as a basis for judging probable trends in prices. This section is concerned only with problems of price forecasting, and it approaches the question of forecasting accuracy from an analytical and statistical point of view. Two main questions are engaged: (1) What are the basic limitations to the accuracy of price forecasts? (2) By what means can the accuracy of such forecasts be improved? These points will be taken up in turn.

The relevance of this section to forecasting in macroeconomic policy models is as follows:

(1) In advance of the season for planting crops or initiating certain

---

[1] This section is based on Fox [7].

livestock production activities, forecasts of the prices at which the resulting products may sell influence the individual farmer in allocating his resources among alternative activities. Resource allocation is the farmer's instrument in attempting to select that set of output quantities which is feasible within his resource constraints and which maximizes the expected value of his objective function — basically or exclusively the net revenue function for his farm.

(2) A government policy maker could use these same price forecasts as a basis for applying policy instruments to *change* the outcomes currently expected — through restrictions on acreages planted or quantities to be marketed from individual farms or through incentives (support prices or subsidies) to increase production of particular commodities.

(3) If the instruments of the government policy maker can control acreages but not per-acre yields, the policy maker's efforts to influence *his* target variables (national outputs, prices and/or net farm incomes, as the case may be) must contend with the irreducible uncertainty of yields.

(4) The disposable income of consumers may affect the farm prices and net farm incomes associated with given outputs. Disposable income is treated in the following section as a variable which is exogenous and noncontrollable from the standpoint of the individuals who are interested in price forecasts — even including (say) the minister of agriculture. From the standpoint of the president or prime minister and his economic advisers, disposable income is an endogenous target variable. The "barter terms of trade" (see Chapter 7) between disposable income and other variables, as seen by the prime minister, may be influenced at least slightly by the fact that a change in disposable income facilitates or hinders the attainment of farm price and income objectives.

The formal structure of the forecasting problem can, however, be illustrated clearly (and numerically) by a simple price-forecasting example which does not need to be imbedded in a policy model.

5.2.1. *Basic Limitations to the Accuracy of Price Forecasts*

The Bureau of Agricultural Economics and its successor agencies have made two general types of advance estimates or forecasts. The first type is made by the Crop Reporting Board and consists in estimating future acreage, production and similar items on the basis of farmers' intentions to plant or of reports on the condition of growing crops. Actual plantings may differ from acreage intentions because of weather conditions at planting time or because of changes in economic conditions and in farmers' evaluations of them subsequent to the date on which the intentions were stated. Advance estimates of production, based upon the condition of growing crops prior to harvest, assume average growing conditions during the remainder of the season. If weather during the remainder of the growing season is more favorable than average, actual production will exceed the advance estimate or early-season indication, and vice versa.

Discrepancies between crop production indications and actual production are largely due to natural phenomena and in many cases cannot be reduced materially unless we develop bases for forecasting the natural phenomena themselves — such as the amounts and time distributions of temperature and rainfall. Moderate improvements may be possible in analyzing the effects of conditions prior to the forecast date upon final production and also in the precision with which crop conditions on the given date are estimated. The precision of final production estimates could also be increased, although in general this would involve more costly procedures for obtaining data.

The other type of forecast is more strictly economic in nature. Price is the variable which we are most commonly interested in predicting. But price forecasts for several months to a year ahead are usually based on estimates of the supply and demand factors which influence price. Although forecasts of consumer demand are derived from economic rather than natural considerations, they are similar to forecasts of supply in the sense that both serve as instrumental or "independent" variables in the

[a] Supply variables in underlying analyses are total or per capita production unless noted.

[b] Represents minimum error range attainable 2 years out of 3 under most favorable conditions *given* the regression equation used. Smaller standard errors could be obtained for some of the prices by data refinements, construction of special series, use of additional explanatory variables and, for some crops, by using deviations from the 1922–1941 average rather than the first differences or year-to-year changes used here.

[c] Unadjusted. Represents the percentage of total year-to-year variation in retail price during 1922–1941 which was "explained" by the combined effects of the other variables.

[d] Supply variables in underlying analyses are per capita consumption.

[e] Based on analyses adapted from George M. Kuznets and Lawrence R. Klein, "A Statistical Analysis of the Domestic Demand for Lemons, 1921–1941." Giannini Foundation of Agricultural Economics, Mimeographed Report No. 84, June, 1943. Prices are measured at the f.o.b. level.

TABLE 5.1

Selected Farm and Food Products: Standard Errors of Price Estimates Based on Regression Analyses for the 1922–1941 Period*

Item[a]	(1) Standard Error of Estimate (Per Cent of Expected Price)[b]	(2) Coefficient of Determination[c]	Item[a]	(1) Standard Error of Estimate (Per Cent of Expected Price)[b]	(2) Coefficient of Determination[e]
Retail prices			Milk, fluid use[d]	3.4	0.91
All meat	2.1	0.98	Condensery milk[d]	9.7	0.76
Pork	4.9	0.92	Milk for cheese[d]	11.6	0.71
Beef	2.4	0.96	Butterfat[d]	7.4	0.85
Lamb	3.4	0.91	Fruits and vegetables		
All meat[d]	1.7	0.98	All fruits	11.5	0.82
Pork[d]	3.0	0.97	All deciduous fruits	9.9	0.82
Beef[d]	2.9	0.95	Apples	6.7	0.96
Lamb[d]	2.9	0.94	Peaches		
Poultry and eggs			(excl. Calif.)	16.6	0.80
Chickens[d]	4.4	0.86	Cranberries		
Eggs	6.8	0.80	(1922–1936)	14.7	0.86
Dairy products			All citrus fruits	11.3	0.92
Fluid milk	2.7	0.87	Oranges	14.0	0.93
Evaporated milk	3.3	0.84	Grapefruit	39.2	0.72
Cheese	4.1	0.84	Lemons, all	36.2	0.61
Butter	5.3	0.84	Lemons shipped fresh		
Farm prices			Summer[e]	16.2	0.79
All meat animals	7.9	0.88	Winter[e]	14.0	0.88
Hogs, cal. yr.	14.8	0.82	Potatoes	16.3	0.93
Hogs, Oct.-Mar.	15.3	0.81	Sweetpotatoes	13.2	0.75
Hogs, April-Sept.	21.5	0.69	Onions		
Beef cattle	6.3	0.90	All	15.2	0.89
Veal calves	5.0	0.93	Late summer	27.0	0.85
Lambs	7.4	0.87	Truck crops for fresh		
Poultry and eggs			market, cal. yr.	5.6	0.85
Chickens	6.2	0.86	Winter	16.3	0.67
Turkeys	9.5	0.90	Spring	11.8	0.49
Eggs	8.5	0.75	Summer	10.4	0.87
Dairy products			Fall	10.1	0.84
All	4.4	0.87	Feed grains and hay		
Milk, wholesale	4.6	0.88	Corn	17.9	0.85
			Hay	8.6	0.90

* See footnotes on p. 126.

estimation of commodity prices. The significance of this fact will appear shortly.

5.2.2. *Limits to Accuracy When Values of Independent Variables are Known*

The form of equation (5.1) is typical of the simpler statistical demand functions which have been derived for farm or food products:

$$X_1 = a_0 + b_0X_2 + c_0X_3 + d_1, \tag{5.1}$$

where $X_1 =$ price,

$X_2 =$ production or supply,

$X_3 =$ disposable consumer income,

all considered as actual or final values of these variables, and $d_1 =$ residual errors or disturbances in X_1 which cannot be attributed to X_2 and X_3.

Equation (5.1) represents the average or expected relationship between a commodity price and the final estimates of the supply and demand variables which influence it. In practice we never find an exact relationship between the final estimates of these three variables. There is always some variation in price which cannot be explained in terms of supply and consumer income. The unexplained price variations may be due to a number of factors, including (1) sampling or measurement errors in any or all variables, (2) mistakes in choosing the form of the regression equation to be fitted to the data (as arithmetic versus logarithmic equation forms) and (3) the effects of variables not included in the analysis. Sometimes variables are omitted intentionally because we believe them to be of minor importance; more often we are forced to leave out possibly significant variables because we have no data on them. For these reasons, any estimate based upon a regression equation will be subject to some error.

Suppose we were to set ourselves the goal of predicting the prices of each of a large number of commodities within a certain percentage limit. More specifically, let us say that we hope to forecast the season average price of each commodity two years out of three within 5 per cent of the actual outcome. From a statistical viewpoint, the possibility of attaining this degree of accuracy for a given commodity will depend upon the basic variability of its price and the closeness with which it is related to other variables, such as its production and consumer income.

5.2.2.1. The Standard Error of Estimate

Table 5.1 presents standard errors of estimate from a considerable number of commodity price analyses for the period 1922–1941. Unless better estimating equations are developed, there will be no way of reducing price forecasting errors below the levels indicated in column 1.[2]

In general, about two-thirds of the prices actually experienced during 1922–1941 (the years included in the analyses) will be found to be within one standard error of estimate of the corresponding prices estimated from the regression equation. Price estimates for other years are almost always subject to a larger error range than this.

Table 5.1 indicates that the prescribed level of accuracy — within 5 per cent in two years out of three — was attainable for annual average *retail* prices of most food livestock products. The 1922–1941 standard errors of estimate for these commodities at retail ranged from 1.7 to 5.3 per cent. In contrast, however, the 5 per cent level of accuracy was not attainable for the farm prices of most of these products with the equations used. Analyses for wholesale milk (total and for fluid use), total dairy products and veal calves gave error levels of 3.4 to 5.0 per cent, but those for most other livestock products ranged from 6 to 10 per cent. Error levels for hog prices and for milk sold to cheese factories exceeded 10 per cent. The analyses of season average farm prices of crops yielded 1922–1941 error levels between 10 and 20 per cent in most cases. Analyses for apples, hay and fresh market truck crops (calendar year total) stayed within a 10 per cent error limit.

The author's exploratory analyses of U.S. average farm prices of grapefruit and lemons gave standard errors of estimate in excess of 30 per cent! Analyses of the California f.o.b. price of lemons by George Kuznets and Lawrence Klein, using specially constructed series including an index of temperatures in consuming centers, gave standard errors of around 15 per cent for the 1921–1941 period. Similarly intensive research for other commodities should also lead to more accurate estimating relationships than those underlying Table 5.1.

5.2.2.2. The Standard Error of Forecast

The figures in Table 5.1 do not cover any errors of the forecasting type. They indicate the minimum level of error with which we might estimate

---

[2] The analyses in Table 5.1 would ordinarily be used in forecasting season average prices several months to a year in advance. Forecasts of a monthly average price made only a few weeks in advance might have smaller forecasting errors than those indicated in column 1.

Additional research would probably yield more accurate estimating equations than those underlying Table 5.1 for most of the commodities listed. In general, the potential improvement is greatest for analyses with the smallest coefficients of determination (column 2).

season average prices *given* the final official postseason estimates of the supply and demand variables used in each analysis. In fact, the Table 5.1 figures slightly understate the actual 1922–1941 error level even in this postseason context. Strictly speaking, the standard error of estimate applies only to the actual observations from which the regression equation was fitted.

For other values, the proper error level is given by the *standard error of forecast*,[3] which may be written, in squared form, as follows:

$$\sigma_{x_{1'}}^2 = S^2\left(\frac{N+1}{N}\right) + \sigma_{b_0}^2 \cdot x_2^2 + \sigma_{c_0}^2 \cdot x_3^2 - 2\sigma_{b_0}\sigma_{c_0}r_{23}x_2x_3 \qquad (5.2)$$

where x_2 and x_3 are deviations from the 1922–1941 average values of the independent variables; S is the standard error of estimate (as in Table 5.1); σ_{b_0} and σ_{c_0} are standard errors of the net regression coefficients of price upon the supply and demand variables and N is the number of observations to which the regression equation was fitted.

Whereas the standard error of estimate measures the variability of observations in the original 1922–1941 sample about the fitted regression, the standard error of forecast also includes an allowance for uncertainty (sampling error) relative to the exact level of the regression surface and the

---

[3] This name is somewhat unfortunate for present purposes. It measures the range of error in an estimate of price based on *actual* or *final values* of the independent variables. In forecasting *over time*, which is the main concern of outlook work, we have the additional problem of forecasting the independent variables themselves.

---

[c] Standard deviations of price for a few crops might be smaller than this in terms of original values, rather than the first differences actually used.

[d] Unadjusted. Represents the percentage of total year-to-year variation in retail price during 1922–1941 which was "explained" by the combined effects of the independent variables.

[e] Standard deviations of supply for a number of crops would probably be smaller in terms of original values (effectively, deviations from 1922–1941 averages) than in terms of the first differences (year-to-year changes) used here. In the case of corn, for example, the standard deviation of the supply variable used would be only 18 per cent based on logarithms of original values. The inertia in livestock production means that variation from one year to the next is usually smaller than variation around a 20-year average.

[f] The demand variable used in all analyses but those for corn and hay is disposable personal income. The standard deviation of this variable during 1922–1941, based on logarithmic first differences, was 12.3 per cent.

[g] Standard error of estimate divided by standard deviation of actual prices.

[h] Supply variable used is per capita consumption of the end product.

TABLE 5.2

Selected Farm and Food Products: Factors Affecting the Accuracy of Price Estimates
United States, 1922–1941

Commodity[a]	Standard Error of Estimate (Per Cent of Expected Price)[b]	Standard Deviation of Actual Prices (Per Cent)[c]	Coefficient of Determination[d]	Standard Deviation of Supply (Per Cent)[e]	Effect on Price of 1 Per Cent Change in		Ratio of Standard Error to Standard Deviation of Price[g]
					Supply (Per Cent)	Demand (Per Cent)	
	(1)	(2)	(3)	(4)	(5)	(6)	(7)
Retail prices							
All meat	2.1	13.2	0.98	7.3	− 1.07	0.86	0.16
Pork	4.9	17.8	0.92	13.2	− 0.85	0.93	0.28
Beef	2.4	12.3	0.96	7.1	− 0.83	0.83	0.20
Evaporated milk[h]	3.3	7.7	0.84	4.8	−	0.59	0.43
Butter[h]	5.3	13.6	0.84	3.3	−	1.01	0.39
Farm prices							
All meat animals	7.9	23.3	0.88	7.3	− 1.60	1.43	0.34
Hogs	14.8	36.1	0.82	13.2	− 1.54	1.63	0.41
Cattle	7.4	18.8	0.90	7.1	− 1.19	1.27	0.39
Condensed milk[h]	9.7	19.6	0.76	4.8	−	1.34	0.49
Butterfat[h]	7.4	19.2	0.85	3.3	−	1.28	0.39
Dairy products, all	4.4	13.4	0.87	1.8	−	0.98	0.33
Apples	6.7	36.3	0.96	44.0	− 0.79	1.04	0.18
Peaches	16.6	37.8	0.80	54.6	− 0.67	0.96	0.44
Oranges	14.0	61.5	0.93	31.1	− 1.61	1.34	0.23
Grapefruit	33.0	67.0	0.72	26.4	− 1.77	1.29	0.49
Lemons, all	36.2	59.8	0.61	23.2	− 1.69	0.78	0.61
Potatoes	16.3	72.9	0.93	15.0	− 3.51	1.20	0.22
Onions							
All	15.2	50.1	0.89	17.5	− 2.27	1.00	0.30
Late summer	27.0	77.9	0.85	21.4	− 2.90	0.72	0.35
Corn	17.9	48.3	0.85	21.4	− 1.93	0.89	0.37
Hay	8.6	28.8	0.90	13.6	− 1.63	0.96	0.30

[a] The supply variables used are total or per capita production unless otherwise noted.

[b] Represents minimum error range attainable 2 years out of 3 under most favorable possible conditions, *given* the particular regression equation used. In some cases, smaller standard errors could be obtained by using original values of all variables instead of first differences. Also, improvements could be obtained in some cases by further refinement of the basic data, by the construction of special series or by the use of additional or different explanatory variables.

exact values of the net regression slopes. The effect of the latter type of error increases as the values of the independent variables depart farther and farther from the center of the 1922–1941 observations. In the analyses underlying Table 5.1, the variables were expressed as year-to-year changes (logarithmic first differences). As changes in consumer income and in livestock production from one year to the next are usually moderate, the standard errors of forecast appropriate to first-difference analyses for livestock products are seldom very much larger than the standard errors of estimate. This is less true of first-difference analyses for crops, where production is more variable. However, if we were to use a 1922–1941 regression based on actual values of price, supply and income (rather than year-to-year changes) to estimate a price for 1952, the standard error of forecast would be extremely large, since money income per person in 1952 was nearly three times its mean value for the 1922–1941 period.

5.2.2.3. Factors Affecting the Standard Errors of Estimate for Selected Products

Table 5.2 indicates some of the factors that influence the standard error of estimate, which represents the minimum error range attainable using the variables included in the given regression equation. A small standard error of estimate requires (1) high correlation between price and the independent variables (column 3) and (2) relatively small variability in the price itself (column 2). This can be seen by comparing the results for beef and apples, where the difference in standard errors results solely from the difference in price variability, and those for meat at retail and dairy products at the farm level, where the difference in standard errors is due almost entirely to a difference in the level of correlation between price and the explanatory variables.

Column 4, 5 and 6 show some factors accounting for differences in the basic variability of the various price series as indicated in column 2. Farm prices of crops (in the absence of price supports) are more variable than farm prices of livestock products, due chiefly to the greater year-to-year variation in crop supplies (column 4).

The price of potatoes is more variable than that of hogs because the former responds more violently to a given change in supply (column 5). In other words, the demand for potatoes is much less elastic than the demand for hogs. Some differences in price variability also result from differences in price responses to consumer income (column 6), the average year-to-year variability of which was about 12 per cent during the 1922–1941 period. Farm prices are more variable percentagewise than retail prices, due to the presence of some relatively stable or fixed elements in marketing charges. This fact is reflected in columns 5 and 6, where price responses to both supply and income changes are indicated to be sharper at the farm than at the retail level.

Column 7 gives a measure of the over-all efficiency of each regression equation in terms of the ratio of the standard error of estimate to the original price variability. In a few cases the standard error of estimate is only a fifth as large as the standard deviation; more commonly it is closer to a third as large for the analyses shown.

5.2.3. *Limits to Accuracy When Values of Independent Variables Must be Forecast*

When we use statistical regression equations to forecast prices several months to a year in advance we introduce major complications. In addition to the standard error of forecast based on final estimates of supply and demand we have the effects of errors or inaccuracies in our forecasts of the independent variables, particularly production and disposable income. These errors, propagated through the net regression coefficients of commodity price upon the independent variables, may be translated into corresponding errors in our price forecasts. To represent this fact, equation (5.1) may be revised as follows:

$$X_1 = a_0 + b_0 X_2' + c_0 X_3' + (b_0 \delta_2 + c_0 \delta_3 + d_1), \tag{5.3}$$

where X_2' and X_3' are forecasts of the independent variables and δ_2 and δ_3 are differences between these forecasts and the actual values or final estimates, X_2 and X_3.

5.2.3.1. Accuracy of Supply and Demand Forecasts

Errors in forecasts of the independent variables are almost always decreasing functions of time. In the case of corn, Clough [6] has shown that the production indication reported in July differs from the final December estimate by less than 300 million bushels in two years out of three. In August the corresponding error band falls to about 180 million bushels and in September to about 100 million. Still further improvements in accuracy are registered in October and November, again using the final December estimate as a criterion.

Similar measures could be calculated for any of the crop or livestock production series for which early season indications are published. A related approach can be used in special analyses, such as Breimyer's [4] study of factors affecting cattle and calf slaughter, which shows how each major piece of new information as it becomes available contributes to the accuracy of slaughter forecasts.

It is more difficult to document the accuracy of forecasts of disposable income, as these forecasts have seldom been published in precise numerical form and files of the unpublished Bureau of Agricultural Economies estimates are available only for a few recent years.

The sheer inertia of disposable income over periods of three to six months is an aid to demand forecasts. During 1946–1952 the standard deviation of changes in disposable income from one quarter to the next was 2.6 per cent and that of cumulative change over two quarters (six months) was 4.6 per cent. The corresponding figures for lags of three and four quarters were 6.4 and 8.3 per cent, respectively. If the economic forecaster allowed correctly for the postwar upward trend in income, these deviations would be reduced to 2.0, 3.2, 4.1 and 4.7 per cent for lags of three, six, nine and twelve months, respectively. The average short-run variability of disposable income during 1929–1937 was nearly twice as great (on a percentage basis) as the postwar variability without adjustment for trend.

The Bureau of Agricultural Economics outlook forecasts of disposable income a year ahead came out within 2 or 3 per cent in four of the six years 1947–1952. The 1947 outlook statement underestimated the inflationary trend into 1948, and the October, 1949 statement, of course, did not anticipate the outbreak of hostilities in Korea.

We can use equations (5.2) and (5.3) to show how the level of price-forecasting error is reduced as the accuracy of our estimates of the demand and supply variables increases. On the average, the latter estimates improve as we draw nearer to the date to which the price forecast applies. At any given time (t) we may define an error for equation (5.3) which corresponds in concept to the standard error of estimate. This error, in squared form, may be written

$$\sigma^2_{x_1'(t)} = \sigma^2_{d_1} + b_0^2 \sigma^2_{\delta_2(t)} + c_0^2 \sigma^2_{\delta_3(t)} \tag{5.4}$$

assuming no correlation between $\delta_2(t)$, $\delta_3(t)$ and d_1.

Remembering that S, the standard error of estimate, equals σ_{d_1} we can convert equation (5.4) into a relative error, dividing through by S^2 and taking square roots as follows:

$$\frac{\sigma_{x_1'(t)}}{S} = \sqrt{1 + \left(\frac{b_0^2 \sigma^2_{\delta_2(t)} + c_0^2 \sigma^2_{\delta_3(t)}}{S^2} \right)}, \tag{5.5}$$

where (t) identifies the date on which the forecast is made and $\sigma_{\delta_2(t)}$ and $\sigma_{\delta_3(t)}$ are standard deviations of the differences between forecasts of (say) production and disposable income made on that date in earlier years and the final estimates of their values prevailing on the date to which the predicted price outcome applies. (For example, using Clough's figures on early season production indications for corn, $\sigma_{\delta_2(t)}$ would be 314 million bushels as of July 10, 178 million as of August 10, 107 million as of September 10 and so on.) Equation (5.5) expresses the error range in price forecasts made at time (t) as a ratio to the standard error of estimate—a ratio always greater than or equal to one.[4]

If we assume $b_0 = -2$, $c_0 = 1$ and $S = 18$ per cent, the ratio in equation (5.5) moves as follows: Previous December, 2.49; July, 1.53; August, 1.23; September, 1.12; October, 1.04; November, 1.02 and December, 1.01.

The expected reduction in price-forecasting errors for corn as the season progresses is due mainly to improvements in the advance estimates of corn production. The July crop report greatly reduces our uncertainty about December corn prices, but the error band is still some 50 per cent larger than the assumed standard error of estimate. For livestock products, the relative importance of improvement in demand forecasts would be considerably greater.

More empirical work would be needed to determine the accuracy with which prices of specific commodities can be forecast at various dates in advance of a given "outcome" period. One possibility would be to calculate the regression of actual prices upon the production and income forecasts existing at each crop reporting date. The net regression coefficients (and even the list of independent variables) might vary from one reporting date to another. As a measure of the improvement of forecasts over time we could compare the standard errors of estimate from the regressions for different reporting dates with each other and with the standard error of

---

[4] Strictly speaking, this ratio should be defined in terms of the standard error of forecast. When the variables are expressed as first differences, the terms in equation (5.2) which depend on departures of the independent variables from their means (i.e., their mean year-to-year changes during 1922–1941) are frequently small, and the standard error of forecast is little larger than the standard error of estimate. This is seldom true of equations based on original arithmetic or logarithmic values and is by no means always true of first-difference equations. If the standard error of forecast were used in the denominator of equation (5.5), the standard error of forecast would also be substituted for σ_{d_1}, in equation (5.4). The resulting error ratios would still be greater than or equal to one but (except at the lower limit) would be somewhat smaller than those based on the standard error of estimate.

estimate obtained by relating prices to the final estimates of the independent variables. For forecasts one to three months in advance of the outcome date, actual prices during the month immediately past might be included in the forecasting equation, with the hope of taking advantage of any inertia that might exist in price-making forces other than those explicitly used in the basic equation.

In concluding this section, one other point should be noted. There may be errors of estimation or measurement in the final figures on price, production and income. To the extent that these errors in the different variables are not correlated with one another, the coefficient of multiple determination will be reduced; also, if the errors lie in the independent variables, the net regression coefficients will tend to be biased toward zero. Thus, improvements in the accuracy of basic statistical series can increase the accuracy and usefulness of the forecasts based upon them.

5.2.4. *Other Factors Affecting the Accuracy of Price Forecasts*

The discussion so far has considered forecasting errors in cases where some specified statistical demand function is known or believed to apply. In practice, we are never completely sure that the structure of economic forces playing upon a commodity price in some future year is exactly the same as during the historical period for which a demand function has been fitted. A close study of the conditions of production and distribution of the commodity may either make us confident that the structure has not changed materially or may strongly suggest that the structure has changed.

Forecasts may be affected by a sudden growth in magnitude of variables the influence of which was previously small. The unprecedented accumulation of liquid assets – particularly cash and demand deposits – in the hands of consumers evidently had a great deal to do with the inflated demand for food during 1945–1948. The influence of this factor during 1922–1941 was probably small, and in any event there were no reliable statistics with which to measure it. Extreme changes in disposable income and in the supply of a given product may take us onto a hitherto unexplored segment of the demand curve in which the elasticities previously experienced do not apply. For example, extremely high prices for a given commodity may lead to a more extensive substitution of competing commodities than would have been estimated on the basis of "normal" relationships.

5.2.4.1. Changes in the Demand and Supply Structure

Forecasts may also go wrong because of true changes in structure, that is, irreversible changes in the net relationships between the price of a commodity and various supply and demand factors. Some changes may arise from trends in consumer tastes. More sudden changes may occur, as when a commodity formerly sold only in fresh form develops a substantial processing outlet. This probably happened to cranberries after 1937 and possibly to oranges during and after World War II. In the first years of such a change the forecaster must apply judgment; in later years the relationships may become subject to statistical measurement. However, the structure of relationships now includes two or three demand curves instead of the original one.

Export commodities have presented special forecasting difficulties in many of the years since about 1933. Export demand has been subject at times to arbitrary shifts because of the actions of governments in importing countries as well as of changes in programs of the U.S. Government. Private forecasters working with export crops, in addition to estimating the normal behavior of farmers and processors, must also try to outguess the policy officials of their own and other countries.[5]

5.2.5. *Methods of Improving the Accuracy of Price Forecasts*

Where full use has not been made of existing data, the first step may be to exploit the remaining possibilities by means of statistical analysis. This analysis can be guided and made more fruitful by more careful *economic* analysis of the factors affecting consumer behavior, the behavior of marketing agencies and the behavior of producers with respect to the commodity in question. This economic analysis may well be formalized into a chart or diagram of the structure of economic forces involved in price determination for the commodity. Every element of the structure should "make sense" in terms of the profit objectives or policies of the economic agents involved, the degree of competition in the various markets and the cost functions and technological characteristics of farms, processing firms and distributing agencies.

Within such a structure, statistical measurement should be made of those relationships — at least the major ones — for which satisfactory data are available and which can be "identified". In many cases, we believe that this approach can be made to yield formal statistical estimating devices which

---

[5] Mathematically, government actions might be considered as changing certain coefficients of an export demand curve which is jointly involved with a domestic demand curve in determining the price of an export crop. Uncertainties regarding government actions could be interpreted as additional terms in equation (5.4).

will give more accurate forecasts than those of a largely intuitive commodity specialist. The possibilities of existing data can also be further exploited in connection with seasonal change, inventory fluctuations and other phenomena a year or less in duration.

Beyond this, the economic relationships between price and other factors may be further refined and illumined by the development of new data, as on inventories at previously unreported market levels. There is a possibility, of course, that the availability of new price-forecasting information will cause marketing firms to alter their behavior to some extent and to make at least a minor change in the structure of economic forces affecting price.

Price forecasts can also be improved by improving our forecasts of the "independent" variables, such as production and disposable income. If weather could be forecast with better than random accuracy for several months to a year in advance, this knowledge would be superior to the universal assumption of "average growing conditions for the remainder of the season" which underlies current crop forecasts.

5.2.6. *Forecasting — Art or Science?*

This section has presented some basic problems of price forecasting. Factors affecting the accuracy of price forecasts were shown to differ widely in magnitude from commodity to commodity. The over-all forecasting problem was broken down into specialized subproblems, such as (1) forecasting crop and livestock production; (2) forecasting disposable income and other demand factors; (3) measuring the net effects of production, income and other factors (in terms of actual values or final estimates) upon price and (4) the recognition of new situations, such as the emergence of hitherto unmeasured or unimportant variables and major changes in utilization or in the basic responses of domestic or foreign purchasers.

Many economists in business and government are inclined to argue that forecasting is and will remain an art rather than a science. Most econometricians hold the opposing view.

Differences over this question sometimes lie more in terminology than in substance. The forecaster who emphasizes "art" may subsume under that term a great many rules of thumb and approximate relationships which were based originally on economic or statistical analysis. He may differ from the self-consciously "scientific" forecaster mainly in the extent to which he relies on mental arithmetic rather than a computer.

Our own belief is that considerable progress in forecasting can be made by the application of formal statistical methods. This leads us to emphasize the role of "science" in economic forecasting. If an "artist" in this field makes a statistically significant improvement over the best formal or "scientific" forecasting devices now in use, we are inclined to look for, and if possible quantify, the additional (and evidently relevant) factors which are used consciously or implicitly to produce this result. There are methods and principles by which science advances and statistical measures by which the significance of reputed advances can be tested. These methods, principles and measurements can be passed on to future forecasters. We know of no sure method for transmitting an "art" from one forecaster to another; if a successful transmission is accomplished, the "art" itself must be basically susceptible to quantitative or statistical procedures.

5.2.7. *Extension to Multi-equational Economic Policy Models*

The principles just discussed can be extended at once to systems containing many equations. If values of all exogenous variables are assumed to be known without error, the uncertainty concerning the values of the endogenous variables is indicated by their respective standard errors of forecast. If the values of the exogenous variables must be forecast, the uncertainty concerning the values of the endogenous variables is correspondingly increased. This topic is developed further in Chapter 6.

5.3. Welfare Consequences of Errors in Data and Imperfections in Data Adjustments

The more important features of this topic as they affect economic policy models have been extensively treated by Theil [16]. A few brief comments seem called for, illustrated in some cases with U.S. data.

5.3.1. *Components of Observed Variation in a Single Variable*

Errors of concept or coverage in a statistical series can be a major source of inaccuracy in the estimation and use of economic policy models. Until recently, the economic data network in the U.S. was not designed for tasks as heavy and demanding as the estimation of an economic policy model of 100 to 300 equations (see Chapter 11). The series on ownership of real property and value of capital stocks—and, indirectly, the estimates of capacity output in different industries— are very weak.

Some commodity flows are relatively well estimated in years when a census of manufactures is taken, but thereafter some very sketchy current data may be used to "move" the census base. Thus, from 1948 to 1957 the

U.S. Department of Commerce's estimates of consumer expenditure for food drifted upward by nearly $10 billion (about 15 per cent) relative to the level implied in the U.S. Department of Agriculture's estimates of quantity of food consumed and the Bureau of Labor Statistics' estimates of retail food prices. Subsequently, the Department of Commerce adjusted its series downward to the level indicated by the USDA series. The major cause of the upward drift was said to be the rapidly widening line of nonfood products sold by supermarkets; the 1948 census-based figure on food sales was apparently sound, but the current data from then until 1957 were based on *total* sales of a sample of food supermarkets rather than on sales of food products only.

Errors of measurement, errors of concept and other systematic biases have been extremely troublesome in the past. Presumably, the error of several billion dollars in estimating consumer expenditures for food led to an opposite error of the same order of magnitude in some other category or categories of consumer expenditures.

Some economic time series are estimated on the basis of probability samples — for example, the U.S. series on labor force, employment and unemployment. Probability samples are not a panacea and are not always the best devices for estimating change. Under favorable administrative and institutional circumstances, a complete count may be more accurate than a probability sample.

Our best method for estimating changes in the population of the U.S. is to take an adjusted base figure for a census year, add births and gross in-migration and subtract deaths and gross out-migration. The statistics on all components of population change are relatively complete and accurate. A probability sample to estimate the total population of the U.S. at monthly intervals would very likely show a decline of 200,000 or 300,000 people on occasion from one month to the next. Yet everyone knows that the actual population does not change in this fashion — the decrease would be a property of the sample and not of the population itself.

More or less random errors of measurement in an economic time series may be thought of as statistical noise. In addition, an economic time series may contain disturbances, or "economic noise." For example, a series on total employment may change from one month to the next because of a strike in the lumber industry or the cessation of a strike in a large automobile manufacturing concern. These short-term changes in total employment may run counter to the basic trend of demand for labor in the economy at that time. It may be necessary to cumulate changes in employment over a period of three or four months before the desired *information* emerges clearly above this kind of economic noise to indicate that the demand for labor is definitely on a cyclical upswing.

Many of our economic time series are seasonally adjusted. In cases where the seasonal swings in the raw data are quite large, seasonal adjustments are no doubt helpful. However, seasonal adjustment factors are based on averages of a limited number of observations and are subject to errors analogous to the standard error of the mean or median. Thus, seasonal adjustment does not eliminate errors; it redistributes them over time.

5.3.2. *Effects of Errors in Variables*

The sources of error in predicting values of the endogenous variables include errors of forecast in future values of the noncontrollable variables, *ex post* errors of measurement in the noncontrollable variables, errors in the coefficients connecting the noncontrollable variables to the target variables, errors in the coefficients connecting the instrument variables to the target variables and *ex post* errors of measurement in the target variables.

The cumulative effect of errors in a multiequation policy model might at least be visualized as follows:

(1) Chart the historical values of each variable which we invest with welfare connotations, that is, each variable which appears in the relevant welfare or objective function (W);

(2) Over the planning horizon specified by the policy maker, draw a preferred time path for each variable with an "error of measurement" zone around it representing simply the estimated level of errors of observation in the target variable *ex post*;

(3) Draw additional "steering tolerance" zones above and below this error band;

(4) Apply weights to deviations of the observed values of each target variable above or below the error band. The weight function will not necessarily be linear; for example, if unemployment rises 2 per cent above the preferred time path, the weight assigned to this deviation might be four times as large as that assigned to a deviation of 1 per cent. Errors in most price and quantity variables could be translated approximately into billions of dollars (or fractions of a billion dollars) of the resulting error in GNP.

This setup would imply a desire on the part of the policy maker to steer the economy in such a way that each of the target variables remained within predetermined limits; in estimating the total loss of welfare, percentage deviations from the preferred time path of each variable would be given a specific weight; given percentage deviations in the more important target variables would result in greater losses of welfare than would similar percentage deviations in less important variables.

The joint (a priori) probability distribution of all noncontrollable variables in the model would summarize the threat to economic welfare inherent in the noncontrollable factors. It should be possible to estimate the prospective variance of the actual (vector) path of the economy about the preferred (vector) path over a specified time horizon on the assumption that the present settings of instrument variables are not changed.

Then, it would be important to determine the sufficiency and efficiency of the instruments available to the policy maker for correcting possible aberrations and reducing the total welfare loss below a specified level. We might also find that legal limitations on interest rates, debt ceilings and other factors would limit the usefulness of an instrument and inhibit or prevent the policy maker from steering the economy back onto a preferred time path if it deviated in a specified direction.

If the effects of all errors in variables and coefficients in the model were converted into equivalent billions of dollars of GNP, we would have a common denominator for appraising the expected welfare gain from reducing any specific source of error.

If certain instruments available to the policy maker were powerful, flexible and acted quickly upon the most important targets, the ultimate limiting factors might be measurement errors in the target variables themselves.

5.3.3. *Estimating Measurement Errors in Economic Variables*

In most econometric investigations, little attention is given to errors of measurement in variables. Unless the series are estimated from probability samples, the econometrician is usually quite reluctant to make any judgments about their measurement error components.

In 1951, while estimating statistical demand functions for a wide range of agricultural commodities and foods, one of the authors tried to arrive at judgment estimates of the levels of *ex post* measurement error in the time series he was using. His procedure was to interview the persons responsible for estimating each of the official published series on commodity prices and production and ask them essentially the following question: Assuming that the annual average of this series in year 1 was measured exactly, within what range do you think you have estimated the corresponding figure for year 2 in two years out of three? Conceptually, the answer to this question is a judgment estimate of the standard error of measurement in the official series.

The persons interviewed were competent applied statisticians, and they responded readily and constructively to the terms of the question. In arriving at their judgments, they took account of the availability of check data (such as regulatory reports on cotton ginnings or on livestock slaughter under federal inspection), of sample sizes and of other problems in estimating acreages and yields of different crops and numbers of different classes of livestock. The results of the 1951 interviews are summarized in Fox [9, p. 121].

In August, 1962 the same author interviewed some of the persons who were most familiar with a number of the time series used in the agricultural sector of the Brookings-SSRC econometric model of the U.S. (see Chapter 11). He supplemented these with some judgments based on knowledge of the data gained during his eight years of service (1946–1954) as associate head and head of the Division of Statistical and Historical Research in the Bureau of Agricultural Economics.

Some of the results, admittedly very rough, are presented in Table 5.3.

TABLE 5.3

Judgment Estimates of Standard Errors of Measurement (ex post) in Published Official Series Compared with Standard Errors of Estimate Obtained When the Same Series are Used as Dependent Variables in Multiple Regression Equations, United States, 1947–1960[a]

	Variable	Judgment Estimate of Standard Error of Measurement (*ex post*)	Standard Error of Estimate in the Agricultural Submodel
P_l	Retail value, food livestock	$4	$15.30
C_c/N	Per capita consumption, food crops	0.4 index points	0.76 index point
$(P_l - P_{la})$	Marketing charges, food livestock	$5	$6.17
$(P_c - P_{ca})$	Marketing charges, food crops	$4	$6.01
P_1	Prices received by farmers, all products	1 index point	4.25 index points
$(A_{gy} - R_{ai})$	Gross farm income	$0.2 billion	$0.60 billion
A_c	Production expenditures	$0.2 billion	$0.21 billion
H_a, H_{aa}	Inventory change	$0.2 billion	$0.44 billion
I_a	Gross investment	$0.25 billion	$0.34 billion
N_1	Employment	150,000 workers	185,000 workers
$C_1/100$	Total consumption, food livestock	0.6 index point	1.64 index points

[a] Quarterly data.

If the judgment estimates of *ex post* measurement error are taken seriously, it will be difficult to reduce the standard errors of estimate of equations explaining A_c, N_1, I_a, $(P_l - P_{la})$ and $(P_c - P_{ca})$. More progress should be possible (partly through disaggregation) in explaining $P_l, C_c/N$, P_1, $(A_{gy} - R_{ai})$, H_a, H_{aa} and $C_1/100$. Some room must presumably be left for bona fide economic "disturbances," but only after we have done our best to allow for the effects of imperfect aggregation, errors of closure between index numbers and value aggregates, seasonal adjustment procedures and interpolation methods. In general, economic time series are combinations of true facts and artifacts. (The true facts include both exact and stochastic components.)

5.3.4. *Errors Arising from the Use of Index Numbers: The Problem of "Perfect Aggregation"*

It is well known that changes in the product of two index numbers, one purporting to measure price and the other quantity of a group of commodities, will in general not correlate perfectly with changes in the corresponding true value aggregate. To avoid this annoying arithmetical problem, the official national income accounts in the U.S. use "implicit GNP deflators." A GNP component in current dollars is divided by the corresponding "real" series measured in 1954 dollars; the quotient is used in lieu of a Laspeyres price index. The net effect is equivalent to a Laspeyres index of quantity and a Paasche index of price. These index numbers satisfy the so-called "factor reversal test,"

$$\frac{V_1}{V_0} \equiv \left(\frac{P_1}{P_0}\right)\left(\frac{Q_1}{Q_0}\right) \equiv \frac{\sum p_1 q_1}{\sum p_0 q_1} \cdot \frac{\sum q_1 p_0}{\sum q_0 p_0} \equiv \frac{\sum p_1 q_1}{\sum p_0 q_0},$$

where V_1 and V_0 are "true" values in current dollars for the given year and the base year (1954), respectively, P_1 and P_0 are values of given year quantities multiplied by given year and base year prices, and Q_1 and Q_0 are values of base year prices multiplied by given year and base year quantities.

Frequently economic policy models include price and quantity indexes of the Laspeyres type, for example, an index of retail food prices and an index of per capita food consumption. It turns out that the time-series regression coefficient of a price index upon a per capita consumption index also depends on the relative variances and covariances of the consumption series for all commodities included in the consumption index.

This can be shown as follows:

Assume that all explanatory variables other than the amounts of different commodities available for consumption (q_i) remain constant. Our problem is to interpret the time-series regression coefficient of an index of retail prices of all food upon an index of per. capita consumption of all food.

For two commodities we may write

$$\begin{bmatrix} p_1 \\ p_2 \end{bmatrix} = \begin{bmatrix} b_{11} & b_{12} \\ b_{21} & b_{22} \end{bmatrix} \begin{bmatrix} q_1 \\ q_2 \end{bmatrix} \tag{5.6}$$

or, in compact matrix notation,

$$p = Bq . \tag{5.6.1}$$

Now, assume the p_i and q_i are price and quantity relatives and are combined into Laspeyres indexes, P and Q, using the same set of expenditure weights, $w_1 + w_2 = 1$. Thus, $P = (w_1 p_1 + w_2 p_2)$ and $Q = (w_1 q_1 + w_1 q_2)$ or

$$p = w'p \qquad \text{and} \tag{5.7.1}$$
$$Q = w'q . \tag{5.7.2}$$

We propose to take time-series observations on P and Q and estimate a least-squares regression coefficient, β.
The formula for β is

$$\beta = \frac{\sum\limits_{t=1}^{n} PQ}{\sum\limits_{t=1}^{n} Q^2} . \tag{5.8}$$

For each time t the appropriate elements in the numerator and denominator of (5.8) are

$$P_{(t)}Q_{(t)} = w'Bqq'w , \quad \text{and} \tag{5.9}$$
$$Q_{(t)}^2 = q'ww'q . \tag{5.10}$$

If we sum these elements over the n time units, the denominator becomes a matrix of variances and covariances of the q_i, with the variances weighted by w_i^2 and the covariances weighted by $w_i w_j$. In the numerator, each structural coefficient b_{ii} and b_{ij} is complexly weighted by combinations of variances and covariances of the q_i with terms in w_i^2 and $w_i w_j$.

If the covariances were all zero and the cross flexibilities of price were zero or small, it is clear that the regression coefficient, β, in different time periods would depend upon the relative variances of the different q_i.

Theil's principle of "perfect aggregation" was designed to explain and under ideal conditions to eliminate this kind of aggregation bias [14]. Empirical applications of this principle, as in aggregating the consumption functions of several or many *functional economic area* models (see Chapters 12 and 16) to arrive at a consumption function for the corresponding national economy, would be most interesting.

5.4. Models, Methods and Data Relevant to
Economic Forecasting: Some Recent Contributions

The main purpose of this section is to supplement the references in Chapter 5 and Sections 6.1 and 6.2 of the first edition by taking account of more recent contributions relevant to economic forecasting. Chapter 11, "Models of Stabilization in Developed Economies: The Case of the United States", has been completely rewritten for the current edition and contains additional material on forecasting with the aid of econometric models.

Improvements in economic data are discussed by Holt [37], Juster [39] and Orcutt [48] in three papers presented at a 1969 symposium on technical aspects of basic data for policy and public decisions. The report of the President's Commission on Federal Statistics [50] contains a great deal of useful information on economic and social data systems in the U.S. as of 1971 and makes a number of suggestions for their improvement.

Three major textbooks on econometric methods by Christ [23] in 1966, Malinvaud [42] in 1966, and Theil [57] in 1971 reflect the increasing maturity and sophistication of this field, which underlies the estimation and prediction aspects of economic policy (and other) models. Klein [41], in a 1971 article, provides an excellent survey of the development of econometrics, its position as of 1970, and its prospects in the 1970's. A mature attitude toward methods of estimation emerged in the early 1960's and was well established by 1971. Klein [40] helped to set this trend with a 1960 paper in which he stated:

> ... The building of institutional reality into a priori formulations of economic relationships and the refinement of basic data collection have contributed much more to the improvement of empirical econometric results than have more elaborate methods of statistical inference. I look toward improvements in precision of econometric judgments of the order of magnitude of fifty percent as a result of a better knowledge of the functioning of economic institutions, through the use of new measurements on variables, and through the use of more accurate data. In contrast, I would expect marginal improvements of five or ten percent through the use of more powerful methods of statistical inference. All routes to improvement must be followed since any gains, no matter how small, are precious, yet different contributions should be kept in proper perspective. The adoption of more powerful methods of mathematical statistics is no panacea.

Evans' textbook on macroeconomic activity [24], published in 1969, integrates macroeconomic theory with econometric formulations and empirical results based on experience with the Wharton-EFU (Economic Forecasting Unit) model and other research. His book is designed for use at the junior and senior undergraduate and beginning graduate levels. From 1969 on it appears that large numbers of advanced undergraduate students have been and will be introduced to macro-economics as a field of applied econometrics using fully empirical stabilization and forecasting models.

Time series analysis is, of course, basic to economic forecasting. The *International Encyclopedia of the Social Sciences*, published in 1968, contains four major articles on time series, including a general survey by Tintner [59], a discussion of cycles by Wold [62], an exposition of seasonal adjustment procedures by Shiskin [52], and a survey of advanced problems by Whittle [61].

A great many recent publications have something to do with economic forecasting. Books centered on forecasting include Theil's *Applied Economic Forecasting* [55] published in 1966, Stekler's *Economic Forecasting* [54] published in 1970, a 1960 Universities-National Bureau Committee conference volume on the quality and economic significance of anticipations data [60], and a two volume work on business cycle indicators edited by Moore [45] in 1961. To these should be added Zarnowitz's *An Appraisal of Short-Term Economic Forecasts* [63] and his article on economic prediction and forecasting [64] in the *International Encyclopedia of the Social Sciences*, published in 1967 and 1968 respectively. There are useful articles on particular aspects of forecasting by Brainard [21], Feldstein [25], Hymans [38], Stekler [53], and Theil and Scholes [58] published at various dates from 1967 through 1971.

A number of new approaches to economic forecasting and time series analysis have been suggested, and in some cases tried, in recent years. Griliches published a survey article in 1967 on distributed lags [35], which have been widely used in econometric models since interest in them was revived by Koyck in 1954.

Spectral analysis aroused considerable enthusiasm among some economists in the 1960's. The first book-length treatment of "the statistical theory of spectral analysis of stochastic processes" was published by Grenander and Rosenblatt [33] in 1957. Its author sought (1) to present a unified treatment of methods that were being used increasingly in the physical sciences and technology, and (2) to direct the attention of theoretical statisticians to this approach; for the latter purpose they emphasized a rigorous mathematical presentation. Granger and Hatanaka [32] published a book on spectral analysis of economic time series in 1964; in the same year

Nerlove [47] published an exposition of the method together with an empirical application to seasonal adjustment in which he believed spectral analysis yielded better results than the method used by the U.S. Bureau of Labor Statistics. However, in a 1970 article, Grether and Nerlove [34] decided that the criteria used by Nerlove in 1964 left much to be desired and that spectral comparisons must be interpreted with great care. Simulations using a minimum mean-square-error criterion of optimality produced "seasonally adjusted series bearing the same relationship to the unadjusted series in spectral terms as that found by Nerlove and others in their studies of BLS and Census methods of adjustment". In 1969 Granger [32] suggested that causal relations between two variables in an econometric model could be investigated by means of cross-spectral methods.

As of 1971, it appears that spectral analysis has provided a constructive challenge to more conventional methods of seasonal adjustment without demonstrating any superiority to them in practice. Grether and Nerlove recommended further research using explicit criteria for the optimality of seasonal adjustment procedures, and expressed surprise that the BLS and Census methods performed so well without such criteria. But conventional procedures do contain implicit criteria for goodness of fit, so improvements over current practice will probably be small.

Theil's 1967 volume on *Economics and Information Theory* [56] presents a novel approach to many economic phenomena. Theil points that, on a formal level, information theory "is actually a general partitioning theory in that it presents measures for the way in which some set is divided into subsets . . . This may amount to dividing certainty (probability 1) into various possibilities none of which is certain, but it may also be an allocation problem in economics." Improvements in forecasts are expressed as gains in information measured in binary digits or *bits.*

J. Marschak published a major article on the economics of information systems [43] in 1971, something quite different from Theil's applications of information theory. Marschak points out that "a large part of our national product is contributed by symbol manipulation—telephoning orders, discussing in conferences, shuffling papers, or just performing some of the humble tasks required of the inspector, or even an ordinary worker, on the assembly line." He states further that:

> I shall study the rational choice-making of an individual from among available information systems, or available components of such systems. The availability constraint specifies . . . the costs and the delays associated with given components . . . of information systems.

It appears that Marschak's approach could be extended to the evaluation of proposed increases in the publication speed and accuracy of data used in economic forecasting.

Merrill [44], in 1965, presented a neat illustration of the value of improved information in the sense of a reduction in uncertainty. Optimal solutions were obtained for a linear programming model of a farm in two successive years. In the first case, price and constraint information available at the beginning of Year 1 was used to determine resource allocation in both years; in the second case, new price and constraint information which became available at the beginning of Year 2 was used in the solution for that year. The excess of total net revenue for the two years in Case 2 over that in Case 1 is the dollar value to the farm operator of the new information provided at the beginning of Year 2.

A 1971 volume on *Price Indexes and Quality Change* [36], edited by Griliches, explores the problem of measuring quality change in price indexes. If the "quality" of consumer goods and services increased by (say) two percent a year, it could be argued that a rise of two percent per year in the Consumer Price Index was consistent with zero increase in the "true" cost of living. If the "quality" of producers goods and government services were also increasing at two percent per year, a two percent rise in the implicit GNP deflator would be consistent with zero inflation. If the conventional price indexes have an upward bias, policymakers will overestimate the rate of inflation and accept a needlessly high rate of unemployment to contain it—the perception will bias the policy. The problem of "quality" measurement is in fact quite complex, but papers by Griliches, Fisher and Shell, Dhrymes, Kravis and Lipsey, Triplett, Cagan and Hall present the state of the art as of 1971.

More accurate forecasts of exogenous variables should permit a policymaker to set his instruments more precisely and approximate his targets for the economy more closely. However, it may be possible to bring some currently exogenous variables under direct or indirect control. Fox [26, 28] illustrated this point with a multi-country world model in which all variables are endogenous except those actually used as instruments by policymakers in the respective countries. Many different degrees of controllability might be achieved by institutionalizing the exchange of forecasts, the use of compatible economic stabilization models by many countries, and even a stabilization model of the world economy.

Schoenman in 1966 published *An Analog of Short-Period Economic Change* [51] which is refreshingly independent of most other work on macroeconometric models. He devotes the first four chapters of his book (pp. 23–151) to a specification of the economic mechanisms of short-period change. The remainder of the book describes the synthesis of these economic mechanisms; the search for data to represent them; and the development of a macroeconometric model. At the final stage he faces the problems of statistical estimation, but not before.

REFERENCES

[1] ALLEN, R. G. D. *Mathematical Economics*. 2nd revised edition, London: Macmillan and Co., 1959, pp. 694–724.

[2] BAKER, JOHN D., and PAARLBERG, DON. "Outlook Evaluation—Methods and Results," *Agricultural Economics Research*, IV, No. 4 (October, 1952), 105–114.

[3] ——. "How Accurate is Outlook?" *Journal of Farm Economics*, XXXIV, No. 4 (November, 1952), 509–519.

[4] BREIMYER, HAROLD F. "Forecasting Annual Cattle Slaughter," *Journal of Farm Economics*, XXXIV, No. 3 (August, 1952), 392–398.

[5] CAVIN, JAMES P. "Forecasting the Demand for Agricultural Products," *Agricultural Economics Research*, IV, No. 3 (July, 1952), 65–76.

[6] CLOUGH, MALCOLM. "Changes in Corn Acreage and Production After Early Indications," *Agricultural Economics Research*, III, No. 4 (October, 1951), 145–146.

[7] FOX, KARL A. "Factors Affecting the Accuracy of Price Forecasts," *Journal of Farm Economics*, XXXV, No. 3 (August, 1953), 323–340.

[8] ——. "Econometric Models of the United States," *Journal of Political Economy*, LXIV (April, 1956), 128–142.

[9] ——. *Econometric Analysis for Public Policy*. Ames: Iowa State University Press, 1958, Chap. 12.

[10] HURWICZ, L. "Prediction and Least Squares," in *Statistical Inference in Dynamic Economic Models*. Edited by T. C. Koopmans. New York: John Wiley & Sons, 1950, Chap. 7.

[11] JOHNSTON, J. *Econometric Methods*. New York: McGraw-Hill Book Co., 1963.

[12] ROOS, C. F. "Survey of Economic Forecasting Techniques," *Econometrica*, XXIII (October, 1955), 363–395.

[13] SENGUPTA, J. K. "Specification and Estimation of Structural Relations in Policy Models." *Quantitative Planning of Economic Policy*. Edited by B. G. Hickman. Washington, D.C.: The Brookings Institution, 1965, Chap. 4.

[14] THEIL, H. *Linear Aggregation of Economic Relations*. Amsterdam: North-Holland Publishing Co., 1954.

[15] ——. "Who Forecasts Best?" Reprinted in *International Economic Papers*, V (1954), 194.

[16] ——. *Economic Forecasts and Policy*. 2nd revised edition. Amsterdam: North-Holland Publishing Co., 1961.

[17] TINBERGEN, J. *Statistical Testing of Business Cycle Theories*. Geneva: League of Nations, 1939.

[18] TINTNER, G. *Econometrics*. New York: John Wiley & Sons, 1952.

[19] BARKER, R. *Ecological Psychology: Concepts and Methods for Studying the Environment of Human Behavior*. Stanford: Stanford University Press, 1968.

[20] BEAL, G. M., BROOKS, R. M., WILCOX, L. D., and KLONGLAN, G. E. *Social Indicators: Bibliography I*. (Sociology Report No. 92). Department of Sociology and Anthropology, Iowa State University, Ames, January 1971. 56pp. (multilithed).

[21] BRAINARD, W. "Uncertainty and the Effectiveness of Policy". *American Economic Review*, Volume LVII, No. 2 (May 1967), pp. 411–425.

[22] CANTRIL, H. *The Pattern of Human Concerns*. New Brunswick, N.J.: Rutgers University Press, 1965, Chapter 16.

[23] CHRIST, C. F. *Econometric Models and Methods*. New York: John Wiley and Sons, Inc., 1966.

[24] EVANS, M. K. *Macroeconomic Activity: Theory, Forecasting, and Control*. New York: Harper and Rowe, 1969.

[25] FELDSTEIN, M. S. "The Error of Forecast in Econometric Models When the Forecast-Period Exogenous Variables are Stochastic", *Econometrica*, Volume 39, No. 1 (January 1971), pp. 55–60.

[26] FOX, K. A. "Critique, Reformulation and Extension: The Nature of 'Exogenous' Threats to Domestic Economic Stability", in *Is the Business Cycle Obsolete?* Edited by M. Bronfenbrenner. New York: John Wiley and Sons, Inc., 1969, pp. 468–474.

[27] ——. "Operations Research and Complex Social Systems", Chapter 9, pp. 452–467 in Sengupta, Jati K. and Fox, Karl A., *Economic Analysis and Operations Research: Optimization Techniques in Quantitative Economic Models*. Amsterdam: North-Holland Publishing Company, 1969.

[28] ——. "Toward a Policy Model of World Economic Development with Special Attention to the Agricultural Sector" in *The Role of Agriculture in Economic Development*. Edited by E. Thorbecke. New York: Columbia University Press, 1969, pp. 95–126.

[29] ——. "Combining Economic and Noneconomic Objectives in Development Planning: Problems of Concept and Measurement." May 18, 1971; 38pp. To be published in Willy Sellekaerts (ed.), *Essays in Honor of Jan Tinbergen*. New York: Macmillan International, 1972. (In press).

[30] ——, and VAN MOESEKE, P. "A Scalar Measure of Social Income". Preliminary draft dated August 12, 1971. To be submitted for publication.

[31] GRANGER, C. W. J. "Investigating Causal Relations by Econometric Models and Cross-Spectral Methods", *Econometrica*, Volume 37, No. 3 (July 1969), pp. 424–438.

[32] ——, and HATANAKA, M. *Spectral Analysis of Economic Time Series*. Princeton: Princeton University Press, 1964.

[33] GRENANDER, V., and ROSENBLATT, M. *Statistical Analysis of Stationary Time Series*. New York: John Wiley and Sons, 1957.

[34] GRETHER, D. M., and NERLOVE, M. "Some Properties of 'Optimal' Seasonal Adjustment", *Econometrica*, Volume 38, No. 5 (September 1970), pp. 682–703.

[35] GRILICHES, Z. "Distributed Lags: A Survey", *Econometrica*, Volume 35, No. 1 (January 1967), pp. 16–49.

[36] ——, (editor). *Price Indexes and Quality Change*. Cambridge: Harvard University Press, 1971.

[37] HOLT, C. C. "A System of Information Centers for Research and Decision Making", *American Economic Review*, Volume LX, No. 2 (May 1970), pp. 149–165.

[38] HYMANS, S. H. "Simultaneous Confidence Intervals in Econometric Forecasting", *Econometrica* Volume 36, No. 1 (January 1968), pp. 18–30.

[39] JUSTER, F. T. "Microdata, Economic Research, and the Production of Economic Knowledge", *American Economic Review*, Volume LX, No. 2 (May 1970), pp. 138–148.

[40] KLEIN, L. R. "Single Equation vs. Equation System Methods of Estimation in Econometrics", *Econometrica*, Volume 28, No. 4 (October 1960), pp. 866–871.

[41] ——. "Whither Econometrics?", *Journal of the American Statistical Association*, Volume 66, No. 334 (June 1971), pp. 415–421.

[42] MALINVAUD, E. *Statistical Methods of Econometrics*. Amsterdam and Chicago: North-Holland Publishing Co. and Rand McNally, 1966.

[43] MARSCHAK, J. "Economics of Information Systems", *Journal of the American Statistical Association*, Volume 66, No. 333 (March 1971), pp. 192–219.

[44] MERRILL, W. C. "Alternative Programming Models Involving Uncertainty", *Journal of Farm Economics*, Volume 47, No. 3 (August 1965), pp. 595–610.

[45] MOORE, G. H. (editor). *Business Cycle Indicators*, Volumes I and II, Princeton: Princeton University Press, 1961.

[46] NATIONAL GOALS RESEARCH STAFF. *Toward Balanced Growth: Quantity with Quality*. Washington: The White House, July 4, 1970, 226 pp.

[47] NERLOVE, M. "Spectral Analysis of Seasonal Adjustment Procedures", *Econometrica*, Volume 32, No. 3 (July 1964), pp. 241–286.

[48] ORCUTT, G. H. "Data Research, and Government", *American Economic Review*, Volume LX, No. 2 (May 1970), pp. 132–137.

[49] PARSONS, T. "Systems Analysis: II. Social Systems", *International Encyclopedia of the Social Sciences*, Volume 15, pp. 452–473. New York: Macmillan and Free Press, 1968.

[50] PRESIDENT'S COMMISSION ON FEDERAL STATISTICS. *Federal Statistics: Report of the President's Commission; Volumes I and II*. Washington: U.S. Government Printing Office, 1971.

[51] SCHOENMAN, J. C. *An Analog of Short-Period Economic Change*. Stockholm: Norstedts, 1966.

[52] SHISKIN, J. "Time Series: IV. Seasonal Adjustment", in *International Encyclopedia of the Social Sciences*, Volume 16, pp. 80–88. New York: Macmillan and Free Press, 1968.

[53] STEKLER, H. O. "Forecasting with Econometric Models: An Evaluation", *Econometrica*, Volume 36, No. 3–4 (July–October 1968), pp. 437–463.

[54] ——. *Economic Forecasting*. New York: Praeger Publishers, Inc., 1970.

[55] THEIL, H. *Applied Economic Forecasting*. Amsterdam and Chicago: North-Holland Publishing Co. and Rand McNally, 1966.

[56] ——. *Economics and Information Theory*. Amsterdam and Chicago: North-Holland Publishing Co. and Rand McNally, 1967.

[57] ——. *Principles of Econometrics*. New York: John Wiley and Sons, 1971.

[58] ——, and SCHOLES, M. "Forecast Evaluation Based on a Multiplicative Decomposition of Mean Square Errors", *Econometrica*, Volume 35, No. 1 (January 1967), pp. 70–88.

[59] TINTNER, G. "Time Series: I. General", in *International Encyclopedia of the Social Sciences*, Volume 16, pp. 47–59. New York: Macmillan and Free Press, 1968.

[60] UNIVERSITIES-NATIONAL BUREAU COMMITTEE FOR ECONOMIC RESEARCH. *The Quality and Economic Significance of Anticipations Data: A Conference*. Princeton: Princeton University Press, 1960.

[61] WHITTLE, P. "Time Series: II. Advanced Problems", in *International Encyclopedia of the Social Sciences*, Volume 16, pp. 59–70. New York: Macmillan and Free Press, 1968.

[62] WOLD, H. "Time Series: III. Cycles", in *International Encyclopedia of the Social Sciences*, Volume 16, pp. 70–80. New York: Macmillan and Free Press, 1968.

[63] ZARNOWITZ, V. *An Appraisal of Short-Term Economic Forecasts.* New York: National Bureau of Economic Research, 1967.

[64] ZARNOWITZ, V. "Prediction and Forecasting, Economic", in *International Encyclopedia of the Social Sciences,* Volume 12, pp. 425–439. New York: Macmillan and Free Press, 1968.

Chapter 6

FORECASTING AND DECISION RULES FOR ECONOMIC POLICY MODELS

This chapter is divided into two parts. The first part deals with the general results, both analytical and empirical, of applying forecasting techniques in econometric models. The second part presents some examples of the derivation of decision rules using economic policy models where forecasting constitutes an essential part of the process. The accuracy and efficiency of a decision rule depends very crucially on that of forecasting the relevant variables: the "data" variables.

6.1. Forecasting in Econometric Models

Following Theil [22], we can distinguish between three essential aspects of forecasting:

(a) Generation of predictions: This stage deals with the particular predictive method or technique used by the forecaster. Alternative forecasting techniques are conceivable in many economic situations. For example, forecasting of endogenous variables may be done through either a very naive model or a multiequation interdependent model.

(b) Verification of predictions: This stage is concerned with the degree to which the forecasts could be imperfect; thus, for example, an interval can be specified within which the empirical variation of predictions around their realized or actual values is tolerated.

(c) The purpose of predictions: This stage is concerned with the evaluation of alternative forecasting techniques and the decision on an "optimal" or best forecasting procedure.

The procedure of selecting a forecasting technique might consist of (1) retaining those techniques which pass the test of verification in terms of a preassigned level of tolerance and (2) choosing one as the "best" with respect to a criterion function based on the specific purposes postulated at the outset. If an interdependent model of linear structural behavior equations is used to

154

generate predictions of endogenous variables, statistical tests can be made by analyzing the errors resulting from the structural equations or reduced-form equations.

> In the former case, one finds which structural equations describe reality well and which do not, but one does not learn much about the ability of the whole model to forecast the endogenous variables when predetermined variables are estimated or known. In the case of the reduced form equation errors, the situation is just the reverse. Thus, for assessing the forecasting ability of the model as a whole, the errors of the reduced form equations are most relevant and for judging individual structural equations, the errors of structural equations are most relevant. [6, p. 10.]

One way to measure the forecasting ability of a simultaneous model is, therefore, to see how closely it approximates the statistical (known) data for the observed period; a natural criterion for this situation seems to be to generalize the concept of multiple-correlation coefficient (R^2) for a simultaneous equation model. Two such generalizations may be mentioned. Assume that we have a linear system in its reduced form:

$$y_{1t} = \pi_{11} z_{1t} + \pi_{12} z_{2t} + \cdots + \pi_{1K} z_{Kt} + u_{1t}$$
$$\dots\dots\dots\dots\dots\dots\dots\dots\dots\dots\dots\dots\dots\dots\dots\dots\dots\dots\dots\dots\dots\dots\dots\dots\dots\dots \quad t = 1, 2, \dots, N \quad (6.1.1)$$
$$y_{Gt} = \pi_{G1} z_{1t} + \pi_{G2} z_{2t} + \cdots + \pi_{GK} z_{Kt} + u_{Gt},$$

where $y_{1t}, \dots, y_{Gt}$ represent observations on G random variables; $u_{1t}, \dots, u_{Gt}$ are G random disturbance terms and $z_{1t}, \dots, z_{Kt}$ denote observations on K nonstochastic variables. This system could be more compactly written as[1]

$$\begin{aligned} Y = Z\pi + U \qquad &Y: GN.1, &(6.1.2)\\ &Z: GN.GK, \\ &\pi: GK.1, \\ &U: GN.1, \end{aligned}$$

where π is a column vector of reduced-form coefficients of GK elements (appropriately derived from the π_i's) and Z is a GN by GK matrix with appropriate submatrices formed by the z's. The least-squares estimate of (6.1.2.) is

$$Y = ZP + \hat{U},$$

where $P = (Z'Z)^{-1} Z'Y$ and prime denotes transposition and $\hat{U}$ denotes the estimate of the true error U. Now consider the matrix

---

[1] For this see, Zellner [28, p. 164].

$$D = (Y'Y)^{-1}\hat{U}'\hat{U},$$

which can be regarded as the matrix generalization of the ratio of the estimated disturbances to the variance of the dependent variables in a single-equation multiple-regression model. This latter ratio is $(1 - R^2)$ in the single-equation case, where R is the coefficient of multiple correlation. Similarly, one could write

$$I - D = (Y'Y)^{-1}P'Z'ZP$$

as the matrix generalization of the ratio R^2 of the variance of the "explained" part of the dependent variable to the total variance of the dependent variable. It is known [25] that the latent roots of the matrix $(I-D)$ are the squared canonical correlations between the predetermined (i.e., independent) variables on the one hand and the jointly dependent variables on the other

$$|(I - D) - r^2 I| = 0 \quad \text{or} \quad |D - (1 - r^2)I| = 0. \tag{6.1.3}$$

One suggestion is to regard the vector of squared latent roots $(r_1^2, \ldots, r_G^2)$ as the vector generalization of the squared multiple-correlation coefficient. A scalar measure suggested by Hotelling is the vector alienation coefficient

$$|(I - D)| = (r_1^2 \cdot r_2^2 \ldots r_G^2). \tag{6.1.4}$$

A more suitable measure in terms of sampling properties is the trace correlation coefficient $\bar{r}^2$ suggested by Hooper

$$\bar{r}^2 = \frac{1}{G}\left(\sum_{i=1}^{G} r_i^2\right), \tag{6.1.5}$$

which is simply the mean of the squared canonical correlations. This can also be regarded as an estimator of the mean of the squared latent roots ρ_i^2 of the parent population. Hooper has shown that under certain assumptions (e.g., normally distributed error terms and the usual assumptions made about the interdependent linear model, etc.) the variance of the sample trace correlation coefficient $\bar{r}^2$ is to the order of N^{-1} given by

$$\text{Var } \bar{r}^2 = \frac{2}{NG^2} \sum_{i=1}^{G} \rho_i^2 (1 - \rho_i^2)^2 (2 - \rho_i^2), \tag{6.1.6}$$

where ρ_i^2's are the squared canonical correlations in the parent population. On the basis of these conditions, it is possible to measure the forecasting ability of the reduced-form model in a way which is analogous to the R^2

criterion for a single-equation multiple-regression model discussed in the preceeding chapter. For instance, assume that the simultaneous model (6.1.2) has errors U with normal distributions, zero means and mutual independence of noncontemporaneous random terms; then the value of the G dependent variables could be forecast simultaneously (Y_F^*), given the estimated regression coefficients ($P = \hat{\pi}$) and a set of values for the independent variables (Z_F)

$$Y_F^* = E(Y_F \mid Z_F) = Z_F P \tag{6.2.1}$$

where Y_F^* is a column vector of G forecast values and P is a column vector of unbiased estimates of the regression coefficients π, i.e., $EP = \pi$. The observed value of Y in the prediction period, say Y_F, is given by

$$Y_F = Z_F \pi + U_F, \tag{6.2.2}$$

where U_F is the column vector of values assumed by the random terms in the forecast period when Z_F is given. By our assumptions on the error variables U and nonstochastic terms Z and the unbiased estimates P, we have $EU_F = 0$. Now the error of forecast (ε) is given by

$$Y_F^* - Y_F = Z_F(P - \pi) - U_F,$$

hence, the expected error ($E\varepsilon$) (i.e., the generalized error of forecast) and the variance-covariance matrix of forecast errors ($E\varepsilon\varepsilon'$) are given by

$$E\varepsilon = E(Y_F^* - Y_F) = Z_F(EP = \pi) = 0, \tag{6.2.3}$$

$$\begin{aligned}
E\varepsilon\varepsilon' &= E\left[(Y_F^* - Y_F)(Y_F^* - Y_F)'\right], \\
&= E\left[\{Z(P - \pi) - U_F\}\{(P - \pi)'Z' - U_F'\}\right], \\
&= EU_F U_F' + EZ(P - \pi)(P - \pi)'Z', \\
&\quad - EZ(P - \pi)U_F' - EU_F(P - \pi)'Z',
\end{aligned} \tag{6.2.4}$$

i.e.,

$$E\varepsilon\varepsilon' = EU_F U_F' + EZ(P - \pi)(P - \pi)'Z', \tag{6.2.5}$$

where the last two terms on the right side of the final equation for (6.2.4) are zero, since U_F and P are statistically independent and $EU_F = 0$ by assumption. Like the t-test in a single-equation multivariable-regression model, we may apply here the multivariate generalization of the t-test, i.e., we may use Hotelling's T^2-statistic for making probability statements [12] about the forecast value Y^* and constructing multivariate confidence regions [1, 20].

This method of forecasting a set of dependent variables simultaneously could be made more flexible by introducing extraneous knowledge or prior information. For example, we may define, after Zellner,[2] a wide class of decision rules (DR) that are alternative to the least-squares forecasting rule given in equation (6.2.1) e.g.,

$$DR = \begin{cases} \hat{\lambda} Y_F^* + (I - \hat{\lambda}) A_U, \text{ for } Y_F^* \geq A_U \\ Y_F^*, \text{ for } A_L < Y_F^* < A_U \\ \hat{\lambda} Y_F^* + (I - \hat{\lambda}) A_L, \text{ for } Y_F^* \leq A_L, \end{cases} \qquad (6.3.1)$$

where $\hat{\lambda}$ is a diagonal matrix with nonnegative diagonal elements, Y_F^* is the vector of forecast values given in equation (6.2.1) based on the least-squares method and A_U, A_L denote, respectively, the upper and lower bounds (vectors) imposed (i.e., known a priori) on the forecast values. In other words, if our calculated forecast value Y_F falls within the range $A_L < Y_F < A_U$, we accept Y_F^* as our forecast. If, however, our calculated forecast vector $Y_F \geq A_U$, we combine linearly Y_F^* and A_U and accept the decision rule $(\hat{\lambda} Y_F^* + (I - \hat{\lambda}) A_U)$ for forecasting purposes. The diagonal elements of the matrix $\hat{\lambda}$ denote the weights in the linear combination, e.g., if $\hat{\lambda} = I$ identically, then $Y_F = Y_F^*$ always, otherwise we accept partly Y_F^* and partly A_U in a linear combination. One reason for obtaining this alternative forecasting decision rule through imposed extraneous bounds (or an imposed coefficient matrix in this mixed-estimation method) is that sometimes the generalized R^2 value could be considerably improved for the whole reduced-form model by such imposition, particularly when the independent variables in the reduced-form model have some degree of intercorrelation, which violates the conditions of classical least-squares method. A second reason might be what has been called the specification bias [21], e.g., the fact that the true model for the real world may be nonlinear and our linear model may hold only as an approximation introduces a bias in our specification. Since linearizing is valid only locally, it may be helpful to vary the bounds around which linearized approximation is made. However, as yet there is no formal method for determining the vector A_L, A_U introduced in (6.3.1).

One of the basic difficulties in simultaneous forecasting is the assumption that the structural equations estimated from a given set of sample observations would remain valid outside the sample. However, in some cases there may be a change of the set of coefficients due to basic structural changes in the economy leading to what has been called a "change of regimes" [18],

---

[2] See Zellner [29]. Several types of decision rules other than that in (6.3.1) are developed here and the expectation and variance of the error of forecast computed.

and these are very difficult to incorporate in a forecasting rule except through the extraneous bounds as imposed in equation (6.3.1). As Christ has observed:

> There are at least two general sorts of questions one can ask about an equation's errors in describing extra-sample data. One is: Are these extra-sample errors so large in comparison with the errors (i.e., residuals) within the sample that the equation does not describe the extra-sample data as well as the sample data? If so, either the equation must be rejected or one must conclude that the structures underlying the two sets of data are different. Even if an equation is not rejected by this test, however, the only thing one can thereby claim for it is that it describes the extra-sample data well or badly in terms of the answer to the second type of question to which we now turn. The second type of question is: Are these extra-sample errors so large as to render the model useless as a practical forecasting device? If so, then obviously the model is not a practical forecaster. Both questions are important in testing a model [6, p. 12].

So far we have been concerned with forecasting the endogenous variables of a simultaneous system. Another part of the problem is to forecast the so-called "data" variables (e.g., part of the exogenous variables) themselves. These variables are generally predicted on the basis of fitted time functions, although there are different methods, e.g., autoregressive or other kinds of stochastic process structures, by which the statistical fitting could be accomplished. One method which has some optimum properties and which has been frequently utilized in control system theory [5] is called the method of exponentially weighted forecasts. Forecasts are here derived by weighting past observations exponentially (i.e., geometrically) as in some distributed lag models. The principal motivation for this kind of forecasting technique has been that it leads to correction of persistent errors without being very sensitive to random disturbances. This method of exponentially weighted moving average forecast is most appropriate when the time series to be predicted involves only two kinds of random components: One lasting a single period of time (transitory) and the other lasting through all subsequent periods (permanent) [11]. The adaptive mechanism implicit in this forecasting process can be better understood by a single variable example. Assume that $y(t)$ represents that part of a time series which cannot be explained by trend, seasonal or any other systematic factors, and let $y_f(t)$ represent the forecast or expected value of $y(t)$ given all the information available through the $(t-1)$st period. Then the exponentially weighted forecasting method changes the forecast value from one period to the next by an amount proportional to the latest observed error, i.e.,

$$y_f(t) = y_f(t-1) + \alpha\big(y(t-1) - y_f(t-1)\big), \tag{6.4.1}$$

where $0 \le \alpha < 1$. Solving (6.4.1) we have

$$y_f(t) = \sum_{i=1}^{\infty} \alpha(1-\alpha)^{i-1} y(t-i). \tag{6.4.2}$$

Equation (6.4.2) gives the rule for an exponentially weighted forecast. Note that the weights $(1-\alpha)^{i-1}$ attached to past values decrease exponentially, and since the weights attached to prior values of y_t add up to unity, the forecasting rule does not introduce any systematic bias in this respect. Our problem is, of course, to get an optimal estimate of the single parameter α in (6.4.2). Several methods[3] have been suggested for estimating such a parameter. Each of these depends on specifying a particular random process underlying the observed time series. A special case, taken from Muth,[4] assumes that the observed time series $y(t)$ has two additive components, the permanent component $\bar{y}(t)$ and the transitory component $n(t)$, such that the two components are statistically independent in each period.

$$y(t) = \bar{y}(t) + n(t). \tag{6.4.3}$$

The transitory components $n(t)$ are assumed to be independently distributed with zero mean and variance σ_n^2. The permanent components $\bar{y}(t)$ are defined by a linear process

$$\bar{y}(t) = \bar{y}(t-1) + \varepsilon(t) = \sum_{i=1}^{t} \varepsilon(i), \tag{6.4.4}$$

where the ε's are serially independent with mean zero and variance σ_ε^2. Further, n's and ε's are also assumed to be independent (although this assumption is not an essential one). The forecasting problem then is to find the coefficients v_j in the equation

$$y_f(t) = \sum_{j=1}^{\infty} v_j y(t-j), \tag{6.4.5}$$

which minimize the error variance V

$$V = E\big(y(t) - y_f(t)\big)^2. \tag{6.4.6}$$

Since by substitutions through (6.4.3), (6.4.4) and (6.4.5) the error variance V can be written as

---

[3] For a summary of these methods see Johnston [13, pp. 211–220].
[4] This case is taken from Muth [17].

$$V = \sigma_\varepsilon^2 + \sigma_n^2 + \sigma_\varepsilon^2 \sum_{j=1}^{\infty} \left(1 - \sum_{i=1}^{j} v_i\right)^2 + \sigma_n^2 \sum_{j=1}^{\infty} v_j^2, \qquad (6.4.7)$$

we set the partial derivative $\partial V / \partial v_k$ equal to zero to obtain the optimal weights, i.e.,

$$\frac{\partial V}{\partial v_k} = -2\sigma_\varepsilon^2 \sum_{j=k}^{\infty} \left(1 - \sum_{i=1}^{j} v_i\right) + 2\sigma_n^2 v_k = 0 \qquad k = 1, 2, \dots. \qquad (6.4.8)$$

Muth has shown that approximately, taking up to second-difference terms, the characteristic equation of the system (6.4.8) is

$$-\frac{(1 - \lambda)^2}{\lambda} + (\sigma_\varepsilon^2 / \sigma_n^2) = 0, \qquad (6.4.9)$$

where λ is the characteristic root. It can be seen that equation (6.4.9) has one root less than unity and the other greater than unity. Only the former, say λ_1, is relevant, because for any root greater than unity the infinite sums in (6.4.7) or (6.4.8) would diverge and the approximation would not hold. Hence, with the value of λ_1 the optimal weights appearing in the forecasting formula (6.4.5) are given approximately by

$$V_K = A\lambda_1^K,$$

where A is an arbitrary constant determined by the condition

$$\sum_{K=1}^{\infty} V_K = 1,$$

i.e.

$$V_K = \frac{1}{\sum\limits_{K=1}^{\infty} \lambda_1^K} \lambda_1^K = \frac{1 - \lambda_1}{\lambda_1} \lambda_1^K = (1 - \lambda_1)\lambda_1^{K-1}.$$

The forecast value $y_f(t)$ is an estimate of the permanent component $\bar{y}(t)$, and hence it has the property that the forecast for all future periods is the same as the forecast for the next period. A multivariable extension of this result has been attempted by a number of writers [3, 7].

6.2. Some Empirical Results on Forecasting

One of the most interesting empirical examples of postwar macroeconomic forecasting is provided by the Dutch and Scandinavian forecasts made during 1949–1952. Theil [22, Chapter 3] has fitted a linear regression of predicted changes (P) on observed actual changes (A) for all the ninety-two Dutch and all eighty-two Scandinavian forecasts, e.g.,

$$P = mA, \text{ where } m = \begin{array}{l} 0.7 \text{ for the Netherlands (1949–1951, 1953)}, \\ 0.55 \text{ for Scandinavia (1949–1952)}, \end{array} \qquad (6.5.1)$$

$$(P - mA)^2 = 10 + 0.10\,A^2. \qquad (6.5.2)$$

The first equation suggests underestimation of actual changes by the forecast values, while the second implies that the variance of the forecasts around the regression (6.5.1) increases linearly with the square of A. This naturally leads to a hypothesis of a persistent underestimation tendency in forecast values. Lips and Schouten [15] analyzed the quality of Dutch forecasts for the period 1949–1954 using the 1955 model of the Dutch economy, which contained twenty-seven equations (twelve definitions, four institutional and eleven behavior equations). This study followed the method of conditional prediction, where the observed changes in exogenous variables are inserted into the 1955 Central Planning Bureau simultaneous-equation model and the corresponding changes in the endogenous variables are then computed and compared with the observed changes in these variables. When such conditional forecasts are compared with the observed changes, the under-estimation bias is much less for the categories of prices (three indices) and values (eleven variables), than for the volume figures (nine volume indices). If we define an inequality coefficient U proposed by Theil as:

$$U = \left[\frac{1}{n}\sum_i \left(P_i - A_i\right)^2\right]^{\frac{1}{2}} \Big/ \left[\left(\frac{1}{n}\sum_i P_i^2\right)^{\frac{1}{2}} + \left(\frac{1}{n}\sum_i A_i^2\right)^{\frac{1}{2}}\right] \qquad (6.5.3)$$

where n = total number of forecast (P_i) and actual (A_i) figures to measure the accuracy of forecasts, the values of U for all the twenty-three variables of the Central Planning Bureau model (1955) were as follows:

Year	U
1949	0.28
1950	0.28
1951	0.28
1953	0.14
1954	0.60
1955	0.65
1956	0.33

Since a high value of $U\,(0 \le U \le 1)$ defined in (6.5.3) indicates a more imperfect forecast ($U=0$ is a perfect forecast and $U=1$ is a most imperfect forecast), it may be seen that the years 1954–1955 were not particularly good. However, some of the forecasts were revised subsequently, and it appears that over 1949–1951 and 1953 the majority of Dutch revisions were successful in the sense that the revisions were generally in the right direction of decreasing U.

The inequality coefficient, as such, does not provide any rule permitting an evaluation of the "absolute" quality of the forecasting technique used. If the same technique (method) is employed over a number of years, U provides an indication of the qualities of the forecasts from year to year. In order to express some judgment about the quality of a given method used to generate predictions, the qualities of the forecasts obtained by different methods should be compared by computing the respective U's.

Such a comparison was undertaken between forecasting on the basis of (1) simple extrapolation and (2) conditional predictions generated by the above-mentioned Central Planning Bureau (CPB) model. The two methods, when compared for all the twenty-three variables by means of an inequality coefficient ($\bar{U}$) which is not normalized,

$$\bar{U} = \left[\frac{1}{n} \sum_i (P - A)^2 \right]^{\frac{1}{2}}$$

give the following results:

Year	$\bar{U}$	
	By Extrapolation	By CPB Method
1949	202	79
1950	175	110
1951	213	106
1953	254	47
1954	84	149
1955	165	84
1956	79	52
All years	178	95

Except for the year 1954, the conditional prediction method had fared better. A more recent study [26] used a somewhat different version of the inequality coefficient to evaluate the quality of the forecasts of all macroeconomic variables appearing in the annual Dutch central economic plans. Table 6.1 provides yearly values for the inequality coefficient from 1953 to 1962 by classes of variables.

TABLE 6.1

Dutch Central Economic Plans — Inequality Coefficients by Plans

	1953	1954	1955	1956	1957	1958	1959	1960	1961	1962
Exogenous variables										
Controlled	0.71	0.74	0.91	0.54	1.06	0.46	0.18	0.38	0.23	0.42
Uncontrolled	0.43	1.06	0.69	0.76	0.38	0.68	0.78	0.57	0.50	0.34
Subtotal	0.63	0.85	0.83	0.63	0.87	0.55	0.50	0.46	0.36	0.39
Endogenous variables	0.86	0.93	0.84	0.66	0.50	0.53	0.58	0.48	0.36	0.22
Targets	0.67	0.90	0.89	0.66	0.39	0.50	0.77	0.28	0.37	0.18
All variables	0.79	0.90	0.84	0.65	0.67	0.54	0.55	0.47	0.36	0.28

The most noteworthy features of Table 6.1 are the amazing improvement in the quality of forecasts over the period under consideration and the greater relative improvements in the quality of the predictions of endogenous as opposed to exogenous variables. It appears likely that this latter phenomenon reflects the refinements introduced in the econometric model used to generate predictions of the endogenous variables (for further discussion, see Chapter 14, Section 14.2.1).

Next we consider a part of statistical decision theory which discusses the problem of deriving optimum decision rules in situations where there are elements of risk and uncertainty. Another part of this problem will be discussed at greater length in Chapter 9.

6.3. The Derivation of Decision Rules for Economic Policy Models

Since 1950, applications of statistical decision theory have extended into more and more fields of science. Many of the more recent applications have not been economic in the usual sense. All applications involve the concept of an objective function. For a business firm — or a particular activity of a business firm — this objective function may simply be a total net revenue curve. In military applications, the penalties for poor decisions might be expressed in terms of losses of men and material or loss of capacity to carry on some further military mission.

The present section will deal with two applications of decision theory to problems of economic policy. The first example, optimal storage decision rules for feed grains, differs from most business examples in that *supply*, rather than demand, is the variable which is subject to stochastic variation. The other application deals with economic stabilization policy; the objective function is specified by a policy maker whose preferences may or may not be supported by any detailed analysis of costs and benefits to individual members of the society. The close formal analogies between decision theory for businessmen and decision theory for government policy makers are suggested by Theil [23].

The derivation of optimal decision rules for national carry-over stocks of feed grains may seem tangential to our primary interest in economic policy models for complete economies. However, the feed grain example has several important virtues, including simplicity, tangibility and numerical quantification in terms of dollars and bushels. Most readers will approach the subsequent derivations of decision rules for macroeconomic stabilization policy with greater insight if they have first carried out the derivation of an optimal carry-over rule. Further, in the United States storage programs for feed grains have been a major component of economic policy with respect to agriculture and have had significant effects on economic stability and on farm-nonfarm income distributions.

6.3.1. *Optimal Inventory Decision Rules*

Modern econometric work on inventory policy dates from two papers, "The Inventory Problem," by A. Dvoretzky, J. Kiefer and J. Wolfowitz, which appeared in the April, 1952 and July, 1952 issues of *Econometrica*. A subsequent expository paper by other authors states the problem thus:

> The inventory problem can be stated very simply: it is to decide how much material to stock in preparation for an uncertain future. Both understocking and overstocking are costly, else there is no problem. If overstocking is not penalized, such large stocks could be held that no conceivable future occurrence would deplete them; if understocking is not penalized, zero stocks could be held. The usual cases, where both understocking and overstocking are costly, are the ones of interest here. [14, p. 717].

Variations in the production of corn in the United States from one year to the next have been attributable primarily to variations in yields per acre; these result largely from variations in weather. Corn is by far the most important feed grain in the United States, and for other reasons as well corn storage has been the principal instrument of government policy in attempting to reduce variatons in feed grain utilization, livestock production and livestock prices.

Gustafson [9, 10] has adapted the "optimal inventory" approach to the analysis of carry-over policy for feed grains. For any given set of assumptions, this approach leads to a simple *storage decision rule* which can be expressed as follows:

"If the total supply of feed grains (carry-in stocks plus current production) is S bushels, the carry-out at the end of the year should be C bushels." The appropriate carry-out could be read off immediately from a chart or table for any given value of total supply.

To derive a storage rule, we must take account of the following elements:

(a) The likelihood of feed grain yields in any given year being above or below average by stated amounts. In practice, this has been based on an analysis of actual yields over a considerable period of years, adjusted for trend and centered near the current trend level of feed grain yields.

(b) The yearly out-of-pocket cost of storing a bushel of grain.

(c) The interest rate (actual or imputed) on working capital tied up in the stored grain.

(d) A schedule of benefits or losses resulting from different rates of feed grain utilization. In a free market economy, the appropriate schedule might be simply the market demand curve, — a schedule of the market prices which would be associated with different levels of feed grain consumption.

If the approach seems complex, it is really no more complex than the considerations confronting any private storage operator. Before storing grain from a big crop at a price of (say) $ 1.40, the operator would presumably ask himself, "What are the chances that the market a year from now will be $ 1.55 or higher? Or that the market two years from now will be $ 1.70 or higher?"

Furthermore, in a sense any year-to-year storage program works against itself. For example, the average farm price for the large 1946 corn crop was $ 1.56 per bushel, while that for the short 1947 crop was $ 2.16. It would certainly have been profitable to carry some corn over from one year to the other. But how much?

Corn utilization_was 3.1 billion bushels in 1946 and only 2.5 billion in 1947. But if 0.2 billion bushels had been transferred from the first year to the second through storage the price in 1946 would have risen and that in 1947 would have fallen. Based on past relationships, the resulting price rise from 1946 (with utilization now at 2.9 billion bushels) to 1947 (with utilization now at 2.7 billion) would have been just about enough to cover storage and interest charges.

As in other economic problems, an equilibrium level of storage is found when the cost of adding one more unit to stocks is equal to the expected level of returns from its subsequent resale or consumption. The cost of adding one more bushel of grain to this year's carry-over may be taken as the current market price plus out-of-pocket storage charges until the following year. The expected marginal return is a more difficult concept. It depends on the probability distribution of feed grain yields over the next several years, translated into their effects on market prices. If the chance to sell at a profit comes two or three years hence, the selling price must cover two or three years of storage costs. Furthermore, the expected prices in future years would be subject to some discount relative to the price which could be obtained by selling the grain today. For the spot cash could be put into other enterprises or investments, and by holding grain we are either foregoing opportunities or paying interest on borrowed funds.

To be specific, let us define the following symbols and functions: $\gamma =$ the out-of-pocket cost of storing a bushel of grain for one year. In this case we assume $\gamma = \$ 0.10$ per bushel per year.

$F(x) =$ the frequency or "probability" distribution of feed grain yields. For simplicity, we shall telescope the actual distribution into three discrete values. As acreage is assumed constant, yield variations are equivalent to variations in production.

X Yield (Bushels per Acre)	$F(x)$ Probability
25	0.2
30	0.5
33	0.3

$p =$ the market demand function for feed grains, expressing price as a function of the quantity consumed. Specifically, we assume $p = \$ 4.50 - 0.10 \ Y$, where Y is utilization expressed in terms of bushels per acre. We assume that the position of this demand curve remains fixed and that prices vary only in association with quantities utilized.

$\alpha =$ the discount factor applied to prospective future returns. In this case we assume $\alpha = 0.95$ (equivalent to a compound interest rate of 5.2 per cent a year).

$C_n =$ the carry-out of feed grains (in bushels per acre) at the end of year n. Realistically, C_n represents only that portion of the carry-over which is in excess of minimum pipeline or working stocks.

$S_n = C_{n-1} + X_n$ is the total supply of feed grains in year n, namely, the carry-out from year $n-1$ plus the production in year n. Certain other accounting relations exist, as that $Y_n = S_n - C_n$.

To derive a storage decision rule, we proceed in what is, at first glance, a surprising fashion. We start with the last year first. We first find a rule R_n which tells us what value of C_n minimizes expected losses (or maximizes expected profits) in year n for each possible value of S_n. We then fall back to year $n-1$ and find a rule R_{n-1} for determining the carry-out (C_{n-1}) in that year which, for each possible value of S_{n-1}, minimizes expected losses for years $n-1$ and n combined. We then work back year by year in this iterative fashion until further steps fail to change significantly the optimum storage rule. For, in most practical cases, the terms of our problem (discount rates, storage costs, yield variations and demand functions) imply a sort of built-in horizon. In the case of feed grains it appears that rules which are optimal with respect to a seven- or eight-year period are almost identical with those which might take account of a theoretically infinite period.

(1) For the n-th year, we simply set $C_n = 0$ for all values of S_n. This sets an arbitrary end-point to the period in which we are interested in maintaining a storage policy.

(2) For the $(n-1)$st year, we find for each possible value of S_{n-1} the value of $C_{n-1} > 0$ which satisfies the following relation:

$$\alpha E \rho (C_{n-1} + X_n - C_n) - \gamma (C_{n-1}) - \rho (S_{n-1} - C_{n-1}) = 0. \quad (6.6.1)$$

The first term is the present (discounted) value of the expected price in year n associated with a given value of the carry-in (C_{n-1}) into that year. The symbol E is the expectation operator. It implies that for any given C_{n-1} we obtain the value of ρ corresponding to each of the three possible values of X and weight these ρ's by their probabilities, 0.2, 0.5 and 0.3, respectively, for yields of 25, 30 and 33 bushels per acre. In technical terms we take the "expectation," or weighted average, of the function $F(x)$ with respect to X_n, the only variable in it which has a probability distribution.

The second term is the out-of-pocket cost of storing the carry-out C_{n-1} until the next season. The third term is simply the market price of grain in year $n-1$, which depends, of course, both on the initial supply S_{n-1} and the carry-out, C_{n-1}.

The expression as a whole for year $n-1$ is actually quite easy to handle.

It results in a function (R_{n-1}) which gives a value of C_{n-1} for each possible value of S_{n-1}. (For values of S_n which would seem to give negative values of R_{n-1}, we simply take C_{n-1} equal to zero.)

(3) The calculation for year $n-2$ brings out the full complexity of this approach. For each possible value of S_{n-2}, we find the value of $C_{n-2} > 0$ which satisfies the following relation:

$$\alpha E\rho \left[C_{n-2} + X_{n-1} - R_{n-1}(C_{n-2} + X_{n-1}) \right]$$
$$- \gamma (C_{n-2}) - \rho (S_{n-2} - C_{n-2}) = 0. \tag{6.6.2}$$

The first term now implies the joint minimization of discounted expected losses in years $n-1$ and n combined, allowing for out-of-pocket costs of storage from year $n-1$ into year n. These factors are carried back cumulatively in the corresponding terms of the calculations for $n-3$ and earlier years. The other two terms relate, as before, to out-of-pocket storage costs and market prices in the current year, $n-2$.

Any remaining confusion can perhaps be solved by working out numerically the optimal storage rule implied by our present assumptions, which are as follows:

$\gamma = 0.10;\ \alpha = 0.95;\ \rho = 4.50 - 0.10Y;$
$X = 25,\ 30$ or 33 bushels, with $F(x) = 0.2,\ 0.5$ and 0.3, respectively.

Step 1. For year n, we take $C_n = 0$.

Step 2. For year $n-1$, we substitute the appropriate numerical values into equation (6.6.1):

$$\alpha E\rho (C_{n-1} + X_n - C_n) - \gamma (C_{n-1}) - \rho (S_{n-1} - C_{n-1}) = 0.$$

As $C_n = 0$, $\rho (C_{n-1} + X_n - C_n)$ is equivalent to $4.50 - 0.10 (C_{n-1} + X_n)$. The expectation, E, of this function taken over the three possible values of X_n is:

$$E(\rho) = 0.2 \left[4.50 - 0.10C_{n-1} - 0.10(25) \right] + 0.5 \left[4.50 - 0.10C_{n-1} - 0.10(30) \right]$$
$$+ 0.3 \left[4.50 - 0.10C_{n-1} - 0.10(33) \right], \text{ or} \tag{6.6.3}$$
$$E(\rho) = 4.50 - 0.10C_{n-1} - 0.10(29.9) = 1.51 - 0.10C_{n-1}.$$

Multiplying this result by $\alpha = 0.95$, the first term of equation (6.6.1) becomes simply

$$\alpha E\rho = 1.434 - 0.095C_{n-1}. \tag{6.6.4}$$

The second term is simply $-0.10\, C_{n-1}$. The third term is equivalent to $-\left[4.50 - 0.10 (S_{n-1} - C_{n-1}) \right]$, or $\left[-4.50 + 0.10\, S_{n-1} - 0.10\, C_{n-1} \right]$. Adding the three terms we have

$$
\begin{aligned}
(\quad 1.434 &- 0.095C_{n-1} \\
(\quad &- 0.100C_{n-1} \\
(-4.500 &- 0.100C_{n-1} + 0.10S_{n-1} = 0, \\
(-3.066 &- 0.295C_{n-1} + 0.10S_{n-1} = 0.
\end{aligned}
$$

(6.6.5)

or

Then

$$
C_{n-1} = \frac{-3.066 + 0.10S_{n-1}}{0.295} = -10.393 + 0.339S_{n-1}.
$$

This last function is the decision rule, R_{n-1}, which for each possible value of S_{n-1} gives us the value of C_{n-1} which minimizes expected losses on storage for years $n-1$ and n combined. As C_{n-1} cannot be less than zero, this function is taken to be zero for all values of

$$
S_{n-1} < S_0 = \frac{10.393}{0.339} = 30.658 \text{ bushels}.
$$

The point of zero carry-out has the following common sense significance: Unless total supply (S_{n-1}) is above the long-run average utilization level $(Y_{n-1} = 29.9)$, the price in year $n-1$ will not be low enough to provide an even chance of "coming out" on a storage venture. If S_{n-1} is very large, the current price will be far below average and there is an excellent chance of profiting on storage (provided that other operators collectively do not store too much).

Step 3. For year $n-2$ we substitute numerical values in equation (6.6.2) as follows:

$$
\alpha E\rho\left[C_{n-2} + X_{n-1} - R_{n-1}(C_{n-2} + X_{n-1})\right] \\
- \gamma(C_{n-2}) - \rho(S_{n-2} - C_{n-2}) = 0.
$$

The second term is $-0.10\,C_{n-2}$, and the third is

$$
\left[-4.50 - 0.10C_{n-2} + 0.10S_{n-2}\right],
$$

just as before except for the change in subscripts.

In the first term, we note that $C_{n-2} + X_{n-1} = S_{n-1}$ and that $R_{n-1}(C_{n-2} + X_{n-1})$ is simply C_{n-1} as calculated from equation (6.6.5). Hence, the whole expression in brackets is equivalent simply to $S_{n-1} - C_{n-1} = Y_{n-1}$, the level of feed grain utilization in year $n-1$. So the first term may be rewritten as follows:

$$
0.95E(4.50 - 0.10\left[C_{n-2} + X_{n-1} - (-10.393 + 0.339C_{n-2} + 0.339X_{n-1})\right].
$$

Noting that the expected value of a constant is the constant itself and that

$E(X_{n-1})$ is simply the weighted average yield of 29.9 bushels per acre, this becomes

$$0.95 (4.50 - 0.10 [0.661 C_{n-2} + 0.661 (29.9) + 10.393]),$$

or

$$0.95 [(4.50 - 1.9764 - 1.0393) - 0.0661 C_{n-2}];$$

or, finally, $0.95 (1.4843 - 0.0661 \; C_{n-2}) = 1.4101 - 0.0628 \; C_{n-2}$

Adding the three terms of equation (6.6.2) we have

$$
\begin{array}{l}
(\quad\ 1.4101 - 0.0628 C_{n-2} \\
(\qquad\qquad\ - 0.1000 C_{n-2} \\
(- 4.5000 - 0.1000 C_{n-2} + 0.10 S_{n-2} = 0, \\
\overline{\quad - 3.0899 - 0.2628 C_{n-2} + 0.10 S_{n-2} = 0.}
\end{array}
\qquad (6.6.6)
$$

or

Hence,

$$C_{n-2} = \frac{- 3.0899 + 0.10 S_{n-2}}{0.2628} = - 11.758 + 0.3805 S_{n-2}.$$

The optimum carry-out C_{n-2} will be zero for any value of S_{n-2} less than

$$\frac{11.758}{0.3805} = 30.901 \text{ bushels per acre}.$$

Step 4. We repeat the step 3 process for year $n-3$, obtaining the storage decision rule

$$C_{n-3} = - 11.983 + 0.3863 S_{n-3}. \qquad (6.6.7)$$

This is the rule R_{n-3} for $C_{n-3} \geq 0$ and $S_{n-3} \geq 31.020$.
This rule is little different from R_{n-2}.

Step 5. For year $n-4$, the storage decision rule is

$$C_{n-4} = - 12.027 + 0.3871 \; s. \qquad (6.6.8)$$

This is rule R_{n-4}, which yields $C_{n-4} \geq 0$ for all values of $S_{n-4} \geq 31.069$.

Step 6. Omitting the calculations, rule R_{n-5} is

$$C_{n-5} = - 12.038 + 0.3873 S_{n-5}. \qquad (6.6.9)$$

If we look back over the rules R_{n-1} through R_{n-5}, they appear to be converging quite rapidly toward final values only negligibly different from R_{n-5}. Thus, for practical purposes R_{n-5} may be taken as the desired optimum storage decision rule.

To illustrate how this rule, R_{n-5}, would operate, consider the randomly drawn ten-year sequence of yields shown in column 2 of Table 6.2.

TABLE 6.2

Decision Rule $C_{n-5} = -12.038 + 0.3873\,S_{n-5}$ Applied to a Hypothetical Sequence of Feed Grain Yields and Resulting Optimal Quantities Stored

Year	(1) Carry-in C_{n-1}	(2) Yield X_n (Bushels per acre)	(3) Total Supply S_n	(4) Carry-out C_n
1	0	33	33.000	0.743
2	0.743	33	33.743	1.031
3	1.031	25	26.031	0
4	0	33	33.000	0.743
5	0.743	30	30.743	0
6	0	30	30.000	0
7	0	30	30.000	0
8	0	25	25.000	0
9	0	25	25.000	0
10	0	30	30.000	0

If stocks at the beginning of the sequence are zero, a yield of 33 bushels in the first year calls for a carry-out of 0.743 bushels per acre. A second year of above-average yield raises the carry-out to 1.031 bushels. A below-average crop of 25 bushels is permitted to reduce the carry-out to zero, and so on. No stocks are built up during a series of average or below average yields.

The effects of rule R_{n-5} on feed grain utilization and prices (Table 6.3) may also be calculated and compared with the situation which would exist if no storage were undertaken in any year. Columns (3) and (4) indicate that during the years which are interspersed with above-average yields, rule R_{n-5} significantly reduces year-to-year fluctuations in market prices. This is directly analogous to the effects of within-the-year storage operations upon the amplitude of seasonal price variations.

Differences in the assumed carry-in in year 1 will, of course, affect the results for all years until stocks are drawn down to zero. For example, an initial carry-in of 7 bushels per acre coupled with a yield of 33 bushels in year 1 would call for a carry-out (C_1) of 3.454 bushels. Given the same sequence of yields as before, the carry-outs for years 2 through 5 would be 2.081, 0.387, 0.893 and 0 bushels, respectively. Thus, if we are faced with an

TABLE 6.3

Consequences of Decision Rule $C_{n-5} = -12.038 + 0.3873 \, S_{n-5}$ for Utilization and Prices of Feed Grains Compared With Utilization and Prices in the Absence of Storage

Year	Utilization (Y_n)		Market Price (p)	
	(1) With no Storage [a]	(2) With Rule R_{n-5}	(3) With no Storage	(4) With Rule R_{n-5}
	(Bushels per acre)		(Dollars per bushel)	
1	33	32.257	1.20	1.274
2	33	32.712	1.20	1.229
3	25	26.031	2.00	1.897
4	33	32.257	1.20	1.274
5	30	30.743	1.50	1.426
6	30	30.000	1.50	1.500
7	30	30.000	1.50	1.500
8	25	25.000	2.00	2.000
9	25	25.000	2.00	2.000
10	30	30.000	1.50	1.500
Average	29.4	29.400	1.56	1.560

[a] Same sequence of yields as in Table 6.2.

initial surplus of feed grains, we might try out a number of random sequences of yields to estimate whether repeated application of rule R_{n-5} would reduce the surplus to normal proportions and, if so, about how many years would be required.

The flexibility of the optimal inventory approach may be illustrated by considering various changes in our initial assumptions. For example, we might set C_n equal to some positive constant instead of zero. In this case, application of our procedure would lead to the (expected) least-cost program for building stocks up to the specified level.

An examination of equation (6.6.2) will indicate the effects of other changes. We note that, with the demand function (p) linear, the resulting storage rule is linear in C and S. Also, the expected value of $p(C, X)$ is simply the market price associated with a utilization of $C + E(X) = C + 29.9$. As the demand function is linear, an increase in the variability of yields (σ_x) about a given average will not change $E(p)$. Hence, it will not change the storage *rule*. However, as the above-average yields are larger than before, the amounts stored in such years will be larger and the average level of stocks will be higher. For example, suppose we double the initial yield variability, so that $X = 20$, 30 and 36 bushels per acre with probability 0.2, 0.5 and 0.3, respectively, and assume the same ten-year sequence of above-average, average and below-average yields as before. The results are as presented in Table 6.4.

TABLE 6.4

Optimal Quantities Stored Under Decision Rule $C_{n-5} = -12.038 + 0.3873\, S_{n-5}$ When Feed Grain Yields Are Twice as Variable as Those in Table 6.2

Year	(1) Carry-in C_{n-1}	(2) Yield X_n	(3) Total Supply S_n	(4) Carry-out C_n
		(Bushels per acre)		
1	0	36	36.000	1.905
2	1.905	36	37.905	2.643
3	2.643	20	22.643	0
4	0	36	36.000	1.905
5	1.905	30	31.905	0.319
6	0.319	30	30.319	0
7	0	30	30.000	0
8	0	20	20.000	0
9	0	20	20.000	0
10	0	30	30.000	0

The maximum carry-over is 2.643 bushels per acre, compared with 1.031 in the earlier example, and the *average* level of stocks is now 0.677 bushels, as compared with 0.252 bushels before.

An increase in out-of-pocket storage costs will reduce the optimum level of storage from any given supply. An increase in the interest rate

$$\left(i = \frac{1 - \alpha}{\alpha} \right)$$

also tends to reduce the optimum level of storage by reducing the present (discounted) value of expected future returns. An upward trend in the demand function (ρ) of k cents per year would be similar in its effects to a decrease in out-of-pocket storage costs.

If the elasticity of the market demand curve were only half as great as was assumed above, the variability of prices (in the absence of storage) would be doubled. If storage costs (γ) and the discount factor (α) are unchanged, this raises the optimum level of carry-out for any given level of supply.

Thus, if ρ is changed to

$$\rho = 7.50 - 0.20Y, \qquad (6.6.10)$$

which is only half as elastic as the original ρ at the point of means (approximately $\rho = \$ 1.50$, $Y = 30$), we obtain the following rule R_{n-5}:

$$C_{n-5} = -15.55 + 0.508S_{n-5}. \qquad (6.6.11)$$

This rule calls for higher carry-out levels than does the previous rule for all values of S_n greater than 30.6 bushels per acre.

If we apply the new rule to the same ten-year yield sequence as before we obtain the results presented in Table 6.5.

TABLE 6.5

Optimal Quantities Stored if Demand Curve for Feed Grains Is Twice as Steep as That Underlying Table 6.2 (New Decision Rule is $C_{n-5} = -15.55 + 0.508 \, S_{n-5}$)

Year	(1) Carry-in C_{n-1}	(2) Yield X_n	(3) Total Supply S_n	(4) Carry-out C_n
		(Bushels per acre)		
1	0	33	33.000	1.214
2	1.214	33	34.214	1.831
3	1.831	25	26.831	0
4	0	33	33.000	1.214
5	1.214	30	31.214	0.307
6	0.307	30	30.307	0
7	0	30	30.000	0
8	0	25	25.000	0
9	0	25	25.000	0
10	0	30	30.000	0

The maximum level of stocks is 1.831 bushels per acre, compared with 1.031 bushels with the original demand function. The average level of stocks is 0.457 bushels per acre, compared with 0.252 bushels under the original assumptions.

If the demand or "penalty" function (ρ) is nonlinear, the calculations become more complicated. For $E\rho(C, X)$ is no longer a linear function of $E(X)$. To obtain $E\rho(C, X)$ we must now calculate a separate value of ρ for each of the possible yields (X) for each chosen value of C. And there is no guarantee that the storage rules (R_{n-i}) will be linear.

The nonlinear case can, however, be handled fairly easily by calculating at each step the appropriate values of C for a few discrete values of total supply (S) and connecting the resulting points graphically. Thus, for year $n-1$ we obtain a graphic approximation to R_{n-1}. For year $n-2$, the value of $C_{n-1} = R_{n-1}(C_{n-2} + X_{n-1})$ is read from this graph for each X_{n-1} and each assumed value of C_{n-2}.

For example, suppose we have a logarithmic demand function passing through the point $\rho = \$ 1.50$, $Y = 30$, with elasticity -0.25. The following values of ρ were read from a graph of this demand curve, drawn on log-log paper:

Utilization (Y) (Bushels per Acre)	Market Price (ρ) (Dollars per Bushel)
25	3.05
26	2.62
27	2.25
28	1.97
29	1.72
30	1.50
31	1.32
32	1.17
33	1.04
34	0.92
35	0.81
36	0.76

We take $C_n = 0$ and calculate the rule for year $n-1$ as follows:

$$0.95 E\rho \left[C_{n-1} + X_n - C_n \right] - 0.10 C_{n-1} - \rho (S_{n-1} - C_{n-1}) = 0. \quad (6.6.12)$$

Now, we choose $S_{n-1} = 30$ and find the value of C_{n-1} which satisfies equation (6.6.12). First, try the value $C_{n-1} = 0$. Substituting in the equation we obtain

$$0.95 \, E\rho \left[0 + X_{n-1} \right] = 0.95 \begin{pmatrix} 0.2\rho(25) \\ + 0.5\rho(30) \\ + 0.3\rho(33) \end{pmatrix} = 0.95 \begin{pmatrix} 0.2(3.05) \\ + 0.5(1.50) \\ + 0.3(1.04) \end{pmatrix},$$

where $\rho(25)$, $\rho(30)$ and $\rho(33)$ are read or interpolated from the table on the preceding page. $E\rho(x)$ is $\$ 1.672$, 95 per cent of which is $\$ 1.5884$. The second term in equation (6.6.12) is zero, and the third is $-\rho(30) = -\$ 1.50$. Hence, the terms on the right-hand side of the equation add to $\$ 0.0884$ rather than zero. This means that we must choose $C_{n-1} > 0$ in order to satisfy the equation.

As C_{n-1} increases, the first term becomes a smaller positive number and the second and third terms become "larger" negative numbers. If we choose $C_{n-1}=1$, the right-hand side of the equation becomes $-\$\ 0.433$. Interpolating, it appears that the value of $C_{n-1}=0.2$ will approximately satisfy the equation.

We repeat this process for $S_{n-1}=32$, 34 and 36, obtaining

S_{n-1}	C_{n-1}
30	0.20
32	0.92
34	1.57
36	2.28

We connect these points graphically to obtain rule R_{n-1}. This process is repeated for years $n-2$, $n-3$,...,$n-i$ until some R_{n-i-1} is not appreciably different from R_{n-i}. In this case, graphic rule R_{n-3} looks like a sufficiently close approximation.

If rule R_{n-3} is applied to the same yield sequence as before, the results are as presented in Table 6.6.

TABLE 6.6

Optimal Quantities of Feed Grains Stored Under Graphically Approximated Decision Rule R_{n-3}, Based on a Non-Linear (Log-Linear) Demand Function

Year	(1) Carry-in C_{n-1}	(2) Yield X_n	(3) Total Supply S_n	(4) Carry-out C_n
1	0	33	33.0	1.6
2	1.6	33	34.6	2.3
3	2.3	25	27.3	0
4	0	33	33.0	1.6
5	1.6	30	31.6	1.1
6	1.1	30	31.1	0.8
7	0.8	30	30.8	0.5
8	0.5	25	25.5	0
9	0	25	25.0	0
10	0	30	30.0	0.4

The demand function underlying equation (6.6.11) had the same elasticity at the point of means as does the present logarithmic ρ. But the logarithmic ρ

TABLE 6.7

Corn, Oats and Barley, Corn Equivalent: Optimal Carry-over Rules Under Specified Conditions and Related Quantities[a]

Item	Unit	Rule θ											
		1	2	3	4	5	6	7	8	9	10	11	12
Condition													
Elasticity, η_0		−0.50	−0.50	−0.50	−0.50	−0.30	−0.30	−0.40	−0.50	−0.50	−0.50	−0.50	−0.50
Cost of storage, γ'	Dol.	0.10	0.10	0.04	0.04	0.10	0.04	0.10	0.10	0.10	0.04	0.04	0.10
Discount rate, α		0.95	0.98	0.95	0.98	0.95	0.98	0.95	0.95	0.95	0.98	0.98	0.95
Variability of yields, σ	Bu.	3.03	3.03	3.03	3.03	3.03	3.03	3.03	5.05		5.05		3.03
Optimal carry-over per acre when supply per acre equals													
28	Bu.	0	0	0	0	0	0	0	0	0	0	0	0
29	Bu.	0	0	0	0	0	0.07	0	0	0	0.33	0	0
30	Bu.	0	0	0	0.33	0	0.77	0	0	0	1.03	0	0
31	Bu.	0	0.34	0.46	0.99	0.55	1.50	0.25	0.28	0	1.75	0.46	0.33
32	Bu.	0.55	0.93	1.07	1.69	1.19	2.25	0.84	0.90	0.39	2.48	1.01	0.87
33	Bu.	1.13	1.57	1.74	2.41	1.86	3.02	1.47	1.53	0.90	3.23	1.70	1.43
34	Bu.	1.74	2.22	2.42	3.15	2.57	3.80	2.12	2.18	1.44	3.98	2.41	2.00
35	Bu.	2.38	2.90	3.12	3.90	3.29	4.60	2.80	2.85	1.98	4.75	3.14	2.57
36	Bu.	3.05	3.61	3.85	4.67	4.02	5.40	3.50	3.55	2.66	5.53	3.92	3.16
37	Bu.	3.74	4.32	4.60	5.45	4.77	6.20	4.22	4.27	3.34	6.30	4.64	3.77
38	Bu.	4.44	5.05	5.35	6.24	5.54	7.01	4.95	4.98	4.04	7.10	5.50	4.39
39	Bu.	5.16	5.80	6.12	7.02	6.31	7.83	5.70	5.70	4.73	7.90	6.31	5.03
40	Bu.	5.89	6.55	6.89	7.82	7.09	8.66	6.46	6.43	5.45	8.70	7.14	5.67

179

TABLE 6.7—Continued

41	Bu.	6.63	7.31	7.67	8.63	7.88	9.50	7.22	7.17	6.18	9.50	7.97	6.31
42	Bu.	7.38	8.07	8.46	9.44	8.68	10.34	7.99	7.93	6.95	10.30	8.80	6.95
43	Bu.	8.14	8.84	9.26	10.27	9.48	11.21	8.77	8.70	7.72	11.12	9.65	7.60
44	Bu.	8.89	9.62	10.06	11.10	10.30	12.08	9.56	9.47	8.50	11.93	10.50	8.27
45	Bu.	9.67	10.41	10.87	11.94	11.12	12.95	10.36	10.23	9.27	12.75	11.35	8.93
46	Bu.	10.45	11.20	11.69	12.79	11.94	13.83	11.16	11.02	10.06	13.58	12.22	9.60
47	Bu.	11.23	12.00	12.52	13.64	12.78	14.72	11.98	11.78	10.84	14.40	13.09	10.28
48	Bu.	12.02	12.81	13.35	14.50	13.62	15.61	12.80	12.58	11.65	15.25	13.96	11.00
49	Bu.	12.82	13.63	14.19	15.35	14.47	16.51	13.62	13.37	12.46	16.08	14.83	11.69
50	Bu.	13.63	14.45	15.03	16.22	15.32	17.42	14.45	14.17	13.29	16.93	15.70	12.38
Related quantity per acre													
k[b]	Bu.	31.04	30.42	30.25	29.49	30.11	28.90	30.58	30.54	31.24	28.53	30.17	30.32
C^*[c]	Bu.	0.3	0.5	0.6	1.4	0.7	2.7	0.4	0.4	0	3.0	0	0.4
C^{**}[d]	Bu.	4.1	5.3	5.7	7.8	6.1	10.1	5.0	5.0	–	10.4	–	4.3
As a national aggregate[e]													
C^*	Mil.bu.	242	270	284	396	298	578	256	256	200	620	200	256
C^{**}	Mil.bu.	774	928	998	1,292	1,054	1,614	900	900	–	1,656	–	802

[a] The marginal value function is assumed to be linear for all rules except the last, where constant elasticity is assumed.
[b] The value of S (supply per acre) below which the optimal carry-over (exclusive of minimum working stocks) is zero.
[c] Point of equilibrium or stationarity; if $C_t = C^*$, $E(C_{t+1}) = C^*$.
[d] Stocks in year $t + 2$ resulting from two successive years of high yields (35 bushels per acre), given $C_t = C^*$.
[e] Obtained by multiplying the per acre value by 140 million acres and adding 200 million bushels, the assumed minimum working stocks.

Source: Gustafson [10, pp. 30–31].

leads to maximum stocks of 2.3 bushels per acre rather than 1.831 and average stocks of 0.830 bushels per acre rather than 0.457.

This happens because the prices associated with low utilizations are much higher if ρ is logarithmic, while the prices associated with high utilizations are only moderately higher. Hence, the arithmetic averaging process of taking expectations leads to a greater excess of marginal returns over marginal costs (for a given carry-out level) when the logarithmic demand curve is used.

In the logarithmic case, an increase in yield variability will raise the level of the optimal storage rule. This is not true in the case of a linear demand function.

Table 6.7 from Gustafson [10] shows an array of optimal carry-over rules derived in a careful and detailed manner from historical data on yields of corn and other feed grains.

In 1953, one of the present authors (Fox) drew upon Gustafson's preliminary results in preparing notes for the United States National Agricultural Advisory Commission, which was then reviewing agricultural price support and related policies for the House of Representatives Committee on

TABLE 6.8

Selected Points on Four Optimal Decision Rules Relating (1) Quantities of Corn Stored to (2) the Total Supply of Corn[a]

Total Supply of Corn (Production plus Carry-in stocks)	Carry-out at Year End Should Be			
	Under Freemarket Policy (1)	Under Highstock Policy (2)	Under Moderate-stock Policy (3)	Under Moderate-stock Policy Disregarding Interest Charges (4)
(Mil. bu.)	(Million bushels)			
4,400	690	1,040	880	990
4,000	440	780	600	720
3,600	200	510	370	450
3,200	150	260	180	190
2,800	150	150	150	150

[a] The first three rules reflect different values set on stability of corn utilization by different policy makers (equivalent to assigning different elasticities to the relevant "marginal penalty function" or "marginal social cost" function. Under free market policy, this is simply the market demand curve. The fourth rule modifies the third rule (moderate stock policy) by assuming a zero interest rate as a further encouragement to storage and stabilization of corn utilization.

Agriculture.[5] Several alternative storage rules derived by the above approach are presented in Table 6.8.

The differences between columns 1, 2 and 3 were expressed as follows:

In a severe drought year, such as 1934, 1936 or 1947, the market price of corn seldom reaches as much as twice the price level of an average crop. But some economists feel that this rise in the market price of corn does not reflect the full extent of the harm or social costs resulting from a drought, some of which might have been averted had additional corn been available from storage. It is hard to set a money value on these other costs, but unless this is done, we have no basis for deciding whether a storage program specifically designed for drought emergencies is really worth the ten years or more of storage costs that might accrue before such a drought occurred. And the first 100 million bushels of corn in such an emergency would cover more urgent needs, and have greater per bushel value, than would a second or third hundred million.

Columns 2 and 3 reflect different arbitrary assumptions as to what such social costs might be. The nature of these assumptions is indicated in Table 6.9.

TABLE 6.9

Selected Points on the "Marginal Social Cost" Functions Incorporating Three Different Values Attached (by Different Policy-Makers) to Stability of Corn Utilization[a]

Amount of Corn Available for Current Consumption (Million Bushels)	Value of an Extra Million Bushels or so Rated at		
	(1) Under Free-market Policy (Per Bushel)	(2) Under High-stock Policy (Per Bushel)	(3) Under Moderate-stock Policy (Per Bushel)
2,000	$3.10	$27.50	$6.20
2,500	2.20	7.00	3.20
3,000	1.70	2.30	1.90
3,200	1.50	1.50	1.50
3,500	1.30	0.85	1.15

[a] See also Table 6.8, footnote a.

[5] See *Long-Range Farm Program: Technical Studies by the United States Department of Agriculture Relating to Selected Farm Price Support Proposals.* Congress of the United States 83rd Cong. 2nd sess. Committee Print for the House Committee on Agriculture, 1954. (Karl A. Fox was (anonymous) editor of and a contributor to this document.) See especially pages 51–56.

Column 1 represents approximately the market prices of corn which would be expected under the given supply conditions, But columns 2 and 3 represent values which might be assigned by an administrator trying to allow for additional storage benefits not reflected in the market place.

If this administrator set a very high value on stability of feed supplies, as in column 2, he would rate the social gain of withholding a bushel of corn from a 3.5 billion bushel crop and adding it to a 3.0 billion bushel crop at $ 1.45 per bushel ($ 2.30 minus $ 0.85), enough to cover several years' storage costs. If he set a more moderate value on stability, as in column 3, he would rate the gain on this transaction at $ 0.75 per bushel ($ 1.90 minus $ 1.14), sufficient to cover storage and interest charges (at 5 per cent) for four years. But the market place itself would return only $ 0.40 per bushel on this transaction ($ 1.70 minus $ 1.30), which would cover storage and interest charges for only a couple of years.

Obviously, larger stocks will be carried under the value scale of column 2 than under that of column 3 or column 1. Feed utilization would be almost completely stabilized under the high-stock policy, and so would market prices. But this very fact would reduce the extent to which storage costs might be recovered as a result of market-price advances. This would further limit the profit possibilities for private-storage operations and transfer almost the entire storage load (except for pipeline stocks) to government.

Table 6.10 summarizes the average levels and ranges of carry-over stocks and prices resulting from different storage rules over a synthetic 25-year period. The carry-in at the beginning of the period is set at 1,000 million bushels in each case. The calculations were made by Robert L. Gustafson in 1953 at the request of one of the present authors (Fox).

One feature of the above notes is important for the following section as well. In all storage decision rules except that based on the free-market demand curve, a policy maker is required to state his preferences for a particular degree of consumption and price stabilization. We do not inquire closely into the logical bases for these preferences, but we can interpret them (at least approximately) into coefficients of the objective function. In generating Table 6.10, the different assumed preferences were identified with different elasticities of demand of arithmetically linear demand functions all passing through a common point. This point was fairly close to the corn price and consumption coordinates existing in 1952–1953.

6.3.2. *Linear Demand Functions Imply Quadratic Total Revenue Functions*

Many applications of decision theory assume quadratic preference functions.

TABLE 6.10

Corn: Summary of Carry-over Stocks and Market Prices Resulting from Alternative Storage Policies over a (Hypothetical) 25-year Period

Nature of Policy	Carry-over Stocks			Market Prices		
	Average Level	Range		Average Level	Range	
		Low	High		Low	High
	(1)	(2)	(3)	(4)	(5)	(6)
	(Mil. bu.)				(Per. bu.)	
Free-market	183	150	388	$1.59	$1.15	$2.37
High-stock	564	150	958	1.47	1.30	1.80
Moderate-stock	306	150	592	1.49	1.25	2.16
Implications of moderate-stock policy if interest charges are disregarded	431	150	830	1.48	1.28	2.04

In the corn-storage case, a preference for very limited fluctuations in the price of corn is equivalent to a preference for very limited fluctuations in total revenue from corn—or, more generally in the *area* under whatever market demand curve or subjectively modified counterpart is specified. Gustafson shows [10, pp. 79–80] that solutions based on the marginal value and the total value functions are mathematically equivalent in the present case.

6.3.3. *Optimal Economic Stabilization Policies*

The application of decision theory to problems of macroeconomic policy was first suggested in the 1950's. Theil (1958) was the first to develop the theory and mathematics of this type of application in a comprehensive way, although Frisch and Tinbergen had made earlier contributions. The following exposition is based on a 1965 paper by Theil [24].

We assume a policy maker who controls a major instrument, government expenditure, and is interested in another variable which he does not control, the gross national product (GNP). However, the two variables are connected by the following equation, which represents the mechanism or structure of the economy:

$$y = a + bx, \tag{6.7.1}$$

where y is GNP and x is government expenditure. Our decision maker considers only one year at a time: On January 1 he must decide on the level of government expenditure for the year and the value of GNP is then automatically determined by equation (6.7.1).

Our decision-maker has a preference function, which may be specified in two steps. First, we assume that he has in mind certain "desired values," η for GNP and ε for government expenditure. For example, he may wish a 5 per cent increase in GNP over last year and a 3 per cent increase in government expenditure. In general, $\eta \neq a + b\varepsilon$, but η and ε are only desires and may or may not prove to be precisely and simultaneously attainable. The second step makes the quite special assumption that the policy maker states his preferences for these two targets as a quadratic function of the deviations between the desired and the actual values, say

$$h(x - \varepsilon)^2 + k(y - \eta)^2.$$

He wishes this sum of squares to be a minimum. He may change the signs of h and k to obtain a function to be *maximized*:

$$w(x, y) = - h(x - \varepsilon)^2 - k(y - \eta)^2. \tag{6.7.2}$$

The actual values of x and y are linked by the equation, $y = a + bx$. Our policy maker must, therefore, choose a value of x which will minimize $w(x, y)$ subject to this constraint.

Theil (1958, p. 433) indicates that this is to be done by means of Lagrange multipliers. We do not really need this technique in the present case, but its application will prepare us for more difficult examples in which there are two or more "linear constraints," such as (6.7.1), and in which the welfare function contains at least two (or more) x's and at least two (or more) y's

In the general case, we must consider the expression

$$w(x_1, ..., x_m, y_1, ..., y_n) - \sum_{i=1}^{n} \lambda_i (q_i y_i - \sum_{h=1}^{m} r_{ih} x_h - s_i), \tag{6.7.3}$$

or in matrix notation

$$w(x, y) - \lambda'(Qy - Rx - s), \tag{6.7.4}$$

where λ is a column vector of Lagrange multipliers. Maximization gives us

$$\frac{\partial w}{\partial x_h} + \sum_{i=1}^{n} \lambda_i r_{ih} = 0 \qquad (h = 1, ..., m),$$

$$\frac{\partial w}{\partial y_i} - \lambda_i q_i = 0 \qquad (i = 1, ..., n), \tag{6.7.5}$$

or

$$\frac{\partial w}{\partial x} + R'\lambda = 0,$$

$$\frac{\partial w}{\partial y} - Q'\lambda = 0.$$
(6.7.6)

We can eliminate λ from the last two expressions. From the second,

$$Q^{-1}Q'\lambda = Q^{-1}\frac{\partial w}{\partial y}, \quad \text{or}$$

$$\lambda = Q^{-1}\frac{\partial w}{\partial y}.$$
(6.7.7)

Substituting this value of λ in the first expression, we obtain

$$\frac{\partial w}{\partial x} + R'Q^{-1}\frac{\partial w}{\partial y} = 0..$$
(6.7.8)

In the present example, $Q = Q^{-1} = 1$ and $R' = b$, so (6.7.8) becomes simply:

$$- 2h(x - \varepsilon) + b(1)\left[-2k(y - \eta)\right] = 0.$$

Dividing by 2 and rearranging terms, we write

$$hx - h\varepsilon = - bk(y - \eta).$$

Substituting $a + bx$ for y, we obtain

$$hx - h\varepsilon = - kb(a + bx - \eta);$$
$$hx - h\varepsilon = - kb(a - \eta) - kb^2 x;$$
$$x(h + kb^2) - h\varepsilon = - kb(a - \eta);$$

$$x - \frac{h\varepsilon}{h + kb^2} = \frac{kb(\eta - a)}{h + kb^2}.$$

Subtracting

$$\frac{kb^2\varepsilon}{h + kb^2}$$

from both sides of the equation we obtain

$$x - \varepsilon\frac{(h + kb^2)}{h + kb^2} = \frac{kb(\eta - a) - kb^2\varepsilon}{h + kb^2};$$

hence,

$$x^0 - \varepsilon = \frac{kb}{h + kb^2}(\eta - a - b\varepsilon),$$
(6.7.9)

where we use the superscript 0 to denote the optimal value of x. The left-hand side contains the optimal decision x^0, measured as a deviation from the desired level of government expenditure (ε). The expression in brackets on the right is the difference between the desired level of GNP (η) and the GNP level that would be realized if the decision maker would decide to set government expenditure at its own desired level $(a + b\varepsilon)$.

To quote Theil [24, pp. 4–5]:

> We can, therefore, regard this expression in brackets as a measure for the "inconsistency" of the decision-maker's desires: he wishes ε for his instrument and η for his noncontrolled variable, but if he decides on ε he does not get η, he gets $a + b\varepsilon$, which is in general different. The formula shows that he should *not* decide on ε if η differs from $a + b\varepsilon$. He should decide on x^0. The value ε is the best instrument value when this variable is considered in isolation; but x^0 is optimal in a more complete sense, *viz.*, when account is also taken of the impact of the instrument on the noncontrolled variable as well as of the preferences regarding this variable. The equation shows further that the difference $x^0 - \varepsilon$ is proportional to the "inconsistency" just mentioned. If we take h, k and b all positive (which is certainly realistic), we find that if the desired GNP level (η) is above the level implied by the desired level of government expenditure $(a + b\varepsilon)$, the optimal decision (x^0) is above the latter desire (ε). This is a plausible result. Note finally that the optimum decision is a complete mixture of the coefficients of constraint and preference function. It contains both a and b, belonging to the constraints and ε, η, h, k, belonging to the preference function. This feature, the mixture of preferences on the one hand and the actual mechanism of the economy on the other hand, is something which one will always find in this kind of analysis.

Suppose now that we introduce a dynamic element into this description of the structure of the economy by stating that GNP depends on government expenditure in both the current year, t, and the preceding year, $t-1$:

$$y_t = a_t + b_0 x_t + b_1 x_{t-1}. \tag{6.7.10}$$

We assume also that a includes random disturbances which cause it to take different values from year to year. To extend the problem further we assume that the policy maker is interested in the values of the variables in two consecutive years, year 1 and year 2. The preference function now becomes

$$w(x_1, x_2, y_1, y_2) = -h\left[(x_1 - \varepsilon_1)^2 + (x_2 - \varepsilon_2)^2\right]$$
$$- k\left[(y_1 - \eta_1)^2 + (y_2 - \eta_2)^2\right], \tag{6.7.11}$$

where ε_1 and ε_2 are the desired levels of government expenditure in year 1 and year 2, respectively, and η_1 and η_2 are the consecutive desired levels of GNP. We may write the "linear constraint" or equation connecting y_t with x_t and x_{t-1} separately for each of the two years:

$$y_1 = a_1 + b_0 x_1 + b_1 x_0, \tag{6.7.12}$$

$$y_2 = a_2 + b_0 x_2 + b_1 x_1. \tag{6.7.13}$$

The inconsistencies of the decision maker's desired values of GNP and government expenditures in the two years are:

$$\text{Year 1:} \quad i_1 = \eta_1 - (a_1 + b_0 \varepsilon_1 + b_1 x_0), \tag{6.7.14}$$

$$\text{Year 2:} \quad i_2 = \eta_2 - (a_2 + b_0 \varepsilon_2 + b_1 \varepsilon_1). \tag{6.7.15}$$

(The value of x_0, government expenditure in the year preceding year 1, is a known number at the time the contemplated decision is to be made.)

We may now substitute the elements of our problem into matrix equation (6.7.4):

$$w(x, y) = \text{equation (6.7.11); or}$$

$$w(x, y) = [(x_1 - \varepsilon_1)(y_1 - \eta_1)] \begin{bmatrix} -h & 0 \\ 0 & -k \end{bmatrix} \begin{bmatrix} x_1 - \varepsilon_1 \\ y_1 - \eta_1 \end{bmatrix}$$

$$+ [(x_2 - \varepsilon_2)(y_2 - \eta_2)] \begin{bmatrix} -h & 0 \\ 0 & -k \end{bmatrix} \begin{bmatrix} x_2 - \varepsilon_2 \\ y_2 - \eta_2 \end{bmatrix},$$

$$Q = \begin{bmatrix} 1 & 0 \\ 0 & 1 \end{bmatrix}; \quad x = \begin{bmatrix} x_1 \\ x_2 \end{bmatrix}; \quad y = \begin{bmatrix} y_1 \\ y_2 \end{bmatrix}; \quad s = \begin{bmatrix} a_1 + b_1 x_0 \\ a_2 \end{bmatrix}; \quad R = \begin{bmatrix} b_0 & 0 \\ b_1 & b_0 \end{bmatrix}.$$

The complete matrix expression to be maximized is:

$$[(x_1 - \varepsilon_1)(y_1 - \eta_1)] \begin{bmatrix} -h & 0 \\ 0 & -k \end{bmatrix} \begin{bmatrix} x_1 - \varepsilon_1 \\ y_1 - \eta_1 \end{bmatrix}$$

$$+ [(x_2 - \varepsilon_2)(y_2 - \eta_2)] \begin{bmatrix} -h & 0 \\ 0 & -k \end{bmatrix} \begin{bmatrix} x_2 - \varepsilon_2 \\ y_2 - \eta_2 \end{bmatrix} + [\lambda_1 \quad \lambda_2] \begin{bmatrix} 1 & 0 \\ 0 & 1 \end{bmatrix} \begin{bmatrix} y_1 \\ y_2 \end{bmatrix}$$

$$+ [\lambda_1 \quad \lambda_2] \begin{bmatrix} b_0 & 0 \\ b_1 & b_0 \end{bmatrix} \begin{bmatrix} x_1 \\ x_2 \end{bmatrix} + [\lambda_1 \quad \lambda_2] \begin{bmatrix} a_1 + b_1 x_0 \\ a_2 \end{bmatrix}. \tag{6.7.16}$$

As the algebra will otherwise be somewhat cumbersome, we must specify what particular arrangement of the final results will have the clearest economic meaning. It seems most useful to seek a solution in the form of equation (6.7.9), which expresses the deviations of the optimal values of the instrument variables from their desired values as functions of the "inconsistencies" between the desired values of the instrument variables and the desired values of the noncontrolled variables:

$$x_1^0 - \varepsilon_1 = f_1(i_1, i_2; h, k; b_0, b_1) \tag{6.7.17}$$
$$x_2^0 - \varepsilon_2 = f_2(i_1, i_2; h, k; b_0, b_1). \tag{6.7.18}$$

The coefficients of the preference function will appear in ratio form, h/k, as it is their *relative* rather than their absolute sizes which prove to be significant for the decision. The multiplicative coefficients b_0 and b_1 from the equation describing the structure of the economy will appear in the solution, but the additive or constant terms $(a_1 + b_1 x_0)$ and a_2 will not, as they do not affect the optimal deviations $x_2^0 - \varepsilon_2$.

The required partial derivatives of matrix equation (6.7.16) are:

$$\frac{\partial w}{\partial x_1} + [\lambda_1 b_0 + \lambda_2 b_1] = -2h(x_1 - \varepsilon_1) + \lambda_1 b_0 + \lambda_2 b_1 = 0,$$

$$\frac{\partial w}{\partial x_2} + [\lambda_1 0 + \lambda_2 b_0] = -2h(x_2 - \varepsilon_2) + \lambda_2 b_0 = 0,$$

$$\frac{\partial w}{\partial y_1} - \lambda_1 = -2k(y_1 - \eta_1) - \lambda_1 = 0,$$

$$\frac{\partial w}{\partial y_2} - \lambda_2 = -2k(y_2 - \eta_2) - \lambda_2 = 0.$$

From the third and fourth equations we obtain at once $\lambda_1 = -2k(y_1 - \eta_1)$ and $\lambda_2 = -2k(y_2 - \eta_2)$. Substituting these values in the first and second equations we obtain:

$$-2h(x_1 - \varepsilon_1) - 2k[(y_1 - \eta_1)b_0 + (y_2 - \eta_2)b_1] = 0,$$
$$-2h(x_2 - \varepsilon_2) - 2k(y_2 - \eta_2)b_0 = 0.$$

We may now eliminate y_1 and y_2 from the equations by substituting for them the right-hand terms of equations (6.7.12) and (6.7.13), respectively; the results are

$$\frac{h}{k}(x_1 - \varepsilon_1) = -[(a_1 + b_0 x_1 + b_1 x_0 - \eta_1)b_0 + (a_2 + b_0 x_2 + b_1 x_1 - \eta_2)b_1],$$

$$\frac{h}{k}(x_2 - \varepsilon_2) = -[(a_2 + b_0 x_2 + b_1 x_1 - \eta_2)b_0].$$

Rearranging to bring all x_1 and x_2 terms to the left sides of the equations, we have

$$\left(\frac{h}{k} + b_0^2 + b_1^2\right)x_1 - \frac{h}{k}\varepsilon_1 + b_0b_1x_2 = -\left[(a_1 + b_1x_0 - \eta_1)b_0 + (a_2 - \eta_2)b_1\right],$$

$$b_0b_1x_1 + \left(\frac{h}{k} + b_0^2\right)x_2 - \frac{h}{k}\varepsilon_2 = -\left[(a_2 - \eta_2)b_0\right].$$

As we wish to obtain solutions in the forms $(x_1 - \varepsilon_1)$ and $(x_2 - \varepsilon_2)$ rather than simply x_1 and x_2, we add the following terms in ε_1 and ε_2 to both sides of the first equation (thus, of course, preserving the equality):

$$- (b_0^2 + b_1^2)\varepsilon_1 - b_0b_1\varepsilon_2.$$

In the second equation, we add to both sides,

$$- b_0b_1\varepsilon_1 - b_0^2\varepsilon_2.$$

Our two equations now become

$$\left(\frac{h}{k} + b_0^2 + b_1^2\right)(x_1 - \varepsilon_1) + b_0b_1(x_2 - \varepsilon_2) = -\left[(a_1 + b_0\varepsilon_1 + b_1x_0 - \eta_1)b_0\right.$$
$$\left. + (a_2 + b_0\varepsilon_2 + b_1\varepsilon_1 - \eta_2)b_1\right] = b_0i_1 + b_1i_2,$$

and

$$b_0b_1(x_1 - \varepsilon_1) + \left(\frac{h}{k} + b_0^2\right)(x_2 - \varepsilon_2)$$
$$= -\left[(a_2 + b_0\varepsilon_2 + b_1\varepsilon_1 - \eta_2)b_0\right] = b_0i_2.$$

The coefficients of $(x_1 - \varepsilon_1)$ and $(x_2 - \varepsilon_2)$ form the determinant

$$A = \begin{vmatrix} \left(\dfrac{h}{k} + b_0^2 + b_1^2\right) & b_0b_1 \\ b_0b_1 & \left(\dfrac{h}{k} + b_0^2\right) \end{vmatrix}.$$

This can be evaluated as

$$A = \left(\frac{h}{k} + b_0^2\right)^2 + b_1^2\left(\frac{h}{k}\right) + b_0^2b_1^2 - b_0^2b_1^2, \text{ or}$$
$$A = (b_0^2 + h/k)^2 + b_1^2(h/k).$$

By Cramer's rule, A constitutes the denominator of the solutions for both $(x_1 - \varepsilon_1)$ and $(x_2 - \varepsilon_2)$.

Also by Cramer's rule, the numerator of the solution for $(x_1 - \varepsilon_1)$ is

$$N_1 = \begin{vmatrix} (b_0 i_1 + b_1 i_2) & b_0 b_1 \\ b_0 i_2 & \left(b_0^2 + \dfrac{h}{k}\right) \end{vmatrix}.$$

This can be evaluated as

$$N_1 = \left(b_0^2 + \frac{h}{k}\right)b_0 i_1 + \left(b_0^2 + \frac{h}{k}\right)b_1 i_2 - b_0^2 b_1 i_2 = \left(b_0^2 + \frac{h}{k}\right)b_0 i_1 + b_1 \left(\frac{h}{k}\right)i_2.$$

The numerator of the solution for $(x_2 - \varepsilon_2)$ is

$$N_2 = \begin{vmatrix} \left(\dfrac{h}{k} + b_0^2 + b_1^2\right) & (b_0 i_1 + b_1 i_2) \\ b_0 b_1 & b_0 i_2 \end{vmatrix},$$

which can be evaluated as

$$N_2 = \left(b_0^2 + \frac{h}{k} + b_1^2\right)b_0 i_2 - b_0^2 b_1 i_1 - b_0 b_1^2 i_2 = -b_0^2 b_1 i_1 + \left(b_0^2 + \frac{h}{k}\right)b_0 i_2.$$

Hence, the policy maker's optimal solutions for the values of government expenditures in year 1 and year 2 are as follows:

$$x_1^0 - \varepsilon_1 = \frac{(b_0^2 + h/k)\,b_0 i_1 + b_1\,(h/k)\,i_2}{(b_0^2 + h(k)^2 + b_1^2\,(h/k)} \tag{6.7.19}$$

$$x_2^0 - \varepsilon_2 = \frac{-b_0^2 b_1 i_1 + (b_0^2 + h/k)\,b_0 i_2}{(b_0^2 + h/k)^2 + b_1^2\,(h/k)}. \tag{6.7.20}$$

As h, k, b_0 and b_1 are all constants (specifying the preference function of the policy maker and the structure of the economy), the deviations $(x_1^0 - \varepsilon_1)$ and $(x_2^0 - \varepsilon_2)$ are linear functions of the "inconsistencies," i_1 and i_2.

If there are no inconsistencies between the policy maker's desired values of GNP and government expenditures *in either year*, $x_1^0 = \varepsilon_1$ and $x_2^0 = \varepsilon_2$. This is indeed a happy result for the policy maker. But note that if an inconsistency exists in *either* year, there will be discrepancies between the desired values and the "optimal solution values" of government expenditures in *both* years. For i_1, the inconsistency between the values of GNP and government expenditures desired in year 1 appears in the solutions for both years, as does i_2, the inconsistency in year 2. Hence, there is a definite interaction between the decision processes of the two successive years [24, p. 9].

Up to this point, we have not introduced uncertainty. This will be discussed at length in Chapter 9.

Theil next assumes that the constant a becomes a stochastic variable. The implications of this new assumption concerning a may be seen in equation (7.9). The optimal value of x, x^0, now becomes a linear function of a, a being a random variable. The desired values η and ε, the coefficients k and h of the policy maker's preference function and b are all known numbers.

We may rewrite equation (6.7.9) in the form

$$x^0 - \varepsilon = \frac{b(\eta - b\varepsilon)}{b^2 + h/k} - \left(\frac{b}{b^2 + h/k}\right)a \, . \tag{6.7.21}$$

The first term on the right-hand side of equation (6.7.21) is a constant. The second term states that a one-unit increase in a will result in a decrease of

$$\left(\frac{b}{b^2 + h/k}\right)$$

units in $x^0 - \varepsilon$. As the coefficients b, h and k are all positive, if the value of a proves to be larger than usual (for example, because private investment is unusually high) the optimal value of x^0 will be *smaller* than usual; the economy will need less assistance than usual from the government expenditures instrument. Conversely, if a is lower than usual, x^0 will be higher than usual; a low level of private investment would have to be compensated in part by a higher than usual level of government expenditure to approach the policy maker's desired level of GNP.

We now see that equation (6.7.21) is a *linear decision rule*, similar to the optimal carry-over decision rules of the previous section. For any value of a, the equation permits us to calculate a value of x^0 which will be the best possible value, given the policy maker's preference function and the value of b.

At the beginning of a year, the policy maker does not *know* what value of a will actually emerge. Hence, equation (6.7.21) must be modified if it is to become an optimal linear decision rule under conditions of uncertainty. Under specified assumptions, Theil indicates that the proper modification is to maximize the *expected value* of the preference function subject to the constraint that $y = a + bx$, the constraint now being stochastic in the sense that a is a random variable. Theil then states the "certainty equivalence theorem," which applies to the particular situation (such as the present example) in which the policy maker's preference function is a quadratic form. The policy maker's optimal decision in this case is precisely the same as the decision that would be made if all uncertainty were to be disregarded right at the beginning by replacing the random coefficient a by its own expected value. (Remember that an "expected value" is essentially the arithmetic mean of a probability distribution.) The only change we must make in equation (6.7.21) is to insert an expectation operator, E, in front of a, as in equation (6.7.22).

$$x^0 - \varepsilon = \frac{b(\eta - b\varepsilon)}{b^2 + h/k} - \left(\frac{b}{b^2 + h/k}\right) Ea . \qquad (6.7.22)$$

As Theil points out, the certainty equivalence theorem holds only under certain conditions. One is that the variance of a should be independent of the instrument x. Another is that the preference function should indeed be quadratic. It is not necessary to believe that the preference functions of policy makers are necessarily and precisely quadratic forms; we may simply use quadratic forms as reasonable approximations to the true preference function over limited ranges on either side of the desired values of the instrument variables. The justification for using quadratic preference functions, says Theil, is analogous to that for using minimum-variance estimation in statistics and mean-square error minimization in engineering, which derived their popularity mainly from considerations of mathematical convenience. A more profound argument in favor of quadratic preference functions is that this form allows us to have decreasing "marginal rates of substitution" between the various instrument variables and noncontrolled variables.

Theil's use of expected values in the macroeconomic policy case is precisely analogous to Gustafson's use of expected values of feed grain yields in deriving optimal carry-over rules. In effect, the expected-value operator, E, permitted us to act in year $n-1$ as though we expected the yield in year n to be equal to the arithmetic mean of the probability distribution of yields.

6.4. Concluding Remarks

In Chapter 1 we commented that the success of mathematical methods in operations research and management science was no doubt hastening the time at which these methods would gain some prestige among "policy men" in the traditional sense and eventually among laymen. In the present chapter we find that the mathematical structure of the corn storage decision model is essentially identical with that of Theil's macroeconomic decision model! Both models make use of quadratic preference functions and of the certainty equivalence theorem.

It is clear that the flow of mathematically similar models across traditional boundaries between disciplines will increase rather than diminish in the years immediately ahead.

REFERENCES

[1] ANDERSON, T. W. *Introduction to Multivariate Statistical Analysis.* New York: John Wiley & Sons, 1958.

[2] ARROW, K. J., KARLIN, S., and SCARF, H. *Studies in the Mathematical Theory of Inventory and Production.* Stanford, Calif.: Stanford University Press, 1958.

[3] BARNARD, G. A. "Control Charts and Stochastic Processes," *Journal of the Royal Statistical Society*, Series B, XXI (1959), 239.

[4] BELLMAN, R., and DREYFUS, S. E. *Applied Dynamic Programming.* Princeton, N.J.: Princeton University Press, 1962.

[5] BOX, G. E. P., and JENKINS, G. M. "Some Statistical Aspects of Adaptive Optimization and Control," *Journal of Royal Statistical Society*, Series B, XXIV (1962), 297.

[6] CHRIST, C. "On Econometric Models of the U.S. Economy," in *Income and Wealth*, Series 6 (International Association for Research on Income and Wealth). Edited by M. Gilbert and R. Stone. London: Bowes and Bowes, 1957.

[7] COX, D. R. "Prediction by Exponentially Weighted Moving Average," *Journal of Royal Statistical Society*, Series B, XXIII (1961), 414.

[8] DVORETZKY, A., KIEFER, J., and WOLFOWITZ, J. "The Inventory Problem," *Econometrica*, XX (April and July, 1952), 187–222, 450–466.

[9] GUSTAFSON, ROBERT L. *Optimal Carry-over Rules for Grains.* Hectographed report prepared at University of Chicago under contract with the U.S. Department of Agriculture, January 31, 1954.

[10] ——. *Carry-over Levels for Grains.* Washington, D.C.: U.S. Department of Agriculture Technical Bulletin No. 1178, October, 1958.

[11] HOLT, C., *et al. Planning Production, Inventories and Work Force.* Englewood Cliffs, N.J.: Prentice-Hall, 1960.

[12] HOOPER, J. W., and ZELLNER, A. "The Error of Forecast for Multi-variate Regression Models," *Econometrica*, XXIX, (October, 1961), 544–555.

[13] JOHNSTON, J. *Econometric Methods.* New York: McGraw-Hill Book Co., 1963.

[14] LADERMAN, J., LITTAUER, S., and WEISS, L. "The Inventory Problems," *Journal of American Statistical Association*, XXXXVIII (1953), 717–773.

[15] LIPS, J., and SCHOUTEN, D. "The Reliability of the Policy Used by the Central Planning Bureau of the Netherlands," in *Income and Wealth*, Series 6 (International Association for Research on Income and Wealth). Edited by M. Gilbert and R. Stone. London: Bowes and Bowes, 1957.

[16] LUCE, R. D., and RAIFFA, H. *Games and Decisions.* New York: John Wiley & Sons, 1957.

[17] MUTH, J. F. "Optimal Properties of Exponentially Weighted Forecasts," *Journal of American Statistical Association*, LV (1960), 299.

[18] QUANDT, R. E. "The Estimation of the Parameters of a Linear Regression System Obeying Two Separate Regimes," *Journal of American Statistical Association*, LIII (1958), 873.

[19] Roos, C. "Survey of Economic Forecasting Techniques," *Econometrica*, XXIII (October, 1955), 363–395.

[20] Roy, S. N. *Some Aspects of Multi-variate Analysis*. New York: John Wiley & Sons, 1957.

[21] Theil, H. "Specification Errors and the Estimation of Economic Relationships," *Review of International Statistical Institute*, XXV (1957), 41.

[22] ——. *Economic Forecasts and Policy*. Amsterdam: North-Holland Publishing Co., 1958; 2nd Revised edition 1961.

[23] ——. *Optimal Decision Rules for Government and Industry*. Amsterdam: North-Holland Publishing Co., 1964.

[24] ——. "Linear Decision Rules for Macrodynamic Policy Problems," in *Quantitative Planning of Economic Policy*. Edited by B. G. Hickman, Washington, D.C.: The Brookings Institution, 1965, Chap. 2.

[25] ——, and Kloek, T. "The Statistics of Systems of Simultaneous Economic Relationships," *Bulletin of International Statistical Institute*, XXXVII (1960), 345.

[26] Van den Beld, C. A. "Short-term Planning Experiences in the Netherlands," in *Quantitative Planning of Economic Policy*. Edited by B. G. Hickman. Washington, D.C.: The Brookings Institution, 1965, Chap. 6.

[27] Zabel, E. "Efficient Accumulation of Capital for the Firm," *Econometrica*, XXXI, (January–April, 1963), 131–150.

[28] Zellner, A. "Econometric Estimation with Temporally Dependent Disturbance Terms," *International Economic Review*, II (1961), 164.

[29] ——. "Decision Rules for Economic Forecasting," *Econometrica*, XXXI (January–April, 1963), 111–130.

Chapter 7

PROGRAMMING ASPECTS OF ECONOMIC
POLICY MODELS

There are different levels at which the programming restrictions play an important role in the quantitative economic policy models. In the Tinbergen approach to economic policy, programming constraints are explicitly introduced through the boundary conditions. To the extent that the optimal solution of a policy model containing an econometric system of equations (rather than inequalities) could be changed through variations in the boundary conditions (and even the preference function), they help to relax the rigidity of an equational model. A second important use of programming is in the area of sensitivity analysis. To what extent is the optimal solution of a model sensitive to slight variations in the coefficients of the problem? In particular, one might analyze the sensitivity of the optimal solution or, in other words, the choice of the optimal instrument vector, when the weights in the preference function are allowed to vary within certain ranges. Alternatively, one could start out with a set of alternative solutions (i.e., targets and/or instruments) as do van Eijk and Sandee [43, p. 1], and present them to the central policy makers so as to estimate a set of reasonable weights for the policy makers' preference function.[1]

However, the most important use of programming in a policy model is that it permits, through duality theorems, the development of a set of "shadow prices" as implicit evaluators or "efficiency indicators."

The programming methods have, however, their own limitations. The most important limitation perhaps is that the optimal solutions cannot, in general, be stated analytically in terms of the parameters of the model. Also, the nonlinear programming methods are as a rule very complicated, both computationally and in terms of sensitivity of their own solutions to vari-

---

[1] See in this connection the discussion of Chenery and Bruno's model in Chapter 13, where the selection of one program among a set of alternatives reveals in a sense the implicit (or explicit) welfare function of the policy maker.

ations of the other parameters of the problem. There are some methods [16], however, by which a class of well-defined types of nonlinear programming may be reduced to a set of equivalent linear programming problems. More-over, for policy models involving economic development and planning in less developed countries, linearity in programming is sometimes a limitation. As a first approximation, it may be tried in those cases where some plausible reasons, a priori or otherwise, are available to justify the linearity assumption (for instance, the linear homogeneous type of production function of the Harrod-Domar models may in some cases be more appropriate than the nonlinear production function, such as the Cobb-Douglas type, appearing in the Solow-type growth model). As Chenery [8, pp. 20–21] has emphasized in the context of less developed economies:

> The principal obstacle to the adoption of the programming solution is the lack of information and the high cost of increasing it. Given the existing lack of data, the mathematical programming formulation does not correspond to the planner's view of his problem. The simplex method and other procedures for solving programming models de-termine the optimum choice among specified activities of production, importing, investment, etc. Only a few of these potential activities can be described by the planner with any accuracy, however, and the avail-able engineering and economic research facilities only permit him to extend his knowledge to a limited degree in formulating a given pro-gramme.[2]

This suggests the need for combining programming techniques with other tools, such as partial models or even individual project-mix analyses, in an over-all policy question. An example of the latter is development planning, which is essentially dynamic in its characteristics and which can, in general, be separated into different phases. Tinbergen [39] has characterized this type of practical problem as follows:

> ... we are in favor of a method of development programming to be called *planning in stages*, which stands at variance with the more am-bitious method of establishing one very complicated model for a simultaneous solution of all problems. In a general way, planning in stages is an attempt first to determine a few of the most important ("strategic") variables and later to determine others, thus coming to greater detail and gradually covering a longer period.[3]

---

[2] Reprinted by permission of St. Martin's Press, Inc., The Macmillan Company of Canada, Ltd., and Macmillan & Co., Ltd.

[3] From *Mathematical Models of Economic Growth* by Tinbergen and Bos, Copyright © 1962, by McGraw-Hill Book Company, and reprinted by their permission.

For policy models with shorter time horizons, linear or even linearized versions of nonlinear programming may be useful in enlarging the domain of feasible solutions whenever it is reasonable to interpret the equational relations of an exact model as weak inequalities. Moreover, certain techniques are now available which allow a considerable degree of flexibility to the otherwise rigid structure of linear programming. Some of these recent techniques which are useful for quantitative policy models include, very broadly:

(a) General methods of sensitivity analysis, which range from stochastic linear programming to the formulation of stability criteria for the set of optimal solutions.

(b) Recursive and multistage programming, which allow variations of optimum policy at different stages.

(c) Methods which characterize, although not completely, optimizing situations where instead of a scalar objective function a vector function is optimized.

Before we consider some of these recent techniques, it may be instructive to refer to some illustrative examples, where programming techniques are explicitly applied to provide answers to questions of optimum economic policy.

7.1. The Specification of Optimum Economic Policy

A most interesting application of programming techniques has been made by van Eijk and Sandee[4] to quantify an optimum economic policy on the basis of a twenty-seven-equation model of the Central Planning Bureau in the Netherlands.[5] Some interesting features of this application are worth pointing out:

(a) It is perhaps the first attempt of its kind to derive an explicit welfare function by "imaginary interviewing" of the policy makers.

> In principle the coefficients of a welfare function can be estimated only by interviewing the policy makers. They would have to answer a series of questions about the marginal rates of substitution for all target variables and in different situations. For the time being, however, such a genuine interviewing of policy makers is impossible ... In short, the presumable outcome of a real interview must be forecast.

---

[4] Some of the quotations to follow are drawn from van Eijk and Sandee [43].

[5] Some new elements have been introduced in the more recent Dutch planning model of 1961, compared with the model of 1955. For a discussion of the recent model of 1961, see Fox and Thorbecke [15]. See also Chapter 14, section 14.2.1, of the present book.

(b) The welfare function utilized in this study is continuous and partitioned into "separable facets," i.e., it is a function in which the partial derivatives depend only on the variable concerned and not on the other ones.

> To take an example: if the price level and investment are targets, the product of these variables does not appear in the function. The partial derivative of welfare with respect to the price level depends only on the price level and not on investment. This implies that in the linear approximation it is possible to pass from one interval to another by changing only one coefficient each time.

This method of linearized (partitioned) facets was used partly to gain computational advantage in applying Frisch's multiplex method of programming, which, unlike the simplex method, specifies a movement from the initial boundary point to the interior of the feasible region for locating the optimal point.

(c) It also shows the need for analyzing a fixed-target policy model in terms of the general framework of a flexible target model. Further, it may be seen how in shorter periods linearizing approximations affect the nature of the optimal solution, which may be either local or global.

To quote van Eijk and Sandee [43]:

> To determine the optimum economic policy for a future period, data for that period must be estimated. Once these have been obtained, ... a forecast can be made by means of the usual model, based on the data and on the assumption of "no change" in economic policy. A provisional survey of that forecast will usually indicate the general direction of a required change in policy. In an interval around such a provisional programme, a linear welfare function can be determined. Linear programming can then be applied to find the optimum programme within the limits of the interval and within the technically possible ranges of the instruments.
>
> The programme thus found need not be the absolute optimum, as other facets of the welfare function may offer better possibilities. This can be systematically explored by determining the welfare function in each of the neighbouring facets, and the optimum policy connected with that function in the facets concerned."

The following six targets were identified as the variables in which the Dutch government as a central policy maker is interested:

(i)   Maximum real income
(ii)   High and stable level of employment, a
(iii) Balance of payments equilibrium, $E - M$
(iv)   High level of investment, i

(v) Stable price level to maintain real income of fixed income earners

(vi) A reasonable income distribution pattern.

After a careful consideration of alternatives and imaginary interviewing of policy makers at different levels such as representatives of trade unions, employers and the government, it was "decided"[6] that against a 100 million guilder balance of payments surplus could be set 400 million of government expenditure (x_G), 500 million of investment (i), 2 per cent increase of real wages (l_R), 1.33 per cent decrease in consumer prices (p_c), 0.5 per cent increase in employment (a) or 200 million of government surplus (S_G). From these marginal rates of substitution, the welfare function in its linear form can be easily written as

$$\phi = 1.0\,(E - M) + 0.25\,x_G + 0.20\,i + 5.0\,l_R - 7.5\,p_c + 0.20\,a \\ + 0.50\,S_G + \text{constant},$$

subject to the limits, i.e., both upper and lower limits, within which the targets (and implicitly the instruments) could be varied.[7]

Two comments may be added to this example. First, it is not dynamic in the essential sense that the solutions would evolve sequentially over time as in a difference equation system. Second, the impact of variations in the bounds of the variables or the parameters (e.g., net prices, resource vector or the coefficient matrix of inequalities) on the optimal value of the objective function is not analyzed, and so the stability characteristics of the solution of the van Eijk-Sandee model are not known.

An alternative approach to the specification of the welfare function by "imaginary interviewing" or reasonable estimates is to assume that the optimizing behavior may be of the satisficing type [7, 36]. In the satisficing case one would be interested in keeping the value of the welfare function W close to a desired value W^* (or alternatively, keeping W equal to or above a reasonable or minimum level). In this case the specification of a loss function is required to indicate how far the deviation of W from W^* will be tolerated. Once this loss function is specified, the selection of the optimum subset of the instrument variables must involve minimization of this loss function in some sense. An interesting taxonomic application of this approach has been made by van den Bogaard and Theil [42], using Klein's six-equation model I [21] for the U.S., which consists of a consumption

---

[6] Analytically, this method has a resemblance to Waugh [45].

[7] For a concrete application of a similar type of welfare function to land redistribution in an underdeveloped country, see Chapter 15, section 15.1.

function, an investment function and a demand-for-labor equation, as well as three identities. It is assumed that starting from 1933, the beginning year of the depression, the government is interested in bringing the depression to an end by 1936. More specifically the following targets were selected: first, immediate welfare assumed to be measured by consumption C; second, future welfare assumed to be measured by net investment I; third, a fair distribution of income assumed to be measured by the ratio of profits (π) to the private wage bill (W_1). Denoting the desired values by asterisks, these targets are then quantitatively specified as

$$C^*_{1936} = C_{1929}(1 + \alpha)^7, \quad \alpha = \text{annual rate of population growth},$$
$$= 0.01 \text{ (estimated)},$$
$$I^*_{1936} = 0.1\, C^*_{1936},$$
$$D^*_{1936} = W_1 - 2\pi = 0.$$

The desired values for the intermediate years are computed by linear interpolation between the actual values in 1932 and the corresponding desired values in 1936:

$$C^*_{1932+i} = C_{1932} + \frac{i}{4}(C^*_{1936} - C_{1932}),$$

$$I^*_{1932+i} = I_{1932} + \frac{i}{4}(I^*_{1936} - I_{1932}) \qquad i = 1, 2, 3, 4,$$

$$D^*_{1932+i} = D_{1932} + \frac{i}{4}(D^*_{1936} - D_{1932}).$$

In addition to including targets in the welfare function, instruments also appear. The desired values of the three instruments (the government wage bill W_2, business taxes T and the government expenditure on goods and services G) were obtained—somewhat arbitrarily—by least-squares linear regressions of W_2, T and G on time during the period 1920–1932:

$$W_2 = 3.531 + 0.215\,(t - 1926),$$
$$T = 5.723 + 0.239\,(t - 1926),$$
$$G = 7.431 + 0.430\,(t - 1926),$$

and by extrapolating these regressions to the period 1933–1936. Since it is impossible in general to realize all desired values exactly by an appropriate choice of the instrument variables, satisfying the six-equation Klein model, it was decided to minimize the differences between actual and desired values in a certain sense, i.e., by forming a quadratic loss function

$$E \sum_{i=1}^{4} (P_i + Q_i) = \text{minimum},$$

where

$$Q_i = (C_{1932+i} - C^*_{1932+i})^2 + (I_{1932+i} - I^*_{1932+i})^2$$
$$+ (D_{1932+i} - D^*_{1932+i})^2 \qquad i = 1, 2, 3, 4,$$
$$P_i = \{(W_2)_{1932+i} - (W_2^*)_{1932+i}\}^2 + (T_{1932+i} - T^*_{1932+i})^2$$
$$+ (G_{1932+i} - G^*_{1932+i})^2,$$

E = expectation operator.

Here the expected value of the sum of squares of the differences between the desired and the actual values is minimized, because the econometric model (Klein's linear difference equation, estimated for 1933–1936) contains stochastic components called residual disturbances. The optimal choice of the instruments follows in this case the certainty-equivalence theorem mentioned earlier.

This example shows the alternative consequences of different policy decisions regarding the instrument variables, particularly when there is scope for estimation error in the econometric model. As van den Bogaard and Theil have mentioned:

> In reality, of course, one will never have at his disposal an equation system fitted over a period which includes the strategy period. The best one can do is to use a system which is estimated from data which refer to a period just before the strategy period. It seems intuitively obvious that such a model lags behind the events in the case of gradual structural changes, so that the deviations between model predictions and reality should be expected to be larger on the average on that account. [42; p. 165].

7.2. An Application to a Domar-type Growth Model

In the aggregative Domar-type model of economic growth, the proportional rate of growth of income is specified by an over-all saving-income ratio and the capital coefficient, which are assumed to be known parameters in the model. In applications to development planning [25, 29], this type of model is generally extended to a multisector framework, each sector having its own saving and capital coefficient. In such cases, it may not be appropriate to consider the sectoral coefficients as sure magnitudes because of the element of uncertainty involved. The latter may be due to the interplay of random forces, the different levels of adjustment in different sectors or even the subjective nature of the extraneous estimates of sectoral parameters. Our object below is to examine the optimum solutions in the intersectoral Domar-type model of growth, when some or all of its parameters are statistically random in the sense of having some known probability distribution functions for a given period of time.

The aggregative Domar model [13] may be specified in its simplest form by its final reduced equation in two related ways

$$G = \Delta Y / Y = \alpha \beta \theta \qquad (7.1)$$

and

$$\Delta Y = I \beta \theta \qquad 0 \le \theta \le 1, \qquad (7.2)$$

where I, Y and G denote investment, income and its proportional rate of growth, respectively, and α, β, θ stand for, respectively, the saving ratio, output-capital ratio and the capacity-utilization ratio.

Now consider the intersectoral generalization of equation (7.1) such that each of the aggregative coefficients α, β and θ may be conceived as a weighted average over different sectors ($i = 1, 2, ..., n$).

$$G = \left(\sum_i \mu_i \alpha_i \right) \left(\sum_i \lambda_i \beta_i \right) \left(\sum_i \eta_i \theta_i \right) = \alpha \beta \theta, \qquad (7.3)$$

where

$$\sum_i \mu_i = \sum_i \lambda_i = \sum_i \eta_i = 1.$$

It is easy to check that sectoral weights are specified by

$$\mu_i = \frac{Y_i}{Y}; \quad \lambda_i = I_i / I; \quad \eta_i = \Delta P_i / \Delta P,$$

where P denotes the productive capacity created by investment. As a successive approximation method, we consider now that β alone is random (hence the β_i's) while α and θ are constants.

We now assume that the objective of the central policy maker is growth with stability. More specifically, we assume that the preference function of the policy maker has two facets, one involving maximization of the expected value of national income and the other involving minimization of the standard deviation of the investment component of national income (e.g., public investment has to offset partly the fluctuations in private investment). So long as reinvestment sets the tempo of growth of national income, the second aspect specifies the need for a steady growth on the average in the investment component itself. Assuming, for simplicity, that the β_i's are mutually independently distributed, our social welfare function Z_2 now becomes a linear combination of the expected value and variance of the rate of growth G, i.e.,

$$Z_2 = w_1 \sum_{i=1}^{3} \lambda_i \bar{\beta}_i + w_2 \sum_{i=1}^{3} \lambda_i^2 v_i \qquad (7.4)$$

where we assume three sectors; w_1, w_2 denote fixed weights (w_1, w_2 may be assumed to absorb the constants $\alpha\theta$), the bar over a variable denotes its expected value and v_i denotes the variance of β_i. The instrument variables are λ_1, λ_2, λ_3, of which two will be independent if we impose the further condition that all investment must be strictly allocated i.e.,

$$\lambda_1 + \lambda_2 + \lambda_3 = 1, \quad \lambda_i \geq 0, \quad i = 1, 2, 3$$

otherwise

$$\lambda_1 + \lambda_2 + \lambda_3 \leq 1, \quad \lambda_i \geq 0.$$

It is easy to show that if w_1 is a nonnegative constant but w_2 is strictly positive (negative) the preference function Z_2 is strictly convex (concave) in the allocation ratio λ_i. Assuming that all investment must be allocated, the optimal values of the instrument variables are easily computed as follows:

$$\lambda_1 = \frac{w_1 \bar{\beta}_1}{2 v_1 w_2} + \frac{v_2 v_3}{\sum\limits_{\substack{i,j \\ i \neq j}} v_i v_j} - \frac{w_1 (v_2 v_3 \bar{\beta}_1 + v_3 v_1 \bar{\beta}_2 + v_1 v_2 \bar{\beta}_3)}{2 v_1 w_2 \sum\limits_{\substack{i,j \\ i \neq j}} v_i v_j},$$

$$\lambda_2 = \frac{w_1 \bar{\beta}_2}{2 v_2 w_2} + \frac{v_1 v_3}{\sum\limits_{\substack{i,j \\ i \neq j}} v_i v_j} - \frac{w_1 (v_2 v_3 \bar{\beta}_1 + v_3 v_1 \bar{\beta}_2 + v_1 v_2 \bar{\beta}_3)}{2 v_2 w_2 \sum\limits_{\substack{i,j \\ i \neq j}} v_i v_j}, \qquad (7.5)$$

$$\lambda_3 = \frac{w_1 \bar{\beta}_3}{2 v_3 w_2} + \frac{v_1 v_2}{\sum\limits_{\substack{i,j \\ i \neq j}} v_i v_j} - \frac{w_1 (v_2 v_3 \bar{\beta}_1 + v_3 v_1 \bar{\beta}_2 + v_1 v_2 \bar{\beta}_3)}{2 v_3 w_2 \sum\limits_{\substack{i,j \\ i \neq j}} v_i v_j},$$

$$q = \left(\sum_{\substack{i,j \\ i \neq j}} v_i v_j \right)^{-1} \{ 2 w_2 (v_1 v_2 v_3) - w_1 (v_2 v_3 \bar{\beta}_1 + v_1 v_3 \bar{\beta}_2 + v_1 v_2 \bar{\beta}_3) \},$$

where q is the usual Lagrange multiplier and we assume that these values of λ_i are feasible, i.e., $\lambda_i \geq 0$. When the fixed weights w_1, w_2 representing marginal rates of substitution are such that $w_1 = 0$ and $w_2 = 1$, the optimal values of the decision variables λ_i in (7.5) are reduced to

$$\lambda_1 = \frac{v_2 v_3}{\sum\limits_{\substack{i,j \\ i \neq j}} v_i v_j} ; \quad \lambda_2 = \frac{v_1 v_3}{\sum\limits_{\substack{i,j \\ i \neq j}} v_i v_j} ; \quad \lambda_3 = \frac{v_1 v_2}{\sum\limits_{\substack{i,j \\ i \neq j}} v_i v_j} ; \tag{7.6}$$

$$q = -2(v_1 v_2 v_3)/\{v_1 v_2 + v_2 v_3 + v_3 v_1\} .$$

It may be seen that our objective function (7.4) is more general than that of van den Bogaard and Theil in that the variance term is explicitly introduced to make it a case of convex (concave) programming. When we allow the slack inequality

$$\sum_{i=1}^{3} \lambda_i \leq 1,$$

and define $\lambda_4 \geq 0$ as the slack variable so that

$$\lambda_1 + \lambda_2 + \lambda_3 + \lambda_4 = 1, \quad \lambda_i \geq 0, \quad i = 1, 2, 3, 4,$$

we may select three instruments out of four in four ways, and we test each possible selection for feasibility, $\lambda_i \geq 0$. In a nondegenerate case (i.e., the case when three instruments are known to enter into the optimal solution), that selection out of four would be optimal, which optimizes the preference function Z_2 in equation (7.4).

Now consider the model (7.2) from the viewpoint of a policy maker interested in optimal selection of the decision variables λ_i, when for simplicity it is assumed that $\theta = 1$, full capacity growth and investment (I) follows an exponential time path given by

$$I = I_0 e^{pt} \tag{7.7}$$

such that the coefficient p in equation (7.7) is stochastic. So long as private investment is a significant component of total investment, as is perhaps true for most less developed economies, the stochastic variations of p may be interpreted as resulting from uncoordinated decisions of individual entrepreneurs and other elements of uncertainty in a market economy. Also, in a less developed economy, the misdirection of investment due to inadequate knowledge and information may be relatively large. Assume for simplicity that the coefficient p is statistically independent of the random variables β_i. Then the variance of income change can be approximately computed as

$$\text{Var } \Delta Y = I_0^2 \left\{ e^{2\bar{p}t} s \left(\sum_i \lambda_i^2 v_i \right) + e^{2\bar{p}t} s \left(\sum_i \lambda_i \bar{\beta}_i \right)^2 + m^2 \left(\sum_i \lambda_i^2 v_i \right) \right\}, \tag{7.8}$$

where $m = $ expectation of e^{pt},
    $s = $ variance of p.

Minimizing the variance given in (7.8) subject to $\sum_i \lambda_i = 1$ for $i = 1, 2, 3$ would specify the optimal levels of the decision variables λ_i as follows

$$\begin{pmatrix} \lambda_1 \\ \lambda_2 \\ \lambda_3 \\ \dfrac{q}{2I_0^2} \end{pmatrix} = R^{-1} \begin{pmatrix} 0 \\ 0 \\ 0 \\ 1 \end{pmatrix},$$

where the matrix R denotes

$$R = \begin{bmatrix} e^{2\bar{p}t}s(v_1 + \bar{\beta}_1^2) & \bar{\beta}_1\bar{\beta}_2 se^{2\bar{p}t} & \bar{\beta}_1\bar{\beta}_3 se^{2\bar{p}t} & 1 \\ \quad + m^2 v_1, & & & \\ \bar{\beta}_2\bar{\beta}_1 se^{2\bar{p}t}, & e^{2\bar{p}t}s(v_2 + \bar{\beta}_2^2) & \bar{\beta}_2\bar{\beta}_3 se^{2\bar{p}t}, & 1 \\ & \quad + m^2 v_2, & & \\ \bar{\beta}_3\bar{\beta}_1 se^{2\bar{p}t} & \bar{\beta}_3\bar{\beta}_2 se^{2\bar{p}t}, & e^{2\bar{p}t}s(v_3 + \bar{\beta}_3^2) & 1 \\ & & \quad + m^2 v_3, & \\ 1 & 1 & 1 & 0 \end{bmatrix}$$

A simplification of this result is possible, if we use the approximation $e^{pt} \simeq (1 + pt)$ and consider only two sectors $i = 1, 2$. In this case, the optimal levels of the decision variables λ_i under the restriction $\sum_i \lambda_i = 1$ are given by

$$\lambda_1 = \frac{v_2\{t^2 s + (1 + \bar{p}t)^2\} - \bar{\beta}_2 t^2 s(\bar{\beta}_1 - \bar{\beta}_2)}{(v_1 + v_2)\{t^2 s + (1 + \bar{p}t)^2\} + t^2 s(\bar{\beta}_1 - \bar{\beta}_2)^2}, \qquad (7.9)$$
$$\lambda_2 = 1 - \lambda_1.$$

In general, however, λ_1 given by (7.9) would be a function of the time period t, which enters explicitly into the planning horizon of the policy maker. Keeping the simplifying assumptions of system (7.9) but considering a more general objective function, we may write

$$Z_3 = w_1 E(\Delta Y) + w_2(-\operatorname{Var}\Delta Y), \qquad (7.10)$$

where E is the expectation operator and w_1, w_2 are fixed weights. Maximization of Z_3 in (7.10) subject to $\lambda_1 + \lambda_2 = 1$ gives, after a little computation, the optimal λ_1 as

$$\lambda_1 = Q^{-1}\left[\frac{w_1(1 + \bar{p}t)(\bar{\beta}_1 - \bar{\beta}_2)}{2w_2 I_0} + N\right], \qquad (7.11)$$

where Q and N denote, respectively, the denominator and numerator of the solution for λ_1 in (7.9) above. It is easy to check that the solution (7.11) reduces to (7.9) when the weights are such that $w_1 = 0$ and $w_2 = 1$. In other cases, the marginal rate of substitution between the two parameters of the distribution (mean and variance) would determine the optimal time path of the decision variable λ_1 when it is feasible.

Now we consider a third type of interpretation of the model (7.1), where for convenience it is assumed that α and θ are known constants while $\beta = \sum_i \lambda_i \beta_i$ is still stochastic. Let us assume now that the probability that at time t the random variable assumes the value β_i is given by an exponential distribution for fixed t,

$$f(\beta_i, t) = e^{-\beta_i/h_{i0}(t)}/h_{i0}(t) \qquad 0 \le \beta_i \le \infty. \tag{7.12}$$

We assume that the mean of the distribution $E\beta_i(t)$ follows a known exponential time trend in the course of development[8]

$$\bar{\beta}_i(t) = h_{i0}(t) = a_i - b_i e^{-c_i t}, \tag{7.13}$$

where a_i, b_i, c_i are known constants. Assuming two sectors $i = 1$, 2 for simplicity and that the β_i's are mutually independently distributed, the objective function may now be specified as

$$Z_4 = \alpha\theta w_1 (\lambda_1 \bar{\beta}_1 + \lambda_2 \bar{\beta}_2) - \alpha^2 \theta^2 w_2 (\lambda_1^2 v_1 + \lambda_2^2 v_2),$$

where v_i denotes the variance of β_i. Maximization of this objective function subject to $\lambda_1 + \lambda_2 = 1$ easily gives the time path for optimal $\lambda_1(t)$ as

$$\lambda_1(t) = (h_{10}^2 + h_{20}^2)^{-1} \left\{ h_{20}^2 + \frac{w_1(h_{10} - h_{20})}{2\alpha\theta w_2} \right\}, \tag{7.14}$$

where h_{10}, h_{20} being functions of t are given in (7.13). It is easy to specify the optimum time path for $\lambda_1(t)$ by considering the initial and asymptotic conditions

$$\lambda_1(t = 0) = [(a_1 - b_1)^2 + (a_2 - b_2)^2]^{-1}$$
$$\left[(a_2 - b_2)^2 + \frac{w_1(a_1 - a_2 - b_1 + b_2)}{2\alpha\theta w_2} \right], \tag{7.15}$$
$$\lambda_1(t = \infty) = (a_1^2 + a_2^2)^{-1} \left\{ a_2^2 + \frac{w_1(a_1 - a_2)}{2\alpha\theta w_2} \right\}.$$

---

[8] A somewhat different type of trend has been estimated for the long-run U.S. data by Klein and Kosobud [22].

We assume that the feasibility conditions $\lambda_i \geq 0$ are not violated for all relevant t. Otherwise, obvious modifications are to be made. By following similar methods, formulas for the general case (7.3) could be developed for specifying the optimal levels of the decision variables λ_i, μ_i and η_i, provided the probability distribution functions for β_i, α_i and θ_i could be specified.

As an empirical application of the model (7.4) outlined before, involving the quantitative determination of the optimum diversification of investment between sectors, we consider the simplest case first, i.e., $w_1 = 0$, $w_2 = 1$, which appears nonetheless very important because of the relative neglect of the stability objective (e.g., minimizing instability through diversification) in the conventional literature on investment allocation. Taking the data from Indian planning statistics [35], the reformulation of our problem is:

Minimize Var $I = 0.1637\, y_1^2 + 0.1435\, y_2^2 + 2\rho\,(0.1533)\, y_1 y_2$
subject to
$$3.6645\, y_1 + 2.6852\, y_2 \leq 104 \text{ (capital)} \qquad (7.16)$$
$$0.0002\, y_1 + 0.0004\, y_2 \leq 0.014 \text{ (labor)}$$
$$y_1 \geq 0, \quad y_2 \geq 0,$$

where y_1, y_2 denote the increase of net output of investment goods and consumption goods over the third plan period, I stands for the reinvestment component and ρ for the population correlation coefficient between the marginal investment output ratios that are assumed to be random. The instrument variables are the proportions of capital and labor allocated to the two activities. The coefficient matrix and other elements are taken from Indian planning statistics. So long as the self-sustaining nature of the growth process depends on maintaining a steady rate of reinvestment out of increased incomes, the objective specified above would help to secure a stable rate of growth of national income. Denoting the above objective function as $R(y_1, y_2) = -\text{Var } I$ and assuming that $\rho = 0$ and in a less developed economy capital is a more binding resource than labor, we may specify the solutions by using the Lagrange multiplier q:

$$
\begin{bmatrix} y_1 \\ y_2 \\ -q \end{bmatrix} =
\begin{bmatrix} 1.1602 & -1.5833 & 0.1692 \\ -1.5833 & 2.1608 & 0.1415 \\ -0.1692 & -0.1415 & 0.0151 \end{bmatrix}
\begin{bmatrix} 0 \\ 0 \\ 104 \end{bmatrix}.
$$

The optimal solutions here turn out to be $y_1 = 17.5980$, $y_2 = 14.7163$ (in billion rupees) and $q = -1.5727$. When checked with the first two restrictions of (7.16), this set of solutions is found to satisfy the capital restriction exactly, and it leaves some unused labor (0.0035 billion man years). To test for local optimality, the Kuhn-Tucker [23] condition may be easily applied Denoting the imputed values of the two resources, capital and labor, by g_1 and g_2, it is apparent that $g_2 = 0$, since there is some unused labor. Using the requirement that the marginal revenue product $(\partial R/\partial y_1)$ must equal its imputed cost at the optimal point, we derive

$$g_1 = 1.5727 = -q_1 \text{ (Lagrange Multiplier)}.$$

Hence, the optimality is necessarily defined by the Kuhn-Tucker theorem. Its sufficiency is easily checked by verifying the solution: $y_1 = 17.5980$, $y_2 = 14.7163$, $g_1 = 1.5727$ and $g_2 = 0$. The absolute value of $R(y_1, y_2)$ is given by 81.7825.

By following the same method, but considering a more general objective function as

$$Z_5 = w_1(y_1 + y_2) - w_2(\text{Var } I)^{\frac{1}{2}}, \tag{7.17}$$

where Var I is given in (7.16) and w_1, w_2 are fixed nonnegative weights such that $w_1 + w_2 = 1$, one may compute the set of optimal values Z_3 for different values of ρ and w_1, w_2. Such a computation is presented in Table 7.1. This shows the interesting result that for certain values of ρ the objectives of minimizing $(\text{Var } I)^{\frac{1}{2}}$ and maximizing $(y_1 + y_2)$ are competitive even when $w_1 = w_2$. The maximum value of Z_5 is reached, however, at 35.9651 for $w_1 = 1$, $w_2 = 0$ and $\rho = -1.0$.

TABLE 7.1

Optimal Values of Z_5 for Different Weights

		Values of Z_5 for different ρ-values								
w_1	w_2	-1.0	-0.75	-0.50	-0.25	0.0	0.25	0.50	0.75	1.0
1.00	0.00	35.96	32.84	32.72	32.56	32.31	31.92	31.14	28.99	0
0.75	0.25	24.82	23.49	22.93	22.99	21.97	21.42	20.63	18.89	0
0.50	0.50	13.68	14.14	13.15	13.42	11.64	10.93	10.11	8.79	0
0.25	0.75	2.53	4.80	3.36	3.86	1.30	0.43	0	0	0
		Values of $(\text{Var } I)^{\frac{1}{2}}$ for different ρ								
		8.61	4.55	6.42	5.70	9.04	10.06	10.92	11.41	0
		Values of $(y_1 + y_2)$ for different ρ								
		35.96	32.84	32.72	32.56	32.31	31.91	31.14	28.99	0

This result could obviously be generalized to allow for dynamic changes in the individual coefficients, for more than two economic sectors, and for cases of discrete programming. One interesting extension is to consider the effect of selecting alternative values for the instrument variables, e.g., the allocation ratios. We define the instrument or decision variables $u_{ij} \geq 0$ as the proportion of the i-th resource (capital or labor) devoted to the j-th activity with the added condition $\Sigma_j u_{ij} = 1$, which implies full utilization of the available resource. The matrix u_{ij} containing decision variables specifies a type of approach [33] known as the "active" approach of programming, contrasted with the passive approach where the implications of alternative choices of these variables are not at all analyzed. One type of specification of an active approach is to maximize the objective function Z_5 given in (7.17) subject to the following model, which now incorporates specifically the instrument variables:

$$3.6645\, y_1 \leq 104\, u_{11}\ (\text{capital})$$
$$0.0002\, y_1 \leq 0.014\, u_{21}\ (\text{labor})$$
$$2.6852\, y_2 \leq 104\, u_{12}\ (\text{capital}) \qquad (7.18)$$
$$0.0004\, y_2 \leq 0.014\, u_{22}\ (\text{labor})$$
$$u_{11} + u_{12} = 1, \quad u_{21} + u_{22} = 1, \quad u_{ij} \geq 0,$$

where Var I in the preference function (7.17) is estimated by

$$\text{Var } I = 0.1637\, y_1^2 + 0.1435\, y_2^2 + 2(0.1407)(0.1533)\, y_1 y_2,$$

with an unbiased estimate for $\hat{\rho} = 0.1407$; w_1 and w_2 are nonnegative weights assigned by the policy maker. Restricting ourselves to cases when w_1, w_2 can take discrete rank-values 1, 2, 3 and u_{11}, u_{21} the following values 0, 0.25, 0.50, 0.75 and 1.0, we compute the alternative solutions in Table 7.2.

It is easily seen that the maximal value of $Z_5 = 90.2177$ is obtained with $u_{11} = 0.50$, $u_{21} = 0.25$ when $w_1 = 3$ and $w_2 = 1$. When more weight is given to the variance, e.g., $w_1 = 1$, $w_2 = 2$, the allocation ratios $u_{11} = 0.50$, $u_{21} = 0.25$ specify a maximum value $Z_5 = 13.6071$, whereas the ratios $u_{11} = 0.2243$ and $u_{21} = 0.1136$ which maximize $(y_1 + y_2)$ alone give a lower value of $Z_5 = 12.3770$.

7.3. Recursive Linear Programming Methods in Economic Policy Models

We will now discuss some methods of linear programming which are very useful for economic policy because they incorporate a recursive relation at one stage or other. Recursiveness here implies a relation of precedence, e.g.,

TABLE 7.2

Optimal Values of Z_5 Under the Active Approach ($\hat{\rho} = 0.1407$)

u_{21}	w_1	w_2	u_{11}				
			0.00	0.25	0.50	0.75	1.00
	1	1	21.0570	18.0439	12.0301	6.0154	0.0
	2	1	54.9553	47.0924	31.3958	15.6982	0.0
0.00	3	1	88.8536	76.1409	50.7614	25.3811	0.0
	1	2	8.2156	7.0394	4.6946	2.3480	0.0
	1	3	0.0	0.0	0.0	0.0	0.0
	1	1	15.7936	22.0882	23.4864	16.5141	8.3352
	2	1	41.2173	54.6070	56.8520	40.1970	22.3352
0.25	3	1	66.6410	87.1259	90.2177	63.8798	36.3352
	1	2	6.1634	11.6574	13.6071	9.3455	2.6704
	1	3	0.0	1.2267	3.7278	2.1768	0.0
	1	1	10.5289	16.6517	21.9438	21.1433	16.6686
	2	1	27.4780	40.6960	53.0832	52.1116	44.6686
0.50	3	1	44.4272	64.7403	84.2227	83.0793	72.6686
	1	2	4.1086	9.2592	12.7481	11.3183	5.3372
	1	3	0.0	1.8666	3.5525	1.4934	0.0
	1	1	5.2652	10.9719	15.7036	20.1543	16.6686
	2	1	13.7397	26.5416	38.3684	49.9142	44.6686
0.75	3	1	22.2143	42.1113	61.0333	79.6742	72.6686
	1	2	2.0558	6.3741	8.7422	10.5485	5.3372
	1	3	0.0	1.7762	1.7809	0.9428	0.0
	1	1	0.0	4.2241	8.4483	12.6721	16.9613
	2	1	0.0	11.3192	22.6386	33.9575	45.3419
1.00	3	1	0.0	18.4144	36.8289	55.2430	73.7225
	1	2	0.0	1.3530	2.7064	4.0587	5.5420
	1	3	0.0	0.0	0.0	0.0	0.0

we may define a sequence of linear programming problems [12] in which the objective function, the constraint matrix and the right-hand side parameters depend upon the primal and/or dual solution variables of the *preceding* linear programming problems in the sequence. Alternatively, we may define a sequence of stages, at each of which a linear programming problem is defined with larger and larger dimensions as we go along the higher and higher stages in the sequence, such that a (lower) block-triangular coefficient matrix may be associated with the entire multistage linear programming problem [10].

The use and implications of recursive structure in a simultaneous-equation model have already beeen discussed in Chapters 2, 3 and 4, and some of these carry over partly to programming models with obvious modifications. Two further comments may be added here. First, a recursive framework of programming permits a wide range of flexibility in the selection of the optimal mix of instruments from one stage to another in a given sequence, e.g., suitable "corrections" or modifications can be made through information available up to the preceding stage; sometimes exogenous information can be combined at some stage with other endogenous information. Second, it emphasizes the need for orienting optimal policy making to the characteristics of each stage in relation to preceding stages, e.g., it may suggest a switchover from one mix of instrument variables to another mix, if the latter has more stabilizing impact at a certain stage and the objective is to minimize the fluctuations, say, of national income and its different components.

Let us consider simple cases, one each for the above two types of recursive linear programming problems.[9] Using the conventional notation, let us write an ordinary linear programming problem in vector-matrix form as

$$\text{Maximize } z(t) = c'x(t) \qquad (7.19.1)$$

under the conditions

$$Ax(t) \leqq b(t) \qquad x: n.1 \qquad (7.19.2)$$
$$c: n.1$$

$$x(t) \geq 0, \text{ all } t \qquad A: m.n \qquad (7.19.3)$$
$$b: m.1 .$$

Here t defines a sequence, e.g., time, $x(t)$ and c are column vectors with m elements, A is an m by n matrix, b is a column vector with m elements and prime denotes transposition. Also some of the elements of the vector $x(t)$ may be target variables and some may be instrument variables.

Now suppose the resource vector $b(t)$ is related to past expectations and performance in the following way

$$b(t) = \hat{\lambda}Ax^*(t-1) + u(t), \qquad (7.19.4)$$

where $\hat{\lambda}$ is a diagonal matrix with m diagonal elements $\lambda_1, \lambda_2, ..., \lambda_m$ and $u(t)$ is a column vector with m components $u_1(t), u_2(t), ..., u_m(t)$ that are

---

[9] The case of multi-stage linear programming will be presented in Chapter 9.

"exogenous" variables (i.e., are not generated recursively). It may also contain instrument variables. The asterisk over a variable indicates its optimum value during that stage, i.e., $x^*(t-1)$ is an optimum vector at $t-1$.

To start the sequence of solutions we find initial conditions from which a given year's data can be derived and from which succeeding solutions may proceed. For example, if the solution vector $x^*(0)$ were known at $t=0$, we could compute $b(t)$ from the relation (7.19.4). Then from the system (7.19.1) through (7.19.3), we could solve for the optimal values of $x^*(1)$, when the vector $x^*(t)$ contains m activities selected out of $(m+n)$, of which m (activities) are "slack". Knowing $x^*(1)$, one could again compute $b(2)$ from (7.19.4), plug into the system (7.19.1) through (7.19.3) to compute the optimal values $x(2)$, and so on. Two cases may be distinguished:

(i) First, suppose at time $t-1$, the vector $x^*(t-1)$ with m components is found to be optimal. Further, with the value of $b(t)$ known from (7.19.4), let the "optimal basic" solution of the linear programming system (7.19.1) through (7.19.3) be given by

$$A^*x^*(t) = b(t) = \hat{\lambda}Ax^*(t-1) + u(t), \qquad (7.20)$$

where A^* is the m by m coefficient matrix associated with the optimal basis. In the first case, the m activities optimally selected at time t are identical with those selected at time $(t-1)$. In this case the system (7.20) represents m difference equations in precisely m unknowns. The stability characteristics of such a system can be determined from the nature of its characteristic roots.

(ii) Second, the $m_1 < m$ elements of the vector $x^*(t)$ may be the same as for the optimal vector $x^*(t-1)$ in year $t-1$, but $(m-m_1)$ elements may be different. The common part (m_1) may be the core part which is chosen in each of the two years, but the remaining part is optimally reshuffled by the optimizing principle in each year. In this case the system (7.20) may be over or underdetermined, i.e., it may contain more or fewer unknowns than equations. One might have to introduce additional restrictions to close the model in some other way.

7.4. An Application to Stabilization Policy

We have already touched upon stabilization policies in the framework of a Phillips-type model (see Chapter 2). We will now further generalize the aggregative Phillips model in several other respects. Other stabilization models are presented in detail in Chapter 8.

First, the multiplier-accelerator coefficients, which are assumed to be fixed constants in the Phillips model, are as a matter of fact subject to monetary constraints, apart from the capacity ceiling and floor restrictions. The interaction of the alternative monetary factors and multiplier-accelerator parameters and the related questions of steady growth of real income with a relatively stable price level may considerably modify, if not alter, the simple feedback-type decision rules of stabilization policy of the Phillips model. Second, government expenditure, which is a control variable in stabilization policy, is usually subject to an upper limit if not also to a lower limit. Hence, in such situations we are interested in that optimal path of the control variable which satisfies the limiting constraints, i.e., of all time paths of the control variable satisfying the upper and possibly lower limits we seek that one which minimizes in some sense the downward shifts in demand and the fluctuations around the desired trend of full employment. Third, the fact that government expenditure, which is the control variable in the Phillips type of stabilization policy, is not always an exogenous variable has interesting implications for an endogenous stabilization policy; this is because the tax component of a given government expenditure policy has alternative patterns of built-in flexibility, according as it is treated endogenously or exogenously.

From an operational standpoint it is useful to consider a difference equation version of the Phillips-type stabilization policies, since empirical data are always discrete, e.g., quarterly or annual data, and the incidence of time lags of adjustment can be more realistically appraised. It is likewise important to make a distinction between the monetary factors and the non-monetary factors in any analysis of disequilibrium, since the fluctuations generated by the usual multiplier-accelerator coefficients are, as has been shown by Hicks [20], Minsky [26], Smith [37] and others [38], greatly conditioned and constrained by the monetary policies and tendencies.

Measuring all variables in real terms, we denote at time t the aggregate variables as follows: private consumption C_t; private investment I_t; net total government spending (on consumption and investment, etc.) G_t; total direct tax payments T_t; other autonomous parts of national income such as net exports A_t; total demand for money L_t; total supply of money M_t; the rate of interest R_t and total national income Y_t. Since we will be concerned with a short-run framework of stabilization policy, we assume that a typical Keynesian model with all its assumptions is a valid description of economic reality. The short-term model may then be presented as follows:

$$C_t = c_0 + c_1(Y_{t-1} - T_{t-1}), \quad (c_1 > 0) \tag{7.21.1}$$

$$I_t = v_0 + v_1(Y_{t-1} - Y_{t-2}) - v_2 R_{t-1}, \quad (v_1, v_2 > 0) \tag{7.21.2}$$

$$Y_t^d = C_t + I_t + G_t + A_t \text{ (definition)}, \tag{7.21.3}$$

$$Y_t = Y_{t-1} - \lambda(Y_{t-1} - Y_{t-1}^d), \text{ if } Y_{t-1} \neq Y_{t-1}^d \text{ (disequilibrium)}, \ (\lambda > 0) \tag{7.21.4.1}$$

$$Y_t = Y_t^d, \text{ if } Y_{t-1} = Y_{t-1}^d \text{ (equilibrium)}, \tag{7.21.4.2}$$

$$L_t = b_0 + b_1 Y_t - b_2 R_t; \quad (b_1 > 0, b_2 > 0), \tag{7.21.5}$$

$$R_t = R_{t-1} - m(M_{t-1} - L_{t-1}), \text{ if } M_{t-1} \neq L_{t-1} \text{ (disequilibrium)} \tag{7.21.6.1}$$

$$R_t = R, \text{ if } M_{t-1} = L_{t-1} \text{ (equilibrium)}, \quad (m > 0). \tag{7.21.6.2}$$

We have, further, the boundary conditions on all our variables, which may be generally written as

$$x_{\min} \leq x_t \leq x_{\max} \text{ for all } t, \tag{7.21.7}$$

where x stands for any variable listed in the above equations and the two-point boundaries are assumed to be predetermined either by real long-run factors or by the practical institutional constraints. For instance, if x is the rate of interest R_t, equation (7.21.7) may imply the liquidity trap where $R_t = R_{\min}$ replaces equation (7.21.6.1) as a disequilibrium relation, since beyond this point increasing money supply is assumed to have no effect on reducing the rate of interest. Similarly, if real income reaches the capacity ceiling $(Y_t = Y_{\max})$, we assume that the excess demand function (7.21.4) has no effect in increasing output and income in real terms, although price changes are still admissible. Further, if x_t is government expenditure G_t, equation (7.21.7) denotes the lower and upper limits or feasibility constraints, which must be institutionally (or practically) satisfied by any policy of public expenditure. For most of our discussions we assume that the boundary conditions given in (7.21.7) are not violated by our relevant variables.

From the standpoint of policy, our system has three instrument variables or control variables, G_t, T_t and M_t, which can be manipulated by the central policy maker to achieve a given objective, such as full employment over time. This objective may be specified by

$$Y_t^* = Y^0(1 + g)^t, \quad g > 0, \tag{7.21.8}$$

where the constants Y^0, g are predetermined and Y_t^* specifies the time path of growth desired by the central policy maker. If the observed growth path Y_t is below the desired path Y_t^* (which is the most important case in the real world and especially so in some underdeveloped countries that are trying to develop through national economic planning either directly or indirectly), the policy problem is how to vary the three instruments G_t, M_t and T_t over time in some optimum manner, so that none of the feasibility constraints (7.21.7) are violated. Of course, other interpretations are possible, particularly when the desired path is determined by a literal projection of past trends.

At this stage it may be necessary to introduce a decision function or preference function of the policy maker, indicating his sensitivity to deviations such as $(Y_t - Y_t^*)$. For example, a simple quadratic preference function (U) may be specified as

$$U = (Y_t - Y_t^*)^2, \qquad (7.21.9.1)$$

where u_1, u_2, u_3 are nonnegative constants, one for each type of policy. Combining equations (7.21.10.1) through (7.21.10.3) and denoting the constant $\lambda(c_0 + v_0 + A - v_2 R)$ by B_1, we get

$$Y_t = \theta_1 Y_{t-1} + \theta_2 Y_{t-2} - \theta_3 Y_{t-3} + B_1, \qquad (7.21.10.4)$$

where

$$\theta_1 = 1 - \lambda - \lambda(u_1 + u_2 + u_3),$$
$$\theta_2 = \lambda(c_1 + v_1 - c_1 n_1 + u_2 - u_3),$$
$$\theta_3 = \lambda(v_1 + u_3).$$

Since $\theta_3 > 0$, the characteristic roots of the homogeneous system corresponding to (7.21.10.4) can all belong to the interior of the unit circle in the complex plane if and only if

$$\theta_2 < 0, \quad \begin{vmatrix} -\theta_2 & 1 \\ \theta_3 & -\theta_1 \end{vmatrix} = \theta_1 \theta_2 - \theta_3 > 0.$$

As the range of variation of the control variable is subject to an upper limit, it would be difficult in general to fulfill the above conditions. In other words, the stabilization policy (7.21.10.3) would in general have the effect of imparting a cyclical explosive tendency to the time series of real income.

Now consider an alternative case in which equations of equilibrium (7.21.4.2) and (7.21.6.2) hold for both the money market and the output market:

$$U = \sum_{t=0}^{n} (Y_t - Y_t^*)^2 \qquad (7.21.9.2)$$

where $t = 0, 1, 2, \ldots, n$ is the planning horizon of the policy maker.

Considering the first case, i.e., equation (7.21.8), we may analyze alternative stabilization policies through either equilibrium relations or disequilibrium relations incorporating either explicitly or implicitly the monetary factors. For example, assume a condition of equilibrium in the money market ($R_t = R$) so that equation (7.21.6.2) holds and, further, assume that equation (7.21.4.1) holds in the output market. By combining the relations (7.21.1), (7.21.2), (7.21.3), (7.21.4.1) and (7.21.6.2) we get a third-order difference equation

$$Y_t = (1 - \lambda) Y_{t-1} + \lambda (c_1 + v_1) Y_{t-2} - \lambda v_1 Y_{t-3} - \lambda v_2 R - \lambda c_1 T_{t-2}$$
$$+ \lambda (G_{t-1} + A_{t-1}) + (\lambda c_0 + \lambda v_0). \qquad (7.21.10.1)$$

For simplicity, we assume further that A_{t-1} is a constant A for all t and that the variable T_t is endogenously determined in a proportional manner

$$T_t = n_1 Y_t, \qquad 0 < n_1 < 1. \qquad (7.21.10.2)$$

Now consider the three types of variations of the control variable G_t which are analogous to the proportional, derivative and integral policies of the Phillips model

$$G_t = - u_1 Y_t - u_2 (Y_t - Y_{t-1}) - u_3 (Y_t + Y_{t-1} + Y_{t-2}). \qquad (7.21.10.3)$$

Making other assumptions, as in case 1, i.e., equations (7.21.10.2) and (7.21.10.3) we obtain,

$$Y_t = k_1 Y_{t-1} - k_2 Y_{t-2} + B_2, \qquad (7.21.11.1)$$

where the constants k_1, k_2, B_2 are

$$k_1 = (1 + u_1 + u_2 + u_3)^{-1} [c_1 (1 - n_1) + v_1 + u_2 - u_3],$$
$$k_2 = (1 + u_1 + u_2 + u_3)^{-1} [v_1 + u_3],$$
$$B_2 = (1 + u_1 + u_2 + u_3)^{-1} [c_0 + v_0 + A - v_2 R].$$

In this case the characteristic equation is of second order and the critical point at which the system shifts from stability to instability (i.e., fluctuations that are oscillatory) is given by

$$k_2 \geq (k_1/2)^2. \qquad (7.21.11.2)$$

To the extent that the tax rate (n_1) can be varied as an anticyclical instrument along with the above-mentioned expenditure policies, it may sometimes be feasible to enforce the equality relation in (7.21.11.2), in which case the stabilization policy itself will be nonoscillatory. This is admittedly not a general result holding in all situations. However, this is a slightly more general result than that of Smith [37], who considered only a proportional money supply policy to infer that the model with monetary factors is more likely to be unstable than the simple Hicksian model. In case the coefficients n_1, u_1, u_2, u_3 are rigidly fixed because the instrument variables T_t, G_t, M_t are treated endogenously, it is more likely that the strict inequality will hold in equation (7.21.11.2).

Other cases could similarly be considered, taking different combinations of equilibrium and disequilibrium relations in the output and money markets; likewise, the incidence of alternative stabilization policies could be analyzed in terms of G_t, T_t and M_t.

The fact that government expenditure policy cannot be changed very abruptly calls for building into the policy a time-recursive relation. Phillips has done this by distinguishing between the planned government expenditure and the realized actual amount in such a way that plans are continually revised recursively in terms of the deviations between the planned and realized magnitudes in the last period.

We might indicate here another type of recursiveness which is independent of the distinction between planned and realized expenditure. For this purpose we present the equations in our earlier model in a slightly modified form as follows:

$$\text{maximize } Z = w_1 C_t + w_2 I_t + w_3 G_t, \tag{7.22.12.1}$$

under the conditions

$$C_t \leqq c_0 + c_1 (Y_{t-1} - T_{t-1}), \tag{7.22.12.2}$$

$$I_t \leqq \bar{v}_0 + v_1 (Y_{t-1} - Y_{t-2}), \tag{7.22.12.3}$$

$$C_t \geqq (1 + r_1)^t C_0, \tag{7.22.12.4}$$

$$I_t \geqq (1 + r_2)^t I_0, \tag{7.22.12.5}$$

$$Y_t = C_t + I_t + G_t \text{ (by definition)}, \tag{7.22.12.6}$$

$$C_t \geqq 0, I_t \geqq 0, Y_t \geqq 0, \tag{7.22.16.7}$$

where the w's are nonnegative weight coefficients, r_1, r_2 and $\bar{v}_0$ are positive constants and C_0, I_0 are initial values at time $t=0$. Equations (7.22.12.4) and (7.22.12.5) specify the lower limits to which consumption and investment are constrained. The objective function is a weighted average of the components of national income. If the desired growth path Y_t^* is determined exogenously, the objective function (7.22.12.1) will minimize the deviation $(Z - Y_t^*)$ by maximizing Z.

We have here three activities I_t, C_t and G_t and three principal constraints (7.22.12.2), (7.22.12.3) and (7.22.12.6). Taking these inequalities only and introducing slack variables S_1, S_2 we may write

$$
\begin{pmatrix} 1 & 0 & 1 & 0 \\ & & & \\ 0 & 1 & 0 & 1 \end{pmatrix}
\begin{pmatrix} C_t \\ I_t \\ S_1 \\ S_2 \end{pmatrix}
= \begin{pmatrix} b_1 \\ \\ b_2 \end{pmatrix},
\qquad (7.22.12.8)
$$

where b_1, b_2 are notations for

$$
b_1 = c_0 + c_1(C_{t-1} + I_{t-1} + G_{t-1} - T_{t-1}),
$$
$$
b_2 = \bar{v}_0 + v_1(C_{t-1} - C_{t-2} + I_{t-1} - I_{t-2} + G_{t-1} - G_{t-2}).
$$

We may have some additional constraints on the instrument variables G_t, T_t which are not introduced explicitly.

The weights corresponding to the slack variables S_1, S_2 are zero, and so the objective function is basically unchanged. The instrument variables G_t and T_t are to be expressed in some optimal sense as a function of the two components of national income C_t and I_t such that the objective function Z in (7.22.12.1) is maximized with the least possible instability. Now there is a definite competitive relation between stability and the optimization goals. A complete absence of fluctuations is possible only if equations (7.22.12.4) and (7.22.12.5) hold with equalities and form the "optimal basis" in the language of linear programming. But this would obviously be the most pessimistic solution. From (7.22.12.8) it is easy to note that there are three important cases of basic feasible solutions.

Case (i). If the first two activities C_t, I_t enter into the optimal basic solution, then we have

$$
C_t = c_1 C_{t-1} + c_1 I_{t-1} + c_1(G_{t-1} - T_{t-1}) + c_0,
$$
$$
I_t = v_1(C_{t-1} - C_{t-2}) + v_1(I_{t-1} - I_{t-2}) + v_1(G_{t-1} - G_{t-2}) + \bar{v}_0.
$$
$$
(7.22.12.9)
$$

If we select G_t and T_t by the rules (7.21.10.3) and (7.21.10.2), we have three difference equations with which to solve for the three unknowns C_t, I_t and G_t. This result has been indicated before.

Case (ii). If the first and fourth activities C_t, S_2 enter into the optimal basic solution for the system (7.22.12.8), we have the first equation of (7.22.12.9), and because of the slack variable S_2, we introduce the minimal investment function given by (7.22.12.5). If, further, we assume proportional policies, e.g.,

$$G_t = -p_1 C_t - p_2 I_t \qquad p_1, p_2 \geq 0,$$
$$T_t = m_1 C_t + m_2 I_t \qquad m_1, m_2 \geq 0, \qquad (7.22.12.10)$$

then we get

$$C_t = c_1 C_{t-1} + c_1 I_0 (1 + r_2)^{t-1} - c_1 (p_1 + m_1) C_{t-1}$$
$$- c_1 (p_2 + m_2) I_0 (1 + r_2)^{t-1}. \qquad (7.22.12.11)$$

One part of the solution of this equation taken up to its homogeneous terms is given by

$$C_t = K_1 [c_1 (1 - p_1 - m_1)]^t, \qquad K_1 = \text{constant},$$

which will be stable (i.e., no oscillations) if the term $c_1 (1 - p_1 - m_1)$ is positive but less than unity. The complete solution of the equation (7.22.12.11) is, however, given by

$$C_t = [c_1 (1 - p_1 - m_1)]^{t-1} \{ \Sigma (B_t / [c_1 (1 - p_1 - m_1)]^t) + K_2 \},$$

where K_2 is an arbitrary constant and B_t denotes the nonhomogeneous terms on the right-hand side of equation (7.22.12.11), i.e.,

$$B_t = c_0 + c_1 I_0 (1 + r_2)^{t-1} - c_1 (p_2 + m_2) I_0 (1 + r_2)^{t-1}.$$

Case (iii). A case very similar to case (ii) occurs when I_t and S_1 enter into the optimal basic solution for the system. In this case the roles of C_t and I_t are reversed as it were. Imposing the conditions (7.22.12.10) and equation (7.22.12.4) we have now

$$I_t = (v_1 - p_2)(I_{t-1} - I_{t-2}) + (v_1 - p_1) C_0 \{(1 + r_1)^{t-1} - (1 + r_1)^{t-2}\} + \bar{v}_0.$$

The solution of the homogeneous part of this equation is given by

$$I_t = A_1 \mu_1^t + A_2 \mu_2^t,$$

where the characteristic roots μ_1, μ_2 are given by

$$\mu = \tfrac{1}{2} \{(v_1 - p_2) \pm [(v_1 - p_2)^2 - 4(v_1 - p_2)]^{\frac{1}{2}}\}.$$

In general, it is likely that this system will have complex roots and hence the associated fluctuations. This is an important difference as compared with case (ii), which cannot in general have complex roots.

The above analysis shows the need for varying expenditures and taxes in different ways for the different components of national income. That component which has a tendency to fluctuate more should evidently be given more weight in the design of stabilization policy.

Also, it is perhaps necessary to consider the sensitivity of a particular type of stabilization policy, especially when the parametric coefficients are likely to vary within a range.

7.5. Sensitivity Analysis for Linear Programming Solutions

The question of sensitivity of the optimal solution of a programming model may be approached in several ways, e.g., (a) by analyzing the impact of the perturbation of the parameters of the problem (i.e., the coefficient matrix, net prices and resource vector) on the extremum value of the objective function,[10] (b) by analyzing the statistical distribution of the extremum value of the objective function under alternative variations in the random components of the parameters of a linear programming problem [1, 33], and (c) by investigating the variation of the spread between the optimum value of the objective function and any other value corresponding to a basic feasible solution vector [34].

From the operational standpoint of a policy model in the nonstochastic case, perhaps the most interesting method of sensitivity analysis of type (a) arises when we consider the sensitivity of the extreme value of the objective function in the neighborhood of the optimum by obtaining a series expansion for the objective function. Let us write the primal and dual linear programming problems in standard notations

$$\text{Primal: max } c'x \text{ subject to } x \geq 0, \quad Ax \leq b, \tag{7.23.1}$$

$$\text{Dual: min } y'b \text{ subject to } y \geq 0, \quad A'y \geq c, \tag{7.23.2}$$

where x and y are column vectors of n and m components, respectively, and the dimensions of A, b, c are the same as in equations (7.19.1) and (7.19.2) before and prime denotes transposition.

Assuming the above to be regular linear programming problems (i.e., abstracting from degeneracy and other peculiarities), let x^0 and y^0 be the optimal solution vectors and $z^0 = (c^0)'x^0$ and $w^0 = (y^0)'b$ be the optimal values of the objective functions, respectively, with the "optimal basis" A^0. By the duality theorem it follows that

$$z^0 = (c^0)'x^0 = (c^0)'(A^0)^{-1}b = (c^{0'}A^0)^{-1}b = (y^0)'b = w^0.$$

----

[10] There are several approaches here of which the most important ones are: Saaty [27], Barnett [2], Courtillot [9], and Williams [47].

Denote by v the common value $z^0 = w^0$ of linear programming and assume now that the matrix A^0 and vectors b and c^0 are functions of a common scalar parameter t; following Saaty's procedure [28, 46], the results below can easily be derived by the rules of vector-matrix differentiation

(i)　　　　　$\partial v/\partial c^0 = x^0 \, ; \qquad \partial v/\partial b = y^0 \, ,$

(ii)　　　　　$\partial v/\partial a_{ij} = - x_j^0 y_i^0 \, ,$

(iii)　　　　　$\dfrac{dv}{dt} = \left(\dfrac{dc^0}{dt} \right)' (A^{0-1} b) + (c^0)' \left(\dfrac{dA^{0-1}}{dt} \right)(b) + c^{0'} A^{0-1} \dfrac{db}{dt}$

$$= \left(\frac{dc^0}{dt} \right)' x^0 - c^{0'} A^{0-1} \left(\frac{dA^0}{dt} \right) A^{0-1} b + y^0 \frac{db}{dt} \, ,$$

since

$$\frac{dA^{0-1}}{dt} = - A^{0-1} (dA^0/dt) A^{0-1} \, ,$$

provided, of course, such expansions around the optimal point (x^0, y^0) are valid, i.e., the vector c has to be interior to the cone associated with the solution vertex.

An application of these sensitivity indices to oil refinery models has been reported by Saaty and Webb, where the formula (ii) averaged over a set of observed solutions gives an idea as to how sensitive the objective value at the optimal point is to possible variations in a_{ij} values. As Webb has observed:

> These practical results are of value in determining the required accuracy of basic data systems, evaluating the significance of management changes in parameters, determining most significant parameters and the detecting of trends in the operation [46, p. 267].

Now consider the second type of sensitivity analysis, i.e., case (b), which is a special aspect of the general technique known as stochastic linear programming [41]. A distinction is usually made here between two related approaches, the passive and the active, respectively. In the *passive* approach the statistical distribution of the optimum value of the objective function is statistically estimated either exactly or approximately by numerical methods and optimum decision rules are based on the different characteristics of the estimated statistical distribution, such as the mean, variance or mode. In the *active* approach a new set of decision variables is introduced which indicates the proportions of different resources to be allocated to the various activities. One effect of introducing the set of new decision variables (i.e., instrument variables) in the active approach is the truncation of the statistical distribution of the optimal value of the objective function of the passive approach. Thus, if U and $\tilde{U}$ are two selections of the decision variables, these can be compared in terms of their effects on the expected value and the variance of the optimum values of the objective function for a set of solutions and an optimum choice between the two policies can in principle be made. An empirical application of this result is shown in Chapter 9 (p. 262).

The third type of sensitivity analysis defines a value of the objective function other than the optimal one which corresponds to a basic feasible solution and is the "next best" in a certain sense. For instance, if $r = 1, 2, ...,$ R denotes the total number of distinct basic feasible solutions (i.e., two basic solutions are said to be distinct if they do not lead to the same value of the objective function), we may define

$$z^0 = \left\{ {}^{\max}_r z_r = c'x \text{ under the conditions } Ax \leqq b, x \geqq 0 \right\},$$
$$z^{(1)} = \left\{ {}^{\max}_r z_r = c'x \text{ under the conditions } z_r \neq z^0, Ax \leqq b, x \geqq 0 \right\},$$
$$z^{(2)} = \left\{ {}^{\max}_r z_r = c'x \text{ under the conditions } z_r \neq z^0, z_r \neq z^{(1)}, Ax \leqq b, x \geq 0 \right\}$$

and so on

Here $z^{(1)}$ may be called the truncated optimal value, truncation being of order one. We note that there is an infinity of solutions between z^0 and $z^{(1)}$, i.e., the convex combination $\lambda z^0 + (1 - \lambda) z^{(1)}$ as λ moves from one to zero. However, we restrict ourselves only to the vertex points (i.e., basic feasible solutions) for the derivation of a decision rule because the set of basic feasible solutions is finite and countable on the one hand and the activity vectors entering into the basic feasible solution are linearly independent, implying that the instrument variables included in the set of activity vectors are linearly independent.

Now we can consider different sample observations $k = 1, 2, ..., K$; compute for each admissible sample (say) $z^0, z^{(1)}$ and $z^{(2)}$ now denoted as $z_k^0, z_k^{(1)}, z_k^{(2)}$ and then compare the statistical distributions of $z_k^0, z_k^{(1)}, z_k^{(2)}$ under certain regularity conditions on the sample space. Since by construction

$$Ez_k^0 > Ez_k^{(1)} > Ez_k^{(2)}, \text{ for admissible } k = 1, 2, ..., K,$$

if we find

$$\text{Var } z_k^0 < \text{Var } z_k^{(1)} < \text{Var } z_k^{(2)} \text{ over sample space } k,$$

the optimal value z_k^0 is said to be stable. If, however, it turns out that

$$\text{Var } z_k^{(1)} < \text{Var } z_k^0,$$

and this difference in variance far outweighs the difference in expected values,

TABLE 7.3

Characteristics of the Distribution of Truncated Maxima of Different Orders

| Character | Truncated Maxima | Sample Size (N) | |
		$N = 25$	$N = 18$
Expected value	z_0	4,955.16	4,755.04
	$z^{(1)}$	1,633.38	1,522.84
	$z^{(2)}$	314.61	300.08
Mode	z^0	6,166.55	5,964.51
	$z^{(1)}$	1,751.47	1,807.26
	$z^{(2)}$	417.25	349.15
Variance	z^0	$10,779 \times 10^2$	$12,492 \times 10^2$
	$z^{(1)}$	$1,504 \times 10^2$	$1,453 \times 10^2$
	$z^{(2)}$	82×10^2	61×10^2

it might be more reasonable to accept the second best solution $z^{(1)}$, which is more stable in terms of variance than the best one, z^0. An application of this latter result has been reported by Sengupta [30, 32]. The results of this application are summarized very briefly in Table 7.3. It may be seen that the variance of $z^{(1)}$ is only one-seventh that of z^0, whereas the expected value of $z^{(1)}$ is about one-third that of z^0.

7.6. Other General Remarks

Concerning the general applicability of programming models to policy situations, two other technical points should at least be mentioned. First, the fact that only a scalar function is optimized in a programming model is a limitation in some cases when there are many goals (targets) and when these can not be combined in terms of common denominators. In systems analysis and operational research methods such possibilities have been encountered frequently. Although not complete, there are some methods for reducing a vector-optimizing problem to a sequence of linear programming problems [4]. Some of the repricing theorems developed by Charnes and Cooper [6] may be helpful in this connection.

Second, nonlinear programming, as we have seen while analyzing van Eijk and Sandee's paper, offers a range of flexibility much greater than linear programming, e.g., locally optimum solutions in different linearized facets. If we incorporate sampling variations and stochastic changes in the parameters of the problem (i.e., the coefficients) in the framework of nonlinear programming, it may be more useful for analyzing the stability of optimal policy solutions. For instance, in terms of expectations, variances and other characteristics, the objective functions corresponding to different distinct local solutions may be tested, compared and evaluated before deciding on the optimum policy.

7.7. Selected Developments in Recent Models of Programming and Economic Policy

Recent years have seen quite a large number of applications of programming models, both linear and nonlinear. Three major reasons may be very clearly traced in the literature. First, the increased use of control theory methods based on Pontryagin's maximum principle and other methods, especially in the theory of economic growth has led to questions of empirically computing optimal control and the associated shadow prices. Second, the development of efficiency of the third generation computer along with the powerful computing algorithms like branch and bound [61], geometric programming [64], SUMT (sequential unconstrained minimization techniques [53]) and the conjugate-gradient [51, 59] and Davidon methods [50] for control problems have played a major role. Third, methods of solving large-scale linear or nonlinear programs by decomposition techniques, which appear to be strikingly similar to the tatonnement processes of a competitive market [61, 63] have been interpreted in recent times as planning by stages through systematic revisions of provisional shadow prices and provisional resource allocations.

Control theory applications of programming models, particularly applications to problems of economic growth, stabilization and monetary-cum-fiscal policy are discussed in Chapter 8. The second major area of application of programming techniques is in development planning either at the economy-wide level or the sectoral level. A brief synopsis of some of the major programming applications in planning is given in Table 7.4; these models are discussed in some detail in Chapters 13 and 14, and it must be emphasized that the models presented in Table 7.4 are selected from a large number of empirical applications with a view to illustrate some of the important characteristics.

It is clear that the range of computing algorithms is quite wide, e.g., from the ordinary simplex method for LP models (case 2B) to mixed integer programming algorithm of branch and bound (case 5). It is very interesting to note some common features of the various programming models. First, since some of the parameters of either the objective function or the model and its constraints are estimated from empirical data, the optimal programming solutions are generally analyzed in terms of sensitivity to variations in some of the important parameters like the elasticity of marginal utility with respect to consumption (case 1), variation in weights or facets of the welfare function (case 3) or variations in the substitution parameter of the CES (constant elasticity of substitution) type production function for sectoral output (it occurs in the model formulation of case 4). This sensitivity analysis provides a guideline for selection of an optimal policy-mix which is in some sense stable for variations of parameters within specified ranges. Sometimes the effects of varying the terminal year requirements are directly allowed for in the boundary condition (as in case 2A). Second, the linkage with intersectoral balances is generally incorporated through the various branches of the open-dynamic input-output model. Since the input-output balances basically provide a consistency framework of demand-supply equilibrium, the programming models in effect shows the impact of this equilibrium being disturbed when a specified welfare function is introduced and optimized. At the optimal solution, it is clear that we observe a new set of demand-supply equilibrium relationships but this is conditional on a specific set of shadow prices which force this new level of equality. This leads to the common third point, e.g., the shadow prices of scarce resources derived from the programming models.

It is clear that shadow prices of resources used in programming models are dependent basically on the form of the objective function, since these measure the marginal contribution to the optimal value of the welfare function resulting from a slight variation of the resources. The relation of shadow prices of resources to their market prices, if markets exist, and the implications when markets do not exist (e.g., contingent future goods [65]) are two major areas where there is some controversy. As it may be seen in Table 7.4 in case 3, the decomposition algorithms proposed for economy-wide planning purposes essentially prescribe a sequence of allocations and price adjustments till an overall optimum is reached; this situation obviously has some meaning when private markets do not exist or the markets do not perform their efficient allocation role due to various imperfections. In cases where private markets do exist, a parametric variation of shadow prices and their comparison with market price trends is certainly very helpful in the sense that the impact of too large a divergence may be traced back either to a misspecification of some relationships in the model or to some exogenous policy constraints (e.g., controlled market prices). However, a high correlation between these two prices should not imply any causality and one should be very cautious in extrapolating shadow prices beyond the period analyzed in the programming model. So long as alternative specifications of constraints for the same model ε ɛe not allowed for in the programming model, even the relative stability of shadow prices cannot always be guaranteed (and indeed in case 5, Westphal [66] reports that he had to reject the maximization of a discounted sum of consumption as an objective function due to instability encountered in computation because of the sensitivity to discount rate). More work seems to be needed in this framework before policy recommendation based on shadow prices can be considered effectively.

REFERENCES

[1] BABBAR, M. M. "Distribution of Solutions of a Set of Linear Equations with Applications to Linear Programming," *Journal of American Statistical Association*, L (1955), 155.

[2] BARNETT, S. "Stability of the Solution to a Linear Programming Problem," *Operational Research Quarterly*, XIII, No. 3 (September, 1962), 219–228.

[3] BELLMAN, R., and DREYFUS, S. E. *Applied Dynamic Programming*. Princeton, N.J.: Princeton University Press, 1962.

[4] CHARNES, A., and COOPER, W. W. "On the Theory and Computation of Delegation Models: K-efficiency, Functional Efficiency and Goals," *Proceedings of the Sixth International Meeting of the Institute of Management Science* (Paris), I (1960), 56–91.

[5] ——. *Management Models and Industrial Applications of Linear Programming*. New York: John Wiley & Sons, 1961, Vol. I.

[6] ——. "Systems Evaluation and Repricing Theorems," *Management Science*, IX, No. 1 (October, 1962), 33.

[7] ——. "Deterministic Equivalents for Optimizing and Satisficing under Chance Constraints," *Operations Research*, XI (1963), 18.

[8] CHENERY, H. B. "The Use of Interindustry Analysis in Development Programming," in *Structural Interdependence and Economic Development*. Edited by T. Barna. London: Macmillan and Co., 1963, pp. 11–27.

[9] COURTILLOT, M. "On Varying all the Parameters in a Linear Programming Problem," *Operations Research*, X (1962), 471.

[10] DANTZIG, G. B. "On the Status of Multi-stage Linear Programming Problems," *Bulletin of International Statistical Institute*, XXXVI, Part 3 (1957–1958), 303–320.

[11] ——. *Linear Programming and Extensions*. Princeton, N.J.: Princeton University Press, 1963.

[12] DAY, R. H. *Recursive Programming and Production Response*. Amsterdam: North-Holland Publishing Co., 1963.

[13] DOMAR, E. D. "Capital Expansion, Rate of Growth and Employment," *Econometrica*, XIV (January, 1946), 137.

[14] DORN, W. S. "Duality in Quadratic Programming," *Quarterly of Applied Mathematics*, XVIII (July, 1960), 155–162.

[15] FOX, K. A., and THORBECKE, E. "Specification of Structures and Data Requirements in Economic Policy Models," in *Quantitative Planning of Economic Policy*. Edited by B. G. Hickman. Washington, D.C.: The Brookings Institution, 1965, Chap. 3.

[16] FRANK, M., and WOLFE, P. "An Algorithm for Quadratic Programming," *Naval Research Logistics Quarterly*, III (1956), 95.

[17] GALE, D. *The Theory of Linear Economic Models*. New York: McGraw-Hill Book Co., 1960.

[18] GRAVES, R. L., and WOLFE, P. (eds.). *Recent Advances in Mathematical Programming*. New York: McGraw-Hill Book Co., 1963.

[19] HADLEY, G. *Linear Programming*. Reading, Mass.: Addison-Wesley, 1962.

[20] HICKS, J. R. *A Contribution to the Theory of the Trade Cycle*. Oxford: Clarendon Press, 1950.

[21] KLEIN, L. R. *Economic Fluctuations in the United States* 1921–1941. New York: John Wiley & Sons, 1950.

[22] ——, and KOSOBUD, R. F. "Some Econometrics of Growth: Great Ratios of Ecomics," *Quarterly Journal of Economics*, LXXV (1961), 173.

[23] KUHN, H. W., and TUCKER, A. W. "Nonlinear Programming," in *Proceedings of the Second Berkeley Symposium on Mathematical Statistics and Probability*. Edited by J. Neyman, Berkeley: University of California Press, 1951, pp. 481–492.

[24] ——. *Linear Inequalities and Related Systems*. Princeton, N.J.: Princeton University Press, 1956.

[25] LANGE, O. "Output-investment Ratio and Input-output Analysis," *Econometrica*, XXVIII (April, 1960), 310–324.

[26] MINSKY, H. P. "Monetary Systems and Accelerator Models," *American Economic Review*, XLVII (December, 1957), 859–883.

[27] SAATY, T. L. "Coefficient Perturbation of a Constrained Extremum," *Operations Research*, VII, No. 3 (1959), 294.

[28] ——, and WEBB, K. W. "Sensitivity and Renewals in Scheduling Aircraft Overhaul," *Proceedings of Second International Conference on Operational Research*. Edited by J. Banbury and J. Maitland. New York: John Wiley & Sons, 1960, pp. 708–716.

[29] SENGUPTA, J. K. "Some Economic Aspects of the Domar-type Model of Economic Growth," *Arthaniti*, V (1962), 26.

[30] —— . "On the Stability of Truncated Solutions of Stochastic Linear Programming." Ames: Department of Economics, Iowa State University, December 20, 1963. Mimeographed.

[31] ——. "Policy Criteria for Stabilization and Growth," *Oxford Economic Papers*, XVI, No. 3 (October, 1964), 407–417.

[32] ——, and KUMAR, T. K. "An Application of Sensitivity Analysis to a Linear Programming Problem," *Unternehmensforschung*, IX, No. 1 (1965), 18–36.

[33] ——, TINTNER, G., and MILLHAM, C. "On Some Theorems of Stochastic Linear Programming with Applications," *Management Science*, X, No. 1 (1963), 143.

[34] ——. "On the Stability of Solutions under Error in Stochastic Linear Programming," *Metrika*, IX, No. 1 (1965), 47–60.

[35] ——, and TINTNER, G. "A Stochastic Programming Interpretation of the Domar-type Growth Model," *Arthaniti*, VI (1963), 1.

[36] SIMON, H. A. *Models of Man*. New York: John Wiley & Sons, 1957, Chap. 14.

[37] SMITH, D. J. "Monetary Factors and Multiplier-accelerator Interaction," *Economica*, XXX (November, 1963), 400–407.

[38] SMITH, P. E. "A Note on the Built-in-flexibility of the Individual Income Tax," *Econometrica*, XXXI (October, 1963), 704–711.

[39] TINBERGEN, J., and BOS, H. C. *Mathematical Models of Economic Growth*. New York: McGraw-Hill Book Co., 1962.

[40] TINTNER, G. "Stochastic Linear Programming with Application to Agricultural Economics," in *Second Symposium in Linear Programming*. Edited by H. Antosiewicz. Washington, D.C.: National Bureau of Standards, 1955, pp. 197–228.

[41] ——. "The Use of Stochastic Linear Programming in Planning," *Indian Economic Review*, V (August, 1960), 159–167.

[42] VAN DEN BOGAARD, P. J. M., and THEIL, H. "Macrodynamic Policy-making: An Application of Strategy and Certainty Equivalence Concepts to the Economy of the United States 1933–1936," *Metroeconomica*, XI (1959), 149.

[43] VAN EIJK, C. J., and SANDEE, J. "Quantitative Determination of an Optimum Economic Policy," *Econometrica*, XXVII (1959), 1–13.

[44] VAJDA, S. *Mathematical Programming*. Reading, Mass.: Addison-Wesley, 1961.

[45] WAUGH, F. V. "A Partial Indifference Surface for Beef and Pork," *Journal of Farm Economics*, XXXVIII (1956), 102.

[46] WEBB, K. W. "Some Aspects of the Saaty Linear-Programming Sensitivity Equation," *Operations Research*, X, No. 2 (1962), 266–267.

[47] WILLIAMS, A. C. "Marginal Values in Linear Programming," *Journal of Society of Industrial and Applied Mathematics*, XI, No. 1 (1963), 82.

[48] CHENERY, H. B. (ed.) *Studies in Development Planning*. Cambridge, Mass.: Harvard University Press, 1971.

[49] ——, and RADUCHEL, W. J. "Substitution in Planning Models", in *Studies in Development Planning*, op. cit., Chapter 2.

[50] DAVIDON, W. C. "Variable Metric Method for Minimization", Argonne National Laboratory Report ANL 5990. Argonne, Illinois, February 1966.

[51] DOBELL, A. R. "Optimization in Models of Economic Growth", in *Studies in Optimization*, Volume I, 1970, pp. 1–27.

[52] ECKAUS, R. S. and PARIKH, K. S. *Planning for Growth*. Cambridge, Mass.: MIT Press, 1968.

[53] FIACCO, A. V. and MCCORMICK, G. P. *Nonlinear Programming: Sequential Unconstrained Minimization Techniques*. New York: John Wiley and Sons, 1968.

[54] FOLEY, D. K. and SIDRAUSKI, M. *Monetary and Fiscal Policy in a Growing Economy*. New York: Macmillan Company, 1971.

[55] KELLER, E. A., Jr. and SENGUPTA, J. K. "Sensitivity Analysis for Optimal and Feedback Controls Applied to Growth Models". Accepted for publication in *Stochastics*.

[56] ——. "Relative Efficiency of Computing Optimal Growth by Conjugate Gradient and Davidon Methods". Accepted for publication in *International Journal of Systems Science*.

[57] KENDRICK, D. and TAYLOR, L. "Numerical Methods and Nonlinear Optimizing Models for Economic Planning", in *Studies in Development Planning*, op. cit., Chapter 1.

[58] KORNAI, J. *Mathematical Planning of Structural Decisions*. Amsterdam: North-Holland Publishing Co., 1967.

[59] LASDON, L. S. "Conjugate Direction Methods for Optimal Control", *IEEE Transactions on Automatic Control,* Volume AC–15, 1970, pp. 267–268.

[60] MACEWAN, A. *Development Alternatives in Pakistan.* Cambridge, Mass.: Harvard University Press, 1971.

[61] SENGUPTA, J. K. and FOX, K. A. *Economic Analysis and Operations Research: Optimization Techniques in Quantitative Economic Models.* Amsterdam: 1969.

[62] SENGUPTA, J. K. "Quantitative Models of Planning for Educational Systems", in *Economic Analysis for Educational Planning,* Chapter 3. Baltimore: Johns Hopkins Press, 1972.

[63] ——. "Economic Problems of Resource Allocation in Nonmarket Systems", in *Economic Analysis for Educational Planning,* Chapter 6. Baltimore: Johns Hopkins Press, 1972.

[64] ——, and PORTILLO-CAMPBELL, J. H. "The Approach of Geometric Programming with Economic Applications". To be published in *Zeitschrift die Gesamte Staats.*

[65] STIGUM, B. P. "Competitive Equilibria Under Uncertainty", *Quarterly Journal of Economics,* Volume 83, 1969, pp. 533–561.

[66] WESTPHAL, L. "An Intertemporal Planning Model Featuring Economies of Scale", in *Studies in Development Planning,* op. cit., Chapter 4.

Chapter 8

OPTIMAL AND ADAPTIVE CONTROL
METHODS IN ECONOMIC POLICY

8.1. Control Theory Approach in Economic Policy

The theory of optimal control has been recently utilized extensively in economic models in several fields of which the following may be particularly mentioned: (a) the elaboration and extension of neoclassical and the related models of optimal economic growth [1, 44]; (b) the implications of optimal fiscal and monetary policies in models of optimal growth [14, 49]; (c) non-linear planning models for intertemporal and intersectoral resource allocation problems [9, 24]; (d) the implications of decomposing a large-scale dynamic model into submodels and the related control-theoretic processes of adjustment in a hierarchical system of decision making [26, 31]; and (e) the problems of stochastic control applied to various economic models under conditions of uncertainty [42, 47].

A comparison of the theory of economic policy with that of optimal control reveals a number of interesting characteristics, some of which may be mentioned here briefly. In our discussion in preceding chapters we noted that the general economic policy problem in the framework of Tinbergen's theory of economic policy may be characterized essentially by (1) a quantitative model involving target (i.e., state variables in control theory language) and instrument (i.e., control variables in control theory language) variables; (2) a specified preference function; and (3) a set of boundary conditions and constraints on the instrument and possibly target variables. If the quantitative model is dynamic in the sense that it is specified by a set of simultaneous differential or difference equations, then the economic policy problem becomes very similar to the optimal control problem, i.e., both problems seek to define a time path of the control (i.e., the instrument) vector which is in some sense optimal in the class of other feasible trajectories.

Once this basic link between the theory of economic policy and that of optimal control is appreciated, we may gain additional insight into the specification, formulation and implementation of the rules of optimum economic policy when these are interpreted in terms of control theory.

Consider first the implications of specification. In control theory, specification or modeling is intimately connected with the problems of (a) computation in terms of algorithmic principles; (b) controllability and observability of the dynamic system in different phases; and (c) the behavior of the optimal trajectory in response to variations in several parameters, like the terminal constraint, a particular coefficient in the dynamic model or the preassigned upper bound on a specific control variable. Broadly speaking, the problem of numerical computation emphasizes the point that in many practical situations one has to truncate the iterative processes of calculation and settle for a suboptimal solution and this is particularly so for large-scale linear and nonlinear models. However, since different algorithms have different degrees of sensitivity to truncation, one has to be careful in selecting a particular type of model specification. The nonlinear models of planning [9, 24] using control-theoretic techniques, some of which are discussed in Chapters 13 and 14 provide some interesting examples along this line.

Controllability and observability [21, 47] with respect to a dynamic control model refer respectively to the points that (a) the model has policy degrees of freedom and (b) that the model has parameters which are statistically identifiable in terms of the observations. Without going into the details of the mathematical conditions defining controllability and observability, we may say in general that these two concepts are closely related to the two well-known results in the Tinbergen-type theory of economic policy, e.g., (1) a fixed-target policy model must have policy degrees of freedom in the sense that the number of instrument variables must not be less than that of the target variables, and (2) a flexible-target policy model must have the parameters of the system equations structurally identified.

The sensitivity analysis for the optimal trajectory due to variations in several important parameters of the dynamic system equations such as the capital-output ratio provides another important means for ranking alternative policies. In the general case when the variations are due to random elements, methods of stochastic control [43, 47] and simulation become relevant here. It is sometimes found in the application of stochastic control methods that there is a trade-off between optimality and stability in the sense that controls which have on the average higher expected pay-offs have also higher variance (i.e., higher instability). For this reason it is preferable sometimes to choose feedback controls as second-best policies [47].

Consider next the welfare function which is maximized in the economic policy model. Besides the alternative forms, which were discussed in the preceding chapters, the control theory approach provides several alternative choices, e.g., (1) minimal time criterion [45] (where the time of transition from an initial state to a terminal state vector is minimized); (2) a two-facet objective function, where one stipulates the cost (or penalty) of deviating from a desired value of the terminal state vector [46]; and (3) other criteria of a stable system behavior [47]. The implications of choosing alternative welfare functions can be better analyzed in control theory framework in terms of their computational convenience, the relative sensitivity of alternative optimal trajectories and their convergence characteristics. In particular, in discrete-time control models, optimization one time-point ahead may be compared with that defined over a planning horizon and thus the decision rules which are restricted to the short-run may be analyzed with those which are committed to the entire planning horizon, which extends beyond the short-run.

As regards the boundary conditions of the economic policy model, the theory of optimal control provides two interesting interpretations of their roles. First, the boundary conditions when appropriately specified may lead to a change-over from one dynamic phase to another, where each phase is characterized by a set of differential (or difference) equations [5, 39]. Thus, from a policymaking framework the boundary conditions provide additional degrees of freedom in choosing a sequence of policies. Second, in optimal control models where the terminal time point is not fixed, a special condition known as the transversality condition is needed as a boundary condition which imposes a restriction on the behavior of the terminal value of the state vector and its associated prices.

It is expected that recent developments in optimal control theory would have far-reaching effects on the problems of optimal policymaking under quantitative economic models. Among others, the following recent tendencies in control theory are likely to prove very important in the development and extension of the dynamic theory of economic policy. First, the recent developments in computing algorithms, e.g., conjugate gradient, Davidon method, geometric programming and SUMT (sequential unconstrained minimization techniques), coupled with the revolution in electronic computer technology are going to have profound effects on the application of control theory methods. However, it turns out that for large systems (e.g., a national planning model on a very large scale an example of which is given in Chapter 14 in the Hungarian model [26]) even the existing computing capacity seems to prove very limited; moreover, the question of computational cost involved in processing information and applying numerical algorithms with varying degrees of efficiency and varying degrees of sensitivity to errors remains wide open. As Bellman [3, p. 25] has pointed out: "An analysis of this situation leads us to conclude that, analogous to the microscopic principle of uncertainty of quantum mechanics, there is a macroscopic principle of uncertainty in control theory. There is no way to control a large system perfectly. This is tied up with the fact that two basic costs are involved, the cost of obtaining data, and the cost of the time required to process and employ this data."

Second, one of the most interesting trends in recent developments in control theory is the emphasis on adaptive control rather than on optimal control designs. An adaptive control system is one where, in addition to the state variables (i.e., target variables) and the performance characteristics of the dynamic system, some means are provided to the policymaker for modifying the control action in order to make it more acceptable (e.g., learning mechanisms may be built in, second-best optimal controls which are restricted to a certain class of feedback controls may be searched, etc. [11, 47]). It is our view that methods of adaptive control could be increasingly applied to economic systems, particularly in fields like planning for educational and other nonmarket institutions and in decision making under conditions of uncertainty [47].

Another most interesting development in recent control theory, which has in our opinion a tremendous scope of application in economic models in the future, concerns the dynamic system when it is described by a set of partial difference and/or differential equations, rather than a set of ordinary differential or difference equations. In control theory the former system (i.e., the system characterized by the partial difference or differential equations) is called "the distributed parameter system"; the problems of characterizing and computing optimal controls for such systems are much more complicated, although some results [29] are now available. Since a multivariable economic policy model generally involves interdependence at different levels (e.g., a national model decomposed into sectoral, regional and spatial decision levels), the marginal concepts like marginal costs, marginal effect of a particular policy ($\partial W/\partial z_i$) on the objective function, etc., which are defined when other variables are held unchanged are frequently used to characterize necessary conditions of optimality in a local sense. It is clear that such marginal conditions of optimality may be analyzed through partial differential equations and the various results on invariant imbedding [2, 3] become applicable here.

8.2. Methods of Optimal Control

Methods of characterizing an optimal control in a dynamic system are somewhat simpler when the dynamic system is deterministic (i.e., nonstochastic) and contains only differential (i.e., continuous time) or difference (discrete time) equations. Methods of stochastic control and systems characterized by mixed differential-difference equations are much more complicated, although some recent results along these lines [12, 18, 29] are now available. From the viewpoint of the theory of optimization, problems of optimal control can be approached from at least three alternative angles, e.g., (1) variational calculus and its extensions through algorithms of non-linear programming [30, 39]; (2) dynamic programming and the associated algorithms [2, 19]; and (3) the maximum principle developed by Pontryagin and his associates [34], which is often called Pontryagin's principle. Since it is impossible here to deal very extensively with all these methods of optimal control, we confine ourselves in this section to presenting a brief outline of the Pontryagin principle for both continuous time and discrete time cases and then indicating very briefly the implications of adaptive control for economic systems.

Consider a continuous-time specification of an economic policy model as follows:

$$\text{Maximize } W = S(y(T)) + \int_0^T f_0(y, z, t)\, dt \qquad (8.1)$$

(cumulative social welfare functional)

under the following conditions

$$\dot{y} = f(y, z, t) \text{ (dynamic model)} \qquad (8.2)$$

$$y(0) = y_0 \text{ (initial conditions)} \qquad (8.3)$$

$$g_k(y, z, t) \geq 0;\ k = 1, 2, \ldots, K \text{ (inequality constrains)} \qquad (8.4)$$

$$y(T) \in R \text{ (terminal period restriction or target region)} \qquad (8.5)$$

$$z \in Q \text{ (region of control).} \qquad (8.6)$$

Here W is a functional depending on the scalar utility function $f_0(y, z, t)$ at each time point $t \in [0, T]$ and the scalar bequest function $S(y(T))$ (which is also called the scrap-value function in a different context [1]) which depends on the terminal value $y(T)$ of the n-element state vector $y = y(t)$. Equation

(8.2) is a vector differential equation containing n equations one for each state variable y_j; $j = 1, 2, \ldots, n$ and the vector function $f(\cdot)$ contains the control variables $z_i = z_i(t)$, $i = 1, \ldots, m$ as components of the control vector (i.e., instrument vector) z. Condition (8.3) states that the dynamic system must start from a given initial state and the remaining conditions (8.4) through (8.6) specify respectively the additional restrictions due to feasibility imposed by the scalar functions $g_k(y, z, t)$ on the system (8.2), the terminal period requirement imposed by the set R to which $y(T)$ is assumed to belong and the requirement on the region of controllability imposed by the closed set Q to which the control vector z is assumed to belong. It will be assumed here that the functions $f_0(\cdot)$ and $f(\cdot)$ in (8.1) and (8.2) respectively are continuous and the first differentials of $f(\cdot)$ exist and are continuous; also the control variables $z = z_i(t)$ are assumed piecewise continuous, since it is known [6] that under these conditions the system of differential equations (8.2) determine the state vector $y(t)$ uniquely, given the initial conditions y_0 and a particular control vector. Any piecewise continuous control vector $z = z(t)$, $t \in [0, T]$ satisfying conditions (8.2) through (8.6) is termed a feasible control and the associated state vector $y = y(t)$, $t \in [0, T]$ a feasible state; the set of feasible controls and that of feasible states define the "policy space" and the associated "state space" respectively. An optimal control and its associated trajectory in the state space are given by any feasible control in the policy space which also maximizes the functional W in (8.1) called the performance criterion.

8.2.1. *The Maximum Principles: Continuous and Discrete Time Systems*

It is clear that the above formulation of the economic policy problem in the framework of control theory can include a wide variety of cases occurring in applied economic models. Some of these cases may be illustrated here as follows:

(1) If the functions $f_0(\cdot)$ and $S(\cdot)$ in the welfare functional (8.1) are constants such that W can be viewed as a cost function depending on the time of transition T, then the performance criterion (8.1) can be interpreted as a "minimal time control problem" [6, 28]. Given the initial $y(0)$ and terminal vectors $y(T)$, the problem then is to choose a feasible control satisfying (8.2) through (8.6) such that the cost of transition time is minimized. Various applications [45, 47] of minimal time control problems are available in economic growth and planning and other problems.

(2) The scrap value function $S(y(T)) = S(y_1(T), \ldots, y_n(T))$, which is used to assign a value in industrial applications to the stock of machines left at

the end of the process T is used in the economic context to imply that the vector of capital stocks left over at the end has some usefulness in maintaining output growth in the future, i.e., after the terminal year T. In the general planning or policy problem where the planning horizon T is not fixed but determined endogenously, we have the case of a moving target region and in this case the function $S(y(T))$ which may then be viewed as a "bequest function" [32] helps to generate a set of shadow prices at the terminal year (i.e., the shadow prices $p_j(T)$ must be such that $p_j(T) = \partial S(H(T))/\partial y_j(T)$, where the latter denotes the marginal variation of the bequest function due to a variation in the terminal state variable; this is called the transversality condition).

Various forms of the bequest function $S(y(T))$ are used in economic growth and planning models and the details of a linear planning model for India due to Eckaus and Parikh comparing the optimal solutions of fixed target and moving target regions are reported in Chapter 13.

(3) The system of differential equations (8.2) which has unique solutions in the state space, given $y(0)$ and any control vector z, can be used to generate various trajectories which may or may not be feasible in terms of the constraints (8.4) through (8.6). For example, one might compare the stability properties of the differential system (8.2) and (8.3), (e.g., whether all its characteristic roots have negative real parts or not) under two feasible controls $z^{(1)}$, $z^{(2)}$, each of which satisfies the remaining constraints (8.4) through (8.6). If one of the feasible controls is identically zero, then this means we are comparing whether the exercise of control improves the stability (or reduces the degree of instability) of the uncontrolled system. Again, if the functions $f(\cdot)$ in (8.2) are linear, then feedback controls and their stability properties can be compared with the optimal control. Noting that the feedback controls are such that the control vector $z(t)$ can be expressed as an instantaneous function of the state vector $y(t)$, we can express the effect of a proportional-cum-derivative feedback control as follows:

$$\dot{y}(t) = Ay(t) + Bz(t) \tag{8.2a}$$

$$z(t) = -Cy(t) - D\dot{y}(t) \tag{8.2b}$$

$$y(0) = y_0 \text{ given,}$$

where A, B, C, D are constant matrices. It is clear that the stability properties

of the controlled system depend on the characteristic roots of the controlled
system

$$\dot{y}(t) = (I + BD)^{-1} \cdot (A - BC)y(t)$$

$$y(0) = y_0$$

and therefore, if the matrix $P = (I + BD)^{-1}(A - BC)$ is such that all its
characteristic roots have negative real parts, then the controlled system
would be stable, even if the matrix A in (8.2a) under conditions of no control
(i.e., $z(t) = 0$) does not have all its characteristic roots with negative real
parts. Since different choices of the elements of the matrices C, D denote
feedback controls with different intensities, one may compare the relative
degrees of stability of alternative feedback controls and hence of feedback
and optimal controls.

A number of economic applications [36, 40] comparing the stability
properties of the Phillips-type models of economic regulation and policies
of economic stabilization in commodity markets [38, 48] are available in
economic literature. Since feedback policies have stabilizing properties, the
theory of stochastic control and its applications [47] deal very extensively
with combining feedback and optimal policies in the sense of a second-best
or third-best policy. Some economic applications in this line are available
in the current literature [1, 47].

It should also be mentioned that other parts of the general control model
can be expressed by suitable transformations in the form of the differential
equation (8.2). For example, one may transform the performance criterion
(8.1) as

$$W = S(y_1(T), \ldots, y_n(T)) + y_{n+1}(T) \tag{8.1.2}$$

$$y_{n+1}(0) = 0. \tag{8.3.1}$$

Thus, the control problem becomes one of maximizing a function W which
depends on the terminal values of the enlarged set of state variables
$y_1(t), \ldots, y_{n+1}(t)$. Similarly, an integral constraint of the type

$$\int^T g(y, z, t) \, dt \geq \alpha \qquad \alpha : \text{constant},$$

which may be a special case of the constraint (8.4) may be replaced by a
new state variable $y_{n+2}(t)$ defined by

$$y_{n+2}(t) = \int_0^t g(y, z, s) \, ds$$

where $g(\cdot)$ is a scalar function of vectors y, z, and scalar s, and then adjoining one additional equation to the system (8.2) as:

$$\dot{y}_{n+2}(t) = g(y, z, t),$$

and suitably modifying the target region restriction (8.5) to include the inequality $y(T) \geq \alpha$. Thus, it is clear that by suitable transformations, a large class of optimal control problems can be reduced to problems of maximizing the terminal year value of a number of state variables and therefore of one state variable.

(4) The inequalities (8.4) which specify the constraints on the state variables and control variables which must be satisfied at any moment t by any feasible control vector $z(t)$ directly introduce the theory of nonlinear programming and the associated Kuhn-Tucker theory, which in this case implies [1, 30] at the optimal control z^0 that there exist multipliers $q_k^0(k = 1, \ldots, K)$ such that

$$q_k^0 \geq 0, \ q_k^0 g_k(y, z^0, t) = 0$$

$$(k = 1, 2, \ldots, K),$$

$$(8.4.1)$$

provided the constraint qualifications [39] are satisfied by the constraints (8.4). The constraint qualifications, loosely speaking, state a condition of nonsingularity when the boundary of the constraint set contains the optimal solution vector.

It is clear that the inequalities (8.4) can indicate the nonnegativity conditions on several economic variables, e.g., if total national output $F(K)$ as a function of aggregate capital stock K is to be allocated between consumption C and investment I, then we need the condition $F(K) - C - I \geq 0$ for economic realism.

(5) The last set of restrictions (8.5) and (8.6) indicates that the sets R and Q to which $y(T)$ and z belong must be suitably defined in order to have meaningful results. For example, the set Q is usually assumed to be closed and bounded for all t in order to indicate that there are definite bounds or limits on the control variables. In economic policy applications government expenditure as a control variable cannot exceed a certain percentage of national income, etc.

It is clear, however, that sometimes the restrictions (8.4) and the bequest function $S(y(T))$ can be subsumed in the sets R and Q suitably defined and the nonautonomous control system indicated by the presence of time variable t in (8.1) through (8.6) can be reduced to an autonomous system by introducing an extra state variable $y_{n+3} = t$, such that

$$\dot{y}_{n+3} = 1, \; y_{n+3}(T) = T.$$

Thus, in enlarged dimension an optimal control problem can be written as follows:

$$\text{Maximize } W = \int_0^T f_0(y, z) \, dt \qquad (8.7.1)$$

subject to

$$y(0) = y_0, \; z \in Q, \; y(T) \in R \qquad (8.7.2)$$

$$\dot{y} = f(y, z), \qquad (8.7.3)$$

where the state vector may be $(n+3)$-dimensional and the sets Q, R are suitably extended to include the cases mentioned before. For the dynamic system given by (8.7.1) through (8.7.3) the maximum principle of Pontryagin [30, 34] states the following necessary conditions for optimal control:

Proposition 1 (Continuous Maximum Principle):

Suppose $\{z^0(t), \; y^0(t); \; t \in [0, T]\}$ constitute an optimal control sequence and the associated trajectory of the state vector. Then there must exist an adjoint (or co-state) vector $p^0(t)$ containing variables $p_i^0(t)$ one for each differential equation (8.7.3) such that the following conditions hold:

(A) Canonical differential equations

$$\frac{dy_i^0(t)}{dt} = \left(\frac{\partial H}{\partial p_i(t)} \right)^0 ; \; \frac{dp_i^0(t)}{dt} = -\left(\frac{\partial H}{\partial y_i(t)} \right)^0,$$

where the superscript zero in the partial derivatives indicates that the latter are evaluated at the optimal trajectory $(z^0(t), y^0(t), p^0(t))$

(B1) $y^0(0) = y_0$; $y^0(T) \in R$

(B2) $p^0(T)$ normal to the set R at $y^0(T)$

(C) Maximization of the current-value Hamiltonian for the optimal control

$$H[y^0(t), z^0(t), p^0(t)] \geq H[y^0(t), z(t), p^0(t)]$$
$$\text{for every } t, \; 0 \leq t \leq T \text{ and all } z(t) \in Q,$$

where the Hamiltonian function $H = H[y(t), z(t), p(t)]$ is defined as

$$H = f_0(y, z) + p'(t)f(y, z), \qquad (8.7.4)$$

where prime denotes transpose.

For a proof of this result the reader may be referred to a number of excellent references [6, 28, 29]. Note, however, that the conditions of the Pontryagin principle are only necessary conditions valid locally. For determining global optimality we need sufficiency conditions like the following: the functions $f_0(y, z)$ and $f(y, z)$ are concave in the variables y, z taken together and the constraint-qualifications of Kuhn-Tucker theory are satisfied (a weaker sufficiency condition is that the function

$$H^0 = \max_{z \in Q} H[y(t), z(t), p(t)]$$

is a concave function of $y(t)$ for given $p(t)$ and t.

A discrete-time control problem analogous to the continuous system (8.7.1) through (8.7.3) may be specified as follows:

$$\text{Maximize } W = \sum_{t=0}^{T-1} F_t(y_t, z_t) \qquad (8.8.1)$$

subject to

$$y_0 = c(\text{given}), \; z_t \in Q, \; y_T \in R \qquad (8.8.2)$$

$$y_{t+1} - y_t = f_t(y_t, z_t), \qquad (8.8.3)$$

where it is assumed that the scalar function $F_t(\cdot)$ and the vector functions $f(\cdot)$ are well defined and continuous for all y_t and z_t and for fixed $z(t)$ the partial derivatives $\partial F_t^t / \partial y_t$, $\partial f_t / \partial y_t$ are continuous and bounded and the sets Q, R satisfy certain conditions of attainability of the optimal control and the associated optimal state. In this framework we have the corresponding discrete version of the maximum principle in terms of the current-value Hamiltonian H_t

$$H_t = H_t(y_t, p_{t+1}, z_t) = F_t(y_t, z_t) + p'_{t+1} f_t(y_t, z_t).$$

Note that the control model here is recursive in the sense that the sequence $\{y_{t+1}, z_t; t = 0, 1, \ldots, T - 1\}$ is the specification of a control policy.

Proposition 2 (Discrete Maximum Principle):

Suppose the sequence $(z_0^0, z_1^0, \ldots, z_{T-1}^0)$ constitutes an optimal control with its associated optimal state vectors $(y_0^0, y_1^0, \ldots, y_T^0)$. Then there must exist a sequence of adjoint (or co-state) vectors $(p_0^0, p_1^0, \ldots, p_T^0)$, one p_t for each difference equation (8.7.3) such that the following conditions hold:

(A) Canonical difference equations

$$y_{t+1}^0 - y_t^0 = \left(\frac{\partial H}{\partial p_{t+1}}\right)^0 ; \ p_{t+1}^0 - p_t^0 = -\left(\frac{\partial H}{\partial y_t}\right)^0$$

(B) Boundary and Transversality conditions

   (B1) $y_0^0 = c$; $y_T^0 \in R$

   (B2) p_T^0 normal to the set R at y_T^0.

(C) Maximization of the current-value Hamiltonian for optimal control

$$H_t[y_t^0, p_{t+1}^0, z_t^0] \geqq H_t[y_t^0, p_{t+1}^0, z_t]$$

   for all $z = z_t \in Q$, all $t = 0, 1, \ldots, T - 1$.

Again, the sufficiency conditions are needed for the global optimality of the sequence $\{y_t^0, z_{t-1}^0 ; t = 1, 2, \ldots, T\}$. In this case, however, the ordinary theory of nonlinear programming can be applied to analyze sufficiency and also we can apply various computational algorithms like conjugate gradient, SUMT (sequential unconstrained minimization technique), multivariable search, geometric programming, etc.

It may be instructive, however, to consider the continuous control model (8.1) through (8.4) and (8.6) once more, since it is explicitly specified in a form applicable to a wide variety of economic systems. Following Arrow and Kurz [1, p. 41] the theorem on optimal control can be stated as follows:

Proposition 3 (Alternative Statement of Continuous Maximum Principle):

Let $z^*(t)$ be a choice of instruments $(0 \leqq t \leqq T)$, which maximizes (8.1) subject to (8.2) through (8.4) and (8.6). If the constraint qualification holds for the constraints, then there exist adjoint (or auxiliary or co-state) variables $p_j(t)$ such that for each t

(a) $z^*(t)$ maximizes $H[y(t), z(t), p(t), t]$ at each t, subject to (8.6), where $H[y(t), z(t), p(t), t] = f_0(y, z, t) + \sum_{j=1}^n p_j(t) f_j(y, z, t)$

(b) $\dot{p}_j = (dp_j(t)/dt) = \partial L/\partial y_j(t)$ evaluated at $(y_j(t), z^*(t), p(t))$, where the Lagrangian function is $L = H[y(t), z(t), p(t), t] + \sum_{k=1}^K q_k g_k(y, z, t)$ and the Lagrange multipliers q_k are such that

(c) $\partial L/\partial z_i \leqq 0$, all $i = 1, \ldots, m$ for $y = y(t)$, $z = z^*(t)$ and $p = p(t)$

$$q_k(t) \geqq 0, \ q_k(t) g_k(y, z, t) = 0, \text{ all } k = 1, \ldots, K$$

and the transversality condition holds at the terminal time point T:

(d) $p_j(T) = \dfrac{\partial S(y(T))}{\partial y_j(T)} (j = 1, 2, \ldots, n)$

It is clear that the transversality condition (d) is necessary only when the target region (i.e., the terminal period) is not fixed. Also, if the bequest function is such that $y(T) \geq 0$, which requires that the end-of-period values of the state variables be nonnegative, then the transversality condition would be transformed as follows:

$$p_j(T) \geq 0, \; p_j(T)y_j(T) = 0; \; (j = 1, 2, \ldots, n).$$

In case where the time horizon T is infinite and there is a discount function $\exp(-\delta t)$ before the function $f_0(y, z, t)$ in the integral of (8.1) with a positive δ such that the discounted integral is bounded for $T \to \infty$, then the transversality condition would further be modified as:

$$\lim_{T \to \infty} \exp(-\delta T)p_j(T) \geq 0, \; \lim_{T \to \infty} \exp(-\delta T)p_j(T)y_j(T) = 0$$

$$(j = 1, \ldots, n).$$

The economic meaning of this result, in a somewhat heuristic sense may be expressed as follows: the value of the state variable (which could be the aggregate capital stock in a neoclassical model of optimal growth [1, 5]) at the terminal year must reach its saturation value (which is zero in this case, i.e., $y(T) \geq 0$, although zero really represents a preassigned constant level) so that the discounted value of $y_j(T)$ is zero. This indirectly suggests that an infinite horizon planning model may have some unrealistic economic implications due to the implicit assumption of saturation underlying the transversality condition.

8.2.2. Illustrative Economic Applications

Economic applications of control theory methods are increasing in recent times due perhaps to the computability of such models using modern electronic computers. Although it is somewhat early to attempt an evaluation of the several types of economic applications of modern control theory methods, broadly speaking the current state of economic applications may be classified under the following groups: (1) optimal investment problems in a neoclassical framework of growth [5, 17] and the related questions of specifying optimal fiscal and monetary policies [14, 44]; (2) investment planning and intertemporal resource allocation problems in the context of

less developed economies [9, 24] and the related implications of specific but
nonoptimal resource allocations; (3) decomposition of multi-level systems
into subsystems so that decentralized decision-making may be possible in
some optimal sense [26, 31]; (4) methods of approximating the optimal
control solution by various suboptimal controls [7, 22] and the related
questions of stability of alternative approximations in the sense of oscillations and convergence properties [11, 24]; and (5) various methods of
simulation applied to problems of stochastic and adaptive control [33, 47].

Since the range of economic applications of modern control theory is
quite extensive, we would consider in this section a selected number of
illustrative applications dealing with the problems of economic growth and
stabilization. A number of growth and planning models using control theory
methods are reviewed in Chapters 13 and 14. Also, a detailed numerical
model of continuous optimal control is presented in Section 8.3 in order to
illustrate the problem of computability, convergence and turnpike behavior.

A. Optimal Control in a Two-Sector Model:

We consider here a two-sector model of investment allocation due to
Arrow and Kurz [1]. The problem is to choose the optimal control variable
$c(t)$ which maximizes (a discounted sum of utilities in an infinite-horizon
framework)

$$W = \int_0^\infty \exp\left(-\lambda t\right) \cdot U\left[c(t), k_g(t)\right] dt \qquad (8.9.1)$$

subject to

$$\dot{k}(t) = dk(t)/dt = f\left[k_p, k_g\right] - \gamma k(t) - c(t) \qquad (8.9.2)$$

$$k(t) \geqq k_g(t) + k_p(t) \qquad (8.9.3)$$

$$k(0) = k_g(0) + k_p(0) \text{ given.} \qquad (8.9.4)$$

Here the two sectors are the public (government) and private sectors employ-
ing capital stocks $K_g(t)$ and $K_p(t)$, respectively, such that the external
effects of public sector investment (i.e., $\dot{K}_g(t) = I_g(t)$) appear in the economy
either as aggregate consumption benefits through direct public services (and
this part enters into the utility function $U[\cdot]$) or as direct production benefits
(i.e., effect of public goods on private sector's productivity) which enter into
the production function

$$Y(t) = F\left[K_p(t), K_g(t), \exp\left(\tau t\right)L(t)\right], \qquad (8.9.5)$$

where τ is the constant rate of labour-augmenting technical progress and the output $Y(t)$ is assumed to be a concave function, homogeneous of degree one and twice differentiable. Defining $\gamma = \pi + \tau$ as the natural rate of growth, where π is a given positive rate of growth of population, the per capita variables are defined as follows: $k_p(t) = K_p(t) \cdot \exp(+\gamma t)$, $k_g(t) = K_g(t) \cdot \exp(-\gamma t)$, $k(t) = K(t) \exp(-\gamma t)$ and $c(t) = C(t) \exp(-\gamma t)$, where $C(t)$ is the aggregate consumption. The relations (8.9.2) and (8.9.3) are then derived from the aggregate relations

$$K(t) = F[K_p(t), K_g(t), \exp(\tau t) \cdot L(t)] - C(t)$$

$$K(t) \geq K_p(t) + K_g(t)$$

and the utility function $U[c(t), k_g(t)]$ in (8.9.1) is assumed twice differentiable and concave and the (i.e., positive and diminishing marginal utility) composite discount rate λ in (8.9.1) is assumed given.

It is clear that the results of Proposition 3 can be directly applied to derive the optimal control, i.e., the instruments $k_p(t)$, $k_g(t)$ and $c(t)$. The current value Lagrangian is

$$L = U(c, k_g) + p[f(k_p, k_g) - \gamma k - c] + q(k - k_p - k_g). \quad (8.9.6)$$

Maximizing this function with respect to the instruments k_p, k_g and c gives us

$$p \cdot (\partial f / \partial k_p) = q \quad (8.9.7a)$$

$$(\partial U / \partial k_g) = p \cdot (\partial f / \partial k_g) = q \quad (8.9.7b)$$

$$\partial U / \partial c = p. \quad (8.9.7c)$$

Eliminating q between the first two equations (8.9.7a) and (8.9.7b) we get

$$(\partial U / \partial k_g) + p \cdot [(\partial f / \partial k_g) - (\partial f / \partial k_p)] = 0.$$

This expresses the equality of value of capital in its two uses at the optimal solution. Also since the functions U and f are assumed strictly increasing in their arguments, the equality relation must hold in (8.9.3), i.e.,

$$k = k_p + k_g. \quad (8.9.7d)$$

Applying Pontryagin's maximum principle we also obtain the differential equation for the adjoint variable $p = p(t)$ as:

$$\dot{p} = dp/dt = \lambda p - (\partial L / \partial k) = (\lambda + \gamma)p - q = [w - \partial f / \partial k_p] \cdot p \quad (8.9.8)$$

(using (8.9.7a) and the definition $w = \lambda + \gamma$).

The other differential equation of the canonical equations is of course given by (8.9.2). The transversality condition is given by

$$\lim_{T \to \infty} \exp\left(-\lambda t\right)p(t) = 0. \tag{8.9.9}$$

Three most important characteristics of this optimal investment model have been emphasized by Arrow and Kurz. First, there is a short-run equilibrium system given by (8.9.7a) through (8.9.7c), which is a static system (i.e., containing no differential terms) obtained through maximization of the current value Lagrangian function L (where $L = H + q(k - k_p - k_g)$, H being the usual current-value Hamiltonian) at each moment t. Since at any given time t, the values of $k = k(t)$, $p = p(t)$ are given (i.e., solved from the canonical equations (8.9.2) and (8.9.8)) then one can solve from this system equations (8.9.7a) through (8.9.7c), the unknowns c, k_p and k_g as functions of k and p. These solutions denoted by

$$c = c(k, p), \ k_p = k_p(k, p), \ k_g = k_g(k, p) \tag{8.9.10}$$

are termed the "derived demand functions". The uniqueness and stability (in the sense of deviations from a given equilibrium point tending to zero) of a solution like (8.9.10) can be easily analyzed, e.g., by totally differentiating the equations (8.9.7a) through (8.9.7c), i.e.,

$$U_{cc}\,dc + U_{cg}\,dk_g = dp \tag{8.9.11a}$$

$$U_{gc}\,dc + [U_{gg} + p(f_{gg} - f_{pg})]\,dk_g + p(f_{gp} - f_{pp})\,dk_p = -(f_g - f_p)\,dp \tag{8.9.11b}$$

$$dk_g + dk_p = dk, \tag{8.9.11c}$$

where the two subscripts on U and f denote partial derivatives with respect to c, k_g or k_p (i.e., $U_{cg} = \partial/\partial k_g(\partial U/\partial c)$ and $f_{pg} = \partial/\partial k_g(\partial f/\partial k_p)$ and f_g, f_p denote the partial derivatives of $f(k_p, k_g)$ with respect to k_g and k_p, respectively. It is clear that if the coefficient matrix of the vector $\begin{bmatrix} dc \\ dk_g \\ dk_p \end{bmatrix}$ is negative definite, then the solution in (8.9.10) is unique [1] and the deviations from the point $(\bar{c}, \bar{k}_g, \bar{k}_p)$ may be locally stable [8].

A second interesting feature is in the dynamic trajectory of the optimal path specified by the canonical differential equations, e.g.,

$$\phi(p, k) = \dot{p}/p = w - f_p; f_p \equiv \partial f/\partial k_p \tag{8.9.12}$$

$$\psi(p, k) = \dot{k} = f(k_k, k_g) - \gamma k - c; \tag{8.9.13}$$

where the variables c, k_p, k_g are understood to satisfy the short-run equilibrium system (8.9.10). It is clear that the stationary solution of the above dynamic system is given by $\phi(p, k) = 0 = \dot{p}$, $\psi(p, k) = 0$. Under certain conditions (e.g., if the locus $\psi(p, k) = 0$ lies above the locus $\phi(p, k) = 0$ for large but finite k) it is known that at least one stationary equilibrium solution exists and if the following conditions are satisfied at this point (p^*, k^*) say

$$\left(\frac{dp}{dk}\right)_{\phi(p^*, k^*) = 0} = -\left(\frac{\partial \phi}{\partial k} \Big/ \frac{\partial \phi}{\partial p}\right) < 0$$

$$\left(\frac{dp}{dk}\right)_{\psi(p^*, k^*) = 0} > 0,$$

then this point has the saddle point property and there are two branches of solution paths which converge at least locally to the stationary point (k^*, p^*). However, in the general case there may be an arbitrary number of stationary solutions and some of them may not satisfy the saddle point property. As Arrow and Kurz [1] have observed: "There will be a unique equilibrium which will be a saddle point, if $w - \gamma$ is sufficiently small and $U_{cg} = \partial(\partial U/\partial c)/\partial k_g$ is nonnegative. In general there will be an odd number of equilibria; every other one beginning with the one with the smallest value of k will be a saddle point, while those remaining are totally unstable."

Note, however, that the balanced growth solution, when the economy is in dynamic equilibrium can be derived from (8.9.12) and (8.9.13) by imposing the conditions $\dot{p} = 0$, $\dot{k} = 0$ and the stability or instability of this solution can be compared with usual equilibrium models of growth (e.g., Solow model [8]). An interesting link between the long run balanced growth solution and a short-run disequilibrium model has been shown by Uzawa [49].

A third interesting feature of this model is that by slightly varying the structure of specification of the model, the role of controllability can be analyzed. In other words, second-best optimal policies and their stability properties may be analyzed, if we assume that government investment is financed by income tax alone and the private sector investment is subject to a fixed ratio of private savings to private disposable income. The optimal control model [1] in this case becomes

$$\text{Maximize } W = \int_{0}^{\infty} \exp(-\lambda t) U[c(t), k_g(t)] \, dt \qquad (8.9.14a)$$

subject to the constraints

$$\dot{k} - sy_d - \gamma k_p \tag{8.9.14b}$$

$$\dot{k}_g = \theta y - \gamma k_g \tag{8.9.14c}$$

$$y = f(k_p, k_g). \tag{8.9.14d}$$

Here s is the fixed savings ratio $(0 < s < 1)$, where personal savings per capita $s_p = sy_d = (1 - \theta)y$ and per capita consumption is $c = (1 - s)y_d$ and θ is the income tax rate as a proportion to per capita national output. It is clear that if the savings ratio s is a fixed constant, then from (8.9.14b) and the definition of c we get

$$s/(1 - s) = (\dot{k}_p + \gamma k_p)/c \rightarrow \gamma k_p^*/c^*,$$

where k_p^*, c^* specify limiting stationary values when $\dot{k}_p = 0$. Since the left hand side of (8.9.14c) is a fixed constant, there is no reason why the control variables (k_p, c, k_g) would satisfy the condition except by chance. Thus, neither the publicly optimal policy nor any other given feasible allocation policy is controllable in general.

It is clear, therefore, that we have to investigate whether a meaningful second-best optimal control exists for the model (8.9.14a) through (8.9.14d). Again, using the Hamiltonian function

$$H = U(c, k_g) + p_p(sy_d - \gamma k_p) + p_g(\theta y - \gamma k_g)$$

we can apply Proposition 3 (the Continuous Maximum Principle) and obtain stationary and other solutions provided they exist.

Two brief comments may be added here. First, a number of similar models involving resource allocation under neoclassical production functions with an intertemporal welfare functional is available in the current literature [5, 11, 23] and the introduction of monetary and fiscal instruments are considered in more generalized frameworks, e.g., multisector and/or heterogeneous capital goods [44, 47]. Second, the economic realism of the stationary solution when it lies on the optimal trajectory may have to be tested on the basis of empirical data. Frequently, it might take quite a long period to reach the stationary state and in that case, following the Keynesian dictum that in the long run we are all dead, the result may be very unrealistic. Very similar objections have been raised by Frisch [15] against the turnpike-type models.

B. Controllability in a Stabilization Model:

A number of attempts has been made in recent times in specifying various types of stabilization policy using optimal control theory [40, 48]. These attempts can be broadly classified into four groups: (1) stabilization models for disequilibrated markets and optimal policy by a central agency like government [42, 48]; (2) stabilization policies for multisector economies [7, 27, 36] under a macrodynamic economic model; (3) analysis of stabilizing tendencies of various feedback control policies using government expenditure through simulation methods [16, 42]; and (4) comparison of alternative policies in dynamic economic models of stochastic and adaptive control [43, 47].

For purposes of illustrating the concept of controllability in a stabilization model we would use a model due to Sengupta [40], which has been analyzed in this aspect in some details by Porter [36] and present the results of Porter and others [35, 37]. Thus we consider a multi-sector multiplier model with n sectors ($i = 1, 2, \ldots, n$) having the following demand (y_{di}) and supply (y_{si}) equations

$$y_{di} = c_i + a_i + u_i \tag{8.10.1}$$

$$\dot{y}_{si} = \mathrm{d}y_{si}/\mathrm{d}t = -\lambda_i(y_{si} - y_{di}), \ \lambda_i \geq 0 \tag{8.10.2}$$

$$c_i = \text{consumption expenditure} = \alpha_i \sum_{j=1}^{n} y_{sj} \qquad 0 \leq \alpha_i \leq 1$$

$$a_i = \text{autonomous expenditure}; \ u_i = \text{government expenditure}$$

Note that the supply equation (8.10.2) expresses the short-run adjustment mechanism which may be in output terms (if unutilized capacity exists) or in price terms (if there is no excess capacity) or in some combination. The above scalar equations can be expressed as a single vector-matrix equation

$$\dot{y} = Fy + Gu + Ga, \tag{8.10.3}$$

where G is a diagonal matrix with elements ($\lambda_1, \ldots, \lambda_n$) in the diagonal and the matrix F has elements f_{ij} given by

$$f_{ii} = -\lambda_i(1 - \alpha_i) \quad \text{and} \quad f_{ij} = \lambda_i \alpha_i \qquad i \neq j; i, j = 1, \ldots, n.$$

In control theory, the controllability of the system[1] (8.10.3) is tested by the rank condition of controllability developed by Kalman and his associates

---

[1] This section which analyzes the controllability of the dynamic model (8.10.3) and the associated stabilizing tendencies of the feedback laws is taken from Porter [36].

[21]. The condition is to test if the rank of the matrix

$$Q = [G, FG, F^2G, \ldots, F^{n-1}G] \qquad (8.10.4)$$

is n, the number of state variables in the system. It is clear that if $\lambda_i \neq 0$ $(i = 1, 2, \ldots, n)$ then the rank of Q is n and hence the system (8.10.3) is controllable, before the introduction of feedback control through the vector u, provided $\lambda_i (i = 1, 2, \ldots, n)$ is not zero.

Now consider that a certain full employment level of income (i.e., a specified vector $\hat{y}$ of sector incomes which is taken to be a constant here, although it is to be understood that in per capita terms this may be quite reasonable) is desired by the policymaker. Then if the vector x denotes deviations from $\hat{y}$, the dynamic model (8.10.3) can be written as

$$\dot{x} = Fx + Gu + Ga \qquad (8.10.3a)$$

and the control problem is to determine a control vector u such that $x = x(t)$ tends to zero as $t \to \infty$ and such that the rate of decay of x may be arbitrarily chosen by the policymaker. If proportional cum-derivative controls are used in the form:

$$u = K_1 x + K_2 z, z = \int_0^t x\, dt; \qquad (8.10.3b)$$

then the augmented system equations become

$$\begin{pmatrix} \dot{x} \\ \dot{z} \end{pmatrix} = \begin{bmatrix} F & 0 \\ I_n & 0 \end{bmatrix} \begin{pmatrix} x \\ z \end{pmatrix} + \begin{bmatrix} G \\ 0 \end{bmatrix} (u + a). \qquad (8.10.5)$$

Again, a necessary and sufficient condition for the controllability of the system (8.10.5) is that

$$\text{rank } G = n \text{ and rank } F^{-1}G = n. \qquad (8.10.6)$$

If the matrix F is singular, the second condition of (8.10.6) is to be replaced by

$$\text{rank } (F + GK)^{-1}G = n,$$

where K is any matrix for which $(F + GK)$ has an inverse. In our model (8.10.3) the determinant of F is

$$|F| = (-1)^n [\prod_{j=1}^{n} \lambda_j (1 - \sum_1^n \alpha_i)]$$

and since $\lambda_i \neq 0$ $(i = 1, 2, \ldots, n)$ by the first condition of (8.10.6), it is clear that F will be nonsingular if $\Sigma \alpha_i \neq 1$. Again, even if F is singular (i.e., $\Sigma \alpha_i = 1$), but G is nonsingular with rank n, then a matrix K must exist such that

$$F + GK = M,$$

where M is an arbitrary nonsingular square matrix of order n.

It is clear, therefore, that independently of the singularity or otherwise of F the augmented system (8.10.5) is completely controllable if $\lambda_i > 0$ ($i = 1, 2, \ldots, n$). Also, it is known [36] that this is the condition of stabilizability of the system (8.10.3a) by the feedback control law (8.10.3b).

Two brief remarks may be made about this type of multiplier accelerator models. First, a discrete-time version of this class of models, in a somewhat more general setting, can be considered where the class of feedback controls could also be more general [37, 47]. Second, it is clear that an optimal control could be specified in this framework if one could specify an objective functional in terms of x and u. The implications of a quadratic functional and the comparison of alternative control policies are discussed by Sengupta [40, 47] and a number of authors. Since an optimal control need not be stabilizing ordinarily, in the sense that the feedback control laws like (8.10.3b) are, adaptive control methods are designed to combine the stability and optimality aspects in an optimal feedback control mechanism, whenever it is possible. Adaptive control methods and their application to economic models are discussed in some detail by Tintner and Sengupta [47].

8.3. A Numerical Application to a Nonlinear Planning Model

This section presents some of the numerical problems of computing optimal trajectories using control-theoretic techniques, e.g., the sensitivity of different algorithms used, the nature of convergence to the turnpike and some approximations to the optimal control mechanism. Two nonlinear planning models which are taken from Keller and Sengupta [22, 23] will be used here for illustration, in order to analyze the sensitivity of two numerical algorithms known as (a) the conjugate gradient and (b) the Davidon method. These two methods are described in detail in [22].

8.3.1. First Numerical Experiment: A Quadratic Model

As an initial sequence of numerical experiments illustrating the control algorithms applied to solve economic models numerically, one may formulate a simple model which has linear production and capital accumulation functions, but the technique of obtaining the numerical solution is in no way restricted to linear cases. These functions were selected only as an initial illustration and will be followed by studies of nonlinear relationships. This model imputes in its objective function a quadratic valuation function of the squared difference between per worker consumption $c(t)$ and a known desired per worker consumption $c^*(t)$ rather than a log function.

Define the following variables: $K(t)$: aggregate capital stock; $C(t)$: aggregate consumption; $(L(t)$: labour force $(L_0 e^{rt})$; $Y(t)$: aggregate output; B: output-capital ratio (parameter); p: penalty constant; (K_0, K_f): initial and final capital stock; $[t_0, t_f]$: fixed planning horizon and $k(t) = K(t)/L(t)$, $c(t) = C(t)/L(t)$, and $y(t) = Y(t)/L(t)$. Then the optimal planning problem $P-1$ can be formulated as follows:

$$\text{minimize } J = \int_{t_0}^{t_f} (c(t) - c^*(t))^2 \, dt + \frac{p}{2}(K(t_f) - K_f)^2 \qquad (8.11.1)$$

subject to:

$$\dot{K}(t) = Y(t) - L_0 e^{rt} c(t) \qquad (8.11.2)$$

$$Y(t) = BK(t) \qquad (8.11.3)$$

$$K(t_0) = K_0, \qquad K(t_f) = K_f. \qquad (8.11.4)$$

The optimal solution for problem $P-1$ may be computed directly from the above formulation or computed after the problem has been stated in per worker terms. For a representative parameter specification let $r=0.01$, $B=0.25$, and $L_0 = 10.00$. Let the desired control $c^*(t)$ be a given as a subsistence level plus a linear time trend, $c^*(t) = 9.0 + 0.5t$, and $t_0 = 0.0$, $t_f = 10.0$. If one allows for a 5 per cent per year rate of growth of output from the economic unit, then $Y(10) = 165.0$, where $Y(0) = 100.0$.

This class of problems, linear dynamics, nonautonomous with quadratic objective functional and state variable terminal constraints, represents one of the easier types of control problems to solve. All numerical computations were made on the IBM 360/40 digital computer using Fortran IV language and double precision arithmetic with accuracy of approximately 16 decimal digits. Both the conjugate gradient and the Davidon algorithms were used to solve the problem $P-1$. In terms of the output variable $Y(t)$ and the adjoint variable $\pi(t)$, the necessary conditions are:

$$\dot{Y}(t) = B(Y(t) - c(t)L_0 e^{rt}), \qquad Y(0) = 100.0$$

$$\dot{\pi}(t) = -B\pi(t), \qquad \pi(10) = p(Y(10) - 165.0)$$

$$g = H_c = 2(c(t) - c^*(t)) - \pi(t)L_0 B e^{rt} = 0,$$

where $H = (c - c^*)^2 + \pi(t)(Y(t) - L_0 c(t) e^{rt})B$.

As the sensitivity indicator for the two algorithms, we use the following norm

$$(g, g) = \int_{t_0}^{t_f} g^T(u(t)) g(u(t))\, dt \,; \quad g(u(t)) = \frac{\partial H}{\partial u} \quad T: \text{transpose}$$

in our computation. This norm is basically related to the Hamiltonian H of the dynamic system. According to Pontryagin's maximum principle, optimal controls $u(t)$ must satisfy for each t the necessary condition $\partial H/\partial u = 0$. Hence, the first-order variation of the functional J can be written as

$$\delta J = \int_{t_0}^{t_f} \left(\frac{\partial H}{\partial u} \right)^T \delta u \, dt.$$

If the variation of the control u is along a direction of search s, then

$$\delta u = s \delta \alpha,$$

where α is a scalar search-parameter. Thus, the derivative of J along s is given by the inner product of $g = \partial H/\partial u$ and s. Also

$$dJ/d\alpha = \int_{t_0}^{t_f} \left[\frac{\partial H^T}{\partial u} \right] s \, dt.$$

TABLE 8.1

Convergence Results for Problem P-1

Iteration Number	Numbers of Integrations	Value of J (obj. function)	Norm (g, g)	$Y(10.0) - 165.0$
Davidon Method:				
1	4	80.5861	263.433	−0.0591
2	7	14.7394	28.205	−0.0988
3	2	14.7370	0.000001	−0.0584
Conjugate Gradient Method				
1	4	80.5861	263.432	−0.0591
2	8	16.2077	16570.00	−0.0103
3	3	14.7370	0.0110	−0.0592
4	9	14.7370	0.00016	−0.0544
5	5	14.7370	0.0246	−0.0572
6	2	14.7370	0.0557	−0.0566
7	3	14.7370	0.0003	−0.0582
8	10	14.7370	0.000003	−0.0584

Therefore, $\partial H/\partial u = g(u)$ is analogous to the gradient vector in finite dimensional analysis and the norm based on the inner product (g, g) defined above can be used as a measure of sensitivity for characterizing the neighborhood of perturbations around the optimal trajectory. In our numerical computations, the penalty constant used was 3.0 and for both algorithms the initial control used was $c_0(t) = 9.0$. The stopping rule was a value of (g, g) less than 1.0×10^{-4}. Values of the functional J, the norm (g, g), and the number of forward and backward integrations per iteration are summarized in Table 8.1. The conjugate gradient method with this and other experiments was much more sensitive to the α-search direction parameter. It required 44 integrations of the state and adjoint differential equations. Most of these were required to determine the search direction parameter.

TABLE 8.2
Optimal Trajectories for Problem P-1 with Time Horizon [0, 10]

t	$Y(t)$	$c(t)$	$C(t)$	$S(t)$	$S(t)/Y(t)$
0.0	100.00000	6.32990	63.29900	36.70100	0.36701
1.2	110.53299	7.59810	76.89827	33.63472	0.30430
2.0	117.08499	8.34780	85.16438	31.92061	0.27263
2.8	123.31299	9.03640	92.92993	30.38306	0.24639
3.6	129.24599	9.67470	100.29329	28.95270	0.22401
4.4	134.89699	10.27130	107.33322	27.56377	0.20433
5.2	140.26900	10.83350	114.11751	26.15149	0.18644
6.0	145.35199	11.36750	120.70422	24.6477	0.16957
6.8	150.11800	11.87800	127.13794	22.98006	0.15308
7.6	154.52800	12.36920	133.45900	21.06900	0.13634
8.4	158.52399	12.84450	139.70041	18.82358	0.11874
9.2	162.02800	13.30660	145.88889	16.13911	0.09961
10.0	164.94199	13.75700	152.03839	12.90359	0.07823

The Davidon algorithm was much less sensitive to the search direction parameter. It converged after three steps and 13 integrations of the differential equations. Both methods gave essentially the same results for the trajectories for problem P-1. Results for various time points are given in Table 8.2. The stepsize for the Runge-Kutta integration was $h = 0.1$. An approximation of the computation time for the Davidon algorithm was 18 seconds per iteration. This includes CPU time and printing time. The time per iteration varies depending on how many linear searches must be completed in the iteration to compute an optimal search parameter.

8.3.2. *Second Numerical Experiment: A Nonlinear Planning Model*

As a second sequence of numerical experiments, we consider the nonlinear planning model (here referred to as problem P-2) studied by Kendrick and Taylor [24], which has a nonlinear welfare function and a linear production function.

The control problem P-2 is formulated as follows:

$$\text{maximize } J = \int_{t_0}^{t_f} e^{-\rho t} \frac{1}{1-n} (C(t))^{1-n} \, dt$$

subject to

$$\dot{K}(t) = e^{zt} \gamma K(t)^B (L_0 e^{rt})^{1-B} - C(t) - \delta K(t)$$

$$K(0) = K_0 \quad \text{and} \quad K(t_f) = K_f$$

Here the variables are:

- J = an index of performance,
- ρ = time rate of welfare discount,
- $C(t)$ = consumption at time t,
- n = elasticity of marginal utility with respect to consumption,
- $\dot{K}(t)$ = capital accumulation,
- $K(t)$ = stock of capital,
- δ = rate of capital depreciation,
- $K(0) = K_0$ is the initial stock of capital,
- $K(t_f) = K_f$ is the terminal stock of capital,
- z = rate of neutral technical progress,
- γ = efficiency parameter,
- B = elasticity of output with respect to capital,
- L_0 = initial labor force,
- r = rate of growth of the labor force,
- $[0, t_f]$ = fixed time horizon.

The form of the production function used is

$$Y(t) = F(K(t)) = e^{zt} \gamma (K(t))^B (L_0 e^{rt})^{1-B} = a e^{gt} (K(t))^B,$$

where $a = \gamma L_0^{1-B}$ and $g = r(1-B) + z$.

The utility function

$$U(C(t)) = \frac{1}{1-n} (C(t))^{1-n},$$

where $n \geq 0$ and $n \neq 1$ has the following properties:

$$U'(C(t)) \geq 0 \qquad\qquad C > 0$$

$$U''(C(t)) \leq 0 \qquad\qquad C \geq 0$$

$$\lim_{n \to 0} U(C(t)) = C(t).$$

We attempted here to gain insight into how nonlinear specification of these functions affects the time paths of the optimal solution trajectories. Penalty functions are used to handle terminal constraints on the state variables. A number of combinations of different parameter values were attempted for this model and a selected optimal trajectory for problem P-2 is given in Table 8.3, when $\delta = 0.05$, $\rho = 0.03$, $n = 0.9$, $r = 0.025$, $K_0 = 15.0$, $z = 0.01$, $Y_0 = 4.27$, $L_0 = 15.0$, $\gamma = 0.285$, and $Y_f = F(K_f) = 7.04$.

The value of the functional was 98.182 and a fixed penalty constant of 5.0 was used with an initial control variable of $C_0(t) = 1.0$. The following features of computation may be summarized:

(a) In all numerical experimentations, the Davidon algorithm was much less sensitive to both the initial control estimate and the search direction parameter. In *every case* it converged with less iterations than the conjugate gradient method.

(b) The shadow price of additional capital measured in terms of utility is seen to start out at 0.479 and decrease to 0.148 as the terminal constraint on capital is satisfied. The savings rate decreases from 0.472 to 0.164 over the ten-year horizon.

(c) The behavior of the savings rate agrees with the expectation that when attempting to hit a certain target rate of growth of output (in the example of problem P-2, 5 per cent per year), an economy with more productive capital should save more in the earlier years of the planning horizon. This example also illustrates the need for obtaining good estimates in the production function parameters as the optimal trajectories change with respect to different values of the parameter B.

It is known [24] that the optimal path satisfies the "turnpike property". As the time horizon $[0, t_f]$ becomes sufficiently long, the optimal time paths for capital per worker and for consumption per worker spend an arbitrarily large portion of the time close to the balanced growth equilibrium. For example, starting from its initial level, k_0 capital per worker moves toward $\bar{k}$ and stays near there, eventually moving away from $\bar{k}$ to satisfy the terminal requirement $k(t_f) = k_f$.

With the parameter values used in Table 8.3 (i.e., $B = 0.6$, $a = 0.8419$, and the growth rate of labor $r = 0.025$ per year), it appears from our computations that the ten-year horizon does not allow the turnpike property to manifest itself for problem P-2. Consumption per worker at $t = 0$ is $c(0) =$

TABLE 8.3

Optimal Trajectories for Problem P-2 with $B = 0.6$, $a = 0.8419$ and Time Horizon of 10

Time t	Output $Y(t)$	Capital $K(t)$	Consumption $C(t)$	Adjoint Variable $\pi(t)$	Savings Rate
0.0	4.275	15.000	2.255	0.479	0.472
0.4	4.395	15.503	2.369	0.457	0.461
1.2	4.636	16.497	2.575	0.415	0.445
2.0	4.878	17.485	2.769	0.377	0.432
2.8	5.122	18.470	2.973	0.344	0.419
3.6	5.367	19.440	3.200	0.314	0.403
4.4	5.610	20.374	3.455	0.286	0.384
5.2	5.845	21.248	3.737	0.260	0.361
6.0	6.071	22.039	4.043	0.238	0.334
6.8	6.283	22.722	4.369	0.217	0.304
7.6	6.477	23.277	4.709	0.197	0.273
8.4	6.651	23.683	5.060	0.179	0.239
9.2	6.798	23.921	5.419	0.163	0.202
10.0	6.917	23.970	5.783	0.148	0.164

$$J = 98.182$$

0.146 and at $t = 10.0$ has increased to $c(10) = 0.27$, where the equilibrium point $\bar{c} = 0.338$ has not been reached. Likewise with $k(t)$, $k(0) = 1.0$ and $k(10) = 1.2$, where $\bar{k}$, the equilibrium point is $\bar{k} = 3.385$. It would appear that a time horizon of approximately 20 years would be needed to exhibit the turnpike property of problem P-2. Note that the balanced growth solution in our case is given by

$$C(t) = (0.338)e^{0.025t}(15.0)$$

$$K(t) = (3.385)(15.0)e^{0.025t}.$$

A detailed analysis of the stationary solution and other characteristics may be found in [23].

8.3.3. Simulation of Optimal Trajectories

Another approach by which one may numerically solve and study optimal economic growth and planning problems relates to simulation, both stochastic and deterministic. The objective of the simulated optimization approach is to develop efficient techniques for locating improved but not necessarily optimum solutions to models where other optimization techniques cannot be realistically applied or are too costly to utilize. A number of methods are available in this area [47]. For example, Fromm and Taubman [16] have applied the technique of simulation via repeated solution of an econometric model to compute the utility of alternative policy actions for evaluating the relative desirability of a set of monetary and fiscal policy actions. Naylor, Wertz, and Wonnacott [33] used stochastic simulation to compare the stability of various policy actions by statistical techniques. Our objective in simulation is to compare the optimal solution (i.e., consumption path) computed from an optimal growth model based on a utility functional with the consumption path computed from various runs of a simulated system based on some sort of feedback relation either deterministic or stochastic. Comparisons may be considered either on the magnitude of consumption, $C(t)$, or its variability, or of the computed utility of the consumption. Experimentation based on the computed optimal paths from problem P-2 were compared with various simulated results, which are reported in detail in [23]. The objective of such simulation, which is extensively discussed in adaptive control methods [47], is to determine that combination of parameter values at which the objective functional (or its deterministic equivalent) is optimized in a suitable fashion.

8.4. Concluding Remarks

From our brief discussion of the control theory methods, it should be clear that these methods provide a very powerful tool for analyzing dynamic economic policies. But insofar as realistic applications to problems of national planning in various countries are concerned, a number of areas exist where difficulties and unsolved problems remain. Some of these areas include, for example, the following: (a) problems of efficient computation of optimal trajectory through decomposition and other methods, (b) development of simpler and approximate methods for choosing controls which are in some sense robust or insensitive in a relative sense to variations in parameters like the capital-output ratio etc., and (c) methods of incorporating what has been called safety-programming by Kornai [26] in the formulation and application of multi-sectoral planning models. Each of these areas presents in our opinion a challenge to the experts specializing in the theory of economic policy currently or in the future.

REFERENCES

[1] Arrow, K. J. and Kurz, M. *The Public Investment, the Rate of Return and Optimal Fiscal Policy*. Baltimore: Johns Hopkins Press, 1970.

[2] Bellman, R., *Adaptive Control Processes: A Guided Tour*. Princeton: Princeton University Press, 1961.

[3] ——. *Some Vistas of Modern Mathematics: Dynamic Programming, Invariant Imbedding and the Mathematical Biosciences*. Lexington: University of Kentucky Press, 1968.

[4] Box, M. J., Davies, D. and Swann, W. H. *Nonlinear Optimization Techniques*. Edinburgh: Oliver and Boyd, 1969.

[5] Bruno, M. "Optimal Accumulation in Discrete Capital Models." In *Essays on the Theory of Optimal Economic Growth*, edited by K. Shell, Massachusetts: MIT Press, 1967, Chap. 11.

[6] Bryson, A. E., Jr. and Ho, Y. C. *Applied Optimal Control*. London: Blaisdell Publishing Co., 1969.

[7] Buchanan, L. F. and Norton, F. E. "Optimal Control Applications in Economic Systems." In *Advances in Control Systems*, Vol. 8, ed. by C. T. Leondes, New York: Academic Press, 1971, pp. 141–187.

[8] Burmeister, E. and Dobell, A. R. *Mathematical Theories of Economic Growth*. New York: Macmillan and Co., 1970.

[9] Chenery, H. B. (ed.), *Studies in Development Planning*. Cambridge, Mass.: Harvard University Press, 1971.

[10] Davidon, W. C. "Variable Metric Method for Minimization." *Argonne National Laboratory Report ANL 5990*. Revised February 1966.

[11] Dobell, A. R. "Optimization in Models of Economic Growth." In *Studies in Optimization*, Part 1, Philadelphia, Pennsylvania: SIAM, 1970, pp. 1–27.

[12] Feldbaum, A. A., *Optimal Control Systems*. New York: Academic Press, 1965.

[13] Fletcher, R. and Reeves, C. M. "Function Minimization by Conjugate Gradients." *Computer Journal*, Vol. 7, 1964, pp. 149–154.

[14] Foley, D. K. and Sidrauski, M. *Monetary and Fiscal Policy in a Growing Economy*. London: Macmillan Co., 1971.

[15] Frisch, R. "Econometrics in the World of Today." In *Induction, Growth and Trade*, edited by W. A. Eltis, M. Fg. Scott, and J. N. Wolfe. Oxford: Clarendon Press, 1970, Chap. 11.

[16] Fromm, G. and Taubman, P. J. *Policy Simulations with an Econometric Model*. Amsterdam: North-Holland Publishing Co., 1968.

[17] Hadley, G. and Kemp, M. C. *Variational Methods in Economics*. Amsterdam: North-Holland Publishing Co., 1971.

[18] Hsieh, H. C. "Synthesis of Adaptive Control Systems by Function Span Methods." In *Advances in Control Systems*, Vol. 2, ed. by C. T. Leondes, New York: Academic Press, 1965, pp. 117–208.

[19] Hsu, J. C. and Meyer, A. U. *Modern Control Principles and Applications*. New York: McGraw-Hill Book Company, 1968.

[20] Kalman, R. E. "Mathematical Description of Linear Dynamical Systems." *SIAM Journal on Control*, Vol. 1, 1963, pp. 152–192.

[21] Kalman, R. E., Falb, P. L. and Arbib, M. A. *Topics in Mathematical System Theory*. New York: McGraw-Hill Book Company, 1969.

[22] KELLER, E. A., Jr. and SENGUPTA, J. K. "Relative Efficiency of Computing Optimal Growth by Conjugate Gradient and Davidon Methods." Accepted for publication in *International Journal of Systems Science*.

[23] ——. "Sensitivity Analysis for Optimal and Feedback Controls Applied to Growth Models." Accepted for publication in *Stochastics*.

[24] KENDRICK, D. and TAYLOR, L. "Numerical Methods and Nonlinear Optimizing Models for Economic Planning." In *Studies in Development Planning*, Cambridge, Mass.: Harvard University Press, 1971, Chap. 1.

[25] KORNAI, J. and LIPTAK, TH. "Two-Level Planning." *Econometrica*, Vol. 33, 1965, pp. 141–169.

[26] KORNAI, J. *Mathematical Planning of Structural Decisions*. Amsterdam: North-Holland Publishing Co., 1967.

[27] KUHN, H. W. and SZEGO, G. P. (ed.). *Mathematical Systems Theory and Economics Vol. I-II*. Berlin: Springer-Verlag, 1969.

[28] LEE, E. B. and MARKNS, L. *Foundations of Optimal Control*. New York: John Wiley, 1967.

[29] LEONDES, C. T. (ed.). *Advances in Control Systems*, Vol. 1–8. New York: Academic Press, 1964–1971.

[30] MANGASARIAN, O. L. 'Sufficient Conditions for the Optimal Control of Nonlinear Systems." *SIAM Journal on Control*, Vol. 4, 1966, pp. 139–152.

[31] MESAROVIC, M. D., PEARSON, J. D., and others. "A Multilevel Stricture for a Class of Linear Dynamic Optimization Problems." *Preprint of Technical Papers*, Joint Automatic Control Conference, Vol. 6, 1965, pp. 93–99.

[32] MORISHIMA, M. *Theory of Economic Growth*. Oxford: Clarendon Press, 1969.

[33] NAYLOR, T. H., WERTZ, K. and WONNACOTT, T. H. "Methods for Evaluating the Effects of Economic Policies Using Simulation Experiments." *Review of International Statistical Institute*, Vol. 36, 1968, pp. 184–200.

[34] PONTRYAGIN, L. S., BOLTYANSKII, V. G., GAMKRELIDZE, R. V. and MISHCHENKO, E. F. *The Mathematical Theory of Optimal Processes*. New York: Interscience, John Wiley and Sons, 1962.

[35] PORTER, B. "Synthesis of Control Policies for Economic Models: A Continuous-Time Multiplier Model." *International Journal of Systems Science*, Vol. 1, 1970, pp. 1–8.

[36] ——. "Stabilization Policies for Multisector Closed Economies." *International Journal of Systems Science*, Vol. 2, 1971, pp. 113–117.

[37] ——, and CROSSLEY, T. R. "Synthesis of Control Policies for Economic Models: A Discrete-Time Multiplier Model." *International Journal of Systems Science*, Vol. 1, 1970, pp. 9–16.

[38] SENGUPTA, J. K. "Cobweb Cycles and Optimal Price Stabilization through Buffer Funds." *Indian Economic Journal*, Vol. 13, 1965, pp. 351–364.

[39] ——, and FOX, K. A. *Economic Analysis and Operations Research: Optimization Techniques in Quantitative Economic Models*. Amsterdam: North-Holland Publishing Co., 1969.

[40] ——. "Optimal Stabilization Policy with a Quadratic Criterion Function." *Review of Economic Studies*, Vol. 37, 1970, pp. 127–145.

[41] ——. "Economic Problems of Resource Allocation in Nonmarket Systems." In *Economic Analysis for Educational Planning*, edited by K. A. Fox, Baltimore: Johns Hopkins Press. 1972, Chap. 6.

[42] ——. "Economic Policy Simulation in Dynamic Control Models Under Econometric Estimation." To be published in *Essays in Honor of Jan Tinbergen,* ed. by W. Sellekaerts, New York: Macmillan International, 1972 (in press).

[43] ——. "Decision Rules in Stochastic Programming Under Dynamic Economic Models." To be published in *Swedish Journal of Economics.*

[44] SHELL, K. (ed.). *Essays on the Theory of Optimal Economic Growth.* Cambridge, Mass.: MIT Press, 1967.

[45] STOLERU, L. G. "An Optimal Policy for Economic Growth." *Econometrica,* Vol. 33, 1965, pp. 321–348.

[46] THEIL, H., *Optimal Decision Rules for Government and Industry.* Amsterdam: North-Holland Publishing Co., 1964.

[47] TINTNER, G. and SENGUPTA, J. K. *Stochastic Economics: Stochastic Processes, Control, and Programming.* New York: Academic Press, 1972.

[48] TURNOVSKY, S. J. "Optimal Government Stabilization Policy in a Single Disequilibrated Market." *Australian Economic Papers,* Vol. 10, 1971, pp. 67–85.

[49] UZAWA, H. "An Optimal Fiscal Policy in an Aggregative Model of Economic Growth." In *The Theory and Design of Economic Development,* edited by I. Adelman and E. Thorbecke, Baltimore: Johns Hopkins Press, 1966, Chap. 5.

Chapter 9

DECISION MAKING UNDER RISK AND UNCERTAINTY IN ECONOMIC POLICY MODELS

There are several ways in which stochastic elements may enter into a Tinbergen-type policy model. First, it is usual for at least some of the structural equations of an economic model to have been estimated statistically, and statistical estimation theory can be interpreted, according to one viewpoint, as a part of statistical decision theory [5]. Second, the weights in the objective function, which are supposed to specify barter terms of trade between the different target variables and different instrument variables (i.e., to bring all important variables to a common denominator through a scalar welfare function) are generally assumed known only within ranges, since the exact specification [1] of these weights is very difficult, if not impossible. Third, the boundary conditions, which are generally implicit in the specification of a policy model, may have variable bounds or, in other words, the bounds specified are only the confidence bounds.

The analytical treatment of such random elements is complicated by several factors, some of which may be mentioned very briefly. First, there is a distinction between repetitive and once-for-all choice (i.e., nonrepetitive) situations which is most relevant for almost all economic decisions. The first case arises where one could assume the specification of a probability distribution for the random elements and decisions are made continually so a learning process is conceivable. In once-for-all choice situations the sampling properties of a decision rule become irrelevant, as it were, because the concept of "average," which is based on a sampling framework, is no longer appropriate. Sometimes this dichotomy is expressed by the distinction which is generally made between risk and uncertainty, where risk presupposes

---

[1] In discussing the attempt of van Eijk and Sandee to quantify the policy maker's preference function, we saw (Chapter 7, Section 7.1) that the weights are only partially determined by imaginary interviewing, because of the assumption of a separable preference function and the possibility of statistical bias in the method of interview.

a known probability distribution whereas uncertainty does not. However, this distinction is not very operational in practice, because in empirical work where the probability distribution itself has to be estimated, it has its own uncertain elements.

Second, any behavior (or decision) which is considered as rational (or optimal) in the presence of random elements is so only in a very well-defined and restricted class. As Arrow [1] has pointed out, we do not really have universally valid criteria for rational behavior under uncertainty. This means not only that we have different classes of decision rules and hence different optima, but also that there is, in general, an element of competitiveness between different optimum decision rules. This has been shown by Milnor [24], who compared alternative principles for ordering risk functions (e.g., minimax and other principles and also the subjective a priori probabilities) and tested against formal but intuitively plausible axioms and proved finally that every conventional ordering principle contradicts at least one intuitively reasonable axiom.

Third, the rationality of an optimal decision, viewed in relation to either the subjective belief of the policy maker or the empirical probability estimated by the technician, is generally evaluated in terms of a scalar preference function rather than a vector function. Hence, decisions which involve many goals, some of which are not comparable in terms of a common denominator (i.e., a certain gain or loss in dollars) are not really facilitated by the existing optimization criteria for risk and uncertainty that are based on scalar functions.

Subject to the above limitations, it is most interesting to analyze some of the broad results on optimal decision making under risk. In its most general form a Tinbergen-type policy model should be viewed as a programming model with inequalities as constraints. The introduction of random elements and the consideration of a linear model leads generally to linear programming under risk, where a number of analytical results are available, though they are not at this stage very operational for large-scale problems. A more specialized form of an economic policy model is in terms of equations containing errors as additive disturbances, usually assumed in the theory of simultaneous-equations estimation. In this case we can discuss different types of decision rules and compare their properties of stability, optimality and even flexibility in a certain sense. The examples of optimum decision rules and the implications of the Simon-Theil certainty equivalence theorem, considered before in Chapter 6, fall in this category. We consider first some simple illustrations of decision rules under repetitive choice situations and then mention some of the simpler results of linear programming under stochastic conditions.

9.1. Decision Rules in Macroeconomic Models

Let us assume that we have either a static macroeconomic model involving the conventional multiplier or a macrodynamic model involving both the multiplier and the accelerator. The static model, which is identical with the static uncertainty model, considered by Holt [14] is

$$Y = C + I + G, \tag{9.1.1}$$
$$C = cY, \qquad 0 < c < 1.$$

The dynamic model (case of dynamic uncertainty) corresponding to (9.1.1) is assumed here to be of the following form

$$
\begin{aligned}
Y &= C + I + G, \\
C &= cY, \\
I &= I_a + I_b, \\
I_b &= b(dY/dt),
\end{aligned}
\tag{9.1.2}
$$

where the first equation specifies the familiar income (Y) identity, with consumption (C), investment (I) and government expenditure (G) as the components of total effective demand. The division of private investment (I) into relatively autonomous (I_a) and nonautonomous (I_b) parts is made to introduce the familiar acceleration principle. Following Holt, we introduce a quadratic disutility function in its most simple form, but in terms of total consumption[2] rather than national income

$$D = (C - C^*)^2, \tag{9.1.3}$$

where C^* is the level of aggregate consumption desired by the central policy maker on the basis of considerations which are largely exogenous. Further, we assume that investment (I) is the only random variable in the problem with a certain probability distribution. We minimize the expected

---

[2] Consumption rather than income may be more appropriate, particularly in the long-run case, where consumption provides the goal of human needs and satisfaction. That is the way the Ramsay-type optimality of growth path is specified as a question of optimal savings and consumption. A more general function corresponding to (7.1.3) would incorporate a term $(I - I^*)^2$ to suggest that different components of national income may have different degrees of instability associated with them. For this problem see Tinbergen and Bos [48, pp. 24–27].

value of D given in equation (9.1.3) with respect to G, where G is related to other variables by the static model (9.1.1). Easy calculations show that minimization is achieved by the following value of G

$$G = \left(\frac{1-c}{c}\right)C^* - EI \qquad (0 < c < 1) \tag{9.2.1}$$

where E denotes the expectation operator. As one would expect, the higher the value of desired consumption (C^*), the higher is the required government expenditure (i.e., the control variable); and the higher the level of average investment (EI), the lower is the required level of control G. The decision rule (9.2.1) is linear, and its advantage is that it requires the knowledge of only the first moment of the probability distribution of the random variable I. Note, however, that in deriving the decision rule (9.2.1) we have chosen to minimize only one type of average disutility, namely, the arithmetic average of D. Suppose now we define by $M(D)$ any type of weighted average of the nonnegative random variable D, including the arithmetic mean, the median and the mode, etc., for which the following equality holds

$$\frac{\partial M(D)}{\partial G} = M\frac{\partial D}{\partial G} \tag{9.3.0}$$

when D is given by (9.1.3). Then for minimizing $M(D)$ with respect to G we must have

$$M(C) = C^*. \tag{9.3.1}$$

But by simple substitution we derive from equations (9.1.1)

$$C = \left(\frac{c}{1-c}\right)(I + G). \tag{9.3.2}$$

By combining (9.3.1) and (9.3.2) and rearranging we get

$$G = \left(\frac{1-c}{c}\right)C^* - M(I), \qquad (0 < c < 1) \tag{9.2.2}$$

where $M(I)$ denotes the set of all "average" values of the nonnegative random variable I for which the transformation defined in (9.3.0) exists. Now if $M(I)$ is taken as the expectation of I, i.e., $M(I) = EI = \bar{I}$, we obtain from (9.2.2) the original decision rule (9.2.1). Now we consider other types of averages included in the set $M(I)$. Let us assume for simplicity that the nonnegative random variable I has the triangular probability density function

$$f(I)dI = (2/A^2)IdI, \qquad (0 \le I \le A < \infty) \tag{9.3.3}$$

then it is easy to show that the modal average of I (denoted as $\breve{I}$) exceeds the median average (denoted as $\tilde{I}$), and the latter exceeds the arithmetic mean (denoted as $\bar{I}$), since $\breve{I}=A=$constant, $\tilde{I}=A/\sqrt{2}$ and $\bar{I}=EI=(2/3)A$. Now we replace $M(I)$ in equation (9.2.2) by these three types of "averages" and denote the corresponding values of G by $\breve{G}$, $\tilde{G}$ and $\bar{G}$, respectively. Under the given assumptions and notations we can state the following proposition:

If the nonnegative random variable I is distributed like the triangular distribution (9.3.3) such that its mode ($\breve{I}$), median ($\tilde{I}$) and arithmetic mean ($\bar{I}$) exist and fulfill the condition (9.3.0), the following inequality holds:

$$\breve{G} < \tilde{G} < \bar{G}$$

between the three alternative optimal values of G given by the linear decision rule equation (9.2.2). To prove the proposition we substitute in equation (9.2.2) the three types of averages of the random variable I, and since C^* is a nonrandom and nonnegative quantity, the inequality $\breve{I}>\tilde{I}>\bar{I}$ immediately leads to $(-\breve{I})<(-\tilde{I})<(-\bar{I})$, from which we obtain finally $\breve{G}<\tilde{G}<\bar{G}$. A corollary to this proposition is that $\breve{G}=\tilde{G}=\bar{G}$ whenever the probability distribution of the random variable I is symmetrical in the sense that $\breve{I}=\tilde{I}=\bar{I}$ (e.g., the normal distribution). This proposition is useful [3] in showing which kind of "average" specifies the minimum amount of government expenditure (i.e., minimum cost) to attain a minimum of "average" social disutility, when the distribution of the random variable is far from symmetrical. However, we should note that the information required about the probability distribution of investment (I) is much more extensive here. Following Simon's approach [38, pp. 74–81], it is useful to classify the hierarchy of different kinds of information a decision maker may have about the future values of certain variables (such as investment I in our case) that are relevant for his optimal decision making. For example:

(a) He might know these values with certainty (with probability one, either subjectively or objectively). This is the nonrandom case.

(b) He might not know these values but be able only to estimate the location parameters, such as expected value, median and mode, from the available observations.

(c) When the size of the set of available observations increases, he can not only estimate the location parameters of the probability distribution

---

[3] A more general result analogous to this has been proved for the case of two-stage linear programming under uncertainty. See Charnes, Cooper and Thompson [9].

but also specify on the basis of nonparametric statistical inference whether the distribution is symmetrical or otherwise.

(d) When the set of available observations expands further, he can estimate both the location and the scale parameters and narrow down the class of distributions which might reasonably be supposed to generate the available observations.

(e) He might know the probability distribution of the future values completely, and so all its parameters could be specified with the highest possible precision.

In case (a) the optimal decision does not involve any static uncertainty. In case (b) there is a problem of optimum choice among the alternative location parameters characterizing the distribution, as we saw before. Note, however, that in case (d) we assume the knowledge of second moments of the probability distribution, and with this knowledge it may be possible in some cases to improve the optimum decision rule (9.2.1) considered before. The fact that the linear decision rule (9.2.1) requires the knowledge of only the first moment of the probability distribution of the random variable I is an advantage only when there is difficulty in estimating the higher moments, but in case higher moments are available or estimable, this decision rule has to be modified to incorporate the effects of higher moments. For instance, if disutility D defined in (9.1.3) is known to be distributed with a certain mean ED and certain information about variance (Var D is available), one may consider the likelihood of distributions such as gamma, chi-square, negative exponential and normal, depending on the relation between mean and variance. For the gamma and chi-square distributions the variance is linearly related to the arithmetic mean. If the distribution of D can be approximated by these distributions, the decision rule which minimizes ED would also minimize the variance. In general, if the variance of C is known to be some function of the expected value of C, we can expand D in a Taylor series, approximately, for small variations of C around its expectation $\bar{C}$, i.e.,

$$\begin{aligned} D = \phi\,(C - C^*) &= (C - C^*)^2\,, \\ &= \phi(\bar{C} - C^*) + (C - \bar{C})\,\phi'(\bar{C} - C^*)\,, \\ &= (\bar{C} - C^*)^2 + 2(C - \bar{C})(\bar{C} - C^*)\,, \end{aligned} \tag{9.4.1}$$

where prime denotes a partial derivative. Hence,

$$\text{Var } D \doteq [\phi'(\bar{C} - C^*)]^2 \text{ Var } C = 4(\bar{C} - C^*)^2 \text{ Var } C\,,$$

where Var C is some function of the expected value $(\bar{C} - C^*)$. Hence, we can now form a new disutility function D_1 as

$$D_1 = E(C - C^*)^2 + \lambda \text{ Var } D, \tag{9.4.2}$$

where λ is a nonnegative weight constant, and we minimize this new disutility function with respect to G to find a linear decision rule. For example, if Var $C = q\bar{C}$, q being a positive constant, we obtain a linear decision rule which would minimize disutility D_1 defined above:

$$\text{(i)} \quad G = [(2q\lambda C^* - 1)/6\alpha q\lambda] - EI$$

whereas in the case of (9.2.1) we obtained

$$\text{(ii)} \qquad G = \alpha C^* - EI,$$

where $\alpha = (1 - c)/c$, $0 < c < 1$.

However, we may choose the lower of the two values of G in (i) and (ii). It is easy to check that if α is such that

$$2q\lambda C^* (3\alpha^2 - 1) + 1 > 0$$

G in (i) is less than G in (ii). It is seen that the linear decision rule (9.2.1) is a special case of a more general situation. Similarly, one may retain higher-order terms in the Taylor expansion (9.4.1) and incorporate higher moments of the probability distribution of D, at least approximately if not exactly. This will also be helpful in testing the sensitivity of a linear decision rule.

It is worth pointing out at this stage that we have discussed, so far, different types of "average" decision rules not because we are concerned with any sampling properties but because this averaging process is one of the most important ways to specify a deterministic equivalent to a completely random (or randomized) decision rule. However, there are reasonable ways other than the averaging process for specifying deterministic equivalents. For instance, we may define a maximum-likelihood-like decision rule $G = G_0$ if the probability distribution of the nonnegative random variable D given in (9.1.3) is known to be such that the value $G = G_0$ maximizes the probability that D lies in the interval $(x < D < x + dx)$.[4] To consider a simple example, assume that the random variable D has a chi-square distribution with mean v, where $v = E(C - C^*)^2$ and the control variable G is related to C by equation (9.3.2). Taking the logarithm of $f(x)$, the frequency function,

---

[4] For the optimal properties of alternative location parameters other than the arithmetic average, see Theil [43].

we maximize $\log f(x)$ with respect to G by equating the partial derivative to zero, i.e.,

$$\frac{\partial \log f(x)}{\partial G} = \frac{\partial \log f(x)}{\partial x} \cdot \frac{\partial x}{\partial G} = 0,$$

and then noting equation (9.3.2) we obtain finally

$$G = G_0 = \frac{C^* + (v-2)^{\frac{1}{2}}}{\left(\dfrac{c}{1-c}\right)} - I_0, \qquad (v \geq 2) \qquad (9.4.3)$$

where I_0 is that value of I which corresponds to the maximum of $f(x)$ with respect to G, which is defined because of the linear relation between the variables I and C in equation (9.3.2).

So far we have considered the desired level of consumption C^* either fixed or preassigned exogenously. Next we may adopt the Bayesian stand-point[5] that C^* is like a statistical parameter having a prior distribution. The Bayesian approach is to choose that decision variable G in our static model which would minimize the expected value of disutility D defined in (9.1.3), given the value of C^*. In a fixed-target Tinbergen-type policy model with random elements this appears to be a plausible assumption for a policy maker who may be certain about the range of C^* without being definite about its actual value.[6] This is in accord with not only the subjective probability interpretation of the prior distribution of C^* but also the fact that desired values themselves are fixed on the basis of some kind of feasibility assumptions about the economic and political climate of an economy. With this interpretation we assume that we have a fixed number of observations N and the parameter C^* is unknown, although its range is known. We have to select a G and, hence, a resulting value of C which is a guess for C^*.

If we are wrong in our guess, we have a loss or disutility (D) which is assumed to be measured by the same disutility function as in equation (9.1.3), i.e.,

$$D = (C - C^*)^2,$$

---

[5] For a discussion of the Bayesian viewpoint and some of its implications for applied decision theory in terms of conjugate distributions, see Raiffa and Schlaifer [26]. For some economic implications of Wald's decision theory for the standard statistical tests, see Arrow [2].

[6] Other interpretations are also possible. The parameters estimated by sample statistics may be postulated to come from a prior distribution, particularly when the structural equations are estimated.

where C is related to investment I and government expenditure G by the static model (9.1.1) above. It should be noted that our interpretation of policy variables is now in accord with classical economic theory, which is in some cases an inversion of Tinbergen's approach to economic policy, so far as the known and unknown variables are concerned. We now argue that the variable C^* is unknown, i.e., the effect of government spending on consumption is unknown, while the instrument variable G and hence C is known except for the random elements. We are required to evaluate the different consequences of choosing different values of G and for that matter different guesses (C) at the value of C^*. The object of such evaluation is to arrive at a decision rule which has some optimum properties in some specific sense.

Following Wald [55], we now define that any rule or relation R by which we arrive at a guess C about the value of C^* is a "decision function." For instance, the following four rules are decision functions:

R_1: $C = k_1$ such that k_1 is a constant, $\qquad\qquad\qquad$ (9.5.1)

R_2: $C = k_2$ such that $EC = Ek_2 = h = C^*$ where h is non- $\qquad$ (9.5.2)
random and hence the variance of C equals $E(k_2^2) - h^2$,

R_3: $C = \lambda k_2 + (1 - \lambda)k_1$ such that λ is a constant $0 < \lambda < 1$ $\qquad$ (9.5.3)
and k_1, k_2 are defined above in R_1 and R_2,

$$R_4: C = \begin{cases} k_2 \text{ with probability } p \\ k_1 \text{ with probability } (1 - p), \end{cases} \qquad (9.5.4)$$

where k_2 and k_1 are defined above.

We note that for a given C^* and a given decision function R the statistical distribution of C and, hence, that of disutility D is fixed so that we may evaluate the expected value of D as a function of C^* and R. This function $p(C^*, R) = ED = E(C^* - C)^2$ is called "the risk function" in Wald's approach. If for two decision functions R_i, R_j, $i \neq j$ having risk functions $p_i = p(C^*, R_i)$, $p_j = p(C^*, R_j)$ we have $p_i \leq p_j$ for all values of C^*, the decision function R_i is said to be "uniformly better" than the decision function $R_j, (i \neq j)$. (We rule out the case here that by increasing N [i.e., by more observations] we may get a better decision rule.) The decision functions which are uniformly better are called "admissible decision functions" in Wald's approach, and a class of decision functions is said to be "complete" if for any decision function $\tilde{R}$ not in the class there is a decision function R in the class which is uniformly better than $\tilde{R}$. To illustrate these optimum properties, let us refer to the decision functions R_1 through R_4 mentioned before and compute the risk functions

$$\rho_k = \rho(C^*, R_k), \qquad k = 1, 2, 3, 4,$$
$$\rho_1 = k_1^2 - C^*(2k_1 - C^*),$$
$$\rho_2 = \mathrm{Var}\ C = \mathrm{Var}\ k_2,$$
$$\rho_3 = \lambda^2(\mathrm{Var}\ k_2) + (1 - \lambda)^2 \{k_1^2 - C^*(2k_1 - C^*)\},$$
$$\rho_4 = p(\mathrm{Var}\ k_2) + (1 - p)\{k_1^2 - C^*(2k_1 - C^*)\}. \tag{9.5.5}$$

Now it is easily seen that the decision function R_1 is the best of all the four if C^* equals k_1, since in this case the nonnegative risk function ρ_1 takes the lowest possible value, zero. Similarly, R_2 is the best of all if C^{*2} equals Ek_2^2. But if $C^{*2} = Ek_2^2$, then R_1 is far from the best decision function. Now consider ρ_3. If there exists a value of $\lambda = \lambda_1$, say, such that $0 < \lambda_1 < 1$ where λ_1 is a constant satisfying the following quadratic equation

$$(\mathrm{Var}\ k_2 - 2k_1 C^* + C^{*2})\lambda^2 + (4k_1 C^* - 2C^{*2})\lambda - (2k_1 C^* - C^{*2}) = 0$$

then ρ_3 will reduce to the following nonnegative expression which is independent of C^*

$$\rho_3 = (1 - \lambda_1)^2 k_1^2 \tag{9.5.6}$$

and this is now uniformly better than ρ_4 given in (9.5.7). Hence, ρ_4 is not an admissible decision function, i.e., for every randomized decision function of the form R_4 there exists another function R_3 with ρ_3 given in equation (9.5.6) which is uniformly better in the sense defined before. But note that ρ_3 given in (9.5.6) is not uniformly better than ρ_1 or ρ_2. Nor is either ρ_1 or ρ_2 uniformly better than ρ_3. Thus, if we restrict our attention to the four decision functions R_1 through R_4 only, the principle of minimizing the expected loss (ρ) enables us to rule out ρ_4 in (9.5.5) from consideration but leaves us with R_1, R_2 and R_3 to choose from, no one of which is uniformly better than another. These three functions R_1, R_2 and R_3 may then be called "admissible decision functions." Now suppose the unknown parameter C^* has a prior statistical distribution and we use Bayes' theorem (which relates the prior and posterior distribution) to minimize the expected value of loss (D) of the posterior distribution; we then obtain a Bayes solution to the decision problem. In an important theorem, Wald proved that under very general conditions the class of all Bayes' solutions constitutes a "complete class" of decision functions, where the term "complete" has been defined before.

But the difficulty with Bayes' solutions is that there are as many of them as there are prior distributions in general. Hence, there remains a further problem of choice among the multiplicity of Bayes' solutions. Here we have a number of criteria available, such as the Bayes-Laplace principle of equal ignorance, Wald's minimax risk approach, Savage's minimax regret and Carnap's probability structure approach. Most of these approaches have been lucidly surveyed in their economic aspects by Luce and Raiffa.[7] The basic difficulty with these alternative criteria is that emphasized by Milnor, which is that each of them violates at least one intuitively plausible axiom.

Now we consider the dynamic model (9.1.2) mentioned before. A decision rule analogous to the static decision rule (9.2.1) could be obtained by minimizing the expected value of disutility D in (9.1.3) subject to the dynamic model (9.1.2). Since investment (I) is the only random variable, it is easy to derive from (9.1.2)

$$\bar{C} = a(\bar{I}_a + G) + ab\{\dot{\bar{I}} + \dot{\bar{C}} + \dot{G}\}, \tag{9.6.1}$$

where $a = c/(1-c)$ is a constant, a dot denotes time derivative and a bar denotes expected value. For the minimization of expected disutility, we should have

$$\bar{C} = C^*, \tag{9.6.2}$$

where C^* is assumed to be predetermined. By combining (9.6.1) and (9.6.2) and solving for the instrument variable G we would obtain the dynamic decision rule. For example, this decision rule can be written as

$$G - (1+b)\theta \exp(\theta t) \int \exp(-\theta t) \dot{G} dt \tag{9.6.3}$$
$$= [(C^* - A \exp(\theta t))/a] - y_a + (1+b)\theta \exp(\theta t) \int \exp(-\theta t) \dot{y} dt,$$

where the expected values of I and I_a are denoted, respectively, by y and y_a, and $\theta = (ab)^{-1}$ is a constant. It is apparent from this decision rule that the higher the preassigned level of desired consumption C^* the higher would be the required government expenditure G, other things being equal. The compensatory relation between the two integrals, one on each side of equation (9.6.3), suggests a number of alternative stabilization policies through government expenditure G, which have been analyzed by Phillips in the case of a deterministic model.

---

[7] See Luce and Raiffa [17]. The statistical aspects of decision theory are treated in Neyman [25, p. 11] and Blackwell and Girshick [5]. For an application of Carnap's probability structure approach, see Tintner [50].

One point common to each of these decision rules is that its efficiency depends on the quality of the forecast for the time curve of expected private investment. Given a poor forecast, dynamic decision rules may behave as poorly as the static decision rule (9.2.1).

A second way of deriving a dynamic decision rule is to consider a planning horizon t_1 to t_2 and select G so as to minimize the cumulative loss functional

$$\int_{t_1}^{t_2} (C - C^*)^2 \, dt$$

under the conditions of the dynamic model (9.2.1). This could be solved [8] by the method of variational calculus or by using Pontryagin's maximum principle, as has been indicated before in connection with the Phillips-type model. For an analysis of this principle and an application see Chapter 8.

In Holt's approach to dynamic uncertainty [14], the macroeconomic model is taken in difference equation terms

$$
\begin{aligned}
Y_t &= I_{t-1} + G_{t-1} + C_{t-1}, \\
C_t &= c Y_t, \qquad t = 0, 1, 2, \dots,
\end{aligned}
\qquad (9.7.1)
$$

where Y is national income (endogenous), I is prviate investment (regarded as exogenous and containing random elements), G is government spending (the instrument variable), C is consumer spending (endogenous), all in real units per period of time, and c is the propensity to consume.

The disutility function adopted is the expected value of the sum of squared deviations of actual from desired values of income and government spending over many periods, the deviations being weighted by the relative importance which the policy maker attaches to them. This is shown in the following equation:

$$\text{Expected disutility} = E \sum_{r=0}^{N} [(Y_{t+r} - Y_{t+r}^*)^2 + g(G_{t+r} - G_{t+r}^*)^2], \qquad (9.1.2)$$

where Y^* and G^* denote the respective desired values. Growth in population, labor force, productivity and the requirements of specific government programs will influence the levels of income and government spending that are *desired* by the policy maker at future points in time.

---

[8] Some simple applications to macrodynamic models of economic growth based on the methods of variational calculus and Pontryagin's maximum principle may be found in Sengupta [30].

By applying the certainty equivalence theorem and replacing the future I_t's with corresponding $\hat{I}_t$'s which are forecasts of the EI_t's, Holt obtains the optimal decision rule

$$G_t = G_t^* - a\left(\sum_{r=0}^{N} z_1^r G_{t+r}^* + \sum_{r=0}^{N} z_1^r I_{t+r}\right) + \left(\frac{1}{gc}\right)\left(\sum_{r=1}^{N} z_1^r Y_{t+r}^*\right)$$
$$- ac(I_{t-1} + G_{t-1} + cY_{t-1}); \quad t = 0,1,2,\ldots, \quad (9.7.3)$$

where the constants a, e, z_1 and b are functions[9] of g and c.

Some feeling for the orders of magnitude involved in this decision rule may be obtained by means of a numerical example. First, we assume a propensity to consume of ($c = 0.7$). Second, we assign g a value of 2, attaching more weight to an undesired deviation of government spending than to an undesired deviation of national income of equal magnitude in terms of billions of dollars at constant prices. The values of the other constants in footnote 9 are as follows:

$$b = 0.7 + 1.4286 + 0.7143 = 2.8429;$$
$$z_1 = \frac{2.8429 - \sqrt{8.0820 - 4}}{2} = \frac{2.8429 - 2.0204}{2} = 0.4112;$$
$$e = \frac{0.7[0.7(0.4112) - 1]}{0.8224} + \frac{1}{4} = \frac{0.2015 - 0.7000}{0.8224} + 0.25 = -0.356$$
$$a = \frac{-0.4112}{2.8(0.356)} = \frac{-0.4112}{-0.9968} = 0.4125.$$

Plugging in these values in equation (9.7.3) gives us

$$G_t = G_t^* - 0.413\left(\sum_{r=0}^{N} 0.411^r G_{t+r}^*, \sum_{r=0}^{N} 0.411^r \hat{I}_{t+r}\right) + 0.714\sum_{r=1}^{N} 0.411^r Y_{t+r}$$
$$- 0.289(I_{t-1} + G_{t-1} + 0.700Y_{t-1}); \quad t = 0,1,2,\ldots. \quad (9.7.4)$$

In this decision rule we see that the optimal level of government spending for the period t depends upon the state of the economy at the time that the decision is made, I_{t-1}, G_{t-1}, and Y_{t-1}, the forecasts that are currently

---

[9] $a = \dfrac{-z_1}{2gec}$, $\quad e = \dfrac{c(cz_1 - 1)}{2z_1} + \dfrac{1}{2g}$, $\quad z_1 = \dfrac{b - \sqrt{-b^2 - 4}}{2}$, $\quad b = c + \dfrac{1}{c} + \dfrac{1}{cg}$.

The values of b and e do not appear in equation (9.7.3) but are required as intermediate links in the solutions for z_1 and a.

available of future private investment, $\check{I}_{t+r}$ $(r=0, 1, 2, ..., N)$ and the desired future time paths of government spending G^*_{t+r} $(r=0, 1, 2, ..., N)$ and national income Y^*_{t+r} $(r=1, 2, ..., N)$.

Of this decision rule, Holt comments:

> The present state of the system is indicated by the last term which is the aggregate external demand in the previous period. This after the one-period lag will determine the level of production in the forthcoming period t. The negative sign on this term reveals the negative feedback of the government spending response. That a forecast of high private investment several periods ahead would "feed forward" to lower government spending or that an increase in the desired level of income would raise government spending presents no surprises. The desired level of government spending has a rather complex influence on the decision. An increase in G^*_t would increase G_t, but an increase in $G^*_{t+\tau}$ $(\tau=1, 2, ..., N)$ would decrease G_t. The latter change would tend to increase government spending in the future and hence, spending in the current period is reduced to avoid over stimulating the economy [14, page 27].
>
> If we expand one of the summation terms in (10) [our equation (9.7.4)] we find that the weights applied to the forecasts decline in six periods to less than one per cent of the initial weight [see our equation (9.7.5)]. Even though the criterion function includes many periods, the weights that are given to forecasts of future investment decline rapidly toward zero. This gives the result one would expect, namely that most of the future is for practical purposes *irrelevant* for today's decisions, even if it could be forecasted perfectly. [14, pages 27–28].

The calculation just mentioned results in the following equation:

$$\sum_{r=0}^{N} 0.411^r \hat{I}_{r+t} = 1.000\hat{I}_t + 0.411\hat{I}_{t+1} + 0.169\hat{I}_{t+2} + 0.069\hat{I}_{t+3} + 0.029\hat{I}_{t+4}$$
$$+ 0.012\hat{I}_{t+5} + 0.005\hat{I}_{t+6} + 0.002\hat{I}_{t+7} + ... + 0.000\hat{I}_{t+N}.$$

$$(9.7.5)$$

A more generalized derivation of this type of linear decision rule in the multivariate case has been made by a number of writers [15, 27, 38, 44].

A number of numerical applications of linear decision theory to economic policy have been made in the Netherlands since 1959. For example, van den Bogaard and Barten made such a study [45] using five instruments and four noncontrolled variables. The noncontrolled variables were employment, the price level of consumer goods, the share of wages in the total national income and the balance of payments surplus (or deficit). The five instruments included tax rates for, respectively, indirect taxes, income taxes for wage earners and income taxes for nonwage earners; government expenditure on goods and services and the wage rate. (The wage rate was regarded as an instrument in the Netherlands during 1957–1959 in that government consent was required for all wage increases.) The application was based on conditions

TABLE 9.1

Classification Scheme of Macroeconomic Decision Analysis [a]

Elements Properties and Features of W and Linear Model	Linear Cases					Quadratic Cases		
	I	II	III	IV	V	VI	VII	VIII
1. Elements entering into W								
a. Targets, fixed	×	×	×		×	× [b]	× [b]	× [b]
b. Targets, flexible				×	×			
c. Instruments					×	× [b]	× [b]	× [b]
d. Institutional limits				×	×			
2. Relationship between number of targets and number of instruments								
e. Number of instruments = number of targets	×			×		×	×	
f. Number of instruments > number of targets		×	×		×			×
3. Decision problem applied to following situation								
g. Static	×	×		×	×	×		
h. Dynamic			×				×	
i. Nonstochastic	×	×		×	×			
j. Stochastic			×			×	×	×
4. Further properties of W								
k. Carry-over amendment								×
l. Smoothing amendment								×

[a] The eight cases shown below (Columns I–VIII) are described in Table 9.2 and most of them are presented in various parts of the book.

[b] Desired value.

TABLE 9.2

Synopsis of a Number of Macroeconomic Decision Models

1 Cases	2 Country. Period of Application, Type of Policy Problems	3 Chapter References in Present Book	4 Welfare Function
I	Mahalanobis Indian Five Year Plan Development Planning	Discussed in Chapter 13	$W = \begin{bmatrix} \Delta Y^* \\ \Delta N^* \end{bmatrix}$ Y^* = given Income N^* = given Employment
II	Japanese Planning Commission Ten Year Plan to Double National Income 1961–1970	Discussed in Chapter 14	$W = \begin{bmatrix} V^*_{70} \\ V^*_{70} \\ S^*_{g70} \end{bmatrix}$ V^*_{70} = given output in primary sector in 1970 V^*_{70} = given level of income in 1970 S^*_{g70} = balanced budget in 1970
III	Duesenberry, Eckstein and Fromm. U.S. Economy in Recession (1957–1959) Stabilization	Not specifically discussed, but referred to in Chapter 2	1) Max $W_1 = - \dfrac{\sum\limits_{t=57:3}^{t=59:2} (DI_{t+1} - DI_t)}{\sum\limits_{t=57:3}^{t=59:2} (GNP_{t+1} - GNP_t)}$ 2) Max $W_2 = - \dfrac{\sum\limits_{t=57:3}^{t=59:2} (GNP_{t+1}^0 - GNP_t^0)}{\sum\limits_{t=57:3}^{t=59:2} (GNP_{t+1} - GNP_t)}$ DI = disposable income; GNP = actual realized value of GNP; GNP^0 = calculated value of GNP assuming discrete changes in personal income tax rates and unemployment compensation.

5 Major Instruments	6 Characteristics of Underlying Model
Investment allocation ratios for consumption goods sectors (λi, $i = 1, 2, 3$)	Simple model: 12 equations 4 identities 4 capital-output ratios 4 capital-labor ratios Investment given exogenously. A priori estimates.
Active instruments: share of government purchases in GNP share of transfer payments in GNP indirect tax ratio Passive instruments: direct tax ratio of wage income direct tax ratio of non-wage income	21 equations, 19 endogenous variables – 2 policy degrees of freedom (i.e., 2 instruments have to be converted to endogenous variables). Least squares estimation.
1. Automatic stabilizers 2. Changes in personal income tax rate 3. Changes in unemployment compensation	Model applies exclusively to fiscal sector. Least squares estimation procedure. Model describes only recession conditions. Main objective is to measure performance of built-in stabilizers.

TABLE 9.2—*Continued*

Synopsis of a Number of Macroeconomic Decision Models

1 Cases	2 Country. Period of Application, Type of Policy Problems	3 Chapter References in Present Book	4 Welfare Function
IV	Van Eijk & Sandee Netherlands (1957) Stabilization	Discussed in Chapter 7	$W = 1.0\,(E - M) + 0.25x_G + 0.20i + 5.0$ $\quad 1_R - 7.5pc + 0.20a + 0.50S_G +$ $\quad + \text{constant}$ $E - M = $ balance of payments surplus $x_G \quad = $ government expenditure $i \quad = $ investment $1_R \quad = $ real wages $pc \quad = $ consumer price index $a \quad = $ level of employment $S_G \quad = $ government surplus
V	Chenery & Bruno Israel Development Planning	Discussed in Chapter 13	$W = f(G^*, u^*, V, C, r, s, L, F)$ $G^* = $ government expenditure (fixed) $u \quad = $ unemployment rate (fixed) $V \quad = $ GNP $C \quad = $ private consumption $r \quad = $ effective exchange rate $s \quad = $ marginal prop. to save $L \quad = $ labor demand $F \quad = $ foreign capital inflow
VI	Van den Bogaard & Theil U.S. Economy (1933–36) Antidepression Optimum Econ. Policy for 1933	Discussed in Chapter 7	$\text{Max } W = - \Sigma\,[(C_{33} - C_{33}{}^d)^2 + (I_{33} - I_{33}{}^d)^2 -$ $\dots + (G_{33} - G_{33}{}^d)^2]$ Variables appearing in W: Targets: $\quad C \quad = $ consumption $\qquad\qquad I \quad = $ Net investment $\qquad\qquad \pi/W_1 = $ ratio of profits to wage bil Instruments: $W_2 \quad = $ government wage bill $\qquad\qquad\quad T \quad = $ indirect taxes $\qquad\qquad\quad G \quad = $ government expenditures $\qquad\qquad\qquad\qquad$ on goods and services

5 Major Instruments	6 Characteristics of Underlying Model
government expenditure; autonomous investment; nominal wage rates, indirect tax rates, wage tax rates, profit tax rates	Dutch Central Planning Bureau Model (1956) 27 equations. Most parameters are based on a priori information.
r, s, F	Development Planning Model 12 equations. Reduced form consists of 4 equations in 8 policy variables (4 policy degrees of freedom).
W_2, T, G	Klein's 6 equations model of the U.S. economy in interwar period.

TABLE 9.2—*Continued*

Synopsis of a Number of Macroeconomic Decision Models

1	2	3	4
Cases	Country. Period of Application, Type of Policy Problems	Chapter References in Present Book	Welfare Function
VII	Same as above except optimum econ. policy for period 1933–36	See Chapter 7	Capital letters refer to actual values. Capital letters with d superscript refer to desired values subscript refer to year $$\text{Max } W = -\sum_{t=1933}^{t=1936}\{(C_t - C_t^d)^2 + \ldots + (G_t - G_t^d)^2\}$$
VIII	Van den Bogaard & Barten; Theil	Not specifically discussed but mentioned in Chapter 9	Three preference functions for Labor Employers, Crown: $$\text{Max } W = -\sum_{t=1957}^{t=1959}\left\{\left(\frac{W_t - W_t^d}{W^0}\right)^2 + \ldots + \left(\frac{B_t - B_t^d}{B^0}\right)^2\right\}$$ Variables appearing in W: *Instruments:* W = % change in wage rate ΔT^{ia} = autonomous change in indirect taxes minus subsidies ΔT^{wa} = autonomous change in direct taxes on wage income ΔT^{oa} = autonomous change in indirect taxes on nonwage income ΔG = change in government expenditure on commodities. *Targets:* n^p = % change in private employment P^c = % change in price level of private consumption Δq^w = change in % share of wages in national income B = surplus in the balance of payments Superscript ^{0} indicates "equivalent deviation"; ^{d} indicates desired value $t = 1957$–1959. Welfare function contains in addition a carry-over and a smoothing amendment.

5	6
Major Instruments	Characteristics of Underlying Model
W_2, T_t, G_t $= 1933$–1936	Same as above
W_t, T_t^{ia}, T_t^{wa} T_t^{oa}, G_t $= 1957$–1959	Macroeconomic model built for the Dutch CPB. 40 equations model in 59 variables.

in the Netherlands in the three-year period 1957–1959. The decision maker was supposed to have a constant horizon of three years in mind. That is, at the beginning of 1957 he planned until the end of 1959; at the beginning of 1958, until the end of 1960 and at the beginning of 1959, until the end of 1961. The constraints were derived from an econometric model consisting of about forty equations (of which twelve were behavioral equations). The uncertainty in these constraints was due partly to the presence of disturbances in the behavioral equations and partly to the presence of exogenous variables in the model which are beyond the decision maker's control (such as the price level of imported goods).

A further feature of the van den Bogaard and Barten study was the application of three alternative preference functions, one representing the standpoint of a "typical" employer, one that of a "typical" trade unionist and one a "neutral" standpoint. The preference functions were all quadratic but slightly more complicated than the ones considered in the previous examples. For example, they contained the sums of squares of the successive differences of the instrument values in order to insure that the instruments did not behave too wildly over time.

In a similar study, van den Bogaard and Theil [54] applied linear decision rules and certainty equivalence concepts to the economy of the U.S. during 1933–1936, using a small six-equation model and specifying such desired targets as a recovery to 1929 levels of per capita income by the end of 1936.

Tables 9.1 and 9.2 above present eight macroeconomic applications of decision rules in summary form. The major features and characteristics of these concrete decision models are given in terms of the form of—and the elements entering—the welfare functions, the structure of the model and the nature of the policy problem.[10] Most of these cases are discussed in greater or less detail in various parts of this book. The specific chapter references can be found in Table 9.2.

The decision rules we have discussed so far are mostly relevant for repetitive choice situations which, of course, are the most important ones. The area of nonrepetitive choice situations has been little explored in an analytical sense, although their role in actual decision making may not be unimportant. Shackle [37] has analyzed the formation of expectation and its relation to the outcomes in individual behavior, and his concept of focus gain and focus loss suggests that extreme values of the outcome, such as extreme disaster or peak level of return, have some effect on the individuals' choice of a

---

[10] For a detailed analysis of these cases see Thorbecke [47].

particular decision. In a slightly different framework, this idea lends itself to the formulation of the decision criterion which minimizes the probability that income level falls below a certain level (e.g., Roy's principle of safety first) [29]. Since the knowledge about probability distribution of the random variables is not directly available in this case, attempt has been made to apply nonparametric inference, e.g., Tchebychef inequality. Simon's concept of a statisficing behavior [39] contrasts partly with maximizing behavior because there is an implication in the former that part of the optimizing policy could be traded for more flexibility and other noneconomic objectives. However, the criteria of rational decision making are far weaker in non-repetitive situations, primarily because of the limited scope of the calculus of subjective probability.

9.2. A Programming Formulation of the Mahalanobis Model

The two-sector Mahalanobis model was presented in Chapter 2. This model lends itself well to a programming framework. In the present treatment, the M-model is generalized in dynamic programming terms by incorporating the variations in the coefficients of the model. In other words, we seek to determine how sensitive the optimal policy or decision rule in the Mahalanobis model is to the observed pattern of changes in the capital coefficients, some of which changes may be due to structural factors.

Let I_t, C_t and Y_t be investment, consumption and national income in year t, λ_i be the proportion of investment devoted to the new investment goods sector and λ_c be the proportion of investment allocated to the consumption goods sector. Further, let β_i and β_c be the marginal output-investment coefficients in the investment goods and the consumption sectors. The programming formulation of the Mahalanobis model is:

$$\text{Maximize } Y_T = C_T + I_T$$

subject to the following restrictions:

$$I_t \leq I_{t-1} + \lambda_i \beta_i I_{t-1} \tag{9.8.1}$$

$$C_t \leq C_{t-1} + \lambda_c \beta_c I_{t-1} \tag{9.8.2}$$

$$Y_t = I_t + C_t, \quad \lambda_i + \lambda_c = 1 \qquad (9.8.0) \tag{9.8.3}$$

$$I_t \geq 0, \quad C_t \geq C_0 > 0, \quad 0 \leq \lambda_i \leq 1 \tag{9.8.4}$$

$$\text{and } \sum_{t=0}^{T} I_t \leq I_s \text{ for all } t = 1, 2, ..., T. \tag{9.8.5}$$

Here C_0 is consumption in period 0 and I_s the total investment available over the whole period 1, 2, ..., T. We assume $t = 1, 2, 3, 4$ and maximize the objective function Y_4 subject to the conditions (9.8.1) through (9.8.5) by choosing $I_1, ..., I_T$ and $C_1, ..., C_T$.

From the long-run planning estimates underlying the Third Five Year Plan in India we obtain the following data: $I_0 = 14.40$, $C_0 = 121.70$, $I_s = 99.00$. All figures are in billions of rupees in constant 1952–1953 prices. Further, the average values $\bar{\beta}_c = 0.706$ and $\bar{\beta}_i = 0.335$ and their estimated variances $\sigma_c^2 = 0.458160$, $\sigma_i^2 = 0.031881$ are obtained from the values of the marginal output-investment ratios for the period 1946–1954 and other estimates reported elsewhere [36].

Following the joint-distribution method, we fit, following the best fitting procedure, independent gamma distributions on the basis of the sixteen value of β_i and β_c. We then select sixteen points in the parameter space and derive the approximate distribution of the objective function Y_4. The results of these calculations are reported elsewhere [33].

We present here (Table 9.3) the expected value $E(Y_4)$ and the variance $V(Y_4)$ computed from the distribution of Y_4 for different values of the decision variables λ_i and λ_c:

TABLE 9.3

Values of $E(Y_4)$ and $V(Y_4)$ as Functions of λ_i and λ_c

	$\lambda_i = 1 - \lambda_c$	
0.33	0.50	0.67
$E(Y_4) = 180.10$	174.20	166.46
$V(Y_4) = 851.88$	519.50	247.23
$g(\lambda_i) = 16.20$	13.08	9.44

Here $g(\lambda_i)$ denotes the coefficient of variation defined as $[100\sqrt{V(Y_4)}/E(Y_4)]$, which indicates in a general way the extent of variability of the end-period national income Y_4. It is obvious from Table 9.3 that if the criterion of minimum variability as measured by the coefficient of variation were followed, the policy $\lambda_i = 0.67$ would be better than the policy $\lambda_i = 0.50$ and still better than the policy $\lambda_i = 0.33$. It may be noted that the last policy, $\lambda_i = 0.33$, was considered to be optimal in the Mahalanobis model, which did not, however, pay any attention to the variability of the marginal output-investment coefficients and the programming restrictions.

It is easy to interpret the dynamic programming model (9.8.0) much in the Mahalanobis fashion by assuming that (9.8.1) and (9.8.2) are strict equalities.

Then we get approximately

$$Y_4 = Y_0 + \frac{(\lambda_i\beta_i + \lambda_c\beta_c)I_0}{\lambda_i\beta_i}\{e^{4\lambda_i\beta_i} - 1\} \qquad (9.8.6)$$

by using the approximation $(1 + \lambda_i\beta_i)^4 \doteq e^{4\lambda_i\beta_i}$ and denoting the initial year national income by $Y_0 = C_0 + I_0$. Retaining the linear and quadratic terms, respectively, of the Taylor development of Y_4 in (9.8.6) and taking expectations we obtain

Linear: $E(Y_4) = Y_0 + 4I_0(\lambda_i\bar{\beta}_i + \lambda_c\bar{\beta}_c),$
Quadratic: $EY_4 = Y_0 + 4I_0[\lambda_i\bar{\beta}_i + \lambda_c\bar{\beta}_c + 2\lambda_i\{\lambda_i(\bar{\beta}_i^2 + \sigma_i^2) + \lambda_c\bar{\beta}_i\bar{\beta}_c\}],$
$$(9.8.7)$$

where a bar over a variable denotes its expected value and σ_1^2 denotes the variance of β_i (the numerical value of which has been given earlier).

If in equation (9.8.6) we replace each random variable β_i, β_c by its expected value $\bar{\beta}_i, \bar{\beta}_c$ and retain only linear and quadratic parts of the Taylor expansion of the series of Y_4, we get the "certainty equivalent values" of Y_4, denoted as $Y_4(E)$ as follows:

Linear: $Y_4(E) = Y_0 + 4I_0(\lambda_i\bar{\beta}_i + \lambda_c\bar{\beta}_c),$
Quadratic: $Y_4(E) = Y_0 + 4I_0[\lambda_i\bar{\beta}_i + \lambda_c\bar{\beta}_c + 2\lambda_i\{\lambda_i\bar{\beta}_i^2 + \lambda_c\bar{\beta}_i\bar{\beta}_c\}],$ $\qquad (9.8.8)$

assuming that β_i and β_c are mutually independently distributed with finite means and variances. By comparing the quadratic cases in (9.8.7) and (9.8.8) it is easy to see that

$$EY_4 \geq Y_4(E) \text{ if } \sigma_i \geq 0.$$

In the linear case, $EY_4 = Y_4(E)$. This result can be proved as a general theorem valid under more general conditions [35].

Now consider the variances of Y_4 in the linear and the quadratic cases respectively. In the linear case, the variance denoted by $V(Y_4)$ is very simple:

$$V(Y_4) = 16I_0^2(\lambda_i\sigma_i^2 + \lambda_c^2\sigma_c^2). \qquad (9.8.9)$$

In the quadratic case we may apply the approximation rule for the variance of a product of two independent random variables

$$V(xy) \doteq V(x)V(y) + (Ex)^2 V(y) + (Ey)^2 V(x),$$

and obtain approximately the variance of Y_4 as

$$V(Y_4) \doteq I_0^2[64\lambda_i^2\sigma_i^2\{(\lambda_i^2\sigma_i^2 + \lambda_c^2\sigma_c^2) + (\lambda_i\bar{\beta}_i + \lambda_c\bar{\beta}_c)^2\} + (\lambda_i^2\sigma_i^2 + \lambda_c^2\sigma_c^2)(4 + 8\lambda_i\bar{\beta}_i)^2]. \qquad (9.8.10)$$

Using these formulae and denoting the coefficient of variation by $g(\lambda_i)$, we obtain Table 9.4:

TABLE 9.4

Alternative Values of $E(Y_4)$ and $V(Y_4)$

0	0.33	$\lambda_i = 1 - \lambda_c$ 0.50	0.67	0.90	1.0
		Linear case			
$EY_4 = 176.76$	169.71	166.08	162.45	157.53	155.40
$V(Y_4) = 1520.06$	693.88	572.54	213.02	100.88	105.77
$g(\lambda_i) = 22.05$	15.52	14.40	8.98	6.37	6.62
		Quadratic case			
$EY_4 = 176.76$	177.55	177.04	175.92	173.43	171.99
$Y_4(E) = 176.76$	177.14	176.12	174.27	164.71	168.32
$V(Y_4) = 1520.06$	1059.96	766.02	499.12	317.08	450.22
$g(\lambda_i) = 22.05$	18.34	15.63	12.70	10.27	12.34

It is apparent from Table 9.4 that the best policy in the sense of minimum coefficient of variation (i.e., the policy of playing safe) is specified by the allocations $\lambda_i = 0.90$ and $\lambda_c = 0.10$; the next best policy is $\lambda_i = 0.67$ and $\lambda_c = 0.33$. Similarly, other conclusions can be derived by applying alternative rules of decision making under uncertainty.

Using the results of (9.7.8), (9.8.9) and (9.8.10), we may also specify the values of the allocation ratio $\lambda_i = 1 - \lambda_c$ so as to either minimize the variance $V(Y_4)$ subject to a given expected value $E(Y_4)$ or maximize the expected value $E(Y_4)$ subject to a given level of variance $Y(Y_4)$. The latter would specify a method of diversification of investment between sectors which would indicate how large an expected value of Y_4 the policy maker may choose, subject to the condition that the variability of Y_4 measured by the variance $V(Y_4)$ be less than or equal to a preassigned level.

For example, taking the linear case of (9.8.9), we may form the objective function F as

$$F = w_1 E(Y_4) + w_2(-V(Y_4)),$$
$$= w_1 Y_0 + 4w_1 I_0 (\lambda_i \bar{\beta}_i + \lambda_c \bar{\beta}_c) - 16w_2 I_0^2 (\lambda_i \sigma_i^2 + \lambda_c^2 \sigma_c^2), \tag{9.9.0}$$

where w_1, w_2 are fixed nonnegative weights such that $w_1 + w_2 = 1$. Maximization of F in (9.9.0) with respect to $\lambda_i = 1 - \lambda_c$ readily gives

$$\lambda_i = (\sigma_i^2 + \sigma_c^2)^{-1} [w_1 (\bar{\beta}_c - \bar{\beta}_i)/8w_2 I_0 + \sigma_c^2] \tag{9.9.1}$$

assuming $\bar{\beta}_c \geq \bar{\beta}_i \geq 0$.

When it is feasible, the allocation ratio λ_i in (9.9.1) specifies one of the optimal ways of decision making in risk situations involving random variation of the output-capital coefficients. This case is similar to the decision rules discussed by Markowitz [3, 21] in his analysis of portfolio investment. If $\bar{\beta}_c = \bar{\beta}_i$, the relation (9.9.1) has an interesting implication, namely, that if the instability of a decision rule is measured by the size of the variance, a policy decision which is optimum in terms of expected value may not be so in terms of variance. However, if it is optimum on both grounds, we have a stable optimum policy.

9.3. Linear Programming with Random Elements

The problem of optimal decision making gets more involved, as one would expect, when there are linear inequalities, either as part of the model or as constraints. The explicit derivation of decision rules in an analytic form is rarely possible in the general case of linear programming, because the latter picks up the optimal solution only among a set of extreme points of a convex set. An ordinary linear programming problem is formulated as follows in vector and matrix notation:

$$\text{maximize } z = c'x \tag{9.10.1}$$

$$\text{under the conditions} \quad c: n.1 \tag{9.10.0}$$

$$Ax \leq b \qquad\qquad x: n.1 \tag{9.10.2}$$

$$x \geq 0 \qquad\qquad A: m.n \tag{9.10.3}$$

$$b: m.1$$

In an economic policy model the vector x contains as subvectors the target and the instrument variables. Our problem can be stated as follows: What happens when the elements of the vectors b and c and of the matrix A are not known constants but random variables? Various approaches are available in this case, which may be classified into three broad types:

(a) Chance-constrained programming [6, 7]. Here we replace conditions (9.10.2) by

$$P(Ax \leq b) \geq \alpha \tag{9.10.4}$$

where P stands for probability and α is a column vector with m elements with $0 \leq \alpha_i \leq 1$, $i = 1, \ldots, m$. The vector α contains a prescribed set of constants that are probability measures of the extent to which constraint violations are admitted.

(b) Two-stage programming under uncertainty [13, 20].

The general structure of a two-stage-programming model may be written explicitly as

$$\text{Minimize } w = c'x + E_y^{\min} f'y \qquad (9.11.1)$$

under the conditions

$$b_1 = A_{11}x \qquad (9.11.2)$$

$$b_2 = A_{21}x + A_{22}y \qquad (9.11.3)$$

$$x \geqq 0, \quad y \geqq 0 \qquad (9.11.4)$$

where A_{ij} are known matrices, b_1 a known vector of initial inventories, b_2 an unknown random vector. It is assumed that whatever be the selection of x in stage 1 (i.e., the first constraint (9.11.2)), there exists at least one feasible y at the second stage (i.e., the assumption of permanent feasibility). The decision process then proceeds as follows: x is chosen to satisfy the first-stage restrictions (9.11.2) only. After the selection is made and the random variable b_2 is observed, one is allowed to compensate with a vector $y \geq 0$ for the infeasibility of the first-stage selection of x at a penalty cost given by $f'y$ where the vector $f \geq 0$ is known, Hence, we change the usual objective function from minimizing $c'x$ to minimizing $c'x$ plus the expected smallest penalty cost, i.e., $w = c'x + E_y^{\min} f'y$.

(c) Stochastic linear programming. A somewhat different line of approach to stochastic linear programming, first suggested by Tintner [49], is concerned with the specification of the statistical distribution of the objective function and the implications for decision making under risk. Here we make the assumption that in the linear programming problem defined in the beginning in equations (9.10.1), (9.10.2) and (9.10.3) the elements of the vectors b, c and the matrix A are random variables with a known probability distribution, say:

$$P(A, b, c). \qquad (9.12.1)$$

We distinguish here between two approaches, termed distribution problems and expected value problems by Vajda [53]. In the expected value problem we consider the optimization of the expected value of the objective function. In the distribution problem we try to derive the statistical distribution of the objective function z.

With the distribution problem as studied by Tintner, we have two approaches: (a) the passive and (b) the active. In the passive approach we derive (by numerical methods, if necessary) the distribution of the objective function z under the assumption of a known probability distribution (9.12.1) of all the parameters of the problem. This approach assumes that in almost all possible situations, i.e., for almost all possible variations of the parameters, the conditions of the simple nonstochastic linear program are fulfilled and the maximum achieved. This approach may be used in order to compare two different production situations, planning in two different countries, etc. We achieve numerically two different probability distributions of the objective function and leave the choice between them to the entrepreneur or the central planner, as the case may be.

Now consider the active approach. This is the following problem:

$$\text{maximize } z = c'x \tag{9.12.2}$$

under the conditions

$$AX \leq BU, \tag{9.12.3}$$

$$x \geq 0. \tag{9.12.4}$$

Here U is a matrix of order $m \cdot n$ with elements u_{ij} and

$$u_{ij} \geq 0, \sum_{j=1}^{n} u_{ij} = 1. \tag{9.12.5}$$

Further, X is a square, diagonal matrix with the elements of the vector x in the diagonal and B is a square, diagonal matrix with the elements of the vector b in the diagonal.

Again the problem [11] is the derivation of the probability distribution of $\{\max z\}$, given the probability distribution (9.12.1). But now the probability distribution of the optimal objective function will depend upon the allocation matrix $U = [u_{ij}]$. We use again the previous examples. Now we have only one production situation. The entrepreneur will consider the probability distributions generated by various allocations of resources u_{ij}. Or in our second example we consider the problem of economic planning. Then the proportions u_{ij} may be allocations to various industries and the central planner will consider the probability distributions of the maximal objective function z generated by these allocations.

Some characteristics of the active approach may be worth pointing out at this stage. In the first place, interpreting the active approach as a policy model, the elements u_{ij} of the allocation matrix U may be considered as instrument variables in Tinbergen's sense, which may be appropriately chosen to optimize a risk preference functional associated with the objective function.

---

[11] This part is based on Sengupta [34].

Let z_a denote the value of the objective function under the active approach, and let U and $\tilde{U}$ represent two different sets of resource allocations that could be selected by the policy maker. Since, in every case, all resources are to be fully allocated by condition (9.12.5), the selections U and $\tilde{U}$ represent only different relative allocations for every resource $i = 1, 2, ..., n$. The resulting probability distributions for "max z_a" induced by these two selections are illustrated in Figure 9.1.

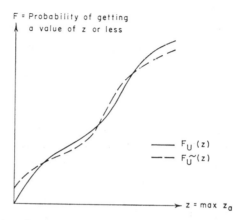

Fig. 9.1. Distribution functions of the maximum value of the objective function under alternative active approaches

Since under stochastic linear programming it is assumed that a utility function (i.e., a risk preference function) is available which permits an ordering between all pairs like F_U and $F_{\tilde{U}}$, on this assumption the problem is formally solved at the "policy level" when the probability distributions are available for each admissible U. In principle, different decision rules could be compared. For instance, if the utility function is such that only linear decision rules which depend by definition on the first moment[12] of the cumulative distributions F_U and $F_{\tilde{U}}$ are considered by the policy maker, the allocation policy U may be said to be "better" than $\tilde{U}$ so long as the first moment (i.e., expected value) of F_U exceeds $F_{\tilde{U}}$. Here we do not consider at all the second moments of the two different distributions. However, even in this case of linear decision rules, an optimum choice problem exists between alternative location parameters characterizing the probability distributions F_U and $F_{\tilde{U}}$ and, hence, between alternative policies U and $\tilde{U}$.

---

[12] That is, more appropriately the location parameters such as the mean, median or mode, etc.

For example, the median, rather than the mean, may offer better decision rules in some cases of nonsymmetric distributions, particularly because it has some specific optimum properties in nonparametric statistical estimation. Similarly, the higher order decision rules, which take into account the second and higher moments, can be ordered and appropriate optimum choice made.

We may also note that the introduction of additional decision constraints by means of the decision variables u_{ij} has the effect of truncating the statistical distribution of the optimal value of the objective function of the passive approach. Let us assume that a particular allocation matrix $U^{(1)}$ is chosen at first on an a priori basis. With further observations of the data and the results of more complete specification of the probability distribution, another allocation matrix $U^{(2)}$ can be selected at the next stage. If the *complete* distribution of the optimal objective function is estimated on the basis of large sample data with a fair degree of reliability, the optimum allocation matrix may have been U^*, which optimizes the utility functional (or the risk preference functional). In case of the optimum allocation matrix U^* we have a complete specification of the probability distribution of the objective function and also of the risk preference functional and consequently we would not benefit from sequential information obtained from new observations. In the case of the active approach we could select a better decision rule, as the probability distribution of the objective function is specified more completely by the additional sequential information. In case of mixed and compound statistical distributions [4], the specification of which is rather complicated on the computational side, this may be difficult, yet very important.

We consider first some of the results of stochastic linear programming, before discussing the other types of linear programming problems with random elements. In a sense the stochastic linear programming problem is somewhat more general than chance-constrained programming or two-stage programming. For example, the random variables of the chance-constrained programming problem may be divided into two sets according as they do or do not violate the stipulated probability measures α. For these two sets, then, the statistical distribution of the optimal objective function could be analyzed separately and then the decision rules could be derived according to a principle of risk ordering.[13]

---

[13] Similarly, the idea of the two-stage programming problem (where a certain x is initially chosen without considering any random variations and later y is chosen to offset the effect of the first-stage decision) is very similar to the different selections of the $U^{(1)}$, $U^{(2)}$ variables in the active approach of stochastic linear programming problems.

We state some results in stochastic linear programming problems as a set of theorems, which should be of interest to research workers in several different policy sciences. Proofs of the theorems and examples of applications will be found in the respective references in footnotes.

Theorem 1.[14] Let $z^{(k)}(x)$ be the objective function (9.10.1) for a selection k of a passive stochastic linear programming problem and $V(k)$ the region in the parameter space (i.e., the space of the matrix A, the vectors b and c) where $z^{(k)}(x)$ is feasible and optimal. If v is a point in V, there is a selection k^* for the dual linear programming problem with corresponding objective function $z^{*(k^*)}(v)$ such that $z^{*(k^*)}(v)=z^{(k)}(v)$ for all x in a certain neighbourhood denoted by $N_e(v)$. Likewise for the active case of stochastic linear programming, assume that the elements of the allocation matrix U can assume only a number of discrete values. Denote a given combination of these values by g and a given selection of U by k. Further, let the objective function for g and k be denoted by $z_g^{(k)}(v)$, where v is a feasible parameter point. Assume now that $z_g^{(k)}(v) \geq z_{g_1}^{(k_1)}(v)$, where k_1 is another selection and g_1 another combination of values of elements of the matrix U. Then there is a neighborhood $N_e(v)$ of the point v such that for all x in $N_e(v)$ we have $z_g^{(k)}(x) \geq z_{g_1}^{(k_1)}(x)$.

Theorem 2.[15] Consider a point v in the parameter space, which is feasible. Let $z_1(v)$ be the maximum value of the objective function in the passive case of stochastic linear programming and $z_2(v)$ the maximum value of the objective function in the active case. Further, we assume a finite number of choices for the allocation matrix U (e.g., we may restrict the variation of the elements of the decision matrix U to discrete values only). Let $z_3(v)$ be the maximum value of the objective function for any choice of U other than that leading to the optimal $z_2(v)$. Then we have

$$z_1(v) \geq z_2(v) \geq z_3(v).$$

Theorem 3.[16] Assume that the elements of the matrix A and the vector b are symmetrically and mutually independently distributed, such that the cross products of two or more random variables are negligible. Then for any feasible x we must have

$$Ex \geq x(E),$$

---

[14] See Tintner, Miller and Sengupta [52].

[15] See Sengupta, Tintner and Millham [34].

[16] See Sengupta, Tintner and Morrison [35].

where E denotes expected value and $x(E)$ denotes the elements of the vector x if all random variables are replaced by their expected values. Likewise, if the vector c is distributed as a nonnegative random variable and the above approximations hold, then

$$Ez(x) \geq z[x(E)]$$

for any feasible and hence optimal x.

Theorem 4.[17] Assume that under the conditions of theorem 2 there exists at least one sample observation for which the strict inequality

$$z_1(v) > z_2(v)$$

holds, so that $Ez_1(v) < Ez_2(v)$. Further, let the random variable $h_{12}(v) > 1$ be defined by

$$z_1(v) = h_{12}(v) z_2(v).$$

Then we have

$$\text{Var}(z_1(v)) > \text{Var}(z_2(v))$$

provided at least one of the following conditions hold:

(i) $h_{12}(v)$ and $z_2(v)$ are statistically independent for all observations.

(ii) $h_{12}(v)$ and $z_2(v)$ are statistically independent only approximately, i.e.,

$$\text{Var}(h_{12}(v) z_2(v)) \simeq [Eh_{12}(v) Ez_2(v)]^2 [G_{12} + G_2 + 2E(d_{12}d_2)],$$

where $E(d_{12}d_2)$ is either nonnegative or negligible and

$$G_{12} = \text{Var}(h_{12}(v))/(Eh_{12}(v))^2; \quad G_2 = \text{Var}(z_2(v))/(Ez_2(v))^2,$$
$$d_{12} = [h_{12}(v) - Eh_{12}(v)]/Eh_{12}(v),$$
$$d_2 = [z_2(v) - Ez_2(v)]/Ez_2(v).$$

(iii) $h_{12}(v)$ and $z_2(v)$ are statistically dependent but the expression $E[(d_{12}^2 + 2d_{12})^2 (d_2 + 1)^2]$ is either nonnegative or negligible.

A few words may be added about the policy implications of these theorems, since detailed empirical applications are reported in the quoted references. The first theorem is useful in studying the characteristics of the statistical distribution of the optimal value of the objective function locally around the neighborhood of the optimal value (e.g., local sensitivity of the optimal solution). Different optimal points may have different local sensitivity characteristics, e.g., the statistical distribution in one case may be highly skew (i.e., linear decision rules may be inappropriate) and in other cases nearly symmetrical (i.e., linear decision rules may be appropriate). Theorem 2

---

[17] See Sengupta, Millham and Tintner [32].

shows the nature and stability characteristics of the optimal objective function when the resource vector is varied parametrically by a decision matrix U. Theorem 2 and theorem 4 taken together show that in terms of variance the optimum solution of the active approach may be preferable to that of the passive approach (i.e., the optimal objective function in the active approach may beat that in the passive approach in terms of a smaller coefficient of variation, e.g.,

$$\frac{\text{Var } z_2(v)}{Ez_2(v)} < \frac{\text{Var } z_1(v)}{Ez_1(v)}.$$

9.4. A Stabilization Model

As an illustration of the use of theorem 4, we consider here a method of generalizing the Phillips-type stabilization policy model in a dynamic programming sense, when some or all the parametric coefficients of the multisector version [18] of the Phillips model are probabilistic in nature. We assume a difference equation version of the model and assume that the policy maker has at his disposal certain nonstochastic instrument (control) variables such as sectoral government expenditure, the values of which in period t are denoted by $u_1(t)$, $u_2(t)$, ..., $u_m(t)$. The policy maker is also interested in certain noncontrolled variables, i.e., the sector incomes as components of GNP, denoted by $x_1(t)$, $x_2(t)$, ..., $x_n(t)$, $m \geq n$, where these are stochastically related to the control variables in a linear way such that the x-variables enter linearly in a parametric fashion during the period $t = 1, 2, ..., T$. We now introduce a linear criterion function for simplicity

$$w = w(x, u) = \alpha'x + \beta'u, \tag{9.13.1}$$

where x and u are column vectors of nT and mT components which can be partitioned as

$$x = \begin{bmatrix} x_1 \\ x_2 \\ \vdots \\ x_T \end{bmatrix}, \quad x_t = \begin{bmatrix} x_1(t) \\ x_2(t) \\ \vdots \\ x_n(t) \end{bmatrix}, \quad u = \begin{bmatrix} u_1 \\ u_2 \\ \vdots \\ u_T \end{bmatrix}, \quad u_i = \begin{bmatrix} u_1(t) \\ u_2(t) \\ \vdots \\ u_m(t) \end{bmatrix},$$

---

[18] For this generalization see Chapter 12, Section 12.2, where we introduced a quadratic functional to represent a preference function. In this section, however, we assume a linear programming framework because of the analytical difficulties involved in studying truncated solutions of quadratic stochastic programming. However, in our case only the objective function is quadratic; hence, it may not be too difficult to formulate an "equivalent" linear programming problem.

and α', β' are corresponding row vectors. The generalized Phillips model can be written as

$$Gx + Hu = s,$$

where s is a column vector and G, H are square matrices of appropriate order. The problem of selecting an appropriate stabilization policy may now be formulated as a problem of choosing the control vector u, which is subject to the model

$$Gx + Hu \geq s \qquad (9.13.2)$$

and the constraints

$$u \geq 0, \quad x \geq 0, \quad \text{for all } t, \qquad (9.13.3)$$

such that it minimizes the scalar function (9.13.1). Here, some or all of the elements of the matrices G, H and vectors s, α, β could be random with a joint probability distribution. The nonnegativity constraints (9.13.3) are not at all essential in any way to our subsequent argument, and these could be replaced by other general constraints with only some minor modifications in our argument. However, for analytic convenience we make the assumption (9.13.3) because our object here is purely to characterize the stability properties of the optimal and nonoptimal policy (i.e., the respective values of the objective function).

Now we make some specific assumptions concerning the joint probability distribution of the elements of the set $S = (G, H, s, \alpha, \beta)$. We assume that we have sample observations for the set S, which we write as S_k, $k = 1, 2, \ldots$, $K \in I_0$, where we have K samples, I_0 being the index set. Any subset of the index set I_0 in the sample space denoted by S_k is defined to be admissible, if and only if it satisfies the following three conditions:

(i) The elements of the vectors α and β are subject only to nonnegative probability distributions. The elements of G, H, s are not subject to any such restriction.

(ii) The sample space generated by S_k is such that it contains more than one basic feasible solution, i.e., if a particular sample value of S_k for some k does not satisfy the restrictions (9.13.2) and (9.13.3), either because it leads to an inconsistent set of equations or because it leads to an unbounded set of solutions, that particular sample is defined as inadmissible.

(iii) The sample space generated by S_k is such that it satisfies the conditions of an ordinary nonstochastic linear programming problem, i.e., a programming problem which has a finite set of basic feasible solutions which are not degenerate and in which the optimal basic solutions are bounded.

Under these assumptions, we may now apply the complete description method of linear programming to the system (9.13.2) to see the total number of basic solutions which are feasible, i.e., satisfy the nonnegativity constraints (9.13.3). Let the total number of basic feasible solutions be denoted by N and the subscript $n = 1, 2, ..., N$. The corresponding values of objective functions are denoted by w_n, $n = 1, 2, ..., N$. The value w_n for a given admissible sample k is denoted by $w_n^{(k)}$. Now we define the following values of the objective function which correspond only to the basic feasible solutions:

$$w_i^{(k)} = \min_n \{w_n^{(k)} \mid n = 1, 2, ..., N\},$$
$$w_j^{(k)} = \min_n \{w_n^{(k)} \mid n = 1, 2, ..., N ; \quad n \neq i\} \qquad (9.14)$$
$$w_l^{(k)} = \min_n \{w_n^{(k)} \mid n = 1, 2, ..., N ; \quad n \neq i, j\}$$

and so on.

By our definition we might interpret $w_j^{(k)}$ as the truncated optimand (i.e., second best optimand) of the first order, $w_l^{(k)}$ as the truncated optimand of the second order (i.e., third best optimand) and so on. To avoid trivial results we assume that for all admissible $k = 1, 2, ..., K$ the optimands $w_i^{(k)}$, $w_j^{(k)}$, $w_l^{(k)}$ are nonzero (i.e., strictly positive). Let us assume also that the expectation (denoted by E) and variance (denoted by V) of the quantities $w_i^{(k)}$, $w_j^{(k)}$, $w_l^{(k)}$ are well defined over the admissible sample space $k = 1, 2, ..., K$. Now, since by construction

$$0 < w_i^{(k)} < w_j^{(k)} < w_l^{(k)}, \qquad \text{for all } k = 1, 2, ..., K,$$

therefore

$$0 < E(w_i^{(k)}) = Ew_i < E(w_j^{(k)}) = Ew_j < E(w_l^{(k)}) = Ew_l .$$

Hence, by the Archimedean property of real numbers, there must exist real and positive numbers $q_{ip}^{(k)} < 1$ such that

$$w_i^{(k)} = q_{ip}^{(k)} w_p^{(k)}, \qquad p = j \text{ or } 1 \text{ and } k = 1, 2, ..., K. \qquad (9.15)$$

Now we can state the following result, which is a special case of theorem 4.

If under the conditions specified in equations (9.14) and (9.15) the variable $q_{ip}^{(k)}$ is statistically independently distributed of $w_p^{(k)}$ over the admissible sample space $k = 1, 2, ..., K$ and the variances $\text{Var}(w_i^{(k)}) = V(w_i)$, $\text{Var}(w_p^{(k)}) = V(w_p)$ for $p = j$, 1; $p \neq i$ are well defined, i.e., they are nonzero and bounded, then $V(w_i)$ is strictly less than $V(w_p)$, if and only if the following two conditions hold simultaneously:

(a) $V(q_{ip}) + (Eq_{ip})^2 < 1$, $p = j, 1$; $p \neq i$

(b) $[(Ew_p)^2 V(q_{ip})/V(w_p)] < 1 - \{V(q_{ip}) + (Eq_{ip})^2\}$

Proof. Since the random variable $q_{ip}^{(k)}$ is statistically independent of $w_p^{(k)}$ for all admissible k,

$$V(w_i) - V(w_p) = \left[\{ V(q_{ip}) + (Eq_{ip})^2 - 1 \} V(w_p) \right] + V(q_{ip})(Ew_p)^2. \quad (9.16)$$

Since $V(q_{ip})(Ew_p)^2$ is strictly positive, this expression (9.16) is negative if the conditions (a) and (b) above hold. Conversely, suppose $V(w_i) < V(w_p)$ for $p = j$ or 1. Then, since q_{ip} is statistically independent of w_p,

$$V(q_{ip}) V(w_p) + (Eq_{ip})^2 V(w_p) + V(Q_{ip})(Ew_p)^2 < V(w_p)$$

from which conditions (a) and (b) of the theorem follow.

Corollary. If q_{ip} and w_p are statistically dependent but other conditions are satisfied, then

$$V(w_i) - V(w_p) \gtreqqless 0, \quad p = j \text{ or } 1; \quad p \neq i$$

according as

$$(Eq_{ip}Ew_p)^2 (1 - r^2 + Q_0) \gtreqqless V(w_p) [(Eq_{ip})^2 - 1],$$

where r and Q_0 are the quantities defined by

$$E(q_{ip}w_p) = r(Eq_{ip})(Ew_p), \quad 0 < r < 1,$$
$$Q_0 = E\left[\{ (q_{ip}/Eq_{ip})^2 - 1 \} (w_p/Ew_p)^2 \right].$$

If the conditions of the above theorem hold good, it implies that the optimal policy vector u is not only optimum in the expected value sense but also optimal in the minimum variance sense, i.e., stable in terms of variance. In case this does not hold, if the truncated optimands exist, the latter may be more stable (i.e., have less variance) than the nontruncated optimand and again we reach a competitive relation between optimality and stability characteristics of a stabilization policy vector, although the stability is measured here by variance.

This leads to a very broad and general conclusion which holds under certain conditions which are not very strict, i.e., if there are two policies (or solutions), if one is optimal in a certain sense it is not more stable than the other, i.e., in most cases it will be less stable. This result may have some interesting implications for alternative approximate solutions (i.e., their stability properties) of nonlinear Euler-Lagrange-type equations for optimization in a variational calculus framework.

9.5. Decision Rules under Chance-Constrained Programming

Now we consider the chance-constrained programming [6, 16, 46] model

(9.10.4) to derive "deterministic equivalents" of the stochastic models analyzed by Charnes and Cooper.[19] The equivalents construct, so to say, equivalent convex programming problems for a general class of linear decision rules under the three classes of objectives: (1) maximum expected value, (2) minimum variance and (3) maximum probability. For simplicity, it is assumed that the matrix A in the change-constrained programming system (9.10.4) is constant (i.e., nonrandom) and the admissible decision rules are restricted to the class

$$x = Db \qquad D: n.m \qquad\qquad (9.10.4.1)$$
$$b: m.1$$

(other classes of rules are, of course conceivable).
The expected value model is then

$$\begin{aligned} &\text{maximize } Ec'x \\ \text{under the conditions}& \qquad\qquad\qquad (9.10.4.2)\\ &P(Ax \leqq b) \geqq \alpha \\ &x = Db. \end{aligned}$$

Substituting (9.10.4.1) into the objective function of (9.10.4.2) we get

$$\text{minimize } -\mu_c' D\mu_b, \qquad\qquad (9.10.4.3)$$

where $\mu_y =$ the column vector Ey. Denoting the i-th row of matrix A by a_i' and $(b-\mu_b)$ by $\hat{b}$ and assuming normality of distribution for the variates $(a_i' D\hat{b} - \hat{b}_i)$, part of the constraints of (9.10.4.2) may be written as

$$\begin{aligned} P(a_i'Db - b_i \leqq 0) &= P(b_i - a_i'Db \geqq 0) \\ &= P(\hat{b}_i - a_i'D\hat{b} \geqq -\mu_{b_i} + a_i'D\mu_b) \geqq \alpha_i. \end{aligned}$$

Assuming $E[\hat{b}_i - a_i' D\hat{b}]^2 > 0$, the above can be normalized and the i-th constraint can be written fully as

$$P\left(\frac{\hat{b}_i - a_i'D\hat{b}}{\sqrt{E[\hat{b}_i - a_i'D\hat{b}]^2}} \geqq \frac{-\mu_{b_i} + a_i'D\mu_b}{\sqrt{E[\hat{b}_i - a_i'D\hat{b}]^2}}\right) \geqq \alpha_i. \qquad (9.17.1)$$

By the assumption of normality, the left-hand side of the argument, i.e., $(\hat{b}_i - a_i' D\hat{b})/\sqrt{E[\hat{b}_i - a_i' D\hat{b}]^2}$ is a standardized normal variable with zero

---

[19] This section is based on the paper by Charnes and Cooper [8].

mean and unit variance, so that (9.17.1) is replaced by

$$F_i\left(\frac{-\mu_{b_i} + a_i' D\mu_b}{\sqrt{E[\hat{b}_i - a_i' D\hat{b}]^2}}\right) \geq \alpha_i, \tag{9.17.2}$$

where

$$F_i(w) = (\sqrt{2\pi})^{-1} \int\limits_w^\infty e^{-y^2/2} \, dy .$$

Usually for normal distributions we take $\alpha_i \geq 0.5$. Then the equation (9.17.2) can be solved as

$$\frac{-\mu_{b_i} + a_i' D\mu_b}{\sqrt{E[\hat{b}_i - a_i' D\hat{b}]^2}} \leq F_i^{-1}(\alpha_i) \equiv -q_i \text{ (say)}, \tag{9.17.3}$$

where $q_i > 0$ for all i, if $\alpha_i > 0.5$.

The system (9.17.3) which involves nonrandom variables (i.e., deterministic values) only can be further reduced to a convex programming problem by introducing new variables v_i and writing (9.17.3) as

i.e.,

$$-\mu_{b_i} + a_i' D\mu_b \leq -v_i \leq -q_i\sqrt{E[\hat{b}_i - a_i' D\hat{b}]^2} \leq 0,$$

$$\mu_{b_i} - a_i' D\mu_b \geq v_i \geq q_i\sqrt{E[\hat{b}_i - a_i' D\hat{b}]^2} \geq 0,$$

which can be further simplified by squaring both sides, since nonnegativity is assigned to all expressions between inequality signs, i.e.,

$$-a_i' D\mu_b - v_i \geq -\mu_{b_i}$$
$$-q_i^2 E[\hat{b}_i - a_i' D\hat{b}]^2 + v_i^2 \geq 0$$

with $v_i \geq 0$ for each i. Hence, the equivalent convex program for chance-constrained programming (9.10.4.2) is

$$\text{minimize} - \mu_c' D\mu_b$$

under the conditions

$$\mu_{b_i} - a_i' D\mu_b - v_i \geq 0, \qquad (i = 1, 2, ..., m) \tag{9.17.4}$$
$$-q_i^2 E(a_i' Db - b_i)^2 + q_i^2(\mu_{b_i} - a_i' D\mu_b)^2 + v_i^2 \geq 0,$$

where the problem (9.17.4) is a convex programming problem in the variables D and v.

Two points may be noted about this method. First, it characterises the problem only within a very restricted class of decision rules, and the operational efficiency of the method must be determined by further experimentation. In other words, one could specify other types of deterministic equivalents [4] which would subsume the cases considered here. Second, the decision rules here are not analytic, i.e., each time they have to be solved as new data come up. An extension of this idea of deterministic equivalent in terms of recursive programming may be helpful, although it will involve nonlinear difference equations that are very difficult to solve.

It has to be noted also that for stochastic linear programming problems in general such constructions in terms of deterministic equivalents have been proposed [40]. The difficulty here is the same as above.

9.6. Two-Stage Programming Methods

Madansky [19] has classified the methods of reducing the effects of uncertainty in a linear programming problem into three types:

(i)   Replacing all random elements by their expected values.
(ii) Replacing the random elements by pessimistic estimates of their values in the hope that they would be "permanently" feasible.
(iii) Reducing the problem to a two-stage (or multistage) problem, where in the second stage one could compensate for the loss due to "inaccuracies" in the first-stage decisions.

He has called these methods the expected value solution, the fat solution and the slack solution, respectively. There is a close similarity of the slack solution to chance-constrained programming.

The difference between the chance-constrained formulation and the "slack" formulation is that in the latter the specific contingency plans of the decision maker for each possible infeasibility are explicitly spelled out, as are the explicit costs for all the possible infeasibilities, whereas in the former these explicit costs of the various types of infeasibility are reflected in the probabilities associated with each of the constraints [18, pp. 106–107].[20]

The two-stage programming problem has usually been analyzed for the case when only the resource vector b is random.[21] One line of work, followed by Madansky, has been concerned with the search for a certainty equivalent, i.e., an equivalent nonrandom problem, by a suitable replacement of the

---

[20] From *Recent Advances in Mathematical Programming*, by Madansky. Copyright © 1963 by McGraw-Hill Book Company and reprinted by their permission.

[21] For multistage extensions and other detailed results of this approach, see Dantzig [12, Chapter 25].

random vector b, such that the solution of the nonrandom problem is also the solution of the two-stage programming problem. Conditions have been derived under which replacing b by its expected value Eb would or would not satisfy conditions of certainty equivalence.

There is a very close link between this approach and the active approach of stochastic linear programming, particularly when in the latter the allocation matrices $U^{(1)}$, $U^{(2)}$, etc. are chosen successively until the complete specification of the distribution of the random variables is known. From this standpoint one could analyze the statistical distribution of $\min_y f'y$ for specified sample selections of x and characterize the deterministic form in which the penalty cost should be added to the usual term $c'x$.

Another important feature of two-stage programming is that it suggests a decomposition principle for large linear programs. For example, if $Eb_2 = \bar{b}_2$ in (9.11.0) above specifies a deterministic equivalent of the two-stage programming problem, the convenient block lower triangular structure of the coefficient matrix of (9.11.2) and (9.11.3) could be utilized in a decomposition algorithm.[22] Since the efficiency and optimality of decision making in a decentralized framework depends so much on the form of the coefficient structure (i.e., the optimal basis in the linear programming language), it is worthwhile investigating the general problem of penalty costs involved in approximating a nontriangular coefficient structure by a near-triangular structure. The special cases of decomposition known so far [23] are also useful in suggesting criteria for aggregating a number of activities, e.g., for a development planning model one might like to aggregate the sectors of a dynamic Leontief model, subject to linear inequalities [41], such that the aggregated activities and the aggregative model have certain stability properties.

9.7. Recent Developments in Decision Models Under Risk

This section presents an outline of selected recent developments in methods of decision-making under risk and uncertainty, which in our view, are operational and, hence, applicable in principle to empirical economic models. Two major areas are briefly reviewed here: A. Recent developments

---

[22] Dantzig has shown how by means of decomposition principles it is possible to plan optimally the over-all operation of a large, central decision-making organization without the central staff having full knowledge of the technology of each part. See Dantzig [12, Chapter 23, also pp. 510–511].

in probabilistic programming; B. Risk and uncertainty in recent economic models.

From a historical standpoint developments in probabilistic programming have occurred primarily in operations research and fields other than economics [75, 79] and this is true for the recent developments also.

9.7.1. *Selected Developments in Probabilistic Programming*

Two major aspects of probabilistic programming applied to LP (linear programming) models have been emphasized in the recent literature. One is the use of nonparametric methods [73] which are relatively distribution free in the sense that these do not depend specifically on the assumption of a specific distribution like the normal, for example. The second development is concerned with methods for incorporating nonnormal distributions in the theory of stochastic programming [74, 77].

The first kind of development is of great practical value since it helps us analyze alternative deterministic transformations of a given stochastic LP problem and choose one that is in some sense more robust or relatively distribution free. Some of the operational methods in this area can be summarized very briefly. First, there is a class of methods which generalizes the safety-first approach based on Tchebycheff-type probabilistic inequalities; some of the generalizations [74, 76, 81] include the following: (a) comparisons [78] with the normal distribution case; (b) comparisons with the IHR (increasing hazard rate) class of distributions and specification of bounds sharper than the Tchebycheff inequality [79] and (c) nonparametric methods of estimation of the resulting distribution [74, 81] of optimal profits. As an example of the first case, consider the LP model given by (9.10.1) through (9.10.3) and assume that the vector c in the objective function is random following a multivariate normal distribution with a mean vector m and a variance-covariance matrix V. In this case we obtain a class of fractile programs if the tolerance measure α $(0 < \alpha < 1)$ is suitably pre-assigned and the lower bound f of the objective function (9.10.1) is maximized, where

$$\text{Prob}\,(z = c'x \geq f) = \alpha. \tag{9.18.1}$$

This fractile approach results in the following concave programming problems

$$\text{maximize } f = m'x - k \cdot (x'Vx)^{1/2}$$

subject to

$$x \in R;\ R = \{x | x \geq 0,\ Ax \leq b\}, \tag{9.18.2}$$

where $k = -F^{-1}(w)$, $F(w)$ being the cumulative probability $\text{Prob}(y \leq w)$ of a unit normal variate y, and k is assumed positive thus implying that α must be greater than 0.50. If instead of preassigning the tolerance measure α, the decision-maker preassigns the lower bound f in (9.18.1), then the following class of nonlinear fractional functional programs [79] are obtained

$$\text{maximize } k = (m'x - f)/(x'Vx)^{1/2}, \; x \in R, \qquad (9.18.3)$$

since maximizing α with $\alpha \geq 0.50$ implies maximizing k with $m'x \geq f$. Note, however, that by Tchebycheff inequality which holds whenever profits $z = c'x$ follow a distribution (not necessarily normal) with finite mean and variance we have the bound

$$0 \leq \text{Prob}(z = c'x \leq f) \leq (x'Vx)/(m'x - f)^2. \qquad (9.18.4)$$

However, if the specific form of the distribution of z is not known, the probability in (9.18.4) cannot be preassigned, i.e., in default of not knowing the probability $\text{Prob}(z \leq f)$ one may suggest a decision rule based on the safety-first principle [73] according to which we minimize the upper bound of this probability:

$$\text{minimize } (x'Vx)/(m'x - f)^2, \; x \in R. \qquad (9.18.5)$$

If this nonlinear program has an optimal feasible solution $\bar{x}$, then this can be used in (9.18.4) to derive a bound on the level of profits. Note that the structure of the two problems, the parametric case in (9.18.3) and the non-parametric in (9.18.5), is very close. However, if the distribution of profits $z = c'x$ is not normal but it satisfies the conditions of the central limit theorem in some form, then our problem is to obtain estimates for the error in approximation through normal distribution and to improve on this result by utilizing asymptotic expansions. Indeed, this is possible for any continuous cumulative distribution $F(t) = \text{Prob}(z \leq t) = \text{Prob}((c-m)'x/(x'Vx)^{1/2} \leq t)$ with finite mean and variance, since it can be expanded around the normal cumulative distribution in terms of the Tchebycheff-Hermite polynomials [73]. Several cases of nonnormal distributions have been worked out [74, 78] in order to analyze sensitivity along this line.

A second approach is to apply methods of distance functions related to the sample and population space. For instance, if we interpret that the sample values of the random variable profit z define a sampling distribution which is an approximation to the unknown population distribution of z, then the degree of reliability of a sampling approximation can be measured in one way at least by the probability of the maximum discrepancy between the two cumulative distributions, the sampling distribution and the population distribution. And, indeed, there are Kolmogorov-Smirnov limit theorems for specifying such probabilities of maximum discrepancy and the results are distribution-free. Using these results, suitable transformations of the stochastic LP model can be made and also alternative empirical distributions fitted to the sample solutions may be analyzed [76].

A third approach considers applying empirical Bayes methods [64, 81] for approximating the parent distribution of a random variable z whose cumulative distribution function $F(z|\theta)$ depends on the parameter θ, say. In the pure Bayesian approach the parameter θ itself is regarded as a realization of another prior random variable with a prior density $g(\theta)$, say, although the prior density may be diffuse or otherwise. Any decision d within a set D about θ is then evaluated by maximizing the expected utility function

$$\bar{u}_g(d) = \int u(d, \theta)g(\theta)\, d\theta, \qquad (9.18.6)$$

where a suitable scalar function called the utility function $u(d, \theta)$ is presumed (note that the utility function is more general than profits in the sense that utility may be a function of profits and other decision variables also). Now with a set of observations t being available, the knowledge of θ is changed by Bayes theorem to a posterior distribution given t, i.e., $G(\theta|t)$ with a density $g(\theta|t)$, say. The new expected utility which is conditional on the observation t then becomes

$$\bar{u}_g(d|t) = \int u(d, \theta)g(\theta|t)\, d\theta. \qquad (9.18.7)$$

Intuitively one expects that any decision based on maximizing the expected utility defined in (9.18.7) which is based on the posterior distribution must be better than that based on maximizing the expected utility defined in (9.18.6), since otherwise the additional observations t on θ have been of no value. Denote the maximum of $\bar{u}_g(d|t)$ over all decisions $d \in D$ by $\bar{u}_g^*(d|t)$. This quantity $\bar{u}_g^*(d|t)$ is a random variable, since the observations t are random being generated by a density function $g(t)$ which is the distribution of t anticipated before the observations were made. This density may be expressed as

$$g(t) = \int p(t|\theta)g(\theta)\, d\theta. \qquad (9.18.8)$$

Hence, the expected value of the quantity $\bar{u}_g^*(d|t)$ is given by

$$E\bar{u}_g^*(d^*) = \int \bar{u}_g^*(d|t)g(t)\, dt.$$

The empirical Bayes procedure makes a frequency distribution interpretation of the prior probability $g(\theta)$ and attempts to estimate it from empirical data [64]. For example, the observations $t_1, t_2, \ldots, t_N$ may be regarded as the realizations from the density function $g(t)$ given in (9.18.8) and the empirical distribution $G_N(t)$ constructed from the ordered sample $t_{(1)} \leq t_{(2)} \leq \cdots \leq t_{(N)}$ as follows:

$$G_N(t) = \begin{cases} 0 \text{ for } t < t_{(1)} \\ k/N \text{ for } t_{(k)} \leq t < t_{(k+1)}, \, k = 1, 2, \ldots, N - 1 \\ 1 \text{ for } t \geq t_{(N)} \end{cases}$$

should provide an estimate of $G(t)$ with a density $g(t)$ given in (9.18.8). It is known from Kolmogorov-Smirnov limit theorems [79] that the estimate $G_N(t)$ converges with probability one to $G(t)$ as N becomes infinitely large. Using this empirical density $g_N(\theta)$ in (9.18.7) in place of $g(\theta|t)$ we can maximize the utility function $\bar{u}_g(d|t)$ for given t, to arrive at optimal Bayes decision rules. Also, one could substitute it in (9.18.8) and compute the expected loss $\bar{L}$ resulting from suboptimal decisions d_* which maximize $\bar{u}_g(d|t)$ given in (9.18.7)

$$\bar{L} = E\bar{u}_g^*(d^*) - \bar{u}_g(d_*|t) \geq 0.$$

It is clear, therefore, that the expected cost of suboptimal decisions or second-best policies can be evaluated by the empirical Bayes methods. Some implications of this method of suboptimality analysis in the framework of normal distribution theory has been recently considered by Aitchison [57]. Other applications of Bayesian methods to stochastic programming are also reported [75].

A number of attempts have been made in recent years to include probability distributions other than the normal in the theory of stochastic and chance-constrained linear programming [77–79]. In particular, the nonnegative distributions like chi-square, exponential, truncated normal, etc., which are potentially more applicable to economic models where the resources and input-coefficients are generally required to be nonnegative have been investigated [77]. Also, for a class of LP problems with random price and resource vectors c and b, a measure of system reliability has been introduced, thereby making it possible to analyze the trade-off between system reliability and optimality [76, 80]. Several economic applications are available in the literature [67, 80].

The theory of two-stage programming under uncertainty referred to in equations (9.11.1) through (9.11.4) before has also been extended in recent

306 DECISION MAKING UNDER RISK

years to include randomness in all the parameters and not simply b_2 defined in (9.11.3). This is now called stochastic programs with recourse which is formulated as follows [87]:

$$w = \inf_{x \geq 0} E_\theta [c'(\theta)x + \{\min_{y \geq 0} f'(\theta)y | A_{21}(\theta)x + A_{22}(\theta)y = b_2(\theta)\}], \qquad (9.19.1)$$

where θ is a point of the joint probability distribution P involving the components of a collection of five matrices, c, f, b_2, A_{21} and A_{22}, and E_θ denotes expectation with respect to θ and inf denotes infimum. If the matrix A_{22} is fixed and constant for all θ, we have a problem of fixed recourse; if A_{22} is square and nonsingular, then we have a problem with stable recourse, i.e., the same set of columns is an optimal basis with probability one [68, 69]. Note that for each value of the decision vector x and for each value of the random variable θ, the term $(\min_{y \geq 0} f'y)$ is the optimal value of the second-stage LP problem

Minimize $f'y$
  subject to

$$y \geq 0; A_{22}y = b_2 - A_{21}x. \qquad (9.19.2)$$

Denote this optimum value of the objective function by $Q(x, \theta)$ and define the sets

$$K_1 = \{x | A_{11}x = b_1, x \geq 0\}$$
$$K_2 = \{x | \text{problem (9.19.2) feasible with probability one}\}.$$

Then the case where K_1 is a subset of K_2 defines stochastic programs with relatively complete recourse. It is clear that this holds if and only if for all values of x in K_1, the set of points defined by $(b_2 - A_{21}x)$ belongs to W^+ with probability one, where W^+ defines the set $W^+ = \{t | t = Wy$ for all $y \geq 0\}$, i.e., by nonnegative weighted sums of columns of W.

It should be clear, however, that although the formulation of stochastic programs with recourse has been very elegant in generalizing the characterization of two-stage programming under uncertainty, the computational problems are still unresolved in respect of (a) the implications of various distributions, normal and nonnormal, and (b) the suitable evaluation of penalty costs, particularly the way these are interpreted in the theory of sequential unconstrained minimization techniques [80].

9.7.2. Risk and Uncertainty in Selected Recent Models

At a general and somewhat aggregate level the treatment of uncertainty and risk in recent economic models has followed three interrelated trends:

(a) It has been argued that the existence, stability and attainability of general equilibrium under a competitive market framework defined in a world of certainty may fail to hold under conditions of uncertainty, since the markets for exchanging contingent claims on future goods may not exist [70, 82]; this has led to investigations about the modifications required to sustain a competitive framework.

(b) It has been argued in the recent theories of optimal growth, particularly by Morishima [66] that under reasonable economic assumptions regarding flexible consumer demand functions and interdependence of production decisions, oscillations and fluctuations cannot in general be avoided and, hence, an element of strong fluctuation-aversion should be built into the dynamic intertemporal utility function in order to indicate the desirability of stability; it is clear that this sort of restriction in effect compels one to choose a second-best rather than the first-best solution [84].

(c) A number of attempts have been made [84] following the approach of Haavelmo to build various types of stochastic processes and controls in the models of economic growth; dynamic portfolio type analysis based on the mean-variance approach has also been considered for lifetime investment allocation problems [72, 84].

At a more operational level some of the following developments are worth mentioning. First, in econometric estimation problems there is some trend in applying Bayesian methods [61, 71, 84], although the main difficulty here is the choice of the appropriate prior distributions. Recent statistical work on empirical Bayes methods may offer some hope here in evolving some systematic procedures besides testing the sensitivity of parametric estimates. Second, it is interesting to note that problems of uncertainty are now incorporated into the detailed intersectoral planning strategy of countries like Hungary where prices are mostly determined by central control and not by market processes, which may have uncertainty due to various adjustments and anticipations. As it has been pointed out by Kornai [63, p. 185]: The magnitude of the effect of divergences from the plans caused by uncertainty will be influenced by three main factors: (a) the elasticity of planning methods and the ability to adapt quickly to unforeseen situations ... (b) the sensitivity and importance of the point of the national economy where a divergence from the plan occurs ... and (c) the supply of stocks and reserves in the national economy." This leads to the modification of the planning model based on input-output type analysis to include the following: (a) a method of safety programming by building appropriate safety levels, i.e., safety levels should be lower for the comparatively less important sectors and higher for those of decisive importance, (b) risk-aversion should be built in the sectoral investment plans, although an equal degree of risk aversion will not be warranted in all sectors of the national economy. By safety programming is meant the class of fractile programs we already referred to in (9.18.2) before. Thus, it is clear how the various methods of stochastic programming would be applicable in national planning situations.

Even in the context of private enterprise economies the need for indicative planning has been emphasized by Meade due to two basic uncertainties, e.g., market uncertainty and environmental uncertainty [65]. Whereas market uncertainty is the relative lack of knowledge of the producer about the future demand pattern by the consumers, environmental uncertainty covers a very wide class of events, e.g., future technical progress may affect the real input cost of energy and, hence, other outputs or the parameters in production or consumption functions may be uncertain. Forward markets and indicative planning provide some mechanisms by which some of the market and environmental uncertainty may be reduced. Indirectly this suggests perhaps the need to analyze an econometric or forecasting model in terms of basic stochastic processes and stochastic controls [84].

Third, recent developments in control theory suggest that methods of adaptive control which incorporate uncertainty by providing various methods of adaptive adjustment are increasingly used for reducing some of stochastic instability associated with optimal control solutions. This area has been recently discussed by Tintner and Sengupta [84] in their application of stochastic and adaptive control methods to various economic models. It may be pointed out that methods of simulation and sensitivity analysis [75] have a considerable scope of application here.

REFERENCES

[1] ARROW, K. J. "Alternative Approaches to the Theory of Choice Under Risk-Taking Situations," *Econometrica*, XIX, No. 4 (October, 1951), 404–431.

[2] ——. "Decision Theory and the Choice of a Level of Significance for the (t)-test," in *Contributions to Probability and Statistics: Essays in Honor of H. Hotelling*. Edited by Ingram Olkin *et al.* Stanford: Stanford University Press, 1960, pp. 70–78.

[3] BAUMOL, W. J. "An Expected Gain-Confidence Limit Criterion for Portfolio Selection," *Management Science*, X (October, 1963), 174–182.

[4] BEALE, E. M. L. "The Use of Quadratic Programming in Stochastic Linear Programming," *Rand Corporation Report* P-2404-1, August 15, 1961.

[5] BLACKWELL, D., and GIRSHICK, M. A. *Theory of Games and Statistical Decisions*. New York: John Wiley & Sons, 1954.

[6] CHARNES, A., and COOPER, W. W. "Chance-Constrained Programming," *Management Science*, VI (October, 1959), 73–79.

[7] ——. "Normal Deviates and Chance Constraints," *Journal of American Statistical Association*, LVII (March, 1962), 134–143.

[8] ——. "Deterministic Equivalents for Optimizing and Satisficing Under Chance Constraints," *Operations Research*, XI, No. 1 (February, 1963), 18–39.

[9] ——, ——, and THOMPSON, G. L. "Chance Constrained Studies for Linear Programming Under Uncertainty: Part I: Constrained Generalized Medians and Two-Stage Problems with General Linear Structure," ONR Research Memorandum No. 106. Pittsburgh, Pa.: Graduate School of Industrial Administration, Carnegie Institute of Technology, December, 1962. (Mimeographed.)

[10] DANTZIG, G. B. "Linear Programming under Uncertainty," *Management Science*, I (April–July, 1955), 197.

[11] ——. "On the Status of Multi-Stage Programming Problems," *Management Science*, VI (October, 1959), 53–72.

[12] ——. *Linear Programming and Extensions*. Princeton, N.J.: Princeton University Press, 1963.

[13] ——, and MADANSKY, A. "On the Solution of Two-Stage Linear Programs Under Uncertainty," in *Proceedings of the Fourth Berkeley Symposium on Mathematical Statistics and Probability*. Vol. I. Berkeley: University of California Press, 1961.

[14] HOLT, C. C. "Linear Decision Rules for Economic Stabilization and Growth," *Quarterly Journal of Economics*, LXXVI (February, 1962), 20–45.

[15] ——, et al. *Planning Production, Inventories and Work Force*. Englewood Cliffs, N.J.: Prentice-Hall, 1960.

[16] KATAOKA, S. "A Stochastic Programming Model," *Econometrica*, XXXI (January–April, 1963), 181–196.

[17] LUCE, R. D., and RAIFFA, H. *Games and Decisions*. New York: John Wiley & Sons, 1957.

[18] MADANSKY, A. "Linear Programming Under Uncertainty," in *Recent Advances in Mathematical Programming*. Edited by R. L. Graves and P. Wolfe. New York: McGraw-Hill Book Co., 1963.

[19] ——. "Methods of Solution of Linear Programs Under Uncertainty," *Operations Research*, X (1962), 463–470.

[20] ——. "Dual Variables in Two-Stage Linear Programming Under Uncertainty," *Journal of Mathematical Analysis and Applications*, VI, No. 1 (February, 1963), 98–108.

[21] MARKOWITZ, H. *Portfolio Selection*. New York: John Wiley & Sons, 1959.

[22] MARSCHAK, T. "Centralization and Decentralization in Economic Organizations," *Econometrica*, XXVII (April, 1959), 399–430.

[23] MATHEMATICA. *Decomposition Principles for Solving Large Structured Linear Programs*. Notes for a course presented by Mathematica, Berkeley, Calif., April 24–26, 1963.

[24] MILNOR, J. "Games Against Nature," in *Decision Processes*. Edited by R. M. Thrall, C. H. Coombs, and R. L. Davis. New York: John Wiley & Sons, 1954, Chap. 4.

[25] NEYMAN, J. "Two Breakthroughs in the Theory of Statistical Decision-making," *Review of the International Statistical Institute*, XXX, No. 1 (1962), 11–27.

[26] RAIFFA, H., and SCHLAIFER, R. *Applied Statistical Decision Theory*. Boston: Division

of Research, Graduate School of Business Administration, Harvard University, 1961.

[27] REITER, S. "Surrogates for Uncertain Decision Problems: Minimal Information for Decision-Making," *Econometrica*, XXV (April, 1957), 339–345.

[28] ROBBINS, H. "An Empirical Bayes Approach to Statistics," *Proceedings of Third Berkeley Symposium on Statistics and Probability*. Berkeley: University of California Press, 1956, Vol. I, pp. 157–164.

[29] ROY, A. D. "Safety First and the Holding of Assets," *Econometrica*, XX, No. 3, (July, 1952), 431–449.

[30] SENGUPTA, J. K. "On the Relative Stability and Optimality of Consumption in Aggregative Growth Models," *Economica*, XXXI (February, 1964), 33–50.

[31] ——. "Some Observations on the Optimal Growth Path for an Underdeveloped Economy," *Metroeconomica*, XVI, No. 2 (1964).

[32] ——, MILLHAM, C., and TINTNER, G. "On the Stability of Solutions Under Error in Stochastic Linear Programming," *Metrika*, IX, No. 1 (1965), pp. 47–60.

[33] ——, and TINTNER, G. "On Some Economic Models of Development Planning," *Economia Internazionale*, XVI, No. 1, (February, 1963), 34–52.

[34] ——, ——, and MILLHAM, C. "On Some Theorems of Stochastic Linear Programming with Applications," *Management Science*, X, No. 1 (October, 1963), 143–159.

[35] ——, ——, and MORRISON, B. "Stochastic Linear Programming with Applications to Economic Models," *Economica*, XXX, No. 119 (August, 1963), 262–276.

[36] ——, ——, ——. "Stochastic Linear Programming with Application to Planning in India." Paper presented to the summer meeting of the Econometric Society, Ann Arbor, Mich., September 8–12, 1962. (To be published in *Indian Economic Review*.)

[37] SHACKLE, G. L. S. *Expectation in Economics*. Cambridge: Cambridge University Press, 1949.

[38] SIMON, H. A. "Dynamic Programming under Uncertainty with Quadratic Criterion Function," *Econometrica*, XXIV (1956), 74–81.

[39] ——. *Models of Man*. New York: John Wiley & Sons, 1957, Chap. 14.

[40] SINHA, S. M. "Programming with Standard Errors in the Constraints and the Objective," in *Recent Advances in Mathematical Programming*, abstract. Edited by R. L. Graves and P. Wolfe. New York: McGraw-Hill Book Co., 1963, p. 121.

[41] SOLOW, R. M. "Competitive Valuation in a Dynamic Input-Output System," *Econometrica*, XXVII, No. 1 (January, 1959), 30–53.

[42] SUZUKI, Y. "On Sequential Decision Procedures," *Bulletin of International Statistical Institute*, XXXVIII, Parts 3–4 (1960), 201–205.

[43] THEIL, H. "Econometric Models and Welfare Maximization," *Weltwirtschaftliches Archiv*, LXXII, No. 1 (1954), 60–83.

[44] ——. "A Note on Certainty Equivalence in Dynamic Planning," *Econometrica*, XXV, No. 2 (April, 1957), 346–349.

[45] ——. *Optimal Decision Rules for Government and Industry*. Amsterdam: North-Holland Publishing Co., 1964.

[46] THOMPSON, G. L., COOPER, W. W., and CHARNES, A. "Characterizations by Chance-Constrained Programming," in *Recent Advances in Mathematical Programming*. Edited by R. L. Graves and P. Wolfe. New York: McGraw-Hill Book Co., 1963, pp. 113–119.

[47] THORBECKE, ERIK. "Research Applications of Quantitative Decision Analysis with

More Specific Reference to Fiscal Policy—A Survey," Paper presented to annual meeting of Operational Research Society of America and Institute of Management Science (ORSA-TIMS), Minneapolis, October, 1964.

[48] TINBERGEN, J., and Bos, H. *Mathematical Models of Economic Growth.* New York: McGraw-Hill Book Co., 1962.

[49] TINTNER, G. "Stochastic Linear Programming with Applications to Agricultural Economics," in *Second Symposium on Linear Programming.* Washington, D.C.: National Bureau of Standards, 1955.

[50] ——. "The Application of Decision Theory of Probability to a Simple Inventory Problem," *Trabajos de Estadistica,* X (1959), 240–247.

[51] ——. "The Use of Stochastic Linear Programming in Planning," *Indian Economic Review,* V (1960), 159–167.

[52] ——, MILLHAM, C., and SENGUPTA, J. K. "A Weak Duality Theorem for Stochastic Linear Programming," *Unternehmensforschung,* VII, No. 1 (1963), 1–8.

[53] VAJDA, S. *Mathematical Programming.* Reading, Mass.: Addison-Wesley, 1961.

[54] VAN DEN BOGAARD, P. J. M., and THEIL, H. "Macro-Dynamic Policy-Making: An Application of Strategy and Certainty Equivalence Concepts to the Economy of the United States 1933–36," *Metroeconomica,* XI, No. 1 (1959), 149–167.

[55] WALD, A. *Statistical Decision Functions.* New York: John Wiley & Sons, 1950.

[56] WOLFE, P. (ed.). *Recent Advances in Mathematical Programming.* New York: McGraw-Hill Book Co., 1963, pp. 113–119.

[57] AITCHISON, J. "Statistical Problems of Treatment Allocation", *Journal of Royal Statistical Society,* Series A, 1970, pp. 206–238.

[58] ARROW, K. J. *Essays in the Theory of Risk-Bearing.* Chicago: Markham Publishing Company, 1971.

[59] BORCH, K. H. *The Economics of Uncertainty.* Princeton: Princeton University Press, 1968.

[60] CHAMPERNOWNE, D. G. *Uncertainty and Estimation in Economics.* Volume III; San Francisco: Holden-Day, 1969.

[61] CHETTY, V. K. "Bayesian Analysis of Haavelmo's Models", *Econometrica,* Volume 36, 1968, pp. 582–602.

[62] HADAR, J. and RUSSELL, W. R. "Stochastic Dominance and Diversification", *Journal of Economic Theory,* Volume 3, 1971, pp. 288–305.

[63] KORNAI, J. *Mathematical Planning of Structural Decisions.* Amsterdam: North-Holland Publishing Co., 1967.

[64] MARITZ, J. S. *Empirical Bayes Methods.* London: Methuen and Co., 1970.

[65] MEADE, J. E. *The Theory of Indicative Planning.* Manchester: Manchester University Press, 1970.

[66] MORISHIMA, M. *Theory of Economic Growth.* Oxford: Clarendon Press, 1969.

[67] NASLUND, B. *Decisions Under Risk.* Stockholm: Stockholm School of Economics, 1967.

[68] PREKOPA, A. "On the Probability Distribution of the Optimum of a Random Linear Program", *SIAM Journal on Control,* Volume 4, 1966, pp. 211–222.

[69] ——. "On Probabilistic Constrained Programming", in *Proceedings of the Princeton Symposium on Mathematical Programming,* ed. by H. W. Kuhn. Princeton: Princeton University Press, 1970, pp. 113–138.

[70] RADNER, R. "Competitive Equilibrium Under Uncertainty", *Econometrica*, Volume 36, 1968, pp. 31–58.

[71] RAIFFA, H. and SCHLAIFER, R. *Applied Statistical Decision Theory*. Cambridge: MIT Press, 1961.

[72] SAMUELSON, P. A. "Lifetime Portfolio Selection by Dynamic Stochastic Programming", *Review of Economics and Statistics*, Volume 51, 1969, pp. 239–246.

[73] SENGUPTA, J. K. "Safety-First Rules Under Chance-Constrained Linear Programming", *Operations Research*, Volume 17, 1969, pp. 112–132.

[74] ——. "Distribution Problems in Stochastic and Chance-Constrained Programming", in *Economic Models, Estimation and Risk Programming: Essays in Honor of G. Tintner*, ed. by Fox, K. A., Sengupta, J. K. and Narasimham, G. V. L. New York: Springer-Verlag, 1969, Chapter 18.

[75] ——, and FOX, K. A. *Economic Analysis and Operations Research: Optimization Techniques in Quantitative Economic Models*. Amsterdam: North-Holland Publishing, 1969.

[76] ——, and GRUVER, G. "A Linear Reliability Analysis in Programming with Chance-Constraints", *Swedish Journal of Economics*, 1969, pp. 221–246.

[77] ——. "A Generalization of Some Distribution Aspects of Chance-Constrained Linear Programming", *International Economic Review*, Volume 11, No. 2, 1970, pp. 287–304.

[78] ——. "A System Reliability Approach to Linear Programming", *Unter nehmens forschung*, Volume 15, 1971, pp. 112–129.

[79] ——, and TINTNER, G. "A Review of Stochastic Linear Programming", *Review of International Statistical Institute*, Volume 39, No. 2, 1971, pp. 197–223.

[80] ——. "Decision Rules in Stochastic Programming Under Dynamic Models", (accepted for publication in Swedish Journal of Economics).

[81] ——. "Fractile Programming Under Extreme Value Distributions for the Stochastic Objective Function" (sent for publication: 1972).

[82] STIGUM, B. P. "Competitive Equilibria Under Uncertainty", *Quarterly Journal of Economics*, Volume 83, 1969, pp. 533–561.

[83] THORE, S. "A Dynamic Leontief Model with Chance Constraints", in *Risk and Uncertainty: Proceedings of a Conference*, ed. by Borch, K. and Mossin, J. London: Macmillan, 1968, Chapter 20.

[84] TINTNER, G. and SENGUPTA, J. K. *Stochastic Economics: Stochastic Processes, Control and Programming*. New York: Academic Press, 1972.

[85] TISDELL, C. A. *The Theory of Price Uncertainty, Production and Profit*. Princeton, N. J.: Princeton University Press, 1968.

[86] TOBIN, J. E. "Liquidity Preference as Behavior Towards Risk", *Review of Economic Studies*, Volume 25, 1968, pp. 65–86.

[87] WALKUP, D. W. and WETS, R. J. B. "Stochastic Programs with Recourse", *SIAM Journal of Applied Mathematics*, Volume 15, September 1967, pp. 1299–1314.

[88] ——. "Stochastic Programs with Recourse: Special Forms", in *Proceedings of the Princeton Symposium on Mathematical Programming*. Princeton: Princeton University Press, 1970, pp. 139–162.

PART II

APPLICATIONS TO ECONOMIC GROWTH STABILIZATION AND PLANNING

Chapter 10

ANALYTICAL MODELS OF ECONOMIC GROWTH AND THEIR IMPLICATIONS

From the standpoint of economic policy, an analysis of the current models of economic growth has two distinct roles to play. First, it aids in the specification of relationships, mostly in a quantitative form, which will describe the economic process or certain essential features of it in a realistic way. Second, the use of models in development planning, either explicitly or implicitly, serves to show, at the least, the weaknesses and limitations of central decision making with or without a naive model. The basic objectives of formulating alternative models of economic growth are essentially operational in character. The word operational is used here to suggest two important recent trends of economic growth models: First, a model is required to analyze and explain the observed process of growth of an economy by means of a set of quantitative variables so that the empirical realism of the model may be tested. A purely formal and strictly logical model based on a set of formal axioms need not be operational as long as we do not set up the criteria of empirical refutability and realism. Hence, the predictive efficiency of a model is essential to its operational character. Second, we require that an operational model must contain a set of policy variables, amenable to control by one or a set of policy makers, such that the observed (or actual) process of growth may be favorably influenced by those policy variables in order to converge to an optimal process of growth when the optimality condition is defined in some meaningful economic sense, e.g., the maximum feasible and sustainable growth rate of per capita real national income. The analysis of the divergence of the actual from the optimal situation may be made in terms of either various characteristics of the optimal situation, such as the stability properties of the optimum equilibrium, the rate and process of convergence of the growth path and the probabilistic aspects of the equilibrium situation, or policy alternatives to ensure the convergence of the observed and actual path to the optimal and idealized time path. The latter objective specifically requires that a growth model

315

must also be a policy model, i.e., it must contain a number of feasible policy alternatives such that the policy maker or a group of policy makers may in some sense choose the optimal set of policy alternatives. This introduces directly the theory of economic policy and various types of linear and nonlinear programming situations that specify the operational contours of growth models.

This section is divided into two sections: Section 10.1 outlines a brief survey of the analytical contents of some of the most important models of economic growth with particular reference to some of their limitations and rigidities. The aspect of trend, which is an essential part of the specification of a growth model, is also examined with reference to some empirical statistical data for the United Kingdom and the U.S. Section 10.2 discusses some of the policy implications of the economic growth models. Since we have attempted a rather detailed analysis of some of the planning models for both developed and underdeveloped economies in Chapters 13 and 14 and of the recent Social Science Research Council (SSRC) model of the U.S. economy in Chapter 11, we confine ourselves to analyzing in this part some of the general analytical implications following from the different ways in which the most important relations of a growth model (e.g., capital accumulation, production function, process of adjustment to disequilibrium, etc.) are specified. For example, it is examined how far a partial model as distinct from a general equilibrium model is useful in specifying the process of growth. Similarly, we explore how far the sequential aspects of policy making could be built into the model in order to facilitate its actual policy application. This has been alternatively called "planning in stages" by Tinbergen and Bos [77, p. 10], which is distinct from the other approach of establishing one master model (i.e., a complicated supermodel) for a simultaneous solution of almost all the economic problems of growth. As these authors pointed out:

> ..., the first stage may consist of a macro-economic study of the general process of production and investment, along the lines suggested by Harrod-Domar models or by similar, somewhat more complicated models. The aim of this first stage should be to determine, in a provisional way, the rate of savings and the general index of production. A second stage may consist then in specifying production targets for a number of sectors over a fairly long period. A third stage, if needed, may go into more detail for a shorter period, giving figures for a larger number of smaller sectors. A fourth stage may consist in "filling the plan out" with individual projects. Intermixed with this succession there may be stages of revision of the previous stages. Thus, the figures

of the second stage may already enable the planner to revise some of the coefficients used in the first stage and to re-do therefore, the first stage. After a fixed interval of time, new data will be available and this may lead to another revision, combined or not with shifting the period of the plan.[1]

10.1. Economic Models of Growth: Their Important Characteristics and Limitations

The models of economic growth can be characterized in a number of alternative ways, depending on the purpose. From our standpoint, we classify growth models into two types: (a) the deterministic type and (b) the probabilistic type. As the name implies, the probabilistic growth models analyze the details of the stochastic process and the underlying probability structure of a set of interacting variables, each of which may represent different measures of the over-all process of growth (e.g., capital, labor, the rate of savings, etc.). Such types of models have important implications for both macroeconomic policy making and the specification of optimum rates of economic development, as is shown, for example, by the recent formulation of inventory models and the applications of the evolutionary stochastic processes [3] in other fields of social science. A typical example [46], drawn from the theory of economic growth, would be the question of deciding the optimum expansion of productive capacity in a certain sector, say, when the future pattern of demand has a probabilistic structure, i.e., an element of uncertainty.

The deterministic models, which are by far the most prevalent, may be further subdivided into two groups: aggregative and disaggregative. The aggregative models are generally based on the assumption of a single sector, whereas the disaggregative models seek to specify the relative rates of growth of several interdependent sectors of an economy. An intermediate case between these two polar types of growth models is provided by an intersectoral model, where the different sectors are completely independent or substantially so. For instance, when the coefficient matrix of an open Leontief model is of a block-diagonal form, we have a system in which the blocks of sectors are relatively independent of one another. As a quasi-disaggregative model, one may also mention the case when the input-output

---

coefficient matrix is triangular or very nearly so and, hence, there is only unilateral dependence between sectors.

Growth models of the aggregative type may be further subdivided into two types: the Harrod-Domar-type and the Haavelmo-type. Apart fron their general similarity, there are two important differences between these two types. The latter has explicitly introduced more general production functions and also the stochastic schemes to which the parameters of a growth model may be subject. The Harrod-Domar model may be regarded, in many ways, as a straight extension of the Keynesian approach insofar as the assumption of savings-investment equilibrium and, hence, the multiplier-accelerator mechanism are concerned. This model, although basically intended to explain growth processes of a mature developed economy, has some important features relating to the development of an underdeveloped economy, such as its emphasis on the capacity-creating and output-creating effects of investment as the main instrument of growth, its stress on the feasibility of investment in terms of saving as a precondition of relative price stability and also its emphasis on reinvestment and a deliberate (planned) policy of public investment as a balancing factor to private investment.

The structure of the Harrod-Domar model can be specified in terms of difference or differential equations, involving single or multiple lags, either with or without some specific shape of the autonomous investment. For theoretical convenience, it is simpler to specify the differential equations system as follows. In Domar's notation [17] we may write

$$\frac{dP}{dt} = I\sigma \text{ (supply side)},$$

$$\frac{dY}{dt} = \frac{dI}{dt} \cdot \frac{1}{\alpha} \text{(demand side)}, \qquad (10.1.1)$$

$$P_0 = Y_0 \quad \text{and} \quad \frac{dP}{dt} = \frac{dY}{dt} \text{ (equilibrium)}.$$

The solution of this system (10.1.1) specifies the full-capacity rates of growth of total income (Y), total investment (I) and total consumption (C) as follows:

$$Y = Y_0 e^{\alpha\sigma t}, \quad I = I_0 e^{\alpha\sigma t}, \quad C = C_0 e^{\alpha\sigma t}, \qquad (10.1.2)$$

where subscript zero denotes initial values, such that the income identity $Y_0 = I_0 + C_0$ is fulfilled. So long as the marginal propensity to save (α) and the potential social average net productivity of investment (σ) are constants, the equilibrium rates of growth of consumption, investment and income differ only by a scale factor. The model (10.1.1) has three other interesting features. The ratio (σ) which refers to increases in potential capacity out of new investment is subject to an upper limit (s), given by the productive capacity of new investment projects. Hence, the difference between σ and s is due to either a misdirection of investment or the lack of balance between the propensity to save (α) on the one hand and the growth of labor and technological progress on the other hand. Even if $\sigma = s$, actual investment (I) may grow at a rate (r), different from the equilibrium rate ($\alpha\sigma$), and so a proportion ($0 \leq \theta \leq 1$) of increased capacity is utilized. The proportional growth rates of income, investment and consumption would be given, in equilibrium, in this case, by ($\alpha\sigma\theta$) except for the scale factor. The ratios of income to productive capacity (Y/P) and income to capital stock (Y/K) would tend, as Domar has shown, to the upper asymptotes $\theta = r/\alpha s = r/\alpha\sigma$ and r/α, respectively, as $t \rightarrow \infty$.

The third characteristic of (10.1.1) refers to cases of instability in the model, when its supply equation is interpreted as a behavior relation of private entrepreneurs, with a corresponding scheme of adjustment to changes in demand. Harrod [28] has emphasized that a divergence of the actual growth rate (G) from the warranted (G_w) or the natural growth (G_n) rate may lead to a cumulative process, upward or downward, with varying degrees of instability. We are not concerned here with the analysis of cyclical phenonena, although the point is worth mentioning which Schumpeter (1934) has emphasized so elegantly, that cyclical phenomena are essentially and possibly inseparably interrelated with the phenomena of long-run growth in a private enterprise economy.

The dynamic growth models developed by Haavelmo [27] are more general in the sense that they incorporate changes in production functions, their parameters being partly technological and partly institutional, changes in accumulation functions showing the rate of growth of capital and technology and a law of population growth which is endogenous to the system. There is neither any specific equilibrium assumption about saving or investment nor any relation in the form of income identity as in a Keynesian model. In his notation, the generalized logistic model of Haavelmo may be written as

$$\begin{cases} \dfrac{\dot{N}}{N} = \alpha - \beta \dfrac{N}{X}, \\ X = a_1 N + a_2 K, \qquad (\beta \geq 0) \\ \dot{K} = \gamma_1 X + \gamma_2 N + \gamma_3 K, \end{cases} \qquad (10.1.3)$$

where the first equation specifies a logistic-type growth equation for population (N), except for its dependence on the time trend of total output (X), which is related to the capital stock (K) and population. For an economy with no capital accumulation, the third equation of the system (10.1.3) can be omitted and the second could be written as a linear function of population alone

$$X = aN + b \qquad (10.1.4)$$

in which case the stationary solutions would be given by

$$\bar{N} = \frac{\alpha b}{\beta - a\alpha} ; \quad \bar{X} = \frac{\beta b}{\beta - a\alpha} . \qquad (10.1.5)$$

For the general system (10.1.3) with capital accumulation, as Haavelmo has noted, there exists no nontrivial stationary solution. Depending on the condition that the roots of the characteristic equation of the system are real and economically meaningful, there exists, however, what Haavelmo has called a "quasi-equilibrium solution" such that the output-labor (X/N) and capital-labor (K/N) ratios remain constant over time, although each of the variables X, N and K develop exponentially. Indirectly this implies a hypothesis about the long-run constancy of the capital-output ratio.

The second important contribution of Haavelmo is to emphasize that dynamic economic models, as an approximate specification of economic reality, must incorporate through the notion of stochastic processes the sequence of random elements which are often called "shocks" to the system. There are different ways to introduce random elements to an otherwise deterministic model. One of the simplest ways, suggested by Haavelmo, is to consider random shocks that are additive to the "exact" part of the solution. Consider a single equation (10.1.6), which may also be written

$$y(t) = a_0 + a y(t - 1) \qquad (10.1.6)$$

in corresponding matrix difference equation form, where we add on the right-hand side a random shock variable $u(t)$ occurring at t. The solution of (10.1.6) would then involve stochastic shifts given by (10.1.7),

$$y(T) = Aa^T + B + \sum_{s=1}^{T-1} a^s u(t - s), \qquad (10.1.7)$$

where

$$y(0) = A + B \quad \text{and} \quad B = \frac{a_0}{1 - a} . \quad (a \neq 1)$$

If the shock variable $u(t)$ can be assumed to be stochastically independent with zero mean and constant finite variance σ^2, independent of t, the mean squared deviation of the exact part of the solution (10.1.7) from the actual value of $y(T)$ would be given by

$$\text{Var } y(T) = \sigma^2 \left(\frac{1 - a^{2T}}{1 - a^2} \right) \quad (a \neq 1). \tag{10.1.8}$$

It is easy to note that if $a > 1$ the variance of $y(T)$ would tend to ∞ as $t \to \infty$ and if $a < 1$ the variance would reach a limiting value $(\sigma^2/(1 - a^2))$. Assuming a discrete Poisson probability distribution for shocks with probability λ/n (where a fixed unit of time is divided into n equal intervals and λ is a constant), Haavelmo has further shown that if $\bar{\sigma}^2$ is the constant variance of a shock when it occurs and the shocks are independent, the asymptotic variance of the sum of all shocks during the year t to $t+1$ tends to the limiting form $(\lambda \bar{\sigma}^2)$ as $n \to \infty$.

The disaggregative models of the deterministic type may be further subdivided into two broad and related types, e.g., the theoretical models largely based on transaction flows of the open or closed, static or dynamic, input-output approach and the operational planning models based on specific policy formulations relating to economic growth and stabilization. Apart from Leontief's basic contributions [42, 43], two other models are worth mentioning in the first category, e.g., the general equilibrium model of von Neumann [80] and its extensions [34, 49, 55] and the model of multisectoral growth of Johansen [31]. In the second category we may mention the planning and programming models for countries such as the Netherlands [5, 6], Norway [4, 32], France [81], etc. at different levels of formalization and actual application and the models for the less developed countries formalized by Chenery [10, 12], Ichimura [30], Lange [39], Mahalanobis [44], Tinbergen [73, 76], Klein [38] and others [56, 71].

In Leontief's notation the open-dynamic balance equation for a sector i is given by (10.1.9), where b_{ik} are the stock-flow or capital coefficients and a_{ik} are the current input coefficients,

$$X_i = \sum_{k=1}^{m} a_{ik} X_k + \sum_{k=1}^{m} b_{ik} \dot{X}_k + Y_i, \quad \text{when} \quad \dot{X}_k = \frac{dX_k}{dt} \tag{10.1.9}$$

$$(i, k = 1, 2, ..., m).$$

Given the assumptions of the Leontief model (10.1.9), two features are specially important from the standpoint of an intersectoral growth model: (1) the relation between sectoral rates of growth and (2) the irreversibility of the capital coefficients. Consider the particular solution of the homogeneous part of the system (10.1.9), which would specify the time rate of growth for each sector

$$X_i(t) = \sum_{j=1}^{m} c_j k_{ij} e^{t\lambda_j} \quad (i = 1, ..., m). \tag{10.1.10}$$

where λ_j are m roots of the characteristic equation of the system. Disregarding complex roots that generate oscillatory fluctuations only, one can see that if all the m characteristic roots are negative, the particular solution for each sector would shrink to zero. But this cannot happen under the regular conditions [19] of a strict Leontief input-output system, where $A = (a_{ik})$ is the input-output matrix such that $(I-A)^{-1}$ exists and is nonnegative (I is the identity matrix) and the capital-coefficient matrix $B = (b_{ik})$ is also nonnegative and nonsingular and the product $B^{-1}(I-A)$ is an irreducible (i.e., indecomposable) [15] nonnegative matrix. Then by Frobenius' theorem [24] $B^{-1}(I-A)$ has a unique positive characteristic vector with a characteristic root which is simple, positive and largest in modulus of all the characteristic roots.[1a] Further, there is no other characteristic vector which is nonnegative. Denote the Frobenius root by λ_1, and if all the other characteristic roots of $B^{-1}(I-A)$ are less than λ_1 in their real parts, λ_1 is eventually dominant over all other roots. In this case, the outputs of any two sectors would be proportional and in the long run the relative rate of growth of all sectors would become the same and identical with the dominant root λ_1 as follows,

$$\frac{\dot{X}_i(t)}{X_i(t)} = \frac{\sum_{j=1}^{m} c_j k_{ij} \lambda_j e^{\lambda_j t}}{\sum_{j=1}^{m} c_j k_{ij} e^{\lambda_j t}} = \frac{c_1 k_{i1} \lambda_1 + \sum_{j=2}^{m} c_j k_{ij} \lambda_j e^{(\lambda_j - \lambda_i)t}}{c_1 k_{i1} + \sum_{j=2}^{m} c_j k_{ij} e^{(\lambda_j - \lambda_1)t}} \tag{10.1.11}$$

$$\lim_{t \to \infty} \frac{\dot{X}_i(t)}{X_i(t)} = \frac{c_1 k_{i1} \lambda_1}{c_1 k_{i1}} = \lambda_1.$$

In other words, the long-run rate of growth and the equilibrium proportions between the sectoral outputs depend only on the structural properties of the system and not on any knowledge about the initial conditions.

The rigid acceleration coefficients b_{ik} in (10.1.9) neglect, however, the irreversibilities of the process of capital accumulation, due to the fact that certain capital stocks are irreducible in nature. This would mean that in the rising phase ($\dot{X}_k \geq 0$) the capital coefficient b_{ik} would be valid for any sector

---

[1a] It has been shown in [33] that for nonnegativity of solutions of (10.1.10) it is necessary and sufficient that there exists a scalar c such that $Q = cI + B^{-1}(I-A)$ is nonnegative. It is understood here that this condition holds, so that Q is nonnegative and irreducible; hence, it has a unique nonnegative characteristic vector and an associated positive characteristic root which is the characteristic root of $B^{-1}(I-A)$ largest in modulus and hence largest in real part. This characteristic root is denoted here by λ_1.

k according to (10.1.9), but in the falling phase ($\dot{X}_k < 0$) it would not be valid and should be equated to zero if it is assumed that the stock of fixed capital (S_{ik}) entering in the definition of b_{ik} is irreducible. Since economic growth involves a rising output sequence for some sectors and a falling sequence for others, a general system represented by (10.1.9) would undergo a switchover from one phase to another, depending on the number of irreversible capital stocks. However, the fact that there are now open ends of the dynamic model to be optimized could be understood better by writing the model (10.1.9) in difference equation terms in vector-matrix notation,

$$X_t = AX_t + B(X_{t+1} - X_t) + Y_t, \qquad (10.1.12)$$

where the vector of capital stocks S_t is such that

$$X_t = AX_t + \varDelta S_t + Y_t, \qquad (10.1.13)$$

$$S_t = BX_t, \qquad (10.1.14)$$

and

$$\varDelta S_t = S_{t+1} - S_t, X_t = (X_i)_t, A = (a_{ik}), B = (b_{ik}), \text{ etc.}$$

We note that equation (10.1.14), relating capital stocks to gross output, implies full utilization of capacity for all sectors. But, as Solow [68] has observed, "that there is nothing in technology to prevent output from falling, i.e.,

$$S_t \geq BX_t \qquad (10.1.14a)$$

this is more than a trivial generalization." With the possibility of excess stocks via (10.1.14a), the output path is no longer unique, i.e., the dynamic system is no longer determinate in the sense of as many equations as unknowns. All we have now is a set of final demand plus capital formation vectors ($Y_t + \varDelta S_t$) as a function of the given capital stocks S_t, i.e., we have a set of feasible but alternative output paths for which an optimal choice problem remains. Solow has considered introducing two types of social welfare functions to determine an optimal path, e.g.,

$$w'S_T = \text{maximum}, \qquad (10.1.15a)$$
$$W(Y_0, Y_1, ..., Y_{T-1}, S_T) = \text{maximum}, \qquad (10.1.15b)$$

where w is a vector of m nonnegative weights assigned to the terminal stock [2] and W indicates a weighted sum of the components of $Y_0, ..., Y_{T-1}$ and S_T, where T is the end year of the planning horizon.

----

[2] Note that the concept of terminal stock could include labor. Further, each stock, including labor, must in the short run be treated as a nonreproducible fixed factor, and so there is more than one resource to be economized.

A more generalized version of the dynamic input-output model is provided by the von Neumann model, which is a closed linear model in which the outputs of one period furnish the inputs of the next period, as in recursive programming discussed in Chapter 7. In this model the terminal stocks of goods are the most important as explicit goods, because these are assumed to be entirely available for investment in the production processes and, hence, growth of output of the next period. Efficiency of a growth path is defined in terms of terminal stocks, i.e., a path of accumulation of stocks lasting a planning horizon of T periods is efficient if no other path starting from the same initial stocks and satisfying other constraints of the model reaches larger terminal stocks of goods after T periods. An efficient von Neumann path of proportional expansion of stocks is the one which achieves the largest possible rate of expansion. The uniqueness of this type of optimal path and the associated ray of shadow prices breaks down, however, as soon as final demand is introduced to make the closed model open, so to say. In its present state the model is not operational for the above reason and other rigid assumptions of the model regarding optimizing behavior, a well-behaved competitive system and no uncertainty or random elements in the system.

The multisector growth model of Johansen is more practical in outlook. Although his model belongs essentially to a dynamic general equilibrium system with a competitive market framework, its important contributions lie in the operational and empirical outlook and the useful features of flexibility, such as the possibility of substitution between labor and capital in each sector with unequal impact of technical change, the feasibility of combining a behavioristic model with a Leontief-type dynamic input-output system and the explicit role of relative prices. The model has been empirically implemented by Johansen on the basis of the statistical data of the Norwegian economy, where the major objective is to explain the long-run growth of the twenty-two sectors (e.g., the first nineteen sectors are domestic sectors, sector 20 is the building and construction sector, sector 21 is the production of other investment goods and sector 22 is a residual, unspecified sector) of the economy, assuming that the over-all growth of the economy as a whole is determined by exogenous variables. (The latter assumption could, of course, be relaxed.) A simplified version [3] of his model could be presented

---

[3] See Zabel [82]. Following Zabel's simplification we consider a twenty-sector version, taking the first nineteen sectors from the original model and combining the twentieth and twenty-first sectors as one sector and neglecting the twenty-second sector of the original model.

in a comparative static framework as:

Sectoral production (X_i) function $: X_i = A_i N_i^{\gamma_i} K_i^{\beta_i} e^{\varepsilon_i t}$ (10.2.1)
(autonomous inputs) $i = 1, \ldots, 20$

Sectoral production function $: X_{ij} = \alpha_{ij} X_j$ (10.2.2)
(intermediate inputs) $i, j = 1, \ldots, 20$

Sectoral profit (π_i) function $: \pi_i = P_i^* X_i - W_i N_i - Q_i K_i$ (10.2.3)
                                           $i = 1, \ldots, 20$

Average consumption expenditure (Y): $\quad Y = P_0 g_0 + P_1 g_1 + \ldots + P_{19} g_{19}$

$$(10.2.4)$$

and the accounting relations

For the first 19 sectors $: X_i = \sum_{j=1}^{20} \alpha_{ij} X_j + V g_i + Z_i$ (10.2.5)

$$i = 1, \ldots, 19$$

For the 20th sector $: X_{20} = \sum_{j=1}^{20} \delta_i K_i + \dot{K} + Z_{20}$ (10.2.6)

For total volume of labor (N): $\quad N = \sum_{i=1}^{20} N_i$ (10.2.7)

For total capital (K) $: K = \sum_{i=1}^{20} K_i$ (10.2.8)

where for sector i, gross output is X_i, employment N_i, fixed capital stock K_i, neutral technical change ε_i and a constant A_i represents other effects in the homogeneous Cobb-Douglas production function;[4] α_{ij} is the current input-output coefficient of the static Leontief system, π_i is sectoral profits, P_i^* is "net price" after adjusting for depreciation and costs of intermediate goods, W_i is fixed wage rate and Q_i is net "cost of using capital" in sector i after allowing for depreciation and rates of return. Z_i is the net exogenous demand for goods of sector i (government demand + exports − competitive imports). Equation (10.2.4) defines at the base point of time Y the average consumption expenditure as a linear sum of prices $(P_0, P_1, \ldots, P_{19})$ and demands $(g_0, g_1, \ldots, g_{19})$, i.e., $g_0 = g_0 (P_0, P_1, \ldots, P_{19}, Y)$ is the demand function for noncom-

---

[4] The implications of this type of production function in an aggregative framework of a Domar-type growth model have been analyzed by a number of writers, e.g., Solow [66], Ott [51], and Eisner [20].

petitive imports and $g_i = g_i (P_0, P_1, ..., P_{19}, Y)$ for $i = 1, 2, ..., 19$ is the demand function for the i-th domestic good. Denoting the total population by V measured from the base period value of unity, total consumption demand is Vg_0 for noncompetitive imports and Vg_i for other domestic goods, $i = 1, 2, ..., 19$. These average demand functions $g_i = g_i (P_0, P_1, ..., P_{19}, Y)$ are considered structurally very important by Johansen because they show the implications of sectoral inequalities in the pattern of consumption demand, i.e., total consumers' expenditure may be apportioned differently between various goods, depending on whether they are expenditures from a large population with a small average consumption or from a small population with a large average consumption.

The static equilibrium conditions are imposed by the assumption that sector profits π_i are maximized with respect to labor (N_i) and capital (K_i) for each sector. Thus, we get

$$\gamma_i P_i^* X_i = W_i N_i,$$
$$\beta_i P_i^* X_i = Q_i K_i. \qquad (10.2.9)$$

For the accounting relations Z_i is the exogenous demand in sector i and in sector 20, the capital goods sector; $K = dK/dt$ is the total net domestic investment and Z_{20} is exogenous demand for capital goods ($\delta_i = $ constant rate of depreciation).

The complete twenty-two sector model has eighty-six equations, eighty-six variables being endogenous and forty-six variables being exogenous. The reduced-form equations of the dynamic model are all obtained by "appropriately" differentiating the original equations with respect to time and making appropriate substitutions and transformations to obtain expressions containing relative growth rates (i.e., $(dx/dt)/x$ for a variable x). Thus, the reduced form of the complete system can be written as,

$$B\xi = L\eta, \qquad (10.2.10)$$

where the column vector of endogenous variables is ξ and that of exogenous variables is η and the coefficient matrices of order 86 by 86 are denoted by B and L, respectively. By assuming total investment, growth in population, growth in productivity and shifts in demand functions as exogenous, the model as a whole seeks to explain broadly the pattern of output, investment and employment in each sector and also the changes in relative prices or terms of trade between sectors. For example, denoting relative growth rates of the variables in the system (10.2.1) through (10.2.8) by lower-case letters, the elements of the endogenous vector ξ and the exogenous vector η are:

$$\xi = (n_1, n_2, ..., n_{20}, k_1, ..., k_{20}, x_1, ..., x_{22}, p_1, ..., p_{22}, r, y)',$$
$$\eta = (k, n, v, z_1, ..., z_{22}, \varepsilon_1, ..., \varepsilon_{20}, p_0)',$$

for the original twenty-two sector model (in our simplification there are twenty sectors and r for the rate of gross return on capital is neglected).

The solution of the reduced-form model (10.2.10) is

$$\xi = B^{-1}L\eta, \qquad \text{assuming } B \text{ to be nonsingular}, \qquad (10.2.11)$$

which shows how the growth rate of each of the exogenous variables influences the growth rate of each of the endogenous variables.

Because of the great potential operational usefulness of this model and the possibility of its adoption with appropriate modifications by less developed economies having reasonable input-output information, it is perhaps of great value to discuss some of the major implications of and the criticisms about this model. From the standpoint of the theory of economic policy there are three important features worth mentioning. First, it is apparent from equation (10.2.10) that this could be interpreted in terms of a Tinbergen-type policy model. For example, assume that the vector η of exogenous variables is decomposed into two subvectors, η_1 for the instrument variables and η_2 for "data" or noncontrollable variables, and, similarly, let ξ_1 and ξ_2 be two subvectors of the vector ξ, representing "targets" and "irrelevant variables," respectively. For consistency of a fixed-target policy model, we assume that the order of the subvector η_1 and ξ_1 is the same and appropriate decompositions of the matrices B and L are feasible. A central policy maker could now solve for the unknown η_1 in order to attain the fixed target $\xi_1 = \bar{\xi}_1$, say by using (10.2.12):

$$\binom{\eta_1}{\eta_2} = L^{-1}B\binom{\bar{\xi}_1}{\xi_2}. \qquad (10.2.12)$$

In a flexible-target policy model we have to introduce a preference function involving a scalar function of ξ_1 and η_1. Second, the effect of linear aggregation of some sectoral variables (i.e., both targets and instruments) could be analyzed to see if there is any gain in terms of stability of policy making or otherwise by taking fewer sectors.[5] This will provide an important link

---

[5] For an analysis of the conditions of aggregation in relation to stability, see Ara [1] and Theil [72].

between a partial model and a general equilibrium model. The simulation aspects of this suggestion are also important. It is, furthermore, useful to emphasize that this model (10.2.12) allows one to track down the effect of errors [54] in estimating the coefficients B and L on the solutions of the policy variables (η_1). Third, the framework of the Johansen model is quite flexible in that (a) with very little modification a sequential division of long-run (i.e., different phases) problems of growth and short-run problems of fluctuation could be made and (b) a set of econometric relations with their statistical estimates could be plugged into the ordinary input-output model through the demand functions and autonomous inputs.

Some suggestions may be offered concerning the applicability of such a model to less developed countries and the required modifications which may be necessary. First, the process of structural change and, in some cases, deviations from balanced or equilibrium growth should be built into the model. The difficulty lies, of course, in the most appropriate quantification of structural change. However, current economic theory has tried several alternatives [25, 36, 57, 77, pp. 84–85] ranging from a practicable concept of productive capacity to discontinuity in the production functions. The recent planning model of the Netherlands' Central Planning Bureau (i.e., "Central Economic Plan" 1961), having thirty-six endogenous variables (some variables being "composite") and as many equations, introduces capacity variables as a certain function of unemployment, and the partial regression coefficients, showing the impact of the capacity variable on export demand $(+1.42)$ and gross investment of enterprises (-7.18) are found to be quite important. (See Chapter 14 and its appendix for a detailed discussion of this model.) As the Central Planning Bureau [6, pp. 113–114] has observed concerning the practical application of their earlier 1955 model and the 1961 model:

> ".... however refined an equation system may be, it always remains a stilted reflection of reality which itself moreover may change its structure every time. When the system is applied in a concrete situation, it may therefore be necessary to change the form of one or more equations, or to revise somewhat the numerical values of the coefficients, including the constant terms, in order to take into account the influence of certain factors which the model does not, or not in an appropriate manner, express. This frequently happened when the 1955 model, on which the estimates were based for a number of years, was applied. The presently published model, although more refined, may also require revisions as mentioned above.
>
> Corrections to a model are needed most in applications outside the range of the observations on which the model is based. The present

model for example, is based on observations in 16 pre-war and nine post-war years, and still in a few of the post-war years only was the general economic situation more or less comparable to the present one. In most of the years of the "sample period", unemployment provided a certain elasticity to the economy which is now entirely lacking. The introduction of the capacity variable $\tilde{w}_1$ was designed especially to meet this difficulty. It remains to be seen how far this attempt has been successful.

For the less developed countries, however, the quantification of structural unemployment [50] may be of considerable difficulty. Further, the dynamic role of additional capital may necessitate a capital-based concept of capacity.

Second, the Johansen model in its present form does not distinguish between short-run and long-run aspects. The equilibrium assumptions (10.2.9) presume a long-run competitive framework for each sector, although the assumptions that total investment is exogenously determined and the input-output coefficients are unaffected by changes in relative prices appear to hold good only in the short run. However, a valid distinction between the short-run and long-run aspects could be built into the model in a planning sense by following two procedures: (a) By redefining the original model in difference equation terms so as to take advantage of a recursive (programming) framework mentioned before in Chapters 4, 7 and 9 and then assuming the appropriate long-run variables to be at their projected trend values, one could build in additional behavior equations, especially for the monetary sector and other dual economies, if any, and then (b) one could follow a strategy of combining the short-run and the long-run model by different rules. An illustration would perhaps make the point clear. Regarding their 1955 model [5] the Central Planning Bureau in the Netherlands used a dichotomy in their planning strategy by dividing the short-run from the long-term planning. The long-term model [79, pp. 429–445]—discussed subsequently—used a macroeconomic model defined by a few aggregative variables over time in order to specify an intertemporal and efficient growth path (i.e., optimizing end period national income, etc.). The solutions derived from this model were then plugged into a detailed input-output table to calculate the intersectoral breakdown of the solutions of the long-term model. In cases of conflict, the short-run intersectoral scheme is given a priority, broadly speaking, and adequate revisions of the long-term macro-model are made accordingly by either specifying additional instruments or modifying the functional relations.

Further, as Johansen has observed, his multisectoral growth model does not necessarily specify a solution that is optimal. In his words:

The main point is that our model represents a formal analogy with the solution which, in theory, is obtained in perfect competition; some of the marginalistic rules of optimal resource allocation as in welfare economics may be much too formal, i.e., it excludes the question of optimal exploitation of technological "know-how." In reality the main difference between an efficient and an inefficient economy may possibly be located here rather than in greater or smaller success in fulfilling certain marginalist rules for the allocation of resources. Hence, it is justified to say that a development path satisfying the equations of our model is not necessarily an optimal one. On the other hand an optimal expansion pattern can be described within the formal framework of the model. (In the above, "optimal" would be interpreted as meaning optimal for given values of the exogenous variables.) If these exogenous variables are controllable by economic policy, we may raise the question of determining their values in an optimal way; .... for planning purposes our model must then be interpreted as indicating a sort of optimal asymptotic model and it should be supplemented by a short-run model which could be used for analyzing the problem by which path we should approach the solution of the long-run model. This is probably a simpler method than merging both the short-run and long-run aspects into one complete model [31, pp. 170–172].

The input-output framework has been utilized for purposes of national planning in ways different from that in the Johansen model. The planning models formalized, for example, for India and the Netherlands adopted a disaggregative approach that is somewhat different from the conventional input-output analysis. The long-term growth model outlined by the Netherlands Central Planning Bureau [5] in the memorandum on "An exploration of economic potentialities of the Netherlands, 1950–1970," seeks to specify the optimal among the alternative growth paths, feasible under the condition of moving equilibrium of demand and supply for each of the three variables: labor, capital and imports. In this method, the parameters and coefficients used in the macromodel are tested for internal consistency and sectoral bottlenecks by means of detailed input-output accounting. In case of disagreement, the boundary conditions and the feasible values of the coefficients of the macromodel are suitably revised. The Indian planning model designed by Mahalanobis is based on a planning horizon of about fifteen years or more, although for each five-year period the marginal output-investment coefficients are recalculated from detailed input-output tables.

The Dutch long-term model, hereafter abbreviated as N-model, contains seventeen equations, fifteen endogenous variables, four instruments and three targets. The four instruments are the savings-income ratio, the rate of emigration, the rate of change of relative export prices and the rate of import substitution. Maximization of per capita real income in the final year (i.e., 1970) is a flexible target, the two other fixed targets being the level of unemployment and the amount of capital export. Assuming a closed economy and the balance of only two factors, e.g., capital (K) and labor (a), the N-model may be written in the notation of Verdoorn [79, pp. 429–445] as,

$$
\begin{array}{lll}
\text{Demand for capital} & : K = ky^x, \\
\text{Demand for labor} & : a = y^p, \\
\text{Supply of capital} & : \dot{K} = \alpha y, & (10.3.1) \\
\text{Supply of labor} & : a = e^{\pi t}, \\
\text{Balance condition (capital)}: kxy^{x-1}\dot{y} = \alpha y, \\
\text{Balance condition (labor)} & : y^p = e^{\pi t},
\end{array}
$$

where $a = y = 1$ for $t = 0$. In consequence of the complementarity hypothesis, the N-model tacitly assumes that the proportional growth of income $(\dot{y}/y)$ will be adapted one way or another to any given level of the saving coefficient (α) by means of monetary measures or other instrument variables that are not incorporated in the system. (See Chapter 3 for a discussion of the relationship between targets and instruments in the above model.)

With different factor endowment and resource structure, the Mahalanobis planning model, hereafter abbreviated as M-model, specifies equilibrium development in terms of capital alone by emphasizing vertical balance more than the horizontal one, to use the concepts of Lange [41]. Assuming the total allocable investment (I_t) to be exogenous, the M-model solves the problem of optimal allocation of investment in two stages, e.g., in the first stage, on the basis of two completely integrated sectors producing investment goods (subscript i) and consumption goods (subscript c), the optimal proportion of allocation to the investment goods sector (λ_i) is specified by the condition of maximization of national income within a specified planning horizon. In the second stage, the allocation of investment between the subsectors of the consumption goods sector is decided by the condition that given targets of employment and national income are attained.[6] It has already been seen in Chapter 2 that the two-sector M-model may be specified as:

$$
\begin{array}{ll}
I_t = I_{t-1} + \lambda_i \beta_i I_{t-1}, \\
C_t = C_{t-1} + \lambda_c \beta_c I_{t-1}, & (\lambda_i + \lambda_c = 1) \qquad (10.3.2) \\
Y_t = C_t + I_t.
\end{array}
$$

---

[6] A detailed discussion of the structure of this model is to be found in Chapter 13, Section 13.1.

After solving the equations for consumption (C_t) and investment goods (I_t), the final income (Y_t) equation can be written as:

$$Y_\tau = Y_0 + I_0 \left(\frac{\lambda_i \beta_i + \lambda_c \beta_c}{\lambda_i \beta_i} \right) [(1 + \lambda_i \beta_i)^\tau - 1]; \quad t = 0, 1, ..., \tau. \quad (10.3.3)$$

An optimal value of λ_i which would maximize Y_t for a given planning horizon can be easily computed from (10.3.3). With an estimate of the parameters $\beta_i = 0.2$ and $\beta_c = 0.3$, the M-model specified the optimal value $\lambda_i = 0.33$ within about a fifteen-year planning horizon.

When the consumption-goods sector is divided into three subsectors (subscripts c_1, c_2, c_3), the model (10.3.2) can be written as:

$$\begin{bmatrix} I_i \\ C_{1t} \\ C_{2t} \\ C_{3t} \end{bmatrix} = \begin{bmatrix} 1 + \lambda_i \beta_i & 0 & 0 & 0 \\ \lambda_{c_1} \beta_{c_1} & 1 & 0 & 0 \\ \lambda_{c_2} \beta_{c_2} & 0 & 1 & 0 \\ \lambda_{c_3} \beta_{c_3} & 0 & 0 & 1 \end{bmatrix} \begin{bmatrix} I_{t-1} \\ C_{1t-1} \\ C_{2t-1} \\ C_{3t-1} \end{bmatrix}. \quad (10.3.4)$$

The triangular coefficient matrix in (10.3.4) implies that the dependence of the consumption-goods sector on the investment-goods sector is unilateral. This eliminates the possibility of effecting via external trade an increase in supply of investment goods by a prior increase in consumption goods.

When λ_i is preassigned an optimal value (λ_i^*) on the basis of maximizing income (Y_t) within a given planning horizon for the two-sector model (10.3.2), the allocation ratios λ_{c_j}, $(j = 1, 2, 3)$ for the subsectors of the consumption goods sector could be chosen to secure balance with marginal proportions of consumption demand. For instance, if α_1, α_2, α_0 denote the marginal propensities to consume of the three types of consumption goods and $\lambda_{c_1} + \lambda_{c_2} + \lambda_{c_3} = 1 - \lambda_i^*$ is the condition of full utilization of investment, the balancing values of λ_{c_j} can be specified as:

$$\lambda_{c_j} = \frac{\alpha_j (1 - \lambda_i^*)}{\sum\limits_j \alpha_j} \qquad (j = 1, 2, 3). \quad (10.3.5)$$

A comparison of the two planning models points out some interesting features about the optimal interpretation of a growth model. First of all, the complementarity hypothesis [81] permitting no substitution of labor and capital, marks a degree of rigidity in both these models. The implication of this inflexibility in the N-model is that the last two equations of (10.3.1) for equilibrium income cannot be simultaneously fulfilled if α, x, k and π are treated as constant parameters. The N-model considered a variable savings-income ratio (α_t) in order to maintain equilibrium in growth:

$$\alpha_t = kx\frac{\pi}{\rho}\exp\{\pi(x-1)t/\rho\}. \tag{10.3.6}$$

But since the savings ratio has a narrower range of variation within zero and unity, a more flexible way would be to solve for a variable elasticity of labor demand (ρ_t) as:

$$\rho_t = (x-1)\pi t/\log_e\left\{y_0^{x-1} + \frac{\alpha(x-1)t}{kx}\right\}. \tag{10.3.7}$$

Alternatively, an appropriate combination of the two flexible instrument variables α_t and ρ_t may be chosen so that the whole burden of adjustment may be shared between them.[7]

Considering the two-sector M-model (10.3.2) now but in differential equation terms and integrating from $t=0$ to $t=\tau$ whenever required, the time path of the marginal investment-income ratio (I_t/Y_t) may be computed as:

$$I_t/Y_t = \frac{\lambda_i\beta_i}{\lambda_i\beta_i + \lambda_c\beta_c}\left[1 + \frac{\lambda_i\beta_iC_0 - \lambda_c\beta_cI_0}{I_0(\lambda_i\beta_i + \lambda_c\beta_c)}\exp(-\lambda_i\beta_i\tau)\right]^{-1}, \tag{10.3.8}$$

where subscript zero indicates initial values. If the intended savings-income ratio does not grow in step with the investment-income ratio given in (10.3.8), there would be an imbalance in the system either in terms of unutilized capacity or commodity-cum-factor gaps. It is evident from the logistic equation for the investment-income ratio in (10.3.8) that as $\tau \to \infty$ the ratio reaches its upper asymptote. Now suppose that total investment (I_t) in the M-model grows at a rate r, which is less than the equilibrium or the target rate $\lambda_i\beta_i$; in this case the annual rate of loss [23], measured in terms of consumption (C_t), would be specified by:

$$C_\tau - C_\tau' = I_0\lambda_c\beta_c\left[\left(\frac{1}{r} - \frac{1}{\lambda_i\beta_i}\right) + \left(\frac{e^{\lambda_i\beta_i\tau}}{\lambda_i\beta_i} - \frac{e^{r\tau}}{r}\right)\right], \tag{10.3.9}$$

of capacity and C_τ equals the supply of consumption goods under full-capacity utilization.

---

[7] Another way which was later adopted by the Planning Bureau is to start with a Cobb-Douglas-type production function permitting substitution between labor and capital.

Taking the parameter values of the M-model, e.g., $\lambda_i = 0.3$, $\beta_i = 0.2$, it is easily verified that for $r = 0.04$, $e^{r(\lambda_i\beta_i - r)}$ exceeds $\lambda_i\beta_i/r$ where $\tau \geq 6$ and hence the terms within parentheses in equation (10.3.9) are all positive. The total loss of consumption goods between period $t = 0$ to $t = \tau$ is obtained by integrating (10.3.9) as:

$$\int_0^\tau (C_t - C_t')\,dt = I_0\lambda_c\beta_c\left[\left(\frac{1}{r} - \frac{1}{\lambda_i\beta_i}\right)\tau + \frac{e^{\lambda_i\beta_i\tau} - 1}{(\lambda_i\beta_i)^2} - \frac{e^{r\tau} - 1}{r^2}\right]. \qquad (10.3.10)$$

The total loss of income (Y) between zero and τ would be given by:

$$\int_0^\tau (Y_t - Y_t')\,dt = \int_0^\tau (C_t - C_t')\,dt + I_0\left[\frac{e^{\lambda_i\beta_i\tau} - 1}{\lambda_i\beta_i} - \frac{e^{r\tau} - 1}{r}\right].$$

This magnitude may be more significant when the integrated investment goods sector is further divided into subsectors and the intra-allocation problem is considered. So long as the volume of savings obtained domestically or otherwise provides an upper bound for the planned total investment, this possibility of income losses must be explicitly incorporated in the model. Some appropriate measures toward achieving price and wage flexibility also need to be investigated, as in the model developed by Uzawa [78] and others [69].

10.2. Use of Models for Growth Planning

The use of input-output models as a programming basis for optimum economic development through a centralized planning agency has been suggested by a number of writers; Lange's contribution [39, 40, 41] may be worth mentioning. Starting from the balance conditions of a Leontief model

$$X_i = \sum_{j=1}^n a_{ij}X_j + Y_i \quad (i, j = 1, 2, ..., n), \qquad (10.4.0)$$

where, for the i-th sector X_i is gross output, Y_i is final demand (or net output) and $a_{ij} = X_{ij}/X_j$ is the usual input-output coefficient, he decomposes Y_i and builds an investment matrix as follows,

$$\begin{aligned} Y_i &= C_i + I_i, \\ I_i &= \sum_j I_{ij} \quad (i, j = 1, 2, ..., n), \end{aligned} \qquad (10.4.1)$$

A set of capital coefficients (b_{ij}) is then postulated to characterize the technological structure of incremental output, i.e.,

$$b_{ij} = I_{ij}/\Delta X_j \quad (i, j = 1, 2, ..., n). \qquad (10.4.2)$$

These are called "investment coefficients" by Lange, and they indicate the amount by which the stock of means of production (i.e., capital stock) produced in the i-th sector and installed in the j-th sector must increase in order that in the latter sector output should increase by one unit per year (assuming a one-year gestation lag, of course).[8] Like the current input-output coefficients a_{ij}, the gross investment coefficients b_{ij} are taken as known constants for the planning period.

Summing the elements of the j-th column of the investment matrix and denoting the sum by

$$I^{(j)} = \sum_{i=1}^{n} I_{ij},$$

we get

$$I^{(j)} = \sum_{i=1}^{n} b_{ij} \Delta X_j \quad (j = 1, 2, ..., n). \tag{10.4.3}$$

This equation indicates the amount of investment that must be allocated to the j-th sector in order to produce in that sector an increase of output equal to ΔX_j per year. It follows from equation (10.4.3) that

$$\sum_{i=1}^{n} b_{ij} = I^{(j)} / \Delta X_j \quad (j = 1, ..., n),$$

and β_j defined as

$$\beta_j = \left(\sum_i b_{ij} \right)^{-1} = \Delta X_j / I^{(j)} \quad (j = 1, ..., n) \tag{10.4.4}$$

is called the sectoral output-investment ratio (for sector j). Further, if we denote total values of investment and output for the whole economy by

$$I = \sum_{i=1}^{n} \sum_{j=1}^{n} I_{ij} \quad \text{and} \quad X = \sum_{i=1}^{n} \sum_{j=1}^{n} X_{ij}$$

and define $\lambda_j = I^j / I$ as the coefficient of sectoral allocation of total investment, the problem of investment planning may be posed as one of optimal choice of the allocation ratios λ_j by a central planning agency, subject to certain reasonable restrictions. For example, Lange considers the problem of maximizing the national output-investment ratio, i.e.,

$$\beta = \sum_{j=1}^{n} \lambda_j \beta_j,$$

---

[8] Further, Lange specifies a relation between b_{ij} and the current input-output coefficient a_{ij} such that $b_{ij} = a_{ij} T_{ij}$, where T_{ij} is the turnover period, which is defined as the period (in some average sense) in which the capital produced in the i-th sector and installed in the j-th sector is used up entirely, assuming a uniform annual rate of use.

subject to the condition that a certain minimal amount of output of each sector remains available for consumption, i.e., maximize $\beta = \sum_j \lambda_j \beta_j$ under the conditions

$$C_i \geq C_i(\min) \geq 0,$$
$$\sum_j \lambda_j \leq 1, \lambda_j \geq 0,$$

(10.4.5)

where C_i is the amount of net output of sector i kept for consumption and $C_i(\min)$ is a constant expressing the minimal consumption requirement for each sector. Maximizing the national output-investment ratio leads to maximizing the rate of increase of gross national product, subject to the minimal consumption standard. The close relation of this type of programming model with the planning model of Mahalanobis is apparent. Some very important advantages of this type of model may be mentioned here. First, other types of realistic constraints due to the foreign exchange, labor market or other institutional conditions can be brought in as additional constraints[9] to the system (10.4.5). Similarly, the objective function can be viewed as a time functional, as in dynamic programming, i.e., either

$$\beta(t) = \sum_j \lambda_j(t)\beta_j(t) \quad \text{or} \quad \sum_{t=0}^{T} \beta(t) = \sum_{t=0}^{T} \sum_j \lambda_j(t)\beta_j(t),$$

where $t = [0, T]$ specifies the planning horizon. Second, as Lange has shown, the growth path of an aggregative Domar-type model could be derived from the optimal solution of sectoral growth-paths in (10.4.5), under appropriate conditions of aggregation. This means that a sequential scheme of planning by stages could be easily built into this framework. For example, assume that in the first stage we have data for only two sectors ($i, j = 1, 2$) and we solve for optimal paths of $X_1(t)$ and $X_2(t)$ and, hence, $X(t) = X_1(t) + X_2(t)$, using the programming scheme (10.4.5). Associated with this optimal solution we would have a set of shadow prices, which may be useful [53, 74] in evaluating resources for growth purposes. At the second stage, assume that we have additional data on a two-region breakdown of each sector. We can now set up a small regional programming model with a different type of objective function, e.g., minimizing an interregional cost function (or even a functional for regional social rents) subject to a set of regional constraints in terms of demand, production and transportation cost and also some equilibrium demand-supply conditions as set up in the usual transportation-type

---

[9] Ichimura, Chenery and others have considered other types of programming problems relating to underdeveloped countries, e.g., Chenery [7] and Chenery and Uzawa [13].

linear programming model. So long as there is no inconsistency between the optimum solutions at the two stages, the first-stage solutions could be either unaltered or improved through optimization at the second stage and so on for the other stages.

A third advantage of this type of model is that it makes a definite distinction between investments by their sectors of origin and their sectors of delivery. For a less developed economy this distinction is very important in a policy sense, because the decisions about allocating investment to certain key sectors in the public sector (e.g., construction, transport, public utilities and industries based on the so-called social overhead capital) would have significant structural impacts and changes, which would be far from either marginal or identical with the preimpact trend. Frisch [22] used this distinction in constructing a model of investment programming for India, which is based on a twenty-two sector input-output table with four additional autonomous sectors and a social welfare function (f),

$$f = 16u + 4v + w,$$

where u equals millions of new jobs created annually, v equals annual rate of investment and w equals net annual increase in India's net foreign assets, liquid or nonliquid, expressed as a percentage of the national income. (Due to the capacity elements and lags, some of the restrictions of this Frisch model are nonlinear and the multiplex method is applied for computing optimal solutions under an alternative set of assumptions.)

However, some caution is needed regarding the limitations, especially of the linear programming model of the type (10.4.5). First, the solutions of a linear programming model always belong to the set of extreme points of a convex set (i.e., the vertices of convex polyhedral cones), which means that the optimal activity mix may exclude some sectors altogether. Further, the addition of new constraints at later stages may change the activity mix if it is not very "stable." Second, the estimates of the sectoral output-investment ratios are in most cases very imprecise for most underdeveloped countries. Their margin of error and the consequent impact on the optimal solution have to be very carefully analyzed. Third, the problem of reliable economic data is so acute in most less developed countries that in some cases a partial approach (e.g., analysis of a set of projects rather than over-all programming) may be justifiable on that ground only. Chenery has emphasized this last point very strongly and on pragmatic grounds [11, pp. 11–21]. In some cases he utilized cross-section data for different underdeveloped countries to derive a norm or average which can be useful as a bench mark for another underdeveloped country [8, 9, 10]. There is, of course, a similarity in input-output structure between countries at more or less the same stage of development, but great caution is needed in assuming comparability of different input-output tables of different countries. The question whether it is valid for certain purposes to divide the economy into two sectors, agriculture and allied industries on the one hand and the rest of the economy on the other, has been examined by Fox and Sengupta elsewhere [21, 58], in the framework of input-output models, which suggested a relative degree of independence of the agricultural complex from the rest of the economy.

10.3. The Trend Problem in Growth Models

Broadly speaking, the analysis of long-term trend has received much attention in the development of growth models during the last decades. This analysis is most useful in characterizing the process of growth of a mature economy, as it evolved from its early stages to the present state. It helps the understanding of the empirical process of historical growth, although it may not be of immediate value in terms of policy making.

Apart from the empirical specification of trends other than the strict exponential growth curve, either through a study of the time trend [33, 37] of the parameters such as the saving ratio and output-capital ratio, or nonlinear elements in the capital accumulation process [29, 63, 64] and production functions [66, 75], two other important analytical aspects emerged from the recent progress in growth models, e.g., a new type of theory of investment characterizing the capital accumulation process and an emphasis on the stochastic elements[10] underlying a process of growth.

In the new view [2, 35], the role of investment is to impart a progressive technology as well as deepen the capital stock. This is different from the old view that capital deepening is the major source of productivity gains and, hence, economic growth of the mature economies. Solow [67] has made one of the earliest attempts to postulate a rate of technological change which is embodied only in new capital goods and affects their efficiency. Every capital good embodies the latest technology at the moment of its construction, but it is assumed not to incorporate subsequent technical progress. Thus, "capital" becomes a continuum of heterogeneous "vintages" of capital goods. Denoting the output rate at time t, resulting from capital equipment

---

[10] A stochastic process interpretation of aggregative growth models and their trend solution may be found in Sengupta [59]. This aspect will not be discussed here.

of vintage v by $Q_v(t)$, the production function takes the form,

$$Q_v(t) = B_0 e^{\lambda v} K_v(t)^\alpha N_v(t)^{1-\alpha}, \tag{10.5.1}$$

where $K_v(t)$ equals amount of equipment (in physical terms) of vintage v surviving at time t and $N_v(t)$ denotes the amount of labor employed on that equipment and α is assumed to be the same for all vintages due to the assumption of neutral technological progress. Under the assumption that labor is allocated optimally over the various vintages, aggregate output (Q_t) can be derived as the sum of the homogeneous outputs of various vintages, i.e.,

$$Q_t = B_0 J_t^\alpha N_t^{1-\alpha}, \tag{10.5.2}$$

where

$$J_t = \int\limits_{-\infty}^{t} e^{\lambda v/\alpha} K_v(t)\, dv.$$

According to the old view, however, the aggregate output under a neutral technical progress rate of μ per year is given by

$$Q_t = A_0\, e^{\mu t} K_t^\alpha N_t^{1-\alpha}, \tag{10.5.3}$$

where, since the difference in vintage per se is unimportant for technical progress, we could write (10.5.3) as

$$Q_t = A_0 \left[\int\limits_{-\infty}^{t} e^{\mu t/\alpha} K_v(t)\, dv \right]^\alpha N_t^{1-\alpha}. \tag{10.5.4}$$

Note that the weighting factor $e^{\lambda v/\alpha}$ in the new theory of investment (10.5.2) changes with the vintages of capital goods, but for the case (10.5.4) it is the same (i.e., $e^{\mu t/\alpha}$ does not involve v). Hence, the implication of the modern theory is that current investment increases output per man partly through affecting the average modernity of the capital stock. A growth model embodying the new type of production function (10.5.2) can be easily built up, as Phelps [52] has shown, by adding the savings-investment relation, an exogenous growth of the labor force and a rate of depreciation of capital stock of a given vintage, e.g.,

$$
\begin{aligned}
\text{Investment:} \quad & I(t) = sQ(t), \\
\text{Growth of labor:} \quad & N_t = N_0 e^{nt}, \\
\text{Depreciation:} \quad & K_v(t) = I(v) e^{-\delta(t-v)},
\end{aligned}
\tag{10.5.5}
$$

where all capital goods are assumed to depreciate exponentially at the rate δ per year. Mathews [48] has considered a similar growth model using, however, a somewhat more general production function than (10.5.1), i.e., he supposes that production functions with constant elasticity of substitution apply to capital goods of each vintage

$$Q_v = (a_v K_v^{-\beta} + b_v N_v^{-\beta})^{-1/\beta},$$

where K_v is the number of machines of vintage v, N_v and Q_v are corresponding values of employment and output and a_v, b_v are constant parameters and the coefficient β is related to the elasticity of substitution (σ) between capital and labor by $\beta = (1 - \sigma)/\sigma$. These growth models have generalized considerably the basic simplicity of the exponential path of the Harrod-Domar-type growth model, although they have a very convenient asymptotic property. The time path of growth of national output, starting from a reasonable initial position, will be asymptotic to a balanced-growth, golden-age equilibrium growth path, along which production, consumption, investment and capital stock of all vintages grow exponentially at the same rate.

Statistical applications of these new types of production functions attempting to estimate the gains in productivity due to both capital deepening and capital modernizing are very difficult because of nonlinearities. Yet the policy implications of some of these results should not be overlooked. First, it is interesting to observe that for the Norwegian economy, which has a relatively high investment-income ratio but a relatively low rate of growth of national product, Johansen [32] showed that the variation of the average durability of capital explains to a large extent the asymmetry between the relatively low growth rate and high investment quota. There is an implicit suggestion that an optimum policy toward investment would attempt to reach the target of an optimum pattern of average durability of capital. Second, this model shows perhaps the contrast that exists between the short-run and the long-run aspects of the growth path. In the long run the average durability of capital goods tends to be independent of the savings-income ratio, whereas in the short run the process of growth of national income depends crucially, among other things, on the responsiveness of output to a policy of greater thrift and investment. For example, it is important to distinguish between the effects of "average age distribution" of capital on the asymptotic growth rate and the immediate effects of a switchover from investment with a lower to a higher mean durability.[11] Third, as Phelps [52, page 560] has emphasized:

The foregoing analysis has some significance for "positive economics." For example, a sustained improvement in the modernity of the capital

---

[11] It seems that this new view of investment and production functions could be incorporated in a multisectoral model. Further, the stochastic aspects of the capital accumulation process, which have been practically neglected in the present growth models except for Haavelmo's work, need, perhaps, to be integrated with this idea of mean durability of capital stock in an economy. See for example Dhrymes [16], Manne [46] and Sengupta and Tintner [64].

stock of a country should be ascribed (proximately) not to the level (rate), nor to the rate of growth of its investment but to a rise of the rate of growth of investment.

Indirectly this may offer a sort of justification for maximizing the proportional rate of growth of national income, as was emphasized in the Lange model (10.4.5) before. In the context of development planning for less developed countries, it is perhaps necessary to investigate the nature and types of interdependence between the investment-income ratio, the capital-output ratio and the productivity implications of the age distribution of new and old capital goods before one suggests an optimum investment program or project mix.

10.4. Recent Developments in Growth Theory

Recent developments in growth theory have followed a number of interesting trends, thanks to the development and use of optimal control theory using Pontryagin's maximum principle and other methods. The analysis of the neoclassical models of growth, the implications for instability of heterogenous capital and disequilibriating factors in models of equilibrium growth and empirical implementation of some of these models for purposes of planning are (applications to planning are discussed in Chapter 13) some of the major areas where important developments have occurred. A major contribution by Morishima [91] discusses some of the basic developments of the modern theory of growth, including some of its major problems and policy implications. A number of other works on the theory of growth have appeared in recent years [83, 84, 95]; however, from a very basic standpoint the contribution by Morishima seems to be very fundamental, since it surveys the whole field from a historical and operational standpoint starting from its very foundation.

It may be useful to review very briefly[12] selected trends in recent growth theory, as they are presented in Morishima's recent book.

10.4.1. *Growth Equilibrium in Neo-Classical and Keynesian Framework*

Morishima begins with a two-good, two-activity model of Walras-type to show the conditions of short run equilibrium and those of the long run equilibrium and whether there exists a path from a short to the long run equilibrium, if the economy starts from a historically given capital labor endowment. The most important assumptions required for establishing

---

[12] This section is based on [92].

short run equilibrium in this two-good (consumption and capital good) neoclassical model include the following: (a) capital good is freely transferable and "malleable"; (b) rule of profitability applies to the price cost relationships for each good and the rule of free goods (i.e., competitive pricing). for each output and factor price i.e. oversupplied good or factor has a zero price; (c) the consumption saving functions satisfy the Harrodian condition, i.e., unit income elasticity and the weak axiom of revealed preference; and (d) the condition of saving-investment balance in the aggregate.

The long run growth equilibrium is analyzed in this two-good framework by assuming real wage rate exogenously fixed and treating the stock of capital and number of workers as variables to be solved for. Suppose $\bar{w}$ is a real wage rate such that the stock of capital and labor increase by the same proportion ρ say. As the consumption-saving functions are assumed Harrodian, a common proportional rise in capital stock and labor leads to an increase in consumption and savings at the same common rate $\bar{\rho}$, provided prices remain unchanged. Such a growth state is called a state of long run or silvery equilibrium growth, where the absolute level of the activities is determined by the condition that the total demand equals total supply. This latter condition implies that the long run growth equilibrium must satisfy the condition emphasized by Harrod that the real wage rate must be fixed at such a level that the warranted rate of growth is equated to the natural rate. If the silvery equilibrium is unique, then any rise in real wage rate above the equilibrium level causes the natural rate of growth to exceed the warranted rate (e.g., in Morishima's treatment the rate of growth of labor force ρ is negative for very low levels of real wage rate, zero for a subsistence level and increases with a rise in real wage rate up to some point), and vice versa. It then follows that any movement away from the silvery equilibrium growth would set up forces causing the system to return to equilibrium; thus it would have global stability. However, when the silvery equilibrium growth is not unique, we may still have at least locally stable growth equilibrium in this two-sector economy, provided the slope of the natural rate of growth curve exceeds that of the warranted rate of growth curve, both curves viewed as functions of the real wage rate w. This local stability may also fail to hold, if the aggregative consumption-saving decision of the community does not satisfy the weak axiom of revealed preference.

In the Keynesian economic framework of a fixed-price model, the rule of free goods (i.e., competitive pricing by which oversupplied goods are imputed zero prices) is violated and the entrepreneurs' investment decisions are guided by a flexible accelerator principle. A deviation from the long run silvery growth equilibrium where the warranted rate equals the natural rate may here be aggravated by insufficient investment (i.e., insufficient effective demand) leading to long run unemployment of labor or capital.

The two-good neoclassical model is easily generalized to include the case of one capital good and many consumption goods, with the stability conditions essentially unchanged. The stability of the real wage rate would still imply the stability of every other variable. But as soon as heterogeneous capital goods are introduced into the theoretical framework, the equality between supply and demand has to be established in each capital market at equilibrium and we can no longer establish definite relationships between the wage stability and the stability of other variables. There arise two other complications in the multi-sector case under the presence of heterogeneous capital goods. Since in the multi-sector case the entrepreneurs' investment decisions are completely independent of the saving decisions of the households, the proportions of total investment allocated to various capital goods need not satisfy the axiom of revealed preference as in the two-sector case; hence, the convergence of the rate of profit to a long run equilibrium state is not guaranteed. Also, even if the convergence of the profit rate to a long run state (i.e., a golden equilibrium, if the consumption by capitalists and saving by workers are neglected) is ensured in some fashion (given the wage rate), the presence of multiple capital goods may cause instability and oscillations (in particular, if the output subsystem is stable, the price subsystem would be unstable, e.g., the dual stability-instability characteristics of the dynamic Leontief model).

Two comments may perhaps be added to this discussion regarding (a) the policy implications of this growth equilibrium analysis, and (b) the question of the most appropriate level of disaggregation to be used in growth analysis under heterogeneous capital goods. From the viewpoint of economic policy, as distinct from economic theory the neo-classical or the Keynesian framework do not completely resolve the question of linking the short run decisions to a long run framework in a satisfactory manner. The general impression we are left with is that in cases where long run equilibrium growth is likely to have stability (local if not global), the short run policies in the public sector may be designed through a detailed multi-sector framework (e.g., input-output framework) to minimize short run deviations from the long run equilibrium trend. Also, since the presence of heterogeneous capital goods increases the chance of instability, it is an open question as to what constitutes the optimum degree of disaggregation of a multi-sector model.

It appears that this question can be usefully resolved only when specific policy-making agencies like the government and the public sector are introduced into the theoretical framework, along with their potential policy instruments. Restricting the discussion to rules of competitive pricing and of profitability has thus been in a sense very abstract and unproductive in a policy framework.

10.4.2. *General Equilibrium Approach to Growth Dynamics*

Following the tradition of the Von Neumann model of economic growth, one could easily analyze joint production through intermediate products and "standardized processes" and also treat capital goods at different ages as different goods. In such a framework the long run growth equilibrium is specified by a state of balanced growth, where prices, wage rate and the interest rate remain stationary over time and the intensities of production grow at a constant geometric rate α. In this state of equilibrium the rate of return of various processes cannot exceed the current rate of interest $(\beta - 1)$, otherwise it would be profitable to borrow from outside. The original Von Neumann model ignores capitalists' consumption and the influence of labor supply on wage rate and then establishes under constant returns to scale the existence of a growth equilibrium satisfying the rule of free goods in goods market (but not in labor market) and the rule of profitability to production processes (but not to consumers). In Morishima's extended version of this model, consumer choice is introduced under a more general saving function for the workers and the capitalists, where their utility functions are assumed to satisfy the condition that the Engel elasticities of all goods is unity. The relationship between the rate of interest $(\beta - 1)$ and the rate of growth $(\rho - 1)$ in this extended framework is found to hold as follows:

$$\rho - 1 = (\beta - 1)s_c, \tag{10.6.1}$$

where s_c = capitalists' savings propensity and the savings propensity of the workers plays no role. This result is identical with the one discovered by Passinetti in the framework of a two-sector model, where the rate of interest (i.e., the steady state of return) is determined by the capitalists' propensity to save in the Passinetti-equilibrium case but by the workers' propensity to save in the anti-Passinetti case.

It is also shown in this framework that the steady state growth equilibrium of the extended Von Neumann model can be given a game-theoretic interpretation in terms of a game between the competitive Market and the Entrepreneur, where the wage rate is set so that the game is fair in the sense that neither player can expect positive (or negative) net gains. In terms of convergence this is basically similar to the Walras-type tâtonnement process between the custodian of the competitive market and the consumers and producers who respond to market price signals. This suggests perhaps the need to characterize the steady state growth by two standards of references, one set by prices, the other by the Harrodian condition of warranted rate being equal to the natural rate. According to the former, we find for any arbitrarily chosen real wage rate the set of prices and interest rate which would induce a perfectly competitive economy to grow in balance at a steady state, which in fact is the warranted rate of growth in the Harrodian framework. But the warranted rate of growth may differ from the natural rate of growth $(\rho - 1)$, leading to continued unemployment unless the real wage rate is appropriately adjusted to obtain silvery equilibrium. In any silvery equilibrium (where the workers and the capitalists are assumed to save constant (positive) fractions of their incomes, i.e., this differs from the golden equilibrium case where workers' saving and capitalists' consumption are both zero) the real wage rate (Ω) determined in equilibrium is equal to the greatest technically permissible wage rate (i.e., the greatest of wage rates consistent with the available technology represented in the model by the set of processes or activities), such that a set of long run equilibrium prices $y = (y_1, \ldots, y_n)$ can be associated with it. This wage-price (Ω, y) system in silvery equilibrium is also unique (implying thereby local stability at the least of the aggregative consumption function of the whole economy) and satisfies the weak axiom of revealed preference.

Although this theoretical construct provides us with a rationale perhaps for analyzing the implicit costs of economic growth which do not follow an equilibrium direction, it fails to resolve some other basic questions, two of which may be briefly mentioned here. First, should we analyze the actual processes of growth of an economy in terms of a sequence of equilibrium growth which may converge to a steady state? Second, what is the relationship between the equilibrium wage price system (Ω, y) and the actual wage price system that may obtain at any given time for a market economy? The first question can be resolved partially by introducing dynamic utility functionals representing the preferences of the policy makers (e.g., the central planning agency), which in effect shows that the game between the Market and the Entrepreneur considered before is fictitious. The second question can be resolved by prescribing a set of rules by which the discrepancy between the two sets of wage price systems can be eliminated. This precisely should be the task of a fruitful research inquiry, which in our opinion remains yet to be undertaken.

10.4.3. *Turnpike Theorems and Norms of Optimum Growth*

The introduction of a dynamic utility functional over a planning horizon (T) for comparing feasible growth paths starting from a historically given initial point raises at least two basic problems, one related to the specification of the form in some ordinal sense which satisfies some reasonable conditions and the other related to the norms or standards by which different growth paths can be compared. The latter question may be particularly important when the planning horizon T gets very large and the optimal path takes on a characteristic which may be similar to a steady state growth equilibrium and may even be independent to some extent of the specific form of the utility functional. It is this sort of question which led Dorfman, Samuelson and Solow [19] to investigate the existence and characteristics of long run growth paths starting with historically given initial endowments and aiming at a terminal stock structure specified by the planning authorities, such that these long run paths are in some sense efficient. The efficiency of such a path, often referred to as Dosso path implies that it is a path which maximizes a scalar index u as follows:

$$\text{maximize } u \qquad (10.6.2)$$

subject to

$$\sum_{i=1}^{m} b_{ij}q_i(t-1) \geq \sum_{i=1}^{m} c_{ij}q_i(t); \ t = 0, 1, \ldots, T-1 \qquad (10.6.3)$$

$$\sum_{i=1}^{m} b_{ij}q_i(T-1) \geq b_j^* u; \ j = 1, 2, \ldots, n, \qquad (10.6.4)$$

where $q_i(t)$ denotes the intensities of m processes at time t having output and input coefficients b_{ij} and c_{ij} respectively (the input coefficient is augmented so as to include consumption of good j by workers employed per unit level of operation of process i) and $b^* = (b_1^*, \ldots, b_n^*)$ are the desired proportions of the stocks of n goods at the terminal time point T prescribed by the planning authorities. Suppose we now restrict our attention only to long run efficient paths, efficiency defined by (10.6.2–10.6.4) which start with historically given initial endowment of stocks of goods and aim at a terminal stock structure specified by the planning authorities. Dorfman, Samuelson and Solow [19] were the first to show that under certain assumptions on the coefficient matrices (b_{ij}) and (c_{ij}) "any" such long run efficient path will arch toward the golden equilibrium path (nicknamed "turnpike" by Dosso) and spend most of its time in a near neighborhood of that turnpike, before finally

moving to the prescribed terminal stock structure, provided the programming (or planning) period T is sufficiently long. Note that the scalar u may
be taken as an index of attainment, i.e., a measure of performance of the
planning system in terms of which all feasible paths are evaluated. Also, the
desired proportions of stock structure $b^* = (b_1^*, \ldots, b_n^*)$ need not be fixed
arbitrarily, if the entrepreneurs' expectations are so guided that this structure
is approached by the competitive system following the rule of competitive
pricing and the rule of profitability. In this case the competitive equilibrium
trajectory (termed Hicks-Malinvaud trajectory) would coincide with the
Dosso path.

Morishima has not only generalized this result but derived an important
oscillatory property of such long run efficient paths, in the particular case
when the assumption of rigid consumption by workers (subsumed as a part
of c_{ij} coefficients in (3) before) is replaced by the more realistic one that the
workers' demand for consumption goods depends on prices and wage
income.

A second type of standard or norm for comparing growth paths starting
from historically given initial endowments is to introduce in an ordinal form
a specific dynamic utility functional defined over a planning (or programming) period T. This leads to a Ramsay optimality problem of order T,
where a level $\bar{y}$ of the posterity utility is specified by the planning authorities
and the utility function of the living generation assumed to be of the form

$$u(T) = \sum_{t=0}^{T-1} \{\theta^{-t} f(e_1(t), \ldots, e_n(t))\} \qquad (10.6.5)$$

is maximized subject to the constraints of technical feasibility. Here θ is the
discount rate (subjective time preference factor), $e_j(t)$ is the quantity of good
j consumed in period t and f is a homogeneous function of degree one in the
variables $e_1(t), \ldots, e_n(t)$ and the additive and period-wise separable form of
the utility function in (5) assumes that the marginal rate of substitution
between any two contemporary goods is independent of consumption in
any other period.

Restricting ourselves to the Ramsay-optimal growth paths we note that
for arbitrary initial starting points, such paths may not be steady, i.e., they
may fluctuate. However, so long as the subjective time preference factor
(θ^{-1}) is set within an appropriate admissible range, there may be a particular
starting point in time, which is relative to θ and which generates a Ramsay-
optimal path coinciding with a balanced growth path from that starting
point onwards. This type of balanced Ramsay-optimal path is called a con-

sumption turnpike and under certain conditions the following result is shown to hold: If a sufficiently long programming period is taken, "any" Ramsay-optimal path spends most of its time in a small neighborhood of the consumption turnpike. Like the Dosso path, this result is subject to one very important qualification (i.e., permanent oscillatory tendency around the turnpike) proved by Morishima, which would arise whenever the system contains complex roots of absolute value unity.

This result emphasizes two very important dangers underlying policy models utilized for growth planning in some optimal manner. First is the need for staying in a zone of stability free from oscillations, i.e., aversion to oscillation and the second is the need to orient short run policies through monetary and fiscal instruments so that the divergence between the actual prices and long run shadow prices can in some sense be minimized. It is of some interest to observe that the control theorists [87] who design optimal controls for the physical systems emphasize also the great necessity for staying in a zone of stability.

10.4.4. Concluding Remarks

Although the theoretical details of Morishima's contributions help greatly in clarifying the linkages which exist between the various phases of model construction in growth economics, they are highly structured in the sense that the following economic problems are either ignored or assumed away: (a) the role of monetary factors and expectations associated with them (problems of money supply and economic growth have been discussed by a number of authors and this is well summarized by Burmeister and Dobell [84]; also problems of optimal fiscal and monetary policies under neoclassical and other conditions are discussed by a number of authors [83, 94]); (b) the divergence from the assumptions of the competitive model (e.g., rule of competitive pricing) and the relationships between adjustments through tâtonnement and nontâtonnement processes; (c) the costs of computation (and foresight) in converging to an equilibrium path, short or long run; and (d) the role of the risk factors behind the entrepreneurial decisions in the short and the long run.

Second, the externalities of the system of growth which are sometimes strongly emphasized by the theory of public goods and the policy towards building social overhead capital, are not very easy to introduce and analyze in Morishima's framework, since the questions of nonprice elements and the lack of any competitive market framework are here prominent by their presence.

Third, in the multi-sector dynamic model where heterogeneous capital goods are explicitly introduced, we have seen how the source of instability may be present when the investment allocation decisions of entrepreneurs are not properly coordinated. However, the important policy question which remains is whether a central planning authority can "efficiently" prescribe and implement appropriate rules of coordination. As it has been recently pointed out that so long as the markets for "contingent goods and contingent claims" do not always exist in the real world, the shadow prices based on the assumption of the existence of such markets may be very unrealistic and uninteresting from the policy-making viewpoint.

Applications of various aspects of growth theory are reported in Chapters 7, 8 and 13. It is interesting to note that it is only very recently that empirical attempts [86, 89, 96] are being made for bridging the large gap between the technical developments in theory and its empirical application.

REFERENCES

[1] ARA, K. "Aggregation Problem in Input-Output Analysis," *Econometrica*, XXVII (April, 1959), 257–262.

[2] AUKRUST, O. "Investment and Economic Growth," *Productivity Measurement Review*, No. 16 (1959), 35–53.

[3] BHARUCHA-REID, A. T. *Elements of the Theory of Markov Processes and Their Applications*. New York: McGraw-Hill Book Co., 1960.

[4] BJERVE, P. J. *Planning in Norway*, 1947–1956. Amsterdam: North-Holland Publishing Co., 1959.

[5] CENTRAL PLANNING BUREAU OF THE NETHERLANDS. *Scope and Methods of the Central Planning Bureau*. "An Exploration of Economic Potentialities of the Netherlands: 1950–1970," The Hague, 1956.

[6] ———. *Central Economic Plan*. The Hague, 1961.

[7] CHENERY, H. B. "The Interdependence of Investment Decisions," in *The Allocation of Economic Resources*. Edited by Abramovitz, *et al.* Stanford: Stanford University Press, 1959.

[8] ———. "Patterns of Industrial Growth," *American Economic Review*, L (September, 1960), 624–654.

[9] ———. "Comparative Advantage and Development Policy," *American Economic Review*, LI (March, 1961), 18–51.

[10] ———. "Development Policies for Southern Italy," *Quarterly Journal of Economics*, LXXVI (November, 1962), 515–547.

[11] ———. "The Use of Interindustry Analysis in Development Programming," in *Structural Interdependence and Economic Development*. Edited by T. Barna. New York: St. Martin's Press, 1963.

[12] ———, and BRUNO, M. "Development Alternatives in an Open Economy: The Case of Israel," *Economic Journal*, LXXII (March, 1962), 79–103.

[13] ——, and UZAWA, H. "Nonlinear Programming in Economic Development," in *Studies in Linear and Nonlinear Programming*. Edited by K. Arrow, L. Hurwicz, and H. Uzawa. Stanford: Stanford University Press, 1958.

[14] CHRIST, C. F. "On Econometric Models of the U.S. Economy," in *Income and Wealth*, Series 6 (International Association for Research on Income and Wealth). London: Bowes and Bowes, 1957.

[15] DEBREU, G., and HERSTEIN, I. N. "Non-negative Square Matrices," *Econometrica*, XXI (July, 1953), 597–607.

[16] DHRYMES, P. J. "A Multi-Sectoral Model of Growth," *Quarterly Journal of Economics*, LXXVI (1962), 264–278.

[17] DOMAR, E. D. "Capital Expansion, Rate of Growth and Employment," *Econometrica*, XIV (January, 1946), 137–147.

[18] ——. *Essays in the Theory of Economic Growth*. New York: Oxford University Press, 1957.

[19] DORFMAN, R., SAMUELSON, P. A., and SOLOW, R. M. *Linear Programming and Economic Analysis*. New York: McGraw-Hill Book Co., 1958, Chap. 9.

[20] EISNER, R. "On Growth Models and Neo-classical Resurgence," *Economic Journal*, LXVIII (December, 1958), 707–721.

[21] FOX, K. A. "The Food and Agricultural Sectors in Advanced Economies," in *Structural Interdependence and Economic Development*. Edited by T. Barna. New York: St. Martin's Press, 1963, Chap. 4.

[22] FRISCH, R. *Planning for India: Selected Explorations in Methodology*. Calcutta: Asia Publishing House, 1960.

[23] ——. "A Reconsideration of Domar's Theory of Economic Growth," *Econometrica*, XXIX (July, 1961), 406–413.

[24] GANTMACHER, F. R. *Application of the Theory of Matrices*. New York: Interscience, 1959. (Translated from Russian edition, 1954.)

[25] GOODWIN, R. M. "A Model of Cyclical Growth," in *The Business Cycle in the Postwar World*. Edited by E. Lundberg. London: Macmillan and Co., 1955, pp. 203–221.

[26] ——. "Optimal Growth-Path for an Underdeveloped Economy," *Economic Journal*, LXXI (December, 1961), 756–774.

[27] HAAVELMO, T. *Studies in the Theory of Economic Evolution*. Amsterdam: North-Holland Publishing Co., 1954.

[28] HARROD, R. F. *Towards a Dynamic Economics*. London: Macmillan and Co., 1957.

[29] HOFFMAN, W. G. *The Growth of Industrial Economies*. Translated from the German by W. O. Henderson and W. H. Chaloner. Manchester: Manchester University Press, 1958.

[30] ICHIMURA, S. "Dynamic Input-Output and Linear Programming Models," in *Programming Techniques for Economic Development with Special Reference to Asia and the Far East*, (U.N. group of experts) Bangkok: United Nations, ECAFE, 1960.

[31] JOHANSEN, L. *A Multisectoral Study of Economic Growth*. Amsterdam: North-Holland Publishing Co., 1960.

[32] ——. "Durability of Capital and the Rate of Growth of National Product," *International Economic Review*, II, No. 3 (September, 1961), 361–370.

[33] JORGENSON, D. "Structure of Multisector Dynamic Models," *International Economic Review*, II, No. 3 (September, 1961), 276–293.

[34] KEMENY, J. G., MORGENSTERN, O., and THOMPSON, G. L. "A Generalization of the von Neumann Model of an Expanding Economy," *Econometrica*, XXIV (January, 1956), 115–135.

[35] KENDRICK, J. W. "Productivity Trends: Capital and Labor," *Review of Economics and Statistics*, XXXVIII (August, 1956), 248–257.

[36] KLEIN, L. "Some Theoretical Issues in the Measurement of Capacity," *Econometrica*, XXVIII (April, 1960), 272–286.

[37] ——, and KOSOBUD, R. "Some Econometrics of Growth: Great Ratios of Economics," *Quarterly Journal of Economics*, LXXV (1961), 173–198.

[38] ——, *et al.* "A Model of Japanese Economic Growth," *Econometrica*, XXIX (July, 1961), 277–292.

[39] LANGE, O. "Some Observations on Input-Output Analysis," *Sankhyā*, XVIII (February, 1957), 305–336.

[40] ——. *Introduction to Econometrics*. New York: Pergamon Press, 1959.

[41] ——. "Output-Investment Ratio and Input-Output Analysis," *Econometrica*, XXVIII (April, 1960), 310–324.

[42] LEONTIEF, W. W. *The Structure of American Economy*, 1919–1929. Cambridge, Mass.: Harvard University Press, 1941.

[43] —— (ed.). *Studies in the Structure of American Economy*. New York: Oxford University Press, 1953.

[44] MAHALANOBIS, P. C. "Approach of Operational Research to Planning in India," *Sankhyā*, XVI (1955), 3–62.

[45] MALINVAUD, E. "Capital Accumulation and Efficient Allocation of Resources," *Econometrica*, XXI (April, 1953), 233–268.

[46] MANNE, A. S. "Capacity Expansion and Probabilistic Growth," *Econometrica*, XXIX (October, 1961), 632–649.

[47] MARGLIN, S. A. *Approaches to Dynamic Investment Planning*. Amsterdam: North-Holland Publishing Co., 1963.

[48] MATHEWS, R. C. O. "The New View of Investment: A Comment," *Quarterly Journal of Economics*, LXXVIII (1964), 164–172. (With a reply by Phelps and Yaari.)

[49] MCKENZIE, L. W. "Turnpike Theorems for a Generalized Leontief Model," *Econometrica*, XXXI (1963), 165–180.

[50] NAVARRETE, A., and I. M. DE. "Underemployment in Underdeveloped Economies," *International Economic Papers*, III (1953), 235–239.

[51] OTT, A. E. "Production Functions, Technical Progress and Economic Growth," *International Economic Papers*, XI (1962), 102–140.

[52] PHELPS, E. S. "The New View of Investment: A Neoclassical Analysis," *Quarterly Journal of Economics*, LXXVI (1962), 548–567.

[53] QAYUM, A. *Theory and Policy of Accounting Prices*. Amsterdam: North-Holland Publishing Co., 1960.

[54] QUANDT, R. "Probabilistic Errors in the Leontief System," *Naval Research Logistic Quarterly*, V (1958), 155–170.

[55] RADNER, R. "Paths of Economic Growth that are Optimal with Regard Only to Final States," *Review of Economic Studies*, XXVIII (February, 1961), 98–104.

[56] ——. *Notes on the Theory of Economic Planning*. Athens: Center of Economic Research, 1963.

[57] RASMUSSEN, P. N. *Intersectoral Relations*. Amsterdam: North-Holland Publishing Co., 1956.

[58] SENGUPTA, J. K. "Models of Agriculture and Industry in Less Developed Economies," in *Structural Interdependence and Economic Development*. Edited by T. Barna. New York: St. Martins Press, 1963, Chap. 5. (With Comments by R. Day.)

[59] ——. "Specification and Estimation of Structural Relations in Policy Models" (Appendix 2), in *Quantitative Planning of Economic Policy*. Edited by R. G. Hickman. Washington, D.C.: The Brookings Institution, 1965, Chap. 4.

[60] ——. "On the Relative Stability and Optimality of Consumption in Aggregative Growth Models," *Economica*, XXXI (February, 1964), 33–50.

[61] ——. "Some Observations on the Optimal Growth-Path for an Underdeveloped Economy," *Metroeconomica*, No. 2 (1964),

[62] ——, and THORBECKE, E. "Some Observations on the Theory of Economic Growth: Balanced and Unbalanced," *Zeitschrift für die Gesamte Staatswissenschaft*, CXX, No. 2 (April, 1964), 243–263.

[63] ——, and TINTNER, G. "On Some Aspects of Trend in the Aggregative Models of Economic Growth," *Kyklos*, XVI, No. 1 (1963), 47–61.

[64] ——. "Ein verallgemeinerter geburten-und todesprozess zur erklarung der entwicklung des deutschen volkseinkommens, 1851–1939," *Metrika*, VI (1963), 143–147.

[65] ——. "An Approach to a Stochastic Theory of Economic Development," (To be published in *Essays in Honor of Professor M. Kalecki*.)

[66] SOLOW, R. "A Contribution to the Theory of Economic Growth," *Quarterly Journal of Economics*, LXX (February, 1956), 65–94.

[67] ——. "Technical Change and the Aggregate Production Function," *Review of Economics and Statistics*, XXXIX (August, 1957), 312–320.

[68] ——. "Competitive Valuation in a Dynamic Input-Output System," *Econometrica*, XXVII (January, 1959), 30–53.

[69] ——. "Note on Uzawa's Two-Sector Model of Economic Growth," *Review of Economic Studies*, XXIX, No. 1 (October, 1961), 48–50.

[70] STONE, R. "Model Building and the Social Accounts," in *Income and Wealth*, Series 4 (International Association for Research on Income and Wealth). Edited by M. Gilbert and R. Stone. London: Bowes and Bowes, 1955, pp. 27–77.

[71] ——, and BROWN, A. *A Programme for Growth: A Computable Model of Economic Growth*. London: Chapman and Hall, 1962.

[72] THEIL, H. "Linear Aggregation in Input-Output Analysis," *Econometrica*, XXV (January, 1957), 111–122.

[73] TINBERGEN, J. *Economic Policy, Principles and Design*. Amsterdam: North-Holland Publishing Co., 1956.

[74] ——. *The Design of Development*. Baltimore: The Johns Hopkins Press, 1958.

[75] ——. "On the Theory of Trend Movements," in *Selected Papers*. Edited by Klaassen, Koyck and Witteveen. Amsterdam: North-Holland Publishing Co., 1959.

[76] ——. "Planning in Stages," *Statskonomisk Tidskrift*, (March, 1962), 1–20.

[77] ——, and Bos, H. C. *Mathematical Models of Economic Growth*. New York: McGraw-Hill Book Co., 1962.

[78] UZAWA, H. "On a Two-Sector Model of Economic Growth," *Review of Economic Studies*, XXIX, No. 1 (1961), 40–47.

[79] VERDOORN, P. J. "Complementarity and Long-Range Projections," *Econometrica*, XXIV (1956), 429–445.

[80] VON NEUMANN, J. "A Model of General Equilibrium," *Review of Economic Studies*, XIII (1945–1946), 1–9. (English translation of an article in German, 1937.)

[81] WELLISZ, S. "Economic Planning in the Netherlands, France and Italy," *Journal of Political Economy*, 68 (June, 1960), 252–283.

[82] ZABEL, E. "A Multisectoral Study of Economic Growth: A Review," *Economica*, XXIX (April, 1962), 284–299.

[83] ARROW, K. J. and KURZ, M. *The Public Investment, the Rate of Return and Optimal Fiscal Policy*. Baltimore: Johns Hopkins Press, 1970.

[84] BURMEISTER, E. and DOBELL, A. R. *Mathematical Theories of Economic Growth*. New York: Macmillan and Co., 1970.

[85] CHAKRAVARTY, S. *Capital and Development Planning*. Cambridge, Mass.: MIT Press, 1969.

[86] CHENERY, H. B. (ed.). *Studies in Development Planning*. Cambridge, Mass.: Harvard University Press, 1971.

[87] FELDBAUM, A. A. *Optimal Control Systems*. New York: Academic Press, 1965.

[88] HICKS, J. R. *Capital and Growth*. London: Oxford University Press, 1965.

[89] KENDRICK, D. and TAYLOR, L. "Numerical Methods and Nonlinear Optimizing Models for Economic Planning", in *Studies in Development Planning*, op. cit., Chapter 1.

[90] MORISHIMA, M. *Equilibrium, Stability and Growth*. Oxford: Clarendon Press, 1964.

[91] ——. *Theory of Economic Growth*. Oxford: Clarendon Press, 1969.

[92] SENGUPTA, J. K. "Foundations of a Dynamic Theory of Economic Growth", *Kyklos*, Volume 24, 1971, pp. 546–556.

[93] ——. "Decision Rules in Stochastic Programming Under Dynamic Economic Models". To be published in *Swedish Journal of Economics*.

[94] SHELL, K. (ed.). *Essays on the Theory of Optimal Economic Growth*. Cambridge, Mass.: MIT Press, 1967.

[95] TINTNER, G. and SENGUPTA, J. K. *Stochastic Economics: Stochastic Processes Control and Programming*. New York: Academic Press, 1972.

[96] UNITED NATIONS ECAFE. *Sectoral Output and Employment Projections for the Second Development Decade*. Bangkok: ECAFE, 1970.

Chapter 11

MODELS OF STABILIZATION IN DEVELOPED ECONOMIES: THE CASE OF THE UNITED STATES

The development of stabilization models has been characterized by inter-actions between data systems, theories and techniques. The first econometric model of the U.S. was completed by Tinbergen in 1939 [39]. It drew upon national income data developed by Kuznets during 1934–37 [31, 32], the macroeconomic theory advanced by Keynes in 1936 [24], and statistical techniques proposed by Frisch in 1934 [14]. Each of the supporting fields had an earlier history and literature of its own; it is significant that Tinbergen's model utilized the most recent and most advanced contributions in each.

The model, in its turn, posed new problems for the supporting fields. It consisted of a set of simultaneous equations, each of which had been estimated separately by least squares. Haavelmo [19, 20] demonstrated that, if the disturbances in two or more equations were significantly correlated, it would be necessary to fit the equations simultaneously to obtain unbiased estimates of population parameters. Haavelmo's theory inspired a flurry of activity on estimation techniques in the late 1940's, culminating in a 1950 volume [30] edited by Koopmans. The new estimation procedures required more elaborate computations than least squares; for some years computation costs and computer capacity presented major obstacles to their use in the estimation of large scale stabilization models. (There was also concern about the small-sample properties of the new estimators, which were known to be unbiased in very large samples but not in small.)

The model, based on annual data for 1919–32, also stimulated demands for more and better data, including quarterly estimates of national income and its components. It cast some doubt on the effectiveness of monetary instruments (which did not yield large or highly significant coefficients in the model but left open the possibility that their true effectiveness was covered up by the insensitivity of annual data, by the inadequacy of certain series to represent the desired theoretical concepts, and/or by special characteristics of the 1919–32 period.

354

The input-output models of Leontief published in 1936 [33] and 1941 [34] created demands for accurate and detailed data on interindustry flows of goods and services in selected years which would be consistent with the national income and product accounts. Somewhat later, work was begun by M.A. Copeland on tracing money flows through the U.S. economy [2]. It is intuitively clear that some master model of the real economy must incorporate input-output relationships, flows of funds, and national income accounts for each time period (year or quarter) and also dynamic econometric relationships explaining the movements of all these variables over time. Input-output features were incorporated in the Brookings quarterly econometric model of the U.S. [6] published in 1965. Substantial improvements in the monetary sectors of stabilization models were reported by de Leeuw and Gramlich during 1968 [3] and 1969 [4]. As of 1971, Klein [28] predicted that macroeconometric model building was bound to culminate in a unified system combining national income accounting, input-output and flows-of-funds all together in a model containing roughly 1,000 equations. At the same time, of course, a variety of smaller models would be used for special purposes.

After World War II, L.R. Klein became the leading figure in developing econometric (stabilization) models of the U.S. He published small scale models of six to twelve equations in 1947 [26] and 1950 [27] and, with the collaboration of A.S. Goldberger, one of 20 equations in 1955 [29]. All of these were based on annual data.

By 1960, several other U.S. economists were experimenting with stabilization models of small to moderate size. Meanwhile, major advances had been made in computer capacity, in quarterly national income accounts and price deflators, in estimation theory, and in computer programs to implement estimation and policy simulation procedures. The most limiting factor had become the capacity of a single investigator, or at most, a two or three member team, to achieve expertise on data systems, market and technological structures, and other peculiarities of every major sector of the economy.

This limitation was removed during 1961–63 by the organization of a major team effort involving 15 or 20 distinguished economists under the leadership of L.R. Klein and J.S. Duesenberry. This effort, sponsored by the Social Science Research Council and funded by the National Science Foundation, produced what was subsequently known as the Brookings quarterly econometric model of the U.S. [6]. The large team completed its work in 1963, and a small staff located at the Brookings Institution carried out further developments, tests and policy simulations for several ensuing years.

Further modeling efforts during 1963–71 at the University of Pennsylvania, the Massachusetts Institute of Technology and the Federal Reserve Board all built to some extent upon experience gained with the Brookings model. By 1971 it was possible for small research groups, at a significant but not insurmountable expense, to obtain access by remote telephone hookup to an extensive data base and to have prescribed simulations carried out on a large scale stabilization model at a central location. Data and programs for small scale models, suitable for instructional purposes in undergraduate economics courses, had also become widely available.

The remainder of this chapter will be organized as follows: (1) the Klein-Goldberger model [29], with subsequent revisions by Goldberger [16], will be used to illustrate some basic features of empirical stabilization models; (2) additional features will be illustrated in terms of the Brookings model [6, 7, 15]; (3) forecasting, multiplier analysis, and policy simulations with stabilization models will be illustrated with results reported by Evans and Klein [9] and Fromm and Taubman [15]; (4) other references will be discussed; and (5) some comments will be made on developments in prospect as of 1971.

11.1. The Klein-Goldberger Model (1955): A Small Scale System Using Annual Data

The Klein-Goldberger model [29] was slightly revised after its initial publication; our discussion is based on the revised version as presented by Goldberger [16] in 1959.

The Klein-Goldberger model attempts to describe the workings of the U.S. economy from 1929 through 1952 in terms of 21 simultaneous equations. Collectively, these equations describe the interrelationships existing among 21 jointly dependent economic variables and among these and a larger number of "predetermined" factors. The jointly dependent variables include components of GNP, such as consumption expenditures, gross private capital formation, and capital consumption allowances. The various components of GNP on both the expenditure and the income side are bound together by a set of accounting identities which are implicit in the national income accounts. Other equations express the determination of money wage rates, prices of farm products, long- and short-term interest rates, employment, the general price level, the stock of fixed capital, and liquid assets held by individuals and businesses.

Fifteen of the 21 equations are fitted by statistical means. These 15 equations do not form a complete and self-contained system; if they did, they would be sufficient to determine the values of 15 of the jointly dependent variables. Actually, the six remaining equations—the accounting identities previously referred to—are needed to "close" the basic statistical set; at the same time they give, by addition and subtraction, the values of six more jointly dependent variables.

The model contained 38 distinct economic variables. However, 26 of these variables also appeared in lagged form such as prices or wages in one or more previous years. From the standpoint of statistical properties and calculations, each lagged series functions as a distinct variable in addition to the original current series. In the statistical sense, then, the 21 equations included 64 variables, which may be classified as follows:

Endogenous	21
Predetermined	
Lagged endogenous	20
Exogenous	17
Lagged exogenous	6
Total	64

11.1.1. *The Model Itself: Variables and Equations*

The 38 basic variables are listed and classified in Table 11.1 and the 21 equations are shown in Table 11.2. As Goldberger remarks, "This system of twenty-one behavioral, technological, and definitional equations ... constitutes a quantitative characterization of the economy of the United States. It provides a self-contained explanation of economic behavior in view of the fact that it is a complete system, that is to say, there are just enough equations to determine the values of the 'unknowns'—the endogenous variables."

Exogenous variables are treated as logically independent variables which do not have to be explained inside of the 21-equation model. The *endogenous* variables are logically dependent upon the exogenous variables and must be explained by them.

Fifteen of the equations are estimated statistically. They may be grouped in the following way:

(1) Equations (11.1), (11.2), and (11.9) represent final demands for components of the gross national product: consumption, investment, and imports.

(2) Equation (11.7) constitutes a production function or supply equation for the total gross national product (less the government wage bill).

TABLE 11.1
List of Variables in the Klein-Goldberger Model

New Symbol, 1959	Brief Definition	Category	Old Symbol, 1955
C	Consumption	Endogenous	
D	Depreciation	Endogenous	
F_1	Imports	Endogenous	
F_R	Farm exports	Exogenous	F_A
G	Government expenditures and exports	Exogenous	$G + F_E$
h	Hours of work	Exogenous	
I	Investment	Endogenous	
i_L	Long-term interest rate	Endogenous	
i_S	Short-term interest rate	Endogenous	
K	Capital stock	Endogenous	
L_1	Household liquid assets	Endogenous	
L_2	Business liquid assets	Endogenous	
L_B	Percentage excess reserves	Exogenous	R
M	National income	Endogenous	Y
N_E	Entrepreneurs	Exogenous	$N_E + N_F$
N_G	Government employees	Exogenous	N
N_L	Labor force	Exogenous	
N_P	Population	Exogenous	
N_W	Employees	Endogenous	
P	Nonwage, nonfarm income	Endogenous	
P_C	Corporate profits	Endogenous	
p	Price level	Endogenous	
p_F	Import price level	Exogenous	p_I
p_R	Farm price level	Endogenous	p_A
Q	Gross national product	Endogenous	$Y + T + D$
R_1	Farm income	Endogenous	A_1
R_2	Farm subsidies	Exogenous	A_2
S_B	Corporate surplus	Endogenous	B
S_C	Corporate savings	Endogenous	S_P
t	Time trend	Exogenous	
T_C	Corporate taxes	Exogenous	
T_E	Indirect taxes	Exogenous	T
T_N	Nonwage, nonfarm, noncoporate taxes, less transfers	Exogenous	$T_P - T_C$
T_R	Farm taxes, less transfers	Exogenous	T_A
T_W	Wage taxes, less transfers	Exogenous	
w	Wage rate	Endogenous	
W_1	Private wage bill	Endogenous	
W_2	Government wage bill	Exogenous	

Source: Arthur S. Goldberger, *Impact Multipliers and Dynamic Properties of the Klein-Goldberger Model.* Amsterdam: North-Holland Publishing Company, 1959, pp. 5–6.

TABLE 11.2
List of Equations in the Klein-Goldberger Model

(11.1) $C = -22.26 + 0.55(W_1 + W_2 - T_W) + 0.41(P - T_C - T_N - S_C)$
$+ 0.34(R_1 + R_2 - T_R) + 0.26C_{-1} + 0.072(L_1)_{-1} + 0.26N_P$

(11.2) $I = -16.71 + 0.78(P - T_C - T_N + R_1 + R_2 - T_R + D)_{-1} - 0.073K_{-1}$
$+ 0.14(L_2)_{-1}$

(11.3) $S_C = -3.53 + 0.72(P_C - T_C) + 0.076(P_C - T_C - S_C)_{-1} - 0.028(S_B)_{-1}$

(11.4) $P_C = -7.60 + 0.68P$

(11.5) $D = 7.25 + 0.10 \dfrac{K + K_{-1}}{2} + 0.044(Q - W_2)$

(11.6) $W_1 = -1.40 + 0.24(Q - W_2) + 0.24(Q - W_2)_{-1} + 0.29t$

(11.7) $(Q - W_2) = -26.08 + 2.17[h(N_W - N_G) + N_E] + 0.16 \dfrac{K + K_{-1}}{2} + 2.05t$

(11.8) $w - w_{-1} = 4.11 - 0.74(N_L - N_W - N_E) + 0.52(p_{-1} - p_{-2}) + 0.54t$

(11.9) $F_1 = 0.32 + 0.0060(M - T_W - T_C - T_N - T_R)\dfrac{p}{p_F} + 0\cdot81(F_1)_{-1}$

(11.10) $R_1(p/p_R) = -0.36$
$+ 0.054(W_1 + W_2 - T_W + P - T_C - T_N - S_C)(p/p_R)$
$- 0.007[(W_1 + W_2 - T_W + P - T_C - T_N - S_C)(p/p_R]_{-1}$
$+ 0.012F_R$

(11.11) $p_R = -131.17 + 2.32p$

(11.12) $L_1 = 0.14(M - T_W - T_C - T_N - S_C - T_R) + 76.03(i_L - 2.0)^{-0.84}$

(11.13) $L_2 = -0.34 + 0.26W_1 - 1.02i_S - 0.26(p - p_{-1}) + 0.61(L_2)_{-1}$

(11.14) $i_L = 2.58 + 0.44(i_S)_{-3} + 0.26(i_S)_{-5}$

(11.15) $100 \dfrac{i_S - (i_S)_{-1}}{i_S} = 11.17 - 0.67L_B$

(11.16) $K - K_{-1} = I - D$

(11.17) $S_B - (S_B)_{-1} = S_C$

(11.18) $W_1 + W_2 + P + R_1 + R_2 = M$

(11.19) $C + I + G - F_1 = M + T_E + D$

(11.20) $h(w/p)N_W = W_1 + W_2$

(11.21) $Q = M + T_E + D$

Source: Goldberger, *op. cit.*, pp. 4, 6, and 7.

(3) The allocation of the gross national *income* (which is equal in value to the gross national product) by distributive shares is described in part by the private sector labor demand equation (11.6), the farm income equation (11.10), and the depreciation equation (11.5).

(4) The important role of the corporate sector in the United States economy is represented in the corporate profits equation (11.4) and in the corporate savings equation (11.3).

(5) A set of four equations relates to the money and securities market: (11.12) and (11.13) describe the demand for liquid assets by households and businesses, respectively; the money supply situation is indicated in terms of long-term interest rates in (11.14), and short-term interest rates in (11.15).

(6) Equation (11.8) relates to the labor market where the money wage rate is, in the immediate sense, determined. This variable is critical in the determination of the absolute general price level, and hence, via (11.11), the level of farm prices. The final demand, production, and income allocation equations refer to real, not money, magnitudes.

The remaining six equations, (11.16) through (11.21), are definitional. Their function in the model is suggested by the fact that equation (11.16) contains only one new endogenous variable *in addition to* endogenous variables appearing on the left hand sides of equations (11.1) through (11.15). This is true also of equations (11.17) and (11.19). The new endogenous variable M in equation (11.19) is needed, in conjunction with some exogenous variables and some left hand endogenous variables from equations (11.1) through (11.15), to determine the value of P in equation (11.18) and Q in (11.21). Equation (11.20) deviates from this simple pattern, as it contains two endogenous variables which do not appear separately on the left hand sides of equations (11.1) through (11.15). This underlines the fact that the set of 21 equations must indeed be solved simultaneously and not sequentially; the definitional equations and the statistically estimated equations are equally necessary to a consistent description of the workings of the economy.

Klein and Goldberger did not refer to Tinbergen's theory of economic policy [40], which was published only two years before their 1955 book went to press. However, we can make an approximate classification of the variables in the Klein-Goldberger model in terms of Tinbergen's categories.

The model includes seventeen exogenous and twenty-one endogenous variables. Seven of the exogenous variables are quite clearly regarded as data. They include time trend, population, labor force, number of entrepreneurs, price of imports, volume of farm exports, and (apparently) number of hours worked per man-year.

The ten other exogenous variables are evidently regarded as potential instruments. They include five kinds of taxes (corporate income, indirect taxes, farm taxes, taxes on wages and salaries, and taxes on nonfarm, noncorporate enterprises); four variables involving government expenditures (government expenditures for goods and services, number of government employees, government wage bill, and farm subsidies); and one monetary instrument, percentage excess reserves.

The classification of the twenty-one endogenous variables into targets and irrelevant variables depends on the value system of the policy maker and the particular set of policies being considered. A plausible selection would include eleven target variables, as follows: the general price level, real consumption, real values of five components of income (private wage bill, nonwage-nonfarm income, corporate savings, farm income, and corporate profits), number of wage and salary earners employed, the wage rate, the farm price level, and gross private domestic capital formation.

The remaining ten endogenous variables, which for completeness we will call irrelevant, include household liquid assets, business liquid assets, depreciation, corporate surplus, imports, short-term interest rate, long-term interest rate, capital stock, real national income, and real GNP. The last two variables are classified as irrelevant only because most of their endogenous components have already been classified as targets; if all the components of a sum are given, the sum itself is automatically determined. In this sense, the number of irrelevant variables in a policy model must be equal to or greater than the number of definition equations.

In brief, the Klein-Goldberger model is evidently concerned with the application of monetary and fiscal policy to the achievement of satisfactory levels of employment, consumption and real income (for five economic groups) together with a concern about wage and price inflation and a satisfactory level of farm prices. The system is driven by population and labor force variables which change quite smoothly over time and is subject to shocks from the international sector.

It is clear that the target variables could be incorporated into a welfare function (as could other variables as well), or that desired time paths of the target variables could be defined; all of the forecasting problems and decision rule derivations mentioned in Chapters 5 and 6 could be elucidated in terms of the Klein-Goldberger model.

11.1.2. *Economic Evaluation as of 1956 : Some Limitations of the Model*

The Klein-Goldberger model was a major achievement under the many kinds of restrictions (of data, computer capacity, computer programs, estimation theory and procedures, and team size) that surrounded such research in the early 1950's. Its authors were very much aware of these limitations, and that this model was simply a step on the way toward more detailed, sophisticated and useful ones. The following paragraphs, based on a 1956 review article by Fox [10], are essentially a critique of the state of the art of econometric model building at that time.

The usefulness of a model for appraising economic policies depends upon the variables included and the accuracy with which their interrelations are measured. Economic theory is largely concerned with explaining the behavior of firms and consumers in terms of demand curves, supply curves, production functions, and so on. It is difficult to think about economic policies systematically without drawing upon these basic concepts. From this viewpoint, the Klein-Goldberger model is limited, since several of its equations are frankly empirical. For example, corporate profits before taxes are expressed simply as a function of nonwage, nonfarm income, of which corporate profits constitute a major share. Changes in wage rates are expressed as functions of time and of earlier changes in the general price level. Net farm income is expressed as a function of real disposable income and the volume of agricultural exports, and farm prices are expressed as a function solely of the general price level. Long-term interest rates are expressed as a function of short-term rates three years and five years previous.

These relationships find little support in economic theory. Other equations, such as those explaining consumption expenditures, gross domestic capital formation, and corporate savings are more in accord with theoretical considerations. The authors were fully aware of these variations in the theoretical appropriateness of the different equations, but some of the expected relationships failed to show up significantly in the data either because they did not in fact hold in the real economy or because the data were inadequate to reflect them.

The level of aggregation in the model is extremely high. This means that we do not have obvious "handles" or points of entry into the equation system for the analysis of some major (and many minor) economic policies. For example, we cannot show the effects on other sectors of the economy of a reduction in support prices for basic crops; we cannot show the effects of a change in aggregate supplies of livestock products (or, for that matter, of all farm products) upon the level of farm prices; we cannot show the effects of changes in down payments and amortization periods upon the volume of residential construction.

The Klein-Goldberger model shares other problems with time series analysis in general, including so-called "latent variables" and intercorrelation. In a few instances coefficients are not statistically significant in 1929–50 but appear to be so when the period is extended by two years. This phenomenon cannot, of course, be explained on the basis of economic theory but only on the basis of technical statistical considerations. For example, the variable "liquid assets of consumers", which did not vary a great deal before

World War II, does not show up as statistically significant in the earlier period but does when two more observations reflecting the huge World War II accumulations of consumer assets are added. The effect of interest rates upon investment is somewhat parallel; although some theories accord it great importance (if properly measured), statistical studies have usually disclosed little or no significant effect.

The high level of intercorrelation in the Klein-Goldberger model creates a hazard from the standpoint of accurate specification of the variables to be included in a given equation. In the consumption equation for example, the coefficient of multiple determination is 0.998, but the largest simple coefficient is 0.991, and three other simple coefficients range from 0.90 to 0.98. Two of the independent variables—lagged consumption expenditures and current disposable income—are correlated to the extent of 0.96. The simple regression of consumer expenditures upon current disposable income fits the historical data quite closely; a combination of disposable income with any or all of the other variables also yields a good forecasting equation, but one with considerably different net regression coefficients. Specifically, the simple least squares regression coefficient of consumer expenditures upon a specially adjusted disposable income variable is 1.035; the corresponding net regression coefficient in the five-variable equation is 0.617. Such differences are highly important if a given policy impinges directly upon only one of the independent variables in an equation.

11.1.3. *Suggestions Made as of 1956 for Further Adaptation of Econometric (Stabilization) Models to the Appraisal of Economic Policies*

The following suggestions were made in the 1956 review article previously mentioned [10]. The reviewer had had twelve years of experience in policy analysis using the extensive data systems of the U.S. Department of Agriculture and one year on the staff of the Council of Economic Advisers. He was optimistic about the possibilities of using information for individual sectors, and analyzing interactions between sectors, at a level of detail that would meet the needs of economic policy makers throughout the federal establishment.

The chief limitation of the Klein-Goldberger model is its level of aggregation. Many applied economists in business and government are sector specialists who take pride in their alertness to a large number of indicators and pressure gauges within their areas of specialization. If models of the economy as a whole are to be useful to such economists and eventually to justify their full acceptance, they must be designed so as to incorporate readily detailed information concerning developments within individual sectors.

The sector specialist tends to be weak in interpreting the effects upon other parts of the economy of developments within his particular area. To measure these effects, we need models which reflect interactions among the different major sectors of the economy. If alternative policies are under consideration in each of several sectors, we should be concerned not only with the effects of each policy upon the area of its immediate application but also with the effects of the group of policies as a whole upon the level of activity achieved by the economy as a whole and in each individual sector.

The impatience of sector specialists with such highly aggregative models as those of the Klein and Goldberger type can be understood in terms of the wealth of detailed sector information which is available and which they see no ready way of incorporating into models of the general economy. For example, leading economists in the U.S. Department of Agriculture have at their disposal an elaborate network of economic and statistical intelligence concerning the agricultural sector. The Klein-Goldberger model, with its single equation expressing the determination of farm income and one other expressing the determination of farm prices, ignores the great bulk of this information.

Similarly, the housing specialist might be interested in such factors as population growth, shifts in age distribution, new family formation, geographical shifts in population, the strength of motivations underlying the movement from central cities to suburbs, and the influence of disposable income liquid assets, down-payment requirements, amortization periods, and mortgage interest rates upon the demand for housing. For some purposes the demand for labor and construction materials by builders (reflected in such series as the number of housing starts) might be considered separately in point of time and price implications from the demand for finished houses on the part of prospective owners or tenants. The housing expert, like the agricultural economist, might use a host of geographical breakdowns, price and construction-cost indices, wage and interest rates, and other factors in order to forecast developments in the housing sector or to appraise the consequences of proposed changes in policies. Here, too, it may be fairly easy to see the direct impact of policy changes upon the housing sector but very difficult to appraise their effects upon other sectors.

We might readily conceive of a model representing the major lines of influence of a set of housing policies upon various economic magnitudes. This model would include wage rates, price indices, disposable personal income, GNP, and perhaps other variables which would also appear, for example, in a model relating agriculture to the nonfarm economy. To the extent that a housing program stimulated employment and raised disposable income, it would lead to a secondary increase in the demand for housing. But it would also increase the demand for farm products, leading to a change in the original situation in that sector. The adjustments involving agriculture might produce still another increase in disposable income, which would result in a further increase in the demand for housing. Thus we could visualize an iterative process whereby two sectors would be brought into a new equilibrium relationship with each other and with the rest of the economy [10]. Prices of building materials would influence the index of prices paid by farmers, increases in farm prices of food products would tend to raise wage rates and construction costs, and so on. The resulting model of two interacting sectors, including some variables relating to the economy as a whole, could be converted into a formally complete system analogous to that of Klein and Goldberger. However, many of the coefficients would have been built up by aggregation from more detailed relationships, and many of the time lags would be based on special analyses. The model as a whole would be built up synthetically from sound components; it would not be limited by the resolving power of a single process of statistical estimation.

This same approach could, of course, be carried out for more than two sectors. Presumably, the model for each sector could be developed in such a way as to leave "handles" or points of entry for each type of policy intervention that might be regarded as worthy of appraisal. The major channels of communication among sectors would also be represented. The logical outcome of this approach would be a model which would permit the advance appraisal of any set of economic policies and programs in relation to any initial positions and trends of the various sectors of the economy. Technical coefficients, which are the mainstay of the interindustry model, would also appear in the model conceived here but would represent only one of several channels of economic interaction.

If we think in terms of the coordination of economic policies and the appraisal of economic developments by the federal establishment as a whole, it is obviously desirable to use the detailed knowledge and skills of specialists in particular economic sectors. At the same time, a more comprehensive and internally consistent model than any now available is needed to anticipate the interactions among sectors and their cumulative effects upon the economy as a whole.

In summary, it seems clear that progress in economic forecasting and the appraisal of economic policies can be hastened by the development of a model or models of the general economy which can encompass our detailed knowledge of the individual sectors. In doing this, we cannot afford to be tied down to a single type of statistical estimation or confined to time series observations drawn from a single limited period. We should not be afraid of the statistical implications of a partly synthetic model if we know the reliability of its basic components. The latter will continue to be useful for intrasector analysis as at present. The major new achievement would lie in the synthesis of these basic components into a model adequately reflecting the interactions among sectors.

11.2. The Brookings Quarterly Econometric Model of the United States (1965)

From 1956 to 1960, books and scientific papers by Tinbergen [41], Theil [38], Duesenberry, Eckstein, and Fromm [5] and other economists in several countries testified to a growing professional interest and sophistication in the construction, interpretation, and use of large-scale macroeconometric models.

In 1959, the Social Science Research Council established a committee on economic stability. That committee approved a proposal for the development of a larger-scale econometric model to be sponsored by the SSRC. J.S. Duesenberry and L.R. Klein were appointed co-chairmen of the project.

The initial development of the Brookings model was sponsored by the Social Science Research Council during 1961-63 under a grant from the National Science Foundation. Beginning in September 1963, responsibility for completing the model and for testing and improving it over a period of years was transferred to the Brookings Institution.

A major volume on the Brookings model was published in 1965, so only a few of its features will be mentioned here [6]. The model is based on quarterly rather than annual data. It is larger than earlier models, containing (as of 1965) approximately 150 statistically estimated equations and a large but unspecified number of definitional equations.

11.2.1. *Research Strategy and Preliminary Results* [7, 15]

The large size of the Brookings model is the outcome of a deliberate research strategy. Previous models of the United States economy had been carried out by one or two principal investigators. Treatment of individual sectors of the economy was highly aggregative. Much empirical knowledge and many sources of data available to experts in particular sectors were overlooked.

During 1961–63, the SSRC group sought to overcome these limitations by dividing the exploratory and developmental work on the model among approximately 20 economists. Each major block of equations in the model was made the responsibility of an economist with special knowledge and previous research experience in that area. The various tasks or sectors included the following: (1) consumption, (2) inventories, (3) residential construction, (4) business investment realization, (5) business investment anticipation, (6) foreign trade, (7) production and final demand, (8) price conversion, (9) price mark-up, (10) wage rates, (11) production and manhours, (12) dividends and other factor shares, (13) labor force, (14) interest and money, (15) agricultural submodel, and (16) government. Functional tasks cutting across sectors included consistent statistical estimation of all equations and simulation tests of various subsystems and the model as a whole.

The work of the sector specialists was coordinated by means of a three-week workshop in August 1961 and another two-week workshop in August 1962. In addition to securing standardization on technical points, the workshop discussions generated a number of insights which could scarcely have emerged from a one- or two-man project.

Figure 11.1 presents a condensed flow diagram of the Brookings model. Its main features, as described by Duesenberry and Klein [6, p. 23] are as follows:

> On the right we have the GNP components, which are fed by the main demand decisions of the economy—consumption, investment, government and foreign. These demands feed back to stimulate orders and more inventories or they work through our input-output mechanism with our final demand regressions and determine the composition of sector outputs. These determine sector labor requirements and with wage-price determination in the left center boxes make up a large part of factor incomes. Another part comes from the money market box. These incomes become disposable through the tax-transfer boxes and feed back into the investment decision, but that will only supplement the output requirements of investment and the capital market facilities in investment planning. Residential investment decisions, like consumption, are fed through population, through the capital market, and through disposable income.

The flow diagram gives visual emphasis to the determination of the GNP and its components and the associated national, personal and disposable income measures (the national income accounting or NIA system). This

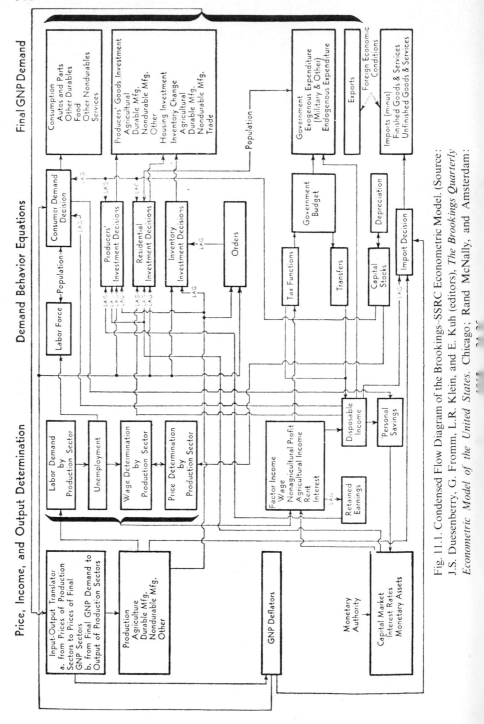

Fig. 11.1. Condensed Flow Diagram of the Brookings–SSRC Econometric Model. (Source: J.S. Duesenberry, G. Fromm, L.R. Klein, and E. Kuh (editors), *The Brookings Quarterly Econometric Model of the United States*. Chicago; Rand McNally, and Amsterdam:

emphasis has characterized earlier stabilization models to an even greater relative extent.

A major innovation in the Brookings model was its incorporation of two input-output "translators". The model contains seven producing sectors. It was necessary to convert time series data on gross sector outputs into estimated time series of sector final demands by a reverse application of the input-output relation in the form

$$f = (I - A)x,$$

where f is the vector of sector final demands, $(I - A)$ the input coefficient matrix and x the vector of gross sector outputs. The resulting estimates of sector final demands were then regressed on the relevant GNP components. The matrix $(I - A)$ was obtained by consolidating rows and columns from a detailed input-output transactions matrix for the year 1947.

Price formation in the Brookings model takes place at the level of the seven production sectors, but prices for nine final demand sectors are used in the analysis of final demand. It was necessary, therefore, to develop a set of weights for translating seven sector prices into nine GNP deflators. These weights (with minor adjustments) were given by the regression coefficients of sector final demands upon GNP components described in the preceding paragraph.

The Brookings effort succeeded, therefore, in integrating the input-output or I-O system with the national income accounting or NIA system in a dynamic econometric model.

The causal ordering structure of the model as a whole proved to be approximately block-recursive or block-triangular, with matrices of nonzero elements in the main diagonal and below. A preliminary, approximate version of the causal structure was given by Duesenberry and Klein as follows [6, p. 28]:

| A | | | Fixed business investment, exports |

| B | C | | Other final demand: consumption, inventories, housing, government expenditures (and receipts), imports, orders |

| D | E | F | Sector outputs |

| G | | H | I | Employment and hours |

| | J | | K | L | Labor supply, unemployment |

| | | M | N | O | P | Wages, prices profits |

| Q | R | | | | S | T | Interest, money, other factor shares |

We will not comment further on estimation problems and statistical properties of the Brookings model; the general principles involved are discussed in Chapters 3 and 4 of this book.

Further study of the flow will disclose other features of the Brookings model. Each arrow, in general, represents several equations. Many of the relationships in the model operate with time lags.

The use of quarterly data should throw more light on the mechanisms of inventory cycles and of monetary and fiscal policy than would be possible with annual data. Several sectors of the economy, including agriculture, foreign trade, housing, money and finance, government, and the labor force, are treated in greater detail than in previous econometric models; this permits a clearer and more operational definition of policy instruments. For example, the equations for the government sector use tax *rates* rather than the amount of tax receipts as the true policy variables; they show that some government expenditures (for example, transfer payments) are endogenously determined; and they clearly separate federal expenditures from those of state and local governments.

An interesting by-product of the workshop discussions in 1961 and 1962 was a greatly increased awareness by the participants of the logical and operational differences between a policy model and a forecasting model. The previous emphasis of most of the individual participants had been either upon forecasting or upon analyzing the effects of policies in particular sectors of the economy. Only gradually did a consensus develop that the model as a whole should be to the fullest extent possible structural and policy-oriented. By the end of the 1962 workshop, there appeared to be general agreement that appropriate equations in the model should express the mechanisms by which specific policy instruments did in fact influence other variables, including those which were the targets of stipulated policies. The model should, of course, forecast adequately, but this was by no means its sole or even its primary objective.

11.2.2. *Some Consequences of the Brookings Model Effort*

Some policy simulations with the Brookings model were reported by Fromm and Taubman [15] in 1968, and further results appeared in 1969 in a volume edited by Duesenberry, Fromm, Klein and Kuh [7].

As of 1971, it appears that the Brookings model effort has drastically and irreversibly changed the nature of research on stabilization models. About 20 economists participated in the 1961 and 1962 workshops and contributed directly to the construction of the model. In addition, several other economists visited the workshops and were stimulated by them. Several of the contributors involved graduate assistants or junior staff members in the work on their sectors, or on the tasks of estimation and simulation. Still other graduate students and colleagues participated vicariously through seminars and progress reports by those directly involved. A number of young economists built up expertise during 1963–71 by working on the Brookings model project as such or by working on other fairly large models that were developed under the supervision of Klein at the University of Pennsylvania, Modigliani and Ando at MIT, and De Leeuw and Gramlich at the Federal Reserve Board. By 1971, research groups at a number of U.S. universities were using stabilization models of moderate to large size and at least one private organization was providing forecasting and simulation services on a fee basis involving the use of a large scale model. A new level of professionalism had been achieved.

This poses a question as to how much can usefully be said about stabilization models of the U.S. in the present book, which must cover a wide range of theoretical topics and applications. It seems best to illustrate a number of points of rather general interest and applicability. A truly professional knowledge of stabilization models can only be gained by using one for forecasting and policy simulation or optimization purposes over a period of time, and by participating in efforts to update or improve it in various ways (new data, different functional forms, different lag patterns, different estimation procedures, different degrees of disaggregation in various sectors, new equations to permit the appraisal of hitherto untried policy instruments, and so on).

In illustrating various points we will draw upon other stabilization models of the U.S. in addition to the Brookings model itself.

11.3. Forecasting with a Stabilization Model

During 1963–67, Evans and Klein [9] met quarterly with economists of a group of major U.S. corporations "to assess the near term outlook through the eyes of an econometric model". Preliminary forecasts of economic activity were prepared before each meeting. At the meeting, assumptions about exogenous variables were discussed, along with specific information on strikes, effects of government regulations, market performance, and the like. After the meeting, forecasts were recomputed on the basis of consensus about exogenous variables and special factors.

At the end of the first month of a current quarter, preliminary data for the preceding quarter would be nearly complete. Constant terms for some equations were adjusted so that the model would nearly duplicate the quarter just completed. Then the model was solved for each of eight quarters, the one just beginning and the next seven.

The predictive record of the Wharton–EFU model for one and two quarters in advance during 1963–66 is summarized in Table 11.3. The record is best for GNP, consumption of nondurables and services, and fixed business investment. The record is worst for inventory investment; part of the error

TABLE 11.3

Predictive Record of the Wharton–EFU Model One and Two Quarters Ahead, 1963–66 (in billions of current dollars)

Variable[a]	One Quarter Ahead:		Two Quarters Ahead:	
	Average absolute change	Average absolute error	Average absolute change	Average absolute error
C_{ns}	5.3	1.6	10.7	1.6
C_d	2.0	1.5	2.3	1.9
I_p	1.5	1.1	2.9	1.3
I_h	0.9	1.0	1.3	1.4
ΔI_i	2.1	2.4	2.1	3.0
F	1.2	1.2	1.3	1.6
G	2.5	1.8	4.9	2.4
GNP	10.8	2.3	21.4	4.3

[a] Symbols are defined as follows: C_{ns} = consumption of non-durables and services, C_d = consumption of durables, I_p = investment in fixed plant and equipment, I_h = investment in residential instruction, ΔI_i = inventory investment, F = net foreign balance, G = government purchases of goods and services, and GNP = gross national product.

Source: M.K. Evans and L. R. Klein "Experience with Econometric Analysis of the U.S. 'Konjunktur' Position," in *Is the Business Cycle Obsolete?* Edited by M. Bronfenbrenner. New York: John Wiley & Sons, 1969, Chapter 12, pp. 366–367.

was attributed to erratic fluctuations due to stockpiling in advance of expected steel strikes and then decreasing stocks when strikes did not occur. Attempts to adjust for this factor were not successful.

TABLE 11.4

Predictive Record of the Wharton–EFU Model Annual Forecasts made during the 4th Quarter of the Previous Year (in billions of current dollars)

Variable	1963[a]			1964		
	Actual change	Predicted change	Error	Actual change	Predicted change	Error
C_{ns}	13.6	14.1	0.5	19.6	19.2	−0.4
C_d	4.6	2.6	−2.0	4.9	0.9	−4.0
I_p	3.2	4.9	1.7	5.6	7.7	2.1
I_h	1.0	−0.8	−1.8	0.8	0.3	−0.5
ΔI_i	1.2	1.9	0.7	−0.7	2.9	3.6
F	0.0	−1.1	−1.1	2.6	−0.5	−3.1
G	6.4	9.4	3.0	5.9	10.4	4.5
GNP	30.0	31.0	1.0	38.7	40.9	2.2

Variable	1965			1966[c]		
	Actual[b] change	Predicted change	Error	Actual change	Predicted change	Error
C_{ns}	23.7	22.9	−0.8	28.5	26.7	−1.8
C_d	5.1	3.9	−1.2	4.3	2.6	−1.7
I_p	5.4	5.9	0.5	9.1	10.6	1.5
I_h	0.1	0.7	0.6	−2.6	−1.2	1.4
ΔI_i	2.9	0.0	−2.9	4.0	−1.8	−2.2
F	−1.3	−0.2	1.1	−1.9	1.1	3.0
G	7.0	5.8	−1.2	17.9	13.8	−4.1
GN	42.9	39.0	−3.9	59.3	55.4	−3.9

[a] Forecast actually made in 1963, as model was not available before then.

[b] Actual data based on extrapolation of old data.

[c] Forecast made at the end of January 1966. For definition of symbols see Table 11.3.

Source: M.K. Evans and L.R. Klein, "Experience with Econometric Analysis of the U.S. 'Konjunktur' Position," in *Is the Business Cycle Obsolete?* Edited by M. Bronfenbrenner. New York: John Wiley & Sons, 1969, Chap. 12, p. 369.

Table 11.4 summarizes the predictive record of the Wharton-EFU model for annual forecasts made during the fourth quarter of the preceding year. The forecasts of GNP and consumption of nondurables and services look very good; so do those for fixed business investment and (on the surface) for government purchases of goods and services. It appears that inventory investment and the net foreign balance are inherently more difficult to predict than most of the other variables. Klein and Evans suggest that the annual forecasts are more important than the others because of the preponderance of calendar-year planning by both business and government. They also note that forecasts made in the fourth quarter of the calendar year are more accurate than forecasts made at other times of the year, because more is generally known at the end of the year than in mid-year about monetary and fiscal policies for the next four quarters.

Tables 11.3 and 11.4 deal with *unconditional* forecasts. Errors in forecasting the endogenous variables reflect (1) errors in forecasting the exogenous variables, and (2) errors in translating specified values of the exogenous variables into corresponding values of the endogenous ones. Once a classification of variables into exogenous and endogenous categories has been made, only errors of the second kind reflect on the model as such.

11.4. Multiplier Analysis with a Stabilization Model

A central feature of Keynes' original model of macroeconomic activity was *the* multiplier [24]. In a large scale econometric model there are many mechanisms formally analogous to the Keynesian multiplier. Some of them are essentially disaggregations of the Keynesian multiplier; others are ratios of final effects to "first round" effects of almost any instrument upon almost any target variable.

Evans and Klein [9; pp. 361–362] state that:

> In modern econometric analysis, the multiplier concept has been extended to encompass the effects of change in any exogenous variable, parameter, or combination of the two. For a simple change in any exogenous variable we compute
>
> $$\frac{Y_{it}^d - Y_{it}^c}{X_{jt}^d - X_{jt}^c}$$
>
> as the multiplier expression that shows the change in Y_{it} (Y_{it}^d = "disturbed" value; Y_{it}^c = "control" value) caused by a change in X_{jt} (X_{jt}^d = "disturbed" value; X_{jt}^c = "control" value). These multipliers can be evaluated at *impact* (first time period), *dynamically* (at points along the simulation path), or in equilibrium (after the simulation has come to long-run equilibrium) . . .

11.5. Policy Simulations with a Stabilization Model

Evans and Klein ran a number of simulations for a (hypothetical) 40 quarter period, starting from the initial position of the U.S. economy in the fourth quarter of 1965. First, a "control solution" was calculated in which values of government expenditures and other exogenous variables were chosen to keep the unemployment rate at about four per cent. Then, a

TABLE 11.5

Changes in Selected Target Variables per $1 Billion Change in Specified Instrument Variables, Measured in Fourth Quarter after Value of Instrument is Changed.

	Target Variables:					
Instrument Variables[a]	GNP (billions of 1958 dollars)	Unemployment rate (per cent of labor force)	Implicit GNP deflator (1958 = 100)	Fixed business investment (billions of 1958 dollars)	Personal disposable income (billions of current dollars)	Corporate profits (billions of current dollars)
I. Measured in Fourth Quarter after Change[b]						
G	2.03	0.23	0.05	0.24	1.27	0.67
G_d	2.10	0.20	0.07	0.30	1.35	0.83
F_e	1.99	0.20	0.00	0.20	1.07	0.64
T_p	1.25	0.07	0.03	0.27	1.71	0.68
T_b	1.54	0.09	−0.10	0.34	0.56	1.43
T_c	0.22	0.02	0.01	0.06	0.27	0.11
FR	1.50	0.15	0.01	0.25	0.77	0.58
II. Measured in Eighth Quarter after Change[b]						
G	2.03	0.22	0.05	0.31	1.25	0.79
G_d	1.88	0.17	0.08	0.38	1.17	0.93
F_e	2.02	0.19	0.01	0.29	1.09	0.71
T_p	1.32	0.07	0.04	0.33	1.72	0.83
T_b	1.54	0.07	−0.07	0.48	0.64	1.49
T_c	0.38	0.02	0.01	0.15	0.38	0.21
FR	2.10	0.12	0.08	1.20	1.08	1.31

[a] For definitions of instrument variables, see text, pp. 376 .

[b] Selected from appropriate rows of Tables 12.6, 12.7, 12.8, 12.9 and 12.10 of Evans and Klein [9].

Source: M.K. Evans and L.R. Klein, "Experience with Econometric Analysis of the U.S. 'Konjunktur' Position," in *Is the Business Cycle Obsolete?* Edited by M. Bronfenbrenner. New York: John Wiley and Sons, 1969, Chapter 12, pp. 370–374.

number of "disturbed" solutions were calculated, in which each of a number of exogenous variables (separately) was changed by $1 billion ($G$, G_d, F_e), or by the equivalent of $1 billion under the conditions of 1965–IV (T_p, T_c, T_b, FR). The symbols stand for the following variables: G = government defense expenditures; G_d = government nondefense expenditures; F_e = value of exports; T_p = personal income tax rates; T_c = corporate income tax rates; T_b = excise tax rates; and FR = free reserves of banks.

In the simulations, expenditure and export variables were *increased* by $1 billion, tax variables were *decreased* by the equivalent of $1 billion, and free reserves (the amount of money banks have to lend) were *increased* by the equivalent of $1 billion.

The resulting changes in constant-dollar GNP per $1 billion change in the above variables are shown in Table 11.5. Similar tables are also presented by Evans and Klein for changes in (1) the unemployment rate, (2) the implicit GNP deflator, (3) fixed business investment, (4) personal disposable income, and (5) corporate profits.

In Table 11.5 the government expenditure and export instruments seem to have very similar effects on real GNP. A reduction in excise taxes seems to have a larger positive effect on real GNP than does a reduction in personal income taxes for the first 8 or 9 quarters but about the same effect thereafter. A reduction in corporate income taxes has a much smaller effect on GNP than do the other instruments. An increase in free reserves seems to have no effect in the first two quarters; from the fifth quarter on, its effect is about the same as those of the government expenditure and export variables.

Table 11.5 shows changes in selected target variables per $1 billion equivalent change in each of several specified instrument variables. (Value of exports, F_e, may be simply a "data" variable, unless we assume that the $1 billion initial increase in exports results from some deliberate ,but unspecified policy action by the U.S. government.) In most cases the multipliers measured four and eight quarters after the initial change are about the same, so we will comment only on the fourth quarter measures.

Each row of Table 11.5 may be viewed as the derivative of a welfare function,

$$W = f(y_1, y_2, y_3, y_4, y_5, y_6),$$

with respect to an instrument variable; thus

$$\frac{\partial W}{\partial G} = \frac{\partial W}{\partial y_1} \cdot \frac{\partial y_1}{\partial G} + \frac{\partial W}{\partial y_2} \cdot \frac{\partial y_2}{\partial G} + \cdots + \frac{\partial W}{\partial G} \cdot \frac{\partial y_6}{\partial G}$$

is the derivative of W with respect to G. The figures in the G row of Table 11.5, Section I, are the values of the $\partial y_i/\partial G$ for $i = 1, 2, 3, 4, 5, 6$; the partial derivatives $\partial W/\partial y_i$, $i = 1, 2, 3, 4, 5, 6$, are not specified. In principle, a policy-maker could assign weights w_i (per unit change in y_i) to each of the y_i; then each row in the table would yield a value

$$\frac{\partial W}{\partial X_j} = \sum_{i=1}^{6} w_i \cdot \frac{\partial y_i}{\partial X_j},$$

where X_j stands for the jth instrument variable.

For reasonable selections of the weights, it appears that the first three rows of Table 11.5 would yield quite similar values of $\partial W/\partial X_j$. The monetary instrument, FR, would apparently have a more favorable effect on fixed private investment (and presumably on economic growth) than would the expenditure instruments when compared at the eighth quarter but not at the fourth. The three tax instruments have widely different absolute and relative effects on personal disposable income and corporate profits. Corporate income taxes have less effect on the targets generally than do other instruments. The initial change (a decrease in excise taxes) leads to a decrease in the price level as measured by the implicit GNP deflator; initial changes in the other instruments all tend to increase the implicit GNP deflator slightly to moderately.

Thus, each section of Table 11.5 is a target and instrument matrix of the Tinbergen-Theil type. The Wharton-EFU model contains some nonlinear relationships, so the $\partial y_i/\partial X_j$ values ($i = 1, 2, 3, 4, 5, 6$) and $j = 1, 2, 3, 4, 5, 6, 7$) would change somewhat as the values of the y_i and X_j changed from one actual or hypothetical situation to another. It also seems likely that the weights $\partial W/\partial y_i$ would change somewhat from one situation to another, as suggested by Van Eijk and Sandee [42] and Theil [38].

Some extensive policy simulations and multiplier analyses with the Brookings model were reported by Fromm and Taubman [15] in 1968. These may be compared with the results obtained by Evans and Klein [9] using the Wharton-EFU model.

Fromm and Taubman also calculated indexes of utility for a number of policies, applying different forms of utility functions and different sets of weights. In addition, they compared actual utility indexes over a number of quarters with averages of utility indexes over the same quarters discounted to the beginning of the simulation period at various annual rates.

Three utility functions were tried, as follows:

(a) Linear $\qquad\qquad u_t = \Sigma_i\beta_i x_i$

(b) Cobb-Douglas $\quad\ \ u_t = \pi x_i^{\beta i}$

(c) CES $\qquad\qquad\ \ u_t = (\Sigma_i\beta_i x_i^\delta)^{1/\delta},$

where u_t is the utility in period t of the ratios of simulation to original solution values (x_i). For the CES, δ was set at 0.5, -0.5, -1.0, and 2.0.

The following sets of weights were used:

(a) Equal weights, $\beta_i = 1$ for all i;

(b) Proportional weights, $\beta_i =$ average share in real GNP for expenditure items (with one exception) and 0.5 for all other items.

Six arguments (x_i) were employed, with the following proportional weights for each:

(a) Real personal consumption expenditures $(\beta = 0.67)$;

(b) Real gross private fixed domestic investment $(\beta = 0.13)$;

(c) Real government expenditures $(\beta = 0.19)$;

(d) The reciprocal of the rate of unemployment $(\beta = 0.5)$;

(e) Current dollar government surplus $(\beta = 0.10)$;

(f) The reciprocal of the implicit price deflator for GNP.

The utility of the outcomes was aggregated over time according to the following formula:

$$u_0 = \sum_{t=1}^{m} \left[\frac{u_t}{(1 + r)^t} \right]$$

where r is a time preference rate (4, 6, 8 and 10 per cent rates were used) and m is a time horizon limit.

Finally, the utility of the variance of outcomes (u_v) was calculated along with a total utility which was equal to the sum of the outcome and variance utilities,

$$u_T = u_0 + u_v.$$

The rationale for this comes from the literature on portfolio selection, which considers trade-offs between the expected values and the variances of alternative investments. The relative weights assigned to u_0 and u_v would, in principle, vary as between policy-makers with different attitudes toward risk aversion.

Table 11.6 presents a few of the calculations by Fromm and Taubman based on a linear utility function. The value of the utility index in 1960–III for "income tax cut plus monetary policy" was taken as 100.0 and the other values were expressed as index numbers on that base.

TABLE 11.6

Examples of Utility Index Calculations and Rank Orders of Alternative Policies, United States, 1960–III through 1962–IV. (Linear utility functions and proportional weights).

Alternative Policies	Utility Indexes		Rank Order of Utility Indexes	
	In 1962–IV	Average of 10 quarters discounted to 1960–II at 6%	In 1962–IV	Average, 10 quarters discounted
	μ_t	$\mu_{0/10}$	μ_t	$\mu_{0/10}$
Government				
Durables expenditures	107.7	97.4	4	4
Nondurables expenditures	107.1	96.7	5	7
Employment	106.4	97.7	6	5
Construction	107.9	97.7	3	3
Income tax cut	104.4	94.7	11	14
Income tax cut plus monetary policy	105.5	95.1	8	12
Reserve requirements reduction	108.6	98.8	1	2
Open market operations	108.6	98.8	2	1
Excise tax cut 1 (small)				
100 per cent pass along	103.8	95.4	12	6
80 per cent pass along	103.7	95.3	13	8
50 per cent pass along	103.3	95.0	14	9
Excise tax cut 2 (large)				
100 per cent pass along	105.6	95.6	7	10
80 per cent pass along	105.1	95.3	9	11
50 per cent pass along	104.6	95.0	10	13

Source: G. Fromm and P. Taubman, *Policy Simulations with an Econometric Model.* Washington: The Brookings Institution, 1968, Tables 5.5, 5.6 and 5.7, pp. 117–119.

The figures in Column (1) refer to a single quarter, 1962–IV. They are not discounted. As every policy resulted in some increase in the target variables relative to the original solution values from 1960–III to 1962–IV, all the index numbers in 1962–IV are greater than 100. The figures in Column (2) are an average for 10 quarters, with the utility index in each discounted back to 1960–II at an annual rate of 6 per cent. Thus, the averages of the original utility indexes would center between 1961–III and 1961–IV at values of about 103 to 106; discounting back from the midpoint of 1961–III and 1961–IV to 1960–II would reduce those values by about 8 per cent to a range of 95 to 98 or so, as in Column (2).

Fromm and Taubman suggest that the indexes in Columns (1) and (2) should not be treated as cardinal measures but should be used only to give the alternative policies a rank order; this is done for Column (1) in Column (3).

Column (4) is not a direct ranking of Column (2), but is based on the sum of the discounted outcome utility in Column (2) and a variance utility. These two operations do not significantly change the relative rankings of different expenditure policies within the set of expenditure policies (first four rows) from Column (3) to Column (4). With one exception, the policies ranked from 6 to 14 in Column (4) had Column (2) indexes within the narrow range of 94.7 to 95.6, less than a single index point; thus the corresponding rankings in Column (4) are inherently somewhat unstable.

The authors summarize their illustrative calculations with utility functions as follows [15, pp. 123–124]:

> ... While the three types of utility functions used to evaluate policies are ones commonly employed, their choice is still quite arbitrary. Unfortunately, there is no evidence available regarding how the forms, arguments, or weights of these functions correspond to the preferences of the Administration, the Congress, or any segment of the public. Thus, only future research will provide a check on the present conclusions.
>
>   These orderings of policies are not to be regarded as a prescription for government decisionmakers. Aside from any questions of the validity and accuracy of the model, neither the multipliers nor the utility functions ... reflect the many other considerations which impinge on a policy choice. Such issues as the degree of government intervention, intergroup and interregional inequities, implications for long-run resource allocation, and other social costs and benefits which are difficult to quantify must be taken into account.
>
>   ... Even within the model framework, the desirability of a *type* of policy is not independent of the initial conditions under which a choice is made, nor is it independent of the degree to which the policy is to be undertaken. (Both these dependencies stem from the nonlinear nature of the behavioral relationships in the economy.) For example, adopting an easy monetary policy when credit is already plentiful will not provide as much stimulus as when credit is highly rationed. ... If the illustrative

utility functions are accepted, the rankings described provide a tentative indication of how policies might fare in general; however, they need not hold in any particular instance.[1]

11.6. Other References on Stabilization Models

A conference volume edited by Bronfenbrenner [1] in 1969, *Is the Business Cycle Obsolete?*, contains useful contributions by economists from many countries. We have already mentioned the article by Gordon [18]; Hickman's paper [21] is a valuable survey and comparison of the dynamic properties of 16 macroeconometric models for 10 countries.

A 1966 article by Nerlove [36] presents a tabular survey of a large number of macroeconometric models. A three volume work by Kirschen and several associates [25], *Economic Policy in Our Time*, published in 1964, describes and appraises the design and implementation of economic policy from 1949 to 1961 in eight European countries and the United States. Volume I, *General Theory*, makes extensive use of Tinbergen's ideas, though with some differences in terminology. All three volumes are valuable both as history and analysis; little official use was made of econometric models during the period covered.

Two articles by de Leeuw and Gramlich in 1968 and 1969 describe the Federal Research Board-MIT econometric model [3] and use it to identify the channels and simulate the effects of monetary policy. The financial sector was displayed in greater detail than in the Brookings and Wharton-EFU models (as they stood in 1968–69), and de Leeuw and Gramlich found higher multipliers for monetary instruments than had appeared in other models of the U.S.

Jorgenson and his associates have done outstanding work on models of investment behaviour; we cite here a 1967 article on investment behavior in U.S. manufacturing by Jorgenson and Stephenson [23] and a 1970 article on the predictive performance of econometric models of quarterly investment behavior by Jorgenson, Hunter and Nadiri [22].

The articles [3] and [4] by de Leeuw and Gramlich, already cited, are also significant in another context. They illustrate the increasing use of econometric models by U.S. government, and quasi-government agencies in the 1960's. The Federal Reserve-MIT model, and a revision or variant called the Federal Reserve-MIT-Penn model, reflects cooperation between an excellent

---

[1] Two other types of simulation in the context of control-theoretic models are discussed in Chapter 2.

staff group in the Federal Reserve Board and leading university economists. A 1966 article by Liebenberg, Hirsch and Popkin [35] reported progress on a quarterly econometric model of the U.S. being developed by the U.S. Commerce Department's Office of Business Economics. A somewhat related achievement of the Office of Business Economics is reflected in a series of articles by Goldman, Marimont, Vaccara [17] and other staff members on the 1958 input-output study of the United States, published during 1964–65.

Another evidence of broadening expertise in the design and use of stabilization models in the U.S. is Evans' textbook, *Macroeconomic Activity: Theory, Forecasting and Control* [8], published in 1969. Designed for Junior and senior undergraduates and beginning graduate students, it integrates macroeconomic theory and policy with corresponding sectors, equations, simulations and predictions based on the Wharton-EFU model.

Fox's submodel of the agricultural sector [13] of the Brookings model contains a number of useful features. One of these is an explicit presentation of the causal ordering matrices for two blocks of equations determining farm prices and farm income respectively and for the 15 equation submodel as a whole. Another is a somewhat sophisticated use of a priori information on elasticities and cross-elasticities of demand for 24 foods to arrive at aggregative equations on consumer demand for food in the Brookings model which would be compatible with a much more detailed model of the agricultural sector in current use by agricultural economists.

A 1956 paper by Fox on the contribution of farm price support programs to general economic stability [11] presented an analysis of the behavior of farm prices and income under alternative price support programs during a simulated severe recession. The econometric structure of the agricultural sector was set forth in considerable detail, based on earlier work on demand analysis and interindustry relationships by the author. Price support measures under consideration by Congress were also applied in detail. Interactions between agriculture and the rest of the economy were represented by a small macroeconometric model containing 11 endogenous variables which were related to one another by 16 coefficients. Exogenous impacts upon the system were limited to changes in the farm price support program. The causal ordering pattern, following Simon [37], was specified. The model included a multiplier of 2.0 connecting exogenous changes in (equivalent) expenditures to changes in GNP. When all of the implicit multipliers in the model were taken into account, a policy which directly increased farm prices by 10 per cent would evidently have led to a total increase in farm prices of 12.3 per cent. This paper, presented at a conference in May 1954, was the earliest attempt to appraise farm price support programs as potential built-in stabilizers by means of a formal (though small scale) macroeconometric model.

11.7. Present Status and Prospects for Large Scale Stabilization Models of the United States as of 1971

The possibilities suggested by Fox [10] in 1956 have to a large extent been achieved. In a 1971 article, Klein [28] refers to "a general 'take-off' in econometric research in the 1960's, possibly beginning with the late 1950 s:

> New estimators were invented; new methods of lag distributions were explored; the methods of spectral analysis were introduced into econometrics; model building became more ambitious; estimated models were being used by many public and private bodies; old nagging problems of nonlinearities were overcome . . .
>
> The great flurry of activity that characterized the ending of the 60's for econometrics has been due in large part to the computer. It is safe to say that this powerful instrument has now been harnessed for the needs of the subject. . . . What formerly seemed out of reach is now accepted practice. The computer has radically changed the lives of econometricians and the bigger part of the change occurred in the latter part of the 60's.

Looking forward into the 1970's, Klein stated:

> At the close of the last decade two significant developments were imminent: (1) the creation of large data banks of economic statistics; (2) the use of remote access computer consoles. As usage of such systems develops, we can look forward to large public data files of consistently defined and completely updated socio-economic statistics . . .
>
> . . . Econometricians are likely to come forward now with applications of their own design and objective from applications of control theory and public policy optimization. Instead of passive observation and prediction, there should be more searching for acceptable loss or gain functions that are to be optimized subject to the restrictions of an estimated model. In this connection, a new problem must be faced soon, namely, on accounting for feedback influences of econometric results on economic performance . . .
>
> With the passage of time, the subtle role of Tinbergen in shaping the development of econometrics emerges in more and more places. . . . His principal theoretical contribution in the postwar era has been in the formalization and quantification of the theory of economic policy, using models to show how instruments can be used to reach macro-

economic targets. . . . The formal use of the Tinbergen approach is now possible for large scale models and should undoubtedly be the focus of a significant amount of future econometric research.

11.7.1. *Some Remaining Problems*

Great progress has been made in the development and use of stabilization models of the U.S. economy since 1955. But problems remain.

R.A. Gordon [18] in a 1969 article considered possible sources of change in dynamic properties of the U.S. economy under the following headings: (1) changes in relationships; (2) changes in behavior of exogenous variables; and (3) changes in pattern of disturbances. He concluded as follows:

> Some structural changes have occurred in the last decade that tend to make the U.S. economy more stable, and recent developments in the field of stabilization policy have moved the economy further in the same direction. But it is important to remember that the economic system is dynamic and subject to almost continuous shock. Imperfect foresight and mistakes of judgment, the strains and stresses of the political process that so often lead to second-best solutions, and limited knowledge of the internal dynamics of the system all suggest that, even with the improvements in stabilization policy of the last six years, the United States has not seen its last recession.

The Brookings model was originally estimated using 1948–60 data. It and similar models are re-estimated from time to time; in principle, earlier years can be dropped as later ones are added, but there remains some uncertainty as to what the true relationships in the economy will be during Years 2 and 3 beyond the last year of data to which the model was fitted.

There have been major cycles in the U.S. birthrate during the past four decades. Once a cohort has been born it is easy to forecast how many will reach t years of age t years hence. But it is not so easy to forecast the political consequences of a major change in the age distribution of voters or the economic consequences of apparent changes in value systems and life styles.

The world political and military postures of the U.S. and other nations have also created major cycles in research and development expenditures for defense, military and space programs. An emphasis in the U.S. from about 1957 to 1967 on expanding scientific manpower also contributed to a major cycle in the training of Ph.D.'s in science and engineering.

The rapid change in the technology of econometric research associated with the computer has been paralleled by changes affecting many other activities and occupational groups. Farm technology in the U.S. has hastened the migration of millions of people from rural to urban locations and has contributed (with other factors) to the concentration of blacks in the central cities of the largest metropolitan areas. Transporation technology has contributed to major redistributions of total population, income groups and types of employment within and between metropolitan areas. Political jurisdictions rarely coincide with commuting fields and their socioeconomic community-of-interest areas.

There was considerable evidence as of 1971 that the executive branch of the U.S. government was not well organized for the formulation and implementation of domestic economic policies. The president proposed in 1971 that a number of departments and independent agencies be regrouped into four major departments concerned respectively with (1) human resources, (2) community resources, (3) natural resources, and (4) economic development. This proposal had not been implemented as of December 1971.

The coexistence in the U.S. during 1970 and 1971 of a 6 per cent rate of unemployment with substantial rates of increase in prices and wages reflected structural problems in the areas of industrial and labor organization and collective bargaining. Collective bargaining was spreading rapidly in the public sector, particularly at state and local levels.

Most of the developments mentioned in this section involve cumulative processes taking place over a period of years. In general, these changes cannot be represented by linear or exponential trends; some may be approximately logistic or at least monotonic; some, like the birthrate, may increase for a while and then decrease.

In principle, the net effects of these developments could be translated into changes in the coefficients (and hence multipliers) of a stabilization model. However, it seems important that the same experts (whether on individual sectors of the economy or on the economy as a whole) should be aware of both the long-term or structural changes and the short-term problems of forecasting and stabilization policy.

The processes we have mentioned may have differential effects upon sectors (industries), occupations, and regions. So far, stabilization models of the U.S. have given some attention to disaggregation by sectors but not by occupations or regions.

Labor unions have some relevance to economic policy at both sectoral and occupational levels. State and local governments have important influences on their own economic and cultural development but do not generally wield instruments of stabilization policy.

Chapter 12 will emphasize a socioeconomic basis for regional disaggregation of the United States into commuting fields or multi-county functional economic areas (FEA's). It will be argued that, while fiscal and monetary instruments will continue to be the mainstays of federal stabilization policy, labor market instruments should be available to responsible officials in each of some 500 multicounty economic areas and metropolitan subareas. A new concept of local government will be emphasized.

Great progress has been made in modeling economic systems. More research is needed in the formulation of objective functions for stabilization models at national, international, and state or regional (FEA) levels. At some point we should experiment with objective functions including noneconomic as well as economic components with an explicit basis in social science research, going somewhat beyond the pragmatic approach taken by Tinbergen [40] in 1952. Some suggestions along this line have been made in Section 5.4.

REFERENCES

[1] BRONFENBRENNER, M. (editor). *Is the Business Cycle Obsolete?*. New York: John Wiley and Sons, 1969.

[2] COPELAND, M. A. "Tracing Money Flows Through the United States Economy", *American Economic Review*, Volume 37, Proceedings Issue, (May 1947), pp. 31–49.

[3] DE LEEUW, F., and GRAMLICH, E. "The Federal Reserve–MIT Econometric Model", *Federal Reserve Bulletin*, Volume 54, No. 1 (January 1968), pp. 11–40.

[4] ——. "The Channels of Monetary Policy", *Federal Reserve Bulletin*, Volume 55, No. 6 (June 1969), pp. 472–491.

[5] DUESENBERRY, J. S., ECKSTEIN, O., and FROMM, G. "A Simulation of the United States Economy in Recession", *Econometrica*, Volume 28, No. 4 (October 1960), pp. 749–809.

[6] DUESENBERRY, J. S., FROMM, G., KLEIN, L. R., and KUH, E. (editors). *The Brookings Quarterly Econometric Model of the United States*. Amsterdam and Chicago: North-Holland Publishing Co. and Rand McNally, 1965.

[7] ——. *The Brookings Model: Some Further Results*. Amsterdam and Chicago: North-Holland Publishing Co. and Rand McNally, 1969.

[8] EVANS, M. K. *Macroeconomic Activity: Theory, Forecasting and Control*. New York: Harper and Rowe, 1969.

[9] ——, and KLEIN, L. R. "Experience with Econometric Analysis of the U.S. 'Konjunktur' Position", in *Is the Business Cycle Obsolete?*. Edited by M. Bronfenbrenner. New York: John Wiley and Sons, 1969, Chapter 12.

[10] FOX, K. A. "Econometric Models of the United States", *Journal of Political Economy*, Volume LXIV, No. 2 (April 1956), pp. 128–142.

[11] ——. "The Contribution of Farm Price Support Programs to General Economic Stability", in *Policies to Combat Depression*. Princeton, N. J.: Princeton University Press, 1956.

[12] ——. "Econometric Models of the United States", in *Econometric Analysis for Public Policy*. Ames: Iowa State University Press, 1958, Chapter 12.

[13] ——. "A Submodel of the Agricultural Sector", in Duesenberry et al. (editors), *The Brookings Quarterly Econometric Model of the United States*. Amsterdam and Chicago: North-Holland Publishing Co. and Rand McNally, 1965, Chapter 12.

[14] FRISCH, R. *Statistical Confluence Analysis by Means of Complete Regression Systems.* Oslo: Universitets Okonomiske Institutet, 1934.

[15] FROMM, G., and TAUBMAN, P. *Policy Simulations with an Econometric Model*. Amsterdam and Washington: North-Holland Publishing Co. and the Brookings Institution, 1968.

[16] GOLDBERGER, A. S. *Impact Multipliers and Dynamic Properties of the Klein–Goldberger Model*. Amsterdam: North-Holland Publishing Co., 1959.

[17] GOLDMAN, M. R., MARIMONT, M. L., and VACCARA, B. N. "The Inter-Industry Structure of the United States—A Report on the 1958 Input–Output Study", *Survey of Current Business*, November 1964, pp. 10–29. (See also May 1965 issue, pp. 13–24, September 1965 issue, pp. 33–49, and October 1965 issue, pp. 7–20, 28).

[18] GORDON, R. A. "The Stability of the U.S. Economy", in *Is the Business Cycle Obsolete?* Edited by M. Bronfenbrenner. New York: John Wiley and Sons, 1969, Chapter 1.

[19] HAAVELMO, T. "The Statistical Implications of a System of Simultaneous Equations", *Econometrica*, Volume 11, No. 1 (January 1943), pp. 1–12.

[20] ——. "The Probability Approach in Econometrics", *Econometrica*, Supplement, Volume 12 (July 1944).

[21] HICKMAN, B. G. "Dynamic Properties of Macroeconometric Models: An International Comparison", in *Is the Business Cycle Obsolete?* Edited by M. Bronfenbrenner. New York: John Wiley and Sons, 1969, Chapter 13.

[22] JORGENSON, D. W., HUNTER, J., and NADIRI, M. I. "The Predictive Performance of Econometric Models of Quarterly Investment Behavior", *Econometrica*, Volume 38, No. 2 (March 1970), pp. 213–224.

[23] JORGENSON, D. W., and STEPHENSON, J. A. "Investment Behavior in U.S. Manufacturing, 1947–1960", *Econometrica*, Volume 35, No. 2 (April 1967), pp. 169–220.

[24] KEYNES, J. M. *The General Theory of Employment, Interest and Money*. New York: Harcourt, Brace and Co., 1936.

[25] KIRSCHEN, E. S. and ASSOCIATES. *Economic Policy in Our Time*. Volume I: *General Theory*; Volumes II and III: *Country Studies*. Amsterdam and Chicago: North-Holland Publishing Co. and Rand McNally, 1964.

[26] KLEIN, L. R. "The Use of Econometric Models as a Guide to Economic Policy", *Econometrica*, Volume 15, No. 2 (April 1947), pp. 111–151.

[27] ——. *Economic Fluctuations in the United States, 1921–1941*. New York: John Wiley and Sons, 1950.

[28] ——. "Whither Econometrics?", *Journal of the American Statistical Association*, Volume 66, No. 334 (June 1971), pp. 415–421.

[29] ——, and GOLDBERGER, A. S. *An Econometric Model of the United States, 1929–1952*. Amsterdam: North-Holland Publishing Co., 1955.

[30] KOOPMANS, T. J. (editor). *Statistical Inference in Dynamic Economic Models*. New York: John Wiley and Sons, Inc., 1950.

[31] KUZNETS, S. S. *National Income, 1919–32*. National Bureau Bulletin 49. New York: National Bureau of Economic Research, 1934.

[32] ——. *National Income and Capital Formation,* 1919–1935. New York: National Bureau of Economic Research, 1937.

[33] LEONTIEF, W. W. "Quantitative Input and Output Relations in the Economic System of the United States", *Review of Economics and Statistics,* Volume 18, (August 1936), pp. 105–125.

[34] ——. *The Structure of American Economy, 1919–1929: An Empirical Application of Equilibrium Analysis.* Cambridge: Harvard University Press, 1941. (See also second edition, enlarged, 1951, including information for 1939).

[35] LIEBENBERG, M., HIRSCH, A. A., and POPKIN, J. "A Quarterly Econometric Model of the United States: A Progress Report", *Survey of Current Business,* May 1966, pp. 13–39.

[36] NERLOVE, M. "A Tabular Survey of Macroeconometric Models", *International Economic Review,* Volume 52, 1966, pp. 127–175.

[37] SIMON, H. A. "Causal Ordering and Identifiability", in *Studies in Econometric Method.* Edited by Hood, W. C., and Koopmans, T. C. (Cowles Commission Monograph No. 14.) New York: John Wiley and Sons, 1953, Chapter 3.

[38] THEIL, H. *Economic Forecasts and Policy.* Amsterdam: North-Holland Publishing Co., 1958, pp. 414–424. (See also second edition, 1961).

[39] TINBERGEN, J. *Statistical Testing of Business Cycle Theories,* Volume II of *Business Cycles in the United States of America, 1919–1932.* Geneva: League of Nations, 1939.

[40] ——. *On the Theory of Economic Policy.* Amsterdam: North-Holland Publishing Co., 1952, revised edition, 1955.

[41] ——. *Economic Policy: Principles and Design.* Amsterdam: North-Holland Publishing Co., 1956.

[42] VAN EIJK, C. J., and SANDEE, J. "Quantitative Determination of an Optimum Economic Policy", *Econometrica,* Volume 27, No. 1 (January 1959), pp. 1–13.

Chapter 12

STABILIZATION POLICY, REGIONAL GROWTH AND PLANNING

This chapter attempts to specify three interrelated aspects of economic policy toward stabilization and growth in a regional framework: (a) the question of useful integration of economic models for small regions with an over-all econometric model of a national economy with special reference to the U.S., (b) the stability and optimality characteristics of a national stabilization policy that has a regional focus and (c) a short review of the general characteristics of the regional growth models that have been developed recently for underdeveloped economies. These three aspects are treated separately in the following three sections.

12.1. Regional Aspects of National Models [1]

This section has only limited objectives, and these are primarily operational rather than theoretical. Our object is to show how a number of lines of empirical research may be brought together to yield a consistent and useful integration of economic models for small areas with an econometric model of a national economy. For concreteness, we will draw on the Brookings-SSRC econometric model described in Chapter 11 and will relate it to actual and hypothetical data for regions and small areas in the U.S. The principles should have general applicability, however, to most countries of sufficient geographic area (relative to the prevailing modes of transportation) to include a number of labor markets which are relatively independent of one another in the short run.

The argument will be developed in terms of quarterly models which lend themselves most readily to a short-run stabilization focus. However, once an integrated set of area models is developed for short-run analysis, it should

---

[1] This section is based on a number of papers written by one of the authors during 1959–1964. See Fox [12, pp. 114–158; 13, pp. 1–34, and 15].

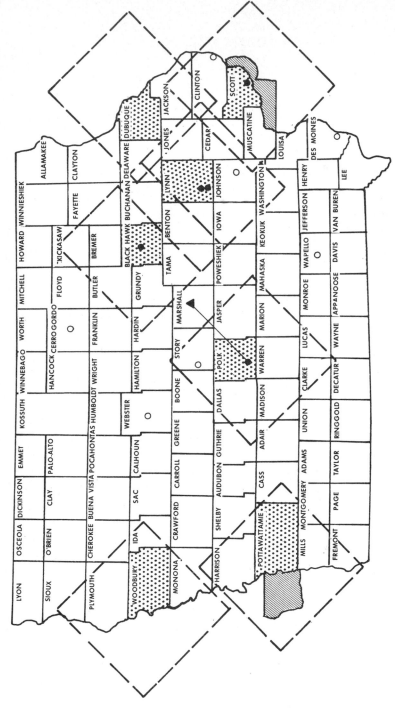

390

Fig. 12.1   50-mile commuting distances from the central business districts of Iowa SMSA central cities of 50 000 people or more in 1960. Each shaded county or pair of shaded contiguous counties is an SMSA.

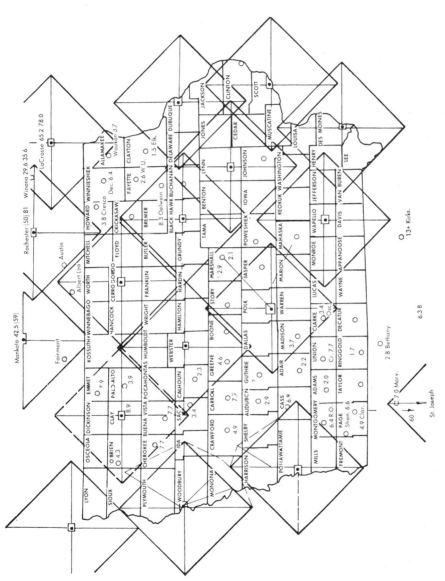

Fig. 12.2. 50-mile commuting distances from the central business districts of all FEA (including SMSA) central cities in or near Iowa. Central cities selected on the basis of range of economic activities performed and relationship to surrounding area.

be relatively easy to develop a consistent set of models for the same areas but adapted to economic planning and development. A network of area (and national) models would give needed focus to the collection, processing and publication of many subsystems of economic data which are currently used for special purposes and in isolation one from another.

The various lines of research which favor such a synthesis for the U.S. in the near future include (1) the Brookings-SSRC econometric model of the national economy discussed in Chapter 11; (2) a tabulation of employment in thirty-one industrial sectors for every county in the U.S. as of 1950 and 1960, to be published in 1965 by the U.S. Department of Commerce; (3) pilot models of state, urban and small area economies published or in process at Iowa State University and other places and (4) the identification by workers at Iowa State University of a principle of area delineation which lends itself to development planning and other kinds of economic policy considerations (see Chapter 1). This principle leads to a policy-oriented set of *functional economic areas* (FEA's) which would cover the entire map of the U.S. in a consistent fashion, consolidating the present standard metropolitan statistical area and state economic area delineations into a single unified system.[2]

Figure 11.1 (p. 323) presents a preliminary flow diagram of the Brookings-SSRC econometric model of the U.S. economy, based on quarterly data for 1947–1960. The Brookings-SSRC econometric model could be treated as a policy model in the Tinbergen sense. The variables could be classified appropriately, and some of them could be formally included in an objective function, linear, linearized or quadratic.

However, all variables in the Brookings-SSRC econometric model are aggregates or averages for the U.S. as a whole. The impiication of a national model seems to be that the regional distributions of variables with welfare connotations are a matter of indifference to the national policy maker. For a country of very small geographic extent this may perhaps be the case. But in a country as large as the U.S., practical politicians are concerned not merely about national totals but also about levels of unemployment and income in fairly small local areas.

So-called structural unemployment has very severe area concentrations. In principle, most economists favor a high degree of labor mobility between industries, occupations and areas. However, occupational modility in the short run may be quite limited and is inherently asymmetrical—i.e., it is

---

[2] Standard metropolitan statistical areas and state economic areas are mutually exclusive. Together, they include the entire area of the U.S.

easier for skilled people to move into unskilled occupations than the converse.

Labor mobility between areas may involve considerable economic, social and psychological costs. Schools, neighborhoods and friends are not changed without effort and (in some cases) trauma. Realistic estimates of such costs would, we believe, justify a good deal of concern about mitigating short-run fluctuations in employment area by area as well as for the nation as a whole.

If so, a national policy maker in the U.S. should include in his objective function not merely one variable representing total national unemployment but perhaps several hundred variables reflecting levels of unemployment in as many areas (or FEA's).

12.1.1. *Size and Delineation of Basic Geographic Units: The Functional Economic Area*

The automobile has profoundly affected the spatial structure of the U.S. economy. Significant numbers of workers are willing to spend as much as sixty minutes' commuting time each way between their homes and their places of work—a total of two hours per working day in transit. In Iowa, this means that some employees in the central cities of labor market areas reside as much as fifty miles away from their places of work. In the congested East, the distances would ordinarily be less; in the more sparsely populated Plains States, workers may be able to travel sixty miles in as many minutes.

In several papers written during 1961–1964, one of the authors has discussed the *de facto* existence and usefulness for policy purposes of a unit which he calls a "functional economic area", or FEA. The principal characteristics of an FEA under U.S. conditions have already been described in Chapter 1. The geographic extent of an FEA is, in most parts of the U.S., determined by the almost universal ownership of passenger automobiles, the rate of travel of such vehicles, and the reluctance of the great majority of workers to spend more than two hours a day commuting between home and work.

If we were to draw a sixty-minute isochrone or "equal travel time" contour line around the central business district of a city of 50,000 or more people, a line extending many miles into the open country in all directions, we would have a first approximation to the boundary of an FEA in the U.S. If we did this for all such cities, the sixty-minute isochrones around some of them would have very irregular outlines.

In Iowa, owing to the relatively homogeneous distribution of the farming population and the almost universal coverage of a rectangular road grid, the sixty-minute isochrones are relatively regular in shape. Figures 12.1 and 12.2 indicate that such sixty-minute isochrones include about 80 per cent of the area and perhaps 90 per cent of the population of Iowa with no further modifications or adjustments. For administrative purposes and economic analysis in the framework of a complete national economic model, it would, of course, be necessary to allocate the remaining areas in some way—probably by extending the minimum commuting time zones outward from each central city until they met in a boundary which was the locus of points requiring an equal number of minutes of commuting time to each city. If the two cities were more closely spaced, persons along some portions of the boundary would be able to reach any central city in less than sixty minutes.

Nearly all the persons who reside within the boundaries of an FEA also work in that area and do the vast majority of their shopping in it as well. Hence, under U.S. conditions, an FEA appears to be a relatively self-contained labor market in the short run. It is also a relatively self-contained area with respect to retail trade, personal and professional services, local government services, and those state and federal services (for example, the postal system) which require face-to-face contact with ordinary citizens. The central city of such an area contains the largest and most varied array of job opportunities and provides the widest and most varied array of consumer goods and services. The central city may also contain a large percentage of those persons, firms and establishments which have a large-region or national cultural or economic orientation.

Having defined such a relatively self-contained area and the cluster of "residentiary" activities with respect to which the FEA is approximately "closed," we may make an approximate separation of the economic activities carried on in the FEA between *residentiary* and *export-oriented*. In relation to an area or small region of this size (about 5,000 square miles under Iowa conditions), agriculture, forestry and fisheries, mining, transportation and manufacturing are preponderantly export-oriented, while all the remaining economic activities are primarily residentiary in nature. As of 1960, about 44 per cent of all employed workers in Iowa were engaged in export-oriented activities and about 56 per cent were occupied with the residentiary cluster. Because the activities have been classified with respect to areas of FEA size, these percentages also apply *approximately* to each of the individual FEA'S in Iowa.

The populations of the central cities of FEA's in or partly in Iowa range from 30,000 to more than 200,000. The population of the FEA's as a whole range from about 150,000 or a little less to 500,000 or more.

Figure 12.3 provides some insight as to the internal structure of an FEA.

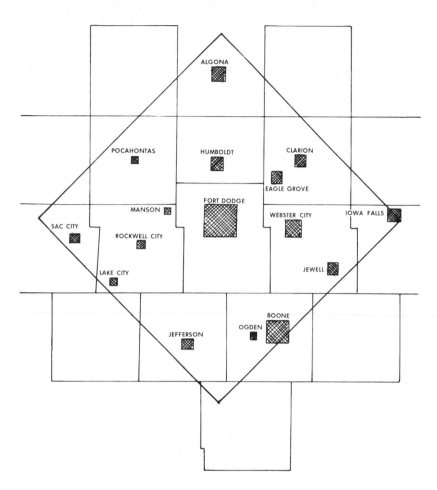

Fig. 12.3. Distribution of town population sizes in the Fort Dodge area. Areas of squares are proportional to 1960 town populations. Only towns with retail sales of $2.5 million or more for year ending June 30, 1964 are shown.

In Figure 12.3 each square has an area proportional to the population of the town or village it represents.

The volume and pattern of retail trade is more indicative of a town's role in the FEA economy than is its resident population, though trade and population are closely related. It is possible to describe the trade centers of an FEA, at least in the American middle west, in terms of four hierarchical stages which we may call (1) full convenience centers, (2) partial retail shopping centers, (3) complete retail shopping centers and (4) FEA central cities.

The range of goods and services, of course, increases with the increasing economic size of the trade center. Almost every resident of an FEA is dependent for certain kinds of goods and services upon the FEA central city. This is simply another indication of the extent to which the FEA as a whole represents a self-contained economy with respect to residentiary activities.

12.1.2. *Models of an FEA Economy*

In practice, we cannot make a perfect separation between residentiary and export-oriented establishments, but the pure case offers significant insights. The intermediate demand section of the input-output model of a three-region economy (each of the regions being an FEA) would be as follows:

Sending Sector:	R_1	R_2	R_3	E_1	E_2	E_3
R_1	×	0	0	0	0	0
R_2	0	×	0	0	0	0
R_3	0	0	×	0	0	0
E_1	×	×	×	×	×	×
E_2	×	×	×	×	×	×
E_3	×	×	×	×	×	×

where R_i and E_i are, respectively, the residentiary and the export sectors of the ith region.

The export-oriented firms in each FEA are part of a national (interregional) trading and manufacturing system. No economic influences (in this model) are transmitted *directly* from the residentiary cluster of one FEA to the residentiary clusters of any others. However, an increase in consumer demand in Region 1 will increase the local demand for outputs of export-oriented firms, directly or indirectly, in all regions.

The structure of an FEA economy and its relations to a national economy can be described more formally in the following model, a national version of which is presented in Chapter 2, Section 2.2.

$$Y_1 = C_1 + I_{1p} + X_{1p} + G_{1c} + G_{1i} + (\lambda_{11} + \lambda_{21} + \lambda_{31})G_f, \qquad (12.1.1)$$
$$M_1 = a_{11}C_1 + a_{21}I_{1p} + a_{31}X_{1p} + a_{41}G_{1c} + a_{51}G_{1i}$$
$$+ (a_{21}\lambda_{11} + a_{31}\lambda_{21} + a_{51}\lambda_{31})G_f, \qquad (12.1.2)$$
$$C_1 = b_1(1 - t_1)Y_1, \qquad (12.1.3)$$

$$N_1 = e_1 Y_1, \tag{12.1.4}$$

$$B_1 = p_{x1} X_1 - p_{m1} M_1, \tag{12.1.5}$$

$$I_{1f} = \lambda_{11} G_f, \tag{12.1.6}$$

$$X_{1f} = \lambda_{21} G_f, \tag{12.1.7}$$

$$G_{1i(f)} = \lambda_{31} G_f, \tag{12.1.8}$$

Federal instruments: $\lambda_{11}, \lambda_{21}, \lambda_{31}, t_1$
Targets: N_1^*, C_1^*.

In these equations, Y is income, C consumption, I_p private investment, X_p private exports, G_c expenditures by local government for current operations, G_i expenditures of local government for investment purposes and G_f expenditures by the federal government. The subscript 1 stands for region or FEA$_1$. The remaining variables are M imports, N employment, B balance of payments, p_x prices of exports, p_m prices of imports, I_f federal investment projects in the local FEA *or* investments induced by federal expenditures, X_f exports purchased by the federal government and $G_{i(f)}$ local government investment activities *induced by* federal subsidies or other expenditures.

The local FEA variables I_p, X_p, G_c and G_i may be regarded as exogenous variables. The endogenous variables of greatest concern to residents of the FEA are presumably N_1, C_1 and perhaps Y_1. The instruments available to the federal government in this model are the personal income tax (t_1), federal expenditures to encourage local private investment (λ_{11}), federal expenditures for "exports" from the FEA (λ_{21}) and federal expenditures to encourage local government investment (λ_{31}). The λ's are allocation coefficients which can presumably be set at different levels for different FEA's. In practice, the personal income tax instrument (t_1) must be applied to all regions simultaneously. The local targets of primary concern to the federal government will most likely be N_1 and C_1.

We have here a simple model in which economic fluctuations and growth may arise from the investment decisions of local businessmen (including farmers) and from the operating expenses of local government. Economic fluctuations and growth patterns in all other FEA's are reflected into the local economy in the form of export demand, X_p.

The federal government could intervene by means of three types of programs affecting, respectively, local private investment, local government investment and "exports" (including sales to the federal government under defense contracts and sales for stockpiling purposes or under agricultural price support programs). The federal government could also influence the level of consumption locally *relative to local income* by varying the federal income tax rate, t_1.

A causal ordering diagram could be worked out for the present model, expressing the eight endogenous variables as functions of the exogenous variables, including the actual or potential instruments of federal government policy. There is an element of simultaneity in this model, as income and consumption (Y_1 and C_1) must be determined at the same causal order. In other words, the model includes a Keynesian multiplier which operates without a time lag.

Without being rigorous or formal in our demonstration, it may be helpful to outline some other features of an FEA economy. Total personal consumption expenditures by residents of the area, C_1, are allocated among the individual firms which comprise the area's residentiary cluster. These firms may sell to or buy from each other to some extent; in addition, they make some purchases from the export-oriented firms in the FEA.

Thus, we might conceptualize a transactions matrix among all establishments in the FEA in the conventional input-output form. However, the transactions would represent flows of money and goods between establishments within the trading sector to a much greater extent than would be the case in national input-output models, which emphasize technological relationships among the production processes in different manufacturing industries. The matrix of transactions could be partitioned into transactions involving establishments (including public schools and other services as well as business firms) in the residentiary cluster and between firms in the export-oriented cluster of activities.

Further, below the column representing purchases by establishment 1 from each of the other establishments in the FEA would be a column representing that firm's autonomous inputs, including its purchases (imports) from firms in other FEA's, its sales at the expense of inventory depletions, its factor payments (wages, interest, rent, dividends and profits), and its indirect business taxes.

In a related process analysis matrix representing the physical organization of production, the alternative levels of output or sales by each firm could be expressed as a demand for workers in each of a number of occupational categories. As workers are specialized much more by occupation than by industry, the occupational distribution of demands for labor by local establishments should be a very important factor in designing short-run policies to stabilize employment.

If the occupationally differentiated demand for labor by each establishment at each alternative level of output were specified, it would in principle
be possible to determine approximately what kinds of policy instruments
would be most effective in balancing the local demand for labor with the local
supply. To the extent that different kinds of establishments used different
kinds of occupational skills (or at least used them in different proportions),

Fig. 12.4. Input-output structure of an economy.

Total Gross Output	Industry / Industry	Interindustry Demands							Final Demands				
		1	2	3	.	.	.	n	C 1	I 2	G 3	ΔH_a 4	E 5
X_1	1	X_{11}	.	.	.	.	.	X_{1n}	f_{11}	.	.	.	f_{15}
X_2	2	.						.	.				.
X_3 =	3	.						.	+ .				.
.	.	.						.	.				.
.	.	.						.	.				.
X_n	n	X_{n1}	.	.	.	.	.	X_{nn}	f_{n1}	.	.	.	f_{n5}

+

Autonomous Inputs		1	2	3	.	.	.	n
ΔH_d	1	S_{11}	.	.	.	.	.	S_{1n}
M	2							.
D	3	.						.
T_b	4	.						.
W	5	.						.
i	6	.						.
R	7	.						.
π	8	S_{81}	.	.	.	.	.	S_{8n}

=

Total Gross Outlay or Income	X_1 X_2 X_3 . . . X_n

the selection of instruments by local and federal governments should be influenced by the pattern of deficiencies in demand for labor on the part of local establishments as a group.

Depending upon the local structure of wages and salaries for each occupation, the distribution of wage and salary income in the FEA could be generated from the occupational distribution of employment. As education and training of appropriate kinds are prerequisites for particular occupations, the local demand for labor also implies a local demand for education and training.

We will not go further into the details of the microstructure of an FEA. However, with very little extension of the scope of our model, we could consider the effects of increased local demand upon the profitability of investments by individual firms, pressures toward change in the locational distribution of workers and economic activities within the FEA and so on. We could, for example, outline a development planning model for the FEA to go along with the microeconomic model described in equations (12.1.1) to (12.1.8).

12.1.3. *Impacts of National Economic Fluctuations upon Local Economies*

Figure 12.4 outlines the structure of an economy in the well-known input-output format. Let us regard it first as representing the national economy as a whole.

In Figure 12.4 total economic activity is divided into n categories. Final demand (F) is divided into five broad categories: personal consumption expenditures (C), gross private domestic fixed investment (I), government purchases of goods and services (G), the increase in inventories in each industry where an increase occurs (ΔH_a) and gross exports (E). Autonomous inputs are divided into eight categories: inventory depletions for those industries showing depletions $(-\Delta H_d)$, gross imports (M), depreciation (D), indirect business taxes (T_b), wage and salary payments (W), interest (i), net rent (R) and before-tax profits (π).

The national income accounts incorporate the following identities:

$$GNP = C + I + G + (\Delta H_a - \Delta H_d) + (E - M) =$$

$$TG \text{ Output} - \Delta H_d - M - \sum_{i=1}^{n} \sum_{j=1}^{n} X_{ij}; \qquad (12.2.1)$$

$$GNI = D + T_b + W + i + R + \pi = TG \text{ Outlay} - \Delta H_d - M - \sum_{i=1}^{n} \sum_{j=1}^{n} X_{ij},$$

$$(12.2.2)$$

and
$$GNI = GNP. \qquad (12.2.3)$$

The double summation term in equations (12.2.1) and (12.2.2) represents the interindustry demands—flows of raw materials, semimanufactures, components and services—which are pronounced and relatively stable features of a mature economy. These intermediate flows are "netted out" in calculating GNP and GNI (gross national income), but they constitute an extremely important mechanism for transmitting changes in activity in a given industry into changes in output and employment in other industries. Whenever economic measures are adopted which stimulate consumption, investment or exports or which increase government purchases of goods and services, this interindustry mechanism is called into play. It also operates when measures are taken to reduce final demands.

In dealing with final GNP demands, the Brookings-SSRC econometric model (Figure 11.1) builds upon the official national income accounts. In the July, 1964 issue of the *Survey of Current Business*, personal consumption expenditures are divided into twelve major components: (1) federal government and (2) state and local government expenditures are each divided into nine major categories. If we subdivide production and employment into thirty-one industrial sectors, there should be room in the final demand columns for investment, inventory changes and exports (net) in each of the thirty-one industries. Hence, the final demand section of Figure 12.4 could logically be expanded into 123 columns (12 for consumption, 18 for government and 31 each for investment, inventory change and net exports). The present Brookings-SSRC econometric model (if conformed) would have to be expanded to include 123 equations explaining the 123 column totals.

Each column (for example, consumer expenditures for food) would include thirty-one elements, some of which could be zero. These elements must attribute total GNP expenditures for each column to various components of the thirty-one producing sectors. With existing published data in the U.S., it is not at all easy to derive the f_{kj}'s in Figure 12.4. However, once we have found them (or forced estimates of them), the sum of the 123 elements in row 1 is the F_1 required for the input-output equation (12.3) below.

We may write
$$X = (I - A)^{-1}F \qquad (12.3)$$

to characterize the dependence of total gross output upon final demand. Equation (12.4) converts deliveries to final GNP demands (f_{kj}, where $k = 1, 2, \ldots 123$ and $j = 1, 2, \ldots 31$) into outputs from thirty-one producing sectors. As a matter of logic, and as indicated in Figure 11.1, employment in each industry is a function of its level of output. Given output and employment, other functional relations can be used to estimate income payments or accruals to each type of factor—wages and salaries, interest, rent, dividends and profits.

Additional functional relationships convert factor payments into disposable income, personal savings and personal taxes. Disposable income figures prominently in the explanation of consumption expenditures for each of the twelve categories to which we have referred. We have thus carried the Brookings-SSRC econometric model through one logical cycle: (1) consumption, (2) production, (3) employment, (4) disposable income and (5) consumption once more.

A classification of the thirty-one industries between residentiary and export-oriented is meaningful for each FEA but not for the U.S. as a whole. If we use the Brookings-SSRC econometric model, expanded to thirty-one producing sectors, to generate impacts upon local area economies, it seems most sensible to use that model as it is (or will be) to obtain consistent national estimates of production, employment and (deflated) incomes and consumption expenditures for all thirty-one industries. Also, most prices and most kinds of wages are determined in integrated national markets and might as well be estimated in the national model.

Table 12.1 is based on data from the U.S. Commerce Department's Business and Defense Services Administration (unpublished as of November, 1963). The classifications in Table 12.1 are crude but instructive.[3] Part of "construction" should probably be allocated to the export industries. "State government" should probably be classed as an export industry in an FEA which includes the state capital and a residentiary industry in other FEA's. "Federal government" should be treated as an export-oriented activity for the Washington, D.C. FEA and as a residentiary activity in other FEA's. Further adjustments could no doubt be made without going so far as to make a special classification for each individual FEA.

It is clear that Androscoggin County's economy is based on manufacturing. It is short on extractive industries, transportation and warehousing. It *appears* short on government employment, but may not be so with respect to state and local government only. It appears somewhat low in the four

---

[3] The classification of industries in Table 12.1 is my own (K.F.). The Business and Defense Services Administration did not attempt to classify the thirty-one industries in this fashion.

TABLE 12.1

Employment by Industrial Sector, United States and Androscoggin County, Maine, April 1, 1960

Industrial Sector	U.S. April 1, 1960 Million Workers	Androscoggin County, Maine April 1, 1960 Thousand Workers
Export-oriented [a]		
Extractive industries (3)	5.0	1.0
Manufacturing industries (10)	17.6	17.0
Transportation and warehousing industries (3)	2.7	0.6
Armed forces (1)	1.7	0.1
Subtotal, 17 export-oriented industries	27.0	18.8 [b]
Residentiary [a]		
Wholesale trade (1)	2.2	0.8
Retail trade categories (3)	9.6	4.8
Finance and service categories (4)	8.2	2.9
Medical, educational and professional services (1)	7.6	3.5
Government, federal, state and local (1)	3.2	1.0
Utilities, communication and entertainment (2)	2.2	0.8
Construction (1)	3.8	1.6
Subtotal, residentiary categories (13)	36.8	15.4
Industry not reported (1)	2.6	0.6
Total, 31 sectors	66.4	34.8

[a] Rough classification with respect to role in a typical FEA.

[b] Individual items may not add to totals because of rounding errors.

Source: U.S. Department of Commerce, Business and Defense Services Administration (unpublished as of November, 1963).

finance and service categories. The county is a standard metropolitan statistical area (Lewiston-Auburn) and evidently has a population of nearly 90,000, and so most of the consumer-oriented activities normally found in an FEA should find sufficient demand to support one or more units within the county. The county employment multiplier derived from Table 12.1 is

$$k = \frac{18.8 + 15.4}{18.8} = 1.82,$$

compared with Powers' estimate of 1.89 for the Tenco FEA in Iowa.

We should note also that workers are trained for *occupations*, not *industries*. One of the most aggregative occupational classifications includes eleven categories. If we had coefficients or simple functions for allocating employment in each of the thirty-one industries among these eleven occupations, we could estimate the impacts of changes in the national economy upon the employment levels and prospects of each of the occupational groups.

The sequential calculations which we have outlined at the national level could also be carried out within each FEA, though with some essential differences. First, let us suggest a consistent basing point for the national economy and for all of its constituent FEA's.

Suppose we take 1960 as a base year, a year in which census data are available at the county level for most variables included in the SSRC model. When directly comparable data are lacking, we could use various "reasonable" and reproducible procedures to allocate each category of consumption expenditures, each category of industrial production and each category of employment among the 400 or so FEA's. In each FEA, the allocation of total consumer expenditures among the twelve categories should again be "reasonable" but need not be based on a special survey of that particular FEA. Within the residentiary cluster of activities, similarities between FEA's are likely to be more striking than differences.

Then, coefficients could be assigned to consumption functions, investment functions and other equations in a model for each FEA such that the functions passed through the estimated 1960 observations for that FEA. The model for a particular FEA could be handled in various ways, but it would (on our assumptions) include thirty industrial sectors. Let us assume, as in Table 12.1, that seventeen of these are export industries in an FEA context and that thirteen are residentiary activities. (Industry 31, "not reported," will be ignored for the sake of verbal simplicity. In practice, it would be prorated.)

12.1.4. *Propagation of National Economic Fluctuations among Industries, Regions and FEA's*

Table 12.2 will give some notion of the behavior of employment in various industries during recent economic recessions in the U.S. The first column indicates the basic magnitude of employment in each industry; the second indicates the severity or mildness of the declines in employment in each industrial category during three recent recessions. As a rule, durable manufactures and mining would be export activities with respect to an FEA; wholesale and retail trade, service and miscellaneous, and finance, insurance and real estate would be residentiary activities.

TABLE 12.2

Nonagricultural Employment: Actual Employment, Average Percentage Change from Peak to Trough and Number of Recessions in which Employment Decreased, Remained Stable or Increased, by Industry Group, United States, 1948–58

Industry Group	Actual Employment, August, 1957	Average Change from Peak to Trough in Three Recessions	Number of Recessions during which employment:		
			Decreased	Remained stable[a]	Increased
	(Millions)	Per cent			
Total	52.5	– 4.0[b]	3	–	–
Manufacturing, durables	9.9	– 13.2	3	–	–
Mining	0.8	– 9.0	3	–	–
Transportation and public utilities	4.2	– 5.9	3	–	–
Manufacturing, nondurables	7.0	– 5.5	3	–	–
Contract construction	2.8	– 3.8	2	1	–
Wholesale and retail trade	11.4	– 1.6	2	1	–
Service and miscellaneous	6.5	0.1	1	1	1
Finance, insurance and real estate	2.4	1.6	–	1	2
Government	7.7	1.6	–	–	3

[a] Changed less than 0.5 per cent.

[b] Equivalent to − 3.1 per cent in terms of total civilian employment, including self-employed persons, persons engaged in agriculture and certain other categories not included in "nonagricultural employment." Note, however, that total civilian employment had a long-run growth trend of slightly more than 1 per cent a year or approximately 0.8 per cent during the average recession period of nine months from peak to trough.

TABLE 12.3

Industrial Production: Changes in Major Groups of Industries from Peak to Trough and Trough to Recovery during Three Cyclical Episodes, United States, 1948–1958

Industry Group [b]	Average Per Cent Changes [a] Peak to Trough (3 cycles)
Industrial production, total	— 11.0
Durable manufactures	— 15.2
Nondurable manufactures	— 5.0
Minerals	— 12.1
Manufactures: special groupings	
Metal manufactures	— 16.8
Consumer nondurables	— 3.8
Miscellaneous manufactures	— 10.4

Sources: Computed from basic data in Business Statistics, 1957 Biennial Edition (A supplement to the Survey of Current Business) and from various issues of Survey of Current Business and Federal Reserve Bulletin.)

[a] Averages for the three special groups of manufacturing industries are based on simple arithmetic averages of published index numbers for 5, 6 and 9 industries, respectively; figures for the "total," "durable manufactures," "nondurable manufactures" and "minerals" indexes are as officially published.

[b] Relative importance of the components may be estimated from 1956 figures on "production and related workers" employed: all manufacturing industries, 13.2 million; metal manufactures, 5.6 million; consumer nondurables, 4.2 million; and miscellaneous manufactures, 3.4 million. (About 0.8 million wage and salary workers were engaged in minerals production.)

Table 12.3 takes standard indexes of industrial production in the U.S. and regroups the various manufacturing industries into metal manufactures, consumer nondurables and miscellaneous. Output of the metal manufacturing industries dropped an average of nearly 17 per cent from peak to trough during three postwar recessions. In contrast, the consumer nondurable goods industries reduced their outputs by an average of less than 4 per cent. The remaining industries could not be neatly classified; the amplitude of their recessions was intermediate between those of the other two categories.

Table 12.4 illustrates a principle which may be used in allocating changes in national employment in particular industries or groups among the various FEA'S. The regression equation reported in the footnote reflects the fact that the decline in nonagricultural employment from July, 1953 to July, 1954

TABLE 12.4

Nonagricultural Employment: Regional Variations in Employment Change Related to Degree of Regional Concentration in Durable Goods Industries, United States, July, 1953 to July, 1954

Geographic Division	(1) Per Cent of Nonagricultural Workers Employed in Durable Goods Industries, July, 1953	(2) Per Cent Change in Total Nonagricultural Employment, July, 1953 to July, 1954	(3) Per Cent Change in Total Nonagricultural Employment, March-April, 1940 to March, 1953
United States	16.8[a]	— 3.7[a]	69.2[a]
Geographic divisions			
East North Central	32.8	— 7.0	69.4
New England	23.1	— 4.6	41.7
Middle Atlantic	20.3	— 4.4	48.3
Pacific	18.6	— 3.1	98.9
East South Central	14.5	— 3.7	59.7
West North Central	13.4	— 2.5	61.0
South Atlantic	10.8	— 3.1	66.7
West South Central	9.8	— 1.9	85.8
Mountain	7.8	— 3.0	90.9

Source: Based on data prepared by Edmond L. Kanwit [25].

[a] Simple arithmetic averages of regional figures.

[b] Simple regression of column (2) upon column (1) is as follows:

$$X_1 = -0.763 - 0.175X_2; \quad r^2 = 0.84$$
$$(0.029)$$

was highly concentrated in the durable goods industries. Hence, the percentage decline in total nonagricultural employment in each geographic division was closely correlated with the percentage of its total nonagricultural workers who were employed in durable goods industries just before the recession started. In the U.S. as a whole, 16.8 per cent of nonagricultural workers were employed in durable goods industries; the coefficient of X_2 implies that a decline of 1 per cent in employment in durable goods industries is associated with a decline of 0.175 per cent in total nonagricultural employment.

The figures in column 3 of Table 12.4 were intended to "partial out" long-run growth trends from the short-run recession effects. The growth factor was not statistically significant in the nine-region analysis but proved to be so in all four of the regression analyses in Table 12.5, which were based upon standard metropolitan statistical areas. The two factors combined accounted for 57 per cent of the variation in nonagricultural employment change among the larger metropolitan labor market areas, compared with 49 per cent and 36 per cent, respectively, in metropolitan areas of medium and small populations. Part of the explanation may lie in the fact that large metropolitan areas tend to be more diversified and hence more like the nation as a whole in their employment patterns than do the middle-sized or small metropolitan areas; a few of the latter might be quite vulnerable to shut-downs by one or two large manufacturing plants. The central impression for our present purpose is one of considerable regional and local variation in employment opportunities during the course of a "national average" recession.

It should be noted that, in the great majority of cases, these eighty-one standard metropolitan statistical areas would be the central cities of corresponding FEA's; in the two larger size classes, the metropolitan area population would strongly dominate the FEA as a whole.

12.1.5. *Short-run Stabilization and "Impact" Model of an FEA*

It remains for us to outline a model by which the impacts of national economic fluctuations could be carried into an FEA and propagated through it.

In the first place, the change in the area output of each of the seventeen export industries could be estimated as (1) a percentage of the change in total U.S. output plus (2) an autonomous component. The proportionality factors for a given industry in the 400 FEA's would sum to 1.0; the autonomous components in any time period (say a quarter of a year) would sum to zero over the 400 FEA's.

Second, area employment in each of the seventeen export industries would be expressed as a function of the corresponding output. Payments from each industry to factors of production would be estimated as in the national model. These payments would give rise to disposable income, taxes and personal savings in respect to persons associated with the export industries. An initial change in the disposable income arising from export industries would increase total income of FEA residents. The causal sequence would then run from consumer expenditures by area residents to increased output of the thirteen residentiary industries; thence to area employment in each of the thirteen residentiary industries and thence to factor payments and disposable income resulting from residentiary activities.

Residential and commercial construction in the area would be influencep by income payments and employment levels in both the export and the residentiary industries. Other functions would deal with local government construction expenditures and tax receipts.

How elaborate the FEA model should be would depend upon its intended uses. Conceivably, one might short-circuit the causal chain through income and consumption expenditures, using simple multipliers or functions to connect changes in total export employment to changes in residentiary employment or in local employment in the thirty industrial sectors as a whole.

Given estimates of FEA employment in each of the thirty industries (plus "unreported") and given functions relating employment by occupation to total employment in a given industry, we could estimate the incidences of local unemployment by occupational groups.

Although one standard classification previously mentioned includes eleven occupational categories, it should be possible to build up much more detailed occupational data for FEA's if it seemed desirable.

12.1.6. *Feedbacks from Area Models to the National Models*

If the models for all FEA's contained values of all variables as of 1960 consistent with 1960 U.S. totals, and if the various consumption and production functions had the same forms as the corresponding national functions, the following procedure should be appropriate.

First, with the national model, calculate consistent national estimates of output and employment in each of the thirty industries.

Second, carry impacts from the seventeen export activities into each of the 400 or so FEA'S. (This should not be a tremendous task, once a suitable computer program was devised. Each of the 400 or so area models would contain the same variables, and the coefficients would be varied only on rational and systematic bases.) The equations and autonomous components used to allocate national employment in each export industry among the FEA's should mean that aggregate export employment in the 400 FEA's would exactly equal the originally estimated national total.

Third, apply a reproducible and rational set of adjustment factors such that employment in each of the thirteen residentiary activities in the FEA's equals or nearly equals in total the consistent estimates from the national model.

Employment, consumption and income associated with the residentiary cluster in a particular FEA need not be *precisely* consistent with the corresponding aggregates estimated from the national model. To some extent

TABLE 12.5

Factors Associated with Changes in Nonagricultural Employment by Geographic Divisions and for Various Size Groups of Standard Metropolitan Areas, July, 1953 to July, 1954[a]

Types of Areas	Per Cent of Total Variation in Nonagricultural Employment Associated with:		Change in Total Nonagricultural Employment, July, 1953 to July, 1954 per Unit Difference in:	
	(1) Employment in Durable Goods Industries (r^2)	(2) Employment in Durable Goods Industries plus Allowance for Growth Trends (R^2)	(3) Per Cent of Total Workers in Area Employed in Durable Goods Industries, July, 1953[b]	(4) Per Cent Increase in Total Nonagricultural Employment, March-April, 1940 to March, 1953[b]
Census divisions (9)	83.6	84.0	− 0.170 (0.033)	0.005[f] (0.013)
Large metropolitan areas (32)[c]	47.0	56.7	− 0.199 (0.041)	0.039 (0.015)
Middle-sized metropolitan areas (31)[d]	28.2	49.4	− 0.098 (0.040)	0.047 (0.014)
Small metropolitan areas (18)[e]	16.2	36.1	− 0.185 (0.077)	0.035 (0.016)
Metropolitan areas, all sizes (81)	27.3	43.0	− 0.150 (0.027	0.036 (0.008)

Source: Basic data for metropolitan areas appear in Kanwit [25]. The selections of areas by size groups were made by Mr. Kanwit in May, 1955, in consultation with Karl A. Fox and the regressions were computed by Martha N. Condee of U.S. Department of Agriculture's Division of Agricultural Economics at that time.

ᵃ This table summarizes the results of regression analyses involving the following variables:

X_1 = Per cent change in number of wage and salary workers employed in nonagricultural industries, July, 1953 to July, 1954.

X_2 = Wage and salary workers employed in durable goods manufacturing as a per cent of total wage and salary workers in nonagricultural industries, July, 1953.

X_3 = Per cent change in number of wage and salary workers employed in nonagricultural industries, March–April, 1940 to March, 1953.

ᵇ Figures in parentheses are standard errors of the regression coefficients.

ᶜ Areas with 1950 population of 500,000 or more.

ᵈ Areas with 1950 population from 275,000 to 500,000.

ᵉ Selected areas with 1950 population of less than 275,000.

ᶠ Not statistically significant.

this begs the question: If the coefficients of FEA consumption functions are not consistent *ex ante* they could presumably be made consistent *ex post*. If all functions were linear, it appears intuitively that exact consistency could be achieved; otherwise, small errors of "closure" might be permitted.

From a policy standpoint, predictions and explanations of levels of employment and unemployment by industry and by occupational group would probably be the most valuable products of short-run FEA models. Prices of nationally traded commodities and wages in industries confronting strong national labor unions should be generated in the national model and multiplied appropriately by the corresponding real production, consumption, income and employment variables in the FEA's. However, prices of local services and wages paid in local service industries could perhaps be generated within the local model. If so, these equations might be formalized for all FEA's so that they would agree closely with the results of the national model.

The so-called autonomous component of local output (and employment) in each of the export industries can be given more concrete meaning. It would be reasonable for the local employment service in the FEA to solicit confidential statements or forecasts from each major employer in the export industries as to their planned net layoffs or net acquisitions, by occupational groups, for specified future periods (from one to six months, or possibly more). These specific forecasts, obtained as part of an "early warning" system, would be propagated through the local FEA model to anticipate probable employment needs and opportunities.

12.1.7. *Further Policy Implications of FEA Models*

It appears that, despite possible weaknesses of data, some very interesting policy questions could be explored if the Brookings-SSRC econometric model were expanded to include specifically some thirty-one production sectors.

There would be considerable policy interest in a consistent set of models for each of the fifty states. This would mean a special partitioning of some FEA's and an aggregation of the various FEA's and parts of FEA's into state totals. Realistic tax functions and tax incidence models (as between occupational and income groups) would be of considerable interest to state government officials and to the economists at state universities and elsewhere upon whom they might call for advice. Some kinds of tax changes would change parameters of a state model in known ways.

State officials should also have considerable policy interest in models for those FEA's which are wholly or partly within their states. Comprehension of the similarity of FEA models in adjacent states might encourage cooperation between states on policy measures for those FEA's which cut across state lines.

At present, few FEA's have legally constituted governing bodies with jurisdictions corresponding to the *de facto* FEA boundaries. It appears that FEA's could be used for policy purposes in at least two different ways: (1) some (perhaps many) powers now allocated by the state to county or municipal governments could be delegated to an officially elected government for the FEA as a whole; (2) without formally eliminating county and municipal offices, the state could use FEA's as its basic units for district offices of the state government and for the planning of various educational and development programs.

Many possible topics of interest have not been touched upon here.

We have defined a certain kind of area and have implied that useful economic models could be constructed for such an area. But useful for what and to whom? Unconditional forecasts of the time paths of important sectors of the area economy (if accuracy were attainable) would help area residents decide whether to "cooperate with the inevitable" *in situ* or to make occupational and geographical moves. But most persons interested in area development believe that things can be done to change the trend of an economy and that information is needed as a guide to public or private groups who wish to change this trend for the better—as they see it.

Logically, this kind of interest leads us into an explicit formulation of the ends and means of area economic policy. In broadest terms, we might conceive of a production possibilities surface in many dimensions comprising all feasible positions of the area economy at a given time or at successive dates over a period of time ("position" being defined as a set of values of all the variables we recognize as worthy of interest in a model of the economy). In principle, any individual might examine this surface and express his preferences as between alternative positions on it—conceivably he might even select a single position as the best of all in terms of his value system or "welfare function." His criteria might be extremely narrow—"which position entails the biggest increase in the value of my real estate"—or they might reflect a very broad concern for the welfare of present and future area residents. In either case, we have the possibility (familiar in economic theory) of juxtaposing a real production possibilities surface and a subjective preference function to define an optimum.

In brief, it should be possible and useful to construct development planning models for FEA's which would be in some sense consistent with the short-run stabilization or impact models of the type discussed here. There are also interesting problems connected with the optimal size and location distribution of firms 'and public service units (schools, for example) within an FEA.

The FEA appears to be an extremely promising and suitable unit for labor market analysis. Education, migration and training all involve changes in the stocks of "human capital." Labor market problems should prove to be highly concrete and tangible at the FEA level, although remedies for some types of problems may require national or at least state-level guidance.

The main contribution of this section is the affirmation that a complete set of impact models for several hundred FEA's could be constructed and integrated with an existing national model at a relatively moderate cost in time and effort. Such a project would provide a real challenge to our present data collecting, processing and publication systems. However, it would enable us to raise the level of understanding of economic policy simultaneously among local, state and national officials. Relations among federal, state and local tax and expenditure policies should be brought into a common framework, and some issues concerning the responsibilities of different levels of government should be considerably clarified.

Models of state or FEA economies could be used unidirectionally without regard to their feedbacks into the national economy. That is, they could be used with the simple intent of tracing impacts of national economic policies or autonomous changes upon the state or FEA economy. So, if the concept of a "complete" model of the U.S. economy containing at least 100 equations for each of 400 economic areas seems appalling, we should remember that only a handful of economists and computer scientists need concern themselves with the details of the complete system.

But in each FEA and in each state there are citizens and leaders whose lives are intimately bound up in, and largely contained within, an FEA. It should not be too difficult to explain the internal mechanism of an FEA economy to officials and lay leaders.

There is also a challenge in terms of realism and tangibility—not to mention data disclosure—at the FEA level which is often lacking in national models. In a national model for the U.S. the steel industry may *perhaps* be regarded as an amorphous collection of firms. But in an FEA the steel "industry" may consist of a single plant. Important private decision makers in the FEA are known to one another in various associational contexts.

Perhaps Wilbur Thompson's comparison of the FEA with a "city-state" best poses both the challenges and the opportunities inherent in the FEA as a unit for economic—and possibly political—action.

12.2. The Stability and Optimality Characteristics of a Regionally Differentiated Economic Policy for Stabilization and Growth[4]

This section analyzes some theoretical aspects of stability and optimality of economic policy for stabilization and growth under a general macro-economic framework of national planning. More specifically, our approach is to consider in detail some important characteristics of alternative stabilization policies which appear when we consider the regional breakdown of such policies for the whole economy.

Analytically, the Phillips-type stabilization policy model will be generalized into a multisector or multiregion framework; if the regions are viewed as FEA's discussed in the earlier section, a multi-FEA analysis of stabilization policy is likely to be useful in showing the alternative implications of a centralized versus a decentralized policy in a certain sense. From an operational standpoint we will discuss the conditions under which the stabilization policy for each region could be aggregated nationally, in the context of a linear dynamic model of the input-output type [19], such that the national policy has those desirable properties of stability and optimality which may be associated with each regional policy.[5]

12.2.1. Analytical Outline of a Stabilization Model

Although the specific assumptions are mentioned whenever required, some of the basic and common assumptions may usefully be noted here for convenience.

(i)   Whenever we refer to optimization with respect to a certain policy, we will restrict ourselves to a criterion function which is assumed to be an integral over time of a quadratic function, the latter being a function of both the state variable (e.g., national income) and the control variable (e.g., government expenditure). In a somewhat simplified form, such a quadratic functional has been used as a performance measure by

---

[4] This part is largely based on the following papers by Sengupta [39, 41, and 42].

[5] In the context of an interregional input-output type of model, this may be reduced to an aggregation problem [1].

Theil [46] and Holt [22] in considering alternative policies for economic stabilization in a multiplier-accelerator type of economic model. More specifically, we assume the criterion function (or the performance integral) to be of the form

$$W = \int_0^T \phi(t) \cdot F(y - y^*, u - u^*) \, dt, \qquad (12.4)$$

where y^* may represent, for example, a desired target value (e.g., full employment level of national income) and u^* a desired value of the instrument variable (e.g., a certain level of government expenditure) under the control of the policy maker. The scalar function F is a quadratic function of the deviations $y - y^*$ and $u - u^*$ such that, in the general case when y and u are vectors, F is assumed to be strictly positive definite. The scalar function $\phi(t)$ is a weighting function which may be viewed as the time discounting of the imputed cost function F in equation (12.4).

(ii) We assume the time horizon T to be fixed and finite and continuous on the positive real axis. The net effect of this assumption could be materially relaxed by considering the stability properties of the solutions of our model when T becomes very large, the integral (12.4) remaining bounded throughout. For most of our discussion, however, we are concerned with short-term problems of stabilization when T is finite and/or small.

(iii) Following Phillips, we may consider two simplified cases of the one-sector model, the first one being based on the multiplier principle and the second one on both the multiplier and the acceleration principle. The first model is:

demand: $y_d = (1 - s) y_s + u + a$,

supply: $dy_s/dt = \dot{y}_s = -\lambda(y_s - y_d)$; $y_s \neq y_d$, (12.5)

hence: $dy_s/dt = \dot{y}_s = -s\lambda y_s + \lambda(u + a)$,

where a denotes autonomous expenditure on investment and consumption together, which is assumed here for simplicity to be given as a constant (although it can be allowed to vary over time), and the lagged response of aggregate supply (y_s) to aggregate demand (y_d) is assumed to be of the continuous exponential type with speed of response $\lambda > 0$. For simplicity, we make the further assumption that there is no time lag between the planned official demand ($\bar{u}$ say) and the actual government expenditure (u), except where it is mentioned explicitly. As in a linear Keynesian model, $(1-s)$ is the propensity to consume.

The second Phillips model, which includes induced investment (I) through the acceleration principle, is of the following type:

$$y_d = (1 - s)y_s + I + u + a,$$
$$I = v(dy_s/dt) - k(dI/dt), \qquad (12.6)$$
$$dy_s/dt = -\lambda(y_s - y_d), \ y_s \neq y_d.$$

If k is zero, there is no feedback relation in the investment demand (I) function, and in this case, by combining all the above three equations, we obtain the reduced-form model

$$dy_s/dt = \dot{y}_s = -\left(\lambda s/(1 - \lambda v)\right)y_s + (u + a)/(1 - \lambda v). \qquad (12.7)$$

In the general case when k is not zero, the final reduced-form equation becomes:

$$\ddot{y}_s + b\dot{y}_s + (\lambda s/k)y_s - (\lambda/k)(u + a) - \lambda\dot{u} = 0, \qquad (12.8)$$

where a dot over a variable denotes a time derivative, first or second according to whether there are one or two dots, and the constant coefficient b is given by

$$b = \lambda s + (1/k) - \lambda v/k.$$

We must point out that these two models (12.5) and (12.6) operate only under the assumptions of a closed economy, with price and monetary factors being only implicit and the persistence of the disequilibrating mechanism being specified by the distributed-lag adjustment function.[6] At the end we will consider the effects of relaxing some of these restrictive assumptions. It should be noted, however, that if $y_s = y_d$ for all $t \geq 0$ the first two equations of the system (12.6) specify the growth path of the system, subject to production and capacity restraints which remain implicit in the Phillips system, although by introducing kinks and nonlinearities the system could be further generalized. We will here consider in some detail only the stabilization aspects in a simplified framework.

Consider now a multisector generalization[7] of the models (12.5) and

---

[6] We will not consider the details of the production function constraint and capacity restrictions to which the above model is subject.

[7] Other related types of generalization may be compared in this context, e.g. Johansen [24] and Lange [28].

(12.6) under the same assumptions as before. The demand and supply pertaining to each sector is now indicated by the subscript $i = 1, 2, ..., n$ and hence, the system (12.5) becomes

$$
\begin{aligned}
y_{di} &= C_i + u_i + a_i, \\
C_i &= \alpha_i \sum_j y_{sj}, \quad 0 \le \alpha_i \le 1, \\
dy_{si}/dt &= \dot{y}_{si} = - \lambda_i (y_{si} - y_{di})(\lambda_i > 0), \\
y_{si} &\ne y_{di}, \quad \text{all } i, j = 1, 2, ..., n,
\end{aligned}
\tag{12.5.1}
$$

where C_i is the final household (consumption) demand in sector i and the second equation specifies the consumption function. The reduced form of this equation is easily seen to be

$$
dy_{si}/dt = \dot{y}_{si} = - \lambda_i (1 - \alpha_i) y_{si} + \lambda_i \alpha_i \sum_{j \ne i} y_{sj} + \lambda_i (u_i + a_i)
$$
$$
(i, j = 1, 2, ..., n).
$$

This equation can be expressed in a vector-matrix form as

$$
dy/dt = \dot{y} = Cy + \hat{\lambda}(u + a), \tag{12.9}
$$

where y denotes the n-component column vector with elements y_{si}, and u, a are corresponding column vectors with elements u_i and a_i, respectively, $\hat{\lambda}$ is a diagonal matrix with elements $\lambda_i > 0$ in the diagonal and C is an $n \times n$ matrix with constant elements c_{ij} defined by

$$
\begin{aligned}
c_{ii} &= - \lambda_i (1 - \alpha_i), \quad i = 1, 2, ..., n, \quad i = j, \\
c_{ij} &= \lambda_i \alpha_i \text{ for } j \ne i, \quad j = 1, 2, ..., n.
\end{aligned}
\tag{12.10}
$$

Following Phillips, if we assume that the full employment level of income, i.e., in our case the column vector y^* of sector incomes, is a constant level desired by the policy maker[8] as it might be for short-term situations not exceeding (say) twelve quarters in a mature economy, we can define a new set of units x in which we express equation (12.9) as

$$
dx/dt = \dot{x} = Cx + \hat{\lambda}(u + a), \tag{12.11}
$$

where, if necessary, the vector of constants y^*, which is purely a translation factor, can be set equal to zero by choosing the appropriate unit of measurement. Now the stabilization policy problem in the Phillips model can be stated as follows: how to choose the time path of the control variable u

---

[8] To get an idea how these desired values are predetermined see van den Bogaard and Theil [49].

(i.e., government expenditure for different sectors) such that the deviation x from the full employment (or desired) level is minimized, if possible to a zero level for all or some t, where $t = 1, 2, \ldots T$ indicates the time horizon of the policy maker.

A generalization of the three types of stabilization policies discussed by Phillips, i.e., the proportional, the derivative and the integral policies, can be easily formalized by the following decision rule:

$$u = -\left(F_p x + F_d \dot{x} + F_i \int x \, dt\right), \tag{12.12}$$

where F_p, F_d and F_i are $n \times n$ matrices of real constant elements indicating the reaction (or impact) coefficients for the proportional, derivative and integral policies, respectively. Assuming nonsingularity of the relevant matrices, we may substitute (12.11) into (12.12) and differentiate both sides to obtain

$$(I + \hat{\lambda} F_d) \ddot{x} = (C - \hat{\lambda} F_p) \dot{x} - \hat{\lambda} F_i x \tag{12.13.1}$$

or

$$\ddot{x} - (I + \hat{\lambda} F_d)^{-1} (C - \hat{\lambda} F_p) \dot{x} + (I + \hat{\lambda} F_d)^{-1} \hat{\lambda} F_i x = 0 \tag{12.13.2}$$

or

$$\ddot{x} - M \dot{x} - N x = 0, \tag{12.13.3}$$

where $M = (I + \hat{\lambda} F_d)^{-1} (C - \hat{\lambda} F_p)$; $N = -(I + \hat{\lambda} F_d)^{-1} \hat{\lambda} F_i$ and I is the identity matrix of order n.

Theorem 1. Given the matrices C and $\hat{\lambda}$ of the Phillips model as defined in equations (12.9), (12.10) and (12.11) there exists an "appropriate" choice of the matrices F_p, F_d and F_i such that the state vector x and the policy vector u defined in equation (12.12) are stable in the sense of Laplace, i.e., each characteristic root has a negative real part and hence, each element of these vectors is bounded for all t including $t \to \infty$.

Proof. Given the matrix C, with its elements defined by (12.10), we can always fix the elements of F_p such that the (ij)-th element of the product $\hat{\lambda} F_p$ denoted by $(\hat{\lambda} F_p)_{ij}$ satisfies

$$(\hat{\lambda} F_p)_{ii} = \alpha_i \lambda_i, \quad i = 1, 2, \ldots, n; i = j,$$
$$(\hat{\lambda} F_p)_{ji} = a_j \lambda_j, \quad j = 1, 2, \ldots, n; \quad i = 1, 2, \ldots, n \text{ and } j \neq i$$

when $(C - \hat{\lambda} F_p)$ turns out to be the diagonal matrix $(-\hat{\lambda})$. Further, F_d and F_i can be chosen to be symmetrical and positive definite so that for the diagonal matrix $\hat{\lambda}$, $\lambda_i > 0$ we have $(I + \hat{\lambda} F_d)$ and $\hat{\lambda} F_i$, each symmetrical and positive definite.

It is sufficient to show that an "appropriate choice" of F_d exists. Assume that F_d is diagonal. Then, since by nonsingularity and symmetry the real matrix $\hat{\lambda}$ is positive definite and since by choice $(I + \hat{\lambda} F_d)$ is symmetrical and positive definite, therefore, the product $(I + \hat{\lambda} F_d)^{-1} \hat{\lambda}$ is symmetrical and positive definite. Similarly, the product $(I + \hat{\lambda} F_d)^{-1} \hat{\lambda} F_i$ could be made symmetrical and positive definite by appropriate choice of the matrix F_i, such that the characteristic equation of the system (12.13.3) with the characteristic root μ

$$\det (I \mu^2 - M \mu - N) = 0 \qquad (12.13.4)$$

has for each characteristic root a negative real part and, hence, $x = x(t) \to 0$ as $t \to \infty$. Therefore, the policy vector $u = u(t)$ is stable in the sense of Laplace. The validity of this result in the single sector Phillips model was shown in Chapter 9 before.

Corollary 1.1. If under the conditions of theorem 1 the matrices F_d, F_p and F_i are constrained to be nonsingular and diagonal with positive diagonal elements such that the diagonal element of the matrix $\hat{\lambda} F_p$ equals $\lambda_i \alpha_i$, i.e., $(\hat{\lambda} F_p)_{ii} = (C)_{ii} + \lambda_i = \lambda_i \alpha_i$ for all i, and, further, if $0 \leq \alpha_i < 1$ and $\lambda_i > 0$ are equal to α_0 and $\lambda_0 > 0$ for all sectors (i.e., all i), the policy vector $u(t)$ is stable in the sense of Laplace, if and only if the number of sectors n be such that

$$\alpha_0 (n - 1) < 1 \text{ for } n \geq 1.$$

Proof. Under the assumed conditions the matrix $(\hat{\lambda} F_p - C)$ can be written as

$$(\hat{\lambda} F_p - C) = \begin{bmatrix} \lambda_0 & -\lambda_0 \alpha_0 \dots -\lambda_0 \alpha_0 \\ -\lambda_0 \alpha_0 & \lambda_0 \quad \dots -\lambda_0 \alpha_0 \\ \vdots & \\ -\lambda_0 \alpha_0 & -\lambda_0 \alpha_0 \dots \quad \lambda_0 \end{bmatrix}$$

from which we can compute its determinant as

$$\det (\hat{\lambda} F_p - C) = (\lambda_0 + \lambda_0 \alpha_0)^{n-1} \{\lambda_0 - (n - 1) \lambda_0 \alpha_0\}$$
$$= \lambda_0 (1 + \alpha_0)^{n-1} \{1 - (n - 1) \alpha_0\}.$$

Denoting the k-th order leading principal minor determinant by δ_k we may derive

$$\delta_k = \lambda_0 (1 + \lambda_0)^{k-1} \{1 - \alpha_0 (k - 1)\}; \quad k = 1, 2, \dots, n. \quad (12.13.5)$$

Now suppose the condition $\alpha_0 (n - 1) < 1$ is satisfied for $n \geq 1$, then $\alpha_0 (k - 1) < 1$ for all $k = 1, 2, \dots, n$ and, hence, $\delta_k > 0$ for all $k = 1, 2, \dots, n$. Hence, the symmetric matrix $(\hat{\lambda} F_p - C)$ is positive definite. Hence, the matrix

M of equation (12.13.3) is negative definite and symmetrical. And further, by the assumed conditions the matrix N is negative definite. Hence, the system has for every root a negative real part. Hence, $x(t)$ and therefore $u(t)$ is stable. As a matter of fact, it is not required that the matrix N be symmetrical, i.e., F_i need not be diagonal, so long as the matrix N is negative definite. But the symmetry condition for the matrix M, along with negative definiteness, is both necessary and sufficient, as has been pointed out by Clower and Bushaw [6].

To prove the necessity of the condition $\alpha_0(n-1)<1$ for $n\geq 1$, assume that the matrix $(\hat{\lambda}F_p - C)$ is positive definite. Then we must have from equation (12.13.5) that $\delta_1 = \lambda_0 > 0$ by positive definiteness and again $\delta_2 = \lambda_0(1+\alpha_0)$ $(1-\alpha_0)>0$ by positive definiteness, which implies $\alpha_0 < 1$ since $\alpha_0 \geq 0$, $\lambda_0 > 0$. Now for $k=n$, we have $\delta_n > 0$, which implies that

$$\alpha_0(n-1) < 1 \text{ for } n \geq 1.$$

Corollary 1.2. If under the conditions of theorem 1 the matrices F_p, F_d and F_i are constrained to be nonsingular, each having nonnegative elements with positive elements in the diagonal, and, further, the matrices C and $\hat{\lambda}$ are as defined by (12.10) before, with $\lambda_i > 0$ for each i, then the n-sector Phillips model (12.13.3) cannot have any characteristic root μ_0 having a nonzero real part such that if μ_0 is a characteristic root $(-\mu_0)$ is also a characteristic root.

The economic meaning of this proposition is interesting. For instance, if there exists at least one pair of roots $(\mu_0, -\mu_0)$ having nonzero real parts, then the state vector $x(t)$ and the policy vector $u(t)$ will be unbounded for $t \to \infty$ and hence unstable in the sense of Laplace.

Proof. From the determinantal equation, i.e., (12.13.4)

$$\det(I\mu^2 - M\mu - N) = 0,$$

it is seen that at least one way in which a pair of roots equal but opposite in sign can arise is if the matrix M is null. This requires $\hat{\lambda}F_p = C$, which is impossible because each diagonal element of $(\hat{\lambda}F_p)$ is positive, whereas that of C is nonpositive by conditions (12.10). Alternatively, if $M = -M$, we can have a pair of roots equal but opposite in sign. This is possible if $\hat{\lambda}F_p = C'$ and $C=C'$ where C is symmetric (and prime denotes a transpose), since $(I+\hat{\lambda}F_d)$ is a nonsingular matrix. But even if the symmetry condition $C=C'$ is possible without violating conditions (12.10), it is not possible to ensure $\hat{\lambda}F_p = C'$, since each of the diagonal elements of $\hat{\lambda}F_p$ is positive, whereas that of C' is nonpositive.

Contrarily, suppose there exists such a root μ_0, where $-\mu_0$ is also a root. Then, since it is non-null, μ_0 is other than zero. Let Q be the characteristic vector, then since μ_0, $-\mu_0$ satisfy the determinantal equation it follows that

$$(\bar{Q}'Q)\mu_0^2 - (\bar{Q}'MQ)\mu_0 - (\bar{Q}'NQ) = (\bar{Q}'Q)\mu_0^2 + (\bar{Q}'MQ)\mu_0 - (\bar{Q}'NQ) = 0,$$

(bar denotes complex conjugate)

which implies that $\bar{Q}'MQ = -\bar{Q}'MQ$ which is impossible on our conditions. Hence, the result.

An economic meaning of the assumption that the matrices F_p, F_d, F_i are nonsingular with positive diagonal elements may perhaps be suggested in the following way. Since the diagonal matrix $\hat{\lambda}$ with diagonal elements $\lambda_i > 0$ expresses the speed of adjustment in relation to an excess supply(or demand) in a given sector, the diagonal form of the F_p, F_d, F_i matrices suggests a rule for concentrating sectoral government expenditure u_i in one sector at most for each $i = 1, 2, ..., n$, such that it permits decentralized decision making for each sector i while guaranteeing the stability of the over-all policy $u = u(t)$. In other words, by appropriate choice of the diagonal elements of F_p, F_i, F_d, the diagonal elements of the matrices $(\hat{\lambda}F_p - C)$, $(I + \hat{\lambda}F_d)$ and $\hat{\lambda}F_i$ may be made dominant in a certain sense [32] such that the convergence $x(t) \to 0$ as $t \to \infty$ may be faster.

Now we consider the same model as (12.11) but introduce a criterion function W as a performance integral, which we assume to be of the form

$$W = \tfrac{1}{2} \int_0^T \phi(t) \cdot (x'Ax + u'Bu)\,dt, \tag{12.14}$$

where $\phi(t)$ is a scalar function continuous in $t \geq 0$ and the matrices A and B are assumed to be symmetric and positive definite. Denoting the column vector of Lagrange multipliers by $m = (m_i)$ we define a scalar function f as

$$f = \tfrac{1}{2}\phi(t) \cdot (x'Ax + u'Bu) + m'(\dot{x} - Cx - \hat{\lambda}u - \hat{\lambda}a). \tag{12.14'}$$

Our variational problem is now to choose that policy vector u which minimizes the integral

$$\int_0^T f\,dt$$

unconditionally, assuming the existence, boundedness and continuity of this generalized integral.

Assuming the problem to be nondegenerate, the Euler-Lagrange equations [11] can be derived easily in vector form as

$$\dot{m} = \phi(t)Ax - C'm,$$
$$0 = \phi(t)Bu - \hat{\lambda}m, \qquad (12.14.1)$$
$$\dot{x} = Cx + \hat{\lambda}(u + a).$$

The homogeneous form corresponding to the equation (12.14.1), after elimination of u and multiplying the two sides of the first equation by -1 can be written as

$$-\dot{m} = C'm = \phi(t)Ax,$$
$$\dot{x} = Cx + Rm, \qquad (12.14.2)$$

where $R = (1/\phi(t))\hat{\lambda}B^{-1}\hat{\lambda}$. Let us denote the characteristic equation of this linear differential equation system by $\delta(\mu)$, where μ is the characteristic root. Then we can state the following result:

Theorem 2 (optimality theorem). If there exists a control vector $u = u(t)$ which satisfies equation (12.11) of the multisector Phillips model and also optimizes the performance integral equation (12.14) in a nondegenerate way, i.e., the Euler-Lagrange equations (12.14.2) are nondegenerate,[9] then the optimal control system has the property that if μ_0 is a characteristic root of the system, $-\mu_0$ is also a characteristic root of the system. In particular, if the root μ_0 has a nonzero real part and the initial condition $x(t)$ at $t=0$ is quite arbitrarily fixed, the optimal control vector $u = u(t)$ is necessarily unstable.

Proof. Let μ_0 be a root. Then, from the characteristic equation $\delta(\mu_0) = 0$ we can write the determinant as

$$\delta(\mu_0) = \begin{vmatrix} C' + \mu I & -\phi(t)A \\ R & C - \mu I \end{vmatrix},$$

whereas the determinant corresponding to $\delta(-\mu_0) = 0$ is

$$\delta(-\mu_0) = \begin{vmatrix} C' - \mu I & -\phi(t)A \\ R & C + \mu I \end{vmatrix},$$
$$= \begin{vmatrix} C - \mu I & R' \\ -\phi(t)A' & C' + \mu I \end{vmatrix} \text{ (by transposition)},$$

---

[9] That is, when the two-point boundary conditions cannot be fulfilled generally, except by chance. For a simple discussion on these aspects see Elsgolc [10].

$$= \begin{vmatrix} C' + \mu I & - \phi(t)A' \\ R' & C - \mu I \end{vmatrix} \text{ (by interchange of diagonal)},$$

$$= \begin{vmatrix} C' + \mu I & - \phi(t)A \\ R & C - \mu I \end{vmatrix} \text{ (by symmetry of } R \text{ and } A).$$

$$= \delta(\mu_0)$$

Note that we do not require the matrix C to be symmetric.

Now suppose there exists at least one root μ_0 with a negative real part. There must then exist a root $-\mu_0$ with a positive real part, and, since the initial vector $x(0)$ at $t=0$ is otherwise arbitrary, the coefficient of $\exp(-\mu_0 t)$ in the explicit solution for $x = x(t)$ could be nonzero and hence, $x(t)$, $t \to \infty$ would be unbounded and unstable for an appropriate choice of the constants of integration and the corresponding characteristic vectors.[9a] In particular, if $\phi(t) = \phi_0$ is constant and all the roots are distinct, the solutions of the system (12.14.1) can be written as

$$x_i(t) = \sum_j \{h_j p_{ij} \exp(\mu_j t) + \bar{h}_j \bar{p}_{ij} \exp(-\mu_j t)\},$$

$$u_i(t) = \sum_j \{g_j q_{ij} \exp(\mu_j t) + \bar{g}_j \bar{q}_{ij} \exp(-\mu_j t)\},$$

(12.14.3)

where h_j, g_j and their conjugates $\bar{h}_j$, $\bar{g}_j$ are constants of integration and p_{ij}, q_{ij} and their conjugates are characteristic vectors of (complex) constant elements. Now let the coefficients of $\exp(-\mu_0 t)$ in the above solution, i.e., $\bar{h}_0 \bar{p}_{i0}, \bar{g}_0 \bar{q}_{i0}$, have positive real parts for at least one i, then for that i, $x_i(t)$ and $u_i(t)$ tend to infinity as $t \to \infty$, if the root $(-\mu_0)$ has a positive real part.

Analytically, the multisector generalizations of the relations (12.7), (12.8) would be very similar to the results obtained in our two theorems. Hence, we will not mention them here specifically.

We have thus far obtained a very broad economic result, e.g., if we consider real roots (or roots having nonzero real parts) to be reasonable on a priori grounds, the optimum policy vector $u(t)$ is not stable because it is optimum in the sense indicated above and the nonoptimal policy vector u defined in equation (12.12) is stable because it is not optimum! It appears that stability and optimality are two competitive characteristics of a desirable policy of stabilization in a generalized Phillips model. At the conceptual level, this leads to a very interesting phenomenon for a multiregional policy model, i.e., the need for emphasizing stabilization policies which are less than perfectly optimal and also less than perfectly stable.

[9a] Note that the performance integral (12.14) may not be bounded in this case and this is why in control theory methods, unbounded controls are either excluded or additional conditions of controllability discussed in Chapter 8 are introduced.

An analogous result, e.g., a competitive relation between the stability and the optimality objectives of a multisectoral stabilization policy, holds under certain conditions when an additive random term is introduced into the generalized Phillips-type model and the stability is measured in terms of variance. In this case the generalized model is interpreted in its optimal aspect as a linear stochastic programming problem.[10]

Some comments on the limitations of the theoretical framework presented before may be useful at this stage. First, it must be noted that the condition of disequilibrium, i.e., $y_{si} \neq y_{di}$ for all $i = 1, 2, \ldots, n$, is an essential condition of the model. This implies, of course, that if for some sector there are bottlenecks and constraints which impede any adjustment on the supply side in real terms the adjustment process for that sector will be only in money terms rather than in real terms. The analytical consequences of some of these difficulties are discussed in a slightly different context by Morishima [34].

Second, it may be more realistic to distinguish between the speeds of adjustment or reactions resulting from three mutually exclusive states for each sector, i.e., $(y_{di} - y_{si}) \gtreqless 0$. The asymmetry between the upward and the downward adjustment of supply may be as important as in the "ratchet effect" of the theory of the consumption function. Of course, if $y_{di} = y_{si}$ for all i, then to indicate a growth sequence we should incorporate the multisector generalization of equation (12.8), which would show the equilibrium growth paths in a balanced growth framework. From the standpoint of development planning and central economic policy, we have investigated elsewhere [43] the broad conditions under which it may be desirable to have imbalance in certain sectors, i.e., $y_{dj} \neq y_{sj}$ for some j, and balance in the remaining sectors, provided the impact of such balance and imbalance is assumed to be known.

Third, the probabilistic aspects of sectoral adjustment have been altogether neglected in this analysis. For example, one might suggest in the lines of inventory control theory that there is a probability p_i for $(y_{di} - y_{si}) > 0$ and q_i for $(y_{di} - y_{si}) < 0$ so that the probability of $y_{di} = y_{si}$ is $(1 - p_i - q_i)$. Following this line of argument, one could analyze the stability and sensitivity of an average optimal control policy in purely stochastic programming terms.

A subject for investigation which might lead to important conclusions regarding the stability and optimality of alternative policies of stabilization

---

[10] See Chapter 9 for some results in this connection. However, it should be noted that absolute stability either in the Laplace sense or in terms of variance may not always be a desirable objective, particularly for a developing economy. On this point see Duesenberry *et al.* [8].

and growth in a multisector model is the extent to which an adaptive mechanism could be built into our policy system through recursive programming. Particularly for spatial equilibrium models, some investigation of the optimizing aspects of the speed of adjustment in different regions is needed [7, 45].

12.3. Models for Regional Growth and Planning in Underdeveloped Countries

This section presents very briefly some general aspects of regional growth and planning primarily in the context of an underdeveloped but developing economic framework. Attention is focused mainly on a review of the formulation of economic models for regional growth and planning and their general characteristics and implications, assuming the existence of a mixed economy with private and public sectors.

We have already indicated in Section 12.1 the theoretical usefulness and practical need for a regional disaggregation of the impact of national economic policy for stabilization. This regional orientation is even more important in the context of economic growth which is basically long run and structural. This is so because the "realistic content" of aggregative growth models that are used for national planning and policy in some underdeveloped countries is provided by their regional interdependence through resource endowments, the transportation network and demand, the regional constraints on production and labor supply and the relations of asymmetry in growth between alternative regions.

From the standpoint of national planning for economic development, the need for an interregional analysis of growth is emphasized all the more by two additional considerations, e.g., (1) economic efficiency through decentralization and (2) the specification of an optimum locational pattern in an economy where transportation cost plays a role as important as the potential capacity of certain industries to spread over a large number of regions for the advantage of scale economies less comparative cost and neighbourhood effects.

The theoretical arguments in favor of decentralized decision making have generally been based on the economy in information processing [2, 27, 31]. If there is a central planning agency at the national level for a country with not too small a geographical area, e.g., India or the U.S., it may not be most efficient for the agency to make all detailed decisions concerning all detailed targets. The agency may have limited knowledge about the detailed parameters at the regional levels, particularly when some of the parameters are subject to dynamic shifts.

One could, however, conceptualize two alternative ways of synthesizing a multiple of regional problems into a single national policy model, assuming that each region appropriately defined can be regarded as a decision-making unit. One is to specify that the national policy problem is a team decision problem [36, 37], so that the optimizing considerations of regional decision-making units are incorporated in the formulation of the national policy model. Alternatively, one can specify a multiphase decision model at the national level, where the various regions form different phases, the central agency itself forming one phase in the sequential scheme of decision making.

In the first case, where we have multiple decision makers, some at the regional levels and some at the center, we need a set of rules of coordination. For example, if each regional policy maker is required to fulfill a part of the national target (e.g., employment) and also a regional target (e.g., output of the so-called residentiary industries) which is specific to the region itself, care should be taken to ensure that the policy instruments chosen by different regional policy makers are compatible among themselves and in relation to the national targets set up.[11] The theoretical framework of analysis for such policy problems is best provided by the combination of a detailed multi-regional input-output model [5, 23, 30, 35, 48] with a more aggregative behavioristic growth model. (The latter generally refers to trend variables which are of key importance at the national level.) The balance equation of a multiregional input-output model in the open-static case can be written with superscripts and subscripts as

$$X_i^k = \sum_m \sum_j X_{ij}^{km} + Y_i^k, \qquad \begin{aligned} i &= 1, 2, \ldots, M, \\ j &= 1, 2, \ldots, M, \\ k &= 1, 2, \ldots, N, \\ m &= 1, 2, \ldots, N, \end{aligned} \qquad (12.15)$$

---

[11] Mathematically speaking, this means that the total policy matrix (assuming a linear or linearized case) must be nearly decomposable into block-diagonal submatrices (or submodels), such that any submatrix (or submodel) may specify, except for a few entries, the decision variables specific to a particular region. The few entries (or variables) that are "extra" in a given block or submatrix (submodel) may be predetermined for that region, either by the central policy maker or the optimal solutions found in other regional submodels. It has already been pointed out in Chapter 11 that the Brookings-SSRC econometric model of the U.S. economy can accommodate this type of flexibility. The Mahalanobis model of development planning for India has a lower-triangular coefficient matrix, but no regional decomposition is available.

where we have M commodities (indices i or j) and N regions (indices k or m) and the notations are

X_i^k = total gross production of the i-th commodity in the k-th region,

X_{ij}^{km} = total amount of commodity i supplied from region k to region m for production of commodity j,

Y_i^k = final demand for the i-th commodity in the k-th region,

This system (12.15) has, however, all the advantages and disadvantages of an open-static input-output model. Linearity of the production structure could at least be introduced as a first approximation so that

$$X_{ij}^{km} = f(X_j^m) \simeq A_{ij}^{km} X_j^m, \qquad (12.15.1)$$

where

A_{ij}^{km} = input-output coefficient, which is treated either as an estimated constant or a known quantity.

The autonomous input structure for the production of a commodity i in region k could be introduced in a number of ways [29, 30], of which one would be

$$X_i^k = F_i^k(L_i^k, K_i^k, \varepsilon_i^k(t)), \qquad (12.15.2)$$

$$M_i^k = \mu_i^k X_i^{k'}, \qquad (12.15.3)$$

where L_i^k, K_i^k, M_i^k denote, respectively, for the i-th commodity in the k-th region the volume of employment, the stock of capital, suitably defined, and other autonomous components, such as imports and depreciation of capital. The term $\varepsilon_i^k(t)$ represents an innovation factor in the production function (12.15.2), and μ_i^k may be taken as a constant or a known quantity.

Following Johansen [24] one may introduce profits (π_i^k) and sector prices (p_j^m), e.g.,

$$\pi_i^k = p_i^k X_i^k - \sum_m \sum_j p_j^m A_{ji}^{mk} X_i^k - w_i^k L_i^k - q_i^k M_i^k - r_i^k K_i^k - G_i^k, \qquad (12.15.4)$$

where the wage rate for labor, price of imports from outside and unit return to capital are denoted, respectively, by w_i^k, q_i^k and r_i^k and G_i^k may denote other autonomous components such as indirect taxes. Similarly, the final-demand term Y_i^k could be decomposed into consumption, exports to outside world and government expenditure, as in a conventional input-output model.

Hence, *in principle* this type of model could be used to build multiregional growth aspects into an over-all national model, provided, of course, transport service is conceived to be one of the sectors and there is an over-all consistency in the number of equations and unknowns. However, such a model has a tremendously large dimension, since we are assuming that a commodity supplied from one region should be considered different from the same commodity supplied from another region and that a separate technical coefficient exists for each of such similar inputs. The most important considerations which remain implicit in the whole framework, i.e., of equations (12.15) through (12.15.4), are the number of constraints, regional, sectoral and otherwise, which must be fulfilled before any solution is obtained. These constraints are generally of four types:

(a) The over-all constraints, e.g., that aggregate demand and supply of a commodity i should not remain out of equilibrium beyond a certain pre-assigned level (here the inventory adjustment process may have to be explicitly introduced);

(b) Capacity constraints in the different sectors and regions, with the associated kinks in the process of adjustment;

(c) Constraints resulting from the feasibility characteristics and expansion of the transport sector;

(d) The optimizing constraints which may be introduced by policy makers for political or other reasons.

These constraints could, of course, be formally incorporated by generalizing the above multiregional model in terms of interregional programming, although the policy solutions could be derived iteratively by stages, as in the well-known spatial equilibrium models.[12] If the structure of relations remains linear, recursive programming methods seem to be very suitable for showing the stability or otherwise of the multiregional pattern of trade. However, in the general case the problem becomes one of nonlinear programming because the constraints are nonlinear, e.g., the production function (12.15.2). Such a framework can be varied in different ways, e.g., (a) to introduce elements of immobility of resources, i.e., transportable (nonresidentiary) and non-transportable (residentiary) factors [29]; (b) to specify optimization conditions such as minimizing the difference in regional incomes per capita [48], minimizing economic rent [44] or maximizing a certain return function for different regions; and (c) to dynamize in other ways in order to study the adjustment process resulting from disequilibrium at any given time.

But two basic analytical difficulties remain which have so far proved to be intractable. First, there is the problem of allocating between regions indi-

---

[12] Short-cut methods for solving spatial equilibrium models involving many commodities and regions and integrating them with linear programming formulations of agricultural production are discussed in Fox [14, Chapter 8].

visible resources which generate external economies and diseconomies; here even the initial characterization of the problem is not complete [26, 38]. Second, there is the problem of introducing the element of uncertainty in the interregional adjustment process; although there has been some work on building stochastic elements into a transportation-type model, the analytical framework is as yet incomplete.

In view of the data requirements, it appears that the formulation of a detailed multiregional growth model is almost an impossible task in most underdeveloped countries. It has been observed by Chenery [4, p. 21]:

> Under these circumstances, it is very likely that project analysis based on informed judgment will give a better first approximation than a mechanical procedure such as the simplex method. One approach that has been used in practice in several countries is to start from an existing input-output model for the base year and to assume a probable value for the maximum rate of growth. This permits the maximizing problem to be converted into a (simpler) problem of minimizing the use of one of the inputs—capital or foreign exchange—subject to restrictions on the final demand and the labour and other resources available. The next step is to utilize the partial analysis of investment projects to guess at the optimum proportions of production and imports in each sector. In some sectors, this estimate may require a revision if the input-output coefficients of the industry did not exist or if it produced a very different set of products; otherwise the initial input coefficients can be used as an approximation to the future structure of the industry. On the basis of these assumptions, an input-output solution can be made in order to test the consistency of the assumptions with the limitations on the balance of payments and the supply of capital and labour.[13]

This approach, however, is very close to what we have mentioned before as a multistage decision problem in a multiregional framework. To emphasize the idea of sequential planning by stages, let us assume that in the first stage the dynamic macroeconomic decision problem at the national level involves national income (i.e., selecting the optimal time path of income) and only a very aggregative growth model of the Harrod-Domar type, with a long planning horizon of (say) ten to twelve years.

At the next stage, we consider problems of optimal decision making at the sectoral levels by disaggregating national income into value added by component industries. An objective function different from that in the first stage (e.g., optimizing productivity through investment allocation between

---

[13] Reprinted by permission of St. Martin's Press, Inc., The Macmillan Company of Canada, Ltd., and Macmillan & Co., Ltd.

industries) could be selected at this stage with a planning horizon of, say, three to five years. Any deviation of the observed solutions from the planned levels at the end of each planning period in this second stage could be utilized to revise the initial first-stage decision. This revised first-stage decision is fed back into the model at the second stage to get an improved decision in the second period.

At the third stage we consider regional disaggregation with a still shorter planning horizon of less than three years and introduce a different optimization function such as minimization of social rent or of interregional difference in per capita income. In this stage, also, any information on the deviation between the optimal and actual values could be fed back into the original model. Such a breakdown of the national policy model brings adaptive flexibility into the decision process through an iterative improvement of the decisions at each stage as more and more information is gained sequententially.[14]

In the interregional phase, however, the detailed data required for a multiregional transaction flows (or input-output) table may not be available; this is particularly likely in countries where "dual economy" structures (e.g., Northern and Southern Italy, which are asymmetric in their growth sequence) prevail. Policy models under such conditions must be largely of an econometric type based on as many behavior equations as can be realistically specified either by direct estimates or through information from other, similar countries.[15] It is, however, very difficult to characterize mathematically the relevant types of asymmetry which may exist between different regions in an economy. Hence, a method of trial and error combined with informed judgement may have to be applied.

12.4. Selected Recent Developments in Regional Models of Stabilization, Growth and Planning

This section presents a brief outline of selected recent developments in regional-cum-spatial models applied to growth and stabilization problems of developed countries and to problems of economic planning in the LDC's (less developed countries). The order of discussion will be as follows: the first subsection presents selected recent extensions and applications of the FEA concept introduced before; this is followed by a subsection on the application of other spatial and locational models to problems of growth in developed economies; the third subsection presents a brief outline of selected aspects of regional and spatial equilibrium models that are empha-

---

[14] A more quantitative specification of sequential planning in relation to an investment planning model of the Mahalanobis type may be found in Sengupta [40].

[15] Chenery [3] has followed this pragmatic procedure in discussing the alternative implications of potential regional development policies for Southern Italy.

sized in current models of development planning in the LDC's.

12.4.1. *Recent Extensions and Applications of the FEA Concept*

The FEA (Functional Economic Area) concept [54, 55] has attracted considerable attention in the U.S. and Canada as a basis for delimiting regions for a number of public sector programs. Similar regions have been recognized and used in other countries under other names. The FEA is a nodal region; its central city is a growth center and occupies a particular level in the national system of cities regarded as a hierarchy of central places. Our illustrations in this appendix refer to the U.S.; however, the basic concepts, derived from central place theory, should apply to any country or region.

The FEA concept seemed to emerge in recent times at a point very near the intersection of several specialized fields such as geography, regional economics, demography and perhaps others.

During the early 1960's Brian J.L. Berry was studying the central place hierarchy of the U.S. from the viewpoint of quantitative geography. At a conference in October 1964, Berry served as discussant of a paper by Fox [76]; his comments, "reflections on the functional economic areas," are included in the conference proceedings [50].

Citing a 1964 paper [51], Berry characterized the spatial organization of the United States in terms of a national system of cities, as follows:

1. We live in a specialized society in which there is progressively greater division of labor and scale of enterprise, accompanied by increasing degrees of specialization.

2. There is an increasing diversity of people as producers. But as consumers they are becoming more and more alike from one part of the country to another, consuming much the same "basket of goods" whereever they may live, as well as increasingly large baskets because of rising real incomes.

3. The physical problem in the economic system is therefore one of articulation—insuring that the specialized products of each segment of the country are shipped to final consumers, seeing that consumers in every part of the country receive the basket of goods and services they demand and are able to purchase, and bringing demands and supplies into equality over a period of time.

4. Articulation requires flows of messages, of goods and services, and of funds. The flows appear to be highly structured and channeled and major metropolitan centers serve as critical articulation points. These flows are as follows: products move from their specialized production areas to shipping points in the locally dominant metropolitan centers; over the nation, products are transferred between metropolitan centers, with each metropolitan center shipping out the specialized products of its hinterland and collecting the entire range of specialized products from other metropolitan centers to satisfy the

demands of the consumers residing in the area it dominates; distribution then takes place from the metropolis to its hinterland through wholesale and retail contacts. In the reverse direction move both requests for goods and services and funds to pay for goods and services received, so that the flows are not unidirectional.

Berry commented further that:

The convergence of the above remarks and those of Fox is evident. I emphasize the critical role of the centers of the FEAs in the articulation of the U.S. economy, while Fox emphasizes how nearly the economy breaks down into FEAs.

Also in 1964, officials of the U.S. Bureau of the Census sought the assistance of the Social Science Research Council in conducting a review of its criteria for delineating metropolitan areas for statistical purposes. This led to the formation of an SSRC Committee on (Geographic) Areas for Social and Economic Statistics under the chairmanship of Fox, and to the direction by Berry of a major study of home-to-work commuting data from the 1960 U.S. census.

The recommendations of Berry and his colleagues, adopted by the committee, were as follows:

As a result of the analysis and evaluation we have undertaken, we recommend the following steps be taken to revise metropolitan area definitional practice beginning in 1970:
1. County building-blocks or equivalent units be retained as the basis of any area classification, in all parts of the country.
2. County-to-county commuting data be the basis of the classification of counties into functional economic areas.
3. Functional Economic Areas be delineated around all central counties satisfying the existing SMSA criteria 1 and 2, and in addition be created for smaller regional centers of populations 25,000 to 50,000 in less densely-populated parts of the country.
4. Where significant cross-commuting takes place, functional economic areas be merged by the creation of a consistent set of Consolidated Urban Regions.
5. Consideration be given, for neatness of social accounting, to allocating all unallocated counties to one of the FEA's or CUR's on the basis of additional criteria of regional interdependence.

While the U.S. Bureau of the Census did not incorporate these recommendations in its plans for printed publication of the 1970 census, it appeared (as of December 1971) that the 1970 data needed for special tabulations on an FEA basis would be available to research workers at a relatively low cost and that such tabulations would almost certainly be made.

Berry delineated some 359 FEAs on the basis of the 1960 journey-to-work data. About 85 of these were merged (in groups of 2, 3, 4, 5 or 6) into 31 consolidated urban regions because of significant cross-commuting; each of the other 274 FEAs was delineated as a single commuting field. The complete set of 359 FEAs included 96 per cent of the total U.S. population as of 1960. Berry presented evidence to show that counties in economic distress by reason of high unemployment and low average income in the mid-1960's were largely concentrated in the gaps between commuting fields (and hence between FEAs).

A few applications of the FEA concept may now be mentioned. It is clear that the central place theory which is closely related to the FEA approach seeks to provide valuable insight into the spatial dispersion of economic activities and for that matter of transportation facilities. Using the framework of central place theory, Fox [56] considered an application to transportation planning where the object is to delineate a set of regions under the following assumptions which are applicable to the present U.S. economy:

1. A transportation system exists to serve a community and is embedded in a community.

2. The communities relevant to transportation planning in the United States consist of a hierarchy of central places (successively larger cities) and their trade and service areas covering successively large peographic territories.

3. Home-to-work commuting fields around cities of (typically) 25,000 or more people are the appropriate units for local transportation planning.

4. Larger regions for transportation planning should be made up of sets of contiguous commuting fields, and the set of larger regions itself should cover the entire continental United States.

5. The most promising large regions for transportation planning appear to be centered on about 24 major metropolitan areas—national metropolitan centers in the Berry-Harris hierarchy [52].

The home-to-work commuting fields, approximated by sets of contiguous whole counties, are FEAs. The larger regions, containing 15 to 25 contiguous FEAs in most cases, will be referred to as national metropolitan regions (NMRs).

We arrive, then, at the following view of the U.S. for purposes of passenger transportation planning:

(a) *Local* transportation planning within each of some 500 multicounty FEAs and metropolitan subareas, involving motor vehicles for the most part;

(b) *National* transportation planning at the level of about 24 widely separated cities, mainly involving air travel; and

(c) *Regional* transportation planning within each of some 24 NMRs, involving motor vehicles, (light) planes, and perhaps some interurban transit by rail.

The bases for these conclusions are presented in a 1971 paper by Fox [56]. If these conclusions are accepted with respect to the planning of passenger transportation, we must still deal (1) with the design of transportation systems for the movement of goods, and (2) with the integration of transportation systems for passengers with those for goods.

The NMR central cities, the regional metropolises next below them in the Berry-Harris hierarchy, and the regional capitals (FEA central cities) are all involved in the wholesale distribution of finished manufactures to retailers. These goods usually move by truck over the same highways used for commuting and other passenger travel within an NMR; i.e., finished goods and people can be accommodated by the same central place-oriented transportation network.

The transportation of raw products from the extractive industries (farm and forest products, coal, crude oil, iron ore and the like) to points of first processing and the transportation of semi-finished goods to points of final manufacture can be planned for the most part independently of transportation systems for passengers and finished goods. The NMR central cities are not primarily manufacturing centers, although much manufacturing takes place in them. At some point, finished *consumers' goods* must be transferred from the extractive and processing system to the wholesale and retail distribution system; the latter system is central place-oriented. *Producers' durable goods* (heavy construction materials, machine tools, heavy equipment, etc.) in a sense never emerge from the extractive and processing system.

Hence, comprehensive transportation planning might logically involve (1) a suboptimization for the central place-oriented subsystem, (2) a suboptimization for the extractive and manufacturing subsystem, and (3) a final joint optimization which should require only moderate revisions in the initial suboptima.

We might be justified in calling the first system a *consumption system* and the second a *production system*. The first system could be viewed as aggregating the demands of final consumers and transmitting them to the manufacturers of finished consumers' goods; the second could be viewed as a multi-stage transformation system which culminates in a production possibilities frontier for finished consumer goods. Equilibrium between the two systems would involve a point of tangency between the aggregate (consumer-derived) preference function of wholesalers and the aggregate production possibilities frontier of final-stage manufacturers.

On a formal level, the central place theory bears obvious relationships to models of decentralization in economic theory which are closely related to the decomposition algorithms of mathematical programming and the theory of hierarchical multi-level systems. We will not go into these matters here; several of them are discussed in [63].

It should be emphasized, however, that under U.S. conditions in the late 1960's and early 1970's, the FEA concept appeared to offer a strategic insight into several major problems that were usually discussed in isolation from one another. The following may be cited as examples:

(1) The depersonalization of human relationships and the breakdown of effective community life in large cities;

(2) The fragmentation of rural areas into thousands of counties and innumerable small towns, each of which was too small to exert any significant control over its economic destiny;

(3) The lack of expanding job opportunities in many rural areas, which forced potential young workers and community leaders to migrate over long distances to secure employment and establish homes in distant cities;

(4) The shortage of job opportunities for many residents of the largest metropolitan areas; and

(5) The extremely high national average level of unemployment.

While each of these problems was partly separable from the others, the FEA concept suggested that they formed an interrelated cluster which could best be solved by using an appropriate set of programs and policies in a coordinated way.

The solutions proposed by Fox in 1968 and 1969 [54, 56] included the following:

1. Metropolitan areas should be restructured to establish civic responsibility within logically-delineated subareas of not more than 500,000 residents each.

2. The cohesiveness of multicounty functional areas should be enhanced and their capacity for civic responsibility recognized and further developed.

3. The United States should be viewed as consisting of approximately 500 semi-independent communities, some of which were physically embedded in, or on the edges of, metropolitan complexes and some of which extended over several contiguous counties containing large stretches of farmland and open country. It was suggested that about 150 of these 500 areas, scattered throughout the United States, should be planned, redeveloped and expanded so rapidly as to generate construction booms and local labor shortages.

4. These 150 or so construction booms would provide a means for achieving maximum employment in at least 150 areas and probably more. Employers in each of the construction boom areas would presumably try to recruit additional workers from nearby functional economic areas or nearby sectors of the metropolis, and state and local labor services could doubtless be organized to facilitate these relatively short-distance moves.

5. The capacity of this set of policy instruments (150 planned growth centers plus programs for inter-area labor transfers) should make it possible to approximate full employment in every labor market area without generating a cumulative wage and price inflation. In effect, inter-area labor transfers would be used to implement specific high employment goals in all labor markets. If the result was to "overheat" the national economy as a whole, the traditional nation-wide instruments such as income surtaxes, excise taxes and tightening of the money supply could be used, relying upon labor market transactions to avert serious or protracted unemployment in any individual area.

This list of problems and possible solutions illustrates the power of central place theory to clarify interrelationships between regional and national policies for stability and growth. The implementation problem remains complex, however, unless the requisite political power is also organized on the basis of central place-oriented regions, notably FEAs and clusters of contiguous FEAs.

12.4.2. *Selected Recent Developments in Spatial Models Applied to Growth and Stabilization Problems*

In recent times several attempts have been made to build some elements of space and regional boundaries in the specification of dynamic equilibrium models of an economic system, where the latter may be the national economy, the world as a whole or a small county or district. Two important reasons are perhaps responsible for this trend. First, the computability of large-scale models in a programming or a consistency framework is no longer a stumbling block, thanks to the efficiency of the third-generation computers and the various decomposition algorithms suitable for solving large-scale models by parts interlinked in some fashion. This does not mean of course that any and every nonlinear programming model of a large order can be solved by the existing computer routines; it only means that at least up to linear approximations, large-scale nonlinear models are now comput-able and by suitable parametric methods a successive sequence of linear approximations may be generated. This provides a tremendous impetus to formulating large-scale multi-region models, e.g., world development planning model [59], interregional trade model [60], spatial market models [62], etc. Second, the empirical specification of multisectoral models of growth, using some form of input-output analysis based on several economic sectors [53] has generally ignored the role of transport costs and inter-regional movement of flows, thus rendering the input-output framework economically less meaningful in situations where interregional flows and transport costs are quite important. Recent times have seen a number of attempts to build some spatial elements into the balance equations of an input-output framework. Some of these attempts include the following:

(a) applications (through numerical approximations and linearization of nonlinear equations) of the Leontief-Strout type gravity trade models into the overall framework of the Leontief model [57, 60];

(b) analysis of consistency of input-output flows with independent regres-sion estimates of production concentration where, for example, for the latter the relative pull or attraction of the three independent factors, (i) final demand; (ii) intermediate demand; and (iii) supply by other industries on the size of a given industry in a given area is examined [58]. (For example, if two or more industries mutually attract each other and frequently so, then they tend to be located in each other's neighborhood.);

(c) applications within an overall input-output framework by decom-posing specific sectors of the input-output table which have significant transportation and communication costs into separate submodels where inter-regional balance considerations can be introduced through transporta-tion-type programming models. (This can be done in a number of ways, e.g., if steel is a sector in the input-output table, we can adjoin a separate submodel for steel which minimizes the total cost of movement of steel subject to specified requirements in different regions and specified production capaci-ties in different locations.) This method of linking through submodels is closely related to the stepwise spatial planning procedure suggested by Tinbergen and his associates [59].

In order to appreciate the difficulties introduced by the spatial elements into the input-output type framework, it may be useful to consider the technical aspects of some of the attempts mentioned before. For example, consider case (a) where the Leontief-Strout type gravity model is specified by the following set of equations [60]:

$$x_i^{0g} = \sum_{j=1}^{m} a_{ij}^{g} x_j^{g0} + y_i^{g} \qquad \text{(balance in region } g) \qquad\qquad (12.16.1)$$

$$x_i^{g0} = \sum_{h=1}^{n} x_i^{gh} \qquad \text{(total production in region } g) \qquad\qquad (12.16.2)$$

$$x_i^{0h} = \sum_{g=1}^{n} x_i^{gh} \qquad \text{(total consumption in region } h) \qquad\qquad (12.16.3)$$

$$x_i^{gh} = ((x_i^{g0} x_i^{0h})/x_i^{00}) \cdot q_i^{gh} \qquad \text{(gravity law)}, \qquad\qquad (12.16.4)$$

where $i = 1, 2, \ldots, m$; $g, h = 1, \ldots, n$; $q_i^{gg} = 0$, and other notations are as follows: a_{ij}^{g} = the amount of input of commodity i required by industry j located in region g to produce one unit of output of commodity j; x_i^{g0} = the total amount of commodity i produced in region g; x_i^{0h} = total amount of commodity i demanded by all final and intermediate consumers in region h; x_i^{00} = total amount of commodity i produced (consumed) in all regions; y_i^{g} = total amount of commodity i demanded by final users in region g; x_i^{gh} = the amount of commodity i produced in region g which is shipped to region h; and q_i^{gh} = a trade parameter which is a function of the cost of transferring commodity i from region g to region h where the transfer costs reflect various factors, including transportation costs.

In this specification the first equation states that a balance exists between total amount of good i demanded by intermediate and final users and the total amount supplied to that region, while the second and third defines total production in region g and total consumption in region h respectively. The fourth equation (e.g., the so-called gravity law) states that the shipment of good i from region g to region h is directly proportional to the total production and total consumption of good i in the two regions respectively and inversely proportional to the total amount of good i produced in all regions. Two interesting features of this equation are to be noted. First, this equation allows simultaneous shipment of the "same good" to occur in both directions between two regions which seem consistent with the observed fact that cross-shipments of a given product do occur (note that in the standard Leontief models the cross-shipments are not admissible since it violates the so-called Hawkins-Simon condition [60]). Second, this equation may be interpreted as a cost function by replacing x_i^{gh} with $T(x_i^{gh})$, where the latter (assumed to be a convex function) denotes the costs of transportation associated with the shipment of good i from region g to region h. This transportation cost function may then serve as the imputed objective function of minimizing total transportation cost defined by $\sum_g \sum_h T(x_i^{gh})$ subject to the constraints (12.16.1) through (12.16.4) and the nonnegativity requirements for the variables. In a more generalized framework it may be possible to impute and maximize an overall social welfare function

$$W = \sum_i \sum_g \sum_h [B(x_i^{gh}) - T(x_i^{gh})] \qquad (12.16.5)$$

by assuming that the welfare functions for n regions are additive and the functions $B(x_i^{gh})$ which denote the net benefit associated with the movement of good i from region g (production point) to region h (consumption point) is assumed to be concave.

Three basic types of problems arise in the application of such models. First, the estimation of the gravity-law relationship (12.16.4), particularly when the relative pull of x_i^{g0} and x_i^{0h} may be different is quite difficult and the data requirement high. (Note that in the "attraction model" [58] referred to in case (b) before, this problem is sought to be resolved through separate regression estimates.) The effect of linear approximations to this relationship has to be carefully evaluated, before one considers its application. Second, if the model is applied in a programming framework with an imputed objective function (12.16.5), then difficulties would arise (a) if the transport cost functions have economies of scale, i.e., diminishing marginal cost in some phase (and in that case the cost function would not be convex), or (b) some of the goods or resources are not shiftable between regions. There are also problems of computing nonlinear programming problems [63]. Third, there are problems of consistency between the regional input coefficients (a_{ij}^g) and the overall input-coefficients (a_{ij}), where the latter indicates the overall requirement of good i as an input for producing one unit of good j. These problems increase when in addition we have capital-account coefficients indicating the investment requirements for expansion of output. Once the regional coefficients a_{ij}^g are fixed, they allow no inter-regional substitution. It seems there is no satisfactory method available as yet to test the stability of the coefficients (a_{ij}^g) relative to the overall co-efficients a_{ij} and this may pose a critical problem in combining regional balance (or imbalance) with the overall balance of an input-output frame-work.

12.4.3. *Selected Developments in Recent Applications of Spatial Elements to Development Planning*

Models of investment planning for underdeveloped economies (which are discussed partly in Chapter 10 and later in detail in Chapter 13) which consider the problems of optimal allocation of investment between sectors under production and demand constraints do not generally introduce the element of space in the design or strategy of planning. This attitude is perhaps defensible if any of the following conditions hold good:

(a) the planning model is at the macroeconomic level, to be followed at the micro level by partial models which would include the locational aspects of production, transportation and consumption (demand);

(b) the interregional differences for industries included in a given "sector" may not be very significant so as to invalidate the optimal investment allocation decision based on sectors only;

(c) the planning model at the macro level is built up on the basis of "sectors", which are themselves constructed as different strata as in stratified sampling, so that the regions included within a given stratum are very similar and more or less homogenous but regions belonging to two different strata are quite dissimilar in their economic characteristics. (It is apparent that the hierarchy of sectors in this case would depend on the type of goods used to define a sector.)

It is clear that in case (a) the planning process is followed by stages: the aggregative model linked with various submodels. In many cases the sub-models (or the partial optimization models) have provided greater flexibility to the decision-maker responsible for macro-economic investment alloca-tion policies. For example, assume that a certain quota of investment x has been centrally allocated for a sector which produces "cement" say. If there are m alternative locations which are technically feasible and if there are significant economies of scale in the sense that cost per unit of output is lower for larger sized plants, then a number of choices is possible. For example, one may concentrate all the investment x into one or two locations to take advantage of the economies of scale but in this case the costs of distribution through transportation would be quite high, if the demand is evenly spread over the whole economy. A second possible solution may be to divide the economy into four or five relatively homogenous regions, then rank them in terms of their expected demand and finally locate at most one plant in a region, giving priority to regions having higher demand. This means that if x units of investment can sustain two optimal size plants, locate these into the first two regions having higher demands for cement than the rest. Similar types of two-stage investment planning problems have been attempted in recent literature, using the algorithms of integer programming [63] and also decomposition [63].

The second case (i.e., case (b) above) may be appropriate for economies having smaller areas more or less in a homogeneous form. But even for larger economies having dissimilar regions, this case may hold in an approximate sense where the costs of interregional flows may be subsumed implicitly in the specification of the model. As an example, consider the following national planning model with regional subdivisions (R regions, H, regional sectors, H_2 national sectors) due to Mennes, Tinbergen and Waardenburg [59]:

$$\text{Minimize } z = \sum_{r=1}^{R} \sum_{h=1}^{H} \tilde{c}_{rh} y_{rh} .$$

subject to

$$y_{rh} = \tilde{n}_{rh} y_r \qquad\qquad r = 1, 2, \ldots, R; \ h = 1, 2, \ldots, H_1$$

$$\sum_{r=1}^{R} y_{rh} = \tilde{n}_h y = y_h \qquad h = H_1 + 1, \ldots, H_1 + H_2$$

$$\sum_{h=1}^{H} y_{rh} = y_r \qquad\qquad r = 1, 2, \ldots, R$$

$$y_{rh} \geq 0 \qquad\qquad r = 1, 2, \ldots, R; \ h = 1, 2, \ldots, H.$$

The notations are defined as follows: y_{rh}=increase in income or value added of sector h in region r; y_r=increase in income of region r; y_h=increase in income or value added of sector h in the country; y=increase in income of the country; $\tilde{c}_{rh}$=total cost per unit increase in income of sector h in region r; $\tilde{n}_{rh}$=increase in total demand for product h in region r, measured in value added, per unit increase of region r's income; and $\tilde{n}_h$=increase in total demand for product h in the country, measured in value added, per unit increase of the country's income. For the equations in the constraint set, the first makes supply and demand (measured in value added) equal to each other in each region and for each regional product, the second does the same for each national sector ($h=H_1+1, \ldots, H_1+H_2$) and for the economy as a whole. The third equation specifies that for each region the sum of the sectoral income increases must be equal to the income target of that region. The nonnegativity restriction on y_{rh} expresses the assumption that it is not efficient for any sector to decrease its output in any region. The international sectors (H_3 in number where $h = 1, 2, \ldots, H_1, H_1 + 1, \ldots, H_2, H_2 + 1, \ldots, H_3$) do not appear explicitly in the constraints, since by assumption they are not used to determine the optimal amounts to be produced (i.e., imports and exports are residuals so to say).

Some of the basic assumptions of the above model (over and above linearity) are the following: (1) each product can be classified as either regional, national or international, the transportation costs being assumed negligible for the national or international goods; (2) for each national product the ratio of income to output is the same in all regions; (3) for each national or regional product the increase in demand is proportional to the increase in national or regional income respectively; and (4) for all products differences in prices between regions can be neglected.

In spite of the simplifying assumptions made in the model specification, several features are worth emphasizing in terms of the economic policy framework. First, the implicit costs of setting particular regional targets can be evaluated through the shadow prices (note that once the regional targets have been set through some form of agreement between opposing regional interests, the allocation of the sectors to the regions must take place on the basis of the efficiency criterion). Second, the above model could easily incorporate regional employment targets, by adjoining to the constraint set a number of inequality restrictions specifying that the level of employment generated in a region must be at least equal to a certain minimum. Also, a detailed input-output matrix system could be adjoined, provided input-output coefficients for each region are separately available.

It is clear, however, that in a dynamic framework the growth in the size of a region and its interdependence are affected by the size of the production units in the sectors belonging to a region. The optimum size of production units in a sector depends on a number of factors like transportation costs, the geographical distribution of demand and the rate of change in technology which are rather difficult to specify or estimate in advance. The relative immobility of some resources, less than flexible demand conditions and the so-called "environmental uncertainties", a term used by Meade to characterize uneven adjustment lags are some of the crucial elements which are not yet well incorporated in regional models of development planning.

A very interesting idea in this framework is to develop regional models in a hierarchy (i.e., the hierarchy models [59] developed by Tinbergen and his associates), and then apply perhaps a decomposition type algorithm to interlink the submodels in the hierarchy. The empirical identification of the parameters of this type of hierarchy models however present a formidable task. It is clear that more empirical investigation is needed in this area before any definitive statements on the hierarchical framework of regional planning can be made.

REFERENCES

[1] ARA, K. "Aggregation Problem in Input-Output Analysis," *Econometrica*, XXVII (January, 1959), 257–262.

[2] ARROW, K. J., and HURWICZ, L. "Decentralization and Computation in Resource Allocation," in *Essays in Economics and Econometrics*. Edited by R. W. Pfouts. Chapel Hill: University of North Carolina Press, 1960, pp. 34–104.

[3] CHENERY, H. B. "Development Policies in Southern Italy," *Quarterly Journal of Economics*, LXXVI (November, 1962), 515.

[4] ——. "The Use of Interindustry Analysis in Development Programming," in *Structural Interdependence and Economic Development*. Edited by T. Barna. London: Macmillan and Co., 1963, Chap. 1.

[5] ——, CLARK, P. G., and CAO-PINNA, V. *The Structure and Growth of Italian Economy*. Rome: 1953, Chap. 5.

[6] CLOWER, R. W., and BUSHAW, D. "Price Determination in a Stock-Flow Economy," *Econometrica*, XXII (July, 1954), 328–343.

[7] DAY, R. H. *Recursive Programming and Production Response*. Amsterdam: North-Holland Publishing Co., 1963.

[8] DUESENBERRY, J. S., ECKSTEIN, O., and FROMM, G. "A Simulation of the U.S. Economy in Recession," *Econometrica*, XXVIII (October, 1960), 749–809.

[9] EGBERT, A. C., and HEADY, E. O. "Interregional Competition or Spatial Equilibrium Models in Farm Supply Analysis," in *Agricultural Supply Functions*. Ames: Iowa State University Press, 1961, pp. 203–227.

[10] ELSGOLC, L. E. *Calculus of Variations*. London: Pergamon Press, 1962.

[11] FORSYTHE, A. R. *Calculus of Variations*. Cambridge: Cambridge University Press, 1927.

[12] FOX, K. A. "Economic Instability and Agricultural Adjustment," in *Problems and Policies for American Agriculture*. Ames: Iowa State University Press, 1959.

[13] ——. "The Study of Interactions between Agriculture and the Nonfarm Economy: Local, Regional and National," *Journal of Farm Economics*, XXXIV (February, 1962), 1–34.

[14] ——. "Spatial Price Equilibrium and Process Analysis in the Food and Agricultural Sector," in *Studies in Process Analysis: Economy-Wide Production Capabilities*. (Cowles Foundation Monograph No. 18). New York: John Wiley & Sons, 1963, Chap. 8.

[15] ——. "Integrating National and Regional Models for Economic Stabilization and Growth." Paper presented to the Conference on National Economic Planning, University of Pittsburgh, March 25–26, 1964. (Mimeographed.)

[16] ———. "Programs for Economic Growth in Nonmetropolitan Areas." Paper presented to the Third Conference on Regional Accounts, Miami Beach, November 19–21, 1964.

[17] ———, and KUMAR, T. K. "Delineating Functional Economic Areas for Development Programs." Paper presented to the Strategy for Regional Growth Conference, Center for Agricultural and Economic Development, Ames, Ia., October 13–14, 1964.

[18] ———. "The Functional Economic Area: Delineation and Implications for Economic Analysis and Policy," Paper presented to the Eleventh Annual Meetings of the Regional Science Association, Ann Arbor, Mich., November 13–16, 1964.

[19] FRISCH, R. "From National Accounts to Macroeconomic Decision Models," in *Income and Wealth*, Series 4 (International Association for Research in Income and Wealth). London: Bowes and Bowes, 1954, pp. 1–26.

[20] HEADY, E. O., and EGBERT, A. C. "Regional Analysis of Production Adjustments in the Major Field Crops: Historical and Prospective," U.S. Department of Agriculture Technical Bulletin 1294, November, 1963.

[21] ———. "Efficient Regional Allocation of Farm Products and Programmed Supply Prices," *Agricultural Economics Research*, XVI, No. 1 (January, 1964), 1–11.

[22] HOLT, C. C. "Linear Decision Rules for Economic Stabilization and Growth," *Quarterly Journal of Economics*, LXXVI (February, 1962), 20–45.

[23] ISARD, W. "Interregional and Regional Input-Output Analysis: A Model of a Space Economy," *Review of Economics and Statistics*, XXXIII, (November, 1951), 318.

[24] JOHANSEN, L. *A Multisectoral Study of Economic Growth*. Amsterdam: North-Holland Publishing Co., 1960.

[25] KANWIT, E. L. "Patterns of Recent Employment Changes–Area and National," *Survey of Current Business*, XXXV (June 1955), 15–20.

[26] KOOPMANS, T. C., and BECKMANN, M. J. "Assignment Problems and the Location of Economic Activities," *Econometrica*, XXV (1957), 53.

[27] LANGE, O. *Introduction to Econometrics*. London: Pergamon Press, 1959.

[28] ———. "Output-Investment Ratio and Input-Output Analysis," *Econometrica*, XXVIII (April 1960), 310–324.

[29] LEFEBER, L. *Allocation in Space*. Amsterdam: North-Holland Publishing Co., 1958.

[30] LEONTIEF, W. "Multiregional Input-Output Analysis," in *Structural Interdependence and Economic Development*. Edited by T. Barna. New York: St. Martin's Press, 1963, Chap. 7.

[31] MARSCHAK, J. "Remarks on the Economics of Information," in *Contributions to Scientific Research in Management*. Los Angeles: University of California Press, 1959, pp. 79–100.

[32] MCKENZIE, L. "Matrices with Dominant Diagonals and Economic Theory," in *Mathematical Methods in the Social Sciences*. Edited by K. J. Arrow, S. Karlin, and P. Suppes, Stanford University Press, 1960.

[33] MEYER, J. R. "A Survey of Regional Economics," *American Economic Review*, LIII (March 1963), 19–54.

[34] MORISHIMA, M. "An Analysis of the Capitalist Process of Reproduction," *Metroeconomica*, VIII (December, 1956) 171–185.

[35] MOSES, L. N. "The Stability of Interregional Trading Patterns and Input-Output Analysis," *American Economic Review*, XXXXV (December, 1955), 803–832.

[36] RADNER, R. "The Application of Linear Programming to Team Decision Problems," *Management Science*, V (January, 1959), 143.

[37] ——. "Team Decision Problems," *Annals of Mathematical Statistics*, XXXIII (September 1962), 857–881.

[38] REITER, S., and SHERMAN, G. R. "Allocating Indivisible Resources Affording External Economies or Diseconomies," *International Economic Review*, III (January 1962), 108–135.

[39] SENGUPTA, J. K. "A Simple Generalization of the Phillips-Type Model of Economic Stabilization," Ames: Department of Economics, Iowa State University, 1963. (Mimeographed.)

[40] ——. "Models of Agriculture and Industry in Less Developed Economies," in *Structural Interdependence and Economic Development*. Edited by T. Barna. London: Macmillan and Co., 1963, Chap. 5.

[41] ——. "Economic Policy for Stabilization and Growth under National Economic Planning." Paper presented to the Conference on National Economic Planning, University of Pittsburgh, March 25–26, 1964.

[42] ——. "On the Relative Stability and Optimality of Consumption in Aggregative Growth Models," *Economica*, (February, 1964), 33.

[43] ——, and THORBECKE, E. "Some Observations on the Theory of Economic Growth: Balanced and Unbalanced," *Zeitschrift für die Gesamte Staatswissenschaft*, CXX (April, 1964), 243–263.

[44] SMITH, V. L. "Minimization of Economic Rent in Spatial Price Equilibrium," *Review of Economic Studies*, XXX (October, 1963), 24.

[45] SOLOW, R. "Competitive Valuation in a Dynamic Input-Output System," *Econometrica*, XXVII (January, 1959), 30.

[46] THEIL, H. "A Note on Certainty Equivalence in Dynamic Planning," *Econometrica*, XXV (July, 1957), 346–349.

[47] TINBERGEN, J. *Centralization and Decentralization in Economic Policy*. Amsterdam: North-Holland Publishing Co., 1954.

[48] ——, and BOS, H. *Mathematical Models of Economic Growth*. New York: McGraw-Hill Book Co., 1962, Chap. 7.

[49] VAN DEN BOGAARD, P. J., and THEIL, H. "Macro-Dynamic Policy-Making: An Application of Strategy and Certainty Equivalence Concepts to the Economy of the United States, 1933–36," *Metroeconomica*, XI (December, 1959), 151–154.

[50] BERRY, B. J. L. "Reflections on the Functional Economic Areas", in *Research and Education for Regional and Area Development*. Edited by W. R. Maki and B. J. L. Berry. Ames: Iowa State University Press, 1966, Chapter 2.

[51] BERRY, B. J. L. "Approaches to Regional Analysis: A Synthesis", *Annals, Association of American Geographers*, Volume 54, No. 1, March 1964, pp. 2–11.

[52] BERRY, B. J. L. and HARRIS, C. D. "Central Place", *International Encyclopedia of the Social Sciences*, Volume 2, pp. 365–370. New York: Macmillan and Free Press, 1968.

[53] BOS, H. C., ed. *Towards Balanced International Growth*. Amsterdam: North-Holland Publishing Company, 1969.

[54] FOX, K. A. "Spatial Equilibrium and Central Place Hierarchies in Agricultural Regions Undergoing Rapid Changes in the Mode of Transport", paper presented at First World Congress of the Econometric Society, Rome, September, 1965 (mimeographed). Abstract in *Econometrica*, Volume 34, No. 5, Supplementary Issue 1966, pp. 28–30.

[55] ——. "Monopolistic Competition in the Food and Agricultural Sectors", *Monopolistic Competition Theory: Studies in Impact*, Essays in Honor of E. H. Chamberlin.

Edited by R. E. Kuenne. New York: John Wiley and Sons, Inc., 1967, Chapter 16.

[56] ——. "Delimitation of Regions for Transportation Planning", *Proceedings of a Conference on Regional Transportation Planning: The Rand Corporation, January 25–27, 1971.* (Report R-706-DOT prepared for the U.S. Department of Transportation). Santa Monica: Rand Corporation, May 1971, Chapter 2.

[57] GHOSH, A. *Planning Programming and Input-Output Models: Selected Papers on Indian Planning.* Cambridge: Cambridge University Press, 1968.

[58] KLAASSEN, L. H. and VAN WICKEREN, A. C. "Interindustry Relations: An Attraction Model, a Progress Report", in *Towards Balanced International Growth*, edited by H. C. Bos, *op. cit.,* pp. 245–268.

[59] MENNES, L. B. M., TINBERGEN, J. and WAARDENBURG, J. G. *The Element of Space in Development Planning.* Amsterdam: North-Holland Publishing Company, 1969.

[60] POLENSKE, K. R. "Empirical Implementation of a Multiregional Input-Output Gravity Trade Model", in *Contributions to Input-Output Analysis:* Proceedings of the Fourth International Conference on Input-Output Techniques; Volume I, edited by A. P. Carter and A. Brody. Amsterdam: North-Holland Publishing Company, 1970, Chapter 7.

[61] PORTER, B. "Stabilization Policies for Multi-Sector Closed Economies", *International Journal of Systems Sciences,* Volume 2, No. 2, 1971, pp. 113–117.

[62] SERCK-HANSSEN, J. *Optimal Patterns of Location.* Amsterdam: North-Holland Publishing Company, 1970.

[63] SENGUPTA, J. K. and FOX, K. A. *Economic Analysis and Operations Research: Optimization Techniques in Quantitative Economic Models.* Amsterdam: North-Holland Publishing Company, 1969.

Chapter 13

ECONOMIC POLICY MODELS FOR
DEVELOPMENT PLANNING

The main purposes of this chapter are to show how policy models can be applied to the process of development planning and thereby provide a link between the theory of economic policy and the theory of economic development and to review in a systematic way some of the major development planning models which have been formulated.

An essential difference which exists between development planning models and the policy models used by countries such as the Netherlands and Japan (which are discussed in detail in Chapter 14) is that the former are mainly concerned with economic development within a medium or long-term time horizon, with little or no attention being paid to stabilization, whereas the latter are usually formulated for short-term stabilization purposes, often within a growth framework.[1]

The essence of a development planning model consists of the integration of a model of economic growth (development) and a policy model. The cornerstones of a planning model are economic theory, which helps to provide the basic behavioral and technical relationships between the various variables, and national income accounting, input-output information, consumer surveys, and a host of other micro and sectoral data. The national income accounts besides supplying the necessary time series yield the macroeconomic and in some cases sectoral identities required to close the model. The input-output tables provide the intersectoral relationships which underly most of the multisectoral models. Consumers' surveys yield estimates of income elasticities of demand and other behavioral parameters; while other data are needed to specify sectoral production and other functions depending on the form of the model.

Ideally, a development planning model should be entirely specified in its

---

[1] The major differences between development planning and stabilization models are discussed in Fox and Thorbecke [10].

equational form before starting the estimation process. In fact, data limitations often preclude strict adherence to the above approach. The more usual procedure is for the technicians formulating development planning models to move back and forth between the formal relationships which they have derived from economic theory and the theory of economic policy, on the one hand, and the available data on the other. The end result of this "ping-pong game" is a model which uses the existing statistical information well, while altering the form of the initial model (either in terms of the variables entering into the model or the shape of the functions relating the latter). In an effort to avoid this last alternative, the model builder will often rely on a priori or cross-section information when the relevant time series are scarce or of questionable quality. This is not to say that a priori or cross-section data are substitutes for the domestic time series of a country for which a development model is prepared. They may be used as such, but in a more general sense they provide a very important additional and complementary type of information even when the relevant historical series are available.

An attempt is made in the following sections to review some of the most important development planning models presently available. These models are subdivided into three major classes. Section 13.1 reviews consistency type models, Section 13.2 deals with optimization models and finally Section 13.3 covers simulation models. Each of these classes is further subdivided according to the degree of sectoral disaggregation. It is felt that the present survey, if not exhaustive, is representative of the present state of the arts.

13.1. Consistency Type Models

A consistency type model, in contrast with an optimization model, does not contain an explicit objective or preference function to be maximized. At the same time, such a model should contain a number of potential target variables among the set of endogenous variables as well as a number of instrument variables among the set of exogenous variables. Thus, even though the preference function of the policymaker is not explicitly formulated, it is possible to follow through the effects of changes in the controlled (instrument) variables and other exogenous variables not under the control of the policymaker on the set of potential targets which are more or less reflective of the policymaker's objectives. In this sense, a consistency type model usually is more flexible than an optimization type model. Various consistent solutions (i.e., development alternatives) can be obtained which correspond to implicit preferences.

This type of model can be broken down into aggregate models which are discussed in Section 13.1.1 and multisectoral models discussed in Section 13.1.2.

13.1.1. *Aggregate (Macroeconomic) Models*

A whole variety of macroeconomic models have been built by individual researchers, planning commissions, international agencies and others. There are at least two major purposes of macroeconomic models. The first one is to explain the major relationships linking the macroeconomic variables over a given period of time, particularly with regard to aggregate consumption, imports, investment and taxes. Another purpose of these models is to obtain consistent projections and test which are the major constraints to economic growth (i.e., balance of payments, investment-savings and in some cases skill constraints). Two important subclasses of macroeconomic models are reviewed here: (a) the export-led, demand-oriented models; and (b) the two-gap models.

A. Export-led, Demand-oriented Models:

In a large number of developing countries exports have provided the proverbial engine of economic growth. In addition, for many of these countries, exports tend to be exogenously determined at least in the short run. Thus, relatively simple Keynesian type models can capture relatively well the growth process. The Thorbecke-Condos [32] model of the Peruvian economy over the period of 1950–66 can be given as an example of this type of model. A version of this model is given in Section 13.5.1. It consists of five behavioral relationships and seven identities. The former were estimated by least squares (one and two stages) on the basis of annual observations covering the period 1950–66 expressed at constant 1963 prices. Out of the six exogenous variables which appear in the system, five relate to the foreign trade sector (i.e., the current and lagged values of exports and the terms of trade effects, and the net inflow of foreign public investment). In this model, private investment is determined by exports and the terms of trade effect lagged one year.[2] Private investment, in turn, is a major determinant of

---

[2] A highly significant statistical relationship was obtained by regressing private investment on lagged exports and the lagged terms of trade effects (see 13.5.1). Thus, private investment is determined exogenously through the changes occurring in the export sector. This would appear to be a reasonable hypothesis given: (a) the relative importance of the export sector; (b) the highly capital intensive nature of export industries; and (c) the relative insignificance of the domestic capital goods-producing sector. It is also relevant, in this connection, to note that UNCTAD used the same relationship as in the Thorbecke-Condos model to explain private investment as a function of lagged exports and terms of trade effects in a large scale econometric model designed to estimate the future trade gap. See UNCTAD [37].

income of which private consumption as well as direct and indirect taxes are functions. Finally, imports are explained by consumption and total investment.

One test of the explanatory power of such a model is to test its predictive ability over the sample period. The first step in such a test is to derive the reduced form of the model by expressing the set of endogenous variables exclusively as a function of the set of exogenous variables and the constant terms.

In symbols, let: A = the coefficient matrix of the endogenous variables, y = the vector of endogenous variables, B = the coefficient matrix of the exogenous variables (including the lagged endogenous variables), x = the vector of exogenous variables, and c = the vector of constant terms.

The estimated model in the Appendix can be expressed as:

$$Ay - Bx - c = 0. \tag{13.1.1}$$

The reduced form of this model is:

$$y = A^{-1}Bx + A^{-1}c. \tag{13.1.2}$$

The matrix $A^{-1}B$ is the matrix of impact multipliers linking the exogenous variables to the endogenous variables. Table 13.1.A in the Appendix gives the reduced form of the Peru model.

The second step, after having derived the reduced form, consists of substituting the actual values of the exogenous variables into equation (13.1.2) above and obtaining the predicted values of the set of endogenous variables (the $\hat{y}$'s) for each year of the sample period. The final step is to compare the values of the predicted exogenous variables with the actual observed values of the endogenous variables (the y's).

The predictive ability of the Peru model on the basis of the above test appeared relatively high. Consequently, this model could be used for short term projection purposes and more specifically to estimate the effects of changes in exports, the terms of trade and the net inflow of public investment on key endogenous variables such as GDP, consumption, private investment and imports.

A model of this type can be useful at the purely macroeconomic level in determining the effects of foreign trade sector variables on GDP growth and the balance of payments (since imports is an endogenous variable). In the short run, the consistency between exogenously determined foreign exchange inflows and GDP growth, on the one hand, and balance of payments equilibrium, on the other hand, can be checked. The major limitation of the above model is the lack of an explicit aggregate production function.

Similar models have been built for a number of countries particularly in Latin-America where the export dependence tends to be substantial. (See for example the models built for Guatemala [11] and Colombia [34].)

B. Two-Gap Models:

Two-gap models try to incorporate into a macroeconomic model the role of foreign assistance. The essence of these models is that two independent constraints may limit economic growth. The first constraint on skills and savings, if it were the binding one, is described as the investment limited growth. Alternatively, when the balance of payments limit is effective, trade limited growth would follow. The underlying assumption is that developing countries are characterized by resource bottlenecks and limited structural flexibility. Either the investment-savings gap or the balance of payments gap may be binding at any one point in time.

An early version of the two gap approach is the Chenery and Bruno model of Israel [6]. The model is given in Section 13.5.2. Eight of the variables appearing in the model are considered as policy variables and divided into classes (which are not mutually exclusive):

Fixed targets (exclusively): government current expenditure (G) and unemployment rate (u).

Variable targets (exclusively): gross national product (V), private consumption (C).

Instrument (exclusively): effective exchange rate (r).

Instrument and institutional limit: marginal propensity to save (s).

Institutional limit (exclusively): labor demand (L).

Variable target, instrument and institutional limit: foreign capital inflow (F).

The logic of the above breakdown is that full employment and services resulting from government expenditures are set up as fixed objectives. Institutional limits or, in other words, judgments concerning the ranges within which the corresponding variables are allowed to fluctuate (without upsetting the economic and political balance) are assigned to F, L and s. In these cases three levels are used for each variable.

Three typical instrument variables are considered—r, s and F—which except for the preassigned institutional limits are under the control of the policymaker. Finally, three variable targets are specified—V, C and F (which is also an instrument).

The reduced form of this model can be obtained by eliminating all the irrelevant endogenous variables, thus ending up with four equations in the eight policy variables. These equations correspond to the three equilibrium conditions for labor, capital and foreign exchange and the last one expresses total consumption $(C + G)$. In a sense the model contains four policy degrees of freedom since four policy variables could be assigned arbitrary values and the values of the remaining four unknowns could be derived on the basis of the four linearly independent reduced form equations.[3] Considering the limitations which have been placed on these policy variables, i.e., (a) government expenditure (G) and the unemployment rate (u) being fixed targets, and (b) the level of capital imports (F), the rise in labor productivity (m), the rate of exchange (r) and the savings ratio (s) being assigned ranges within which they can move, the policy problem reduces itself to specifying the alternative sets of values of these eight variables which satisfy the equations of the reduced form and the above "policy constraints".

The flexibility which is introduced in this model, through the above discussed degrees of freedom, appears to be a real advantage. Indeed, the policymaker can be presented with a set of different—but internally consistent—alternative policy programs (defined as a set of values of the eight policy variables satisfying the model and the boundary conditions). The policymaker can then select one program among this set. In the selection process the policymaker will have to use an explicit or an implicit welfare function. If he employs the latter, which would seem to be more likely and typical, his choice among alternative programs reveals, essentially, the preference function of the government. It is, of course, true that the welfare function of the policymaker is already bounded in the above model by the imposition of fixed values to government consumption and the rate of unemployment and by the assignment of maximum and minimum values to s, m, F and r. Nevertheless, there remains a feasible area, and it is in selecting among the feasible alternative programs that the policymaker further reveals his welfare function and, more specifically, his evaluation of the incremental benefits (mainly in terms of V and C) and incremental costs of the various policy variables.

The Chenery-Bruno model lends itself to a linear programming formulation. The various constraints, i.e., s, e and F as well as the institutional limits

---

[3] This statement has to be qualified in at least two ways. First, once fixed values are assigned to the fixed targets G and u, only two policy degrees of freedom are left. Secondly, any "arbitrary" values selected for the institutional limit (r, s, L, F) should fall within the predetermined ranges for these variables.

on other variables and parameters yield a feasible set. An optimal solution within this set could of course only be obtained after specifying explicitly an objective function to be maximized.

The two gap approach is formalized in a somewhat later article by Chenery and Strout [7]. The essence of the Chenery–Strout framework is a proposed method for the estimation of the foreign aid required by a typical developing country in the course of growth. The main features of the theory are, first, that foreign aid can be used to fill either a saving gap or a foreign exchange gap and, secondly, that a typical less developed country will normally move through three distinct consecutive stages of growth which can be identified by a difference in the gap filling function of aid, i.e., a skill-limited phase, a saving-limited phase, and a trade-limited phase.[4] At the outset of the development process the absorptive capacity of a developing economy in terms of investment is limited by skill shortages, which is incorporated in the model by the postulation of an exogenously determined maximum growth rate of investment. In a sense this growth rate reflects the rapidity of the learning-by-doing process. After investment has reached a certain level, the saving constraint becomes binding. In both of these cases the gap between needed investment and the available domestic savings can be measured and is to be filled through foreign aid. Finally, in the third phase the trade gap becomes larger than the saving gap and is thus binding.

The Chenery and Strout model is in fact overdetermined. It is this over determinacy which allows the existence of a "gap between the two gaps" [9, p. 905] in an ex ante sense while ex post these two gaps should be of equal magnitude. The process which is described is a disequilibrium process which implies structural inflexibilities. While this type of model can be criticized on methodological and on operational grounds, e.g., that it does not necessarily describe the development process of an aid recipient and that the sequence of phases may be different than the one postulated by the authors, the approach can be useful in measuring the productivity of foreign aid and in providing criteria for the allocation of foreign aid.

The two gap approach has been applied retrospectively to build structural models of, e.g., Pakistan [7], Greece [2] and Israel [6], covering the last two decades. In addition, the United Nations Conference on Trade and Development (UNCTAD) prepared detailed projections of the trade prospects and capital needs of a series of developing countries [37] using the two gap methodology.

[4] Fei and Ranis [9] give a systematic and formal evaluation of the Chenery-Strout model which clarifies some of the issues brought out in the latter.

The models described above are representative of aggregative development planning models, where the object is to follow through the impact of changes in a few policy (controlled) variables and exogenous variables on key noncontrolled (target) variables. The corresponding effects of disaggregation, such as a sectoral, regional, choice of techniques and decentralized policy implications, can only be arrived at with the help of adjunct disaggregative models which are integrally related to the macro model or embrace the latter.

13.1.2. *Multisectoral Models*

There are basically two types of consistency type multisectoral models: (a) models broken down in a few major sectors, not relying on an input-output table; and (b) models based on input-output information. The former type contains usually sectoral production and consumption functions for major sectors and categories of goods, while abstracting from the intersectoral links. The latter type of model on the other hand is based on a much greater degree of disaggregation and incorporates specifically the intersectoral relationships.

A. Models Disaggregated in a Few Major Sectors:
   This class of model represents an extension of the macroeconomic model reviewed previously. The main difference is that instead of having one aggregate production or consumption function, for example, these functions are specified for a few major sectors. Two examples of such models will be given here, i.e., the Adelman-Mahn Je econometric model of the Korean economy [3] and the Thorbecke-Field Argentina model [33].
   The Korean model consists of twenty-six equations (14 behavioral relations and 12 identities). The model was estimated on the basis of annual observations covering the relatively short period of 1956–66. As is typical of such a model, all values are expressed in constant prices. The system includes 26 endogenous variables, 5 exogenous policy variables and 14 other exogenous and predetermined variables. Five groups of behavioral (structural) equations were estimated: production functions, consumption functions, investment equations, import demand equations and some tax and monetary equations.
   Production functions are specified to explain sectoral value added for, respectively, the primary sector, mining and manufacturing, social overhead, and services. In each case a major determinant of sectoral value added is the stock of capital. Consumption expenditures were disaggregated into food and nonfood private consumption, and government consumption. The first

two types of consumptions are explained by disposable income and a measure of the internal terms of trade while government consumption is regressed on domestic taxes. The sectoral breakdown for the investment function is similar to that of the production function. These equations describe how the desired level of investment is determined in each sector. These relations are of the "accelerator" type and includes some financial variables. The final set of structural relations explains imports of, respectively, machinery and equipment, goods and services other than machinery, and intermediate raw materials.

This model is in fact of the two gap variety in that ex ante inequalities arise between the saving-investment gap and the import-export gap. A simple algorithm is worked out to equate these two gaps ex post. For instance, if the saving-investment gap is the larger of these two, the adjustments may take the form of extra imports, fewer exports, or lower consumption levels than were desired on the basis of the behavioral relationships. The reduced form of the model and the corresponding dynamic multipliers were obtained which made it possible to follow through the impact of the major policy instruments and other exogenous variables on the whole set of endogenous variables. Again, an interesting feature of this model is that partial dynamic multipliers, resulting from such policies as increasing the money supply, have an impact upon aggregate demand or aggregate supply or upon both, revealing the possibility for ex ante inequalities between the two factors. Various alternative development strategies can be simulated by varying exogenous instruments such as taxes, government investment budget, money and time deposits, agricultural prices and the foreign exchange rate.

The Thorbecke-Field of the Argentina economy [33] is designed to describe the interrelationships between the foreign trade and the productive sectors of the economy, investigating sector by sector the effects of policy actions on the structure and levels of current exportables and on the composition and destinations of current imports. The importance of this sectoral follow-through is borne out by the experience of Argentina, where the failure of policymakers to promote exports and the emphasis on import substitution of consumer goods industries (which required indirectly a large amount of capital-machinery and equipment imports) contributed heavily to disequilibrium between the foreign sector, other sectors, and certain targets of growth and development.

The model—given in Section 13.5—consists of 23 equations explaining 23 endogenous variables. Eight of the equations (Nos. 2, 3, 4, 5, 6, 7, 13 and

22) are behavioral, with the remaining 15 definitional or technical. A brief discussion of these equations follows. The first is the income identity equation relating gross domestic product, (Y_s) to the sum of its components. Equation 24 defining GDP from the demand side can be obtained through a substitution process involving equations 1, 8, 9, 10, 11, 12 and 18 and is therefore not an independent relation in the model. In this sense the model is an equilibrium model, in contrast with a two gap type model. Equations 2–4 are the sectoral production functions for agriculture, industry and services, respectively. Equations 5–7 relate consumption of agricultural products, industrial goods, and services to changes in disposable income, the internal terms of trade, and a variable reflecting changes in income distribution, respectively.

Sectoral exports are specified in equations 8–10 essentially as the surplus available for export after consumption and investment requirements have been deducted from available supply. This assumes that the foreign demand for Argentine exports is infinitely elastic with respect to price, an assumption that appears reasonable at least for the country's major export products (the share of agricultural exports to total exports fluctuated between 80 and 90 per cent during the sample period). The form of these export equations is interesting in that a reconciliation between the expenditure variables and the value added variables is necessary to explain exports at a residual part. The parameters appearing in the export equations were derived directly from input-output relationships (see [33, pp. 189–90] for an explanation of the methodology).

Imports are broken down into the basic categories in equations 11–14, i.e., imports of raw materials and intermediate goods, capital goods, and consumption goods (the latter being specified exogenously). The rationale for this stems from the fact that in Argentina, and most developing countries, imports of consumption goods are regulated almost entirely by government import controls. Imports of raw materials (equation 13) are specified endogenously as a function of the level of output in the industrial sector and of the purchasing price as reflected by the external terms of trade. The remaining import equation, 14, defines imports of capital goods residually after all claims on foreign exchange earnings have been deducted. This implies that Argentina's capacity to import is always fully utilized and that the demand for imports of capital goods is bounded only by the availability of foreign exchange. The first claimant on foreign exchange will be raw material imports to utilize existing capacity to the fullest before applying foreign exchange to the importation of capital goods. Equations 15–17 are

self explanatory. The alpha, beta, and gamma coefficients are policy parameters that reflect the shares of total investment to be allocated to the three
major sectors. In the case of Argentina, it is important to note that the
supply of exports can mainly be affected through increases in alpha. Equations 18–21 provide the definitions of the investment components. A
behavioral relationship explaining the output of domestic investment goods
as a function of the lagged capacity variable and the annual change in
industrial value added is given in Equation 22.

The causal links between the major variables in the above model can be
expressed.[5] The causal interpretation is relatively straightforward. The
distribution of total investment among the three productive sectors (by
varying the alpha, beta and gamma shares discussed above) determines
the sectoral capital stocks which in turn affect the sectoral value added
magnitudes. The supply of investment funds is simultaneously determined by the domestic production of investment goods and the capacity
to import capital goods. The capacity to import, in turn, explains the
level of agricultural and nonagricultural output available for export.[6]
An increase in alpha would imply the channeling of additional investment
into the agricultural sector, thereby increasing agricultural output and,
potentially, the quantity of agricultural products available for exports. The
exportable surplus would also be increased by reducing domestic consumption of agricultural commodities. There is fairly strong evidence that in the
forties and fifties the stagnation in agricultural production was the result
of a relatively low allocation of investment to that sector and of price
policies which discriminated against it. Indeed, the internal terms of trade
were moved against agriculture, partially to favor the import substitution
process in the consumer goods industries and partially to provide low cost
food to the urban workers. In turn, these price policies led to a very substantial increase in agricultural consumption. Hence, a combination of
relatively low levels of investment into agriculture and price policies unfavorable to agriculture led to, respectively, a stagnation in agricultural
output and a substantial increase in agricultural consumption resulting in a
decline in the exportable surplus. The latter, in turn, affected the capacity to
import and constrained the growth process strongly.

---

[5] See [33] for this causal diagram.

[6] Since historically the agricultural sector has accounted for 90 per cent or more of total
exports, the amount of agricultural products available for export becomes the principal
determinant of the capacity to import and, hence, of capital goods imports.

Whereas most multisectoral models of the above type use a sectoral breakdown along productive lines, other breakdowns are possible as well. For example, it would be reasonable in a number of developing countries to use a dual breakdown either at the level of the economy, or better at the sectoral level, whenever appropriate. In this latter case sectors such as agriculture, services and certain branches of industry would be broken down into a traditional and a modern subsector to reflect the substantial differences in the production functions of the subsectors. One interesting example of a two-sector model of a hypothetical economy along dual lines, which would appear to be applicable to at least small dual economies, is that of Sandee [30]. Sandee builds a relatively simple macroeconomic model along dual lines and uses programming techniques to measure the impact of changes in instrument variables, tax changes, urban food rationing, and food subsidies in urban areas on potential targets such as GNP, the rural and the urban standards of living.

B. Multisectoral Input-Output Type Models:

In general, models of this type are used not only to explain the underlying multisectoral structure of the economy but, more importantly, to project sectoral output (and in some cases employment) in a way consistent with the structure of production (given by the linear sectoral production function in the input-output matrix) and the behavioral demand relationships for domestic and imported goods. Thus, such models are very useful in testing the feasibility, at the disaggregated level, of attaining given target growth rates of GNP and of revealing the sectoral implications with respect to supply and demand of macroeconomic plans.

Since the characteristic feature of this type of model is the reliance which is placed on input-output information, a few comments about the alternative forms which the I–O information may take appear in order. According to the relationship which is specified between inputs and outputs, three different alternative models can be constructed: (1) the constant average coefficients model which is based on the original Leontief formulation and which is still the most widely used version. Input-output coefficients, consumption coefficients, and even capital-output ratios are assumed constant over time; (2) the constant marginal coefficients model, where the marginal rather than the average coefficients are assumed constant. Usually these models necessitate at least two input-output tables to derive the marginal coefficients; and (3) the constant elasticity coefficients model where elasticities are used to relate inputs to outputs, household demand to income and capital requirements to production.[7]

The treatment of imports is also subject to alternative formulations. In each case imports may be separated into competitive and noncompetitive types.[8] In the first approach, imports of the noncompetitive type are distributed according to the end-use and the inter-industry flows are considered as inputs with fixed input coefficients in each sector. The competitive type of imports is treated as a negative column vector in the final demand matrix and is estimated exogenously.[9] A second approach divides the input coefficients a_{ij} between domestic input coefficient d_{ij} and the import input coefficients m_{ij} ($a_{ij} = d_{ij} + m_{ij}$). The final demand vector F (consumption, investment and exports) is also divided into two vectors, that is F_d (the components of final demand met by domestic production; and F_m, the components of the final demand met by imports. Then the balance equations can be written as $(I - D)X = F_d$, where D is the matrix of d_{ij} coefficients, and

$$M = (m_{ij})X + F_m, \qquad (13.1.3)$$

where M is a vector of imports, $[m_{ij}]$ is the matrix of m_{ij} coefficients. Imports are now endogenous to this system, and the interindustry table has to be "double-celled", one cell corresponding to the domestic component, and the other cell corresponding to the imported component.

Finally, a third method is to consider the imports of a commodity as a given proportion of the domestic production of that commodity. Thus, the ratios of sectoral imports to sectoral output are postulated and imports can be treated as a negative column vector among the components of final

---

[7] This last method is the one which van Rijckeghem [39] used in building a model of Brazil which is subsequently discussed. As van Rijckeghem indicates, the relative magnitude of measurement error increases considerably as "the move is made from average to marginal coefficients or to elasticities". At the same time, it should be noted that a formulation in terms of elasticities is the most general one since it can be made to embrace constant coefficients (in which case the elasticity coefficients will be unitary) or any given marginal coefficients.

[8] This distinction is somewhat arbitrary. In some cases the import of a commodity is defined as competitive if less than half the supply available is imported. Furthermore, in other cases complementary imports are distinguished between use-specific and non-use-specific. The use-specific component can be considered of a technological nature while the non-use-specific component can be thought of as amenable to import substitution in a given period of time (though both types are complementary in the initial period). See ECAFE [38] for specific detail.

[9] The present discussion on alternative ways of treating imports in an input-output framework is based on ECAFE [38] which should be consulted for a more detailed technical discussion.

demand. This method permits one to make assumptions regarding the possible degree of import substitution.

Two of the most interesting attempts at building intersectoral consistency models are those of van Rijckeghem for Brazil [39] and Tims for Pakistan [36]. Both of these are variants of the closed dynamic Leontief approach. As was previously pointed out, instead of using constant or marginal average coefficients in projecting input-output coefficients, consumption co-efficients and capital output ratios, van Rijckeghem uses elasticities. van Rijckeghem explains clearly the various steps involved in constructing his intersectoral consistency model which, in general, might apply to most models of this type. These steps are: (1) the determination of the overall growth rate for GNP—preferably within a macroeconomic framework or based upon a simple macroeconomic model; (2) the determination of the growth rates of consumer demand for the products of the various sectors consistent with the overall growth rate (various types of consumption func-tions based on aggregate or per capita income elasticities or expenditures elasticities can be used to estimate consumer demand); (3) the determination of the sectoral growth rates of the other components of final demand (invest-ment, government consumption and exports) which at that stage are taken exogenously;[10] (4) the determination of the sectoral growth rates of gross output consistent with the growth rates of final and intermediate demand weighting each of the latter's components by "product distribution co-efficients", reflecting the relative distribution of supply in the input output table at the outset of the planning period; (5) the specification of the prevail-ing degree of self-sufficiency for each sector at the beginning of the planning period; (6) the determination of the import substitution targets—expressed by a relationship between the growth rate of competitive imports and of total supply; (7) the specification of the input-output elasticities; (8) the derivation of the growth rates of sectoral output through the substitution of steps 7, 6, 5, and 2 into 4 as function of a set of predetermined variables; (9) the determination of the sectoral growth rate of capital stock correspond-ing to the growth rates of sector outputs and the specification of the growth rates of total investment demand for capital goods supplied by each appro-priate sector. "Investment distribution coefficients" reflecting the distribu-tion of investment at the beginning of the planning period are used to allocate investment by sector of destination to investment by sector of

---

[10] As a first approximation, the growth rate of total investment is derived from the macro model used in step 1.

origin. At this stage, the calculated sectoral growth rates of investment demand can be compared to those assumed at stage 3 and 4 of the model. This leads to an iterative procedure which leads the system to converge rapidly. Finally, the last step (10) consists of a check of the feasibility of the global growth rate selected initially at stage 1. If the initial growth rate is not feasible, either it or the import substitution targets may have to be revised.

The above model was applied to Brazil—making use of the 1959 input-output table which is broken down into 32 sectors, consumption functions derived from family budget surveys and extraneous information about investment requirements and the capital matrix. Two interesting features of this model, in addition to the logical consistency sequence described above, are the treatment of investment and import substitution.

Regarding the former the growth rate of total investment demand (i.e., one of the components of final demand) for capital goods supplied by sector i is given in step (9) as:

$$z_i = \sum_j \varepsilon_{ij} z_{ij} + \varepsilon_{ic} z_{ic} + \varepsilon_{ig} z_{ig}, \tag{13.1.4}$$

where z_i = the growth rate of total investment demand for capital goods supplied by sector i; z_{ij} = the growth rate of investment demand from sector j for investment goods supplied by sector i; z_{ic} = the growth rate of consumer demand for investment goods supplied by i; and z_{ig} = the growth rate of government demand for investment goods supplied by i.

The ε_{ij} are the "investment distribution coefficients" which reflect the initial conditions. In the case of Brazil—as in that of most developing countries—there are three major sectors of origin, i.e., machinery, transport equipment, and construction (thus i above stands for each one of these sectors). It is clear that these distribution coefficients have to sum up to unity for any given i,

$$\sum_j \varepsilon_{ij} = 1,$$

where i = machinery, transport equipment, construction.

The Tims model of Pakistan has many of the same characteristics as that of van Rijckeghem. It is meant to check the feasibility and effects on the system of given growth rates of GNP, agriculture, and exports taken exogenously. It makes use of marginal coefficients (rather than constant coefficients or elasticities) to describe anticipated changes over a five year planning period. These marginal coefficients are based on two existing input-output tables—the assumption being that the future trends will correspond to those observed between the two "snapshot" years. The model itself is broken down into seven major sectors and contains 98 equations (98 endogenous and 8 exogenous variables). One of the key policy questions addressed by the model is that of the consistency between the investment-savings and balance of payments gaps for given GNP growth rates. Import substitution becomes a policy variable to relax the balance-of-payments constraint when the latter becomes binding. The treatment of investment is essentially similar to that of the previous model. Investment by sector of origin is explained as a linear function of investment by sector of destination, e.g.,

$$I_i = \sum_j \varepsilon_{ij} I_j, \tag{13.1.5}$$

where i represents the sector or origin (i.e., investment goods industries, construction, transport and communications and "all other services") and j represents the sector of destination. I_i is the final demand investment column vector and I_j is the investment row—reflecting the investment requirements per unit of output for sector j. The ε_{ij} are investment distribution coefficients. Thus, investment is essentially determined from the required demand side; there is no mechanism to explain the sectoral contribution to capital formation.

The two consistency models reviewed above stopped short of deriving explicitly the sectoral employment effects. For that purpose some additional logical steps are required. A number of studies have concentrated more explicitly in deriving the sectoral employment effects for specific countries within an overall consistency framework. Among the contributions are those of Boon for Mexico [4]; Thorbecke and Stoutjesdijk for Peru [35]; ECAFE [38] for a number of ECAFE countries; Hazari and Krishnamurty for India [12] and Thorbecke-Sengupta for Colombia [34].

The last reference above [34] goes beyond the formulation of a consistency model to project sectoral output and employment in that it attempts as well to project changes in income distribution. It addresses itself to one of the key problems of this decade in the developing world, namely, that of increasing unemployment and greater inequality in the distribution of income which many countries are experiencing inspite of a reasonably high GDP growth performance. It is becoming clear that economic growth *per se* (at least over the feasible range) is not sufficient to insure full employment and a socially desired income distribution. Consequently, many governments are placing a higher relative weight on the objectives of increasing employment and achieving a more equal income distribution relative to an increase in aggregate output. Colombia is a good example of such a country. The employment objective became the primary planning goal and an ILO mission was invited to help formulate a full employment strategy to be implemented between 1970 and 1985. The resulting strategy [16] was not based on any formal consistency model and therefore some of the assumptions could not be checked for internal consistence. This provided the starting-point of the Thorbecke-Sengupta framework [34].

The study is divided into two major parts. The first part attempts to describe quantitatively the macroeconomic and sectoral structure of the Colombian economy over the period 1950–67 in terms of output, employment and income distribution. The second part projects these variables to 1980 within a consistent framework and under different assumptions regarding export growth and technological change.

Part I entailed the following steps. The first step consisted in building a macroeconometric model of Colombia over the period 1950–67. This model proved capable of explaining accurately the macroeconomic structure and performance of the Colombian economy over the sample period. The model itself determines the paths of the endogenous variables consisting of gross domestic product, consumption, investment and imports as functions of exogenous variables such as exports, changes in the terms-of-trade and public expenditures.

The second step consisted of obtaining input-output and employment information on a comparable basis within a 10–12 sector breakdown. From the above information it proved possible to derive the sectoral income distribution and to design a methodology which provided a mapping between the sectoral and personal income distribution prevailing in the mid-sixties.

The second part of the study was devoted to the design of an analytical framework capable of generating a set of internally consistent projections to 1980. First, projections of the major macroeconomic variables were undertaken within the context of the macroeconomic model mentioned above under two alternative assumptions regarding exports and public expenditure variables (i.e., "high" and "low" growth alternatives). Next, the various components of sectoral final demand were projected in a way consistent with the macroeconomic projections. Thus, for example, final demand consumption for the various sectors was computed as a function of GDP growth given likely values of the sectoral income elasticities of consumption demand. Likewise, the sums of the sectoral final demand components (i.e., consumption, changes in stocks, investment, exports and imports) were consistent with, namely add up, to the projected values of the variable appearing in the macroeconomic model.

Thirdly, the sectoral gross output and value added vectors were projected to 1980 given projected final demand and the consolidated input-output table of 1966. Furthermore, on the basis of magnitudes of the growth rates of labor productivity by sector likely to prevail over the projection period, the sectoral employment and income distributions were derived. The methodology designed in Part I was then used to map the personal income distribution resulting from the sectoral distribution. At that stage, it could be determined whether the changes in the composition of output and employment affected the personal income distribution. To the extent that changes in the latter were projected to prevail in 1980, revised projections of the final demand components (specifically consumption of agricultural and manufacturing goods) were undertaken to insure consistency with the new income distribution.

In addition, a fairly rudimentary test was conducted to check whether the alternative output combinations resulting from the projections to 1980 could be produced given the total investment funds generated by the macroeconomic model. It was determined that the investment availability would not constrain the attainment of the projected sectoral output and value added combinations reached under the two growth alternatives.

The whole set of projections described above reflects the likely consequences of a maintenance of the productive structure of the Colombian economy since the input-output matrix prevailing in the base-year (1966) was used to generate these projections. The value of these projections for policy purposes is that they may provide the policymaker with a quantitative view of the consequences of essentially neutral technological policies.

The final section of Part II was devoted to a simple analysis of the effects of technological changes in agriculture on employment and income distribution.

13.2. Optimization Models

Optimization models, in contrast to consistency type models, postulate explicitly an objective function to be maximized. Policy experimentations can take place by a number of methods such as (a) varying the form of the objective (preference) function; (b) varying the values of the exogenous variables which appear in the model; and (c) varying the specification of the model itself. Even though most optimization models in the development planning field are multisectoral, at least one example of a highly aggregated model [26] is reviewed.

13.2.1. *Aggregative Models*

Probably the simplest optimization planning model is the one devised by Mahalanobis[11] at the outset of India's planning activities. His first attempt was a two-sector model where the economy is divided into two sectors, one producing consumption goods and the other investment goods:

$$I_t = I_{t-1} + \lambda_i \beta_i I_{t-1}, \qquad (13.2.1)$$

$$C_t = C_{t-1} + \lambda_c \beta_c I_{t-1}, \qquad (13.2.2)$$

$$Y_t = C_t + I_t, \qquad (13.2.3)$$

where I_t = Investment in year t, assumed endogenous, C_t = Consumption in year t, Y_t = Income in year t, λ_i = Proportion of total investment allocated to produce investment goods, λ_c = Proportion of total investment allocated to produce consumption goods, $\lambda_i + \lambda_c = 1$, β_i = Output/capital ratio for investment goods, and β_c = Output/capital ratio for consumption goods.

It has already been seen in Chapter 10 (Section 10.1) that the policy problem which this planning model was to help solve was the proportion of total investment which should be allocated to produce investment goods (λ_i) in order to maximize aggregate income (Y_t) given the planning horizon τ (thus, where $t = \tau$).

The output/capital ratios are assumed known, i.e.,

$$\beta_i = 0.2 \quad \text{and} \quad \beta_c = 0.3.$$

These parameters were based on the production situations of each sector. Thus, the division of the variables in terms of a policy breakdown is:

Data: C_0, I_0, Y_0 (the initial values of these variables),
Instruments: λ_i (only one instrument since $\lambda_c = 1 - \lambda_i$),
Target: maximize Y_τ,
Irrelevant variables: C_τ, I_τ.

---

[11] See Mahalanobis [26]. See also Chapter 10, Section 10.1 for a discussion of the two- and four-section Mahalanobis models.

The reduced form of this system can easily be derived:

$$I = (1 + \lambda_i \beta_i)^\tau I_0, \tag{13.2.4}$$

$$C = C_0 + I_0(\lambda_c \beta_c / \lambda_i \beta_i)[(1 + \lambda_i \beta_i)^\tau - 1], \tag{13.2.5}$$

$$Y = Y_0 + I_0 \left\{ \frac{\lambda_i \beta_i + \lambda_c \beta_c}{\lambda_i \beta_i} \right\} [(1 + \lambda_i \beta_i)^\tau - 1]. \tag{13.2.6}$$

Once the planning horizon τ has been specified, i.e., $\tau = 15$ years, equation (13.2.6) can be solved for λ_i, which yields $\lambda_i = \frac{1}{3}$, $(\lambda_c = \frac{2}{3})$. The meaning of this last result is that the proportion of total allocable investment to be invested in investment goods which will maximize income in about 15 years is one-third. It should be noticed that in the above example the implicit welfare function includes only one element, namely, the maximization of Y_τ. The maximization of C_τ from period 0 to period τ or some other appropriate criterion could have been substituted for the maximization of Y_τ.

13.2.2. Multisectoral Programming Models

National planning models are relying increasingly on linear, nonlinear and dynamic programming techniques within multisectoral frameworks in order to specify the resource allocation and distribution alternatives in a developing economy. Even though the operational usefulness of these models is still relatively limited, they can be of some value in exploring the consequences of alternative development plans. It should be noted that the development of new computational algorithms and the use of third generation computers have made the large scale programming models solvable in terms of approximate or even exact numerical solutions.

We have discussed in Chapter 7 (Section 7.7) the general nature and characteristics of some of the recent programming models in development planning. Table 7.4 summarizes their important features, e.g., nature of objective function, types of computing algorithm used and other important characteristics.

In this section a sample of these programming models based upon the set summarized in Section 7.4[12] is reviewed in some detail. More specifically, these models are analyzed from the standpoint of specification, computation and pricing implications. The following models are explicitly discussed: (a) Sandee's linear programming demonstration model of India [29]; (b) Kendrick and Taylor's nonlinear control-theoretic model [21]; (c) Westphal's planning model for South Korea featuring economies of scale [41];

---

[12] Four of the five models discussed in this section are summarized in Table 7.4. The only additional model evaluated in this section is that of Sandee [29].

(d) Eckaus and Parikh's dynamic linear programming model of India [8]; and (e) MacEwan's interregional linear programming model of Pakistan [24].

Although the present set of models is either actually or potentially applicable to national planning problems, it should not be inferred here that these models were actually used by any national government or planning commission for policy purposes in more than a purely illustrative fashion. The main purpose of this review is to present the broad features of these models referring whenever necessary to the technical relationships which are given in the appendix for some of these models. The final section of this chapter is devoted to a general appraisal and comparative evaluation of development planning models.

A. Sandee's Demonstration Planning Model of India [29]:

Sandee's model is one of the earliest attempts at building a linear programming planning model. As such, it has the real advantage that the underlying methodology and empirical assumptions are spelled out in great detail and is therefore very useful for expository purposes.

The starting-point of Sandee's model is a thirteen-sector input-output table for 1960. On the basis of the derived input-output table for 1960,[13] twelve balance equations[14] were specified. They show how the output of each branch is divided among inputs and the various categories of the final bill of goods (consumption, investment, net exports and changes in stocks). All of the variables in these balance equations are expressed as increases in flows between 1960 and 1970, corresponding to the planning period.

Given a knowledge of the sectoral capital-output ratios of the heavy engineering, other equipment manufacturing and construction sectors, as well as the stock-to-output ratios with respect to all sectors, and assuming that the sectoral growth rates of output prevailing in 1960 are maintained to 1970, it is possible to express a set of investment relations. These relations indicate the amount of increased investment (between 1960 and 1970) required to produce the increase of total output of each sector and can be substituted for the increased investment terms in the balance equations above.

---

[13] At the time of preparation of this model, the only input-output table available was that for 1953–54. Consequently, the 1960 table was derived from the previous one and includes only a few changes in the coefficients of the interacting part.

[14] No balance equations were necessary for the thirteenth sector (housing), since the total increase in output is assigned to consumption.

In addition to the twelve balance equations, four other equations appear in the model; one is a super production function for agriculture where the increase in agricultural output is made a function of the increase in fertilizer applied, irrigation projects executed and agricultural extension.[15] The last three relations are identities necessary to close the model: (1) one defining total investment in terms of its components; (2) one specifying a balance of visible trade equal to that of 1960; and (3) the final equation, expressing total consumption, as in the case of investment above, in terms of its components (agriculture, good manufacturing, transportation, large-scale industry and small-scale industry).

Since the model consists of sixteen independent linear equations in thirty variables, this leaves fourteen degrees of freedom, which signifies that if fourteen variables are given arbitrary values, the other sixteen (unknown) variables can be computed.

In order to eliminate as much as possible unrealistic alternatives, a number of constraints are added to the model. These constraints relate to foreign trade, investment—providing an upper limit to total investment and lower limits to sectoral investments—and consumption. The investment constraints are interesting in that an upper limit is placed on the marginal propensity to save (24.5 per cent) and a lower limit to the sectoral growth rates based on the existing growth rates in 1960. Finally, the consumption constraints indicate upper and lower limits of 13 per cent above or below the Engel curve for the various sectors.

In the maximization process, given the fourteen degrees of freedom which exist, fourteen variables (or linear combinations of them) can be used as coordinate axes, spanning a fourteen-dimensional space in a linear programming framework. In such a space a point would be defined by its fourteen coordinate values and would, thus, represent definite (determinate) values for all thirty variables, which in turn would stand for an entire plan in the context of the model. The rationale for the constraints is to prevent the occurrence of completely unrealistic, impossible or undesirable values for given variables. The constraints are introduced in the form of slack variables.

In the above form, a linear function of the variables in the sixteen basic equations can be maximized. The target to be maximized was taken as the level of consumption in 1970. Given the structure of the model, the maximization of consumption also implies the maximization of investment, since

---

[15] For a quantitative specification of this function see Chapter 15.

the savings function takes the following form[16]:

$$I \leq 0.32\,C.$$

Thus, the welfare function to be maximized in this model includes solely one element, consumption (and through the linearity relationship investment). The justification which is given for not incorporating other elements in the welfare function is that a consideration of these variables, such as employment and income distribution, may be done with the help of adjunct models.[17] The maximization process or, in other words, the location of the optimum was done with the help of linear programming.

B. Kendrick and Taylor's Nonlinear Control Theoretic Model [21]:

This model is a highly aggregative illustrative version of a larger model.[18] The present version of the model contains two goods, consumption and investment, where the former enters nonlinearly in the specification of the welfare function and the latter enters nonlinearly in the specification of a production function. A discrete-time formulation of the model is used to approximate the continuous time differential-equation model which in turn is used to illustrate the problems of numerical computation of the control-theoretic models.[19] In this very highly aggregative version of the model there are no binding constraints on labor supply, although the initial capital stock and terminal output level are preassigned. The basic elements[20] of this nonlinear model consist of:

(1) the objective function, which specifies a utility function of the following type

$$u(c) = (1 - \eta)c_i^{1-\eta}; \eta \geq 0, \eta \neq 1, \qquad (13.2.7)$$

which, therefore, has the convenient property of being linear when the

---

[16] An upper limit of 24.5 per cent assigned to the marginal propensity to save implies that out of every additional unit of income 0.245 is invested and 0.755 consumed, or that for every additional unit of increase in consumption, investment rises by $0.245/0.755 = 0.32$ unit.

[17] The following quotation from Sandee is symptomatic in this respect: "Equality has not found a place in the model either (employment being the other target previously discussed). This worthy cause and the means to further it can probably be analyzed and planned on its own and without reference to the details of the model in hand" [29, p. 39].

[18] A detailed version of this control theoretic model including input-output balance relations was considered in the context of the Korean economy [20].

[19] Such as several recent computing algorithms (i.e., conjugate gradient) which are closely related to the maximum principles developed by Pontryagin and others.

[20] The complete model is given in Section 13.5.4.

parameter η tends to zero (i.e., comparison with linear or piecewise linear utility functions can thus be made qualitatively and quantitatively);

(2) the production function, which specifies output (y_i) as a loglinear function of capital stock (k_i) in every period i so that the effect of variations in the capital elasticity of output on the optimal output-trajectory can be observed and analyzed;

(3) a finite planning horizon (n), which implies that "the so-called turnpike property" of the neo-classical growth paths is not evidenced for realistic parameter values, until the value of n is quite large, i.e., $n \geq 50$ years in this illustration. (For example, it has been emphasized [21, p. 18] that "a 20-year planning horizon would not have allowed the turnpike behavior to manifest itself to the same extent as in the 50-year horizon, with a consequent loss on the part of all generations—assuming no parameter changes of course.");

(4) the dynamic shadow prices of capital (i.e., the adjoint variables) associated with the investment demand equation (for each time period i), whose initial value (i.e., at $i = 0$) is such that for growth rates far from the turnpike, the final capital stock is very sensitive to it; and

(5) a comparison of alternative methods of numerical computation (e.g., neighboring extremal methods, gradient techniques and quasilincarization methods) of the optimal trajectory, which shows that different computation techniques have different degrees of convergence and sensitivity to alternative parameter settings.

Whereas the present model is expressed in terms of one sector, it appears that it could be generalized [20] to include: input-output type intersectoral balance relations, a consumption vector with each of its components (denoting consumption of goods of sector k) proportional to aggregate consumption and, finally, inequality constraints on the state and control variables.

C. Westphal's Model of South Korea [41]:

This planning model features economies of scale in capacity expansion for plants in petrochemicals and steel.[21] It contains nonlinearities at two stages, e.g., in the specification of the welfare function and in the nonlinear cost function showing decreasing marginal costs due to the scale of the plant. However, the nonlinear objective function is approximated by a piece-wise linear function by suitable choice of weights and the nonlinear cost function

---

[21] The complete model is given in Section 13.5.5.

(total cost $= ay^b$, where y is capacity output, a and b are suitable positive parameters $0 < b < 1$) is linearly approximated as:

$$\text{Total cost} = \bar{B}\delta + By,$$

where $\bar{B}$ denotes the fixed cost required only if capacity is built (i.e., $\delta = 1$), B, the variable cost of constructing a unit of capacity and y is capacity output level.

This planning model has among others two distinct objectives. First, it has a part called KPEM (Korean Project Evaluation Model) which is designed to specify as a part of the optimal solution, the optimal timing and scale of capacity expansion in petrochemicals and steel and their implications for other sectors. This KPEM submodel was built to test the proposition "that serious resource misallocation would result if either the petrochemicals complex or the steel mill were built. KPEM demonstrates that in competition with the expansion of traditional production neither would result in serious resource misallocation" [41, p. 86]. Second, the implications of the terminal period constraint with respect to the consumption-investment choice and the implicit cost of production (i.e., shadow price) are analyzed in great detail using empirical data and alternative specifications of "plan parameters". The implicit cost of production in the terminal period (which is available from the dual problem) includes both an implicit change (i.e., shadow price) for constructing capacity during the plan (following from constraint (4) in the Appendix) and the implicit cost of expanding and replacing the capacity in the future (following from the terminal constraint (11) in the Appendix). Since these implicit costs differ for different sectors, there is no reason why a balanced expansion of all the sectors at a given fixed rate would be optimal. It is in this sense that one can test with this model the implications of balanced versus unbalanced growth in a multisectoral framework.

It is interesting to note that the discounted sum of consumption was rejected as an appropriate welfare function in this model, since it was found to result in the all-or-none solution for consumption-investment choice thus exhibiting the so-called "flip-flop" property (i.e., "for high discount rates consumption is at its upper bound in the initial periods; for low rates consumption is initially at its lower bound"). Thus consumption growth "flips" from the terminal periods to the initial periods as the discount rate is increased over a narrow region [41, p. 63].

A few other interesting features of this model may be briefly mentioned.
(1) The complete model has a 10-year planning horizon 1967–68 to

1975–76 (i.e., five 2-year periods) in which production and trade variables for eleven sectors (each having sets of various economic activities) are endogenously determined along with sectoral investment and aggregate consumption. The two scarce resources in the model are foreign exchange and domestic savings and there are no labor constraints;

(2) For the petrochemicals and steel sectors where investment allocation decisions are especially affected by "lumpiness" and the associated characteristics of decreasing marginal costs as the scale of the plant increases, special aggregation schemes are proposed. The latter gives rise to more operational optimal solutions which correspond more closely to concrete choices;[22]

(3) The piece-wise linear objective function allows for post terminal consumption by providing capacity immediately after the plan period (in this aspect it is basically similar to the "transit model" version of the Eckaus-Parikh formulation contained in the Appendix);

(4) The computing method used to solve this linear mixed integer programming model is a variant of the branch and bound algorithm, which appears to be quite expensive to run.

D. Eckaus and Parikh's Dynamic Programming Model of India [8]:

This model, in its "target" and "transit" versions, is intended to determine the optimal levels of savings and investment over time, including the use of foreign exchange resources and their intersectoral and intertemporal distribution subject to a number of constraints on the production processes and other economic activities in different sectors. Private consumption is a composite commodity and is consumed in proportions that are fixed in each period (the shares of sectoral consumption to total private consumption are fixed within a planning period). Aggregate consumption must increase monotonically with time and it is assumed that there is a uniform time-lag of three years for investment—creating new capacity. As in Westphal's model, labor supply is assumed to be unlimited and, hence, not binding on output. The economic model has the following important elements:

(1) The objective function to be maximized is assumed to be the sum of aggregate consumption in each of the plan periods, discounted by a social discount rate. To prevent the "flip-flop" property (i.e., concentrating consumption at the end or the beginning of the planning period) mentioned

---

[22] Thus, the proposed aggregation scheme places the "principal users" of petrochemicals (or iron and steel) within the same sector and the principal supplier of its intermediate products within another sector.

previously, a consumption growth constraint is added, which requires that aggregate consumption grows by at least a stipulated minimum rate;

(2) Production accounting relationships in the model specify that the total requirements for each commodity in each period not exceed its availability in that period;[23] Similarly capital accounting relationships are specified by means of consistent capital-output ratios subject to capacity constraints for each sector;

(3) New capital creation is allowed in each production sector with a separate gestation lag for each of the capital goods producing sectors;

(4) Other constraints such as an aggregate limit on the maximum permissible level of net savings as a proportion to net national product and balance of payment constraint were intended to make the model more realistic;

(5) Terminal conditions are laid down in terms of the final capital stocks on hand and in process of completion. In the version called the "Target Model", the terminal conditions are stipulated from some source outside the model[24] in the form of required minimum terminal capital stocks in each sector. In the version called the "Transit Model", the terminal conditions are set endogenously from a specification of the required post-terminal growth rates of consumption, exports and imports. Thus, while the "target model" version is useful in testing the feasibility and the implicit costs (i.e., shadow prices) of prescribing a given target set of output capacities in the plan formulation, the transit model is used to compute the optimal time path (or sequence) of transition to the required post terminal growth rates of consumption, exports and imports, starting from the initial conditions given by initial production capacities, stocks of inventories and other variables.

(6) In addition to the "Target Model" and "Transit Model" versions, the implications of extending the planning horizon to eighteen and thirty years, respectively, are examined in Guidepath Models, which embody partial procedures for endogenously changing consumption proportions and for shifting resources from traditional to modern methods of production in the agricultural sector.[25]

---

[23] This part uses input-output balance equations, where the 50-sector input-output matrix (for the year 1955–56) is consolidated into eleven aggregated sectors to stay within computational limits.

[24] For example, in the calculated solutions the target stocks are taken from the Third Five Year Plan (1961–62 to 1966–67) and the proposed Fourth Five Year Plan in India.

[25] Thus, the effects, of new production technologies such as the use of high yielding varieties and intermediate inputs reflecting the Green Revolution are introduced.

It is interesting to note that the model recognizes explicitly that there may be different degrees of uncertainty associated with various intersectoral parameters: "In the models presented here, all sectors were treated as if data of equal quality were available. This was done mainly because stochastic programming is not sufficiently developed for the purposes of these models and partly because the significance of errors in specification could be explored by testing the sensitivity of the solutions to changes in parameters" [8, p. 19].[26]

E. MacEwan's Interregional Linear Programming Model of Pakistan [24]:

This model is interregional in addition to being multisectoral. Production processes and demand in the two major regions[27] of Pakistan are considered separately. Thus, two complete but separate submodels are built for East and West Pakistan using the same equational specification. The model is multisectoral, relying on a thirty-five sector input-output breakdown, one for the eastern wing and one for the western wing of the country.

The model is comparative static, variables being defined as changes between 1964–65 and 1974–75. One interesting technical feature of this model is the use of marginal input-output coefficients for projection which attempt to anticipate the important structural and technical changes that will take place. In the manufacturing sectors, technical coefficients have been adjusted to incorporate the changing relative importance of small- and large-scale activity. In agricultural sectors, and particularly in food grains production, explicit account has been taken of the simultaneous existence of modern and traditional techniques and the increasing importance of the former over time.

The welfare function to be maximized is a weighted function of increments in per capita consumption in East and West Pakistan. By varying the weights it is possible to see the implications of various regional distributional

---

[26] Yet in the detailed LP type planning model for Hungary developed by Kornai and Liptak [22] which is discussed in some detail in Chapter 14, methods of building safety margins were explicitly considered for individual sectors by following the method of safety programming. Their results indicate that the optimal ranking of sectors is greatly conditioned by the extent to which the constraints allow the specification of risk aversion measures.

[27] The eastern region has become a sovereign state, Bangladesh, since this model was prepared. Hence, the two region classification is no longer politically meaningful. Since we are more interested in reviewing the methodology and specification than in the numerical results or policy implications, this model presents a good example of some of the interregional and distributional aspects of development planning.

preferences on the system. The explicit choice variables of the linear programming problem are the increments over the planning period of: (1) the
level of consumption in each region; (2) the quantity of capital flowing
between the regions; and (3) the source of supply of each commodity, i.e.,
production in East Pakistan, production in West Pakistan or importing
from abroad.

The complete model is given in Section 13.5.6. The main characteristics in
the specification of this model are: (1) increments in sectoral consumption
(c_i) are linearly related to increments in total consumption (c) through
equations of the following form for each region separately:

$$c_i = \gamma_i + B_i c. \qquad (13.2.8)$$

These functions are linear approximations of Engel's functions, where
$\sum_i \gamma_i = 0$ and $\sum_i \beta_i = 1$ to insure that $\sum_i c_i = c$; (2) balance equations are
specified for goods and services, foreign exchange and capital, respectively.
It should be noted that in the first two balance equations, imports and
exports into each wing are broken down into a regional and an international
component; (3) both foreign and regional imports are further broken down
into competing and noncompeting parts; (4) export limits are imposed at the
sectoral and at the aggregate levels for each region, reflecting the difficulties
inherent in entering new markets and expanding old ones rather than supply
limitations; (5) the treatment of savings is extremely simple. All agricultural
sectors are assumed to contribute the same proportion of value added (i.e.,
12 per cent) to savings with all nonagricultural sectors contributing a high
proportion (i.e., 24 per cent). It is probable that data limitations did not
permit a more realistic treatment. More specifically, it would have been
theoretically sounder to apply different marginal saving propensities to
wage and nonwage value added (income) in the different sectors or at least
for major sectoral groupings.

Perhaps the most interesting conclusion reached from running the model
is that disparity reductions (as between East and West Pakistan) are consistent with an economically optimal program. This follows from the higher
projected consumption of food grains in the East (which is the poorer region)
and the productivity advantage which it is expected to enjoy in producing
the latter. The model shows clearly that regional productivity and comparative advantage—given limited trade opportunities—are related not only to
supply forces but also in an essential way to the structure of final demand. A
final observation regarding the specification of the model is that it does not
contain any effective labor or skill constraints.

Before completing this section on multisectoral programming models, it is important to note that experimentation is proceeding with a substantially different approach than the one underlying the previously reviewed models. This approach is based on multilevel planning, that is, the formal linkage of different models representing different parts of the economy. Perhaps the best example of such models is the multilevel planning model of Mexico which is presently being built under the auspices of the Development Research Center of the World Bank.[28] The main characteristic of this type of model is the formal linkage of a multisectoral, economy-wide model with an agricultural model which is further decomposed into a number of district submodels. This model is discussed in some detail in Chapter 15 (Section 15.2.1).

13.3. Simulation Models

Simulation of an economic system has been defined as "the performance of experiments upon an analog of the economic system and the drawing of inferences concerning the properties of the economic system from the behavior of its analog. The analog is an idealization of the generally more complex real system, the essential properties of which are retained in the analog" [1, p. 268]. In addition, simulation requires a high speed or analog computer and involves some stochastic elements. The solutions obtained on the basis of simulation techniques tend to be quite specific. Changes in initial conditions or parameters require separate simulation experiments yielding different sets of time paths for the endogenous variables. Thus, on the basis of various runs some of the properties of the relationships between input and output quantities in the system under investigation can be inferred.

Conceptually, a simulation model of an economic system can be viewed in the following general mathematical form (see [27, pp. 30–32]):

$$\psi(t + 1) = F[\psi(t), \alpha(t), \beta(t), \gamma(t)] \qquad (13.3.1)$$

where:

$\psi(t)$ = a vector (set of variables) which defines the state of the *simulated* system at any given time. State variables usually involve the level of a variable

---

[28] The work which is reported here is to be published in a forthcoming book on *Multilevel Planning: Case Studies in Mexico*. The main architects of this approach were A. Manne who constructed the multisectoral economy-wide model (entitled Dynamico); John Duloy and Roger Norton, who worked on the agricultural sector model [15].

at a given time and might be such things as production capacities, land allocated to various activities, prices, population by subgroups, and levels of technology;

$\alpha(t)=$a set of parameters that defines the structure of the system. Structural parameters usually involve rates of change of variables between levels, or input-output coefficients. For example, technical coefficients, response co-efficients, price elasticities, migration rates, birth and death rates (some of these may be subject to variation within the model);

$\beta(t)=$a set of exogenous variables that influence system behavior; e.g., world prices and weather;

$\gamma(t)=$a set of variables which can be controlled to alter the system's performance in various directions; e.g., investment alternatives, tax policies and import duties.

This equation illustrates how the variables which define the state of the simulated system in time period $t+1$ is a function of the initial state of the system, and the values of the parameters (α), the exogenous variables (β) and the policy variables (γ) at time period t.

There are at least three major characteristics which distinguish simulation models from the other type of models reviewed above. First, they do not incorporate any explicit preference or welfare function to be maximized; secondly, they are not based as most consistency models on sets of simultaneous linear equations, rather they are formulated in terms of difference equations; and, finally, in at least some applications non-linearities can be introduced in the system.

There are very few simulation models in the development planning field. Two pioneering attempts [14, 27], neither of which is a development planning model as such, are evaluated here.

The Holland-Gillespie simulation experiments [14] were performed on a 250 equation dynamic model which is supposed to represent a typical under-developed economy. To add some realism to the specification of the model, data from the Indian economy were used in the selection of a number of parameters.[29] The model divided production activities into six categories. Besides relationships describing production and consumption over time, the model includes equations reflecting monetary and fiscal variables, inter-

---

[29] Nevertheless, the model as built does not depict India but rather a hypothetical economy which has some of the characteristics of that country.

national trade and finance, capital and stock formation and many other forces. Even though the total number of equations is large, the number of behavioral relationship (in contrast to identities or purely physical or time trend relationships) is relatively low. The state of the economy at the beginning of a run is specified by a set of initial values which are "plugged" in the equations. The computer proceeds to determine the new set of values for the endogenous variables at the end of each time period which is taken as one-twentieth of a year. The process is repeated, interval by interval, over five hundred periods adding up to 25 years. The course of the variables can thus be followed over time in a recursive fashion.

There are two major questions which can be raised and answered by this type of model. First the model can be used to simulate the results of changes in "instrument" variables (under the control of the policymaker) on the whole system. Thus, for example, the effects of a devaluation, a change in the sectoral allocation of public investment or a population control policy can be estimated. This type of simulation may be useful to the policymaker in providing him with the alternative consequences of different policies on the major objectives which he is trying to achieve (e.g., growth of income, price stability, full employment, balance-of-payments equilibrium). Secondly, experiments can be undertaken on the model to test how sensitive the system is to various alternative specifications of both equations and parameters. Such experiments will help identify those equations and parameters which have the greatest impact on the system. This information is of utmost importance to the model-builder in deciding on what parts of the model need to be respecified or improved.

The main contribution of this pioneering attempt is clearly not in the policy conclusions which are drawn but rather in its thorough description of the applicability of the simulation technique to development planning. Other macroeconomic simulations models of developing countries are those of Holland applied to Venezuela [13] and of Kresge applied to Pakistan [23].

The second simulation model which is reviewed in detail here is not strictly speaking a national model. It consists of a generalized simulation approach to agricultural development in Nigeria [27].[30] This major effort was undertaken by an interdisciplinary group at Michigan State University.

---

[30] In fact this model is a sector model. For a discussion of agricultural sector models see (Section 15.2) Chapter 15 and particularly Table 15.4 for major characteristics of this model.

This group built a very large-scale model of Nigeria's agriculture, broken down into three interacting submodels corresponding to, respectively, (a) northern Nigerian agriculture; (b) southern Nigerian agriculture; and (c) the rest of the economy.

The two regional agricultural submodels contain production, marketing and consumption activities for a number of crops which provide income to each respective population. In turn, changes in income and population levels determine demand functions and labor movements within each regional model. The regional submodels are linked with the nonagricultural submodel through incoming flows of consumer goods and producer inputs and outgoing flows of raw materials. The model can, thus, simulate interregional trade and food and labor migration. Land and so called "modernizing" inputs are combined into the sectoral submodels to reflect technological alternatives.

Basically the model was built in an eclectic fashion from a large number of "building blocks" representing the physical, biological, economic, social, political and cultural relationships existing within and among the major sectors of the economy. These building blocks, as the authors indicate "are composed of interrelated functional relationships which can be broken apart into more manageable components because of their recursive nature (i.e., one function necessarily follows another in time and is dependent upon the output of the previous function) or the seeming independence (geographic, behavioral) at any point in time [27, p. 33]. The specification of these various relationships appears to be done on an ad hoc basis; in some cases parameters are selected on a priori grounds, in other cases they may be based on statistical estimation, in still others on researchers' judgments.

The overall model consists of over two thousand equations, only a fraction of which are presented in symbolical form in [27]. The nonagricultural submodel is the only submodel explicitly presented—at least functionally. The latter is based on a ten sector input-output table of the Nigerian economy for 1959. Examples of policy problems which can be potentially addressed within the model are the impact of changes in such policy means as prices paid to export crop producers, research, public investment allocation, and import substitution on such policy objectives as farm and nonfarm income, per capita nutrition, balance of payments, and employment. Even though, a number of tests have been run to check the ability of the model to replicate changes which occurred during the historical (sample) period, considerably more work might be required before the model can be used by policymakers. The sheer size of the model, combined with the impossibility of checking the underlying assumptions, quantitative specifications and the explanatory power of the multitude of building blocks forming the model make it very difficult, at this time, to evaluate the quality and overall performance of the model critically. Nevertheless, it is clear that some important methodological contributions are resulting from this project particularly with regard to the design of interacting submodels, the cross fertilization of different disciplines and a critical determination of these relationships and parameters with regard to which results are sensitive.

Before completing this section on simulation models, it should be noted that a very recent simulation model has just come out at the global level on the Limits to Growth [28]. The major conclusion of the simulation experiments run on the model is that given finite resources and population growth, a continuation of past economic growth is likely to have catastrophic results. More specifically, one can speculate that a major implication of the results of this model is that countries can no longer be oblivious to the negative effects of their own economic growth on the rest of the world. Conceivably, the welfare functions of countries would need to be altered to take into account the negative effects of their own growth on the rest of the world.

13.4. A General Appraisal of Development Planning Models

Three types of development planning models have been reviewed and discussed in this chapter: consistency models, optimization models and simulation models. An appraisal and critical evaluation of these three types is undertaken in this section. The main characteristics of consistency models is that (1) the structure of the economy is described by way of a set of simultaneous linear equations, and (2) no explicit welfare function is postulated. The major purpose of consistency models is to identify the major relationships between variables at either the macroeconomic or multisectoral levels over a given historical period in which there is reason to believe that the underlying structure of the economy remained relatively fixed. Two other important purposes of consistency models are (a) to use them within the historical period to simulate the alternative effects of changes in exogenous variables (both data variables and potential instrument variables) on the set of endogenous variables, a subset of which might consist of potential target variables; and (b) to undertake projections outside the sample period.

In the classification used in this chapter we divided consistency models into a macroeconomic type and a multisectoral type. The former type was further subdivided into export-led and two-gap models. The main usefulness of export-led models from a policy standpoint lies in measuring and predicting the effects of changes in the export sector, the net inflow of foreign capital, and highly aggregate public sector variables on GDP, imports (and indirectly the balance of payments) and other endogenous macroeconomic variables. Two-gap models go further in the sense that they permit the ex ante identification of the bigger (binding) gap, namely, the saving or the balance of payments gap.[31] It is the overdetermined character of these models (the fact that they contain one more equation than endogenous or unknown variables) which permits the identification of the binding gap ex ante. Again, the above determination can be helpful in the allocation of foreign assistance and of policy measures appropriate to relieving or relaxing the binding gap.

The multisectoral models make it possible to check the sectoral implications of given macroeconomic paths. The feasibility of given GDP growth targets can be checked from the standpoint of sectoral constraints and the model, in a general sense, insures that the sectoral growth paths are consistent from both the demand and supply sides. The sectoral components of final demand are related to income and population growth whereas sectoral value added is based on linear production functions. It has been seen that in many instances multisectoral consistency models rely on simple macroeconomic models to obtain initial assumptions regarding the likely growth of macroeconomic variables. The feasibility and consistency of these initial assumptions is then tested at the intersectoral level and if necessary, altered until a consistent solution is obtained. Thus, when such models are used for projection purposes, a few iterations may be required until consistency is obtained. Policy questions which can be examined within the context of these models, in addition to those already referred to, are: the effects of import substitution, the effects of sectoral investment allocation and in a limited way so far, the effects on employment and income distribution.

Optimization models made out the second class of development planning models reviewed here. The great majority of these models are of a programming type. These models tend to display some common characteristics, which are brought out in the review undertaken in Section 13.2: they are basically consumption-maximizing models, with or without some other constraints imposed on other policy objectives; they make use of shadow prices of the constraints which should be interpreted as the implicit cost of

---

[31] In a general sense a third gap, i.e., skill constraints, can also be measured and identified.

maintaining equilibrium in the balance equations; they experiment with alternative sets of values of parameters such as capital-output ratios or terminal output targets in order to gain some idea of the sensitivity of the optimal solution to a fixed set of parameters and exogenous variables; and they tend to compare the optimal solutions of the algebraic model with some benchmark or reference plan calculations.

Although the consumption-maximizing objective may be quite reasonable as a social welfare function, there are other objectives such as employment and income distribution which might well have been incorporated in the welfare function. In some cases, threshold levels or desirable ranges for objectives not included in the objective function can be specified by way of specific constraints included in the model. However, when conflicting rather than complementary relationships exist between major objectives, it may be desirable to express the welfare function in terms of these objectives with appropriate weights. The form of the welfare function does not necessarily have to be linear, it could be quadratic to reflect, for instance, the diminishing marginal contribution to welfare of each individual objective (see Theil [31]). The only model in which a distributional objective is explicitly incorporated in the preference function is that of MacEwan where the latter is expressed in terms of two regional per capita consumption variables with appropriate variable weights.

A second important question which should be raised with regard to programming models concerns the meaning and usefulness of shadow prices computed from them. Since the shadow prices are dependent on the specific objective functions and the way the constraints are set up, one should be very cautious in interpreting their use and applicability in general situations. Thus, as was pointed out in the review of the Kendrick and Taylor model [21], the terminal condition (i.e., terminal capital stock) may be very sensitive to the initial value of the shadow price of the capital stock. This type of sensitivity is known to be present in multisectoral models with heterogeneous capital goods (see Chapter 10 for more details). It is also relevant to note that comparisons of shadow prices with existing market prices is not generally made in planning models probably because the actual markets may have various noncompetitive characteristics which are ignored in the model specifications and also because of aggregation problems. The only systematic attempt in this direction has been made by Kornai [22] in his planning model for Hungary, which is discussed in some detail in the next chapter.

With regard to the sensitivity analyses usually performed on these planning models, two important aspects which are usually ignored should be pointed out. First, the computing algorithm itself may generate some kind of sensitivity in the computation of optimal trajectories.[32] Secondly, it is known from the decomposition experiments on the linear programming planning model of Kornai [22], that part of the sensitivity and convergence problems may be generated through inadequate disaggregation and decomposition procedures. The geographical decomposition of an overall central plan versus the integration of separate area or regional plans raise important questions regarding the organization of the planning machinery with two or more planning levels organized at least partially in a hierarchical fashion. The problem of linking the submodels into an overall plan (or the decomposition of the latter into submodels) is yet to be solved in a satisfactory manner in the optimization models and incorporated into the planning strategy of developing countries.[33]

A final typical characteristic of programming models is the assumption of unlimited supply of labor. The fact that this assumption may not hold for different skill levels and for different technologies would certainly alter the nature of the optimal solution. The planning model for Israel constructed by Bruno [5] shows this very clearly. A planning model in which the skill levels (including education beyond the school leaving age) are endogenous and employment generation is expressed as a function of production characteristics (including the growth of labor productivity) and the demand pattern over time (as determined by income growth and distribution) would be more meaningful from a policy standpoint in most developing countries where unemployment is an increasingly serious problem.

Very few simulation models have been built for developing countries. It appears likely, however, that the future will see a large upsurge of simulation studies in the development field. There are at least three major characteristics which are distinctive of simulation models in contrast with other types of models. First, they do not contain an explicit preference function to be

---

[32] Some experiments [18, 19] with applying conjugate gradient and Davidson algorithms to control models applied to economic growth have shown that sensitivity analysis in the sense of robustness has to be tested much more carefully than is usually done. Thus, for example, the analysis of sensitivity in different phases is required, since the types of instability may be different.

[33] At least one major effort at formulating a multilevel planning model applied to Mexico, which was touched upon in Section 13.2.2, is presently under way [15]. Another model, of the simulation type, which is discussed in Section 13.3 is based on the interaction of three submodels [27].

maximized. Some of the endogenous variables which are simulated over time by the system can be considered as potential target variables in a similar way as in consistency type models. The second major characteristic is that the specification of these models can be very flexible. Since the set of endogenous variables is solved recursively from period to period through a set of difference equations, nonlinearities can be introduced in the specification of the equations. A third feature, typical of these models, is that they lend themselves readily to the inclusion of, and the experimentation with stochastic terms. Thus, through Monte-Carlo type procedures the probability distributions of endogenous variables can be obtained through the random selection of values for exogenous variables conforming to given probability distributions for the latter.

Likewise, the sensitivity of the resulting values of the endogenous variables over time to the equational and numerical specifications can be tested. Both of these elements can be very useful to the policymaker and model builder. It is definitely valuable for the policymaker to obtain the consequences of some policy action in probabilistic rather than deterministic terms.

At this stage, a major limitation in the construction of simulation models is the scarcity and uneven quality of micro and macro information in developing countries. Another limitation follows from the sheer size of most of these models which makes it practically impossible to evaluate the behavioral or technical relationships underlying them.

13.5. Appendix on Development Planning Models

13.5.1. *Thorbecke-Condos Peru Model*[34]

Behavioral Relationships: R^2

1. $C^p = 11050.0 + 0.56936X^D$ 0.96
   $\quad\quad\quad\quad (0.02917)$

2. $I^p = 2886.95 + 0.77306E_{-1} + 0.65972\bar{Z}_{-1}$ 0.90
   $\quad\quad\quad\quad (0.07773)\quad\quad (0.29103)$

3. $M = -3512.20 + 0.15456C + 0.58033I$ 0.97
   $\quad\quad\quad\quad (0.03946)\quad (0.11374)$

4. $T^d = 143.46 + 0.04071X$ 0.76
   $\quad\quad\quad\quad (0.00706)$

5. $T^i = 4444.11 + 0.14877X$ 0.98
   $\quad\quad\quad\quad (0.00625)$

---

[34] [32], based on version in [17]. Standard errors are given in parentheses.

TABLE 13.5.1

"The Reduced Form" of the Peru Model (1965)

Exogenous Variables / Endogenous Variables	Constant Term	F	R	$\bar{E}_{-1}$	$\bar{Z}_{-1}$	$\bar{E}$	$\bar{Z}$
X	27,342.66	1.09502	2.13422	0184652	0.72241	2.60929	2.60925
X^p	26,464.42	−0.11246	0.72983	0.68612	0.58553	2.11485	2.11485
X^g	880.23	1.20748	1.40439	0.16040	0.13688	0.49440	0.49440
X^D	26,086.08	1.05044	2.04733	0.81206	0.69300	2.50302	2.50302
C	26,725.76	0.79217	2.47937	0.61239	0.52261	1.88759	1.88759
I^g	56.85	1.01340	0.09070	0.01036	0.00884	0.03193	0.03193
I	2,943.81	1.01340	0.09070	0.78342	0.66856	0.03193	0.03193
C^p	25,902.37	0.59808	1.16567	0.46235	0.39457	1.42512	1.42512
I^p	2,886.95	0	0	0.77306	0.65972	0	0
M	2,326.91	0.71054	0.43584	0.54929	0.46876	0.31028	0.31028
T^d	1,256.58	0.04458	0.08688	0.03446	0.02941	0.10622	0.10622
T^i	−376.34	0.16291	0.31751	0.12594	0.10747	0.38818	0.38818

Identities:

6. $\ X = C^p + I^p + X^g + \bar{E} + \bar{Z} - M$
7. $\ X^p = C^p + I^p + \bar{E} + \bar{Z} - M$
8. $\ X^g = T^i + T^d + \bar{F} + \bar{R}$
9. $\ X^D = X - T^d$
10. $\ \ C = C^p + X^g - I^g$
11. $\ \ I^g = s^g X^g + (1 - s^g)\bar{F}$
12. $\ \ I = I^p + I^g$

Endogenous Variables:

$C^p, I^p, M, T^d, T^i, X, X^p, X^g, X^D, C, I^g, I$

Exogenous Variables:

$\bar{E}_{-1}, \bar{Z}_{-1}, \bar{E}, \bar{Z}, \bar{F}, R$

List of Variables:

The symbols represent the following variables expressed in millions of soles in 1963 prices:

Endogenous Variables:

    X = Gross domestic income

    X^p = Private gross domestic income

X^g = Government gross domestic income
X^D = Disposable gross domestic income
C = Total consumption
C^p = Private consumption
I = Total gross investment
I^p = Private gross investment
I^g = Public gross investment
M = Total imports of goods and services
T^d = Direct taxes
T^i = Indirect taxes

Exogenous Variables:

$\bar{E}$ = Total exports of goods and services
$\bar{Z}$ = Terms-of-trade effect
$\bar{E}_{-1}$ = Total value of exports of goods and services, lagged one year
$\bar{Z}_{-1}$ = Terms of trade effect, lagged one year
$\bar{F}$ = Net inflow of foreign public investment $(F = E^x - A^x - i^x)$
E^x = New inflow of foreign public investment
A^x = Amortization of foreign public investment
i^x = Interest payment on foreign public investment
R = Net revenue from non-tax, non-foreign source

13.5.2. *Chenery-Bruno Israel Model* [6]

Production function:

1. $V_n = V_0 + \bar{\beta}(\bar{K}_0 - \bar{K}_n) + \beta(K_n - K_0)$.

The subscript 0 stands for the initial period and n for the final year. β represents the average product per unit of increase in capital stock. The second term allows for the possibility of reducing excess capacity.

Labor demand:

2. $L_\tau = \lambda_0(1 - m)^\tau V_\tau$

λ_0 is the average labor input per unit of output at the beginning of the period and m is the annual rate at which it decreases.

Import demand:

3. $M_\tau = u_c^r C_\tau + u_g^r G_\tau + u_i^r (I_\tau + R_\tau) + u_e^r E_\tau$

Each import coefficient (u^r) is derived from an input-output model.

Replacement:

4. $R_\tau = R_\tau(K_\tau, K_{\tau-1}, K_{\tau-2}, \ldots)$,

Savings:

5. $S_n = S_0 + s(V_n - V_0)$,

Labor supply:

6. $N_\tau = N_0(1 + \gamma)^\tau$,

Exports:

7. $E_\tau = \Sigma_i E_\tau(r, P_{ei}, \tau)$.

These seven equations are of a behavioral technical type, whereas the remaining five specify the equilibrium conditions for $S - I$, balance of payments and employment equilibrium and identities:

Savings-investment equilibrium:

8. $S_\tau + F_\tau = I_\tau + R_\tau$,

Balance-of-payments equilibrium:

9. $M_\tau = E_\tau + F_\tau$,

Employment equilibrium:

10. $L_\tau = (1 - u)N_\tau$,

Total net capital formation:

11. $\sum_{i=0}^{n-1} I_\tau = (K_n - K_0)$,

Gross national product:

12. $V_\tau = C_\tau + G_\tau + I_\tau + R_\tau + E_\tau - M_\tau$.

List of Variables:

Endogenous (uncontrolled) variables:

V_τ = Gross national product

C_τ = Private consumption

I_τ = Total investment net of replacement

R_τ = Replacement

E_τ = Exports of goods and services

M_τ = Imports of goods and services

S_τ = Gross domestic savings

K_τ = Total capital stock

N_τ = Labor supply

L_τ = Labor demand

Instrument and controlled variables:

G_τ = Government current expenditure

F_τ = Foreign capital inflow
u = Unemployment rate $(N_\tau - L_\tau)/N_\tau$
s = Marginal propensity to save $(\Delta S/\Delta V)$
r = Effective exchange rate
m = Annual increase in labor productivity

Exogenous (predetermined) variables:
Initial values of all variables
τ = Time
P_{ei} = Export price in sector i
K_0 = Initial unused capital stock
K_n = Final unused capital stock

13.5.3. *The Thorbecke-Field Model of Argentina* [33]

$$
\begin{aligned}
&(1) && Y_s && = V_a + V_b + V_o \\
&(2a) && V_a && = v_a(\bar{L}, \bar{N}_a, K_a, \overline{RF}) \\
&(2b) && V_a && = v'_a(\bar{L}, \bar{N}_a, \bar{K}_{a-1}, \overline{RF}) \\
&(3) && V_b && = v_b(N_b, K_b) \\
&(4) && V_0 && = v_o(\bar{N}_o, K_o) \\
&(5) && C_a && = c_o + c_1 Y^d + c_2 \bar{t} t_i + c_3 \bar{y} \\
&(6) && C_b && = c_4 + c_5 Y^d + c_6 \bar{t} t_i + c_7 \bar{y} \\
&(7) && C_o && = c_8 + c_9 Y^d + c_{10} \bar{t} t_i + c_{11} \bar{y} \\
&(8) && X_o && = \frac{d_o}{b_o} V_o - C_o - I_0 + \frac{1}{b_o}(\bar{M}_o + \bar{T} i_o) \\
&(9) && X_a && = \frac{d_a}{b_a} V_a - C_a - I_a + \frac{1}{b_a} M_a + \frac{1}{b_a}(\Delta \bar{S} t_a + \bar{T} i_a) \\
&(10) && X_b && = \frac{d_b}{b_b} V_b - C_b - I_b + \frac{1}{b_b} M_b + \frac{1}{b_b}(\Delta \bar{S} t_b + \bar{T} i_b) \\
&(11) && M_b && = M_k + \bar{M}_c + e M_{rm} \\
&(12) && M_a && = (1 - e) M_{rm} \\
&(13) && M_{rm} && = m_o + m_1 V_b + m_2 \bar{t} t_e \\
&(14) && M_k && = X_a + X_b + X_o + \bar{I}_f - M_{rm} - \bar{M}_c - \bar{M}_o \\
&(15) && K_a && = \bar{K}_{a-1} + \alpha I_t - \bar{D}_a \\
&(16) && K_b && = \bar{K}_{b-1} + \beta I_t - \bar{D}_b \\
&(17) && K_o && = \bar{K}_{o-1} + j I_t - \bar{D}_o \quad (\alpha + \beta + j = 1) \\
&(18) && I_t && = I_a + I_b + I_o \\
&(19) && I_a && = \Delta S t_{an} \\
&(20) && I_o && = O
\end{aligned}
$$

(21) $I_b = I_d + M_k$
(22) $I_d = i_1 + i_2 \overline{CAP}_{-1} + i_3(V_b - \bar{V}_{b-1})$
(23) $Y^d = Y_s - T_y$

It should be noted that through substitution the definition of GDP from the demand side can be obtained:

(24) $Y_d = Y_s = C_a + C_b + C_o + I_t + X_a + X_b + X_o$
$$- M_k - M_{rm} - \overline{M}_c - \overline{M}_o - \overline{T}i - \Delta \overline{St}$$

LIST OF VARIABLES IN MODEL
(all national-income variables expressed at constant prices)

Endogenous Variables:

C_a = consumption of agricultural commodities
C_b = consumption of manufactured commodities
C_o = consumption of "services"
I_a = contribution of agriculture to gross capital formation
I_b = contribution of industry to gross capital formation
I_o = contribution of the service complex to gross capital formation
I_d = value of domestically produced gross investment
I_t = gross investment
K_a = capital stock in the agricultural sector
K_b = capital stock in the industrial manufacturing sector
K_o = capital stock in the service complex
M_a = agricultural imports
M_b = industrial imports
M_k = imports of capital goods
M_{rm} = imports of primary and intermediate goods used in the current production process (raw materials)
V_a = value added in the agricultural sector
V_b = value added in the industrial manufacturing sector
V_o = value added in the service complex (all remaining sectors)
X_a = agricultural exports
X_b = industrial exports
X_o = service exports
Y^d = disposable income
$Y_s = Y_d$ = gross domestic product

Exogenous Variables:

$\overline{CAP}_{-1}$ = capacity in machinery and equipment industry lagged one year

$\bar{D}_a$ = replacement investment (depreciation) in agriculture

$\bar{D}_b$ = replacement investment (depreciation) in industry

$\bar{I}_f$ = net foreign investment plus any changes in holdings of foreign currency

$\bar{K}_{a-1}$ = capital stock in agriculture lagged one year

$\bar{K}_{b-1}$ = capital stock in industry lagged one year

$\bar{K}_{o-1}$ = capital stock in remaining sectors of the economy lagged one year

$\overline{RF}$ = index of yearly average rainfall

$\overline{St}$ = over-all change in stocks

$\Delta \overline{St}_a$ = change in stock in agriculture sector

$\Delta \overline{St}_b$ = change in stock in industrial sector

$\Delta \overline{St}_{an}$ = change in stock of livestock $(\Delta \overline{St}_{an} = \overline{St}_{an} - \overline{St}_{an-1})$

$\bar{T}_y$ = direct taxes

$\overline{tt}_e$ = external terms of trade (ratio of the price of imports to the price of exports)

$\overline{tt}_i$ = internal terms of trade (the ratio of agricultural to non-agricultural prices)

$\bar{V}_{b-1}$ = value added in industry lagged one year

$\bar{y}$ = the share of wage income in total income

$\bar{T}_i$ = indirect taxes

$\bar{L}$ = number of hectares used in production in agricultural sector

$\bar{M}_c$ = imports of consumption goods

$\bar{M}_o$ = service imports

$\bar{N}_a$ = size of labor force in agriculture

$\bar{N}_b$ = size of labor force in industry

$\bar{N}_o$ = size of labor force in service complex

13.5.4. Nonlinear Planning Model Using Control-Theoretic Methods of Solution: An Illustrative Case Due to Kendrick and Taylor [20, 21]

A. Welfare function:

(1) Maximize $J = \sum\limits_{i=0}^{n-1} (1 + \rho)^{-i}(1 - \eta)^{-1} c_i^{1-\eta}$

under the following restrictions (2)–(6).

B. Behavioral relations (over time, $i = 0, 1, \ldots, n$):

(2) Production equation: $y_i = f(k_i) - (1 + g)^i \cdot a k_i^\beta$

(3) Investment demand: $k_{i+1} - k_i = f(k_i) - c_i + (1 - \delta)k_i$

C. Definitional and policy constraints:

  (4) Initial capital stock (given): $k_0 = \bar{k}$
  (5) Terminal condition (given): $y_n = f(k_n) = \bar{y}$
  (6) Nonnegativity conditions: $(c_i, k_i, y_i) \geq 0$, all $i = 0, 1, \ldots, n-1$

D. List of symbols. Variables:

  c_i: instantaneous consumption at time i
  k_i: stock of capital at time i
  y_i: output at time i $(i = 0, 1, \ldots, n)$

E. Parameters and other symbols:

  ρ: time rate of welfare discount
  η: elasticity of marginal utility with respect to consumption
  δ: rate of depreciation
  $g = r(1-\beta) + z$; $a = \gamma l_0^{1-\beta}$
  z = rate of neutral technical progress
  γ = efficiency parameter
  β = elasticity of output with respect to capital
  l_0 = initial labor force (given)
  r = rate of growth of labor force.

F. Illustrative values used in calculation:

  $\delta = 0.05$
  $k_0 = 15.0$
  $\rho = 0.03$
  $\beta = 0.75$
  $y_0 = 4.275$
  $y = 85.5$ (denoting approx. 6 per cent geometric growth rate over the planning horizon $n = 50$)
  $\eta = 0.9$
  $a = 0.5609$
  $r = 0.025$
  $z = 0.01$.

For sensitivity analysis other complementary values of a and β are used as follows:
 $a = 2.1723, 0.8419, 0.5609, 0.4900, 0.285$
 $\beta = 0.25, 0.60, 0.75, 0.80, 1.00$

13.5.5. *A Planning Model for South Korea Featuring Economies of Scale* [40, 41]

A. Welfare function:

(1) Maximize $W = \sum\limits_{t=1}^{6} \sum\limits_{i} \phi_{i,t} w_{i,t}$

where $\phi_{i,t} = (2.10)(P_t/2)^{0.5}(1.10)^{-2t} \log \overline{C}_{i,t}$ $(t = 1,\dots, 5)$
(in-plan welfare)

$\phi_{i,6} = (1.95)(P_5/2)^{0.5} \log \overline{GDP}_{i,6}$

under the following restrictions (2)–(15).

B. Behavioral and policy constraints:

(2) Material balances: constraint (A)

$$m_i + x_i^* = \sum\limits_{j=1}^{12} A_{ij}x_j + \sum\limits_{j=1}^{11} B_{ij}y_j + \sum\limits_{j=10}^{11} B_{ij}\delta_j + c_i + e_i + g_i + s_i$$

where $x_i^* = x_i$ for $i = 1,\dots, 6, 8, 9{-}10$ and $x_7 = x_{11}$ for $i = 7$ and x_{12} for $i = 11$.

(3) Foreign exchange balance: constraint (B)

$$\sum\limits_{i=1}^{12} M_i x_i + \sum\limits_{i=1}^{11} N_i y_i + \sum\limits_{i=10}^{11} \overline{N}_i \delta_i + \sum\limits_{i=1}^{11} m_i + f_t + r_t \le \sum\limits_{i=1}^{11} F_i e_i$$
$$+ f_{t-1} + b_t$$

(4) Capacity utilization: constraint (C)

$$x_{i,t} \le 2(1 - D_i)^{2(t-1)}k_{i,1} + 2 \sum\limits_{s=1}^{t-1} y_{i,s}$$

(2 year gestation lag between capacity construction and use assumed)

(5) Marginal savings propensity upper bound: constraint (D)

$$\sum\limits_{i=1}^{11} B_i \Delta y_{i,t} + \sum\limits_{i=10}^{11} \overline{B}_i \Delta \delta_{i,t} + \sum\limits_{i=1}^{11} \Delta s_{i,t} + H\Delta C_t + \Delta f_t - \Delta f_{t-1}$$
$$+ \Delta r_t - \Delta b_t + \Delta sl_{Bt} \le 0.30 \sum\limits_{i=1}^{12} V_i \Delta x_{i,t}$$

(6) Commodity export upper bounds: constraints (E) and (F)

$$\text{(E)} \ e_i \leq \varepsilon_i; \quad \text{(F)} \ \sum_{i=1}^{11} e_i \leq 217.5 \prod_{s=1}^{t} (1 + \gamma_{\varepsilon,s})^2; \ \gamma_{\varepsilon,1} = 0$$

(7) Primary production growth limit: constraint (G)

$$x_{1,t} \leq (1.06)^2 x_{1,t-1}$$

(8) Import substitution limit: constraint (H) (nontraditional iron and steel)

$$A_{7,12} x_{12,t} \leq (1 - A_{7,11}) x_{11,t}$$

(9) Integer requirements: constraint (I)

$$y_i \leq Y_i \delta_i; \ \delta_i = 1 \text{ or } 0$$

(10) Terminal debt: constraint (J)

$$\sum_{t=1}^{5} (1.10)^{2(5-t)}(b_t - r_t) = 726$$

(11) Terminal investment: constraint (K)

$$(1.08)^2 \Delta x_{i,5} + \tfrac{1}{2}[1 - (1 - Di)^2] x_{i,5} \leq 2y_{i,5}; i = 1, \ldots, 9$$
$$(1.08)^2 \Delta x_{i,5} + \tfrac{1}{2}[1 - (1 - Di)^2] x_{i,5} - (1.08)^2 m_{i,4} \leq 2y_{i,5}$$
$$+ ek_{i,5}; i = 10, 11$$

(12) Private consumption demand

$$c_i = (P_t/P_0) \cdot \bar{S}_i + S_i C_t$$

(13) Inventory accumulation conditions: constraint (L)

$$s_i = E_i y_i \quad i = 1, \ldots, 9 \text{ (producing sectors)}$$
$$s_i = E_i \Delta x_i \quad i = 10, 11, 12 \text{ (decreasing cost industries)}$$

(14) Housing investment (HC_t) implicitly allowed for in the demand side of the constraint (A) for the construction sector ($i = 6$); H denotes the requirement for housing construction per unit of consumption.

(15) All variables (endogenous and exogenous) are required to be nonnegative.

C.   Definitions and explanatory statements:

1. (a) $w_{i,t}$: nonnegative weights $\sum_i w_{i,t} = 1$; $t = 1,\ldots, 6$ (1967–68
       to 1975–76 used to approximate the nonlinear welfare
       function

$$\tilde{W} = \sum_{t=1}^{\infty} (1 + \varepsilon)^{-t} P_t^{\alpha} \log_e (C_t/P_t); \rho = \text{discount factor}$$

   (b) $\rho = 0.10$; $\alpha = 0.5$;
       Capacity is measured in yearly output, whereas total con-
       sumption (C_t) over 2 years.
   (c) Gross domestic product (GDP) in the post-terminal year is
       used in the objective function as a proxy for post-terminal
       consumption.

2. A_{ij}: current account input-output coefficients
   B_{ij}: variable charge input-capacity coefficient for domestic goods
   $\bar{B}_{ij}$: fixed charge input-capacity coefficient for domestic goods

3. $B_i = \displaystyle\sum_{j=1}^{11} B_{ij} + N_i$; $i = 1,\ldots, 11$

   $\bar{B}_i = \displaystyle\sum_{j=1}^{11} \bar{B}_{ji} + \bar{N}_i$; $i = 10, 11$

   V_i = value added per unit of production in sector
       $i = 1 - \displaystyle\sum_{j=1}^{11} A_{ji} - M_i$

   $\gamma_{\varepsilon,t}$ = annual growth rate of aggregate exports between period t
       and $t - 1$
   Y_i = scale of the largest plant that can be constructed in sector i
   $\bar{S}_i$ = intercept term in the consumption demand for commodity i
   S_i = marginal propensity to consume commodity i (out of total
       consumption expenditure)
   $k_{i,t}$ = capacity in sector i, period t
   E_i: own output inventory accumulation coefficient, sector i
   S_i: inventory accumulation in sector i

4. Number of constraints in constraint groups (A) through (L) are as follows: (A)=55; (B)=5; (C)=55; (D)=5; (E)=50; (F)=5; (G)=4;(H)=4;(I)=20;(J)=1;(K)=11;(L)=12; and total=228

D.   List of symbols (except those already mentioned):

Endogenous activity variables (each defined to be a sum over 2 years at constant 1965 prices):

$x_{i,t}$ = gross production in sector i, period t; (60) (Note: the number in parentheses indicates the total number of the variable in the system.)

$y_{i,t}$ = gross capacity increase; (55)

$\delta_{i,t}$ = fixed construction for capacity creation in sector i; (10)

$e_{i,t}, m_{i,t}$ = exports and imports of commodity i, period t; (50 + 50)

C_t = aggregate consumption in period t; (5)

f_t = foreign exchange accumulated since 1966 ($t = 1,\ldots, 5$); (5)

b_t = foreign capital inflow; (5)

r_t = foreign debt repayment; (5)

$w_{i,t}$ = weights in objective function approximation; (132)

$e_{ki,t}$ = excess capacity in sector i; (46)

sl_i = slack variable in equation i; (84)

Total endogenous variables = (507)

Exogenous variables:

$g_{i,t}$ = government consumption demand for commodity i

Other symbols:

M_i = total noncompetitive import-output coefficient for sector i

N_i = variable charge noncompetitive import-capacity coefficient

$\bar{N}_i$ = fixed charge noncompetitive import-capacity coefficient

F_i = conversion factor for exports of commodity i

D_i = annual depreciation coefficient for ith sector's capacity

ε_i = upper bound on exports of commodity i

$$GDP = \sum_{i=1}^{12} V_i x_i = \sum_{i=1}^{11} (c_i + g_i + e_i + z_i - m_i) - \sum_{i=1}^{12} M_i x_i$$

= gross domestic product less product originating in household and government sectors

c_i = consumption demand (nongovernment) for commodity i

13.5.6. *A Regional Planning Model for Pakistan* [24, 25][35]

A. Welfare function:

(1) Maximize $W = \dfrac{N^e}{N^e + N^w}\left(\dfrac{c^e}{N^e} + Q^e\right) + \dfrac{N^w}{N^e + N^w}\cdot\left(\dfrac{c^w}{N^w} + Q^w\right)$

under the following restriction:

B. Behavioral relations (by sectors and regions)

(2) Structure of consumption: $c_i = \gamma_i + \beta_i c$

(3) Intermediate demand: $x_{ij} = a_{ij}x_j$

(4) Fixed capital requirements: $h_{ij} = \alpha b_{ij}x_j - H_{0ij}$

(5) Working capital requirements:

$$w_i = \alpha \sum_i \omega_{ij}x_j + \alpha\omega_{ic}c + \alpha\omega_{ih}h_i + \alpha\omega_{ir}r_i^2 + \alpha\omega_{ie}e_i - W_i^0$$

where $w_i = \sum w_{ij} + w_{ic} + w_{ih} + w_{ir} + w_{ie}$

(6) Noncompetitive imports: $\bar{m}_i = \sum_j \mu_{ij}x_j + \mu_{ic}c$

(7) Regional noncompetitive imports: $r_i^{-1} = \sum_j \mu'_{ij}x_j + \mu_{ic}c$

C. Definitional and policy constraints:

Supply and demand balances for

(8) Goods and services (by sectors):

$$x_i + m_i + r_i^1 \geq c_i + \sum_i x_{ij} + \sum_j h_{ij} + \text{rep}_i + w_i + e_i + r_i^2 + \text{gov}_i$$

(9) Foreign exchange:

$$\sum_i p_i e_i + \sum_i p'_i r_i^2 + f = \sum_i q_i m_i + \sum_i q'_i r_i^1$$

(10) Total capital:

$$S + f + \sum_i \text{tar}_i = \sum_i \sum_j h_{ij} + \sum_i w_i + \sum_i \text{rep}_i + \sum_i \text{gov}_i$$

Definitional and feasibility limits

(11) Over-all supply of funds: $f^e + f^w = F$

---

[35] The two regions in this model, the East and West, have no political relevance anymore, after the declaration of independence of the Eastern region, which is now the independent and sovereign nation of Bangladesh. Hence, the relations of this model are to be taken for illustrative purposes only, i.e., for showing the difficulties of building regional elements.

(12) Availability of foreign funds: $F = \bar{F}$

(13) Foreign imports (by sectors receiving: $m_i = \hat{m}_i + \bar{m}_i$

(14) Regional imports (by regional sectors receiving): $r_i^1 = \hat{r}_i^1 + \bar{r}_i$

(15) Exogenous demand elements: (a) $rep_i = \overline{rep}_i$

                                     (b) $gov_i = \overline{gov}_i$

(16) Export limits: (a) by sectors: $p_i e_i \le \bar{e}_i$

                           (b) total: $\Sigma \bar{e}_i > \bar{E}$

(17) Limits on total savings: $S = \sum_{i=1}^{6} s_1 v_i + \sum_{i=1}^{35} s_2 v_2$

       where $v_i = (1 - \sum_{j} a_{ji}) x_i$

(18) Limits on agricultural growth:

       $x_i \le x_i^*[(1.05)^{10} - 1]$, for i, a nonfood grain agricultural sector

(19) Limits on importing in order to export: $x_i \ge r_i^2 + e_i$

(20) Specific constraint for interregional paper trade:

       $r_{14}^1 \le 0.33(x_{14} + m_{14} + r_{14}^1)$

(21) Specific constraint for cottonseed oil: $x_{08} \le x_{04}$ for the Western region only.

D.   List of symbols:

Variables (specified separately for each region):

Increments over the Plan period (1964–65 to 1974–75)

c = aggregate regional consumption (c^e, c^w for eastern and western regions respectively)

c_i = regional consumption of products of sector i

x_i = regional gross output of sector i

m_i = imports to the region from abroad of goods classified under sector i

r_i^1 = imports to the region from the other region of goods classified under sector i

x_{ij} = current deliveries to sector j of goods classified under sector i

h_{ij} = net fixed capital deliveries

rep_i = deliveries of goods classified under sector i for replacement investment

w_i = working capital deliveries of goods classified under sector i. (Note: that the demands for working capital and inventories for production, consumption, investment and exports are determined separately as follows:

$$w_{ij} = \alpha \omega_{ih} h_i - W_{ij}^0; \; w_{ic} = \alpha \omega_{ic} c_i - W_{ic}^0;$$

$$w_{ih} = \alpha \omega_{ih} h_i - W_{ih}^0; \; w_{ir} = \alpha \omega_{ir} r_i^2 - W_{ir}^0; \text{ and}$$

$$w_{ie} = \alpha \omega_{ie} e_i - W_{ie}^0.)$$

e_i = export of goods of sector i from the region to abroad
r_i^2 = export of goods of sector i from the region to the other region
gov_i = government public administration and defense expenditure on the products of the ith sector (zero except for $i = 34$)
f = net regional inflow of funds
S = aggregate regional savings
tar_i = total tariff earned on imports of goods classified under sector i
F = net inflow of funds to the nation from abroad
v_i = value added in sector i

Predetermined base-year variables and exogenous variables:

N = population in 1974–75
Q = a negative constant indicating the decline in per capita consumption which would take place due to population growth were there no growth of consumption
H_{0ij} = deliveries of net fixed investment to sector j of goods classified under sector i in base year
W_{0ij} = deliveries of working capital investment to sector j of goods classified under sector i in base year
$\overline{\text{rep}}_i$ = exogenously specified increment over the plan of replacement-investment of type i
$\overline{\text{gov}}_i$ = exogenously specified increment over the plan of government expenditures on public administration and defense
$\bar{e}_i$ = upper limit on foreign exchange earned from exports abroad of type i products
$\bar{E}_i$ = upper limit on foreign exchange earned from total exports abroad
$\bar{F}$ = exogenously specified limit on increment over the plan to net inflow of funds from other nations from abroad
x_i^* = peak output attained up to 1964–65 in nonfood grain agricultural sectors

Parameters and other symbols:

γ_i, β_i: parameters of the ith consumption function

$p_i(p_i')$: f.o.b. price of foreign (regional) exports of type i

$q_i(q_i')$: c.i.f. price of foreign (regional) imports of type i

a_{ij}: marginal input-output coefficient

α: stock-flow conversion factor

b_{ij}: incremental capital-output ratio

$w_{ij}, w_{ih}, w_{ir}, w_{ie}$: incremental working capital required per unit of product delivered to the jth sector, where $j =$ consumption, investment, regional and foreign exports respectively

$\mu_{ij}(\mu_{ij}')$: increment of noncompetitive foreign (regional) imports of type i required per unit of production in sector j

$\mu_{ic}(\mu_{ic}')$: increment of noncompetitive foreign (regional) imports of type i required per unit of consumption

$\hat{m}_i$: competitive regional imports of type i products

s_1, s_2: marginal savings rates for agricultural and nonagricultural sectors respectively.

13.5.7. *The Eckhaus-Parikh Dynamic Programming Model of India* [8]

The complete model is too long to reproduce here. It is given in a consolidated form in [8].

REFERENCES

[1] ADELMAN, I. "Simulation, Economic Processes", *International Encyclopedia of the Social Sciences,* The Macmillan Co. and the Free Press, 1968.

[2] ——, and CHENERY, H. C. "Foreign Aid and Economic Development", *The Review of Economics and Statistics,* February 1966.

[3] ——, and MAN JE, K. "An Econometric Model of the Korean Economy (1956–66)", in *Practical Approaches to Development Planning.* Edited by I. Adelman, Baltimore, The Johns Hopkins Press, 1969.

[4] BOON, G. K. "Factor Intensities in Mexico With Special Reference to Manufacturing", in *Towards Balanced International Growth.* Edited by H. Bos, Amsterdam: North-Holland, 1969.

[5] BRUNO, M. "Optimal Patterns of Trade and Development", in *Studies in Development Planning.* Edited by H. B. Chenery, Cambridge, Massachusetts; Harvard University Press, 1971, Chapter 8.

[6] CHENERY, H. C., and BRUNO, M. "Development Alternatives in an Open Economy: The Case of Israel", *Economic Journal,* LXXII (March, 1962).

[7] CHENERY, H. B., and STROUT, A. M. "Foreign Assistance and Economic Development", *American Economic Review,* September, 1966.

[8] ECKAUS, R. S., and PARIKH, K. S. *Planning for Growth: Multisectoral Intertemporal Models Applied to India.* Cambridge, Massachusetts: MIT Press, 1968.

[9] FEI, J. C. H., and RANIS, G. "Foreign Assistance and Economic Development: A Comment", *American Economic Review,* September, 1968.

[10] FOX, K. A., and THORBECKE, E. "Specification of Structures and Data Requirements in Economic Policy Models", in *Quantitative Planning of Economic Policy.* Edited by B. G. Hickman, Washington, D.C.; The Brookings Institution, 1965, Chapter 3.

[11] FLETCHER, et al. *Guatemala's Economic Development, The Role of Agriculture.* Ames, Iowa: Iowa State University Press, 1970.

[12] HAZARI, B. R., and KRISHNAMURTY, J. "Employment Implication of India's Industrialization: Analysis in an Input–Output Framework", *Review of Economics and Statistics,* 1970.

[13] HOLLAND, E. P., et al. *Dynamic Models for Simulating the Venezuela Economy.* The Simulmatics Corporation, 1966 (Mimeo).

[14] HOLLAND, E. P., and GILLESPIE, R. W. *Experiments on a Simulated Underdeveloped Economy: Development Plans and Balance-of-Payments Policies.* Cambridge, Massachusetts: The M.I.T. Press, 1963.

[15] INTERNATIONAL BANK FOR RECONSTRUCTION AND DEVELOPMENT. *Multilevel Planning: Case Studies in Mexico.* (Development Research Center Draft, February, 1972, mimeo).

[16] INTERNATIONAL LABOR OFFICE. *Towards Full Employment.* (A Programme for Colombia, prepared by an interagency team organized by the ILO) Geneva, 1970.

[17] IOWA UNIVERSITIES MISSION TO PERU. *Peruvian Macroeconomic and Agricultural Prospects and Strategy, 1967–1972.* Iowa–Peru Program, Lima, December 1967.

[18] KELLER, E. A., Jr., and SENGUPTA, J. K. "Relative Efficiency of Computing Optimal Growth by Conjugate Gradient and Davidon Methods". (Sent for publication, 1972).

[19] ——. "Sensitivity Analysis for Optimal and Feedback Controls Applied to Growth Models". (Sent for publication, 1972).

[20] KENDRICK, D., and TAYLOR, L. "A Dynamic Nonlinear Planning Model for Korea", in *Practical Approaches to Development,* op. cit. Edited by I. Adelman.

[21] ——. "Numerical Methods and Nonlinear Optimizing Models for Economic Planning", in *Studies in Development Planning,* op. cit. Chapter 1. Edited by H. B. Chenery.

[22] KORNAI, J. *Mathematical Planning of Structural Decisions.* Amsterdam: North-Holland Publishing Co., 1967.

[23] KRESGE, D. T. *A Simulation Model for Economic Planning, A Pakistan Example.* (Economic Development Report 81, Development Advisory Service). Cambridge, Massachusetts: Harvard University Press, 1967. (Mimeographed).

[24] MACEWAN, A. *Development Alternatives in Pakistan.* Cambridge, Massachusetts: Harvard University Press, 1971.

[25] ——. "Problems of Interregional and Intersectoral Allocation: The Case of Pakistan", in *Studies in Development Planning,* op. cit., Chapter 7. Edited by H. B. Chenery.

[26] MAHALANOBIS, P. C. "The Approach of Operational Research to Planning in India", *Sankhya,* XVI (December, 1955), 3–62.

[27] MANETSCH, T., et al. *A Generalized Simulation Approach to Agricultural Sector Analysis, With Special Reference to Nigeria.* East Lansing, Michigan: Michigan State University, November 30, 1971.

[28] MEADOWS, D. H., et al. *The Limits of Growth*. (A Report for the Club of Rome Project on the Predicament of Mankind), Potomac, 1972.

[29] SANDEE, J. *A Demonstration Planning Model for India*. Calcutta: Indian Statistical Institute, 1960.

[30] SANDEE, J. "A Programming Model for a Dual Economy", in *The Role of Agriculture in Economic Development*. Edited by E. Thorbecke, New York; Columbia University Press, 1969.

[31] THEIL, H. *Optimal Decision Rules for Government and Industry*. Amsterdam: North-Holland Publishing Co., 1964.

[32] THORBECKE, E., and CONDOS, A. "Macroeconomic Growth and Development Models of Peruvian Economy", in *The Theory and Design of Economic Development*. Edited by I. Adelman and E. Thorbecke, Baltimore, Maryland; The Johns Hopkins Press, 1966.

[33] THORBECKE, E., and FIELD, A. "Quantitative and Policy Relationships Between Agriculture, Non-Agriculture and Foreign Trade Throughout the Growth Process: The Case of Argentina and Peru", in *The Role of Agriculture in Economic Development*. Edited by E. Thorbecke, New York; Columbia University Press, 1969.

[34] THORBECKE, E., and SENGUPTA, J. K. *A Consistency Framework for Employment Output and Income Distribution Projections Applied to Colombia*. (Paper prepared for Development Research Center of IBRD, January 1972, mimeo.).

[35] THORBECKE, E., and STOUTJESDIJK, E. *Employment and Output, A Methodology Applied to Peru and Guatemala*. (Organization for Economic Cooperation and Development, Development Center, Paris, 1970.)

[36] TIMS, W. "A Growth Model and Its Application—Pakistan", in *Development Policy, Theory and Practice*. Edited by G. Papanek, Cambridge, Massachusetts; Harvard University Press, 1968.

[37] UNITED NATIONS CONFERENCE ON TRADE AND DEVELOPMENT (UNCTAD). *Trade Prospects and Capital Needs of Developing Countries*. New York, 1968.

[38] UNITED NATIONS, ECONOMIC COMMISSION FOR ASIA AND THE FAR EAST (ECAFE). *Sectoral Output and Employment Projections for the Second Development Decade*. (Development Programming Series No. 8, Bangkok, 1970.)

[39] VAN RIJCKEGHEM, W. "An Intersectoral Consistency Model for Economic Planning in Brazil", in *The Economy of Brazil*. Edited by H. S. Ellis, Los Angeles; University of California Press, 1969.

[40] WESTPHAL, L. E. *Planning Investment With Economies of Scale*. Amsterdam: North-Holland Publishing Co., 1970.

[41] WESTPHAL, K. E. "An Intertemporal Planning Model Featuring Economies of Scale", in *Studies in Development Planning*. Edited by H. B. Chenery, op. cit., Chapter 4.

Chapter 14

NATIONAL PLANNING MODELS IN DEVELOPED ECONOMIES

The purpose of this chapter is to review and analyze the main features of national planning models which have been formulated and used in a few developed mixed and centrally-planned economies.[1] The discussion will proceed in the following way: First, a brief introductory part will attempt to bring out the essential difference between the use which planning models can serve in developed, as opposed to underdeveloped, countries; second, the planning models used by the Central Planning Offices of the Netherlands, Japan, France (in the preparation of the Fourth and Sixth Plans, respectively) and Hungary will be presented and examined critically.

The 1961 model of the Dutch Central Planning Bureau is analyzed in more detail than the other two models. Reasons for this are that the former model is tighter and more rigorous from an econometric and policy standpoint and lends itself, as a result, better than other planning models to generalizations about the operational use of the theory of economic policy.

14.1. Difference in Types of Planning Models

The first distinction which should be made with respect to planning models is that between long, medium and short-term models [6]. Long- and medium-

---

[1] Even though the emphasis in this chapter is on the evaluation of national models of mixed economies one model relating to a centrally-planned economy (i.e., Hungary) is discussed in detail. In general, it does appear that the theory of economic policy, as such, can be extended to any economic system. The main difference between a planning model in a centrally planned country and in a mixed economy would appear in the behavioral equations and in the constraints. It is likely that the parameters of the former would be influenced by the directives and the direct controls imposed by the central planner and that the constraints would be more rigid (than in a mixed economy) in reflecting direct controls. In a sense, a planning model in a mixed economy is more open-ended, since besides fixing values of instrument variables to attain policy goals it relies, in addition, on the equilibrating forces of the market mechanism.

term policy models are only concerned with trends and the specification of the future macroeconomic equilibrium conditions, usually in terms of the balance between the availability of and the requirements for resources. This type of model is often limited to checking only the physical equilibrium, but it sometimes incorporates, also, a financial equilibrium check. Most long-term models assume complementarity in the production function (in some instances the possibility of limited substitutability is introduced). If these models are used for policy, as opposed to purely forecasting purposes, quantitative recommendations with respect to the policy instruments will depend, in large measure, on the length of the planning horizon. For example, we saw before that in the two-sector Mahalanobis model the magnitude of λ_i (the proportion of total investment to be allocated to investment goods) which maximizes national income varied depending upon the time horizon, i.e., whether national income is to be maximized five, ten of fifteen years hence.

The uncertainty factor becomes compounded as the time horizon is moved further into the future. More specifically, the assumptions concerning the exogenous conditions as well as the invariances in the structural equations are more likely to be invalidated as the planning horizon increases. The long- and medium-term models are used mainly to ascertain the feasible range of growth rates of aggregate (or per capita) income and the nature of the long-run manpower balance (i.e., the level of the long-run equilibrium between demand for and supply of labor). It is, therefore, not surprising that most development planning models, as was seen in Chapter 13, are of a medium- or long-term type. The overriding importance which is attached to the goals of economic growth and increased employment, as well as the rather fluid institutional and economic structure which usually prevails in developing countries, explains the reason for the adoption of the above type of model. The inference should not be drawn, however, that underdeveloped countries do not suffer from or care about short-term economic instabilities. The typical balance of payments fluctuations, resulting from highly variable foreign exchange receipts for areas exporting primary products (and caused by low demand and supply elasticities), as well as the persistent, but often erratic, behavior of inflationary pressures caused by external (as in the above case) or internal factors, testify to the contrary. The main reason why policies to cope with these sources of instabilities tend to take the form of *ad hoc* measures (such as direct import controls) is that the economic, financial and institutional structure of these countries is usually not susceptible to short-term quantitative economic policy.

First, the underlying structure is relatively flexible, and so a macro-economic model would be difficult to specify quantitatively in the short term (the parameters of the behavioral relations would tend to fluctuate significantly over a relatively short period of time), and second, the typical instruments used for stabilization purposes in mature economies, such as changes in the discount rate, tax rates and public transfers, are, generally, fairly ineffective in reducing or alleviating short-term fluctuations in key targets, such as the price level of consumer goods and the state of the balance of payments. It is because of the nonreceptivity of macrotargets to short-term changes in monetary and fiscal instruments, in addition to the reasons given above, that short-term quantitative planning models have, typically, not been constructed for developing countries.

It is important to note that not only developing countries need long or medium-term models for development planning purposes. A number of developed countries built long-term models which are complementary to their short-run stabilization models. Perhaps the best known of these models is the one prepared by Verdoorn [20] for the Dutch Central Planning Bureau (CPB) ,which is presented and discussed in Chapter 10 (Section 10.1) and briefly in Chapter 3. It will be seen that other countries (i.e., France and Japan) also developed long-term models, essentially as an adjunct to their short-run stabilization models. In a sense, it can be said that the former models are concerned with growth and employment prospects in a trend sense, whereas the latter deal with the alleviation of the (short-run) fluctuations around the trend.

These long-run planning models take the form in their cruder version of projections amounting essentially to the extrapolation of a few macro-variables on the basis of past trend. In their more sophisticated version these models include a few instrument variables, such as the savings ratio and the emigration rate, as in the case of the previously mentioned Verdoorn model.

In contrast to long- and medium-run models, national planning models with a short time horizon have typically been formulated and used for stabilization purposes. Each endogenous variable in the system is expressed as a function of other endogenous, lagged endogenous and exogenous data and instrument variables. The incorporation of lagged endogenous variables as explanatory variables makes it possible to build into the model some of the more significant dynamic and cyclical features of the economic system. Changes in the external conditions can be incorporated in the model by plugging in new values (i.e., forecasts) of the exogenous data. Likewise, the impact of changes in the instrument variables can be followed through the whole set of endogenous (targets and irrelevant) variables. Thus, on the above two counts, the model can be almost continuously readapted to changing external stimuli. The first type of stimuli would be originated by any change in the exogenous variables outside the control of the policy maker, such as changes in income abroad, in price level of imports and even in weather (which appears as an explanatory variable in the unemployment equation of the 1961 Dutch CPB model discussed subsequently); whereas the second type of stimuli would be triggered by any change which the policy maker would make in the policy instruments appearing in the model.

The welfare losses resulting from imperfectly specified models as well as the losses from the use of out-dated parameters can be approximated quantitatively and rules formulated about the optimum timing of new estimates, the best use of additional information and a revision (or a new specification) of the model.

Short-run stabilization models have been designed for and used mainly by the Dutch government. These will be discussed in some detail below. It will also be seen in the analysis of the Dutch CPB model that the introduction of a curvilinear capacity equation provides the short-term model with an element of built-in flexibility. In a sense the explicit introduction of capacity offers a bridge between the long-term planning and the stabilization models.

In the former the growth of output is a function of such invariances as the elasticity of capital with regard to GNP and the supply elasticity of labor. Complementarity among resources being customarily assumed, the long-term growth path becomes a balanced full-employment type of path. Likewise, stabilization models which do not allow for capacity changes do not permit one to follow through the differential impact of relative input shortages or ceilings on investment and other endogenous variables. However, where capacity is explicitly included as a variable, it implies the possibility of examining the impact of different ratios of inputs on the system. For instance, in the Dutch CPB model capacity is expressed in terms of the percentage of unemployed ($\tilde{w}$). Thus, an increase in $\tilde{w}$ ceteris paribus amounts to a decline in the effective labor-capital ratio.

The next section is devoted to an analysis of a number of national models used for planning purposes. The structure of the models is emphasized, while as much as possible is abstracted from the institutional factors.

14.2. National Planning Models in the Netherlands, Japan, France, and Hungary

14.2.1. *The Netherlands Model*

The first published model used by the Dutch Central Planning Bureau (CPB) appeared as an Appendix to the 1955 Plan [8].

At that time the model contained twenty-seven endogenous variables and equations. These equations were divided into (a) definitional relations which represent identities between variables (eleven in number), (b) balance equations expressing an (national income accounting) equilibrium condition which must be fulfilled (one equation), (c) institutional equations which reflect the control which the government can exert on transfer payments and various tax bills and contain a number of instruments (four equations), (d) technical equations which are derived essentially from production function (input-output) data (two equations) and (e) behavior equations reflecting the behavior of economic agents (nine equations).

The model was completely static, and no lags appeared anywhere in the system. All relations were linearized and expressed in terms of initial values of the variables and first differences, the product of changes in two variables being ignored throughout. Most of the structural coefficients had been fixed a priori.

The above model was used for stabilization purposes. In addition, a simple long-term planning model (the Verdoorn model)[2] discussed subsequently, was also constructed to examine the growth and employment prospects.

The 1955 model was gradually improved and revised on the basis of additional information, and in 1961 the Dutch CPB published its new model [10, Annex 1], which is reproduced in Section 14.3.1 of this chapter.

The 1961 model exhibited a number of differences and innovations compared to the earlier versions which are brought out by the CPB [10, Annex 1]. First, the new model expressed variables not as first (absolute) differences but rather as percentage changes from year to year. The notation which has been chosen for these percentage changes (and which should be kept in mind when the actual model in Section 14.3.1 is studied) is the following:

$$x_t = 100 \frac{\Delta \tilde{x}_t}{\tilde{x}_{t-1}},$$

where, $\tilde{x}_{t-1}$ = absolute value of the variable in the base year,

$\Delta \tilde{x}_t$ = absolute difference,

x_t = percentage change.

---

[2] See Chapter 10, Section 10.1, and Chapter 3.

Consequently, the parameters which represent the relationship between two symbols without ~ are elasticities.

Second, a very significant change was the introduction of lagged endogenous and lagged exogenous variables. For instance, in the consumption function (equation (1))[3] the value of consumption (C) is determined by disposable wage income with a lag of four months and by disposable nonwage income with a lag of eight months. The shortest lag appearing in the model is four months, and the longest is two years.

Third, quasiaccelerators and distributed lags appear in some relations, and the influence of monetary variables, liquidities and the rate of interest has been taken into consideration.

Fourth, whereas in the 1955 model parameters had been assigned on a priori grounds, in the 1961 model they were statistically estimated by the two-stage least-squares method. Of particular interest from a stabilization viewpoint is the fact that the base periods used to derive the coefficients covered the years 1923–1938 and 1949–1957. All time series were on an annual basis, and so for each series sixteen annual prewar observations and nine annual postwar observations were available.

Since years of high economic activity were more frequent and the quality of the statistical data substantially better in the postwar period, observations for that period were counted twice as heavily as for prewar years in calculating the coefficients. The theory of this procedure is that the use of periods characterized by very different levels of economic activity in estimating the parameters increases the range of situations with which the model can cope. Moreover, weighting observations according to the quality of the underlying statistical time-series inputs will, in principle, improve the estimates of the structural parameters. Further, a change of considerable importance, which has already been alluded to, was the incorporation of a capacity equation.

The model, which is reproduced in Section 14.3.1, contains thirty-six endogenous variables and thirty-six equations, which are divided into two general types: the so-called reaction equations and the definition equations. The former are further subdivided into clusters determining, respectively, (a) expenditure categories (consumption, private investment, stock formation and exports), (b) demand for factors of production and capacity (demand for labor and for imports, capacity equation) and (c) prices of, respectively, consumption, export, investment and "autonomous expenditures" goods.

---

[3] Equation numbers in this section correspond to the original model given in Section 14.3.1 of this chapter.

The total number of reaction relationships amounts to eleven. The definition equations, in turn, are subdivided into (a) relations between value and volume variables, (b) expenditure totals, (c) costs and margins, (d) unemployment, (e) incomes, (f) taxes and (g) lagged influences (for a total of twenty-five definition equations).

The variables appearing in the model can be subdivided into the following categories:

1. Endogenous variables
   a. Possible targets and irrelevant variables.
2. Data
   a. Lagged endogenous:
      (i) with lags of less than one year,
      (ii) with lags longer than one year.
   b. Exogenous variables:
      (i) instruments,
      (ii) other exogenous data (thus not under the control of the policy maker).

The classification of the variables appearing in the 1961 CPB model in terms of the above categories is as follows:

1. Endogenous variables
   a. Possible targets and irrelevant variables:
      Resources: a, L, Z, T_K, m, M,
      Expenditures: c, p_c, C, p_x, X, i, p_i, I, N, b, p_b, B, v', $p_{v'}$, V', V,
      Unemployment: $\Delta \tilde{w}$,
      Secondary incomes and taxes: l^B, Z^B, T''_z,
      Composite variables: v_a, v_m, H, $p_{m-v'}$, K, $\tilde{w}_1$, π_w, Ψ_i, Ψ_a, Λ.
2. Data
   a. Lagged endogenous:
      (i) with lags of less than one year,

$$
\begin{array}{ll}
L^B_{-1/3} & \Delta p_{v'}, p_{v'-1/2} \\
Z^B_{-2/3} & \Delta v_m \\
\Delta p_c & (v'-a)_{-1/2} \\
 & (v'-m)_{-1/2} \\
\Delta \tilde{w}_{1-1/2} & T'_{K-1/3}
\end{array}
$$

   (ii) with lags of one year or more and thus, known variables: ΔC_{-1}, Z_{-1}, $\tilde{N}_{-1}$, $\tilde{V}_{-1}$, p_{x-1}, $\Delta \tilde{Z}_{-1}$ and all the variables with lags of at least one year appearing in the three relations specifying the composite variables Ψ_i, Ψ_a and Λ.
   b. Exogenous variables:

(i) possible instruments;

x	=autonomous expenditure (government expenditure, investment by government and residential construction),
l	=average gross wages per standard year of 300 days,
O'_L	=income transfers with regard to wage income, including government wages and direct taxes on cash basis (expressed as a percentage of wage bill of enterprises),
O'_Z	=income transfers with regard to nonwage income, including direct taxes on cash basis (expressed as a percentage of total nonwage income),
$\tilde{T}_z$	=direct taxes on nonwage income (on cash basis),
Δa_0	=change (second difference) in number of persons employed in government sector (man years),
$\tilde{T}'_K$	=indirect tax rate.

(ii) other exogenous variables (thus not under the control of the policy maker):

c^r_{-1}	=time and demand deposits at the end of the year
t^*	=prewar decreasing trend (1933 = 15, 1938 = 0) (in equation 3),
b_c	=competing exports,
$p'_b, \Delta p'_b$	=prices of competing exports,
k	=quantitative import restrictions (1932–1937),
k'	=rate of liberalization (1949–1955),
$\Delta \tilde{P}, \tilde{P}_{-1}$	=population in working ages,
$\Delta \tilde{P}_{B-1}, \tilde{P}_{B-1}$	=dependent working population
$\Delta \tilde{T}_c$	=minimum temperature below 0° centrigrade,
$r_{k-1/2}$	=short-term rate of interest (discount rate of the Central Bank),
$P_{b-1/2}$	=export prices,
$p_m, p_{m-1/2}$	=import prices,
D	=net invisibles,
$\tilde{w}$	=registered unemployment as a percentage of dependent working population,
F	=depreciation of enterprises.

It should be noted that since the model is specified on the basis of annual time series, the lagged endogenous variables with lags of less than one year (category 2.a. (i), above) are, in fact, a linear interpolation of the (unknown) current value of the endogenous variable and of the (known) value of that variable in the previous year. It will be seen below that this procedure has important consequences from the standpoint of the structure of the model, its interpretability and its statistical specification.

An examination of the complete model (in Section 14.3.1), together with the list of possible instruments and targets given above, makes it possible to understand how the model can actually be used for policy purposes. For instance, changes in government transfers (O'_L and O'_Z) can be used in equations (30) and (31) to affect disposable wage and nonwage income (L^B and Z^B) which might be policy targets in an income distribution sense. Likewise, a change in the volume of government expenditures (x, which includes also residential construction) will alter the value of total output (V) through equations (15) and (22).

A fundamental question in the construction and the analysis of any econometric model is whether the set of economic relationships to be incorporated is of a recursive or interdependent (simultaneous) type [6].

The model is recursive[4] if by proper rearrangement of the relationships a triangular matrix of coefficients, relating current values of the endogenous variables to one another, can be obtained so that only zero elements appear above the main diagonal. The concept of causal ordering developed by Simon and discussed in Chapter 3 and Chapter 11 is based on the property of recursiveness.

In an attempt at analyzing the structure of the 1961 CPB model and illustrating the properties of recursiveness and interdependency in stabilization models, a nearly triangular coefficient matrix of the endogenous variables was obtained by proper rearrangement of the equations (see Figure 14.1). Furthermore, the complete causal ordering of the whole set of endogenous variables could be worked out on the basis of the above matrix.

It should be made clear at the outset that the 1961 system as a whole is interdependent, though the coefficients determining this interdependence are only eight in number. These coefficients appear above the diagonal in Figure 14.1. Two reasons account for the interdependence. First, a number of lagged endogenous variables have lags shorter than a calendar year. For instance, total private consumption (C) is expressed as a function of disposable wage income lagged four months ($L^B_{-1/3}$) and disposable nonwage income lagged eight months ($Z^B_{-2/3}$).

---

[4] See Chapters 3 and 4 for details of the exact model and its stochastic part in the recursive case.

Since the model is estimated exclusively on the basis of annual observations, the lagged endogenous variables with lags of less than a year are approximated on the basis of the (known) value of the variable in the previous year and the current (unknown) value. Thus $Z^B_{-2/3}$ is arrived at through linear interpolation:

$$Z^B_{-2/3} = \frac{2Z^B_{-1} + Z^B}{3}.$$

If time series were available on a quarterly or perhaps monthly basis, all of these lagged endogenous variables would be truly predetermined instead of a combination of predetermined and current endogenous variables, as is the case here. As can be seen from an examination of Figure 14.1, this procedure is responsible for a major part of the interdependence in the CPB model, seven of the eight nonzero coefficients above the diagonal of the matrix in Figure 14.1 resulting from these lagged endogenous variables.

The second factor accounting for the interdependence is that capacity is explicitly introduced through a generalized capacity-impact curve $(\tilde{w}_1)$, which is expressed as a function of the percentage of unemployed $(\tilde{w})$. If the percentage of unemployed were assumed to be predetermined and if the lagged endogenous variables with lags of less than one year were truly predetermined, the model would become wholly recursive.[5]

The incorporation of a capacity equation (equation (26)) provides the model, as was previously pointed out, with an element of built-in flexibility, since the responses of key endogenous variables, such as aggregate investment and exports, will be greatly influenced by the level of capacity at which the economy operates. Capacity is measured in terms of the percentage of workers unemployed $(\tilde{w})$ on the basis that labor and not capital is the limiting factor. (Capital goods and raw material shortages can be removed in the Netherlands through additional imports.) A generalized capacity-impact curve $(\tilde{w}_1)$, which is highly curvilinear, is postulated as a function of the percentage of unemployed. Regression coefficients are next computed for a number of endogenous variables (i.e., exports, price level of exports, investment, imports) as a function of the impact curve.

Since $\tilde{w}_1$ is a function of $\tilde{w}$ of the form $\tilde{w}_1 = \ln(\tilde{w} + \eta) - \alpha\tilde{w}$, where η and α are parameters and ln stands for natural logarithm, it follows that different levels of unemployment will affect $\tilde{w}_1$ in a nonlinear way, the impact of which in turn will be transmitted to a number of endogenous variables

---

[5] For a detailed scheme and arrow diagram analysis of causal ordering (from first to tenth-order) of the Dutch CPB model (1961) in a recursive case, see Fox and Thorbecke [6].

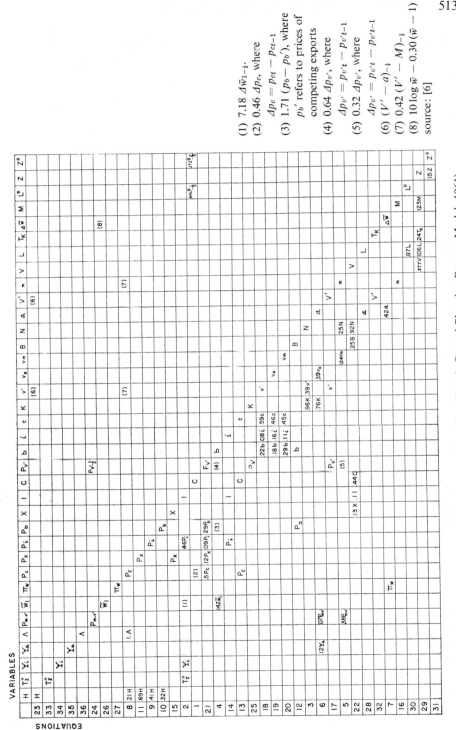

Fig. 14.1. Coefficients Matrix of Endogenous Variables (Dutch Central Planning Bureau Model, 1961)

(1) $7.18\, \Delta\bar{w}_{t-\frac{1}{2}}$.
(2) $0.46\, \Delta p_c$, where

$$\Delta p_c = p_{ct} - p_{ct-1}$$

(3) $1.71\,(p_b - p_b')$, where p_b' refers to prices of competing exports
(4) $0.64\, \Delta p_{v'}$, where

$$\Delta p_{v'} = p_{v't} - p_{v't-1}$$

(5) $0.32\, \Delta p_{v'}$, where

$$\Delta p_{v'} = p_{v't} - p_{v't-1}$$

(6) $(V' - a)_{-\frac{1}{2}}$
(7) $0.42\,(V' - M)_{-\frac{1}{2}}$
(8) $10 \log \bar{w} - 0.30(\bar{w} - 1)$
source: [6]

through the regression coefficients, linking $\tilde{w}_1$ or $\Delta\tilde{w}_1$ to them. The annual changes in $\tilde{w}$ and $\tilde{w}_1$, namely, $\Delta\tilde{w}$ and $\Delta\tilde{w}_1$, are both treated as endogenous variables. It should be noted that the inclusion of the capacity-impact curve introduces some difficulties in the solution of the model. A linearized form giving $\tilde{w}_1$ as a function of $\tilde{w}_{-1}$ (last year's percentage of unemployment) can be used.

Where the changes in $\Delta\tilde{w}$ are small or where only one value of $\tilde{w}_{-1}$ is used, as in the preparation of annual plans, simple adjustments can be worked out. Alternatively, when considering different initial levels of employment or larger changes in $\Delta\tilde{w}$, the coefficients of the inverse and the reduced form will be altered. Methods have been worked out to cope with this situation by deleting $\Delta\tilde{w}_1$ from the class of endogenous variables and including it among the predetermined variables [21].

It might be noted in this connection that the selection of labor as the limiting factor is strictly based on the special circumstances prevailing in the Netherlands. In many lesser developed countries the limiting factors, in both the short run and the long run, tend to be capital and the availability of foreign exchange to purchase development goods and necessary inputs. In contrast, in countries where the population density is low (Australia, Canada) a labor scarcity could be overcome, at least partially, through a proper immigration policy.

Up to this point the Dutch CPB model has been analyzed in some detail, without any attempt at assessing its qualitative performance in a policy sense. One way in which this can be done is to compare the forecasts with the actual realization for the various classes of variables.

The quantitative concept which has been developed and used for this last purpose is the so-called inequality coefficient,[6] which is a measure of predictive accuracy. In general, noncontrolled variables, such as the price level of imports, volume of world trade and competitive price level on foreign market showed relatively high inequality coefficients, indicating thereby fairly inaccurate forecasts [19]. This is not surprising, since these variables are very difficult to predict accurately.

On the other hand, the quality of the forecasts of the instrument variables was fairly good during the more recent period (1958–1962), showing a very substantial improvement in predictive quality compared to the previous five years (1953–1958). The significant reduction in the magnitude of the inequality coefficient in the recent past is probably the most noteworthy

---

[6] This has been defined before in Chapter 6.

feature, reflecting, as it does, the improvements in the planning model itself and in the ability to forecast noncontrolled variables (see Chapter 6).

After completing the analysis of the short-term CPB model which is used for stabilization purposes, a few comments will be made about the long-term models used by the Dutch Planning Bureau. The 1955 long-term model [9] took as its planning horizon 1950–1970. It sought to specify the optimal growth-path compatible with a moving equilibrium of demand and supply for three basic variables, labor, capital and imports. The complete model consisted of seventeen equations, fifteen endogenous variables, four instruments and three targets. The four instruments were the savings ratio, the rate of emigration, the rate of change of relative export prices and the rate of import substitution. The targets included two fixed ones, the level of unemployment and the amount of capital exports, and one flexible one, the maximization of per capita real income in 1970. The model is based on the assumption of fixed proportions (invariances) being maintained, and it does not allow for substitutability among resources. A simplified version of this model, discussed by Verdoorn [20], has been presented in Chapter 10, which assumes balance between only two factors, capital and labor.

The above model has certain features in common with the two-sector Mahalanobis model, discussed before, such as the maximization of income at some specified future date. A comparison of these two long-term models reveals some interesting implications of the planning process resulting from different initial model specifications [13].

Finally, it should be pointed out that the long-term growth prospects are not analyzed exclusively with the help of completely aggregative models of the above type. It has already been seen in Chapter 13 that a number of development planning models take a disaggregative (input-output) form. Likewise, developed countries will often use fairly detailed input-output projections to ascertain the growth perspective in terms of sectors and final-demand categories. Often, such a disaggregated procedure can provide an important check on the accuracy of the parameters of the long-term (macro) planning model and on the feasibility and validity of the instrumental values arrived at by solving the macromodel as a function of the targets. A good example of a disaggregated attempt at assessing the possible economic growth in the Netherlands is by Sandee.[7] The basis of the projections rests

---

[7] See Sandee [11]. Further Sandee [12] has developed a seven-sector linear programming model with 1963 as a base year and 1967, 1970 and 1975 as reference years, which includes the usual input-output coefficients and consumer demand elasticities.

on an input-output table for 1960, broken down in terms of four major sectors—agriculture, manufacturing, construction and services—and five categories of final demand—exports, private consumption, government consumption, investment in fixed assets and stock increases.

The input-output table was projected to 1965 and 1970 through a detailed and specific appraisal of the growth prospects of the various sectors and the likely changes in the final-demand categories. (Sectoral employment is made an integral part of these projections.) It should be noted that, in the case of the Netherlands, the initial stock level and state of the balance of payments are elements which may have an important inpact on the future projections of the input-output table and thereby be a possible source of error because of their essentially volatile nature.

It is, of course, obvious that developed countries have a very substantial advantage over developing countries in the formulation of such projections because of the availability of much better disaggregated statistical information.

14.2.2. *The Japanese Planning Model*

The planning process in Japan dates back to the beginning of the postwar (World War II) period. A number of more or less ambitious plans for reconstruction, self-support and long-term growth purposes were formulated and drawn between 1946 and the present.

The 1956 five-year plan for economic self-support used essentially the Colm approach [4] in making growth a function of the rates of increase of, respectively, the labor force and labor productivity. This plan was revised in 1957 when the "new long-range plan" for 1957–1962 was conceived, which emphasized the role of the private sector and which permitted the selection of an optimal rate of growth among the various alternatives consistent with relative full employment, balance of payments equilibrium and a minimum desirable level of domestic savings.

These various plans suffered from a number of shortcomings of a technical and institutional nature, which will not be reviewed here. The one extremely unusual feature which practically all the postwar Japanese plans shared in common was that the target growth rates were consistently exceeded by the actual growth rates.

In 1960, the Economic Planning Agency started work on an elaborate long-term growth "Plan for Doubling National Income" in ten years (1960–1970). This plan was to be based on a fairly detailed econometric policy model and is, therefore, discussed in some detail below.

There is a paucity of information about the technical aspects of the Japanese planning process in the Anglo-Saxon literature. Much of the informational background used here is consequently based on the papers by Shishido [14] and Watanabe [22].

The major objectives of this ten-year plan were (a) rapid expansion in social overhead capital facilities to fill a real need caused by large scale private investment since 1955, (b) high rate of industrial growth of the secondary sector, (c) promotion of exports, partially through financial help to underdeveloped countries, (d) investment in human resources, advancement of science and technology and (e) reducing the dual structure of the economy and improving income distribution.

The first step in the preparation of the ten-year plan consisted of the determination of the target growth rate with the help of long-range projections to 1980, examining specifically (a) the limiting factors, such as labor, energy, foreign exchange and domestic savings, and (b) the supply and demand balance of key commodities. As a result of this preparatory study, it was found that a growth rate of 7 per cent over the period 1961–1970 was possible. On this basis, the "Ten Year Plan for Doubling National Income" was formulated, which implies an annual rate of growth of 7.2 per cent over the period under consideration. In order to allow for some flexibility, it was decided not to specify exactly the target date, the plan stating that "the doubling of national income should be attained in and around ten years."

The second step was the construction of the quantitative planning model. The original model consisted of about fifty equations, including minor structural relations. A simplified version of this model is presented in Section 14.3.2, based on Shishido's presentation. The original model includes all transactions in the conventional national accounts, which makes it somewhat unwieldy from an expository viewpoint. The major simplification included in the model presented in Section 14.3.2 and discussed here is the integration of the household and private enterprise sectors which were treated separately in the original model.

The ten-year planning model is presented in Section 14.3.2, together with the relevant list of symbols. It can be seen that the model consists (in its simplified version) of twenty-one equations which can be subdivided into the following categories: (a) national income accounting identities (equations (1) to (6)), (b) structural and behavioral relations (equations (7) to (16)), (c) labor balance identity (equation (17)) and (d) institutional (policy) relations (equations (18) to (21)). The variables appearing in the model can be broken down into three general classes as follows:

Classification of variables in Japanese ten-year plan

1. Endogenous variables (19 variables)
   a. Income variables: $V_2, V_3, C, G, I, E, M, W, R, S_p, B$;
   b. Capital stock: K;
   c. Taxes and transfers: T_i, T_d, A;
   d. Employment: L, L_1, L_2, L_3.
2. Exogenous variables (5 variables)
   $\bar{V}, \bar{V}_1, \bar{S}_g, \bar{F}, \bar{N}$.
3. Policy variables (5 variables)
   a. Active instruments: α, β, γ,
   b. Passive instruments: δ, ε.

Since the model contains twenty-one independent equations and nineteen endogenous variables, two of the policy variables have to be converted into endogenous variables in order to obtain a solution for the system. In the above case it was decided by the planning agency to convert the tax ratio δ and ε into endogenous variables.

Thus, category 3.b. becomes endogenous variables and category 3.a. exogenous variables. To distinguish between the two types of policy variables above, the term *active* instruments [8] was coined here to apply to the exogenous subset of policy variables: the share of government purchases in GNP (α), the share of transfer payments in GNP (β) and the indirect tax ratio (γ). In contrast, the endogenous policy variables (δ and ε) are here called passive instruments to denote the fact that the equilibrium magnitudes of these variables are obtained only after the system has been solved as a function of the eight exogenous variables (five noncontrolled exogenous variables and three policy instruments).

The relationships appearing in the model require, on the whole, little explanation, and so only some of the major features of this model will be examined here.

In the first place, it should be noted that among the set of exogenous variables are found GNP ($\bar{V}$), gross value added in primary industry ($\bar{V}_1$) and the government surplus $\bar{S}_g$.

These first two variables are in fact targets: $\bar{V}$ reflecting the target growth rate decided upon (7.2 per cent or a doubling of national income in ten years) and $\bar{V}_1$ standing for the previously mentioned objective of reducing the discrepancies caused by the existence of a dual economy (objective e. above)

---

[8] This distinction is not made by the Japanese planning commission.

Income distribution, employment and social considerations all played a role in the specification of value added in the primary sector. Government surplus in the above model is also equivalent to a policy target, reflecting the traditional objective (and policy) of maintaining a balanced budget. In a broad theoretical sense, $\bar{S}_g$ could just as well have been considered an instrument. The fact that it was not is a direct consequence of the institutional environment within which the plan was conceived, the reduction of S_g being strongly against the traditional fiscal policy of the country.

The other two noncontrolled exogenous variables representing world trade $(\bar{F})$ and population $(\bar{N})$ are typical exogenous variables.

The model lends itself well to the analysis of the policy consequences (on the set of endogenous variables) of changes in external conditions ($\bar{F}$ and $\bar{N}$), changes in certain fixed targets ($\bar{V}$, $\bar{V}_1$ and $\bar{S}_g$) and changes in instruments (α, β, γ). It should be noted that a decision about the quantitative specification of the policy instruments α and β was only reached after several experiments were made of their impact on δ and ε (direct tax ratios on wage and nonwage income, respectively).

The model was statistically estimated using annual observations. A few relationships in the model deserve additional explanations. Equation (11) expressing exports as a function of world trade is of crucial importance for Japan, given its dependence on foreign trade.

The plan assumes exports to grow at 10 per cent annually, the volume of world trade being estimated to grow at 4.5 per cent per year and the elasticity of Japanese exports with respect to world trade being set at 2.2.

Equation (9) represents an estimate of the capital-output ratio. This global ratio was obtained after having derived and examined sectoral capital stocks and coefficients. An incorrect specification of this ratio can have serious consequences for planning, as will be pointed out subsequently. Since both total output and value added in the primary sector are predetermined, only the outputs of the secondary (V_2) and tertiary sectors (V_3) are determined by the system. V_2 is obtained from equation (7) and V_3 from equation (1) as a residual. It is interesting to notice that the labor force in tertiary industry is expressed as a function of output in that sector and labor productivity in the secondary sector (equation (16)), the assumption here being that the latter magnitude may affect productivity in the tertiary sector. Finally, labor demand in the primary sector is arrived at as a residual after the global and the other two sectoral labor forces have been derived.

The model as a whole is quite simple, since a large number of the endogenous variables are connected with $\bar{V}$. The significance of using $\bar{V}$ as a key explanatory variable in the structural and behavioral relations is that it permits an asssesment of the alternative effects of different global growth rates on the set of endogenous variables. Experimentation as a function of given growth rates is thus made relatively easy.

It is essential to remember that the above model is no more than a global long-term planning model, which explains why it was referred to as the "framework model." It provides a first quantitative basis for a number of more detailed disaggregated analyses such as trade projections by regions and commodities, supply and demand projections for many goods and forecasts of sectoral investment requirements. It appears that these detailed submodels were all linked to the framework model and coordinated into a single economic system. This represents a good practical example of the need and desirability for the linkage of disaggregated submodels to the macropolicy model.

What appears, however, to be intrinsic to the Japanese planning process —in contrast, for instance, to the Dutch process—is that the underlying planning framework is a long-range one. Consequently, recommendations with respect to quantitative stabilization policy can only be arrived at on the basis of some adjunct and, most probably, partial short-term model. The lack of a complete and explicit short-term (or medium-term) stabilization model of the Dutch CPB type (see the previous section of this chapter) appears to be a possible shortcoming of the Japanese planning process. The study by the Japanese planning agency, at the present time, of a quarterly and annual model in addition to the long-term and perspective models indicates interest in trying to build a short-term model able to cope with cyclical problems.

By solving the long-term planning model for the (unknown) values of the endogenous variables as a function of the eight exogenous variables, one obtains the terminal (around 1970) values of the former set. One purpose of the plan was to determine the sectoral outputs by 1970, consistent with a doubling of national income between 1961 and 1970. At the time of preparation of these sectoral projections, no input-output consistency check was undertaken. However, such a check was subsequently performed by Watanabe. As a result of it, a number of fairly important inconsistencies were discovered which are summarized here.

First, use was made of Chenery's cross-section study [3] to determine how the 1970 sectoral projections in the plan compared with the calculated ones applying Chenery's growth parameters. It was found that the two sets of figures were quite close, implying a pattern of relative balanced growth over the ten-year period. This correspondence would have been expected, were it not for the fact that one of the objectives of the ten-year plan was an accelerated development of the secondary sector (objective b. above).

This raises the question of whether the objective of rapid further industrialization was indeed quantitatively reflected in the projections.

The second and more fundamental consistency check consisted of calculating sectoral production from the demand side, i.e., to compute for each sector total output by assuming the final demand bill (minus imports) given in the plan and deriving the intermediate demand corrected for possible technological changes by iterative methods. Substantial differences appeared between the projected and the computed sectoral output values. For example, projected output was significantly overestimated in the following sectors: machinery, construction, metals and nonmetallic mineral products. In contrast, agricultural and mining outputs were underestimated.

The conclusion which can be drawn from the above check is that serious miscalculations can result from macropolicy models when their parameters and the resulting values which they give rise to are not carefully compared to the results of disaggregated submodels. The type of consistency check undertaken above illustrates well the desirability and usefulness of relying on input-output (or other forms of disaggregation) to provide more accurate and detailed quantitative policy recommendations. It should be noted that in the Japanese example above, an excess supply in the construction, machinery, metals and some mineral sectors would have resulted in 1970 on the basis of the macroprojections. This discrepancy leads one to question the accuracy of the sectoral capital-output ratios employed in the model.

A final feature of the Japanese planning setup is that the private sector was never formally involved in the formulation of plans. The private sector appears, however, to take the targets appearing in the plan as guideposts or directives for their own actions. A move is presently under way to involve the private sector more in the planning process and for the planning agency to express directives more explicitly.

14.2.3. *The Planning Model used in the French Fourth Plan*

The methodology which has evolved in the preparation and the formulation of the French Five-Year Plans since the end of World War II is unique and presents important differences from the planning process of both the Netherlands and Japan.

The present analysis will concentrate on an examination of the fourth plan (1959–1965), which appears to have formalized many factors which were treated on an *ad hoc* basis in the previous plans. In 1959, work started on the preparation of the fourth plan. Two types of projections were envisaged: first, long-term (framework) projections to 1975, and second, projections within the term of the plan, i.e., to 1965, the former projection being the framework (*plan d'encadrement*) within which the actual projections of the fourth plan could be drafted. This is why the year 1975 was called the horizon of the plan and 1965 its term.

The base year which was selected was the year 1959, not 1960, because of the greater statistical information available in the former year.

As will become clear from the subsequent analysis, the French planning process follows an iterative method which is broken down into a number of steps. It is in some cases difficult to distinguish clearly between these steps because they may take place simultaneously or an initial step (or hypothesis) may be altered on the basis of further analytical checks leading to a new round of projections consistent with the revised hypothesis.

The first step was the selection of a global growth rate of Gross Domestic Product (GDP). The long-term projections (to 1975) were prepared on the basis of three alternative growth rates of GDP, covering the range of feasible situations, namely 3, 4 and 6 per cent. An appraisal of the consequences of these rates plus an examination of the past historical trend resulted in the selection of an initial growth rate[9] (p) of 4.5 per cent (which was later changed to 5 per cent) for the period of the plan. Once this rate is chosen, two types of checks could be undertaken: the physical equilibrium check and the financial equilibrium test. The present discussion will center primarily on the former procedure because it precedes the test of financial feasibility in a sequential sense and, as will be pointed out subsequently, monetary and fiscal policy can be used within limits to make the financial conditions conform to a given physical equilibrium.[10]

A complete scheme of the model used in the formulation of the plan is presented in Section 14.3.3 of this chapter. This model was used to determine the physical equilibrium. Since the planning procedure in France is essentially iterative, it is very difficult to present a formal closed model. The schema in Section 14.3.3 ought to be interpreted as an *ex post* rationalization of an iterative procedure which ultimately converges to a set of equilibrium values. Since every relationship is both presented symbolically and discussed in

---

[9] The symbols used here are those contained in the analytical model, or schema, of the fourth plan presented in Section 14.3.3.

[10] For a thorough discussion of the preparation of the fourth plan, see [7]. Our present review is based on this text.

For the methodology underlying long-term projections, see Benard [1].

Section 14.3.3, the latter should be consulted and carefully studied as a necessary complement to the analysis in the text. Likewise, the list and classification in terms of the exogenous and endogenous categories of the major variables contained in the model appear in Section 14.3.3.

Physical equilibrium can be expressed within the national income accounting framework as follows: production plus imports equals consumption of households plus government consumption plus capital formation plus exports. Given the selected global rate of growth and assuming a zero balance of trade, the above macrovariables were first projected within a simple three-sector breakdown (agriculture, industry and services), which was later expanded to seventeen branches.

It should be noted that the modernization commissions, discussed below, make use of an even more detailed breakdown, consisting of twenty-eight branches.

Given the preselected rate of growth, the first set of projections deals with the final-demand components. Government expenditures (consumption and capital formation) are determined partially on the basis of the welfare function of the policy maker regarding such functions as education, health, housing and national defense and partially as a function of the rate of growth of GDP and population growth. Thus, only one part of government expenditure (A) by major function depends on p, the remainder being specified autonomously (see equation (8)).

Household consumption by products for the terminal year of the plan is estimated on the basis of (i) demographic information concerning the rate of growth of population, the active labor force, the population pyramid, etc.; (ii) studies (i.e., econometric and statistical among others) of income elasticities of demand for the French economy based on time series as well as cross-section information— other parameters than elasticities are also used; (iii) changes in income distribution and in relative prices (taken into account to a limited extent). The first projection broke down consumption by broad functions which were subsequently converted through a transformation matrix into a classification according to twenty-eight product groups (see equations (9), (10) and (11)).

Investment was projected using the same breakdown (twenty-eight branches) as above. Three types of methods were used to predict investment by branch:

(i) Direct estimation and judgements by the commissions and by experts in each branch. This method was applied in those sectors where clearly defined investment programs existed, as for solid fuels, petroleum and natural gas, iron, nonferous minerals and metals and transport and communications. In the case of agriculture and residential construction, the output in 1965 was fixed as a target and thus the investment needs could be directly specified.

(ii) The second method calculated the investment requirements with the help of marginal (gross) capital-output ratios by sectors. This was done for the mechanical and chemical industries.

(iii) Finally, for the other branches the ratio of investment to business turnover, corrected for anticipated technological change, was applied to estimate sectoral investment (see equation (4)).

Detailed studies of export prospects by regions of destination and by commodities were undertaken to derive export projections which are taken as exogenous. For imports, noncompetitive imports were first estimated as a function of the growth rate of gross domestic output and other variables, and second, competitive imports were projected assuming a certain relation between domestic output and imports by branch (the breakdown was according to the twenty-eight sector classification) (see equations (12) and (13)).

Once the above components of final demand have been determined for the terminal year of the plan, it is possible to derive the intermediate demand by branch necessary for and consistent with the final bill of goods arrived at by summing C, F, E-I, A and S. The addition of final demand and intermediate demand provides gross output for each branch.

The intermediate demand requirements were arrived at with the help of the existing input-output table, which was modified to reflect technological change and likely input substitution. (If inconsistencies appear in the above projections, attempts are made at correcting them in an iterative way.)

The final step in the initial projection round consists of checking the employment effects of the above structure of output. Detailed demographic studies are employed to derive total population and total active labor force in 1965. Since full employment is a policy goal, the changes in the supply of labor by branches are checked against the demand for labor, given the projected output by sector. One of the first conclusions which was reached upon performing this test was that the initial rate of growth which was chosen was too low to ensure full employment. Consequently, the target growth rate was increased to slightly above 5 per cent. In the process of estimating labor supply and demand by sector, the realizable increases in labor productivities and the "necessary" productivities (to give rise to the planned output) are determined and compared *inter se* to derive the projected labor productivities (ε_j) by branch (see equations (14) and (15)).

Once consistent physical projections have been reached, the financial feasibility of the plan is assessed. Financial revenues and expenditures tables are drawn for the households, enterprises and the government. Minor inconsistencies between planned savings and planned investment resulting from an examination of these tables are corrected by way of monetary and fiscal tools.

The planning procedure which is described above is iterative, as was already pointed out. The formulation of projections is arrived at through a method of successive approximations which implies a continuous movement back and forth between the initial hypotheses and their consequences, which if not totally desirable leads in turn to changes in the initial set of hypotheses. It is interesting to notice that convergence was obtained fairly rapidly in the preparation of the fourth plan. The main reasons for this appear to be that the planning machinery which has been developed since the end of the war is now working fairly efficiently. The reports of the modernization commissions —containing representatives of management, labor and technical experts and government—have been unified and can now be fairly easily translated into the national income accounts and input-output frameworks. The latter two systems, in turn, have evolved in a direction which makes them conform closely to the planning needs. The "Commissariat au Plan," finally, has gained a great deal of experience in the essential procedure of synthesizing information and projections coming from many highly decentralized sources.

A unique feature in the French planning process, which can only be touched upon here, since the present treatment does not go into the institutional aspects of planning, is the involvement of the private sector in the formulation of the plan. Through representation of management and labor in the vertical (by branch) and horizontal (manpower, financing, etc.) commissions, the private sector plays a key role in the preparation of the plan. In the above treatment, three distinctive types of planning procedures have been analyzed in detail.

14.2.4. *The Planning Model Used in the French Sixth Plan*
It is only in the preparation of the French Sixth Plan (1971–75) that for the first time a completely formalized model was used.[11] The model, as such, is

---

[11] The model itself entitled FIFI (which stands for Physical-Financial) was constructed by a number of mathematical economists from I.N.S.E.E. Given the size of the model, there is no comprehensive version giving all of the equations available at this time. The model, however, is described in some detail by its major architects: Courbis [25]; and Aglietta and Seibel [23]. In addition, Bénard [24] provides a very good analysis of the model on the basis of the above sources and others. A compact version of the model in equational form is given in Section 14.3.4.

essentially a multisectoral consistency model which can be used to simulate the effects of alternative assumptions regarding exogenous variables not under the control of the government and policy variables which are under the control of the government. The model is very large consisting of approximately 1500 equations and 3500 variables.

The builders of FIFI opted rather strongly against the construction of an optimization type model. They felt that no objectives should be imposed a priori. As Courbis put it, "It is only through successive tâtonnement that one can determine the appropriate economic policy to attain the desired objectives" [25, p. 5].

A very important feature of this model is that prices are endogenously determined. Since variables are expressed both in quantitative and value terms and prices are endogenously determined, it follows that the model is nonlinear (i.e., values are obtained by multiplying volumes by prices). In addition, there are other nonlinear behavioral relations. The nonlinear character of the model requires the use of decomposition algorithms and iteration procedures to solve it. At the same time FIFI is not strictly speaking a dynamic model. It is comparative-static in the sense that it describes an equilibrium state for the economy for a given year of the Plan, generally the last year, but not the dynamic process within the Plan period.

Conceptually, the model can be used for policy purposes by specifying *given* values of the exogenous variables not under the control of the government and varying the set of policy instruments. Thus, corresponding to each set of predetermined values of the exogenous variables not under the control of the government, variations in policy variables provide different solutions to the model which in a sense trace an efficiency frontier for the set of potential policy objectives. By altering the assumptions made at the outset about the exogenous variables and again varying the policy instruments a new efficiency frontier can be obtained. The choice can then be made as to where the government wants to be on each one of these efficiency frontiers. The choice itself is, of course, dependent on the explicit or implicit preference function of the government which the model builders do not attempt to postulate. Rather, they consider the purpose of the model to provide the policymaker a range of alternative choices regarding feasible values of the policy objectives on the basis of which the latter can decide which combination he prefers.

Three types of sectors are distinguished in the model: (a) administered sectors for which prices are fixed by the public sector and which include energy, transports and communications, agriculture and housing; (b) the protected sectors which are shielded from foreign competition and which include agricultural and food industries, construction and public works, commerce and services; and (c) the sectors which are exposed to foreign competition and which include all the other branches of industry. In the administered sectors prices are fixed by the government, while in the exposed sectors prices are determined largely as a function of the foreign price (see (c) in Section 14.3.4 which explains the price determination relationships). More specifically, the various supply curves of goods and services (in all three types of sectors) are determined by the cost of intermediate inputs and labor, the appropriate tax rate and a minimum markup required to generate a sufficient flow of undistributed profit to self-finance the required investment (see equation (6) in Section 14.3.4). The behavioral assumption which is made here is that entrepreneurs will only undertake the required investment to produce specific goods and services if they can finance a certain minimum fraction of the investment cost from within the enterprise. Given the supply and demand functions equilibrium prices are obtained for both the administered and protected sectors. With respect to the exposed sectors it is assumed that the domestic price will be equal to the foreign price and that imports will be equal to the difference between the quantity demanded at that (foreign) price and the quantity domestically supplied.

The final demand of households for goods and services is based on linear expenditure functions (see equation (10) in Section 14.3.4). Exports of industrial products depend on foreign demand, domestic production, domestic consumption and the ratio of foreign to domestic prices. Imports of noncompeting (complementary) products are directly related to the domestic output of the sector using these imports as inputs. Thus, complementary imports are treated essentially in the same way as all other domestic inputs—the form of the sectoral production function being linear of the Leontief-type (see equations 1–3). Competing imports are determined as indicated above by the difference between the prevailing domestic demand and the domestic supply at the prevailing foreign price. The model contains also a wage rate equation which explains the latter as a function of the changes in the price level and the unemployment rate (see equations 4 and 5). Finally, the model includes a series of administrative (public sector) relations, identities and balance relations and financial operations.

The FIFI model was used in the preparation of the Sixth Plan essentially in a simulation-cum-forecasting sense, as we have seen it, rather than in a decision (e.g., optimization) sense. In this connection, the following quotation from one of the architects of FIFI is revealing:

The inclusion of the state in the model is abstract. The state is assumed to be an economic agent which is endowed with a behavior pattern, but whose aim is sufficiently different from those of the other agents to receive special treatment. This agent sets itself general aims and seeks to achieve them by applying many and various means of intervention whose direct impact is felt in different parts of the economic system. The coordination of these means of intervention is not a matter for a predetermined pattern of behavior having all the earmarks of a mechanism. The opposite point of view prevails; that of freedom in the the use of intervention in order to determine by trial and error, the combination that fits the aims pursued in each situation. Here, then, we appear to have come back to a global finalism, with a method of trial and error replacing that of direct optimization. [23, p. 12]

14.2.5. *Planning Method in Hungary*

As an illustrative example the planning method developed in Hungary resulting from the work of Kornai [27], Kornai and Liptak [28] and others [32] provides perhaps the most interesting attempt at specifying the basic problems of investment planning in a centrally controlled socialistic economy.[12] In these economies the role of the competitive market forces so prominent in the private enterprise economies is unimportant if not negligible. Reasons for selecting the case of Hungary instead of other countries such as, e.g., the U.S.S.R. or Poland, are two-fold. First, the Hungarian model is perhaps one of the first to introduce two-level planning in a decomposition framework between the center and the team of sectors, such that the shadow prices of central resources evaluated at successive stages could provide an optimizing direction. Second, the application of linear and nonlinear programming in individual sectors (e.g., sector programming) is quite widespread in economic planning in Hungary and the experiences in sector programming in the absence of explicit market prices as in a private-enterprise economy, having revealed certain features of the planning process which are quite novel and in many ways fundamental. For example, some of these features include the following: (a) methods for allowing safety factors through safety programming due to the presence of various elements of risk and uncertainty; (b) sensitivity analysis through parametric variation of certain prices or productivity indices which may affect all the important sectors of the economy; and (c) comparison of programming solutions with traditional accounting rules and consistency models using the balance relations of the input-output table.

---

[12] The model is given in equational form in Section 14.3.5.

It is interesting to note that the method of two-level planning applied to linear programming models is basically related to the decomposition algorithms developed by Dantzig and Wolfe [26] and others [32] for possible applications in large decentralized systems of decision-making, e.g., a large corporation with various levels of decision-making. Although the Kornai-Liptak algorithm differs from the Dantzig-Wolfe algorithm in several respects [30], it has the basic similarity with the latter that it prescribes Walras-type tâtonnement processes whereby the original central problem is decomposed into sector programs in order to evolve an allocation pattern where the sum of the maximal yields or profits of the sector programs is the greatest. Two interesting points about the applications of this two-level technique to national planning in Hungary may be worth mentioning. First, this technique helped to build a facet of optimization to the consistency method of macroeconomic planning that was followed by the National Planning Bureau in Hungary using the detailed input-output matrix of the economy to check the inner coordination of the annual and five year plans. Second, since the optimization objective leads to a very large-scale linear programming model, even for the existing computer capacities, special methods of solution using a fictitious play of the polyhedral game are applied. The players are the center and the team of sectors. The strategies of the center are the feasible allocation patterns for the central resources, those of the sectors, the feasible shadow price systems in the duals of the sector programs. The pay-off function is the sum of the dual sector objective functions. As Kornai and Liptak note [28, p. 143]

> Actually the inspiration for the development of the allocation technique of the OCI (overall central information) problem and the iterative method of solution was derived from the present planning practice in a socialist economy. The method to be described is in some degree an imitation of the usual course of planning. The National Planning Bureau, acting on the basis of the requirements of economic policies and of general information about the various sectors, works out a preliminary draft plan which contains general targets (quota figures) for the sectors. The center makes a provisional distribution of the available resources, material, manpower, etc., among the sectors and at the same time also allocates their output targets. The sectors then proceed, through their own detailed calculations made on the basis of their concrete conditions, to give "substance" to the quotas and to lend concrete meaning to the central targets. In so doing, they also make recommendations for changes to the Planning Bureau. This is what is in economic usage called "counter-planning." On the basis of the counter-plans the National Planning Bureau modifies its original

targets and again sends them down to sectors. The method proposed here is an attempt to aid this process of planning and counter-planning by means of objective criteria.

Without going into the technical details of computing algorithms implicit in the two-level scheme of planning which is in the form of a "pyramidal network" of linear programming models, the essential feature of the two-level planning may be easily illustrated by a two-sector model of allocation of investment by the center. Denote by the vector x_i the activity vector of sector $i(i = 1, 2)$ with respective coefficient matrices A_i, objective functions (cost) $C_i(x_i)$ and sectoral resources b_i; then the problem of allocation of total investment (B) between sectors 1 and 2 may be posed as an optimization problem as follows:

Minimize $C_1(x_1) + C_2(x_2)$ (14.1)
    subject to

$$A_1 x_1 = b_1; \; A_2 x_2 = b_2 \qquad (14.2)$$

$$a'_{B1} x_1 + a'_{B2} x_2 = B; \; x_1 \geq 0; \; x_2 \geq 0. \qquad (14.3)$$

Here a'_{B1}, a'_{B2} denote vectors of coefficients relating to new investment allocated to the respective sectors (note that the resource constraints in (14.2) do not include new investment resources) and the objective function is to minimize the sum of the costs for the two sectors. Denote by λ the investment quota allocated to sector 1, the remaining, i.e., $(B - \lambda)$, to be allocated to sector 2. By parametric programming it may be possible to determine an optimal value λ^* for which the total costs $C_1(\lambda) + C_2(\lambda_2)$ have a minimum value. But this possibility is limited to the case when the overall model is not very large. For large-scale models it may be impossible to determine the optimal value λ^* even for LP models since it may surpass the existing computing capacities [27]. Hence, the need for a decomposition algorithm.

It should be pointed out, however, that the decomposition algorithm of the two-level planning procedure has been utilized in planning discussions in Hungary for a number of purposes other than as a numerical computing technique. Some of these purposes include the following: (1) the meaning and interpretation of various shadow prices computed from the programming model and the implications of their divergencies from the official price system; (2) the comparative appraisal of alternative planning techniques applied to specific sectors like cotton textiles industry, e.g., traditional accounting calculation of efficiency of investment compared with official plan allocations for the sector and with the programming solutions derived from the decomposition algorithm; and (3) methods for incorporating safety factors through fractile programming (see Chapter 7) using risk-aversion measures so that the solutions derived from the programming model are not greatly sensitive to the uncertainty and errors in estimating the parameters like the input-coefficients.

TABLE 14.1

Divergencies Between the Actual Price System and the Computational Evaluations

Description of Characteristics	Actual Price System	Official Evaluations Used in Investment Efficiency Calculations	Computational Evaluation Used in Long-Term Programming
1. Is there any rent charged on the use of fixed capital? If so, at what rate?	None (Recently the actual payment of rent on capital was established, but this does not affect the price)	Yes; 20 per cent	Yes; 8 per cent
2. What rental is being charged on the use of working capital?	3 per cent	20 per cent	8 per cent
3. Are wages taken as constant over time?	Yes (With the actual price system, this is evident)	Yes	No
4. Are the calculations based on a uniform rate of foreign exchange?	No; the rate of foreign exchange varies according to product group	Export returns and material input costs are calculated at a uniform rate of exchange. The costs of investments are calculated in terms of actual prices which vary according to product-group	A uniform rate of exchange is employed

It is clear that in economies where private markets do not exist, the so-called invisible hand of the competitive free market solution may be very difficult to identify. The determination of the most appropriate relationship between the shadow prices and the official prices constitutes one of the most fundamental yet unresolved problems in the theory of economic planning today. The information of Table 14.1 reproduces only a part of the table given in Kornai [27, p. 312] which reveals clearly how the divergences between the two prices may be very important in the case of Hungary:

The second aspect referring to the comparative analysis of alternative variants of planning is greatly facilitated by the parametric sensitivity analyses applied to objective functions. For instance, in case of the cotton textile industry the effects of varying rental rates on capital (used in old or new machines) are analyzed by varying the parameter γ in the objective function

$$\text{Minimize } C(x) = c'x = (\gamma p' + r')x \tag{14.4}$$

of the parametric LP model, where p = vector of investment costs per unit of activity, r = vector of operation cost per unit of activity, and x is the activity vector. Thus by parametric programming it is investigated whether the different plan variants are consistent with each other in the technological development of the cotton textile industry.

The third aspect referring to safety programming in the sector models of planning is also analyzed through another class of parametric programming methods. Let $C_Q(x)$ denote the Q-quantile of the objective function $C(x)$ in (14.4) assuming that it is stochastic due to randomness in the parameters p or r. Then $C_Q(x)$ indicates the value at which the probability of the event $C(x) \leq C_Q(x)$ equals Q. If $C(x)$ is normally distributed for all x with expectation $\bar{C}(x)$ and standard deviation $\sigma_C(x)$, then it follows that

$$C_Q(x) = \bar{C}(x) = \theta_Q \cdot \sigma_C(x), \tag{14.5}$$

where θ_Q is given by the inverse function $\Phi^{-1}(Q)$ where $\Phi(\cdot)$ is the cumulative distribution function of a normal variate. In the general case the parametric program becomes:

$$\text{Minimize } C_Q(x) \tag{14.6}$$

subject to

$$Ax = b; x \geq 0; 0 \leq Q \leq 1. \tag{14.7}$$

For all values of Q between zero and unity, one seeks to determine a vector $x^* = x_Q^*$ which is feasible according to (14.7) and where the objective function (14.6) is at a minimum. The value of Q selected in any decision situation is called the safety level, the index θ_Q the safety factor and the resulting parametric program (14.6)–(14.7) the safety programming. Since $\theta_Q \geq 0$ for $Q \geq 0.50$ it is clear that the expression $\theta_Q \sigma_C(x)$ in (14.5) can be interpreted as penalty for uncertainty for $Q \geq 0.50$. For the case $Q = 0.50$ the criterion (14.5) reduces to the Laplace criterion of minimizing the expected value. In case of $Q = 1.0$ we get the maximum criterion of Wald [32]. Thus the role of the safety level index Q in safety programming is similar to that played by the optimism-pessimism index of Hurwicz's decision criterion [32]. Methods of building suitable safety levels for different sectors through safety programming vary according to the sector's role in the likely divergences from the plans caused by uncertainty, e.g. the flexibility of sectoral planning and the ability of the sector to adapt quickly to unforeseen situations, the expected national impact of the divergence from the plan occurring at the sector level and the expected supply of stocks and reserves to take care of the unforeseen situations.

It is worthwhile at this stage to add a few concluding remarks on the overall method of two-level planning and the decomposition algorithm attempted for Hungarian planning. First, the similarity of the decomposition algorithm with the competitive market process is very superficial to say the least, since the competitive framework is only hypothetical, invented in the account book of the center. The risks of management failure when a sector has to transfer (or sell) some central resource to another sector internally (i.e. in the absence of a private market) at a marginal cost price below its average costs may induce biased and exaggerated reporting of sectoral marginal productivity to the center. This may destroy the neutral competitive behavior of the center and the sectors altogether. Second, the problem of resource allocation in nonmarket systems is greatly conditioned by the presence of indivisibility and joint costs, the nature and importance of public goods (having externalities) produced in the system and the various subgoals considered by the sector-level decision makers. This is one of the most active areas of current research [31, 32].

The choice of the countries selected for review purpose was, perhaps, felicitous in the sense that it covered the gamut from short-term to long-term planning models. Indeed, it was seen that (a) the Dutch CPB model is essentially a short-run stabilization model; (b) the French system relies on intermediate (five-year) plans; (c) the Japanese Ten-Year Plan provides a good example of a long-term planning model; and, finally, (d) the Hungarian model is an excellent prototype of the planning process in a centrally-planned economy. The operational use of planning models covering a range of problems from short-term stabilization resource allocation in centrally-planned economies to long-term growth could be illustrated with concrete examples.

14.3. Appendix on Planning Models

14.3.1. *The Dutch Central Planning Bureau Model (1961)*[13]

A. *Reaction equations*

Expenditure categories:

(1) $\quad C = 0.64\,L^B_{-1/3} + 0.17\,Z^B_{-2/3} + 0.46\,\varDelta p_c - 0.16\,\varDelta C_{-1}$
$\qquad + 0.05\,c'_{-1} - 0.63$,

(2) $\quad I = 0.82\,(Z_{-1} - T''_z) + 0.46\,p_i + 0.80\,c'_{-1} - 7.18\,\varDelta\tilde{w}_{1-\frac{1}{2}} - \varPsi_i$
$\qquad + 29.62$,

(3) $\quad N = 0.39\,v' - 1.34\dfrac{\tilde{N}_{-1}}{\tilde{V}'_{-1}} + 0.96\,K + 0.18\,p_m + 0.41\,t^*$,

(4) $\quad b = 1.46\,b_c - 1.71\,(p_b - p'_b) - 1.11\,(p_b - p'_b)_{-1} - 0.64\,\varDelta p'_v$
$\qquad + 1.42\,\tilde{w}_1 - 7.52$.

Factors of production and capacity:

(5) $\quad m = 1.24\,v_m + 0.29\,\varDelta v_m + 2.50\,N - 0.38\,p_{m-v'} + 0.32\,\varDelta p_{v'} - 0.30\,k$
$\qquad + 0.11\,k' - 0.08$,

(6) $\quad a = 0.39\,v_a + 0.76\,K + 0.07\,p_{m-v'} + 0.12\,\varPsi_a + 0.66$,

(7) $\quad \varDelta\tilde{w} = -0.42\,a + 0.39\dfrac{\varDelta\tilde{F} - \varDelta\tilde{a}_0}{\tilde{P}_{B-1}} - 0.04\,\varDelta\tilde{T}_c + \varPi_w - 4.49$.

Prices:

(8) $\quad p_c = 0.21\,H + 0.20\,p_{m-\frac{1}{2}} - 0.42\,(v' - m)_{-\frac{1}{2}} + 0.17\,T'_{K-1/3}$
$\qquad + 1.82\,r_{k-1/2} + \varLambda - 2.26$,

(9) $\quad p_i = 0.41\,H + 0.39\,p_m + 0.33\,p_{i-1} + 1.03$,

(10) $\quad p_b = 0.32\,H + 0.43\,p_m + 0.23\,p'_b + 0.25\,\varDelta p'_b + 0.15\,p_{b-1} - 0.65$,

(11) $\quad p_x = 0.69\,H + 0.31\,p_m + 0.27\,p_{x-1} + 1.22$.

B. *Definition equations*

Relations between value and volume variables:

(12) $B = b + p_b$,

---

[13] See [10, Annex 1].

(13) $C = c + p_c,$

(14) $I = i + p_i,$

(15) $X = x + p_x$

(16) $M = m + p_m,$

(17) $V' = v' + p_{v'}$

Expenditure totals:

(18) $v' = 0.59\,c + 0.11\,x + 0.08\,i + 0.22\,b,$

(19) $v_a = 0.46\,c + 0.20\,x + 0.16\,i + 0.18\,b,$

(20) $v_m = 0.45\,c + 0.15\,x + 0.11\,i + 0.29\,b,$

(21) $p_v = 0.50\,p_c + 0.12\,p_x + 0.09\,p_i + 0.29\,p_b,$

(22) $V = 0.44\,C + 0.13\,X + 0.10\,I + 0.92\,N + 0.25\,B + 0.06\,D.$

Costs and margins:

(23) $H = l - (v' - a)_{-1/2},$

(24) $p_{m-v'} = p_m - p_{v'-\frac{1}{2}} + 0.06\,T'_{K-1/3},$

(25) $K = p_{v'} - 0.27\,l - 0.30\,p_m - 0.06\,T'_{K-1/3}.$

Unemployment:

(26) $\tilde{w}_1 = 10\log \tilde{w} - 0.30\,(\tilde{w} - 1),$

(27) $\Pi_w = 1.68 \left\{ \dfrac{\tilde{P}_{-1}}{\tilde{P}_{B-1}} \right\}^* + 2.18 \left\{ \dfrac{\tilde{P}_{-1}}{\tilde{P}_{B-1}} \right\}^{**}.$

* Period 1923–38.

** Period 1949–57 and ff.

Incomes:

(28) $L = a + l,$

(29) $Z = 3.77\,V - 1.06\,L - 0.24\,T_K - 1.23\,M - 0.24\,F,$

(30) $L^B = 0.87\,L + 0.87\,O'_L,$

(31) $Z^B = 1.50\,Z + 1.50\,O'_Z,$

Taxes:

(32) $T_K = V' + T'_K,$

(33) $T''_z = \Delta \dfrac{\tilde{T}_z}{\tilde{Z}_{-1}}.$

Lagged influences:

(34) $\Psi_i = 2.30 \log \tilde{I}_{-1} - 1.06 \log \tilde{p}_{i-1} + 7.18\,\tilde{w}_{1-1\frac{1}{2}} - 1.88 \log$
$(\tilde{Z}_{-2} - \tilde{T}_{z-1}) - 1.84 \log \tilde{c}^r_{-2},$

(35) $\Psi_a = \log \tilde{z}_{-1} - 1.59 \log \tilde{a}_{-1}$,

(36) $\Lambda = -0.35 \log \left\{\dfrac{\tilde{v}'}{\tilde{m}}\right\}_{-1\frac{1}{2}} + 0.56 \log \tilde{H}_{-1} + 0.17 \log \tilde{p}_{m-1\frac{1}{2}}$
$+ 0.65 \tilde{r}_{k-1\frac{1}{2}} + 0.14 \log \tilde{T}'_{K-1-1/3} - 0.83 \log \tilde{p}_{c-1}$.

The endogenous variables of the system are:

Resources: a, L, Z, T_K, m, M,

Expenditures: $c, p_c, C, p_x, X, i, p_i, I, N, b, p_b, B, v', p_{v'}, V', V$,

Unemployment: $\Delta \tilde{w}$,

Secondary incomes and taxes: L^B, Z^B, T''_z,

Composite variables: $v_a, v_m, H, p_{m-v'}, K, \tilde{w}_1, \Pi_w, \Psi_i, \Psi_a, \Lambda$.

C. *List of symbols*

Symbols with $\sim$ refer to absolute figures. Unless otherwise stated, symbols without $\sim$ represent percentage changes. In the expenditure categories, incomes, etc., capital letters refer to values in current prices, lower case letters to volume figures and prices.

a = Number of persons employed in enterprises (man years),

a_0 = Number of persons employed in the government sector (man years),

B, b = Exports of commodities,

b_c = Competing exports,

C, c = Total private consumption,

c^r = Time and demand desposits at the end of the year,

D = Net invisibles,

F = Depreciation of enterprises,

H = Labor costs per unit of total output (equation (23)),

I, i = Gross investments of enterprises (excluding government, enterprises and residential construction),

k = Quantitative import restrictions (1932–1937),

k' = Rate of liberalization (1949–1955),

K = Gross profits per unit of output (equation (25)),

l = Average gross wages per standard year of 300 days,

L = Wage bill of enterprises,

L^B = Disposable wage income,

M, m = Imports of commodities,

N = Stock formation (expressed as a percentage of total output less stock changes and net invisibles),

O'_L = Income transfers with regard to wage income, including government wages and direct taxes on cash basis (expressed as a percentage of wage bill of enterprises),

O'_Z =Income transfers with regard to nonwage income, including direct taxes on cash basis (expressed as a percentage of total nonwage income),

P =Population in the working ages (14–65 years),

P_B =Dependent working population,

p_b =Export prices,

p'_b =Prices of competing exports,

p_c =Consumption price,

p_i =Investment price,

p_m =Import price,

$p_{m-v'}$=Margin between import price adjusted for the incidence of indirect taxes and the price of total output (with a lag of half a year, see equation (24)),

$p_{v'}$ =Price of total output (less stock changes and net invisibles),

p_x =Prices of autonomous expenditure,

r_k =Short-term rate of interest (discount rate of the Central Bank),

$\tilde{T}_c$ =Minimum temperature below 0° centigrade (sum of monthly averages),

$\tilde{T}_K$ =Indirect taxes minus subsidies,

$\tilde{T}'_K$ =Incidence of indirect taxes minus subsidies ($\tilde{T}'_K=\tilde{T}_K/\tilde{V}'$),

t^* =Prewar decreasing trend (1923=15; 1938=0),

$\tilde{T}_z$ =Direct taxes on nonwage income (on cash basis),

T''_z =Variation in the incidence of direct taxes on nonwage income (equation (33)),

V =Total output,

V', v' =Total output less stock changes and net invisibles,

v_a =Total output less stock changes and net invisibles (reweighted with intensity of labor demand; equation (19)),

v_m =Total output less stock changes and net invisibles (reweighted with import quota; equation (20)),

$\tilde{w}$ =Registered unemployment as a percentage of dependent working population,

$\tilde{w}_1$ =Curvilinear indicator of available capacity (equation (26)),

X, x =Autonomous expenditure (government expenditure, investment of government enterprises and residential construction),

Z, z = Nonwage income,

Z^B = Disposable nonwage income.

14.3.2. *Japanese Long-Term Planning Model: "Ten-Year Plan to Double National Income" (1961–1970)* [14]

A. National income identities:

(1) $\bar{V}_1 + V_2 + V_3 = \bar{V}$,

(2) $\bar{V} = C + G + I + E - M$,

(3) $W + R = \bar{V} - T_i$,

(4) $C + T_d + S_p = W + R + A$,

(5) $G + A + \bar{S}_g = T_i + T_d$,

(6) $E - M = B$.

B. Structural and behavioral relations:

(7) $V_2 = f_1(\bar{V})$,

(8) $I = f_2(K)$,

(9) $K = f_3(\bar{V})$,

(10) $M = f_4(\bar{V})$,

(11) $E = f_5(F)$,

(12) $W = f_6(\bar{V}_1, V_2, V_3)$,

(13) $S_p = f_7(W, R, T_d, A)$,

(14) $L = f_8(\bar{N})$,

(15) $L_2 = f_9(V_2)$,

(16) $L_3 = f_{10}\left(V_3, \dfrac{V_2}{L_2}\right)$.

C. Labor balance identity:

(17) $L = L_1 + L_2 + L_3$.

D. Institutional (policy) relations:

(18) $G = \alpha \bar{V}$,

(19) $A = \beta \bar{V}$,

(20) $T_i = \gamma \bar{V}$,

(21) $T_d = \delta W + \varepsilon R$.

E. List of symbols:

$\bar{V}$ = Gross national product,

$\bar{V}_1$ = Gross value added in primary industry,

---

[14] See [14].

V_2 = Gross value added in secondary industry,

V_3 = Gross value added in tertiary industry,

C = Private consumption,

G = Government purchases of goods and services (including government investment),

I = Private investment,

K = Private capital stock at the end of year

E = Exports,

M = Imports,

$\bar{F}$ = World trade,

W = Wages and salaries,

R = Nonwage income,

T_i = Indirect taxes,

T_d = Direct taxes,

A = Transfer payments,

S_p = Private saving,

B = Net exports

$\bar{S}g$ = Government surplus (government current saving minus government investment),

α = Share of government purchases in GNP,

β = Share of transfer payments in GNP,

γ = Indirect tax ratio,

δ = Direct tax ratio of wage income,

ε = Direct tax ratio of nonwage income,

L = Total labor force,

L_1 = Labor force in primary industry,

L_2 = Labor force in secondary industry,

L_3 = Labor force in tertiary industry,

N = Total population.

Symbols with a bar on the top are exogenous variables; Greek letters are policy variables; $f_1, ..., f_{10}$ stands for functional relations. All other variables are endogenous.

14.3.3. *Schema of the Model Used in the Preparation of the Fourth French Plan (1959–1965)* [15]

The following notation has generally been followed:

Small case letters: scalars.

---

[15] See [7].

Capital letters: vectors.

Capital letters with two bars: matrices.

Subscript i refers to products.

Subscript j refers to branches.

See list of symbols below.

This schema is based on "La Comptabilité Nationale dans la Préparation du IV: Plan" [7]. The notation and symbolism have, however, been altered in places to avoid possible confusion. Since the system is solved essentially through an iterative method, the model is very difficult to formalize. It is essentially open-ended in an axiomatic sense, and what is presented here is nothing but an *ex post* rationalization of a series of converging iterations.

(1) $[1 - |A'|] X + I = C + A + E + L + F + S = D.$

This is the straightforward national income identity, expressing the equality of total supply and demand for all products. A' is the intermediate demand matrix obtained from the interacting part of the input-output table.

(2) $p = P'[D - I]/P'_0[D_0 - I'_0].$

P' is the transpose of the unity vector, $[1, 1 \ldots 1]$ and so is P'_o since constant prices are assumed. Higher prices for certain types of goods, i.e., housing and services, could be handled through P'. $[D-I]$ gives the vector of domestic output by types of goods. (Since $D - I = [1 - |A'|] X$.) The sum of value added by sectors in the final year of the plan divided by the sum of the sectoral value added in the base year is equal to the index of gross domestic product (p).

(3) $s_i = s_i(x_i, i_i, x_i^0, i_i^0, u_i).$

s_i represents stock formation of product i. It is some function of the level of gross production and imports of i in the final and the initial years of the plan and of the average stock turnover period (u_i).

(4) $f_j = f_j(x_j^0, x_j).$

f_j represents the functions determining investment by branches j (j=agriculture, foodstuffs, petroleum, etc. for 17 branches). The f_j functions take three different forms:

(a) **Direct estimates** made by commissions or experts. This can be done in branches having well-defined investment projects, such as petroleum, natural gas, iron, minerals, metals, transportation and communication. Likewise for residential construction and agriculture where target output levels determine the investment needs.

(b) Estimates based on marginal (gross) capital-output ratios. This was done for the mechanical and chemical industries.

(c) Estimates based on the ratio of investment to business turnover, making allowance for technological changes, a method which was employed for the remaining industries.

In general, the levels of output in the initial and in the terminal year of the plan (x_j^0 and x_j) appear in f_j.

(5) $f_{ij} = k_{ij} f_j$.

The division of investment is done in terms of only two products: (i.e., i=construction and equipment). The k_{ij}'s are not necessarily constant; they may vary with the level of investment.

(6) $F = |f_{ij}| U$.

The amount of capital formation by product (F) is equal to the f_{ij} matrix multiplied by the unit vector U. Thus, for every sector one obtains the total capital formation in construction and equipment.

(7) $L = \bar{L} + \bar{\bar{L}}_p$.

Residential construction consists of two parts: a $\bar{L}$, which is independent of the rate of growth, and (b) $\bar{\bar{L}}_p$, which represents the qualitative changes which are a function of p.

(8) $A = \bar{A} + \bar{\bar{A}}_p$.

Total government expenditures by broad functions. A (consumption and gross capital formation) is determined on the basis of social and political considerations.

The welfare function of the policy maker will determine government expenditures on health, education, national defense, etc. Here again, one part is independent of the selected rate of growth.

(9) $c = P'C$.

Total consumption by households (c) is equal to the sum of household consumption by products (the C vector).

(10) $\phi_k = \phi_k(c)$.

The ϕ_k's are relations (i.e., certain functions) of different types which can be used to derive household consumption by broad functions (clothing, food, housing, etc.). These relations take the form of constant income elasticities, variable income elasticities, etc., depending on the group of products.

(11) $C = |T| \phi.$

The vector of household consumption by products (C) is derived from the vector of household consumption by functions, i.e., clothing, food, etc. (ϕ) by way of a transformation matrix function-product $(|T|)$ (*grille de passage fonction-produit*). ϕ itself is a function of the growth rate (p) and income elasticities and other coefficients based on time-series or cross-section studies. It should be noted that the transformation matrix is not entirely independent of c and thus of p.

(12) $$X = \begin{vmatrix} X_1 \\ X_2 \end{vmatrix} \quad I = \begin{vmatrix} I_1 \\ I_2 \end{vmatrix} \quad E = \begin{vmatrix} E_1 \\ E_2 \end{vmatrix}.$$

Gross production by branches may be predetermined, as in the cases where (a) definite projects exist (i.e., for aluminum, natural gas and crude petroleum) and (b) domestic output is nonexistent (i.e., raw cotton). X_1 is thus given. By analogy the same distinction applies to imports and exports.

(13) $I_2 = \bar{I}_2 + |X_2|\bar{\bar{I}}_2.$

The imports of commodities for those branches where the level of imports is not already predetermined (the vector I_2), can be divided into competitive and noncompetitive imports. $\bar{I}_2$ stands for the latter category, whereas competitive imports are related by way of the vector $\bar{\bar{I}}_2$ to the level of gross domestic output.

It should be noticed that $|X_2|$ represents the diagonal matrix constructed from the vector X_2. In this fashion the competitive import requirements $\bar{\bar{I}}_{21} X_{21}, \bar{\bar{I}}_{22} X_{22}, ..., \bar{\bar{I}}_{2n} X_{2n}$ can be derived.

(14) $\varepsilon_j = \bar{\varepsilon}_j \pi + \bar{\bar{I}}_j (x_j).$

Labor productivity by branch (ε_j) depends on the impact of production on productivity (i.e., scale economies), which is indicated by the functions $\bar{\bar{\varepsilon}}_j (x_j)$, and on the effect of the rate of growth on productivity, reflected by $\bar{\varepsilon}_j \pi$, where π is the so-called productivity adjustment coefficient by branch varying with p. In a way, it can be said that $\bar{\varepsilon}_j \pi$ measures the necessary productivity by branch, given the labor resources, in order for the target growth rate (p) to be attained. The functions $\bar{\bar{\varepsilon}}_j (x_j)$, on the other hand, measure the realizable productivity changes, given the rise in output branch by branch. Results obtained from the two above methods are then compared to determine ε_j. Statistical information and expert advice are used to derive the $\bar{\varepsilon}_j$ vector and the $\bar{\bar{\varepsilon}}_j$ functions. The working time is assumed constant.

$$(15) \quad e = \sum_j \varepsilon_j x_j .$$

The total available labor force (e) has to be equal to the sum of the products of labor productivity by branch (ε_j) or, better said, its reciprocal, and the branch output (x_j).

Classification and List of Variables

Exogenous (predetermined) variables:

p = Index of gross domestic product,

X_1 = Given productions (see equation (12)),

E = Exports by products,

e = Labor force available,

$|A'|$ = Input-output coefficient matrix (in some cases the ratio of intermediate demand to total output by sector is used. In this way not all of the a_{ij} coefficients have to be known).

Vectors: L and $\bar{L}_p$ (equation (7)),
$\bar{A}$ and $\bar{\bar{A}}_p$ (equation (8)),
$\bar{I}_2$ and $\bar{\bar{I}}_2$ (equation (13)),
$\bar{\varepsilon}_j$ (equation (14)).

Transformation matrices: $|T|$ (equation (11)), $|k_{ij}|$ (equation (5)).

Functions: f_j (equation (4)), ϕ_k (equation (10)),
$\bar{\bar{\varepsilon}}_j$ (equation (14)).

Endogenous variables:

X_2 = Production for those branches where output is not already predetermined (i.e., X_1 is predetermined in equation (12)),

ϕ = Household consumption by function (lodging, clothing, food, etc.); varies with p and parameters such as income eleasticities

C = Household consumption by product,

c = Total (global) household consumption,

A = Government expenditures by product (consumption and gross capital formation),

I = Imports by products, varies with p,

L = Residential construction, varies with p,

F = Capital formation by products, varies with X,

S = Stock formation, varies with X,

π = Productivity adjustment coefficient by branch, varies with p (equation (14)),

ε_j = Labor productivity by branch.

Variables relate to the final year (1965) of the plan (except when otherwise indicated).

14.3.4. *Structure of FIFI, i.e., The Model Used in the Preparation of the French Sixth Plan* (1971–1975)

Only the principal relations of FIFI are presented here, following Bénard's interpretation and nomenclature [24].[16]

a) Production Relations:

    (1) Intermediate Demand

$$m_{ij} = a_{ij}x_{ij}$$

    (2) Labor Requirements

$$L_j = n_j x_j$$

    (3) Fixed Capital Requirements

$$K_{ij} = b_{ij}x_j,$$

where x_j = output of product (sector) j, L_j = labor requirements in j, K_{ij} = fixed capital requirements in sector j by sector of origin i, a_{ij} = the Leontieff static input-output matrix, n_j = labor-output ratio in j, and b_{ij} = capital-output ratios (i.e., units of capital goods i required to produce one unit of output of j).

The above relationships assume fixed proportions and, thus, do not allow for any substitution between inputs.

b) Determination of the Nominal Wage Rate:

$$(4) \ TXH_m = 8.10 + 0.38 \ TPG - 2.47 \ U,[17]$$

where TXH_m = percentage average annual growth rate of the nominal hourly wage rate, TPG = percentage annual average growth rate of the general price level (the general price level itself is assumed endogenous), and $\bar{U}$ = percentage average unemployment rate (i.e., proportion of unemployed in labor force).

---

[16] This section follows closely Bénard's interpretation, which should be consulted for more details [24, pp. 588–600]. It should be noted that Bénard's version is very similar to that of Courbis [25] one of the major architects of FIFI.

[17] It should be noted that this relationship is based on the Phillips curve and, as such, is similar to the capacity equation (equation 26) in the Dutch CPB Model (see Section 14.2.1).

The wage rate itself for the target year of the Plan (year T) is given by the following relation:

(5) $W_T = W_0(1 + TXH_m)^T$.

It is relevant to note that the growth rate of the wage rate is assumed constant throughout the planning period and therefore not subject to short-term fluctuations, which would appear to run counter to the Phillips relation.

c) Determination of Prices:

Three types of sectors are distinguished depending on the forces affecting price formation; i.e., administered, protected and exposed sectors. The former category would be either public or strongly influenced by the government. The protected sectors are shielded from foreign competition in contrast with the exposed sectors.

1. For all three types of sectors there is a cost relationship determining prices for each branch j within a sector (p_j):

(6) $p_j = \sum_i p_i a_{ij} + w_L a_{Lj} + \dfrac{\beta_j}{\alpha_j} \sum_i p_i b_{ij} + \theta_j$.

The first two terms on the right hand side of equation (6) represent the cost of production of, respectively, intermediate inputs and labor. The third term represents gross profits after taxes and the last term (θ_j) is the tax rate applying to firms in branch j.

An essential feature of FIFI is the importance which is attached to self-financing. Entrepreneurs will only undertake investments amounting to $\sum_i p_i b_{ij} x_j$ if they can finance from within a fraction B_j of a share (α_j) of (nondistributed) profits π_j. Thus,

$$B_j x_j \sum_i p_i b_{ij} = \alpha_j \pi_j.$$

Hence profit per unit in j can be expressed as

(7) $\dfrac{\pi_j}{x_j} = \dfrac{\beta_j}{\alpha_j} \sum p_i b_{ij}$.

In matrix notation equation (6) becomes:

(8) $P'\left[I - A - \left(\dfrac{\beta}{\alpha}\right)B \right] = W'[A'_L] + \theta$.

2. For sectors exposed to foreign competition, there is a link between internal and external prices of the following type:

(9) $p_e = \pi_e + h_e m_e,$

where p_e = price of product in the exposed sector e, π_e = external (foreign) price of the same products, considered as an exogenous variable, m_e = import volume of product e, and h_e = marginal propensity of import prices to increase as a function of import volume.

d) Household Demand:

This demand can be broken down into savings and final consumption by product. Household savings are linked to disposable income, the overall price level and investment in housing.

Household consumption is derived from linear expenditure relations based on Stone's model of the following form:

(10) $C_i = \beta_i p_i + \gamma_i [C - \sum_j \beta_j p_j]$ $i, j = 1, 2, \ldots, n,$

where C_i = value of consumption of product i, p_i = price of product i, and C = total disposable income after taxes and savings and where $\sum_i \gamma_i = 1$.

This last equation satisfies Slutky's conditions, i.e., consumers are assumed to maximize a utility function of the following type:

(11) Max $U = \prod_i (q_i - \beta_i)^{\gamma_i}$

     under the budget constraint $\sum p_i q_i = C,$

where q_i = quantity consumed of good i, so that $C_i = p_i q_i$, and $\prod_i$ is a multiplier.

e) Foreign Trade Relations.

Competing imports are determined on the basis of market shares, non-competing (i.e., complementary) imports are either determined exogenously or endogenously in which case they are related to the level of domestic production.

Exports of industrial products are based on an econometric relation which measures foreign demand (D_e) and domestic production (X), both of which encourage exports, and domestic consumption (C) which slows exports down. The ratio of foreign prices (p_{ex}) to domestic prices (p) represents the extent to which exports are competitive. Thus, export demand can be expressed as:

(12) $E = k D_e^{\alpha} X^{\beta} C \dfrac{p_{ex}}{p}$

where α, β and δ are positive elasticities and γ is negative.

f) Administrative Relations:

These constitute a submodel describing five types of administrations (the state, the social security administration, local administrations, semi-public agencies and private or foreign administrations). These entities have to follow certain institutional rules. Within limits discretionary policy measures can be introduced in these relations and their effects on the whole model can be simulated.

g) Identities and Balance Relations:

A number of such relations appear in the model, e.g., with respect to resource and product availability and use, and a whole set of relations translating volumes into values for goods and services.

h) Financial Operations:

These operations are essentially exogenously projected. The availability of capital from various sources (household savings, nondistributed profits, etc.) are compared to the capital required. Through successive iterations a financial equilibrium is obtained.

14.3.5. *Two-Level Long-Term Planning Model in Hungary* (1962) (*LP form* [28])

(1) Maximize $J = \left[\displaystyle\sum_{i=1}^{n} \sum_{t=1}^{T} \sum_{\substack{k=\mathrm{repr,}\\ \mathrm{exp,}\\ \mathrm{imp}}} c_{ikt} x_{ikt} + c_{i0} x_{i0} + \sum_{k=\mathrm{inv}} c_{ik} x_{ik} \right]$

(2) $\displaystyle\sum_{\substack{j=1\\ j\neq i}}^{n} z_{jit} + Q_{it} = r_{it} \leqq R_{it}; \ (i = 1,\ldots,n; t = 1,\ldots,T)$

(3) $\displaystyle\sum_{i=1}^{n} w_{it} = W_t; \ (t = 1,\ldots,T)$

(4) $r_{it} \geqq 0, z_{ijt} \geqq 0, w_{it} \geqq 0; (i = 1,\ldots,n; j = 1,\ldots,n;$
$j \neq i; t = 1,\ldots,T)$

(5) $r_{it} \leqq \displaystyle\sum_{\substack{k=\mathrm{repr,}\\ \mathrm{exp,}\\ \mathrm{imp}}} f_{ikt} x_{ikt} + f_{i0t} x_{i0} + \sum_{k=\mathrm{inv}} f_{ikt} x_{ik} \leqq R_{it}; (t = 1,\ldots,T)$

(6) $\displaystyle\sum_{\substack{k=\text{repr,}\\ \text{exp,}\\ \text{imp}}} g_{ijkt}x_{ijkt} + g_{ij0t}x_{i0} + \sum_{k=\text{inv}} g_{ijkt}x_{ik} \leq z_{ijt}; (j = 1,\ldots, n;$
$\qquad\qquad\qquad\qquad\qquad\qquad\qquad\qquad j \neq i; t = 1,\ldots, T)$

(7) $\displaystyle\sum_{\substack{k=\text{repr,}\\ \text{exp,}\\ \text{imp}}} h_{ikt}x_{ikt} + h_{i0t}x_{i0} + \sum_{k=\text{inv}} h_{ikt}x_{ik} \leq w_{it}; (t = 1,\ldots, T)$

(8) $\displaystyle\sum_{t=1}^{T} \sum_{\substack{k=\text{repr,}\\ \text{exp,}\\ \text{imp}}} a_{iskt}^{0}x_{ikt} + \sum_{k=\text{inv}} a_{isk}^{0}x_{ik} \leq b_{is}^{0}; s = \text{special condition}$

(9) $\displaystyle\max c_{ikt} \leq \min\left\{ \min_{k=\text{imp}} (-c_{ikt}), -c_{i0}\right\}$

(10) $x_{ikt} \geq 0; x_{ik} \geq 0; x_{i0} \geq 0$

The variables are defined as follows:

Central program decision variables:

$i, j = 1, 2,\ldots, n$ (sectors); $t = 1, 2,\ldots, T$ (planning horizon); $k =$ index of activities

   1. r_{it} = domestic requirement of output produced in the ith sector in the tth period (supply assignment by the center)
   2. z_{ijt} = materials quota in terms of jth product available to sector i in period t by central assignment
   3. w_{it} = manpower quota for sector i in period t

Constants in the central program:

   4. Q_{it} = consumption by individuals and public bodies of the ith product in period t
   5. R_{it} = upper bound on the ith sector supply assignment
   6. W_t = manpower quota available in the whole economy in period t
   7. The feasible central programs are those which satisfy the constraints (2), (3), (4).

Sector program decision variables:

   8. (a) x_{ikt} = the level of the kth activity planned for the ith sector in period t
      (b) x_{ik} = level of kth investment activity in period t;
      (c) x_{i0} = unbounded import activity for sector i
   9. k = repr., exp., imp. = denote respectively the reproductive activities for continued operation of output capacity for the ith product (i.e., ith sector), export activities and import activities; k = inv denotes invest-

ment activities including both the establishment of new capacities and the production in these new facilities.

10. f_{ikt} = output coefficients such that (a) $f_{ikt} = 1$ for k representing reproductive activities; (b) $f_{ikt} \geq 0$ for k representing investment activities with at least for one t, $f_{ikt} = 1$; (c) $f_{ikt} = -1$ for k representing export activities; and (d) $f_{ikt} = 1$ for k representing bounded and unbounded import activities.

Sector program constants:

11. g_{ijkt} = input coefficients such that (a) $g_{ijkt} \geq 0$ for reproductive activities and investment activities and (b) $g_{ijkt} = 0$ for all foreign trade activity.

12. k_{ikt} = manpower coefficients such that (a) $h_{ikt} > 0$ for reproductive activities; (b) $k_{ikt} \geq 0$ for investment activities; and (c) $h_{ikt} = 0$ for all foreign trade activities.

13. a^0_{iskt}, a^0_{isk}, b^0_{is} = constants representing either input and output coefficients or availabilities which satisfy the special condition characteristics of the particular circumstances of the sector, e.g., output in some sectors may be bounded by the country's natural resources, etc.

14. (a) c_{ikt}, c_{ik} = foreign exchange returns of the corresponding activities such that (a) the returns are zero for reproductive and investment activities (b) the noncompetitive imports are regarded as negative foreign currency returns; and (c) the foreign currency returns of export (import) activities are positive (negative).

    (b) c_{i0} = net foreign exchange returns from import activities x_{i0} for which there are no effective upper bounds.

15. Sector program constraints are given by (5) through (10) and the sectoral objective function is given by the expression under the sign $\underset{t\ k}{\Sigma\Sigma}$ in relation (1). The central macroeconomic program is regarded as optimal only when the sum of the maximal values of the sectoral objective functions is at a maximum.

REFERENCES

[1] BENARD, J. "Production et Dépenses Intérieures de la France en 1970," in *Europe's Future in Figures*. (ASEPELT) Edited by R. C. Geary. Amsterdam: North-Holland Publishing Co., 1962.

[2] BENTZEL, R., and HANSEN, B. "On Recursiveness and Interdependency in Economic Models," *Review of Economic Studies*, XXII, No. 59 (1954–1955), 153–168.

[3] CHENERY, H. B. "Patterns of Industrial Growth," *American Economic Review*, L (September, 1960), 624–654.

[4] COLM, G., and GEIGER, T. *The Economy of the American People: Progress, Problems, Prospects*. Washington, D.C.: National Planning Association, 1962.

[5] ECONOMIC PLANNING AGENCY OF JAPAN. *New Long-Range Economic Plan 1961–1970*. (Plan for Doubling National Income), Tokyo, 1961.

[6] FOX, K. A., and THORBECKE, E. "Specification of Structures and Data Requirements in Economic Policy Models." in *Quantitative Planning of Economic Policy*. Edited by B. G. Hickman, Washington, D.C.; The Brookings Institution, 1965, Chap. 3.

[7] "La Comptabilité Nationale dans la Préparation du IVème. Plan," *Etudes et Conjonctures*, No. 4 (1963).

[8] NETHERLANDS CENTRAL PLANNING BUREAU. *Central Economic Plan 1955*. The Hague, 1955.

[9] ——. *Scope and Methods of the Central Planning Bureau*. The Hague, 1956.

[10] ——. *Central Economic Plan 1961*. The Hague, 1961.

[11] SANDEE, J. "Possible Economic Growth in the Netherlands," in *Europe's Future in Figures*. (ASEPELT) Edited by R. Geary. Amsterdam: North-Holland Publishing Co., 1962.

[12] ——. "A Long-Term Phased Policy Model for the Netherlands." Paper presented to the Econometric Society, Boston, December, 1963.

[13] SENGUPTA, J. K., and TINTNER, G. "On Some Economic Models of Development Planning," *Economia Internazionale*, XVI (February, 1963), 34–50.

[14] SHISHIDO, S. "Japanese Experience with Long-Term Economic Planning." in *Quantitative Planning of Economic Policy*. Edited by B. G. Hickman, Washington, D.C.; The Brookings Institution, 1965, Chap. 9.

[15] SIMON, H. A. "Causal Ordering and Identifiability," in *Studies in Econometric Method*. (Cowles Commission Monograph 14.) Edited by W. C. Hood and T. C. Koopmans. New York: John Wiley & Sons, 1953.

[16] STROTZ, R. H. "Interdependence as a Specification Error," *Econometrica*, XXVIII (April, 1960), 428–442.

[17] ——, and WOLD, H. O. A. "Recursive Versus Nonrecursive Systems: An Attempt at Synthesis," *Econometrica*, XXVIII (April, 1960), 417–427.

[18] THEIL, H. *Economic Forecasts and Policy*. Amsterdam: North-Holland Publishing Co., 1961.

[19] VAN DEN BELD, C. A. "Short-Term Planning Experience in the Netherlands," in *Quantitative Planning of Economic Policy*. Edited by B. G. Hickman, Washington, D.C.: The Brookings Institution, 1965, Chap. 6.

[20] VERDOORN, P. J. "Complementarity and Long-Range Projections," *Econometrica*, XXIV (October, 1956), 429–450.

[21] ——, and POST, J. J. "Capacity and the Short-Term Multipliers." Paper presented to the 25th European meeting of the Econometric Society, Copenhagen, July, 1963.

[22] WATANABE, T. "National Planning and Economic Growth in Japan," in *Quantitative Planning of Economic Policy*. Edited by B. G. Hickman, Washington. D.C.: The Brookings Institution, 1965, Chap. 10.

[23] AGLIETTA, M. and SEIBEL, E. "Use of the Model FIFI in French Planning", United Nations, Economic Commission for Europe, Varna, 1970.

[24] BENARD, J. *Comptabilité Nationale et Modèles de Politique Economique*, Paris: Presse Universitaire de France, 1972.

[25] COURBIS, R. "Le Modèle Physico-Financier de Projection Economique à Moyen Terme FIFI", Nations Unies, Commission Economiques pour l'Europe, Varna, 1970.

[26] DANTZIG, G. B. and WOLFE, P. "The Decomposition Principle for Linear Programs", *Operations Research,* Volume 8, 1960, 101–111.

[27] KORNAI, J. *Mathematical Planning of Structural Decisions.* Amsterdam: North-Holland Publishing Company, 1967.

[28] ——, and LIPTAK, T. "Two-Level Planning", *Econometrica,* Volume 33, 1965, 141–169.

[29] MARTOS, B. and KORNAI, J. "Experiments in Hungary with Industry-Wide and Economy-Wide Programming", in *Mathematical Optimization Techniques:* Proceedings of an International Conference held in CIME August 30–September 7, 1965, Rome, 1966.

[30] SENGUPTA, J. K. "Economics of Decomposition and Divisionalization Under Transfer Pricing", *Zeitschrift Gesamte Staatswissenschaft,* Volume 127, No. 1, January 1971, 50–71.

[31] ——. "Economic Problems of Resource Allocation in Nonmarket Systems", in *Economic Analysis for Educational Planning,* edited by K. A. Fox, Baltimore: Johns Hopkins Press, 1972, Chapter 6.

[32] ——, and FOX, K. A. *Economic Analysis and Operations Research: Optimization Techniques in Quantitative Economic Models.* Amsterdam: North-Holland Publishing Company, 1969.

Chapter 15

THE AGRICULTURAL SECTOR AND
ECONOMIC DEVELOPMENT

This chapter is divided into two parts. The first and longer section (15.1) relates agrarian reform to the process of economic development for an underdeveloped economy through an operational application of the theory of economic policy. The remaining section (15.2) is devoted to a critical review and classification of agricultural models which have been built for a few developing countries.

15.1. Agrarian Reforms Policy Toward Economic Development

The standpoint which is taken in this section[1] of the chapter is that of an economist interested in determining the role which changes and reforms in the agricultural sector can perform as a *means* to the attainment of the *end* of economic growth and other major policy objectives. Agrarian reform is defined here as:

> Changes in rural institutions with the objective of improving rural levels of living. These institutions include those of holding and transmitting rights in land, allocating returns to land between owners and tenants, extending credit for land purchase, farm operation and improvements, taxing land values and land income, conserving and developing agricultural and other resources, marketing of farm and other products, broadening opportunities for educating and training rural people and promoting rural health and welfare services.

The various means that are explicitly stated as constituting agrarian reforms are not all institutional in character, as the above quotation implies. Certain means, such as public investment in fertilizer plants and irrigation

---

[1] This section is based on Thorbecke [22].

552

schemes—which would presumably come under conservation and development of agricultural resources—are not structural or institutional changes in the same way as changes in land tenure. The term "reform" connotes changes in the foundations or institutions of an economy and is therefore exclusive of changes in quantitative means or instrument variables, which are under the control of the policy maker and which do not necessitate changes in either the structure or the institutions of the economy.

For our purpose, economic growth is defined very broadly as the changes in the economy that permit the creation of an increased capacity to satisfy the physical wants of individuals. Aggregate output will be used as an index or measure of economic growth, keeping in mind the following qualifications: (1) The rate of increase in aggregate output should be higher than the rate of population growth, so as to negate the possibility of a lower per capita output figure associated with a higher aggregate output,[2] and (2) the increase in aggregate output should not be accompanied by more than a specified worsening of the income distribution.[3]

15.1.1. *Policy Framework*

The purpose of this section is to formulate a conceptual and operational framework within which agrarian reforms are viewed as means toward the attainment of certain given ends and, in particular, the objective of economic growth.

The rigorous analytical structure which Tinbergen designed in the area of the theory of economic policy will form the starting point of this attempt. The essence of Tinbergen's approach to the theory of economic policy can be summarized in terms of three basic elements which have been rigorously presented in earlier chapters: a welfare function, a division of economic variables in four classes and a structural model. The first element of his framework is the postulation of an objective welfare or preference function reflecting the general interest of the people. To circumvent the difficulties inherent in any attempt at making interpersonal and intertemporal utility comparisons, as well as the possible intransitivity of the community welfare function,[4] Tinbergen replaces the actual aggregate social welfare function

---

[2] Under this definition, a decline in aggregate output, compensated by a larger decline in the size of the population (and thus leading to an increase in per capita output) is not considered as evidence of economic growth.

[3] This could be done quantitatively by specifying a certain Gini ratio on the basis of the Lorenz curve.

[4] This point is sometimes referred to as the voting paradox, first established by Arrow.

of the community by the policy maker's preference function, which normally should approximate the welfare function of the citizens rather closely. If this were not the case, the government (of the party in power) would be replaced in the next general election by a more representative state. The objective preference function of the policy maker contains the ends of society, which are taken as given by the government. The elements entering the welfare function can appear in the form of either flexible targets (i.e., maximum output) or fixed targets (i.e., at least 97 per cent of labor force employed).

The second element of this Tinbergen framework is the division of variables into four general classes. The exogenous variables, which are the data, are considered to influence the endogenous variables, which are the economic phenomena per se. There are two classes of data: (1) those over which the policy maker cannot exert any influence (*other data*) and (2) those under the control of the latter (*policy means*). The policy means under the control of the government can be further subdivided into (a) *instrument variables*, which are of a quantitative character and are used to adapt the economy to small and frequent changes in some of the other data (Examples of policy instruments would be tax rates, discount rates and the foreign exchange rate.), (b) *structural changes*, which are means altering the underlying structure of the economy, such as quantitative restrictions, built-in stabilizers, antitrust legislation and allocation of public investment as between projects in a developing economy and (c) *reforms*, which are changes in the foundations of the community in terms of spiritual values and the essential relations between individuals. (Examples of these are voting rights, property rights, opportunity for education and existence of some form of social security.)

The next two classes of variables, consisting of the endogenous variables in the theory of economic policy, are first, the *target variables*, which incorporate the immediate goals of the policy maker. These target variables reflect the policy maker's welfare function. They can be either fixed or flexible. As was pointed out previously, the goal of full employment, for instance, could be stated in terms of a minimum level of unemployment or in terms of maximizing the level of employment. Second are the so-called *irrelevant variables*, which are the economic phenomena in which the policy maker is not primarily interested at the time of decision making. In a sense, these variables are the side effects caused by changes in the means of economic policy.

The third major element of the Tinbergen approach consists of the specification of a system of structural relationships, reflecting the technical (i.e., production functions), behavioral and institutional relationships in the economy. The set of causal relations constitutes the "model."

If the period under consideration is relatively short (say six months), the structure of the economy can be assumed to remain constant and can be approximated quantitatively. The parameters (structural coefficients) of the behavioral demand, supply and other relationships can be determined statistically (through least squares and multiple regression analysis, for instance) or on a priori grounds.

Given the model and assuming that the policy maker is operating in the short run, the problem of economic policy becomes quantitative in the sense that instrument variables are used to achieve the specified economic goals (usually given in terms of predetermined fixed targets) despite the disturbances arising from the noncontrollable factors.

The use of quantitative economic policy has been pushed relatively far, particularly in the Netherlands and in Norway. In the former country, the Central Planning Bureau makes use of a system of thirty-six simultaneous equations relating the various variables. (See Chapter 14 for a detailed presentation of this model.) The structural parameters are revised at regular intervals and at least once a year.

When the means of economic policy alter the prevailing structure or foundations of the economy, the nature of the problem becomes much more complex, since the model itself will be affected.[5] Economic policy becomes a much more arduous and tenuous task, taking the form of qualitative economic policy and reforms. It will be argued later in this part that the goal of economic growth at a relatively early stage of development will require the use of policy means that will alter both the foundations and the structure of the economy. It is only after an economy has reached a fairly advanced stage of economic development that economic policy can become quantitative in the above described sense.

A further characteristic of the Tinbergen approach that should be mentioned here is that the basic methodology can be applied, first, to any level of government—from regional to international—second, to the study of any sector or industry and third, to any time period from short run to long run. The extent of the spatial, sectoral or temporal partitioning would depend exclusively upon the nature of the economic policy problem under consider-

---

[5] This might take the form of new structural coefficients or a different mathematical shape for the equations entering the model or additional variables and equations.

ation. Similarly, selection of the targets and of the means (instruments, structural changes and reforms) is done on an *ad hoc* basis consistent with the problem at hand.

The framework summarized above appears to be quite relevant and applicable to the study of agrarian reforms. It has the great merit of providing a conceptual frame of reference within which (1) various types of agrarian means can be distinguished, (2) the mutual compatibility and consistency of the ends of agrarian reforms can be explicitly analyzed and (3) the causal relationships between agrarian reforms, as means and predetermined targets, and, more specifically, economic growth, can be established via the model. In the present context, the model should be conceived as a set of relationships linking the various economic variables. Even though these relationships could be quite sophisticated (which might be the case in a mature economy), in the case of most underdeveloped nations, the "model" would take the form of rough empirical input-output, cost-benefit types of relationships between agrarian means and policy objectives.

The first two steps are essentially of a methodological and taxonomic nature and will be discussed in the remainder of this section. Step 3, on the other hand, requires both a theoretical knowledge of the impact of agrarian changes on economic development, efficiency, distributive justice or whatever the aims of the agrarian reforms are and some knowledge of the empirical relationships which prevail in a developing economy. An attempt at illustrating the effects of one specific agrarian mean—land redistribution— on the welfare function is undertaken subsequently.

Agrarian reform as a concept is open to a large number of interpretations, and no widely accepted definition of it exists. The reason for this may be that this term is essentially an institutional and not an analytical one and that historically it was defined on the basis of its components. As Gittinger [7] pointed out:

> Every reform must be suited to the culture that it is intended to serve. The success of an agrarian reform is to a large measure dependent upon the degree it can be made to harmonize with the cultural matrix and to adapt existing social and economic institutions to promote progress toward fulfilling the necessary conditions of economic development.

In any case, it appears that a breakdown of agrarian reforms into types of policy means might have some operational value, as will be shown subsequently, and would not be simply an exercise in idle taxonomy. Any classificatory scheme is, to a certain extent, arbitrary, and the present is no exception to the rule (for instance, a few means can be classified under more than one heading). The following breakdown does not claim to be exhaustive, but it does include most agrarian policy means:

A. *Instruments* (essentially quantitative policy parameters requiring no changes in the structure of the economy).
   1. Changes in tax rates and in tax incidence, e.g., for and as between tenants and landlords in the agricultural and industrial sector.
   2. Direct or indirect subsidies, such as those on fertilizers, tillage equipment and pesticides.

B. *Changes in structure.*

B. 1. The introduction of price support and credit programs. (It should be noted that a change in parities or support levels within an existing program would be considered an instrument.)
   2. The allocation of funds and facilities for research on improved seeds, farm management, fertilizer, etc.
   3. Public investment in irrigation and fertilizer plants.
   4. Public investment in social overhead capital (infrastructure), e.g., the building of intravillage and intervillage roads.
   5. Reclamation and settlement.
   6. Improvements in credit and marketing facilities. (The actual institution of these facilities where none existed before should be considered as truly a reform.) These changes could take the form of publicly supported rural credit banks, state cooperatives, etc.
   7. Education; larger public support of education, for example, higher salaries for teachers, subsidization of teacher training school construction. (A change in the opportunities for education resulting from a change in the compulsory school age would be more in the nature of a reform.)
   8. Extension service, which would include the dissemination of new information concerning farm management, farm technology, crop diversification and adult education.
   9. Training of rural population in the acquirement of new industrial skills.
   10. Promoting rural health and welfare.[6]

C. *Reforms* (changes in the foundations of the economy).
   1. Changes in the tenancy arrangements, relating to distribution of the

---

[6] Here again it should be noted that the actual institution of such programs — as opposed to changes within — alters the institutional setting of a country and is therefore a reform.

product (as between owners and tenants), terms of the lease, security of the tenants, water rights, etc.

2. Land redistribution; change in the property rights of various groups and individuals.

3. Land consolidation; reduction in fragmented and noncontiguous tracts.

4. Nationalization of agriculture; collective farming.

It is self-evident, but bears repeating, that the selection of agrarian means depends upon the objectives to be achieved. Therefore, an examination of the most important objectives (ends) which a society or a government may have in mind is relevant at this stage. An answer to this question involves specifying the elements entering the social welfare function of the community or the objective preference function of the policy maker. Tinbergen [27; pp. 15–17] gives the following list of the major aims of economic policy in modern times:

a) Maintenance of international peace.

b) Maximum real expenditure per capita with "full" employment and monetary equilibrium.

c) Improvement of distribution of real income or expenditure over social groups and countries.

d) Emancipation of certain underprivileged groups.

e) As much personal freedom as is compatible with the other aims.

These, of course, are the broadest aims. For purposes of this discussion, it seems desirable to specify the principal objectives of agrarian reforms per se. A review of a number of reform acts indicates four major objectives; (a) *productive efficiency*, (b) *economic growth*, (c) greater *equality* in the opportunity to have access to and ownership of resources, in income distribution and in status and security and (d) *justice*, the rule of law and the elimination of exploitation.[7] It is clear that the simultaneous attainment of all four objectives is only possible in a very limited way. Means designed to enhance the achievement of one objective may affect other objectives negatively. For instance, if some form of progressive taxation is used to equalize the income distribution, beyond a certain point the use of this instrument will affect growth negatively by reducing total private savings and ultimately capital formation in the economy. Another example may suffice to indicate the kind of conflict that may exist in the goals. The choice of investment

---

[7] For an interesting discussion and interpretation of the objectives of agrarian reforms applied to a specific act (The Bombay Tenancy and Agricultural Lands Act), see Wunderlich [33], pp. 83–96.

programs in a densely populated, underdeveloped economy is a difficult one. The highest rate of growth will be achieved if the available resources are allocated to the investment program which leads to the largest increase in national income. Now the choice of the process will depend on the prices of the factors. If the actual market prices are taken as the relevant parameters, the choice of project will tend to be more capital-intensive than is warranted on the basis of the opportunity costs of factors. The reason for this is that the institutional wage rate (often akin to the subsistence wage rate) is higher than the equilibrium wage rate, which in a number of underdeveloped countries would approximate zero. On the other hand, the scarcity of capital and entrepreneurial ability is such that the prevailing profit and interest rates are often below their equilibrium levels (marginal value product). Consequently, the use of accounting or shadow prices reflecting the opportunity costs (equilibrium prices) of these factors provides a better criterion for the choice of investment projects and programs for economic growth than if market prices were used. At the same time, it might violate the static conditions of productive efficiency, which are determined on the basis of the market prices.

Therefore, whenever the ends are not mutually consistent or compatible, it is essential that relative weights be attached to the ends and that all substitution rates, as between ends, be stated (i.e., indifference of the policy maker as between an increase of 1 per cent in the annual rate of growth and a 2 per cent change in the Gini income-distribution ratio). In the absence of such quantitative (or even ordinal) weighting of the ends, it is difficult to formulate policies when at least some of the ends are competitive.[8] Admittedly, some of the ends are essentially of a qualitative nature (i.e., justice) and thus not subject to quantification. Nevertheless, it is almost always possible to state whether a competing or complementary relationship exists between targets and to offer estimates—sometimes very rough—of the degree of substitutability between them. The least that a policy maker should be expected to state is a priority as between the aims, which in turn can be translated into the welfare function. Besides making possible a more rational choice of the means of economic policy, the specification of the welfare function in the above sense has the added advantage of forcing the policy maker to state his ends in such terms that the electorate can compare

---

[8] If all the targets were complementary and the barter terms constant (thus, independent of the level of goal achievement), the maximization of one of the ends would be equivalent to maximizing the objective welfare function.

campaign promises (contained in the party platforms) to the actual goals pursued once he is in office. Later in this section a quantitative attempt is made at relating agrarian means to policy objectives.

It should be mentioned in passing that governments in power are not necessarily motivated by their own image of the welfare function of the community. Their main purpose may be to maximize the chance of being reelected, and they will therefore behave according to some sort of "vote-fare" function. The vote maximization function would entail a strategy by which policy means would be used as long as the total votes gained from this action were larger than the total votes lost [3]. It would seem that this behavior pattern fits a number of land reform acts undertaken by newly independent countries, and it may help to explain the heavy emphasis which these reforms placed on distributive justice and equality as opposed to economic growth. At the same time, it does not appear that the welfare function and the vote-fare function would need to be too different. It is true that the latter would need to take into consideration the strategies of the opposition party, which could lead to short-run, essentially transitory, factors entering this function.

After this examination and classification of the policy means and major objectives of agrarian reforms the next section is devoted to the analysis of the contribution that agrarian means can make to the end of economic growth. It is thus assumed that the other ends are of a subsidiary nature, unless otherwise stated.

In analyzing the growth process of underdeveloped areas, it is customary to use a two-sector model (agriculture and industry). It can be said, very succinctly, that the path of development consists of a general transformation from an economy characterized by abundance of labor and extreme scarcity of capital—and a very small modern industrial sector superimposed upon but not integrated to a large native agricultural sector (economic dualism)— to an economy in which the proportion of the labor force employed in agriculture has become small (for instance, one-fourth or less) and the two sectors have become integrated.

The Lewis treatment [14] of development in terms of two sectors opened up a meaningful new theoretical framework that is most useful in assessing the role of agriculture in growth. Two recent attempts built upon Lewis's model performed the type of synthesis described above.[9]

---

[9] See Ranis and Fei [17] and Johnston and Mellor [13]. It is interesting and curious to note that both of these articles (appearing in the same issue of the *American Economic Review*) arrived at similar general conclusions after following quite different approaches.

Of particular interest in the present context is the fact that the general transformation from a rural underdeveloped economy to a developed industrial economy is analyzed by both sets of authors in terms of three distinctive phases which, although not coincidental, appear to overlap greatly. The characteristics inherent in each phase —corresponding to a certain stage of development— will be discussed briefly first. Next, the agrarian policy means most appropriate to each phase and most conducive to the general transformation will be analyzed.

If each phase is looked at from the standpoint of agriculture, the first phase would be called the stationary or stagnation stage, the second phase would be the take-off stage and the third phase that of commercial agriculture. Phase I is characterized by labor redundancy; it will exist as long as part of the labor force has a marginal physical productivity of zero. The institutional wage rate can be thought to be determined by the average product of the total labor force (including the redundant part) and can thus be assumed to be equal to the total agricultural output per capita.[10] (At the beginning of phase I, the total population is assumed to be employed in agriculture.) Throughout phase I, the supply curve for labor in the industrial sector is infinitely elastic at the institutional wage rate, since the opportunity cost of labor is zero. As agricultural workers are withdrawn and added to the industrial sector, a surplus of agricultural goods begins to appear. The reason for this is that since some labor is redundant, throughout phase I at least, total agricultural output remains unchanged as the redundant workers move to the industrial sector. At the same time, the total consumption of the remaining workers (the institutional wage rate times number of remaining workers) declines, since by definition their wage rate (equals consumption) is assumed to be constant. The difference between the total agricultural output and the total agricultural consumption is the total agricultural surplus. This surplus can be viewed as agricultural resources released to the market through the reallocation of agricultural workers. Conceptually, the agricultural worker moving to the industrial sector during this first stage can be thought of as carrying over his own bundle of food (and consumption needs). Thus, the transfer of workers from the rural to the industrial sector during this first phase provides a potentially important source of domestic capital formation. In order for capital formation, as such, to be realized, the

---

[10] The maintenance of this wage level is possible only under institutional or nonmarket forces, since under competitive conditions the wage rate would be zero and starvation would result.

released (free) resources making up the agricultural surplus need to be embodied in the creation of capital or social-overhead capital goods in the industrial sector. This question is subsequently examined in some detail.

Phase II begins as soon as all of the redundant agricultural labor force has been absorbed in industry. The marginal physical product (MPP) of labor in agriculture is positive and increases as additional workers leave the land. Throughout this phase, however, the MPP is less than the institutional wage rate. Thus, both phase I and phase II show evidence of disguised unemployment (MPP less than wage rate). The supply curve of labor in the industrial sectors turns upward at the outset of this second period, since the marginal agricultural surplus is declining whereas it was constant before. The farm worker can now be imagined as carrying over to the industrial sector his own wage rate from which is deducted his foregone contribution to total agricultural output (his MPP). It is this increasing opportunity cost that turns the industrial labor supply curve upward. This phase continues until the MPP has reached the level of the institutional wage rate.

Phase III is truly the commercialization stage. The MPP of labor in agriculture is equal to or above the institutional wage rate, and the supply curve of labor in agriculture, which during the earlier phases had been infinitely elastic at the going institutional wage rate, slopes upward, indicating for each level of real wage rate the amount of labor that may be released from the agricultural sector. Since disguised unemployment has disappeared, the two sectors are fully integrated (economic dualism no longer exists) and market forces are allowed to operate. More specifically, market prices reflect opportunity costs and resources can be allocated efficiently on the basis of these prices. The agricultural surplus, in the sense defined above, has vanished, and the wage rate in the industrial sector is determined on the supply side by the MPP of labor (the opportunity costs) in the agricultural sector.

The first phase is one in which the preconditions for take-off, to use Rostow's terminology, have not been met. The concept of progress and the acceptance of the desirability of change are often foreign to the majority of the peasants at the outset of this period. Even when the goal of progress is desired, the great reluctance to change traditional farming methods, indicating a high risk-aversion, provides an effective obstacle to the implementation of change. In many respects, this high risk-aversion to new farm management methods is perfectly rational from the standpoint of the individual farmer, given the environment with which he operates. He must weigh the cost of a new method against the future net benefits resulting from it. In evaluating and estimating those future benefits, the farmer is greatly handicapped by his lack of knowledge, and even when he is convinced that the expected value of the net benefits is substantially larger than their immediate costs, the distribution of outcomes around the mean is of great importance. It is sufficient to discourage him from the application of chemical fertilizer, for instance, to know that in 1 per cent of the cases the application of this fertilizer results in losses. The fact that this farmer is living on a subsistence wage prevents him from taking any risk (in terms of a new technology) that could lead to starvation (the marginal utility of a rupee lost is substantially higher than that of a rupee gained at the subsistence level). The position of the farmer during this phase can be compared to that of the gambler who knows that the odds are heavily in his favor but who is prevented from betting because of lack of funds.

It is probably during this stage that the most important changes in the foundations and the structure of the economy will need to take place, since no endogenous forces appear to be at work in the direction of growth. In this sense, economic backwardness can be considered a quasistable equilibrium system and growth a disequilibrium system, as Leibenstein has pointed out. What is needed is to introduce exogenous stimuli that will provide a framework which will be conducive to growth.

During phase I, agrarian policy means can play an important role as a conditioning influence to growth. More particularly, a number of land reforms seem desirable. First, under most circumstances, a land-redistribution scheme from tenants to owners (C.2. in the list of policy means)[11] would improve the accretionary process, besides improving the efficiency of resources.[12] It would give the actual cultivators the full exercise of managerial and operational powers. As Raup argued convincingly:[13] "Agricultural policy for maximum growth in this phase of development would seem to call for the creation of patterns of production, consumption and investment that will maximize the accretionary (capital formation) process." At the same time, a conversion from tenant-occupiership to owner-occupiership would improve the tax collection problem, since the link between the payments of taxes and public services received would become more direct

[11] Letters and numbers next to agrarian means refer to the list given previously.

[12] For a theoretical discussion of the impact of different types of land reforms on the production function (and the efficiency of resources), see Heady [8].

[13] Raup [18, p. 16] makes a strong case for land reforms at an early stage of development without specifying exactly at what stage. It seems that phase I in the present analysis would correspond to that stage.

under the latter system. (Raup points out that the landlords might be reluctant to pay taxes in order to contribute to the education of their tenants' children.)

It is clear that a number of complementary means should be provided in order to facilitate the accretionary capital formation of the individual owners and make use of the existing agricultural surplus during this phase. These means will be discussed subsequently.

An alternative reform to a redistribution of land consists of changes in the tenancy arrangements themselves (C.1.). Changes that would be conducive to growth would be a shift from share rents to cash rents for the tenants and a considerable lengthening of the terms of the leases, which would increase the security of the tenants and make the planning period longer.

In general, this alternative would not be as effective an inducement to growth and efficiency of production as would the promotion of owner-occupiership, although it might have a greater positive impact on some ends of the welfare function. This would be true, for instance, if under the end of justice the inalienable right of private property was deemed important. It is interesting to note that as long as agricultural production takes place under conditions of constant returns to scale a change in the size of the farm unit will not improve productive efficiency. Somewhat differently expressed, this means that a process of land consolidation and subdivision (i.e., through the breaking up of absent landlords' estates) would not affect total agricultural output. Thus, here is an example of one agrarian means (land subdivision) that would enhance the end of equality and leave the goal of productive efficiency unaffected. In the case of decreasing return to scale, the reorganization of agriculture to include more and smaller farms would, over a range, permit the simultaneous attainment of the goals of equality, productive efficiency and, indirectly, growth. It is only under conditions of increasing returns to scale that the strictly economic objectives of agrarian reforms are clearly competitive with the distributive ends.[14]

The evidence suggests that it is only in highly developed countries where agriculture is commercialized (U.S., Canada) that increasing returns to scale exist. The present meager empirical evidence in underdeveloped areas would suggest that production is taking place pretty much under conditions of constant returns to scale [8, pp. 16–21: 10, Chapter 17].

To come back to the two land reforms suggested earlier as appropriate

---

[14] See Heady [8, pp. 16–21] for an interesting analysis of the relationship between "food production" and "other goals of reform" under various returns conditions.

to phase I, it should be clear that the efficiency of each would be a function of its impact on the welfare function, and specifically on growth, and its costs in monetary and nonmonetary terms. A program of land redistribution to encourage cultivation by owners would be more conducive to economic growth than a change in land tenancy. On the other hand, the cost of the former in terms of material and nonmaterial resources would appear to be larger.[15] In view of the relatively scarce administrative resources available to governments of most underdeveloped areas, it would seem that a reform altering the tenancy arrangements would be more feasible. At the same time, the administrative costs of enforcing these tenancy arrangements would prevail over time, whereas in the case of land redistribution from tenants to owners the cost of administering and implementing the reform (abstracting from the payments of compensation which can be considered to be direct costs) would not be spread over the long run. Thus, besides the total costs of these alternative programs, another element entering into the decision-making process is the distribution of costs over time.

It was mentioned earlier that the success of a land redistribution scheme was dependent on the implementation of complementary measures. This is equally true for a change in land tenancy arrangements. The most important of these measures in this first phase would seem to be the institution of an agricultural extension service (B.8.), which could take the form of a community development program. The aims of this extension service during the first period could be relatively modest and consist essentially of the dissemination of simple information with the view of improving farm management on the assumption of only very slight increases in the resources available. The additional inputs could be fertilizer, tillage tools and equipment, seeds and pesticides made available to the cultivators at subsidized prices (A.2.).[16] There is a strong presumption, supported by firsthand investigations, that improvements in productivity are possible with only slight changes in the input mix.

---

[15] An index of the efficiency of a policy mean might be the ratio of the change in the objective welfare function caused by it to the cost of the policy mean in terms of material and nonmaterial resources. One of the costs of a land redistribution scheme is the inflationary pressures that could be released by a land-bond compensation scheme. It is relatively difficult to devise a compensation scheme that would be both equitable and noninflationary, since to a large extent an equitable scheme would require a prompt cash redemption of the land bonds to the old owners, which in turn would be more inflationary than a slower redemption scheme.

[16] Extension services would become a much more important policy mean in phase II, as is shown subsequently.

It was pointed out that as the redundant labor force moves to the capitalist sector during this phase, an agricultural surplus is released. Potentially, this agricultural surplus is an important source of capital. In order to realize this surplus, the government should proceed on two fronts. First, it needs to provide or induce alternative employment opportunities in the nonagricultural sector to make the actual transfer possible, and second, it needs to siphon off the actual surplus (or part of it) by means of taxation to prevent increased per capita consumption (and thus a higher wage rate in agriculture). These measures—like the blades of a pair of scissors—can be successful only if they are undertaken jointly and in the sequential order stated above. The undertaking of public projects in social-overhead capital areas (B.4.), mainly in irrigation schemes, rural roads and schools, would provide the necessary employment opportunities for the redundant workers, and direct taxation (A.1.) could be used to finance at least a part of the capital cost of these projects and, more specifically, the food needs of the transferred workers. The remaining capital needs could, to some extent, be met through foreign investment grants and aid (including U.S. surplus-disposal program) from international agencies and public sources in the developed countries. The magnitude of these social-overhead capital (infrastructure) projects (SOC) would depend upon the size of the redundant labor force. On the assumption that the truly redundant labor force (MPP equals zero) forms only a small proportion of the population in most under-developed areas, the over-all scope of these projects could be relatively limited.[17]

A number of agrarian policy means appropriate to phase I have been discussed and analyzed above, and a final comment concerning their mutual compatibility seems in order. It was argued that a land-redistribution scheme would strengthen the link between benefits received and taxes paid and thereby ease the task of collecting taxes. Thus, some "external economies" exist in the use of certain policy means, the use of one improving the effectiveness and the efficiency of others.

Therefore, in conlusion, the best package of means during phase I appears to be a combination of land redistribution (with changes in land tenure as a less desirable alternative), direct taxation, investment in social-overhead capital, subsidies for simple agricultural inputs and a modest extension service (C.2, alternatively C.1, A.1, B.4, A.2 and B.8). (See Table 15.1 for a

---

[17] It will be subsequently argued that the scope of social-overhead capital projects will be much larger in phase II.

schematic representation of agrarian policy means and the process of economic development.)

The transition from the stagnation stage to the take-off stage (phase II) is difficult, if not impossible, to discern in practice. Whereas, in theory, phase II begins as soon as the MPP of agricultural workers becomes positive, turning the supply curve of labor in the industrial sector upward, "this shortage point" cannot, in practice, be established with any degree of precision. The implication of this is that in the formulation, execution and timing of public policy no absolute distinction can be made as between these phases. Certain measures might be undertaken at the end of phase I instead of at the outset of phase II or vice versa. In general, an earlier institutional change might have some advantages, since many policy means appropriate to phase I are also appropriate, usually with a greater intensity of use, to the take-off phase.

Phase II is the crucial phase in the development process. Johnston and Mellor list what they consider the most important nonconventional inputs for increasing agricultural productivity. They are as follows: (1) research to develop improved production possibilities, (2) extension-education programs, (3) facilities for supplying inputs of new and improved forms (particularly improved seed and fertilizers) and (4) institutional facilities for servicing agricultural production, such as credit and marketing agencies and rural government bodies for fostering collective action, such as building feeder roads [13].

During this phase, the efficiency of resources in agriculture needs to be increased, with heavy reliance on new techniques (often imported from abroad) of a labor-intensive, capital-saving nature.

Historically, the impact of agricultural research (B.2.) during this period has been very great in some countries.[18] The effect of this type of research is to move the production possibility surfaces upward without a large change in the actual quantities of conventional inputs. Through the addition of small doses of nonconventional inputs and relatively minor changes in factor proportions, agricultural output can be raised substantially. One major problem in agricultural research is that it cannot be imported *in toto*. It is true that innovations occurring in industrialized countries in terms of chemical fertilizers, improved seeds, etc. can often be used in less well-developed regions. Nevertheless, most of these innovations are made on the basis of the institutional and physical environment existing in these developed

---

[18] This has been substantiated by Johnston [12] for Japan, Taiwan and Denmark.

TABLE 15.1

Agrarian Policy Means and the Process of Economic Development

Economic Development Phase	Characteristic Features	Major Objectives	Principal Agrarian Policy Means Appropriate to Period and Conducive to Growth
Phase I Stagnation	MPP labor = 0 (labor redundancy) Supply of labor in agriculture infinitely elastic at institutional wage rate Supply of labor in industrial sector infinitely elastic at institutional wage rate Economic dualism Preconditions to take-off not met Existence of agricultural surplus	Distributive justice Equality of opportunity Economic development	Land redistribution (C.2.) Changes in land tenancy (C.1.) Taxation (A.1.) Social-overhead capital (B.4.) Subsidies (A.2.) Extension (B.8.) *Reforms* most important policy means
Phase II Take-off	0 < MPP labor < institutional wage rate Supply of labor in agriculture infinitely elastic at institutional wage rate Supply of labor in industrial sector upward sloping	Economic development Productive efficiency Equality Justice	Research (B.2.) Public investment in social-overhead capital and farm implements (B.4., B.3.) Education (B.7.) Extension (B.8.) Credit and marketing facilities (B.6.) Taxation (A.1.) *Structural changes* most important policy means
Phase III Commercialized agriculture	MPP labor ≥ institutional wage rate Agricultural and industrial sectors fully integrated	Productive efficiency Economic growth	A number of *instrument* variables

countries, where commercial agriculture prevails. There is truly no susbtitute for local agricultural research, starting with the existing physical-agronomic structure and developing innovations that are specifically applicable to this structure. It would appear that decreasing costs characterize research, and so the returns to research per unit of funds spent on research might increase considerably throughout this period and phase III. In any case, the absolute cost of research is small. The scarcity of trained agricultural researchers is, in the short run, an important bottleneck, but it can be overcome by an educational program.

The importance of education (B.7.) and investment in the human agent has been greatly emphasized in the literature recently, and it is not necessary to dwell on it further here [21]. Extension services (B.8.) can be considered as a form of adult education. In a few presently underdeveloped countries, agricultural extension has taken the form of community development programs. The attempts at setting up experimental farms using farm management methods that differ from traditional methods might, after some time, trigger "demonstration effects" on the production side. It is still too early to evaluate the effectiveness of community development programs of this kind in India[19] and other countries, but the likelihood is that extension services can perform a major role in disseminating information and increasing the over-all knowledge of the rural population. In this phase, the amounts of public funds allocated to extension services could be substantially higher than in the preceding stage. Two additional tasks under supervision of the extension service might consist of training rural population to acquire new skills (B.9.), thus facilitating the transfer and promoting rural health and welfare (B.10.).

It was indicated earlier that the characteristic feature of phase II is that the MPP of agricultural labor is positive but below the prevailing institutional wage rate. Now, on the assumption of constant technology and population size (which were the implicit assumptions made in the model presented above) the transfer of farm labor from the agricultural to the industrial sector would entail the release of a declining agricultural surplus per worker. At the outset of phase II, the agricultural surplus of the first workers to move would be almost equal to their wage rate, but as more workers

---

[19] The Ford Foundation is financing an experimental development program of this sort. The Ford Foundation has selected areas where the potentials for increased productivity are high, and presumably it hopes to induce changes in production methods by showing the results that can be achieved on experimental farms.

transferred, their positive foregone MPP in agriculture has to be subtracted from their wage rate.

At the end of the take-off phase, the MPP of agricultural labor is equal to the institutional wage rate and the marginal agricultural surplus disappears entirely. Thus, under static conditions, the potential capital formation per worker is lower in phase II as compared with phase I and, furthermore, declines, reaching zero at the end of this second stage.

The assumption of static conditions—constant technology and population size—is relatively valid in phase I, but certainly it cannot be maintained in the take-off phase. More specifically, it would seem that at least two counteracting forces are likely to influence considerably the two-sector model and more specifically the size of the marginal agricultural surplus (the potential capital formation per transferred worker).

The first force would result from the improvements in sanitation, medical knowledge and availability of drugs which would tend to reduce the death rate, thus leading to a substantial increase not only in the size of the population, but also in the rate of population growth. It is obvious that this force would tend to reduce the agricultural surplus, since it can be assumed that the institutional wage rate prevailing in phase I is very rigid downward, being presumably close to the subsistence level. In a sense, part or all of the potential capital formation (the total agricultural surplus) is used up to feed the additional population.

The second force that is likely to take effect during phase II is an increase in total agricultural output resulting from the measures undertaken during this period. Increased agricultural output will also mean a larger total agricultural surplus, as long as the institutional wage rate can be prevented from rising.

The net effect of these two forces on the size of the agricultural surplus during the take-off phase depends upon a large number of factors. It is clear however, that the more positive the net effect is, the closer the economy will get to the commercialization point and phase III.

The increase in population is usually related to the improvements in output and resource productivity. The absolute size of the labor force in agriculture is likely to remain very high throughout the take-off period and not decline [2]. A relative decline in the share of the population in agriculture will, however, take place as the migration from agriculture to the industrial sector proceeds.

During this phase, it is essential that new employment opportunities in the nonagricultural sector open up. Here again, public investment in social-overhead capital projects (B.4.) and specifically in irrigation and fertilizer plants (B.3.) would perform this task and at the same time contribute to the supply of strategic inputs that could raise farm productivity. Taxation (A.1.) will loom more important in phase II than in the preceding one. The agricultural surplus released by the migrating workers needs to be channeled into investment activities instead of higher consumption.

Finally, the development of a number of services is crucial in the take-off phase. Credit facilities and improvements in the marketing structure (B.6.) appear to be structural changes that are possible in phase II and that will further the transformation process to commercial agriculture.

The most appropriate agrarian means in phase II would appear to be a combination of research, public investment in social-overhead capital, including irrigation and fertilizer plants, education and extension and new institutional credit and marketing facilities, together with taxation (B.2., B.4., B.3., B.7., B.8., B.9., B.10., B.6. and A.1.).

The integration of the two sectors is achieved and a relatively high degree of development is attained once the economy enters the commercialization stage (phase III). The structure of the economy during phase III is much less flexible than during the take-off period and changes are much more gradual. Whereas at the start of the general transformation no endogenous force inducing economic growth existed, a number of growth factors have become built into the system in the commercialization stage. Economic policy can become quantitative in the Tinbergen sense (described in section II), and the predetermined targets, such as a predetermined rate of growth of national income, can be achieved with the help of instrument variables.

The major problem the policy maker faces in the first two phases is the lack of specific empirical information concerning the quantitative (and sometimes even qualitative) impact of agrarian means on economic growth. A modest attempt at examining the quantitative impact of land redistribution (C.2.) on the welfare function is undertaken in the next part of this chapter. The amount of empirical work on input-output relationships, capital-output ratios and, in general, of the structural changes in an input-output matrix conducive to economic growth is still quite limited and subject to wide

---

[20] One interesting attempt at trying to maximize the target of national income over a 10-year period (1960–1970) subject to constraints and solving the model for those measures most conducive to this maximization process is contained in Sandee [19]. Sandee uses a super production function for agricultural output of the following form:

$$O = 4.0f + (2.4i + 514) + (3.7e + 520),$$

margins of error.[20] The potential social contribution of empirical research in this area is undoubtedly extremely high and should have a very high priority in development planning. It is not an unfair appraisal of the state of development planning at this date to say that the refinement of the tools and methods used is in dire contrast to the quality of the empirical relationships and data used.

15.1.2. *An Illustrative Application*

In what follows, an attempt is made at applying and illustrating the methodology developed in the first part of this book with reference to a specific agrarian mean, namely, land redistribution (C.2.).

It should be clear in this connection that this amounts to a "partial equilibrium" approach, since the impact of only one policy mean on the welfare function is analyzed. In a generalized treatment of the impact of instrument variables on the preference function of the policy maker, as, for instance, in the case of development planning models, the simultaneous effects of changes in one or more instrument variables can be calculated for the whole set of endogenous variables (the target and irrelevant variables). Another difference between the present analysis and development planning models, which are discussed in Chapter 13 (growth models) is that in these models the policy means take the form typically of instrument variables, whereas in the present context the policy mean under consideration amounts to a reform which, as was pointed out previously, is much more difficult to analyze within a quantitative framework than when the structure of the economy is assumed unaltered.

A final qualification should be made explicit before starting the actual analysis. Land redistribution by itself, in the absence of other reforms or changes in the policy means enumerated above, is not likely to have any real impact on the welfare function. If land redistribution is not combined with the whole set of complementary measures discussed earlier, it may simply take the form of a legal change of land titles without any economic or social improvements resulting from it. Therefore, in order to make the following discussion meaningful and operational (at least potentially so), land redistribution should be understood to include a minimum of complementary

---

where

O = increase in agricultural output between 1960 and 1970,
f = increase in the application of fertilizer between 1960 and 1970,
i = irrigation projects executed between 1960 and 1970,
e = expenditure on agricultural extension between 1960 and 1970.

measures, such as the extension of credit and technical assistance to the new farmers and changes in the marketing system. In a more thorough treatment, the individual as well as the combined costs of the whole set of agrarian means would have to be weighed as against their quantitative benefits on the welfare function.

In summary, the present discussion offers an example of the way in which a quantitative framework can be formulated within which decisions can be reached with respect to the policies involving changes in structure and reforms.

The analysis will proceed according to the following steps:
(i)   The major elements entering into the welfare function will be specified as well as the marginal rates of substitution between these elements.
(ii) The effects of land redistribution (interpreted in a broad sense) on the targets included in the welfare function will be estimated.
(iii) The costs of land redistribution will be calculated.

The second and third steps are essentially attempts at measuring, respectively, the welfare benefits and the costs of land redistribution. To reduce somewhat the hypothetical and arbitrary character of the analysis and to add an element of concreteness it was decided to use Peru as the frame of reference. It should be perfectly clear that the determination and specification of the above steps, and particularly of the first two steps, is the proper function of the ruling government. The welfare weights which were selected here represent at best, the judgment and opinion of an observer about the relative importance of different targets and their marginal contributions to the welfare function.

Very few attempts at the quantitative specification of the welfare function appear in the literature. The simplest form which this function can take is probably linear, a partitioned and continuous one, which is the form van Eijk and Sandee used in approximating the welfare function of the Netherlands in 1957.[21]

With respect to an underdeveloped country, the major elements entering the welfare function would appear to be (1) the rate of growth of real income (on either a per capita or aggregate basis), (2) the level of employ-

---

[21] See van Eijk and Sandee [31]. The welfare function which was obtained on the basis of interviews with different groups (relating to 1956–1957) was the following:

$$\pi = 1.0\,(E - M) + 0.25\,x_G + 0.20\,I + 5.0\,l_R - 7.5\,p_C + 0.20\,a + 50\,S_G + \text{Constant}.$$

Since $\dfrac{d\pi}{d(E - M)} = 1$ and $\dfrac{d\pi}{dX_G} = 0.25, \ldots$ etc.,

ment, (3) the income distribution, (4) the state of the balance of payments, (5) the price level and (6) a minimum threshold of political and social stability, in the absence of which democratic planning could not be carried out.

In a certain sense, this threshold can be interpreted as the minimum level of the desires of the society (or the various groups in the society) for certain key factors (to be specified below) which, if not granted, would trigger a social or political revolution.

The above targets, with the exception of the last one, can be expressed without too much difficulty in a quantitative form. Political and social stability is a very elusive concept which would appear to overlap both material and psychic welfare (i.e., the minimum demands for education, freedom, etc.). Nevertheless, an attempt is made below to relate this goal to the welfare function and express it in a quantitatively comparable form to the other targets.

If the welfare function of the policy maker were to be stated in terms of the above targets and in a linear and partitioned form, the following would obtain:

$$W = aY + bE + cY_\sigma + d(X - M) - eP + fPS, \qquad (15.1)$$

where,

W = the level of welfare,
Y = aggregate real income,
E = the level of employment,
Y_σ = income distribution,
$X - M$ = the balance of payments,
P = the price level,
PS = political and social stability,
$a, b, c, ..., f$ are the welfare weights attached to the targets.

---

the interpretation of the above function is that against a 100 million (guilders) balance of payments surplus $(E - M)$ could be set as follows:

400 million	government expenditures (x_G),
500 million	investment (I),
2 per cent increase	in real wages (l_R),
1.33 per cent	decrease in consumer prices (p_C),
0.5 per cent increase	in employment (a),

or

200 million	government surplus (S_G).

This function was only supposed to be valid over a narrow range of the various targets and instrument variables. For further discussion of this function see Chapter 7.

Recognizing that the determination of the weights is the proper domain of the government, one might nevertheless assign possible weights for Peru on the basis of 1962 figures. As an example,

$$W = 5/6Y + 50E + cY_\sigma + 1.0(X - M) - 100P + fPS, \qquad (15.2)$$

where the numéraire for the balance of payments $(X-M)$ is taken as 20 million dollars and where E refers to the level of the active population in 1962, P to the price level (base $= 100$ for 1962) and the weights attached to the income distribution (c) and to political stability (f) are, for the time being, left unspecified. Since the partial derivatives in the above function depend only on the variables concerned and are independent of the other targets, it follows that the marginal rates of substitution between targets can easily be obtained. Thus, if the above example reflected the views of the policy maker, the latter would set up against a 20 million dollar balance of payments surplus:

$24 million: growth in real income (Y).

2 per cent: increase in the level of active population employed (E).

1 per cent: decrease in the price level (P) (or alternatively a reduction of the rate of inflation by 1 per cent).

$1/c$:   improvement in the income distribution (Y_σ).

$1/f$:   improvement in the index of political stability (PS).

These "barter terms" between the targets are readily derived from the ratio of the partial derivatives. Indeed, since

$$\frac{dW}{d(X-M)} = 1 \quad \text{and} \quad \frac{dW}{dY} = \frac{5}{6},$$

it follows that

$$\frac{dW}{d(X-M)} \div \frac{dW}{dY} = \frac{6}{5},$$

and that to maintain the level of welfare constant a sacrifice of 24 million dollars in Y would compensate a 20 million dollar surplus in the balance of payments. Likewise,

$$\frac{dW}{d(X-M)} \div \frac{dW}{dE} = 0.02$$

which means, given the choice of units, that a 2 per cent increase in the amount of active population employed is set up against a 20 million dollar surplus in the balance of payments, as is a 1 per cent decrease in the (consumer) price index.

It is, of course, obvious that the selected welfare weights refer to a very specific time period and are only valid for that (short) period. This is particularly true given the form of the above preference function. Since no products of targets appear in the above formulation, the contribution to welfare of any one target is assumed independent of the level of attainment of the set of other targets. This assumption is only tenable for slight changes in any target and for a narrow range within which the targets can be altered.

Some justification might be given for the quantitative weights used in the previous example. Aggregate real income in Peru in 1962 (at 1960 prices) amounted to about 2.350 billion dollars and the level of active population employed to roughly 3.4 million. Thus, real income *per member of the active population* equaled about 700 dollars. A 1 per cent increase in active population would add 34,000 people, and assuming the marginal income equal to the average income of the active population, the corresponding income creation would be of the order of 23.8 million dollars (34,000 times 700 dollars). Given the tremendous income distribution disparity, the likelihood is that the marginal income of the newly added members of the actively employed population would be substantially below the average. Thus, if the estimated income of the new workers were set at 350 dollars the welfare weight attached to E could become 50 and the necessary increase in the level of E to compensate for a 20 million dollar balance of payments surplus or a 24 million dollar increase in Y would be 2 per cent (equivalent to 68,000 times 350 dollars equals 23.8 million dollars). In this same fashion, a 1 per cent decrease in the GNP price index would increase real income by 23.5 million dollars.

The marginal rate of substitution which is taken here between aggregate income and the balance of payments was meant to imply a strong balance of payments position and a relatively weak multiplier effect on both domestic income and employment which are characteristic features of the Peruvian economy at this time.

So far no specific weights were given to the goals of more equal income distribution and political and social stability. The first goal can be easily quantified. In a country with good income distribution statistics, an index of income distribution would be the Gini coefficient (the ratio of the area circumscribed by the Lorenz curve and the line of perfect income distribution equality to the area of the triangle). The limits of this ratio are one (complete inequality) and zero (perfect equality), and a move toward more equal income distribution could be expressed as a percentage reduction in this ratio. Since income distribution statistics are notoriously lacking in most lesser developed countries, a much rougher index than the Gini coefficient has to be selected. In the case of Peru, for example, the dualistic nature of the economy is so pronounced that a rough, yet meaningful, index of income distribution might be the ratio of "Costa" income to "Sierra" income (the third natural region of Peru "Selva" contributes such a small share of national income that it can safely be abstracted from at this time).[22] A given transfer of income from Costa to Sierra should help bring about the integration of the economy (which happens to be a major political goal) and the creation of a national market. Economies of scale on the production and consumption sides would appear to depend on a more equal distribution of income between these regions as well as between individuals.

Political and social stability is a much more difficult goal to specify quantitatively than any of the above-mentioned ones. It depends on the level of availability of certain material and nonmaterial services to the community. In a very general way these services can be identified and their relative political and social importance ascertained. These services will typically flow from certain programs. For instance, the material and non-material desires of the community necessary to the maintenance of political and social stability may include land ownership, education, health, shelter and improved transportation and communication. These desires have their counterpart in concrete programs in land redistribution, schools, public health, housing and roads. The government can measure the relative political importance of each program nationally and regionally. For instance, if land ownership is considered a 10-point issue, the importance of housing can be expressed relative to land reform (i.e., 2 points); the 10 points for land reform should reflect the maximum amount of public support obtainable, namely, to the point where public support is evenly divided for and against further land reform measures.[23]

Each major program can be expressed in terms of tangible criteria or specific accomplishments, such as "percent of six to ten year olds for whom schools and teachers are available within one mile of home or by free bus."

Table 15.2 provides some hypothetical measurements of program potentials and goals for an economy or given region. In Table 15.3 the differ-

---

[22] It is not overly exaggerated to speak of two almost independent economies with two quite distinct income levels. The per capita income of Peru in 1960 was estimated at 207 dollars. Estimates would tend to indicate that this is the combined result of 0.7 of the population in the Sierra with an average income of 82 dollars per capita and 0.3 of the population with a per capita income of 494 dollars.

[23] This discussion and the hypothetical tables which follow are based on Fox [6].

TABLE 15.2

Hypothetical Measurements of Program Potentials and Goals for an Economy or a Given Region

Programs	Actual Situation in 1963	Maximum Possible Achievement	Goal for 1968
1. *Land redistribution*[a]			
A. Per cent of total land area subject to expropriation	36	0	18
B. Per cent of area transferred to campesinos	0	100	50
C. Per cent of total land (not A.)	64		82
2. *Schools*			
A. Per cent of 6 to 10-year-olds for whom buildings and teachers are available within one mile or by free bus	30	100	80
B. Same for 11 to 15-year olds	10	100	80
C. Per cent of schools offering school lunch	40	100	80
3. *Public health*			
A. Per cent of population having "safe" water	20	100	40
B. Per cent of births attended by physician or trained nurse	30	100	50
C. Per cent of population having "adequate" access to doctors and hospitals	20	100	50
4. *Housing*			
A. Per cent safe running water within 100 feet from house	30	100	50
B. Per cent with "adequate" number of rooms for family size and age-sex composition	20	100	40
C. Electric lights	20	100	40
D. "Suitable" cooking facilities	20	100	40
E. "Adequate" heat	40	100	60
5. *Roads, rural*			
A. Per cent of farm population within one mile of all-weather road	20	100	40
B. Per cent of child-days school attendance missed because of roads	20	0	15
C. Per cent of adult-days work lost because of roads	20	0	15
D. Per cent of days of year impossible to get goods to market because of roads	30	0	20

[a] These figures are consistent with estimates made of the land area subject to expropriation under the Peruvian Reform Bill (1960).

TABLE 15.3

Hypothetical Calculations of Contributions to Well-Being (W)[a]

| | Weight within Subgroup (1) | Relative Importance of Subgroup 1963 (2) | Increase in W (well-being) | |
			If 1968 Goal is Reached (3)	If Maximum Value of Issue is Realized (4)
1. *Land*	1.00	10	5.00	10.00
A. Per cent of total land area subject to expropriation				
B. Per cent of area transferred to campesinos	1.00		5.00	10.00
2. *Schools*	1.00	3	1.62	2.22
A. Per cent of 6 to 10-year-olds for whom buildings and teachers are available within one mile or by free bus	0.5		0.75	1.05
B. Same for 11 to 15-year-olds	0.3		0.63	0.81
C. Per cent of schools offering school lunch	0.2		0.24	0.36
3. *Public health*	1.00	3	0.75	2.31
A. Per cent of population having "safe" water	0.2		0.12	0.48
B. Per cent of births attended by physician or trained nurse	0.3		0.18	0.63
C. Per cent of population having "adequate" access to doctors and hospitals	0.5		0.45	1.20
4. *Housing*	1.00	2	0.40	1.48
A. Per cent safe running water	0.2		0.08	0.28
B. Per cent with "adequate" number of rooms for family size and age-sex composition	0.3		0.12	0.48
C. Electric lights	0.2		0.08	0.32
D. "Suitable" cooking facilities	0.1		0.04	0.16
E. "Adequate" heat	0.2		0.08	0.24

TABLE 15.3—Concluded

	Weight within Subgroup (1)	Relative Importance of Subgroup 1963 (2)	Increase in W (well-being)	
			If 1968 Goal is Reached (3)	If Maximum Value of Issue is Realized (4)
5. *Roads, rural*	1.00	2	0.49	1.84
A. Per cent of farm population within one mile of all-weather road	0.4		0.16	0.64
B. Per cent of child-days school attendance missed because of roads	0.1		0.05	0.20
C. Per cent of adult-days work lost because of roads	0.3		0.15	0.60
D. Per cent of days of year impossible to get goods to market because of roads	0.2		0.13	0.40
Recapitulation:				
Land			5.00	10.00
Schools			1.62	2.22
Public health			0.75	2.31
Housing			0.40	1.48
Roads			0.49	1.84
Total increase in *W*			8.26	17.85

[a] An example might clarify this table. Taking Program 2A, above, the relative importance of the school program (subgroup 2) as a whole is given a weight of 3 (column 2). Since the weight of 2A within the school subgroup is 0.5 (column 1), the maximum welfare weight attainable if program 2A is completed in its entirety (i.e., 100 per cent of the 6 to 10-year-olds have access to buildings and teachers within one mile or by free bus) is 1.5 ($= 3 \times 0.5$). Given the fact that 30 per cent of these school children are assumed to have had access to the above facilities in the base year (1963), the maximum potential incremental welfare gain is equal to 70 per cent of 1.5 = 1.05 (see column 4), and if the welfare goal set for 1968 (i.e., 80 per cent of above school children with specified facilities) is attained, the increment to welfare would be ($80 - 30$ per cent) $\times 1.5 = 0.75$ (see column 3).

ences between the actual 1963 levels and the 1968 goals are converted into estimates of increases in well-being. The relative importance weights are supplied by the government (or political observers). Differences between observers can be stated quantitatively and possibly reconciled into "consensus" weights. The changes in W resulting from each program provide a subjective measure of the benefit of the program. It is obvious from Table 15.3 that increases in the level of welfare can result from a large number of combinations of program mix. The marginal benefits of each program in terms of W can be weighed against their marginal costs.

The end result of the hypothetical example used above is that the increase in welfare caused by political stability can be translated into a quantitative index. The parameter f $(dW/dPS=f)$ in the welfare function above (15.2) is no longer left unspecified, and it can now be stated in relative units. It becomes possible to express the marginal rates of substitution between the other targets appearing in the welfare function above (such as Y and E) and the objective of political stability. For instance, an 0.50 increase in the index given at the end of Table 15.3 might have the same welfare contribution as a 20 million dollar balance of payments surplus or a 24 million dollar increase in Y. Again, the determination of the barter terms between political stability and the other targets requires the trained judgments of the government leaders.

Three final comments should be made with respect to the target of political stability. First, in this case, perhaps even more than for other targets, a minimum threshold is a necessary precondition to planning. It is only after this threshold has been provided that the question of substitution between targets becomes relevant and applicable. The second comment is that the elements which contribute to political stability, i.e., the five community desires listed above, can be satisfied through the five programs corresponding to them. The programs themselves are instrumental in nature. It is possible that the community attaches welfare implications to the instruments as well, i.e., that it is not indifferent as to which instrument or set of instruments is used to attain given targets. In this case, the welfare function might be expressed in terms of both targets and instruments.[24] This type of function is encountered and discussed in Chapter 13 on development planning models.

---

[24] An interesting attempt at formulating quadratic welfare functions corresponding to the different preferences of three groups (labor, employers and the government) in terms of four targets and five instruments was undertaken in the Netherlands by van den Bogaard and Barten [30].

Finally, it can easily be deduced from the programs influencing political stability that the relative weights of these programs or, in other words, their urgency and priority will be altered as the implementation of the programs gets under way. The relative importance and contribution to well-being of any one program will tend to decline as a certain level of achievement has been attained. Thus, as was pointed out above, the welfare weights in the welfare function are only valid over a narrow range of values which the targets can take (which may imply a short period of time).

After having specified quantitatively the welfare function, an attempt can be made at measuring the impact of land redistribution (C.2.) on the welfare function. This necessitates the formulation of the various relationships relating land redistribution, interpreted fairly broadly, to the targets appearing in the preference function. If land redistribution (which is defined as including a minimum of complementary agrarian means) is denoted by L (instead of the more narrow C.2.), the marginal benefits of L can be derived from these relationships.

Indeed, if here again for simplicity a linear form is assumed for the above relationships, one would obtain:

$$Y = \alpha_0 + \alpha L,$$
$$E = \beta_0 + \beta L,$$
$$\vdots \quad \vdots \quad \vdots$$
$$PS = \lambda_0 + \lambda L,$$

where the marginal impact of L on Y is measured by $dY/dL = \alpha$, and similarly for $dE/dL = \beta$, and so on.

Some of these relationships may be fairly difficult to calculate. Even the direction of the impact of L as a policy mean on any given target is not always obvious. For instance, the effect of L on aggregate income (Y) may be zero or even negative in the short-run ($dY/dL \leq 0$). Similarly, the impact of L on B, E and PS is very much dependent on the specifics of the agrarian reform bill or system followed. In the case of Peru it would appear that the impact of L on the above targets is not likely to be significantly different from zero, given (a) the protection which is provided in the bill for large commercial agricultural farms on the "Costa" which cater to the export market and (b) the relatively slow bond redemption scheme envisaged ($dB/dL = 0$, $dE/dL = 0$, $dP/dL = 0$). On the other hand, no doubt exists that $dY_\sigma/dL > 0$ and $dPS/dL > 0$, i.e., that land reform will contribute to improving the distribution of income and political and social stability.

As an exercise the incremental benefits to welfare of land redistribution might be approximated. On the basis of the proposed agrarian reform bill in Peru, the amount of land subject to expropriation was estimated at 34 per cent of the total cultivated, cultivable and natural pasture land area. If the goal between 1963 and 1968 is to redistribute 50 per cent (see Table 15.2) of the land subject to expropriation and given the welfare weight of 5.0 points attached to the completion of this program (i.e. the successful expropriation of 50 per cent of the land subject to expropriation; see tables 15.2 and 15.3), it follows that an increase of 1.0 in the political stability index would correspond to a change of ownership of 10 per cent of the above land each year. The opportunity welfare weight of 1.0 in political stability means 48 million dollars in terms of foregone aggregate real income, given the marginal rate of substitution previously specified. In other words, given the welfare function which has been postulated above, annual expropriation of 5 per cent of the land subject to expropriation would have the same impact on welfare as 24 million dollars of additional income, 20 million dollars of payments surplus, a 2 per cent increase in active population and so on.

Once the incremental welfare benefits of land reform have been expressed quantitatively, it becomes necessary to compute the incremental costs of land reform in order to compare the relative efficiency of this policy mean. This was done in a detailed study, the essence of which is summarized below [23]. First, the total value of land by categories and by departments was calculated on the basis of the Agricultural Census of 1961 and tables used by land assessors. Second, the amount and value of land subject to expropriation on the basis of the proposed agrarian reform bill was estimated. The total value of land subject to expropriation came to 308 million dollars and amounted to 1.7 million hectares of cultivated and cultivable land and approximately 3 million hectares of natural pastures (representing about 34 per cent of the total land area in those two classes).

The costs of land reform can be divided into the direct costs of land redistribution and a number of indirect costs which have to be incurred simultaneously with land transfers and are basic to their success. The direct costs are a function of the financing scheme used by the government. These costs were estimated on the basis of the following assumptions (which appeared consistent with the proposed agrarian reform bill): (a) It was assumed that the total value of land subject to expropriation amounts to 370 million dollars (this figure includes a margin for administrative costs of executing the program and for a few essential inputs to new settlers, which explains the apparent discrepancy with the previously stated total land value); (b) it was assumed that land would be transferred over a 10-year period so that each year 37 million dollars worth of land would change ownership and therefore that bonds totaling 37 million dollars would be issued annually for 10 years; (c) these bonds would be redeemed over a 20-year period from their date of issue and carry a 5 per cent interest rate; and (d) the new landlords would purchase their land over a 30-year period and pay 2 per cent interest on the unpaid balance. A "grace period" of four years was provided to the new landlords before they started repaying the principal on their land. On these assumptions, the fiscal implications of this land transfer scheme could be worked out over time. The annual excess of government outlays (bond redemption and interest payment) over income (principal repayment and interest receipt from new landlords) increases between year 0 and year 9, at which time they reach a peak of almost 17 million dollars. After that they decline gradually until year 22, after which the net outflow is replaced by a net inflow which is maintained until year 43, the length of time necessary to complete the above scheme. Given the annual fluctuations which occur under this scheme over time, it is difficult to determine a proper way of discounting the future net flows to their present values. Nevertheless, it appears clearly that the direct costs of this land transfer scheme would be relatively low. The average annual cost over the first five years, for instance, amounts to about 8.7 million dollars. Proper discounting would reduce this figure further.

The next step is to compute the minimum indirect costs. It seems essential, before a rough estimate of these costs can be made, to attempt to estimate the number of families which might be involved in the resettlement process. The total *active population* employed in agriculture is, according to the 1961 Census, 1.6 million. A fairly reasonable assumption is that a farm family consists of approximately 1.6 *active* persons (i.e., between four and five persons in total). Thus, the total number of farm families might amount to approximately one million. The main criteria included in the bill and governing the determination of the average size of the farm are, first, family labor employment and second, a farm family income level above the subsistence level.

These criteria are quite vague, and it is therefore difficult to translate them into quantitative terms. As a broad approximation it was assumed that the average farm size, corresponding to the above criteria, would vary between 10 and 15 hectares for cultivated and cultivable land and between 100 and 150 hectares for natural pastures. On the basis of these judgments it is possible to obtain an order of magnitude of the number of families which could be resettled. The total land area in cultivated and cultivable land, as previously mentioned, was estimated at 1.7 million hectares, while the estimate for natural pastures was 3 million hectares. Given these figures it means that, respectively, between 116,000 and 174,000 families could be granted new ownership on the former type of land and between 20,000 and 30,000 on the latter type. Since the land transfer process is assumed to take *10 years*, it follows that between 13,600 and 20,400 families could be resettled every year for 10 years.[25]

Estimating the indirect costs connected with land redistribution is at least as difficult and as risky as estimating the average farm size. As a minimum these costs would include (1) short-term production credit to purchase inputs such as fertilizers, insecticides, seeds and cattle, (2) medium or long-term credit for construction, irrigation, farm improvement and other purposes and possibly (3) public expenditures for technical assistance and extension. A tentative estimate of at least the first two types of indirect costs would be, as a strict minimum, around 500 dollars per family. Thus, the annual indirect costs of transferring land to between 13.6 and 20.4 million families would amount to between 6.8 and 10.2 million dollars.[26]

After these somewhat tedious calculations it becomes possible to compare the incremental costs of land redistribution to their incremental benefits in terms of welfare. Recapitulating, it was determined that a 10 per cent transfer of the land subject to expropriation would contribute 1.0 point to the political stability index, which on the basis of the hypothetical welfare function previously specified is equivalent to 48 million dollars in terms of real income. The incremental costs of a 10 per cent transfer of land subject to expropriation add up to between 15.5 and 18.9 million dollars, inclusive of the direct and minimum indirect costs. The conclusion which can be reached following the above analysis is that the level of land redistribution assumed is socially efficient with respect to political stability, since the welfare contributions to

---

[25] An observation which is conveyed by these last figures is that the land reform scheme is only going to affect between 13.6 and 20.4 per cent of the total number of farm families in Peru. The estimates further strengthen the almost self-evident presumption that the employment alternatives in Peruvian agriculture and, more generally, in the agricultural sectors of most underdeveloped countries are very limited. In this sense, the land reform is not a panacea, yielding a solution to population pressures in agriculture and is not a substitute for a well-conceived industrialization scheme.

[26] It should be remembered that the purpose of this exercise is to compute the incremental costs of land redistribution, including a minimum level of other services and not the incremental costs of a complete agrarian reform program.

the latter goal are greater than the costs of the specific scheme under consideration. Before any generalization can be made about the over-all impact of land transfer on the welfare function, it is necessary to estimate not only dPS/dL or $\Delta PS/\Delta L$ (as was done above) but also the effects of L on all the other targets entering the preference function.

If, as was assumed previously, the impact of L on the balance of payments, the price level and employment is not significantly different from zero, while improving the goal of income distribution equity and political stability, it would follow that the over-all welfare benefits would exceed the costs of the level of L specified in this example. Therefore, the above policy of land redistribution would be socially desirable and should be undertaken.

It should be remembered that the welfare weights chosen in the welfare function were hypothetical and in this sense arbitrary. The purpose of the above discussion and example was to formulate a simple operational framework within which quantitative policy decisions could be made. The major difficulties which have to be overcome before the present approach can be used are (1) the quantitative determination of the marginal rates of substitution between objectives by the government and (2) the estimation of the quantitative effects of the policy means (particularly when they take the form of changes in structure or reforms) on the goal attainment level of the targets.

The choice of a linear and partitioned welfare function, implying that the contribution to welfare of any one target was independent of the level of other targets (within a narrow range), simplified the presentation. There is no reason why a different form cannot be selected if it fits and reflects the views of the government. The quadratic form, as was pointed out in the first part of this book, facilitates the maximizing process and, as such, may be superior to the linear form.

The conclusions that follow from the preceding analysis can be stated briefly. It was argued that the methodology developed by Tinbergen in the area of the theory of economic policy provides a valuable framework in the examination of (1) the various types of agrarian reform considered as means of economic policy, (2) the various objectives of agrarian reform, (3) the relationship between agrarian means and the end of economic growth, more specifically, and (4) the marginal rates of substitution between objectives entering the welfare function and the relationships between policy means and targets.

It was seen that three phases could be distinguished in the general transformation from an essentially stagnant rural economy to a well integrated economy in which commercial agriculture prevails. As a broad generalization, it was shown that the agrarian means most appropriate to growth are likely to be land reforms in the stationary phase, structural changes in the take-off phase and instrument variables in the commercialization period.

In one sense, the complexity of decision making throughout the process of economic development is inversely related to the administrative skill of the government. This can be stated somewhat differently by saying that the effects of the policy means available at an early stage of development are much more uncertain than at a later stage, while the administrative skill of the policy maker improves over time. The convergence of interests, however, would appear to be higher at an early stage, and so the specification of the welfare function, at least, is a much easier task.

15.2. A Typology of Agricultural Sector Models in Developing Countries

There are very few models which describe quantitatively the agricultural sector of developing countries.[27] An attempt is made here to review and evaluate critically a selected number of the more representative of these models and, in that process, provide a classification scheme.[28]

It is important, at the outset, to specify conceptually the domain of sector analysis and models and the hierarchy of linkages which can, and should ideally, be incorporated into an agricultural sector model. Starting at the most micro level, the unit of observation is the farm (F) as a producing firm and as a consuming household. Farms can be grouped together on the basis of certain criteria (e.g., technique of production, size of the land holding, quality of land) into districts (D) which represent the first level of aggregation. Agricultural districts, in turn, can be consolidated together to form a region (R) according to climatic, economic or even administrative factors. The agricultural sector (A) can be composed of a number of regions. Finally, agriculture has to be linked to the rest of the national economy (E) as well as to the world economy (W).

Figure 15.1 shows this hierarchy of linkages in a schematic way. Ideally, the sector model should embrace explicitly the relationships within and as

---

[27] There are a number of national and regional agricultural models, which have been built for developed countries. For a review of these see Heady [9]. The operational usefulness of these models for policy purposes appears to be limited at this time in both East and West.

[28] This section is based on Thorbecke [25].

between agricultural subsets (F–D; D–R, or at least F–R; and R–A) and the links with the rest of the economy (A–E) and the outside world (i.e., foreign trade and investment linkage) directly (i.e., A–W) or through the national

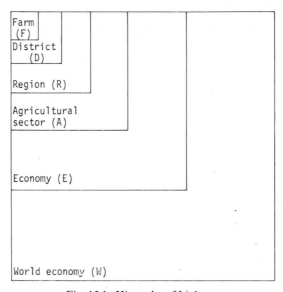

Fig. 15.1. Hierarchy of Linkages.

economy (A–E–W). In a sense, the system to be modelled is one in which each set is a subset of a higher order set.[29]

It will be seen in the review of sector models that the above scheme is a useful one and an important criterion in classifying models according to the sets (domains) and links which are emphasized. Thus, some models are built from the "bottom up", i.e., they start by describing the purely micro-behavior of farms and proceed to aggregate at the district and regional level, whereas other models are built from the "top down" starting at the macro-economic level; which is subsequently disaggregated into an agricultural sector, component regions and so forth.

Table 15.4 provides a breakdown of sector models into the following four distinctive classes according to a number of characteristics and criteria: (a) multilevel planning models; (b) microeconomic-dynamic models; (c)

---

[29] A complication in the above scheme is that districts and regions are spatial units in which agricultural and nonagricultural activities take place. Thus, the latter have to be described in the specification of rural districts and regions.

TABLE 15.4

Classification of Sector Models

Characteristics	Conceptual Framework / Type of Model — Multilevel Planning		Micro-Economic-Dynamic	Simulation Systems	General Equilibrium Consistency Framework	
Examples[a]	[11]	[32]	[1]	[15]	[4]	[24]
Consistency vs. Optimization	√		√	√	√	
One-Period Dynamic	√		√	√	√	
Micro-orientation			√			
Macro-orientation	√			√	√	
Formal Links:						
Farm-Region			√			
Farm-Sector						
District-Region	√					
Region-Sector	√			√		
Sector-Economy	√			√	√	
Methods and Techniques:						
Programming	√					
Recursive Programming			√			
Recursive Systems Analysis				√		
Various Methods,				√	√	
(including non-quantitative						√
description)						
Technological Alternatives:						
incorpoated at						
Farm Level			√	/		
District or	√					
Regional Level				√		
Sector Level					√	
Migration Activities:						
included at						
Regional Level	√		√	√		
Sector Level						√

[a] Numbers in brackets refer to specific models (see list of references at the end of the chapter). Source: [25].

simulation-systems models; and (d) general equilibrium-consistency models. The major characteristics and criteria used in Table 15.4 refer to the form of the model i.e., (i) is it of an optimization or consistency type?; (ii) one-period or dynamic?; (iii) does it have a micro- or macro-orientation? In addition, the models are classified according to the major links (such as farm-region or sector-economy) which they emphasize, the techniques and methods which they use, and the ways in which technological alternatives and migration activities are incorporated into them.

Prototype examples corresponding to each class are presented next and reviewed critically on the basis of the above set of criteria and others such as the form of the preference functions, and major policy objectives contained in the various models; the principal policy problems addressed in the sector models and their operational usefulness to policymakers.

15.2.1. *Multilevel Planning Models*

Perhaps the best examples of such models are those being built presently by the Development Center of the IBRD and applied to Mexico [11] and the Ivory Coast [32]. It has been mentioned in Section 13.2.2 that the main characteristic of these models is the formal linkage of a multisectoral economy-wide model with an agricultural model which is further decomposed into a number of district submodels which are grouped together into four regions. Thus, the E–A–D links (see Figure 15.1) are formally introduced. Since there are three levels of planning, solutions can be obtained at the economy-wide level, at the agricultural sector level or at the district level.

The Mexican model designed by Duloy and Norton [11] with the help of the Mexican government is basically a programming model of the agricultural sector. Agriculture is subdivided into 20 district submodels on the basis of climatic conditions (e.g., irrigated vs. rain-fed areas, soil fertility, and elevation). These submodels in turn, are grouped into four main geographical regions. Cropping and investment activities are specified for each submodel.

Certain inputs, such as land, water and the farmers' own labor, are supplied and specified as constraints at the district level, other inputs such as hired labor and chemical inputs appear as regional constraints and still others (e.g., credit and machinery services) are treated as sectoral constraints (e.g., balance-of-payment, total investment) are specified at the national level. The nature of the constraints makes it possible to express the model in a block-diagonal way with respect to the districts. For any activities (e.g., crops produced according to a given technology) certain inputs are supplied and constrained at the national, sectoral, regional or district levels. Thereby each district submodel can be solved independently or the whole agricultural model can be run and solutions obtained at the sectoral level.

The sector-wide model contains about 2,500 cropping activities to describe alternative technologies (e.g., mechanized and nonmechanized) for producing the 40 major Mexican crops. Demand functions are specified nationally taking transportation costs into consideration. However, it is not assumed that each submodel area can equally well supply the "national" market. Spatial price differentials are used to reflect the differential transport costs faced by each submodel. Product prices are endogenously determined. The sector model contains a detailed treatment of employment and seasonal migration.

At least two different objective functions can be postulated and the model solved accordingly to simulate the agricultural sector behaving either as a monopolistic supplier of products or, more realistically, as a collection of competitive producers.

At this stage the model is designed to address itself to questions of pricing policies for both inputs and outputs, trade policies, employment programs and the effects of certain investment projects. At a later stage when the agricultural sector model is formally linked to the economy-wide model (DYNAMICO)[30] the effects of investment projects on a district could be analyzed within a general equilibrium framework. In other words, the impact of a large project or set of projects could be followed through logically and quantitatively on the district, the region, the sector and ultimately the national economy. If the above linkages could be accurately captured and reflected in the marriage of CHAC (the agricultural model) and DYNAMICO, such a general equilibrium treatment of the effects of projects could potentially revolutionize the methodology of project analysis.

So far only limited numerical results have been obtained. The study is not yet operationally useful to policymakers. Further work is in process which might lead to useful policy results. In the meantime, some methodological elements of the model might well be transferable in the design of other sector analyses. Among these would appear to be the decomposition algorithm (e.g., the treatment of central and district constraints), the treatment of labor supply and migration (e.g., different reservation prices are postulated for different labor skills and types) and perhaps some aspects of the substitutability between labor and capital in production activities.

15.2.2. Microeconomic, Dynamic Models

This class of models is represented by the collaborative work of Day [1],

---

[30] The formal linkage between the multisectoral, economy-wide model (DYNAMICO) built by A. Manne and the agricultural model is presently under way [11]. The agricultural model—baptized CHAC for the rain god of the Maya—was started after DYNAMICO has already been specified which makes the linkage between the two more difficult.

Mudahar [16] and Singh [20].

In contrast to other sector models, this type of model is built entirely from the "bottom up". The unit of observation is the farm as a producing firm, on the one hand, and as a consuming household on the other. The model was applied to Punjab agriculture—in that sense it is a regional rather than a national sector model. The two most important and distinctive features of this approach are the form of the preference function of the farmer as decision-maker and the way the model is made dynamic. The preference (objective) function of the farmer is postulated in a lexicographic way. In other words, four major objectives are specified at the micro-level, ranked in terms of absolute priority (lexicographic ordering): (a) satisfying subsistence consumption needs; (b) a utility function comparing cash consumption and future income; (c) a safety-first objective; and (d) maximization of net cost returns. Thus, the model is solved through maximizing a lexicographic utility function subject to stringent constraints. What is truly distinctive in this model is that the maximization procedure is undertaken at the farm level. It is felt by the authors that the traditional behavior of farmers is well captured and described by the above function.

The dynamic elements are introduced through recursive programming. Thus, for example, the farmer's decisions in year t are influenced by past output prices, past realized sales and savings, and, in general, depend recursively on the previous period's solutions. As Mudahar pointed out "This intertemporal recursive interdependence generates environmental feedback functions which, once explicitly included, . . . (make) the model a 'short-sighted' dynamic model of decisions" [16, p. 14].

The model contains the following activities: (a) production activities by type of technology, by crop and by season; (b) investment activities for variable inputs and capital; and (c) household activities which include subsistence consumption, commercial consumption, cash savings, and labor supplying on and off farms. As was pointed out previously the above activities recognize the farm unit as a household and a firm which has linkages to external sectors. Various constraints are imposed on inputs, borrowing, adoption, subsistence, consumption-savings, and safety.

There are certain questions which do not appear to be adequately treated to qualify this type of model as a full-fledge sector analysis, i.e., the aggregation of production and demand; and the interaction between Punjab agriculture, the rest of Indian agriculture and the economy, as a whole. Some limited empirical results have been obtained—although no run has yet been made on the complete model. For these reasons, the operational usefulness of this type of model has not yet been tested. However, work is proceeding on the specification and estimation of the model and it may one day prove useful for policy purposes.

15.2.3. *Simulation, Systems-Science Model*

The prototype of this class of model is that developed over the last four years by an interdisciplinary group at Michigan State University under the direction of Glenn Johnson [15]. It is a very large scale model of Nigeria's agriculture, broken down into three interacting submodels corresponding to, respectively, (a) northern Nigerian agriculture; (b) southern Nigerian agriculture; and, (c) the rest of the economy. The model is basically a consistency-type model. The results of changes in exogenous variables, policy instruments, and technology can be simulated within the model. In that way, a number of alternative "development plans" can be generated. This model is discussed in detail as an example of a simulation model in Section 13.3 which should be consulted.

15.2.4. *General Equilibrium-Consistency Framework*

Sector analyses of this type tend to be much more "open ended" than the previous models, using a variety of methods and techniques.[31] Representative examples of such sector analyses are the Fletcher-Merrill-Thorbecke [4] study of Guatemala and sector studies FAO is presently engaged in, in connection with its Perspective World Agricultural Development program in Latin America (for underlying methodology see [24]) and particularly in Colombia.

The framework used in preparing the sector study of Guatemala is of a general equilibrium type. It is a broad based study and analysis of Guatemala agriculture within the context of the national economy. Thus, it is an attempt at describing and analyzing the agricultural sector within a consistency setting, emphasizing the role of agriculture in the overall process of economic development of the country.

The sector analysis is built essentially from the "top down". A relatively simple macroeconometric model of the economy was constructed to describe quantitatively the major structural and behavioral relationships between macroeconomic variables—and particularly the impact of exports, changes

---

[31] In that sense they can be better described as conceptual frameworks rather than "closed" models.

in the international terms-of-trade and foreign investment on Gross Domestic Product (GDP), domestic investment and the balance of payments —during the recent historical period (1960–67). This model was subsequently used to obtain consistent macroeconomic projections over the planning period (to 1975). Thus, the above macroeconomic model provided the link between the world economy and the national economy (the E–W link in Figure 15.1) so essential in a country as dependent on trade as Guatemala.

The macroeconomic projections obtained through the model provided, furthermore, a cadre within which agricultural production and consumption had to be consistent.[32] In other words, agricultural demand projection by commodity groups had to be consistent with the projected growth rates of GDP and population and the prevailing income elasticities of demand and exogenously determined foreign demand. Likewise, agricultural production had to be consistent with the overall growth of the economy in terms of e.g., availability of capital and intermediate inputs. In this way, the link between the economy and agriculture was established (E–A).

No formal quantitative model of the agricultural sector was built. The approach used can be described as an attempt to study and analyze the contributions of agriculture to the major national policy objectives, i.e., output, employment, income distribution and the balance of payments. The nature of the sector study was strongly policy-oriented. Within the agricultural sector, the framework consisted of a quantitative analysis of the structure of agricultural production; the marketing system; government policies and programs; projections of demand for and supply of goods and considerations of alternative policies to improve the performance of the sector. The lack of data and time as well as the necessity for operational usefulness imposed serious limitations on building a complete quantitative model.

The central concern of the study was to identify policies to promote

---

[32] The lack of any input-output table for Guatemala made it impossible to perform a formal input-output consistency check. Such a check would help insure that the sectoral growth rates of gross output and value added are mutually consistent with and correspond to a given (projected) growth rate of GDP obtained from the macro-model. Thus, agricultural demand projections would have to be consistent with given income elasticities of demand for food and raw materials and agricultural production would have to be in line with the intersectoral production structure of the economy as given by the I–O coefficients. This type of I–O consistency check was undertaken in a study of Peru which used a very similar methodology (see [26]).

development and welfare in the large subsistence agricultural subsector consistent with overall economic and social objectives. An agricultural stragety to achieve these goals was formulated and used as a basis for a sector program by the Guatemala government.

Another example of the consistency-framework to analyze agricultural development is given in [24], the methodology of which was applied to the case of Colombia by FAO [5].

REFERENCES

[1] DAY, R. H., SINGH, I. J., and MUDAHAR, M. S., "A Dynamic Microeconomic Model of Agricultural Development", paper presented at Iowa State University, May 1971.

[2] DOVRING, F. "The Share of Agriculture in a Growing Population," *FAO Monthly Bulletin of Agricultural Economics and Statistics,* VIII (August–September, 1959), 1-11.

[3] DOWNS, A. *An Economic Theory of Democracy.* New York: Harper & Bros., 1957.

[4] FLETCHER, L., MERRILL, W., GRABER, E. and THORBECKE, E. *Guatemala's Economic Development: Role of Agriculture,* Ames, Iowa State University Press, 1970.

[5] FOOD AND AGRICULTURE ORGANIZATION, "Alternative Output and Employment Projections for Colombian Agriculture", (internal working paper, Rome, October 1971).

6] FOX, K. A. *Quantifying the Expected Political Consequences of Economic and Social Programs.* Ames: Department of Economics, Iowa State University, 1963, (Dittoed.).

[7] GITTINGER, J. P. *Economic Development Through Agrarian Reform.* Unpublished Ph.D. dissertation, Iowa State University, 1955.

[8] HEADY, E. O. "Techniques of Production, Size of Productive Units and Factor Supply Conditions." Paper presented to Social Science Research Council Conference, Stanford, Calif., November, 1960.

[9] HEADY, EARL O., (ed.), *Economic Models and Quantitative Methods for Decisions and Planning in Agriculture,* Ames: Iowa State University Press, 1971.

[10] HEADY, E. O. and DILLON, J. L. *Agricultural Production Functions.* Ames: Iowa State University Press, 1961.

[11] INTERNATIONAL BANK FOR RECONSTRUCTION AND DEVELOPMENT. *Multilevel Planning: Case Studies in Mexico.* (Development Research Center Draft, February, 1972, mimeo).

[12] JOHNSTON, B. "Agricultural Development and Economic Transformation: Japan, Taiwan and Denmark," Paper presented to Social Science Research Council Conference, Stanford, Calif., November, 1960.

[13] JOHNSTON, B. F., and MELLOR, J. W. "The Role of Agriculture in Economic Development," *American Economic Review,* LI (September, 1961), 566–593.

[14] LEWIS, W. A. "Development with Unlimited Supplies of Labour," *The Manchester School,* XXII (May, 1954), 139–191.

[15] MANETSCH, T., et al. *A Generalized Simulation Approach to Agricultural Sector Analysis, With Special Reference to Nigeria.* East Lansing, Michigan: Michigan State University, November 30, 1971.

[16] MUDAHAR, M. S., "A Dynamic Microeconomic Analysis of the Agricultural Sector: The Punjab", SSRI, University of Wisconsin, December 1970.

[17] RANIS, G., and FEI, J. C. H. "A Theory of Economic Development," *American Economic Review,* LI (September, 1961), 533–565.

[18] RAUP, P. M. "The Contribution of Land Reforms to Agricultural Development: An Analytical Framework." Paper presented to Social Science Research Council Conference, Stanford, Calif., November, 1960.

[19] SANDEE, J. *A Demonstration Planning Model for India.* Calcutta: Indian Statistical Institute, 1960.

[20] SINGH, I. J., "The Transformation of Traditional Agriculture, A Case Study of Punjab India," paper presented at the Winter Meetings of the Econometric Society and AAEA, Detroit, December 1970.

[21] SCHULTZ, T. W. "Investment in Human Capital," *American Economic Review,* LI (March, 1961), 1–17. (Presidential address).

[22] THORBECKE, E. "Agrarian Reforms as a Conditioning Influence in Economic Growth," in *Agrarian Reform and Economic Growth in Developing Countries.* Washington, D.C.: U.S. Department of Agriculture, Economic Research Service, March, 1962.

[23] ——, "Some Notes on the Macroeconomic Implications and the Cost of Financing Agrarian Reform in Peru." Lima, Peru: Instituto Nacional de Planificacion, November, 1963. (Mimeographed study prepared for the INP.)

[24] THORBECKE, ERIK, "A Methodology to Derive Consistent Agriculture Projections under Technological Change within the Context of Overall Economic Growth and Alternative Income Distributions", paper prepared for the Policy Advisory Bureau of FAO, Rome, July 1971.

[25] THORBECKE, E., "Preparing Sector Programs for Agriculture: Sector Analysis, Models and Practice." (Prepared for the Conference on Strategies for Agricultural Development in the 1970's, December 1971, Stanford University.)

[26] THORBECKE, ERIK and STOUTJESDIJK, E., *Employment and Output, A Methodology Applied to Peru and Guatemala,* Paris, Development Center, OECD, 1971.

[27] TINBERGEN, J. *On the Theory of Economic Policy.* Amsterdam: North-Holland Publishing Co., 1952.

[28] ——. *Economic Policy, Principles and Design.* Amsterdam: North-Holland Publishing Co., 1956.

[29] ——. *Design of Development.* Baltimore: Johns Hopkins Press, 1958.

[30] VAN DEN BOGAARD, P. J. M., and BARTEN, A. P. "Optimal Macro-Economic Decision Rules of the Netherlands, 1957–1959." Paper presented to the Econometric Society, Amsterdam, September, 1959.

[31] VAN EIJK, C. J., and SANDEE, J. "Quantitative Determination of an Optimum Economic Policy," *Econometrica,* XXVII (1959), 1–13.

[32] VAURS, RENE, CONDOS, APOSTOLOS, and GOREUX, LOUIS, "A Programming Model of Ivory Coast," Development Research Center, IBRD, summer 1971.

[33] WUNDERLICH, G. L. *The Bombay Tenancy and Agricultural Lands Act as a Means of Agrarian Reform.* Unpublished Ph.D. dissertation, Iowa State University, 1955.

Chapter 16

CONCLUDING REMARKS

We have ranged over a wide territory. Part I has touched upon a number of the major problems and techniques of modern econometrics in addition to those specifically developed in connection with the theory of economic policy. Part II has suggested applications of the theory of quantitative economic policy to national economies, to regional economies and functional economic areas and to sectors of a national economy (such as agriculture), and at national, regional and sector levels we have presented models of economic growth, of economic planning and development and of economic stabilization.

The theory of economic policy in the sense of this book grew up in a macroeconomic context at the national level. Initially, it also had an economic stabilization focus.

Tinbergen [4] distinguished between quantitative policy, qualitative policy and social reform. Quantitative policy consisted simply in changing the values of certain members of a set of instrument variables. Qualitative policy would involve the introduction of a new instrument not included in the original set. The decision to introduce a personal income tax in a country which previously had had none would thus be classified as a qualitative policy. But the boundary between quantitative and qualitative policy is by no means clear, nor does a qualitative policy change necessarily have a bigger impact upon the economy than a quantitative policy change. Consider, for example, the qualitative change involved in raising the personal income tax from 0 to 2 per cent of personal income, as compared with that of raising the rate of the existing tax from 2 to 10 per cent of personal income.

Reforms, according to Tinbergen, are changes in the foundations of a society. Some of the more dramatic of these have been associated with civil war or revolution. Others have been contained within constitutional bounds but have nevertheless involved serious and widespread social unrest.

597

By far the largest portion of this book has been concerned with quantitative economic policy in Tinbergen's original sense. We have made a few references to phase changes or changes in regime which would probably embrace Tinbergen's concept of qualitative changes in policy. We have discussed reforms only in the context of economic planning in less developed countries and in a straightforward, pragmatic way.

16.1. Qualitative Policy and Economic Models

Model building for analyzing qualitative policy poses a great challenge to the analytical economist who wants to extend the theories of quantitative economic policy. There are three levels at which further research appears to be needed most, e.g., the specification of the objective function, the development of a sensitivity analysis for changes that have medium or long-term implications and the question of integration of a set of submodels, each with different but partially related optimizing criteria.

The basic analytical difficulty with the specification of an objective function (i.e., preference function) is that the latter is invariably a scalar, i.e., every variable, whether a target or an instrument, must be expressible in a common denominator through a scalar function. For a policy maker who has multiple objectives or goals, not all of which can be translated into a common denominator, the relevant preference function should be a vector. But the techniques required for the general case of vector optimization have not been established, although some work has been done to characterize the problem, e.g., to consider the analogous problem of a family of programming models or, in some cases, to allow noncomparability between optimal subsets [2, 6]. One of the interesting consequences that follows from this approach is the need to define criteria for suboptimization, in most cases of which the general concept of an optimum is less meaningful. This apparently has very important implications for a scheme of decentralized planning through different submodels, each with different objective functions at different stages, so to say.

This problem in at least its regional aspects has a formal resemblance to the problem of translating the utility functions of different individuals into some aggregative measure of social welfare. Samuelson (1947), as interpreted by R. G. D. Allen, suggested a social welfare function of the vector of the k individual utility functions:

$$W = f\left(U_1, U_2, \ldots U_k\right).$$

Samuelson visualized W as *ordinal* like the individual utility functions.[1] Each U_i is assumed to depend only on the individual's own consumption of goods and services. Then W sets a consistent social ordering of all possible situations, as valued by a particular policy maker or according to some specified viewpoint or system of ethical beliefs. The last $k-1$ equations needed to make the general equilibrium for the economy determinate are derived from the condition that W must be a maximum subject to the restraints set by the rest of the system.

We may think of each U_i in the present context as an objective function specified by a policy maker responsible (in part at least) to the residents of the ith region and $W = f(U_1, U_2, \dots U_k)$ as that of a national policy maker who sees his responsibility as one of optimizing some function of the utility levels realized and perceived by each of the k regional policy makers. We might conceive of the U_i's and W as vote-fare functions. Or, we might simply regard the requirements for basic political stability or re-election as setting constraints within which each regional policy maker must seek to optimize his objective function expressed in terms of the regional economic variables. The political constraints under which the national policy maker must operate will be related to those operative upon the regional policy makers in a manner which depends upon the electoral system of the particular country.

In brief, it is not *necessary* that the separate U_i be judged equal or comparable or that they should be aggregated into a form such as

$$W = \sum_{i=1}^{k} w_i U_i.$$

If the latter type of aggregation is indeed undertaken, it still does not imply that the individual economic variables which enter the *regional* objective functions will enter W in the form of simple summations or Laspeyres indexes of the regional magnitudes.

Theil's principle of "perfect aggregation" may be of value here.[2] We assume that the *weights* applied to deviations of actual regional employment from the desired regional level vary from one regional policy maker to another. Now suppose the national policy maker wishes to express his own objective function in terms of the macrovariable *national* employment. Suppose further that the required change in the value of the selected instru-

[1] See Allen [1, p. 722].

[2] See Theil [3]. See also the interpretation of Theil's approach in Allen [1, pp. 694–724].

ment in each region, e.g., expenditures made in that region by the national government, is an exact linear function of the deviation in regional employment:

$$G_i - G_i^* = b_i(N_i^* - N_i), \quad i = 1, 2, \ldots k,$$
(16.1)

where b_i may vary from one region to another, depending on the structures of their economies; G_1^* and N_1^* are desired values.

If the k equations (16.1) are to be aggregated into a single macrorelation such that the equation

$$\sum_{i=1}^{k} (G_i - G_i^*) = G - G^* = B(N^* - N)_{req}$$
(16.2)

will give the same "perfect prediction" of the required value of $(G - G^*)$ as the k regional relations, it turns out that

$$B(N^* - N)_{req} = \bar{b} \sum_{i=1}^{k} \left(\frac{b_i}{\bar{b}}\right)(N_i^* - N_i), \quad \text{and}$$

$$\sum_{i=1}^{k} (G_i - G_i^*) = G - G^* = \bar{b}\left[\sum_{i=1}^{k} \frac{b_i}{\bar{b}}(N_i^* - N_i)\right],$$
(16.3)

where

$$\bar{b} = \frac{1}{k}\sum_{i=1}^{k} b_i.$$

In brief, the right-hand term in (16.3) is the sum of the deviations of actual from desired employment in each region *weighted by* the regional "effectiveness coefficient" b_i, which gives the dollars of increase in government expenditure required in that region to accomplish a unit increase in employment. If we suppose further that the subjective weights w_{gi} and w_{ni} are attached to $(G_i - G_i^*)$ and $(N_i^* - N_i)$, respectively, by the regional policy maker, it appears intuitively that the *optimal deicision rule* for determining government expenditures in the ith region would take the form

$$G_i - G_i^* = \left(\frac{w_{ni}}{w_{gi}} \cdot b_i\right)(N_i^* - N_i).$$

Substituting

$$c_i = \left(\frac{w_{ni}}{w_{gi}}\right)b_i,$$

the principle of "perfect aggregation" leads us to

$$\sum_{i=1}^{k} (G_i - G_i^*) = G - G^* = \bar{c}\left[\sum_{i=1}^{k} \frac{c_i}{\bar{c}}(N_i^* - N_i)\right], \tag{16.5}$$

where

$$\bar{c} = \frac{1}{k}\sum_{i=1}^{k} c_i .$$

The expression in brackets now includes a multiplicative combination of the constraints b_i reflecting the real structures of the regional economies and the relative subjective or vote-fare weights (w_{ni}/w_{gi}).

The development of sensitivity analysis applied to policy models has been mostly concerned with very small changes in a local neighborhood. So far, no general method is available for the analysis of sensitivity to finitely large changes, although in another field, e.g., control engineering, involving microdecision units such as a single plant manager, the impact of unforeseen changes is incorporated indirectly through what is called "homeostatic control" [5]. In economic models, the range of uncertainty and imprecision is much greater than in control engineering, and that may partly explain why there has been very little effort toward building some links between short-run and long-run policy models.

There is a great need for characterizing the so-called "structural break" and its external effects through the whole economy. Analytically, there is some need for going into the nonlinearities of the mathematical structure of policy models, although it is doubtful whether this would be a productive venture.

In our discussion of quantitative policy models we assumed implicitly that the preference function of the policy maker is always independent of the constraints. If this assumption does not hold, it is likely that there is some relation between the "net prices" in the objective function and the so-called resource vector in programming language. There is need for a quantitative characterization of this relation, which seems to be of great importance for our insight into the process of growth of a less developed economy.

16.2. Remarks on Quantitative Economic Policy

Few economists would question the desirability of developing more and more accurate models of an economy. If we refrain from this attempt, we forego opportunities to extend the boundaries of economic science. But economists, like other scientists, are not content to leave problems un-investigated. They must investigate them "because they are there."

Modern governments have almost everywhere assumed a considerable degree of responsibility for steering their economies in the interests of various social and political objectives. At the least, almost all governments stand ready to intervene in the economy if its performance, as reflected in the levels and trajectories of major variables such as unemployment and real income, deteriorates badly. Hence, though national governments, and political parties within nations, approach the problem of economic steers-manship with varying degrees of reluctance and sophistication, they must all stand ready to steer their economies in time of need and to make at least moderate adjustments in economic instruments (and institutions) from time to time.

The central problem is to describe the economy of a nation in such a way that the effect of an initial change in any unit or sector of it can be traced into all other units or sectors, quantitatively as well as qualitatively. Quantifi-cation is most important, for without it we can hardly rise above the statement that "everything affects everything else."

Prior to 1950, few economists would have held out much hope of achieving useful models of complete economies. Today a considerable number would be optimistic about this. Recent developments within economics and in computer technology have set the stage for dramatic improvement in the study of complete economies. The continuing improvement of national income and product accounts is a facilitating factor. The recent burgeoning of macroeconomic theory, the successful use of economic policy models in the Netherlands and the growing use of macroeconomic models in other countries are providing larger areas of firm ground upon which operational models can be erected.

The makers of public economic policy are (as such) political decision makers rather than economists. However, they are quite conscious of the process of decision making, and in general it is much easier for them to think in terms of the probable reactions of individual firms, consumers, or state or local governments than to think in terms of relationships between aggregative variables. Nor is the economist justified in placing much confidence in aggregative economic relationships unless he can rationalize them in terms of actual or probable responses of individual decision-making units to proposed economic policies. An economic policy generally involves some change in the incentives or rules of the game for a sizeable class of economic units—for example, all wheat farmers. The goal of the policy may be a specified change in the national production of wheat. But the success of the policy depends upon the decisions made by each individual wheat farmer as he studies its price and income implications for his own farm.

Hence, to anticipate the effects of policies upon economic aggregates we must anticipate the responses of economic units. Each unit will respond in the light of its goals and the limitations or constraints upon its actions.

We may visualize an economy as made up primarily of households and firms. A household buys consumer goods and services, it pays taxes to support public services and it supplies or sells factors of production to firms. For some types of economic policies (as free public education) the individual, rather than the household, is the unit of primary concern.

Perhaps the word "firm" should be confined to a private enterprise, farm or nonfarm, operated for profit. However, public enterprises such as municipal power plants, water works, and the like are in many respects almost indistinguishable from private firms in terms of technology, employment relationships and motivations.

The various public enterprises in an area may be regarded as trying to maximize the output of services from a given budget expenditure. The private nonprofit organizations may be regarded as trying to maximize net benefits rendered to their members: this would be attained (in a temporal sense) if the services provided by the last $100 of "input" were worth precisely $100 to the supporting members.

Finally, the policy-making officials of national, state and local government may be viewed either as trying to maximize the welfare of the residents of their jurisdiction (as perceived by the policy makers) or as trying to .naximize expected votes for their parties in the next election. In a democracy, the policy maker's welfare function and his vote-fare function may lead to quite similar decisions on taxes, expenditures and other matters of economic consequence.

Any economic unit has to accept as given many aspects of the economy of which it is a part. These "data" generated by the economy may be regarded as contingent upon the goal-maximizing activities of the unit. We are suggesting that logical and potentially verifiable bridges between macro-relations and microrelations are needed in the further development of quantitative economic policy models. Unless we know why individual firms or consumers respond in ways suggested by aggregative data, we are not sure that they will respond this way if a deliberate policy change is introduced.

For example, attempts have been made to estimate normative supply functions for types of farms and for small agricultural regions on the basis of linear programming analyses of a sample of individual farms. Similar studies should be attempted with samples of firms in other kinds of industries and samples of local and state governments. (In this kind of research, each observation may be a case study of significant dimensions and considerable interest to the proprietor or director of the unit studied.)

The work of maintaining reliable bridges between microrelations and macrorelations will never be finished, so long as the individual firms are free to adopt new techniques and so long as the size distributions and internal organizations of firms and other decision-making units are constantly changing.

The problem of "sectoring" a national economy in terms of industries is of long standing. In input-output studies and in standard industrial classification systems industries are made up of establishments (plants) producing a fairly well-defined cluster of goods or services. Perhaps the logical extreme of this kind of disaggregation is process analysis, which begins its description of the production process in terms of the operating characteristics of individual machine tools and the time and the material requirements for highly specific unit tasks.

At the process analysis level of detail, production processes are independent of political ideologies. Thus, it should not surprise us that economists and plant managers in socialist countries are beginning to find uses for linear programming (and potentially quadratic programming) techniques. With changing technology, the work of classifying industries and keeping input-output or process analysis models up to date also can never be completed and laid aside.

It is possible, of course, to disaggregate a national economy into an exhaustive set of regions and to maintain a uniform industrial sectoring within each region. But further attention should be given to the role of the diversified multi-industry firm, which operates in several different industries. For example, a firm once specialized in the meat packing industry has recently branched out into (1) the production and distribution of chemical fertilizers and (2) the sale of life insurance. It may be that the insurance division responds to economic conditions and policy changes as does an independent insurance firm and that the responses of the meat packing division and the fertilizer division are also similar to those of independent firms specialized to their respective industries. Nevertheless, the normative and the actual responses of multi-industry firms deserve analysis, specifically from the point of view of their probable responses to the various instruments of quantitative economic policy.

We could conceive of an economic model which might be sectored first by firms for each of the 200 or so largest firms in the economy and second by industry (establishments producing specified clusters of products) within each firm. Formally, this would be no more difficult than sectoring first by regions and then by industries. In economic policy applications, a national policy maker might be portrayed as attempting to maximize a preference function in terms of national aggregative variables while each individual firm tried to maximize its own position subject to the actions of the federal policy maker and the actions of other firms specifically individuated in the model.

But the structure of a supermodel, once it is so large in dimension, raises its own problems, some of which are only beginning to be investigated by research workers; for example, decomposability or near-triangularity, different aspects of flexibility and also the effects of errors at one place or another. The question of linking the submodels through a recursive relation built into the over-all model is still at its initial stage of investigation, and problems of the real world are seldom completely recursive but only approximately so. Different types of approximate recursiveness, both statistical and economic, offer a line of further research. A problem which is closely related is the question of optimum aggregation of a large model into a smaller one by defining, for example, some rules of aggregation. If the submodels are already programming models in regular form, the situation becomes complicated, as one can imagine. Several implications and insights will be mentioned briefly in the following section.

16.3. Additional Light on Economic and Political History

We have felt for some years that light might be shed on certain aspects of a nation's economic and political history by attempting to reconstruct economic policy models at (say) twenty-year intervals during centuries of rapid economic development. Among the advanced economies, changes in the U.S. during the last two centuries have been particularly great.

For every twentieth year, an attempt could be made to construct a model of the economy, a rough classification of the population into incidence groups and a classification of economic variables according to Tinbergen's scheme. The usual historical sources could be examined in an attempt to estimate terms of trade between different target (and instrument) variables.

"Rational" political decisions would not depend directly upon economic incidence groups but perhaps upon these groups weighted by their relative political influence. With economic development, transactions matrices would change, the coefficients of major behavioral equations would change, new targets would become explicit and new instruments would be introduced. Certain important issues would be resolved and disappear from the explicit target variable set.

As each country has only one history, it should not take an inordinate amount of work to exhaust this particular suggestion.

16.4. Insights with Respect to Economic Development

The historical exercise just described might provide valuable insights into the political implications of economic development.

Suppose we compare planned cross-section structures of a developing economy at five-year intervals. Certain reductions in employment in the agricultural sector may be planned along with certain increases in employment in other sectors. Regional shifts of population may be projected, along with growth rates of population in particular cities and other political jurisdictions. Land reform programs would also change the distribution of people among tax and public service incidence groups or incidence groups defined with respect to these plus other policies.

Implicitly, this concern with the redistribution of the population among incidence groups assumes that a welfare function could be devised by measuring the actual incidences of alternative policies upon each group and then letting the policy maker apply such weights as he pleases to a change of (say) $10 per capita in the "position" of each group. As the impacts of many policies could be defined in terms of real income, one of the challenges would be to assign equivalent dollar values to benefits not priced in the market place (for example, the vocational or earning power contribution of public education). Different policy makers would assign different weights to increases of $10 in average per capita incomes of the different groups. If this suggestion seems crude, let us simply regard it as the first phase of an exploratory process which could subsequently lead to more sophisticated formulations.

In Tinbergen's scheme, we take the policy maker's preference function as given. But, in a developing economy, actions taken as a result of the existing preference function of the existing policy maker will encourage a redistribution of policy incidence groups which will almost certainly change the vote-fare (and, as a practical matter, the preference) functions of future policy makers or even of the present policy maker if he stays in office for a long time.

Given a static and permanent preference function, we can measure the efficiency of an instrument in terms of the changes in target values (and hence in an index of welfare) which it produces along the surface of the existing preference function. But this concept must now be extended to include the efficiency of an instrument in changing (1) the coefficients of the economic model which will prevail five or ten years hence and (2) the coefficients of the preference function which will exist at various future times! Is it possible to give a quantitative meaning to an optimal rate of change in the preference function of a policy maker? The presumption is that a policy maker who acts in 1965 on the basis of certain barter terms of trade between variables is capable of stating that, if the structure of the economy and its policy incidence groups changed according to his projections, he would act as of 1970 in accordance with another and different set of values of the barter terms of trade between variables.

REFERENCES

[1] ALLEN, R. G. D. *Mathematical Economics*. 2nd revised edition. London: Macmillan and Co., 1959.

[2] CHARNES, A., and COOPER, W. W. "On the Theory and Computation of Delegation Models: K-efficiency, Functional Efficiency and Goals," in *Management Science, Models and Techniques*. Edited by C. W. Churchman and M. Verhulst. London: Pergamon Press, Vol. I, 1960 pp. 56–91.

[3] THEIL, H. *Linear Aggregation of Economic Relations*. Amsterdam: North-Holland Publishing Co., 1954.

[4] TINBERGEN, J. *On the Theory of Economic Policy*. Amsterdam: North-Holland Publishing Co., 1952; revised edition, 1955.

[5] TOMOVIC, R., and RADANOVIC, L. "Homeostatic Control of Dynamic Systems," in *Proceedings of the First International Symposium on Optimizing and Adaptive Control*, Rome, Italy, April 26–28, 1962. Pittsburgh, Pa.: Instrument Society of America, 1962, pp. 57–67.

[6] ZADEH, L. A. "Optimality and Nonscalar Valued Performance Criteria," *IEEE Transactions on Automatic Control*, Vol. AC–8, No. 1 (1963), pp. 59–60.

INDEX